Contextual Approaches in Communication

Corina Daba-Buzoianu/Hasan Arslan/Mehmet Ali Icbay (eds.)

Contextual Approaches in Communication

PL ACADEMIC RESEARCH

Bibliographic Information published by the Deutsche Nationalbibliothek
The Deutsche Nationalbibliothek lists this publication in the Deutsche Nationalbibliografie; detailed bibliographic data is available in the internet at http://dnb.d-nb.de.

Library of Congress Cataloging-in-Publication Data
Contextual approaches in communication / Corina Daba-Buzoianu, Hasan Arslan, Mehmet Ali Icbay (eds.).
pages cm
Includes index.
ISBN 978-3-631-66609-8
1. Communication--Social aspects. 2. Interpersonal communication. 3. Mass media--Social aspects. 4. Information technology--Social aspects. I. Daba-Buzoianu, Corina, 1983- editor. II. Arslan, Hasan, editor. III. Icbay, Mehmet Ali, editor.
HM1206.C6665 2015
302.2--dc23

2015033445

This book is the scholar work of International Association of Social Science Research (IASSR). It is also printed with the financial support from IASSR. The manuscripts in this book are compiled from the full texts from the annual conferences organized by International Association of Social Science Research. They are first reviewed by the independent reviewers, and then proof-read and edited by the editors.
The opinions and views expressed in articles are not necessarily those of this volume's editors.

ISBN 978-3-631-66609-8 (Print)
E-ISBN 978-3-653-05967-0 (E-Book)
DOI 10.3726/978-3-653-05967-0

PL Academic Research is an Imprint of Peter Lang GmbH.

Peter Lang – Frankfurt am Main · Bern · Bruxelles · New York · Oxford · Warszawa · Wien

This publication has been peer reviewed.

www.peterlang.com

Foreword

Contextual Approaches in Communication gathers studies addressing communication not only from different perspectives, but also referring to different contexts. Thus, the current volume acknowledges the importance that context has in communication studies, regardless of the topics or methodology. The volume brings together studies on media, new media and social media, with a focus on journalism, television and radio. Corporate social responsibility together with marketing and advertising are being addressed through field research and theoretical reflections. The volume also gathers papers on gender studies, identity and image analysis, and intercultural communication. *Contextual Approaches in Communication's* papers use both quantitative and qualitative methodologies and underline the importance that context has in deciphering communication processes.

A significant number of papers address media, new media and social media, but they do not only refer to their mechanisms and structures, but also discuss consequences of their usage and lack of regulation. For instance, Emre Osman Olkun's paper *Change in the structure of media ownership in Turkey: Example of Milliyet and Vatan newspapers* concludes that the Turkish press was shaped according to economic and politic conditions. Thus, the economic and political changes in Turkey can easily be observed in media ownership and implicitly in the media discourse. F. Betul Aydin and Sukuru Balci's paper *Political effect and ideology in the news discourse: an example of the 2014 local elections* reveals how national newspapers protrayed politicians, by referring to the 2014 elections. Readers' habits are being changed by new media, as is revealed by Baris Bulunmaz's paper *Changing reading habits together with the new media and the case of newspaper practices in Turkey.* Cerem Yegen and Baki Yegen propose a discussion under the topic of communicative reality.

The idea of community radio is being addressed by Figen Algul, who discusses Greek community radio in Turkey, drawing on the literature on the field and on qualitative research. According to Algul, community radios develop in well-established democracies and need significant financial support. At the same time, community radios transform into internet radio. Metin Kasim and Ozlem Gulec Kinali discuss children's exposure to food and beverage advertisements broadcast on television. In their study *Measuring effects of children-oriented food advertisements on primary school freshmen, broadcast on television,* Kasim and Kinali conclude that the state should get involved and introduce clear regulations. Also, they mention that media-literacy lessons should be included in the education curriculum. Mehmet Ogulcan Turan addresses an ethical issue in terms of television broadcasting. In his study *The use of the images of Mobese cameras in television news: a new type or source?*, Turan aims to analyze the basic features of news in which Mobese (=CCTV-camera) images are being used. The author underlines the lack of regulation and the fact that the images are being used unethically. The need of regulation of audio and visual media is also being presented by Kemal Cem Baykal's paper *Self-regulation in audio-visual media field in Turkey.* Cank Ates proposes *Historical transformation of gift and presentation on television as consumer product in modern era: instance of Valentine's Day,* by looking into the transformation of gifts of mutual give-and-take and give back. Ates also points out that the emergence of capitalism has influenced the perception of gifts. Songul Omur discusses television habits of Turks living in Germany and mentions that the ratio of German TV preference tends to be higher in the case of the third generation of immigrants. The discussion on migration is continued by A. Nevin Yildiz Tahincioglu in *The effects of 'Honor' on communication between Turkish immigrants and Swedes: an example of Stockholm and Uppsala.* The paper studies the relation between honor and gender among Turkish migrants in Sweden. The results show that honor is seen as an important cultural element. Turkish migrants view honor as protecting them from cultural influences of other ethnic groups. *Differences between male and female brains and their influences on effective behaviors in organizations* by Sultan Basaran points out the relation between gender studies and organizational studies. Gender is also being addressed from a perspective of interpersonal communication in the paper *Does gender reflect on interpersonal communication? Women's and men's communication style* by S. Didem Ozsenler. Finally, interpersonal communication is discussed in relation with communicative ecology and a digital environment by Demet Guruz and S. Didem Ozsenler.

Social media is more than a new form of media. It represents a significant shift in the way communication is being perceived and used. A very interesting feature of social media is its influence on corporate image as it empowers the public to a significant extent. Sevda Denecli's paper *Impact of viral marketing through social media on corporate image,* together with Ceyda Denecli's *Impact of companies Facebook pages on consumer brand preferences* show that companies still need to learn how to communicate with the public in social media. In their quantitative studies on Facebook, the two researchers show that the development of technology has created new forms of communication, which implicitly generate new forms of corporate images. The concept of gatekeeping is put in relation with online journalism by Nurettin Guz, Hayrullah Yanik and Ozan Kocabas. The paper reveals that in new media organizations news-making is not limited to delivering news to the public. Comments and criticism can also shape news.

Derya Erdem proposes *A study on new media studies in Turkey*, drawing on previous research, while Betul Onay Dogan discusses the importance of online marketing in the study *Representations of cities in new media in the context of website*, by investigating both textual and visual elements. According to Dogan's study, online videos contribute to the construction of cities' identity. Understanding online behavior helps companies to develop better applications and to better communicate with the public. Murat Yetkin Yasar and Yigit Kacmaz' paper *Do we need mobile applications in 3's tourism: the case of Alanya* aims to reveal the mobile device usage of Alanya's tourists. Their results show that tourists are mostly interested in leisure and food and less interested in historical places. Adem Burak Cakmak and Baris Yavuz propose a paper to discuss mobile subscriber location density data for social benefits, not only for business purposes. In their study *A recommendation of using location density gathered from wireless networks for human sciences* the two researchers show that mobile subscriber density data can be used and applied in medicine, transportation, employment and disaster management.

Going online also poses serious risks, especially for teenagers. As studies show, the number of teenagers who are addicted to online games is dramatically increasing. Taking this into account, Bunyamin Ayhan and Selahattin Cavus aim to investigate the level of addiction to online gaming of early-adolescence high-school students. The study underlines the fact that especially boys are in serious danger, and that education both at home and in school, together with society as a whole should find better ways to respond to this risk. The students' internet and social media usage is also addressed by Emel Basturk Akca and Idil Sayimer, in their paper *Secondary school students' attitudes to and awareness of cyberbullying in Turkey: a scaling method case study in Ankara*. The study reveals that there are significant gender differences in terms of cyberbullying experiences and perceptions. Boys were more likely to approve of cyberbullying-related behavior and get involved in online hate-groups. Cyberbullying is also addressed by Alsi Karaarslan in the paper *Cyberbullying and child abuse: parents' awareness of cyberbullying and child abuse in Facebook practices*. Ceyda Tetik, in turn, describes the role that social media plays in the identity crisis of the young.

As Feride Akim discusses in *Academicians' use of social media tools for education: an assessment on communication faculties in Turkey and in Baltic*, social media can also be used for education and learning. Akim's study reveals that Facebook is frequently used by academicians, unlike Twitter or other social media. The study *Personality factors that affect the use of Facebook: a research on university students* by Murat Kocyigit and M. Nejat Ozupek focuses on personality factors and social media. The authors conclude that individuals who have extrovert personality traits use Facebook intensely for sharing photos, while individuals with open personality traits comment frequently. Emel Karagoz' and Guiden Ozkan's paper *Presidency as a new political field of power: the reflection of field-habitus relation on Twitter* is the only paper in this volume addressing political communication on Twitter.

Through a semiotic study on brand positioning, Ilknur Dogu Ozturk's paper states that both universal cultural and local cultural signs must be taken into consideration when communicating. According to Ozturk, universal cultural signs must be merged with the local ones in order to gain a clear brand positioning. Talking about brand memorability, Oyku Ezgi Yildiz investigates the role that advertising music has in this respect. Yildiz aims to understand whether music creates associations with brands and whether this associations have an effect on brand memorability. The study concludes that it is important to associate music with brands as it creates positive attitudes. *The effect of corporate personality and credibility on organizational commitment* by Eylin Babacan and Ozge Mutlu aims to analyze the perceptions of Rotary's corporate personality and corporate credibility on organizational commitment to Rotaract clubs. Cansu Aydemir's paper *In the context of branding: using gender roles, creating criteria and analysis of advertisements broadcast in Turkey* mention that advertisements with cultural content are easily remembered. Sifa Elcil addresses the *Strategic role of leadership approach in corporate communication*, and concludes that senior managers and corporate employees leading with a sense of quality and excellence will tend to appreciate corporate communication. The internal public is valued through the relation with internal marketing and branding, as Dincer Atli's paper points out. Brand equity is studied through field research in Ozge U. Yurttas's paper *A field research on the brand equity of internet and social media applications.*

Departing from theoretical considerations on social responsibility, Ahmet Tarhan and Mustafa Bal conclude in their paper *Corporate social responsibility practice implications in new communication platforms* that industrial companies fail to properly communicate their corporate social responsibility strategy. The paper *Fostering social networks for corporate social responsibility communication: an exploratory study on Twitter* by Selin Turkel and Ebru Uzunoglu discusses corporate social responsibility in a less studied social media channel: Twitter. Corporate social responsibility is also being addressed by Senem Gungor in the paper *Advancement of the awareness of social responsibility at universities: a research on a lesson of "social responsibility campaigns" at Baskent University.*

Based on Maslow's theory, Cuneyt Gok presents the paper *Body: a means of expression* in which he points out that there are significant differences in the perception of needs, taking Amazon, Africa and some well-developed countries as examples. Nonverbal and written communication are analyzed in the film

Dr. Zhivago by Nukhet Eltut Kalender, while Gul Coskun Degrmen discusses *The representation of PR as a profession in Turkish cinema after 2000.* Cinema is also being investigated in Tugba Elmaci's paper *Militarism in new Turkish cinema as a mechanism for constructing masculinity.*

Corina Daba-Buzoianu[1]

---

1 Her work was possible with the financial support of the Sectorial Operational Programme for Human Resources Development 2007–2013, co-financed by the European Social Fund, under the project number POSDRU/159/1.5/S/134650 with the title "Doctoral and Postdoctoral Fellowships for young researchers in the fields of Political, Administrative and Communication Sciences and Sociology".

Contents

A. Nevin Yıldız Tahincioğlu

The Effects of 'Honour' on Communication Between Turkish Immigrants and Swedes: An Example of Stockholm and Uppsala

Introduction

The variations in the sex regime are the most important among the parameters that shape the communication between the individual members of different ethnic, religious, and cultural groups. In fact, moral norms that undertake important roles in intercultural communication are associated with gender regimes. Honour as a norm that regulates sexual morality is an important aspect that has to be considered while examining the problems that are experienced by Turkish immigrants while communicating with other cultures. Looking at the discussions related to honour will make the importance of this study, the subject of which is the effects of the perception of honour to the intercultural communication of the immigrants from Turkey who are living in Stockholm and Uppsala, easier.

Honour, which includes the moral norms and prohibitions related to the sexuality of women and the fertility of women in the Meditteranean and Middle Eastern communities where Turkey is also included, describes the woman with shame and the man with glory (*sheref*). The sphere of influence and the degree of honour that forms the relationship of the individual with society, as well as forming the self-respect of an individual, increases with immigration and multiculturalism (Peristiany, 1965). The main reason that gave birth to honour, the roots of which goes back as far as the ancient ages, is the geographical position of the Mediterrenanean and the Middle East Regions which is open to invasions. This is because the inhabitants of this geography had to share their land and their living space with foreigners along with the invasions. The locals, who could not fight against the invaders because of their structures that are divided into tribes, have misguided their women in order to protect their biological and cultural assets from foreign blood. This fear stemming from foreign blood (i.e. from different cultures) has increased once again in multicultural structures in today's conditions (Tillon: 2006, p. 198).

According to this logic, the protection of honour and accordingly, the affiliation and the culture, requires the isolation of women relatives from other cultures. The external interventions, which aim to convert the cultural values of minorities or immigrant groups, often cause an increase in the pressure on women who are members of this group.

These strengthen the reflex of protecting the private domain, which has been marked as the domain of birth, cultural, and moral values, from foreigners (Chatterjee, 2002). Additionally, this reflex is creating a strong resistance that rises against change (Kymlicka, 1998). So, the intercultural communication, which causes the differences as well as the similarities to come to light, causes the formation of a new common culture or can cause the transformation of each culture which interacts within itself (Knoblauch, 2001, p. 24).

Methods

This study is part of the big research study which has been carried out in Uppsala and Stockholm between February and July 2013 with the support of The Scientific and Technological Research Council of Turkey. Within the scope of this study, the deep-interview technique has been selected as a research method which was used for collecting data about the effect of honour on communication between the Turkish migrants and Swedish people.

All questions were projected to understand whether or not honour has been considered as a barrier for intercultural communication between Turkish migrants and Swedish people. The following questions are examples of some basic-key questions used in in-depth interviews: (1) What are the cultural and moral differences between migrants who come from Turkey and Swedish people in aspects such as family life, marriage rules and ceremony, and sexual rules?; (2) What kind of cultural differences lead to conflict and segregation between Swedish and migrant people who come from Turkey?; and (3) What are the cultural and moral differences between Turkish and Swedish women?

The participants are 15 males and 15 females who have immigrated from Turkey. The age average of the people who were interviewed varied between 21 and 57 years. Half of the interviewees were male, while the other half were female. Eighteen of the 30 interviewees consisted of first-generation migrants (FGM) and rest of them were member of the second-generation migrants group (SGM). Half of the interviewees were members of the middle class (First Group: FG) and the other half of them were members of the lower-class (Second Group: SG).

Table 1: List of interviewees

Name	Sex	Age	Social economic status: FG[1] SG[2]	Migrants generation: FGM[3] SGM[4]	City
Nazmi	Male	30	SG	SGM	Stockholm
Zehra	Female	26	SG	SGM	Stockholm
Hasan	Male	50	SG	FGM	Stockholm
Neriman	Female	57	SG	FGM	Stockholm
Hamdiye	Female	55	FG	FGM	Stockholm
Nermin	Female	57	SG	FGM	Stockholm
Semih	Male	23	SG	SGM	Stockholm
Elif	Female	36	SG	SGM	Stockholm
Fatma	Female	26	SG	SGM	Uppsala
Recep	Male	21	FG	SGM	Stockholm
Tümay	Female	51	FG	FGM	Stockholm
Hüseyin	Male	24	FG	SGM	Uppsala
Şahika	Female	35	FG	FGM	Uppsala
Gülsürn	Female	23	FG	FGM	Uppsala
Sevil	Female	26	FG	FGM	Uppsala
Canan	Female	55	FG	FGM	Uppsala
Sinan	Male	25	FG	SGM	Uppsala
Ahmet	Male	30	SG	SGM	Stockholm
Bilal	Male	41	SG	FGM	Uppsala
Zafer	Male	50	SG	FGM	Uppsala
Hayri	Male	50	SG	FGM	Uppsala
Şenay	Female	30	FG	FGM	Uppsala
Hatice	Female	23	FG	SGM	Stockholm
Hayriye	Female	45	FG	FGM	Uppsala
Suavi	Male	55	FG	FGM	Uppsala

1 FG: First group interviewee who is a member of the middle-class.
2 SG: Second group interviewee who is a member of the lower-class.
3 FGM: First-generation migrant.
4 SGM: Second-generation migrant.

Name	Sex	Age	Social economic status: FG[1] SG[2]	Migrants generation: FGM[3] SGM[4]	City
Serhat	Male	29	SG	SGM	Uppsala
Fırat	Male	27	SG	SGM	Uppsala
Halil	Male	23	FG	SGM	Uppsala
Berna	Female	52	SG	FGM	Uppsala
Halise	Female	42	FG	FGM	Uppsala
Rıza	Male	35	FG	FGM	Stockholm
Şehnaz	Female	54	FG	FGM	Uppsala
Total: 30	Female: 15 Male: 15		FG: 15 SG: 15 Total: 30	FGM: 18 SGM: 12 Total: 30	

Findings

All of the participants in this study claimed that honour is an important cultural value for them and that they separate their culture from dominant culture and other co-culture with the norm of honour. Hayri, who is a FGM and father of two, has married someone from his hometown Ankara because of 'honour' which he considers as a cultural difference: "Honour is important for us. For example, we are all equal, but regarding honour, men and women are not the same. Swedes tell us, I don't care about your honour. Our customs and manners do not mean anything to them. They do not understand, the more pressure they put on us, the more we are connected to our values. Because for us, woman means honour and this is the difference between us" (Hayri, SG, FGM).

Married, father of two, and pizza baker Sinan has stated that honour, which he sees as a "cultural difference," is seen by all the Turkish migrants and not just by himself as a commitment to the motherland, to the nation, and to the family: "If we forget the territory, the customs and traditions from where we came, we will be destroyed. The Swedes do not understand this and we are exposed to constant pressure about this issue. They keep asking as where our women are. Women are everything for us. First of all, they are mothers for us, they are holy, they are our honour, and they are at home where they should be. This is the greatest humane difference between us anyway" (Sinan, SG, SGM).

The people who were interviewed, suffering from the efforts of the Swedes who try to convert the immigrants, are turning to ethnic and cultural groups who possess the closest value systems to them. Şenay, who came to Sweden as an imported bride, stated that she did not get used to Sweden at all and that the expectations of the Swedes from the immigrants is one of the top issues that she complained about the most: "First of all, they do not accept us as we are. They tell us 'your culture is more backwards than ours.' I do not know what they want from us. They keep talking about 'woman, honour.' They tell us 'Come on be like us, go out, drink, have fun in the disco, and beyond that go out and be men and women together outside.' They do not have a concept of honour and they do not want us to have any either" (Şenay, SG, FGM).

As the above transmitted data has indicated, the immigrants from Turkey also consider the concept of honour as a cultural item which provides cultural superiority over other cultures. A SGM, 23-year-old university graduate Semih, is among the interviewees who expressed the cultural differences between the two communities by a hierarchical ranking: "The Swedes are more educated than us, they work at good jobs. But one thing is missing there… …this is the absence of honour. So, in that respect, we are superior to them" (Semih, FG, SGM).

Honour, which is seen as a means of establishing superiority at first glance, is actually the expression of the subaltern position of the immigrants against the dominant culture. This is because the dissolution of honour would mean the disintegration of family which is the only power domain left in their hands.

Also for Suavi, married and father of three children who has been living in Sweden for nearly 30 years and lives on with unemployment benefits, the existence of honour is sufficient to cover up all deficiencies: "We came here, we left everything behind us… We were respectable families from where we came. Here you are just an immigrant. Everything from our language to our culture and even our professions became worthless. What have we got in our hands now? Only our culture and our morals. If we can not preserve them, we will be destroyed. Because here we work in jobs where they do not want to work, we collect their trash, we take care of their sick and their elderly, and we clean their dirt. But my daughter, their dirt is more than ours, let it be, they do not have any honour in the first place" (Semih, SG, FGM).

Bilal, a specialist doctor, married, and father of two children, believes that the family institution has to be protected from the Swedes in order to protect honour which is considered as the only thing left in hand. According to Bilal, "the family concept has crashed in Swedes and this collapse is also threatening their family integrity" (Bilal, FG, SGM).

The family institution in Sweden and the social status of the women is extremely scary for all the remaining male interviewees, such as this interviewee who is scared to lose what he has in his hand. At the centre of this fear that is felt towards the Swedish culture are the 'sexually unsatisfied' Swedish women in who are "masculinised" because of the "extreme freedom."

But Zafer, who was married to a Danish lady for ten years, is extremely annoyed with this language which has been developed against the Swedish ladies. The actual issue according to Zafer is that the immigrants from Turkey have developed a racist and discriminating view towards different cultures. This view, which ensures that the immigrants survive who themselves feel weak against the Swedes, is actually damaging the communication between the two cultures: "Turkish immigrants say that Swedes or the Northern ladies have no morals. Actually the ones who have no morals are themselves. For these people morals are to be honest, to be clear and sincere. And if you talk about family, their family bonds are stronger than ours, everyone from us is leading a double life. And whoever wants to live their freedom like Fadime Şahindal is being killed by her father. Turkish men have locked their own wives at home. But they themselves are on the streets, looking for Swedish women. The Swedes have seen this dishonesty and they do not want to be abused. They ask us, where are your wives, your daughters, and your sisters?" (Zafer, FG, FGM).

The above transmitted data also indicates that the communication between two different cultures is also functioning as a cultural negotiation and as a result of this, transformations occur in both cultures. According to the expressions of the immigrants, the 'relaxed manner' of women is being discussed as an issue in Swedish society unlike in the past. The families advise their daughters not to be friends with the immigrants in order to not be 'abused.'

Şahika, who is a mother of three, stated that the sexuality age in Sweden is quiet low and that this is affecting her own children: "The Swedes who were looking down on us have started to learn how to protect the 'honour' of their daughters from the Turkish immigrants" (Şahika, SG, FGM). What is interesting is that the Swedes are protecting their 'honour' from Turkish male immigrants.

This frame finds an answer in both societies which has been named as a use-being abused relation by a vast majority of the immigrants from Turkey. This is because the Swedish State, with the expression of an interviewee, has started a war against 'honour.' According to the majority of the interviewees, along with this war, the male immigrants from Turkey have increased the honour based pressure on female relatives even more: "If the Swedes would not talk about honour all the time and if they would not insist that our women should be like their women, neither my husband nor his family would put so much pressure on me" (Şengül, SG, FGM).

According to Zehra (26), who is a SGM and has one child, there are two parameters which are the cause of obsession of the Swedish State and society with 'honour and the fact that the immigrant women are locked up in homes.' One of the parameters is 'the fact that the male immigrants treat the Swedish women with whom they had an affair like a dirty piece of cloth, and the second parameter is the murder of Fadime Şahindal by her father because she was living together with a Swedish man': "The gossips which were being talked behind closed doors before and which were targeting Swedish women are now spilled. And the murder of Fadime has put the image of the Swedish in the heads of the immigrants. In other words, they said if that issue was so important for you as to kill Fadime and her lover, why did you do the same to our women for years? And this is not just living simply together and having an affair, our men do sambo with these women for years and they leave these women after many years once they got pregnant. They never call the woman or the child. I have such friends, they are 20 years old and they have not seen their fathers once" (Zehra, FG, SGM).

Unlike Zehra, the majority of the interviewees justify both these attitude towards the Swedish woman and the murder of Fadime. This frame also displays the point of views of both societies regarding the concepts of morality and violence. According to the interviewees, one of the biggest segregation points of the Swedes and the immigrants from Turkey is the approach of both societies to violence. All of the interviewees with a low education and income level, as well as many interviewees with a higher education and income level, have stated that 'they could not explain to the Swedes that violence is from time to time a necessary method even if the issue is regarding honour.'

But according to lawyer Recep, who is also a SGM, the assertiveness of the Swedes is actually the reason of these murders: "Here, the request of the state and the community from you is quite clear: change your culture, leave your wives free. Ok it is nice, but is this mentality issue something that can be changed simultaneously? Look, Fadime's family let their daughter study, they have sent her to another city… But she went and started to live in the same house with a Swede without being legally married and as if this was not enough, she went off to the parliament and said 'immigrant women lead a double-life.' The murderer here is not the uneducated father of Fadime, but the Swedish State who let Fadime go to the parliament and let her talk there. This state should try to understand the immigrants rather than forcing them" (Recep, FG, SGM).

According to the majority of the interviewees, the Swedish State has used the incident of Fadime in order to display the differences of the two cultures that emerged at the level of civilisation. A SGM, Halil, studying at the university who is a second grade relative of Fadime, calls the aftermath of the murder as a 'cultural lynch' as well as before the murder. According to Halil, the incident of Şahindal is a process where the Swedes have announced their own culture as more civilised and humane over the Eastern cultures. However, the Swedes are not the only ones that are ethnocentric. The father of Fadime who has killed her has focused on the importance of honour in terms of his culture in his defense at the court and has openly stated that he 'has killed his daughter as she choose a Western lifestyle' (http://bianet.org. last viewed: 08.12.2011).

These statements will become more meaningful when considered along with the language that has been developed by the immigrants against the moral values of the Swedes: "Turkish immigrants smile at the faces of the Swedes, once they turned their back they looked down on them saying that they are sluts and have no morals. They used to see their women as a prey and they did not have any respect for their men" (Nermin, FG, FGM).

Discussion

This study is part of the wide scoped study on honour and gender perspective of Turkish migrants living in Sweden, which has been realised with the post PhD research scholarship, which has been allocated to myself by The Scientific and Technological Research Council of Turkey 2013 between the months February and July. I have interviewed the immigrants who have participated in this research study within the framework of a guideline which consisted of five questions. The research data have foremostly revealed that the transformations that occurred at the immigration and multiculturalism centre line of the honour perception of Turkish immigrants affected the communication between the two cultures in an adverse manner.

The results of this research study show that all of interviewees seen honour as the important cultural right and they think that honour helps them to protect their genealogy both culturally and biologically from other ethnic and cultural groups. So, Turkish immigrants perceive honour as natural, normal, and even further as a precondition to be a human being and they take it as a basic reference point in their communication with other cultures. The absence of honour from the point of view of the immigrants is equal to the absence of culture, morals, and faith. This point of view leads to a cultural segregation which emerges from the honour centre line and consequently affects the communication between these two cultures in a negative manner.

According to this, while Turkish immigrants were criticising them on the grounds that the Swedes were "devoid of sexual morality," the Swedish were criticising the Turkish immigrants because of their honour norms. The Swedish State and society has brought the concept of honour and the life conditions of the Turkish women for discussion, which were formed around the concept of honour along with the view points which were subjects of this discussion. These discussions led to the induration of the honour perception of the Turkish immigrants. The immigrants were reading the discussions and criticism in question as an intervention and attack to their culture. The negotiations between the two cultures cause various transformations in both cultures and we could even say that a new culture emerges from these two. The data that has been acquired within the context of the research study show that the concept of honour does not only affect the communication between the Turkish immigrants and the Swedes, but also cause transformations in both cultures. It is obvious that the aforementioned transformations widen the distance between the two cultures. What is more important is that the transformation that moves over 'our women-your women' discussions has caused the marking of the women members of both cultures as a sexual commodity and has led to the narrowing of the area of freedom.

References

Kymlicka, Will (1998). *Multicultural Citizenship/The Liberal Theory of Minority Rights*. Abdullah Yılmaz (Translation), Ayrıntı Publications: İstanbul.

Knoblauch, Hubert (2001). Communication, Contexts and Culture: A communicative constructivist approach to intercultural communication, In. Aldo Di Luzio (Eds.), *Culture in Communication: Analyses of Interculturel Situations* (pp. 3–34). John Benjamin Publising Company: Amsterdam.

Partha Chatterjee (2002). *Nation and its Pieces*. İsmail Çekem (Translation), İletişim Publications: İstanbul.

Peristiany, J. G. (1965). Honour and Shame in a Cyprıot Highland Village, In. J. G. Peristiany (Eds.), *Honour and Shame the Values of Mediterranean Society* (pp. 171–191). The University of Chicago Press: Chicago.

Tillion, Germiane (2006). *Harem ve Kuzenler.* Şirin Tekeli and Nükhet Sirman (Translation), Metis Publications: İstanbul.

Honor crisis between the State and the municipalities in Sweden, http://bianet.org.

Adem Burak Çakmak & Barış Yavuz

A Recommendation of Using Location Density Gathered from Wireless Networks for Human Science

Introduction

Deploying big data analytics methods on mobile network subscriber's location data not only gives an opportunity for mobile operators to bring new revenue generating products to the markets but can also be used for social benefits purposes. In this study, we will briefly explain how huge and precious mobile subscriber location density data is used for social benefits besides for business purposes, such as in the medical, disaster, and transportation planning areas. For example, if location data such as how many people has travelled from one specific area to another within a city during rush hour and which routes they have preferred can be gathered from mobile network subscriber data, then the best transportation plans can be created for city residents in order to decrease time wasted and money. We will share the statistic results for the use cases in which we have performed big data analysis on real mobile subscriber data.

Methods

Deploying business logics on big data systems is one of the popular topics among the information technology (IT) community. Services on top of data warehouses are especially common usage examples of big data technologies. By this way, corporations can easily analyse their customers regarding past expenses, behaviours, usage, etc. This makes companies eligible to offer new campaigns for extra services, to increase customer loyalty, and to conduct internal analysis.

A year ago, Turkcell launched a new service called Smart Map which is a new approach to the location based services business in which population density is considered. It is targeted to be an enriched geomarketing platform with unique Turkcell capabilities.

Turkcell has several advantages to produce such a platform. First of all, it is the biggest GSM operator in Turkey with 35 million subscribers. Turkcell also has advanced data processing know how to generate valuable information like profile, economic status, gender, marital status, and so on.

Another great capability of Turkcell is their network monitoring probes. These probes gather mobile signalling activities from 30,000 2G/3G base stations which cover 99.13% of the population. Activities like location update, SMS/MMS signalling, call origination/termination, and establishing data sessions are monitored by these probes and related signalling data is consolidated in a central system.

Finally, Turkcell runs periodic coverage simulations in order to calculate real coverage areas of every individual base station. After obtaining the results, the whole country is partitioned into tiny grids. Another partitioning is performed for the neighbourhoods in the residential areas. Coverage percentages of these base stations are shared into grids and neighbourhoods by also considering road networks and residential populations living in those areas.

By bringing up coverage ratios, profile information from data warehouses, and network activities from the central system for every part of the country together, the Turkcell Smart Map emerges.

One of the great advantages of the Smart Map is user lists. The system accepts custom MSISDN lists which are prepared in external platforms and produces a density map for those lists. For now, this feature is used for commercial purposes like obtaining a density map of a customer list of an enterprise.

Besides serving the geomarketing industry, this service can be used for several social problems. In this article, we will cover several social problems that Smart Maps can contribute to for research and analysis.

Findings

The main use cases for Smart Maps in social perspectives are as follows:

- Medical
- Employement
- Disaster Management
- Transportation Planning

For each case, our research details information and benefits which are given below.

Medical Research Studies

For many epidemics and other diseases, determining the location of the start point is crucial to discover the source. Such kind of investigation is mostly started from the home address of the patients. However, this sometimes causes researchers to miss the correct location source. In 1854, Dr. Jon Snow discovered that cholera was spread from a water pump in Soho district in London which killed 127 people. Dr. Snow first created a map regarding the addresses of the victims. Most of the victims were near Broad Street but some of them were far away from that location. He then conducted interviews with the relatives of the victims and he discovered that every victim drank water from the pump on Broad Street. However, some of them were sitting far away from that location. He made several more interviews and learned that those victims also filled their buckets from the same pump as it was the only well operating pump within a few square kilometres. Figure 1 shows the cholera map of Dr. Snow which was obtained from the addresses of the victims.

Figure 1: Cholera map of Dr. Snow

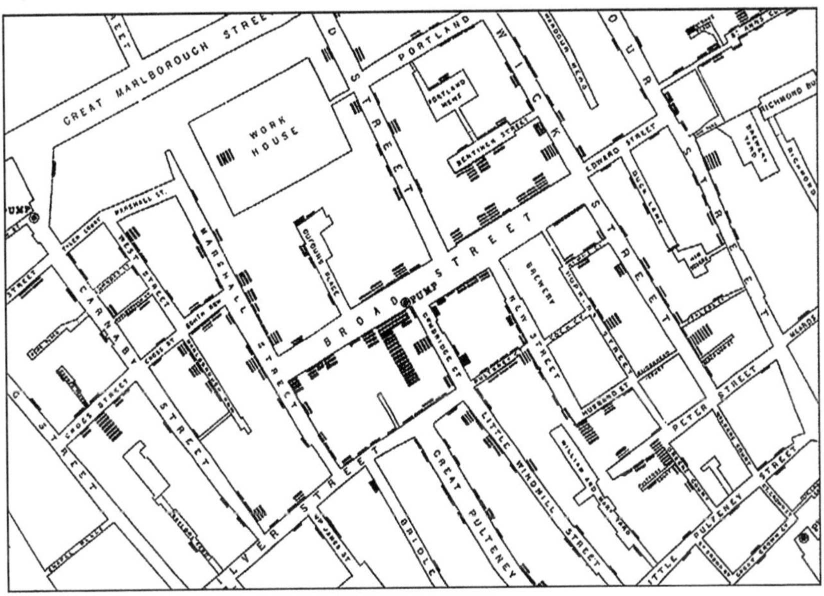

In order to identify the source for such kind of epidemic, GSM signals can be used to determine the exact location. If such kind of disease happens in our times, every victim's common presence location in any time can easily found.

Besides epidemic cases, GSM signals can also be used for hereditary and subsequently acquired diseases. For example, in Dilovasi city in Turkey, a lot of cancer incidents are observed. This region is highly industrialised and a lot of chemical facilities operate together. Micro detailed analysis can be performed in order to determine the exact locations that all victims are subjected to the oncogenic material. The map in Figure 2 is created on the macro scale. Maps which use GSM signals will not be static as in this example. It would be on a micro scale and have a dynamic density layer in the time domain.

Figure 2: World cancer map in 2008

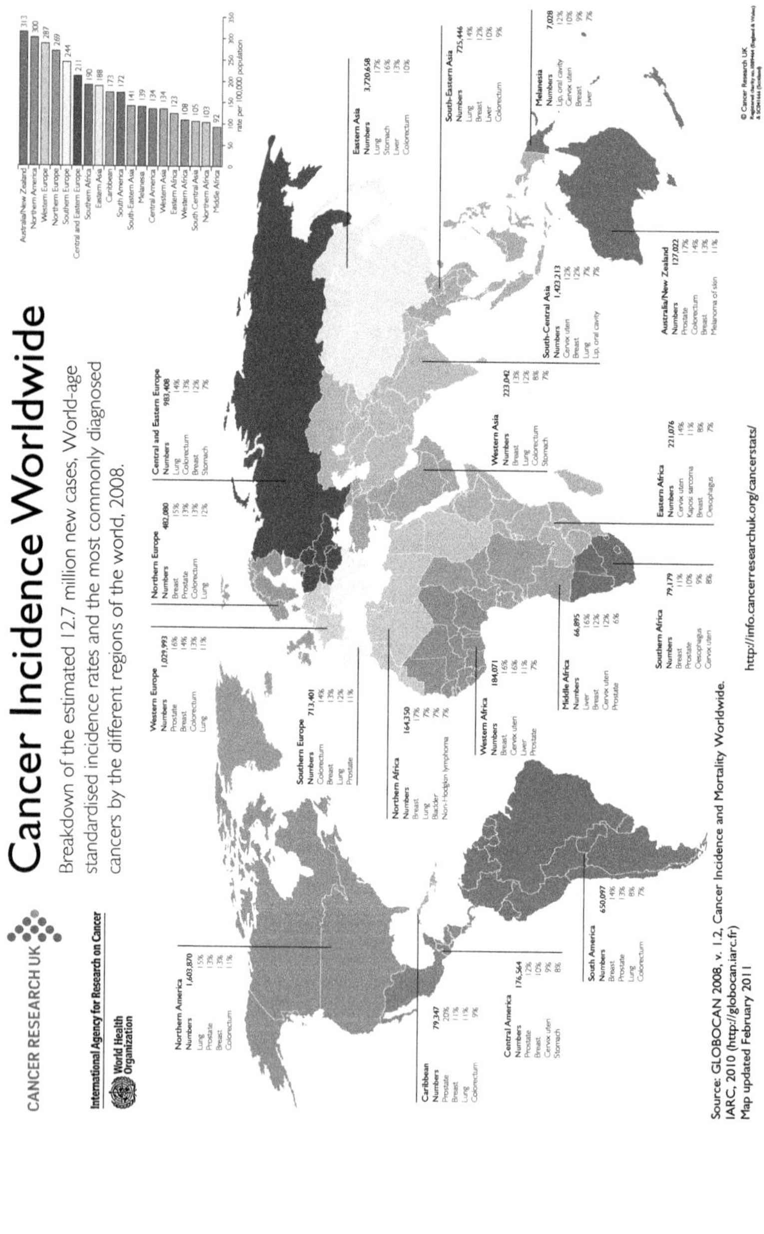

Unregistered Employment

In third world countries, a lot of workers are employed without being registered to social security agencies. This makes those people and their families vulnerable to handle medical problems and unemployment and prevents them from making retirement plans for older ages.

GSM signals can also be used to detect such kind of unregistered employment. People who are not informed about the social security agency and make periodic location changes in the morning and evening times can be suspicious to be employed illegally and those people and the workplaces should be investigated deeply in order to uncover such kind of incidents.

Disaster Management

Turkey is a country of 74 million people that straddles the continents of Europe and Asia. More than 80% of the land surface is rough, broken, and mountainous, and of limited agricultural value. Nearly 85% of the land is at an elevation of at least 450 metres and the median altitude of the country is 1,128 metres [3]. As is shown in Figures 3, Turkey is one of the most seismically active countries in the world, situated at the meeting point of multiple tectonic plates. Since 1900, an estimated 90,000 people have lost their lives in 76 earthquakes, with a total affected population of seven million people and direct losses of over 25 billion United States (US) dollars [4]. Most of these earthquakes occurred along the North Anatolian Fault, which cuts across northern Turkey from east to west. Many seismologists believe that the next big earthquake will strike close to Istanbul with a reported 75% chance that a magnitude 7.0 earthquake will occur within 40 years [5].

Figure 3: Map showing seismic activity and earthquakes in Turkey during November 2013

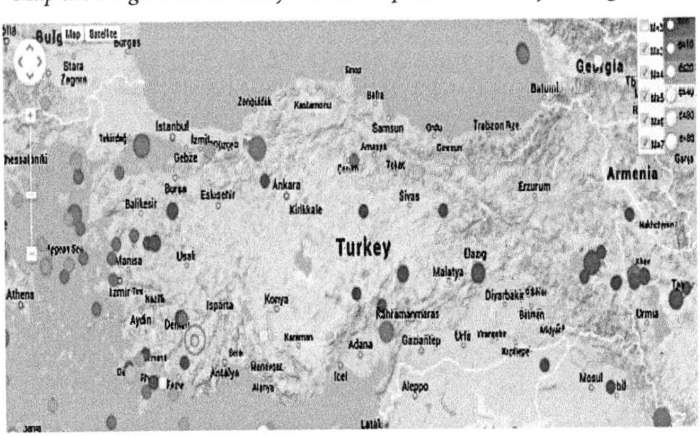

Earthquakes are one of the most critical natural disasters which Turkey is faced with. There are also floods, forest fires, and landslide risks. Each natural disaster is different and presents a unique set of challenges which cannot be fully planned or prepared for. However, in order to minimise the impact of a disaster, preparation is very critical. However, organising and supporting the affected people after a disaster is fundamental. Missing people and the reporting of such is a major issue after all disasters so the Smart Map product can be very effective as governmental agencies such as the Republic of Turkey Prime Ministry Disaster and Emergency Management Presidency (AFAD) seek to locate affected people in affected areas. The Smart Map can provide the locations of population masses in which increments are based on province, district, neighbourhood, and even grids (400×400 metrrs) smaller than neighbourhoods, for a period of time in the past (as is shown in Figure 4). Therefore, the AFAD or other search and rescue organisations can decide where the possible targeted places are located based on the most crowded places before the disaster has happened. In addition to that, after a disaster, Smart Map analysis can also run and evaluate the new populated places in order to send support teams. Finally, Smart Map based location density big data analysis facilities can bring a precious asset for developing comprehensive disaster management plans in such countries like Turkey that carry tremendous natural disaster risks.

Figure 4: Smart Map population density before disaster (a simulation example)

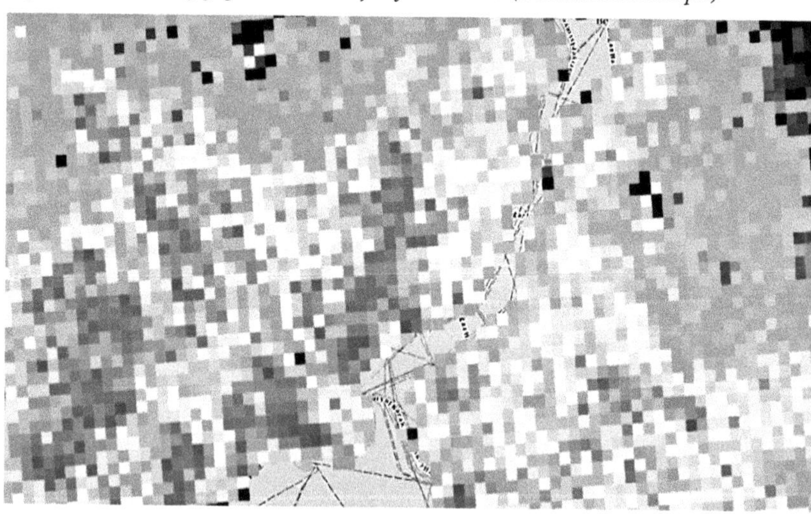

Transportation Planning

Today, transportation has significant importance for countries for their economic and social development. A good and well-planned transport system may substantially increase agricultural and industrial production as it enables products to reach markets at competitive prices. It may also boost foreign trade and enhance tourism revenues and ultimately national income [6]. On the other hand, there is a very high level of migration into cities and there are of course increasing demands of residents causing problems for metropolitan areas around the world that are grappling with transportation congestion. Since transportation planning is not being done efficiently, the biggest problem Turkey will face in the near future is not maintaining a liveable environment as their populations grow. Even if there are efforts on the municipality side and efforts on the central government side, technological improvements and innovations should be considered and tried for smart efficient transportation. In that case, our Smart Map application, which provides location density and movement analysis using GSM mobility data, can be a solution for smart efficient transportation. Some use case metrics which we have extracted from the real GSM data (40 million subscribers) using the Smart Map application and their benefits from Turkey transportation point of view are as follows:

According to our analysis, 1,250,000 people have left Istanbul during the Feast of Sacrifice in 2013. 83% of them went to the Anatolia side and 17% of them went to the Europe site. Based on visitors in the Anatolia direction, 76% of them went via the Sakarya route and 24% went via the Yalova route. These statistics can give us an idea of what the direction of traffic intensity for the Feasts in Turkey would be and the transportation plan can be shaped according to this analysis. For example, new roads or additional trains, planes, or bus voyages are provided to travelers.

In Istanbul, there are two bridges that connect the European and Asian sides. Many people cross these bridges every day for business or traveling purposes. Most of the traffic congestion occurs on these bridge roads. If we can figure out which districts or micro areas (400m × 400m grids which Smart Map provides density information in a minimum area) people uses on their travel as a start and destination point every day, then all public or private transportation can be planned efficiently and the number of transporters on time basis can be decided upon using that movement analysis data provided by Smart Map application. For example, based on one of our smart map analysis:

- Place: "Buyaka Mall" in Ümraniye, Istanbul
- Time period: Sunday between 14:00–19:00
- People which have visited the mall came from;

- o 37.5% Ümraniye
- o 10% Üsküdar
- o 7.6% Kadıköy
- o 6.7% Çekmeköy
- o 5.8% Ataşehir
- o 5.4% Sancaktepe
- o Others

Finally, we have run an analysis for Istanbul Atatürk and Adana Airports. As is shown Figure 5, according to the Smart Map movement analysis, travelers that go from Istanbul to Adana generally pass to Mersin, Hatay, and Kahramanmaras. This direction information will certainly give an idea for transport companies.

Figure 5: Smart Map analysis for Istanbul - Adana flights

Discussion

As a conclusion, this paper has shown how mobile subscriber density data can be used and applied to different demands beside business purposes such as in medical, transportation, employment, or disaster management. It can also bring a precious asset to human life in order to prevent the wasting of time and money.

References

Geology of Turkey - http://en.wikipedia.org/wiki/Geology_of_Turkey
The International Disaster Database - www.emdat.be

Shigeko Segawa (2012), Turkey Prepares for the Inevitable Big Earthquake -, The Asahi Shimbun Science and Medical News Section

Transportation in Turkey, Country Report, 2011, Republic of Turkey Ministry of Transport and Communication

Steven Johnson (2007), John Snow Famous Cholera Map - http://flowingdata.com/2007/09/12/john-snows-famous-cholera-map/

World Cancer Map - http://cancercareunited.org/worldcancermap/

Ahmet Tarhan & Mustafa Bal

Corporate Social Responsibility Practice Implications in New Communication Platforms

Introduction

Nowadays, it seems rather difficult to maintain the companies through only seeking profit. As well as the profit motive, the companies also should show themselves in other fields to their target groups. One of those fields is corporate social responsibility. Bowen (1953: 6) defined social responsibility as the whole of obligations and necessities related to improving social life through deciding and determining the policies related to social values and expectations as well as their own purposes. Some of the obligations that lead companies to social responsibility applications are as follows: the increasing level of income in Turkey, the consumers who gain awareness, similarity of almost all the products and services except small differences in the markets (Ülger, 2003: 118), increasing levels of social expectations and sensitivity to environment, and the companies which desire to locate themselves next to the target groups different from their rivals (Tarhan, 2011: 540).

The leading factor that provides the enterprise with a competitive advantage against rivals is the positive impression gained with corporate reputation and brand value. The images and brand names, which are intangibles and enable the companies to communicate with their target groups, gain strength through social responsibility activities and provide a competitive advantage via their rivals (Crowther and Aras, 2008: 61). Thus, the social responsibility activities which the companies will execute through gaining awareness about their responsibilities will turn them back into a positive image (Peltekoğlu, 2012: 189). According to a survey published in the Fortuna Journal by the Hay Group, an international consulting company, the corporate social responsibility activities, as well as financial and administrative factors of the companies, are also regarded a criteria for the list of "The Top Admired Companies of the United States of America." In the study which was carried out in such an important field, the study clearly shows that the presentation of corporate social responsibility as a criterion affects the corporate image (Kotler and Lee, 2006:15).

When it is considered from the point of the benefits of the internet and corporate web pages in presenting the social responsibility messages of the companies and applications, the most important benefits are as follows: the companies may present the messages they desire to the groups without agents or delays and filtration of other people (Ihator, 2001:18); the use of it in establishing a positive image against traditional mass communication media (Insch, 2008:141); it enables companies to make contact with target groups through collecting necessary information about them (Cooley, 1999:41); it provides the companies, which send their messages without being exposed to any limitations and obstructions, the power of "determining the agenda" (Esrock and Leichty, 1999:457); and provides an opportunity for a dialogue for higher interaction, as well as accessing the groups through the internet and social media (Cooley, 1999:42). Despite the advantages it provides, the activities which the companies execute are only announced through their web pages and this isn't enough for them to express themselves completely.

The companies have to adapt themselves to the social networks which have gained significance and usage in recent years. This is because social networks revolutionise the communication methods which companies traditionally developed, the ways to distribute their products, the services, potential customer attracting methods, the methods to establish brand experience, and the methods to support and provide customer relations (Fisk, 2009:292). Thus, the companies have to follow social media accounts which billions of people use all over the world and express themselves in those accounts. According to the studies executed in Spain, for example (Vicente and Araceli, 2012:47; Lina and Ivette, 2011:166), it is seen that companies use their Facebook and Twitter accounts in social media accounts with the purposes of business and advertisements which the companies use; however, it is seen that they don't use those social media accounts for corporate responsibility messages, although those social media accounts provide numerous interaction and dialog alternatives.

Methodology

In this chapter, the model, population, and sampling method of the research study and the evaluation related to the method to be used in the collection of data are employed. In this research study, the social responsibility messages collected from the web pages and corporate social media accounts of the top 500 industrial companies determined by the Istanbul Chamber of Industry were analysed through content analysis.

Within the scope of the research study, generally, we analysed the distribution of industrial companies according to their sectors, whether they employ social responsibility messages on their corporate social media accounts, the ways they presented those messages in their corporate web pages and the ways those messages are presented, and the distribution of those messages according to their sectors. Moreover, we analysed the corporate social media instruments of companies that employ social responsibility messages in their corporate web pages, the time and frequency of time which they share those messages, the distribution of those messages according to their social responsibility fields, and the distribution of those messages according to sectors.

In accessing this data, the first 100 companies among the top 500 companies of Turkey in 2013, which were declared by the Istanbul Chamber of Industry, were handled and the data of the research study were obtained by forming a coding scale. Moreover, the content typing scale by Esrock and Leichty (2000), the basic categories used by Kalender and Bakan (2006) in their study, and the study by Tarhan (2011) related to environmental social responsibility were used to gather the data showing the ways that the messages of social responsibility were presented on web pages and social media accounts. After the sampling and related categories were determined, we evaluated whether the top industrial companies employ messages related to social responsibility on their corporate web pages and their corporate social media accounts and the ways they submit their messages. The coding process was executed between August 16–26, 2014.

Findings

The distribution of industrial companies according to sectors, the quality of the links which employ messages related to social responsibility on the corporate web pages, the ways which the messages on the web pages are presented, the social responsibility fields of the messages on the web pages, and the distribution of those messages according to their sectors are presented. Among the findings given below, moreover, issues such as whether industrial companies employ the links which lead to social media accounts from their corporate web pages, the distribution of messages in the corporate social media accounts of the industrial companies which employ those links, the social responsibility fields which they apply messages to, and their distribution according to sectors were also included.

Fields of Activity for the Industrial Companies

When the sectoral distribution of industrial companies is considered, the sectors are as follows: food, iron/steel, automotive, energy/petrol, construction/building, electrics/electronics, chemicals/drugs, mines, glass/ceramics, textile/garment industry, machinery, and transportation. Among the companies which were taken as samples, the food sector is the most represented sector with 23 companies, the iron/steel sector follows it with 21 companies, and the third rank belongs to the automotive sector with twelve companies. The transporting and machinery sectors are only represented with one enterprise each. Moreover, it is striking that 94 of those companies are private companies, while only six of them are public industrial companies.

The Distribution of Social Responsibility Messages on Corporate Web Pages

It was determined that 84 (84%) of the industrial companies which were evaluated within the scope of the research study announced the activities they executed related to social responsibility fields through their corporate web pages, while 16 (16%) of them applied no message related to the social responsibility activities. It may be regarded as a significant development that the applications which occupy an important place for the companies in constructing and solidifying a positive image, as well as social responsibility, are applied by the majority of industrial companies determined as the sample of the study.

Table 1. The ways of transmitting social responsibility messages on corporate web pages

	Exist		Absent		Total	
	F	%	F	%	F	%
Text	80	95.2	4	4.8	84	100.0
Media release	60	71.4	24	28.6	84	100.0
Annual report	32	38.1	52	61.9	84	100.0
Brochure text	2	2.4	82	97.6	84	100.0
Corporate journal	13	15.5	71	84.5	84	100.0
Audio-visual materials	60	71.4	24	28.6	84	100.0

The communication type where industrial companies submit their messages related to social responsibilities to target groups through their corporate web pages was evaluated. It was observed that the companies simultaneously use more than one communication type in transmitting their social responsibility messages. When the ways of transmitting social responsibility messages by the companies are considered, almost all the companies (95.2%) use texts in transmitting their messages. The majority of companies (71.4%) benefit from both press bulletins and announcing activities through audio-visual activities. Those instruments are followed by annual activity reports with a rate of 38.1%, corporate journals with a rate of 15.5%, and brochure texts with a rate of 2.4%.

When the findings showing that the social responsibility messages announced by the industrial companies through their corporate web pages are related to the social responsibility fields are considered, it is striking to see that almost half of the 1,607 messages are related to activities of the environment (23.0%) and education (20.5%) and the sensitivities related to them. They are followed by culture and art (9.3%), social responsibility (9.0%), and support to individual sportsmen (8.3%). The least executed and announced social responsibility fields are printing-publication and program-broadcasting with a rate of 0.1%.

Table 2. The distribution of messages according to their social responsibility fields

	F	%
Environment	370	23.0
Education	330	20.5
Culture and art	149	9.3
Public responsibility	144	9.0
Individual sportsmen	133	8.3
Health	99	6.2
Activities related to workers	94	5.8
Science	76	4.7
Sports teams	52	3.2
Festivals/contests	43	2.7
Sports organisations	42	2.6
Exhibitions	30	1.9
Activities related to physically handicapped people	26	1.6
Protection of cultural and historical artifacts	13	0.8
Visual arts	4	0.2
Printing-publication	1	0.1
Program-broadcasting	1	0.1
Total	**1,607**	**100.0**

It can be said that, from the point of findings, industrial companies give more place to activities and announcements related to the environment in order to remove the general opinion about the harm they give to the environment while they produce, a good perspective turning it into a favourable impression. Moreover, it is also seen that the efforts to fill this gap when public funding is insufficient in education in our country, which has a young population, have priority from the point of constructing and maintaining a positive image of industrial companies.

Another topic to be analysed is the distribution of the messages which the industrial companies presented through their corporate web pages. Almost one fifth of the messages which industrial companies presented through their corporate web pages (319, 19.9%) belong to the industrial companies in the automotive sector. It is followed by the food sector with 279 messages (17.4%) and the iron/steel sector with 248 messages (15.4%). When the sectors which employ the social responsibility messages the least are considered, it is seen that the machinery sector has 6 messages (0.4%) and transportation sector has 4 messages (0.2%).

The Distribution of Social Responsibility Messages in Corporate Social Media Accounts

The distribution of messages of industrial companies related to social responsibility activities were also evaluated from the point of social media instruments. The corporate social media accounts of the 84 industrial companies, which give social responsibility messages through their corporate web pages, were also analysed.

It was determined that some of the 84 industrial companies which forward to their social media accounts from their corporate web pages only use either their Facebook or Twitter accounts, while some of them forward to both social media accounts. Accordingly, the number of industrial companies which forward to both Facebook and Twitter is 40. The number of industrial companies which forward to only Facebook is six, while the number of industrial companies which forward to only Twitter is one.

When the distribution of Facebook and Twitter social media instruments is considered, it was found that 46 of 84 industrial companies (54.8%) forwarded to Facebook and 41 of them (48.8%) forwarded to Twitter social media means.

Table 3. The companies which present social responsibility messages through their corporate social media accounts

	Exist		Absent		Total	
	F	**%**	**F**	**F**	**%**	**F**
Twitter	18	43.9	23	56.1	41	100.0
Facebook	24	52.2	22	47.8	46	100.0

Among the 46 industrial companies which forward to Facebook from their corporate web pages, 24 of them (52.2%) employ social responsibility messages, while 22 of them (47.8%) don't employ messages related to social responsibility activities at all. On the other hand, among 41 industrial companies which forward to Twitter from their corporate web pages, 18 of them (43.9%) share their social responsibility messages through this instrument, while 23 of them (56.1%) don't prefer this instrument in sharing their social responsibility messages.

Another topic to be analysed is the temporal distribution of the messages of the industrial companies whose corporate social media accounts were analysed for a period of three months (15 May–15 August). Total quantity of the messages which industrial companies presented through their corporate social media accounts is 195. Of those messages, 90 of them (46.2%) were forwarded between the dates of 15 May and 15 June, 56 of them (28.7%) were forwarded between the dates of 16 June and 15 July, while 49 of them (25.1%) were forwarded between the dates of 16 July and 15 August.

It is seen that almost half of the corporate social media messages (46.2%) were shared between the dates of 15 May and 15 June. The most important factor in this result is the sharing executed by the industrial companies in connection with the World Environment Day on 5 June. This data corresponds to the finding that the messages are highest in quantity in the distribution of the social responsibility messages presented in social media.

Table 4. The distribution of the messages presented in social media according to social responsibility fields

	Facebook	**Twitter**	**Total**	**%**
Environment	26	22	48	24.6
Activities related to workers	18	17	35	17.9
Public responsibility	13	14	27	13.8
Education	13	8	21	10.8
Festivals/contests	13	4	17	8.7
Sports teams	9	3	12	6.2
Sports organisations	6	3	9	4.6
Culture and art	5	4	9	4.6
Science	4	3	7	3.6
Health	2	4	6	3.1
Activities related to disabled people	3	1	4	2.1
Total	**112**	**83**	**195**	**100.0**

The distribution of the messages which industrial companies forward through their corporate social media accounts according to fields was also analysed. It is followed by the activities related to the workers with 35 messages (17.9%), social responsibility with 27 messages (13.8%), and education with 21 messages (10.8%). The least forwarded social responsibility messages belong to health with six messages (3.1%) and the support to disabled people with four messages (2.1%). It is striking here that the environment and education occupy the first rank on the corporate web pages and the highest rank of messages on social media accounts were related to the environment and the activities for the workers.

The distribution of messages which industrial companies forwarded through their corporate social media accounts was analysed. In light of this information, 38 of 195 messages (19.5%) presented in the corporate social media accounts were given by the companies in the energy/petrol sector. It is followed by the food sector with 37 messages (19.0), constructing/building sector with 35 messages (17.9%), and iron/steel sector with 34 messages (17.4%). The sector which forwards the least social responsibility messages from corporate social media accounts is glass/ceramic with one message (0.5%), while sectors such as chemicals/drugs, textile/ready wear, machinery, and transport were seen to employ no social responsibility messages on their corporate social media accounts.

It was determined in the research study that almost all the social responsibility messages (87.2%) in the corporate social media accounts that were obtained during the period of three months where the account of social media was analysed came from five basic industrial sectors. These are energy/petrol, food, construction/building, iron/steel, and electrics/electronics. Nevertheless, the industrial companies which carry on business in important sectors such as chemistry/drugs, textile/ready wear, machinery, and transportation were seen to share no messages related to their social responsibility fields from their social media accounts. The non-existence of messages shared by the industrial companies which occupy an important place both in Turkey and around the world may be regarded as a deficiency.

Finally, the rates of incidence in the social responsibility messages presented by the industrial companies through their corporate web pages into their corporate social media accounts were analysed. Accordingly, only 26 messages (21.7%) among the 120 social responsibility messages shared by the industrial companies which function in the electrics/electronics sector are forwarded through corporate social media accounts. It is followed by the energy petrol sector which employs 38 messages in social media among 201 messages shared (18.9%) and the industrial companies which serve in the construction/building sector which employ 35 messages in social media among the 205 messages shared. Moreover, another striking topic is that industrial companies in the chemistry/drugs sector, which shares 94 messages in their corporate web pages, and the textile/ready wear sector, which shares 36 messages, both don't announce such activities through their social media accounts.

Conclusions

Nowadays, social responsibility activities possess great significance from the point of public relations. The companies provide support to the society that they give products and services to in order to form an impression that they provide support except for their activity fields and develop positive perceptions. It is important to gain the expected favour from the activities announced to the target group. Especially after the popularisation of new communication technologies, the companies prefer announcing those activities through the corporate web pages where they can control their content and their corporate social media accounts.

At the end of the research study, it was determined that the industrial companies fail in announcing the social responsibility activities they executed using their corporate web pages. It was also determined that social responsibility activities were concentrated in fields such as the environment and education; however, the applications related to other social responsibility fields were insufficient. Another significant finding is that the messages presented through corporate web pages aren't reflected into the social media accounts of the companies enough. The corporate web pages and social media instruments, which are frequently preferred in the fields such as advertisement and announcement, aren't used enough in announcing social responsibility activities which provide a contribution to the image of companies and have positive effects on their reputation. This is viewed as a deficiency.

The companies should more actively benefit from corporate web pages and social media accounts which provide an opportunity for them to determine the content, instantly access broader groups, and engage in interactive communication. Moreover, the increase in the diversity of the executed social responsibility applications may be regarded as an obligation for both companies and society.

References

Bowen, H. R. (1953). Social Responsibilities of the Businessman, *Harper & Brothers Publishers.*

Cooley, T. (1999). Interactive Communication – Public Relations On The Web, *Public Relations Quarterly, Summer*, 144(2), P: 41–42.

Crowther, D. and ARAS, G. (2008). Corperate Social Responsibility, *Ventus Publishing.*

Esrock S. L. and Leichty G. B., (2000). Organization of Corporate Web Pages: Publics and Functions, Public Relations Review, 26(3), pp: 327–344.

Fisk, P. (2009). Customer Genius, *Capstone Publishing* Ltd., UK.

Ihator, A. (2001). Corporate Communication: Challenges and Opportunities in a Digital World, *Public Relation Quarterly*, Winter, P:15–18.

Insch, A. (2008). Online communication of Corporate Environmental Citizenship: A study of New Zealand's electricity and Gas Retailers, *Journal of Marketing Communication*, 14(2), P:139–153.

Kalender, A. ve Bakan, Ö. (2006). Kurumsal Sosyal Sorumluluğun Web Sayfalarındaki Görünümü: Sanayii Kuruluşlarının Web Sayfaları Üzerine Bir İnceleme, *New Media and Interactivity International Conference*, November 1–3, İstanbul.

Kotler, P. and Lee, N. (2006). Kurumsal Sosyal Sorumluluk, Çev: S. Kaçamak, *MediaCat*, İstanbul.

Lina, M. G. V. and Ivette, S. V. (2011). Social Media as a strategic Tool for Corporate Communication, *Revısta Internacıonal De Relacıones Publıcas*, No: 2, Vol. I, Spain.

Peltekoğlu, F. B. (2012). Halkla İlişkiler Nedir?, 7. Baskı, *Beta Yayınları*, İstanbul.

Rajendra, Bandi, P. D. Jose, Malini Mehra, (2003). "Corporate Social Responsibility in the Information and Communication Technologies Sector: Discussion", *IIMB Management Review*, 15(4), 61–77.

Tarhan, A. (2011). Kurumsal Çevre Sorumluluğu: Sanayi Kuruluşlarının Web Sayfarı Üzerine Bir Değerlendirme, *E-Journal of New World Sciences Academy*, V:6, N:3, ISSN:1306-3111, P:539–558.

Ülger, B. (2003). İşletmelerde İletişim ve Halkla İlişkiler "The Big Business", *Der Yayınları*, İstanbul.

Vicente J. R. D. and Araceli C. M. (2012). CSR Communication Through Online Social Media, *Revista Latina de Comunicación Social*, ISSN 1138-5820, P: 047–067, Spain.

Aslı Karaarslan

Cyberbullying and Child Abuse: Parent's Awareness of Cyberbullying and Child Abuse in Facebook Practices

Introduction

Telecommunications, media, and the integration of the information technology industry are related with the main factors behind the formation of new business models, modern people's position, and entity in network society. The relation and the communication between network community members and mass media differentiated and became very oriented and especially interactive. People of the network want to subsist all the time and everywhere in network society beyond all traditional forms of communication. Briefly, they want to constantly stay connected (Kandemir, 2015). These developments in communication technology have been an important and indispensable element of our life with some problems such as to access, store, and share information (Baker & Kavşut, 2007).

Besides these benefits of communication technology, some problems may occur when it is misused. These problems are unidentified malicious or infected e-mails, anonymous calls, sounds, images, and texts which include insults and threats and are emitted by e-mail or text messages (Arıcak, 2009). One of the problems, which is a result of the malicious use of communication technology, is cyberbullying.

Cyberbullying is defined in many ways, including: the misuse of communication technology by an individual or group in order to harm people and repeat this act (Li, 2006; Belsey, 2007; Hinduja and Patchin 2009); sending annoying messages or using social aggression (Willard 2007); a kind of psychological bullying using electronics such as mobile phones, websites, chat rooms, or web logs (Shariff and Goa in 2005); using intentional aggressive movements repeatedly over time by an individual or group where the victim cannot defend himself or herself against these aggressive actions (Smith et al., 2008); and receiving death threats via e-mail and messages, unauthorised picture sharing, and dissemination of shameful and false allegations (Lenhart, 2007).

Looking at the studies on cyberbullying such as Estévez et al. (2009) and Marsh et al. (2004), similar results are reached: When the cyber victimisation increases, self-confidence is low and there is a negative relationship between cyber victimisation and self-confidence. When the adolescent victim has a good relationship between his or her parents, this victim also has self-confidence. These studies stated that adolescents who faced less cyber victimisation have good communication with their parents.

Ybarra and Mitchell (2004) stated that cyberbullying and victimisation seem to be a common problem among young people. In this study, whose participants use the internet regularly, it is seen that 15% of participants are cyberbullies and 14% of participants make rude comments when they are online. These participants' ages range between ten and 17 years. In the study of Noret and Rivers (2006), in which participants are between eleven and 15, it is seen that 7% of participants received an offensive e-mail at least once in their lifetime. In the study of Raskauskas and Stoltz (2007), in which participants are students between the ages of 13 and 18 years, it is seen that 49% of students were victims of cyberbullying and 21% of students were cyberbullies.

If we look at the research studies conducted by Siyahhan, Uzunhasanoğlu, Sarıbeyoğlu, Çıplak, Yılmaz, and Memmedov (2008), it appears that 36% of Turkish students are cyberbullies. Topcu (2008) stated that 16% of secondary school students are cyberbullies and 17% of secondary school students were exposed to cyberbullying.

23% of college students have been a cyberbully at least once and 55% of college students have been exposed to cyberbullying at least once (Dilmac, 2009); however, another research study suggests that 20% of college students have been a cyberbully at least once and 54% of college students have been exposed to cyberbullying at least once (Arıcak, 2009). Peker, Eroglu, and Citemel (2012) suggested that cyberbullying shows significant differences in the sexes and it appears that men are more likely to be involved in cyberbullying compared to women.

There is a study, which is conducted regarding the comparison of Europe and Turkey, about the risks faced by children on the internet. This study has shown that 46% of children are disturbed by sexual photos in Turkey. In Europe, this rate is 33%. 8% of children, who are between nine and 16 years of age and live in Turkey, had received sexual messages and 3% of these had sent similar messages. 12% of children in Europe had received sexual messages and 3% of children said that they had sent similar messages. 50% of children in Turkey who said that they had received sexual messages feel uncomfortable, but only 25% of children in Europe who said that they had received sexual messages feel uncomfortable. 14% of children between nine to 16 years of age in Turkey had met face to face with strangers on the internet that they did not know and only 2% of these children said that they had met these strangers outside. 25% of children across Europe had met with strangers on the internet and 6% of these children had met outside with these strangers (http://www.socialmediatr.com/blog). The discomfort ratio of sexual content messages in Europe (33%) is lower than in Turkey (46%). At the same time, the ratio of people who bullied is 20% in Europe and 9% in Turkey. We have seen in this study that children who don't feel uncomfortable from the exposure to sexual content messages are more likely to be exposed to cyberbullying.

Children's internet usage in Turkey is an important area of ethical debate in terms of risk and loss. The main online risks brought by the internet are pornography, bullying, sexual messages, interacting with unknown people, meeting online established relationships with strangers, misuse of personal information, and harmful content (Aydın, 2013). These harmful components as a result of misuse can lead to child abuse.

Child abuse is a comprehensive serious problem which has complex causes and tragic consequences and includes medical, legal, developmental, and psychosocial things (Ziyalar, 1999; Polat, 2002). Child abuse is defined by the World Health Organization as a behaviour that is conducted intentionally or unintentionally and that negatively affects the health of adults and children, as well as the physical and psychosocial development of children (The First İstanbul Children Congress; Children Reports in İstanbul, 2000; Dubowitz, 2002).

Cyberbullying means hurting someone emotionally with abusive messages that are sent from mobile phones, photos that are put on internet, rude article that are published on personal blogs, and untrue rumours that are spread by e-mails rather than by directly inflicting physical harm to children (Huang and Chou, 2010).

The protection of children's privacy and privacy rights on the internet is one of the most fundamental ethical issues (Aydin, 2013). Privacy and confidentiality are described as a situation where a person's or group's personal life and personal affairs are far from being open to the public or where a person or group does not have the right to control the flow of information about themselves. There are two important elements in this issue. The first element is that only an individual should have the power to check his or her own personal information. The second element is that an individual should have the right to control the information which conflicts with his or her values and interests (Aydın, 2013).

The impact of cyberbullying can be much more severe. For example, Rebecca Ann Sedwick, who was twelve and lived in Lakeland, Florida in the United States of America, committed suicide due to her exposure to cyberbullying more than one year ago. About 15 girls frequently said to her that "you must die" and "why are you not dead yet?" on the internet and the mobile environment. Before the suicide, she had replied to her one friend: "I will jump!" Authorities said that this cyberbullying issue started about one year ago because of the boyfriend effect (http://www.milliyet.com.tr/).

To buy something is now very easy with developing technology. It is not surprising for many people to read this kind of news: "14 month old girl accidentally bought a 1962 model classic car from a shopping application on her father's smart phone while she was playing with the device."

When the work which is related to virtual bullying is checked, it can be easily seen that the relationship between children and parents is very important. However, there is no study about this issue. In this study, we research the level of parent's awareness of cyberbullying and child abuse in Facebook practices. We examine whether or not a parent's education level is important to this issue.

Methods

Research Model

One of the scanning models, the relational scanning model, was used in this study. This model's purpose is to find the presence and degree of existence between two or more variables. This model does not give real cause-effect relationships and at the same time, if the situation in a variable is known, it is known that the other can be estimated (Karasar, 2006).

Working Group

The sample of the study is 200 student's parents. These students, who are between seven to 14 years of age, are still studying at Istanbul Primary School. 96 of the 200 parents have received higher education.

Data Collection Tool

A questionnaire was used in the study which was prepared using a Likert scale. The Likert scale's main purpose is to ratie the attitudes of individuals to replay a certain attitude. The Likert scale determines whether participants approve of some points (Karasar, 2006). Parents, who have or do not have higher education, were used as independent variable and the effects of having higher education on parent's awareness of cyberbullying and child abuse in Facebook practices were used as dependent variables. We researched whether or not having received higher education has any effects on parent's awareness. Parent's awareness in Facebook practices and parents' knowledge of the social network and internet relationships were measured with a questionnaire which includes 44 questions.

Data Collection and Analysis

Research data were obtained through questionnaires which were administered face to face. The collected data were analysed using Excel.

Findings

Table 1: Findings of cyberbullying and parental awareness of child abuse of Facebook practice

		Parents who have higher education	Parents who don't have higher education
1	Before accepting something or installing something or becoming a member, the parent reads the condition of using the social network	75%	97%
2	The parent checks the information, which is published, at different sources before believing	95%	93%
3	The parent knows and implements the privacy setting in the social network	80%	88%
4	The parent uses the same password on different social networks (Facebook, Instagram, Twitter, Swarm, etc.)	16%	38%
5	The parent regularly changes the password of social media accounts (Facebook, Instagram, Twitter, Swarm, etc.)	53%	58%
6	The parent shares his or her passwords for social media accounts with other people (Facebook, Instagram, Twitter, Swarm, etc.)	6%	10%
7	The parent uses an updated anti-virus program and firewall and thinks that these are enough for protection	74%	71%
8	The parent said that he or she has information about internet relationships and virtual life	72%	69%
9	The parent thinks that virtual life makes the relationship between them and friends/family stronger	30%	28%
10	The parent gives his or her social media identity to his or her family and his or her co-workers (Facebook, Instagram, Twitter, Swarm, etc.)	33%	38%
11	The parent thinks that using Facebook is a part of social life	34%	26%

		Parents who have higher education	Parents who don't have higher education
12	The parent uses his or her real identity on Facebook	79%	86%
13	The parent thinks that the contents of Facebook negatively affect life	10%	15%
14	The parent said that he or she checks whether or not the content is safe before he or she shares photos and videos on Facebook	90%	94%
15	The parent thinks that friend request which are sent by strangers are not a threat for his or her security	21%	32%
16	The parent accepts friend requests which are sent by strangers	7%	2%
17	The parent reads messages which are sent by strangers	13%	13%
18	The parent replies to messages which are sent by strangers	3%	2%
19	The parent thinks that sharing his or her personal photos, videos, writings, and information is safe	23%	71%
20	The parent said that he or she uses Facebook's privacy settings carefully ('just me,' 'just friends,' 'public,' 'friends of my friends,' and 'special')	78%	88%
21	The parent is friends with his or her child on Facebook	50%	70%
22	The parent said that he or she shares his or her child's personal photos, videos, writings, and information and that sharing these is safe	36%	37%
23	The parent is aware of the fact that other people can follow his or her sharing that is about his or her child	71%	76%
24	The parent is happy when someone makes a good comment about his or her child's photo	48%	58%
25	The parent gets permission from his or her child before sharing his or her child's photo	49%	65%
26	The parent said that his or her child doesn't become vulnerable when he or she shares his or her child's photo	22%	27%

		Parents who have higher education	Parents who don't have higher education
27	The parent doesn't think that sharing the family members which can be shared in the "About-Family Relations" section on Facebook isn't a threat/risk	27%	37%
28	The parent tags everything such as people, place, and time in the picture	34%	36%
29	The parent said that it is not an opportunity for self-seeking people when he or she shares picture and photos which contain something about wealth	42%	55%
30	The parent shares information which is related to internet relations and virtual life with his or her child	35%	47%
31	The parent thinks that anti-virus programs and firewalls protect his or her child from harmful content	50%	52%
32	The parent speaks with his or her child about social networks and internet risks	84%	97%
33	The parent controls his or her child's computer	83%	90%
34	The parent is aware of his or her child's friends on Facebook	74%	88%
35	The parent forbids using the internet when he or she is concerned about something	92%	96%
36	The parent said to his or her child to not accept the friend requests which are sent by strangers	93%	98%
37	The parent said that his or her child says something to him or her when the child is exposed to bullying such as messages, videos, photos, etc.	80%	87%
38	The parent thinks that he or she is a good role-model about using the Internet to his or her child	75%	88%
39	The parent concerns that freedom of expression is important for communication between he or she and his or her child	94%	99%
40	The parent was exposed to behaviour that could damage (insulting, humiliating, etc.)	14%	10%

		Parents who have higher education	Parents who don't have higher education
41	The parent said that his or her child was exposed to cyberbullying	5%	12%
42	The parent is aware of the fact that cyberbullying is a crime and everybody can be sentenced because of cyberbullying	83%	86%
43	The parent knows that people can denounce behaviour like cyberbullying to this website: "www.ihbarweb.tr"	68%	82%
44	The parent denounced before these kind of behaviours	10%	13%

Discussion

This study explored the parent's awareness of cyberbullying and child abuse. This awareness of parents is researched in Facebook practices which is the most popular social network.

According to research conducted at California State University, Facebook users may have become sensitive to respond to positive impulses which are associated with social networks. These expressions are used by the Live Science website: "Facebook addicts can control their behavior, but they have no motivation to control their behavior which born with impulses. The reason for this would be that they don't believe that results will be bad for them." One of the effects which is caused by Facebook is the "fear that they are missing the opportunity" (FOMO). This situation appears when they see pictures of their friends which are taken at a party, in a café, or of their meal. Researchers have stated that "Facebook addiction," which is increasing in recent years, means that they check what is going on whether or not they want to (http://t24.com.tr/haber/). 42% of parents who have higher education and 55% of parents who do not have higher education said that it is not an opportunity for self-seeking people when they share pictures and photoss which contain something about wealth. People's increasing desire to share something on social media reveals the standard of living that users have.

Cyberbullying does not only target adults. Content, which are created by us about our children, can be used in a bad way by malicious people. Parents feel safer than children and parents think that their children are more prone to risks. 71% of parents who think that sharing their personal photos, videos, writings, and information is safe, but only 37% of parents who have higher education said that they share their child's personal photos, videos, writings, and information and that sharing these is safe.

It is important that parents get permission from their child before sharing their child's photo. 49% of parents who have higher education and 65% of parents who do not have higher education get permission from their child before sharing their child's photo. However, Lenhart (2007) said that sharing photos without permission is cyberbullying. When we set out from this definition, we can easily say that children are exposed to cyberbullying if their parents do not get permission from their children before sharing their child's photo.

Furthermore, if parents do not use their real identity on Facebook, they are considered a cyberbully. Aricak (2009) defined cyberbullying as being "unidentified" and "anonymous." This study stated that 79% of parents who have higher education and 86% of parents who don't have higher education use their real identity on Facebook.

6% of parents who have higher education and 10% of parents who don't have higher education share their password for social media accounts with other people (Facebook, Instagram, Twitter, Swarm, etc.). Although parents' awareness of this issue is high, because of the lack of experience, children's awareness isn't. Children share their personal information to be member of a club. At this point, parents should share their experience to protect children.

21% of parents that received higher education and 32% of parents that did not receive higher education think that friendship invitations from unknown people on Facebook create a security threat. 7% of parents that received higher education and 2% of parents that did not receive higher education accept invitations from unknown accounts on Facebook. Nevertheless, even though both parent groups do not think that the invitations from unknown accounts do not create a security threat, they still reject these invitations.

The internet, mobile phones, and SMS communications make life easier; however, they can be turned into harmful instruments by malicious people (Arıcak, 2009). In order for the users to decide the audience of the information they are sharing, there are settings, such as: "only me," "only friends," "public," "my friends' friends," and "Custom." 78% of parents that received higher education and 71% of parents that did not receive higher education use these settings carefully. When we choose the "my friends' friends" option, people in the friend list of our friends will be able to see the information we share. We may choose people carefully on any social media platform but one of our friends may not. That is, when you use this option, it is easier for a malevolent person in your friend's friend list to reach your content.

Furthermore, the misuse of information and communication technologies causes internet addiction, plagiarising of assignments, cheat exchange via mobile phones, easy access to bomb making web pages or to racist/discriminative web pages, pornographic web pages, or sexual abuse via electronic-based communication devices (Erdur-Baker & Kavşut, 2007; Morahan-Martin & Schumacher, 2000; Valkenburg, Karen, & Soeters, 2001; Wright, Joy, Christopher & Heather, 2009). Therefore, the security settings of social media which we use should be carefully and properly set.

27% of parents that received higher education and 37% of parents that did not receive higher education think that adding family members in the "family and relationships" option of the "about" section of their account does not cause any security risk/threat. Adding our uncle to the "about" section means that we give our mother's maiden name. Our mother's maiden name is information that we should not share with everyone.

72% of parents that received higher education and 69% of parents that did not receive higher education claim that they know about internet relations and virtual life. 35% of parents that received higher education and 47% of parents that did not receive higher education share their internet relations and virtual life information with their children. Although they claim that they know about internet relations and virtual life, parents that received and did not receive higher education have failed to share this type of information with their children. In addition, parents that think that they are role models for using the internet are confident about their "information."

50% of parents that received higher education and 52% of parents that did not receive higher education think that having virus/security-wall precautions on their computer can protect their children from harmful content. There are many things that may cause a threat while using the internet. Virus containing e-mails, advertisement messages and pop-ups, harmful software, online or offline violent games, immoral web pages, illegal organisation web pages, and misleading information containing web pages require users to consciously use the internet and parents to get informed about this subject. By using content filters, encryption, digital signatures and certificate use, security walls, antivirus software, and tracking software, it is possible to avoid the harmful sides of the internet and to protect children (Kuzu, 2008).

Nonetheless, using internet security programs are not enough by itself to protect ourselves from hacktivism. According to Professor Dorothy Dunning, hacktivism is the conflict of activism and computer piracy that is the exploitative unconventional and generally illegal operations for computers through special software (Demirkıran, 2013). Hacktivism's journey that started in late 1980s, has improved because of the developments in technology, has been popularised, and has found new supporters day by day (Demirkıran, 2013). Although, in hacktivism, actions are done digitally and on the internet, the purpose is to draw attention to a certain social problem and to cause a change in the real world. The main aim is to create a difference through the digital world. Hence, hacktivism and hacktivists are not virtual and should not be underestimated (Demirkıran, 2013).

The research studies on cyberbullying show that cyberbullying affects individuals in many ways. The people harassed by cyberbullying have problems such as depression, crime, drug use (Mitchell, Ybarra & Finkelhor, 2007), disappointment, sadness (Raskauskas & Stoltz, 2007), anger, worry, demotivation towards lessons, academic failure, school absenteeism (Beran & Li, 2005), and even suicide (Hinduja & Patchin, 2009).

92% of parents that received higher education and 96% of parents that did not receive higher education forbid the use of the internet for their children when they worry about a situation. The prohibitions of using the internet for children may break the bound between children and parents. The communication between children and parents should be more constructive than destructive for their development. Communication is like a wall or an artwork that is constructed ever since the individual's childhood. Each day, he or she adds a new brick, widens, reshapes, and raises it but if there are missing bricks or holes, the walls that are raised day by day will be weak. Healthful construction of the wall from the start will lead to good self, interpersonal, intergroup, and social communication. A solid foundation of a building gives self-confidence to a person and causes him or her to approach people with trust. Otherwise, the individual often lacks self-confidence and fails to think and act healthily in mutual or multiple relations (Pembecioğlu, 2014). It is way better to have certain precautions than to forbid things for children. The recommendations below have been given by Şendağ and Odabaşı (2006) to families for them to consider when their children use the internet:

1. Children should never give their names, addresses, credit card numbers, and password information and they should not fill out any online form without their parents permission.
2. They should not install any software on a computer without the permission of their parents or a trusted adult.
3. They should not meet strangers if their parents are not with them.
4. Children should not enter any chat room without their parents' permission. This is because children could encounter individuals who are not their compeers and conversely, malicious people.

5. They should not tell any person on the internet where their family will be or what they will do.
6. If children meet a new person on the internet, they should not answer instantly or communicate. Children also ought not to communicate via e-mail, etc. without the permission of their parents.
7. They should be cautious when they enter a new online space.
8. Children should not send any e-mail or pictures without the permission of their parents.
9. They should not purchase online or not to give their credit card numbers without permission of their parents.
10. They should not reply to chat conversations or e-mails that are disturbing.
11. Children ought to know, knowing or not knowing, that all kinds of disturbing contexts that are encountered should be reported to their parents.

On the other hand, many types of software, which are used to protect children, can block e-mails which have harmful content and that can warn adults about recordings are available. In addition to the use of this software, identifying the rules of using the internet can be very effective (Kuzu, 2008). 60% of children in Turkey connect to the internet in the school and 51% of children in Turkey connect to the internet in internet cafes. Due to this fact, parents cannot control how their children use the internet (Pembecioglu, 2012).

In one episode of the "truth always wins," which is prepared by Aamir Khan in India, the subject is the concept of privacy. In this episode, there is a scene where Aamir Khan is sitting with children and talking about "danger" and "trust." At the end of the conversation, one child replied to Aamir Khan: "If life is in danger, tell this to bodyguard" (https://www.youtube.com/).

Having the opportunity to send messages any time from everywhere and having the opportunity to hide your identity via mobile phones and the internet make it easier to send insulting, degrading, and threatening messages (Greene, 2006). 14% of parents who have higher education and 10% of parents who don't have higher education were exposed to behaviour that could damage (insulting, humiliating, etc.). Parents should consider that people who want to harm others can reach many people in a short amount of time (Slonje & Smith, 2008).

83% of parents who have higher education know that cyberbullying is a crime; however, 68% of them know to notify ihbarweb.com. It should be known that cyberbullying is a crime and we must not forget to notify ihbarweb.com in case of encountering any threat.

References

Arıcak, O. T. (2009). Psychiatric symptomatology as a predictor of cyber bullying among university students. Eurasian Journal of Educational Research, 34, 167–184.

Arıcak, T., Siyahhan, S., Uzunhasanoğlu, A., Sarıbeyoğlu, S., Çıplak, S., Yılmaz, N., & Memmedov, C. (2008). Cyber bullying among Turkish adolescents. Cyber Psychology & Behavior 11(3), 253–262.

Ayas, T. (2011, Ekim). Lise öğrencilerinin sanal zorba ve mağdur olma yaygınlığı. 11. Ulusal Psikolojik Danışma ve Rehberlik Kongresi'nde sunulmuş sözlü bildiri. İzmir.

Aydın, İ, Çocuk, İnternet ve Etik, Gençlik Araştırmaları Dergisi, 2013-2, s-1, 100–119.

Baker, Ö. E., & Kavşut, F. (2007). Akran zorbalığının yeni yüzü: Siber zorbalık. Eurasian Journal of Educational Research, 27, 31–42.

Belsey, B. (2007). Cyberbullying: A real and growing threat. ATA Magazine, 88(1), 14–21.

Beran, T., & Li, Q. (2005). Cyber harassment: A study of new method for an old behavior. Journal of Educational Computing Research, 32(3), 265–277.

Birinci İstanbul Çocuk Kurultayı İstanbul Çocuk Raporu. İstanbul: İstanbul Çocukları Vakfı Yayınları, 2000: 138–146.

Dilmaç, B. (2009). Sanal zorbalığı yordayan psikolojik ihtiyaçlar: Lisans öğrencileri için bir ön çalışma. Educational Sciences: Theory & Practice 9(3), 1291–1325.

Dubowitz H. Preventing child neglect and physical abuse. Pediatr Review 2002; 23: 191–196.

Estévez, E., Murgui, S. & Musitu, G. (2009). Psychological adjustment in bullies and victims of school violence. European.

Greene, M. B. (2006). Bullying in school: A plea for measure of human rights. Journal of Social Issues 62, 63–69.

Journal of Psychology of Education, 24(4), 473–483.

Demirkıran, P., Hacktivizm, Hack Kültürü ve Hacktivizm: Yeni bir Siyaset Biçimi, 2013, 27–33.

Hinduja, S., & Patchin, J. W. (2009). Bullying beyond the schoolyard: Preventing and responding to cyberbullying. California: Carwin Pres.

Huang, Yun-yin., Chien Chou. (2010). An analysis of multiple factors of cyberbullying among junior high school students in Taiwan. Computers in Human Behavior. Volume 26, Issue 6, November 2010, Pages 1581–1590.

Kandemir, C. IPTV Yayıncılığının Sorunları ve Geleceği, İstanbul, Derin Yayınları, 2013: s-1.

Karasar, N. (2006). Bilimsel araştırma yöntemi. Ankara: Nobel Yayın Dağıtım.

Kuzu, Abdullah. (2008). İnternet Kullanımı Ve Aile Araştırması. Ankara: T.C. Başbakanlık Aile Ve Sosyal Araştırmalar Genel Müdürlüğü Yayınları. Genel Yayın No: 133.

Lenhart, A. (2007). Cyber bullying and online teens. PEW Internet & American Life Project.

Li, Q. (2006). Cyberbullying in schools: A research of gender differences. School psychology international, 27, 157–170.

Marsh, H. W., Parada, R. H., Craven, R. G. & Finger, L. R. (2004). In the looking glass: A reciprocal effects model elucidating the complex nature of bullying, psychological determinants and the central role of selfconcept.

Mitchell, K. J., Ybarra, M. L., & Finkelhor, D. (2007). The relative importance of online victimization in understanding depression, delinquency, and substance use. Child Maltreatment, 12, 314–324.

Morahan-Martin, J., & Schumacher, P. (2000). Incidence and correlates of pathological internet use among college students. Computer Human Behavior, 16, 13–29.

In C. S. Sanders & G. D. Phye (Eds.), Bullying: Implications for the classroom (pp. 63–106). Florida: Academic Press.

Noret, N., & Rivers, I. (2006). The prevalence of bullying by text message or email: Result of a four year study. poster presented at British psychological society Annual Conference, Cardifft.

Raskauskas, J., & Stoltz, A. D. (2007). Involvement in traditional and electronic bullying among adolescents. Developmental Psychology, 43, 564–575.

Pembecioğlu, N., Etik-İletişim-Çocuk, Kutupyıldızı Yayınları, İstanbul, 2012.

Pembecioğlu, N., TRT Uluslararası Çocuk ve Medya Kongresi II, TRT Eğitim Dairesi Başkanlığı, Ankara, 2014:14.

Polat O. Çocuk ve Şiddet. İstanbul: Der Yayınları, 2002: 85–97.

Raskauskas, J., & Stoltz, A. D. (2007), Involvement in traditional and electronic bullying among adolescents, Developmental Psychology, 43, 564–575.

Shariff, S., & Gouin, R. (2005). Cyber - dilemmas: gendered hierarchies free expression and cyber-safety in schools, presented at safety and security in a networked world: Balancing Cyber-Rights and Responsibilities. Oxford Internet Institute Conference, Oxford, U.K.

Smith, P. K., Mahdavi, J., Carvalho, M., Fisher, S., Russell, S. & Tippett, N. (2008). Cyberbullying: Its nature and impact in secondary school pupils. Journal of Child Psychology and Psychiatry, 49, 376–385.

Slonje, R., & Smith, P.K. (2008). Cyberbullying: Another main type of bullying? Scandinavian Journal of Psychology, 49, 147–154.

Topçu, Ç. (2008). The relationship of cyber bullying to empathy, gender, traditional bullying, internet use and adult monitoring. Unpublished master dissertation, Middle East Technical University, Ankara.

Valkenburg, P.M., & Karen, E., Soeters (2001). Children's positive and negative experiences with the internet. Communication Research, 28, 652–675.

Wright, V.H., Joy, J.B., Christopher T.I., & Heather, N.O. (2009), Cyberbullying: Using virtual scenarios to educate and raise awareness. Journal of Computing in Teacher Education, 26(1), 35–42.

Willard, N. (2007). Cyberbullying and cyberthreats. U.S.A: Research Pres.

Ybarra, L.M., & Mitchell, K.J. (2004). Youth engage in online harassment: Associations with caregiver-child relationships, internet use, and personal characteristics. Journal of Adolescence, 27(3), 319–336.

Ziyalar N. Çocuk istismarı ve ihmalinin önlenmesi. Çocuk Forumu 1999; 2: 31–33.

http://www.socialmediatr.com/blog/turkiyede-9-16-yas-arasindaki-cocuklarin-yuzde-47-si-sosyal-paylasim-sitelerini-kullaniyor/.

http://www.milliyet.com.tr/abd-yi-karistiran-intihar/dunya/detay/1763540/default.htm.

https://www.youtube.com/watch?v=vr2zFBNxD1o.

http://t24.com.tr/haber/facebook-aliskanliklari-beyinde-kalici-izler-birakiyor,285313.

Aysen Temel Eginli & S. Didem Ozsenler

Does Gender Reflect on Interpersonal Communication?: Women's and Men's Communication Styles

Introduction

Communication takes part in every aspect of life and life without communication is unimaginable. Quite often, the process of communication is disrupted by misunderstandings. These misunderstandings are particularly frequent in communication between women and men. Do women and men communicate in different forms and ways? If they do, what is the main reason(s) of this difference? Even though women and men speak the same language, it is perceived as if they speak different languages, since there are differences in terms of the words they choose and the their points of focus. The reason of this difference is explained by the functional approach to interpersonal relationships and by the fact that the communication skills of the people are somehow related to the functions that they expect from the aforementioned relationship. In this context, it can be stated that the communication, which is established when there are gender-related, cultural, etc. differences, is closely influenced by the differences in communication values of the person (Holmstrom, 2009, pp. 225–226).

Literature Review

Gender communication is a very specific field in communication works. Gender communication focuses on explaining women's and men's communication forms, communication styles, and the differences between their verbal and non-verbal communication. The term "gender" is preferred over the term "sex." The reason for this preference is that "sex" refers to a person as a genetic factor, while "gender" refers to the form or style identified by society and that is preferred by the person (Eunson, 2012).

The effect of psychological and sociological processes, which have been experienced by women and men from the primitive ages until today, lie at the bottom of the communication differences between women and men. The reasons of communication differences between women and men are explained both sociologically and psychologically. When reviewed sociologically, it is stated that the differences between female and male communication stem from learning from infancy. Each baby is born into a gendered society and develops a gender-related identity within society. While men learn values peculiar to males, such as not being feminine, being successful, venturous, self-confident, and being interested in tangible subjects within the social structure, women learn other attributions, such as being emotional, meeting the expectations of others, forming and maintaining interactions, etc. (Wood, 2011 cited by Cinardo, 2011, pp. 4–5). Besides, girls and boys are raised differently in their childhood and the games, toys, selection of words, tone of voices, and non-verbal messages get involved. While girls are expected to be silent, speak softly, and play games by singing songs, boys play more clamorous games. While the games played by boys are intended for competition and defence, games played by girls are intended for showing interaction and communication (Mohindra and Azhar, 2012, p. 18). All of these learned and gender-related values reflect directly on communication style. When reviewed psychologically, it is stated that the parents' communication with their children affects the communication differences between women and men and girls and boys are raised differently and driven towards different expectations. Since boys and girls imitate the same sex in terms of communication behaviour, their communication forms are also transferred by imitation (Stevens et al. 2008). In addition, whilerequiring females to communicate more since they take over domestic and household responsibilities from the primitive ages until today, males need less communication since they take over other tasks, such as hunting, problem solving, etc. in the external environment. In this case, the communication differences between women and men have emerged (Eunson, 2012). In addition to these statements, Holley et al. (2010) state that the communication differences between women and men are typically associated with gender-stereotype behaviours and they explain this as demand-withdraw. Accordingly, when one of the parties, for example, the female, tries to solve a problem or to explain something, the other party, the male, criticises, makes requests, changes the subject, and tries to grow away or walk off from the subject by making her angry or ashamed. Stereotypically, the essence of this behaviour is the reflection of social and psychological summations acquired by women and men in the process of socialisation.

Tannen (1991) indicates that the communication differences between women and men manifest itself in the use of different languages. In this context, she describes the female communication form as rapport and the male communication form as report. Rapport communication style focuses on relationships and its main function is to build empathy and understanding in relationships. On the contrary, report communication style is task and goal-oriented and its main function is to create solutions for problems. Due to its "focus on content" characteristics, the report communication style of men focuses on obtaining information regarding the subject. The rapport communication style of women focuses on feeling intimacy in relationships and on building relations. While women put emphasis on details and disclosure of family and love affairs, men focus on the essential point and centre upon the incidents, news, and realities by growing away from the personal matters. Women refrain from using threatening and aggressive language; men prefer to use direct and target-oriented language. The rapport communication style of women and report communication style of men, their characteristics, and focus points are shown in Table 1.

Table 1: Women and men's communication style and behaviour

Women	Men
Communication Style	
Rapport Communication Style	***Report Communication Style***
• Indirect communication • Apologising • Use of qualifiers • Succinct style • Thanks • Maintaining an Appearance of Equality • Considering the other person and Relationship • Downplaying authority	• Direct communication • Giving advice to solve problems than showing support • Avoiding one down position • Downplaying doubts • Rarely give compliments • Ritual fighting, banter • Direct requests
Communication Behaviour	
• Feeling • Harmony • Closeness • Relationships • Feeling • Sharing • Cooperation • Group • Intuitive	• Logic • Reason • Power • Rank • Status • Competition • Winning • Team • Think
Communication Strengths	
• Ability to read body language and pick up nonverbal cues • Good listening • Effective display and empathy	• Physical presence • Direct and to the point interactions. • Body language signals of power.
Communication Weakness	
• Overly emotional • Meandering • Not authoritative	• Overly blunt and direct. • Insensitive to audience reactions • Too confident in own opinion.

Source: Adapted from Tannen (1991); Mohindra et al., 2013, p. 4.

Gray (1999) explains this as follows: "men usually want to talk about their daily experiences; women prefer to talk about problems. Women focus on talking about incidents and situations in detail, men focus on finding solutions simplistically or think they are expected to find a solution. Women only want sharing and empathy."

In 14,000 written documents analysed in 70 different studies performed on female and male language, it has been understood that the words used by women were mostly related to psychological and social processes, while the words used by men were on impersonal topics and object properties (Newman et al., 2008, p. 211). Besides, there are some points where women and men show linguistic differences; in other words, they express and give different meanings to the same topic in different ways and show differences in verbal communication (McQuiston and Morris, 2009, pp. 56–57).

In a research study conducted by Newman et al. (2008) on 14,000 documents regarding female and male language, it has been determined that compared to males, females use more pronouns, words that refer to psychological state (crazy, lazy, remembering, etc.), social words (such as friend, sister/brother, etc.), and intensely give references to psychological processes. It has also been seen that compared to females, males are more interested in longer words, numbers, and tangible objects, and focus more on current issues.

One of the differences between female and male communication is related to the way they ask questions. Females ask questions in a communication process to learn about the details about the topic, and therefore, they might ask too many questions regarding the reasons related to the topic. That being said, females also ask questions to verify the information that they obtained. In addition, females use tag questions to clarify the ambiguous points of the conversation, to emphasise important points of the topic, and to reveal other aspects of the topic (Netshitangani, 2008). At this point, a difference is seen between males' and females' way of acquiring information. It is observed that males are more linear and try to apprehend the fundamental points when obtaining information, whereas, females tend to obtain deep and detailed information in order to understand the relationship and give a meaning to it (Cinardo, 2011, p. 16).

There are also differences between women and men in non-verbal communication. When using personal space, females want to define their own space in public or in crowded places and thus, they rule out the intruders from their personal space with equipment such as books, purses, etc. Women usually stick their arms close to their bodies, while men stick out their arms angularly in order to look strong, to protect others, to draw a line, etc. Women frequently touch their hair, lips, and clothes. Males use their hands and fingers to point out, to warn, etc. in the communication process. Men touch others less than women. While men consider touching as intrusion of privacy, women consider it as a way of being friendly, being sweetness and light, and as an explanatory behaviour (Eunson, 2012). Besides, it is observed that women smile far more than men in the communication process and perceive smiling as an indicator of friendship and intimacy, rather than an indicator of happiness in relationships. Men smile when they genuinely feel happy and are pleased and they do not consider smiling as an expression of reflecting positive feelings. Eye contact has different meanings for women and men. While women interpret eye contact as a way of showing intimacy and trust, men usually interpret eye contact as threat, power, and status, in addition to intimacy and trust (McQuiston and Morris, 2009, p. 68).

Methodology

It is observed that women and men mostly show different approaches to the same topic in the communication process or ascribe different meanings to the same expression, and thus, they have disagreements and discrepancies. The starting point of this research study is to reveal whether the main reason of these disagreements and discrepancies is really a difference and to determine whether the differences identified in previous studies regarding communication exist in young people. So the study has two main questions. These are:

(1) Do women and men communicate in different ways?
(2) At which points do women and men differ in the communication process?

For this purpose of the research study, the focus group interview and observation methods were selected. For the purpose of the research study, the participants were particularly selected among young people/college students between the ages of 19 and 23 years using the random sampling method based on voluntary participation. As a result, six female and five male students participated in this study. Videos were recorded in this research study by the permission of the participants. Two researchers deciphered and encoded the video footages separately and the data were also controlled by a separate encoder. On this basis, the results were put through a qualitative evaluation and interpretation methodology. For encoding the results, the codes set forth by "Deborah Tannen (1991), How to Close the Communication Gap between Men and Women, McCall's May, Vol. 118, N.8, pp. 97–100" and "Vinita Mohindra, Samina Azhar, Vikas Jaoolkar, A Study of Communication with Reference to Male and Female Approaches and Perceptions, An International Journal in English, Issue 12, February 2013, pp. 1–6" were utilised and new codes were also created and added by the researchers. The codes utilised in this research study bear qualifications that classify the report communication style of men for obtaining information and the rapport communication style of women for agreement-harmonisation by Tannen. These codes take part under the communication style and focus points in communication titles in Table 1 above. In addition to these codes, the researchers added the following codes: physiological needs, tangible objects and authority for men, trust, ambiguity, and intimacy for women.

The study began with the distribution of the NASA space survival exercise form (NASA exercise: Survival on the Moon), following a briefing given to the students by one of the researchers regarding the research. The NASA exercise form was selected to determine whether the students communicate differently on the same topic. Each participant expressed his or her own personal opinion for about ten to twelve minutes regarding the articles on the form, and from time to time, they also criticised or contributed to each other's statements. Interactions were formed between female and male participants during focus group interview and it was observed that these interactions occasionally turned into conflicts and that they sometimes involved approval.

Findings

Communication Style

When the statements of female and male participants were analysed in terms of direct and indirect communication, it was observed that the male participants used direct and clear statements and that the female participants preferred statements based on further explanation.

Statements of female participants: "I normally love to eat. I am sure I would think of food in such a case, but since I am lost and trying to reach the ship, I would think of magnetic compass and celestial map after the oxygen tube. I would think of trying to find my direction first, so instead of eating what I have available, I would eat more when I reach there…" and "How can you not know that lifting a parachute is no joke? There are different sizes, and many different types. Which one would we get? We need to think accordingly"

Statements of Male Participants: "the track of time is critical;" "why would you use 'instead,' use it alternatively;" "no need to argue, there are certain things, let's focus on them;" "mind the order of importance;" and "there must be someone to take initiative, we argue too much even on that nylon rope."

When the statements of male participants were analysed, it was observed that they focused on versatile thinking and tried to handle the situation in different ways. In this context, the **statements of male participants** are as follows: "Look, it could be in two ways, it will be cliché but you can either shoot someone to protect each other, which is less likely in space, or as you said, it can be from the outside. But it would not be a problem if we save it for the last for safety" and "Just a second, can I ask a question? Will we use the flare and the gun at the same time?"

A conspicuous characteristic in the communication style of the **female participants** was that they focused on relationships and expressed their thoughts on other people. **For example**, "I think we should get the first aid kit, after all, something bad might happen to us. We might need to help, if something bad happens to one of us while walking. I cannot go on if something bad happens to somebody, like one of us might get a slight wound, we can dress the wound. And then we can go on together" and "It would be risky to go across without any communication. Instead of risking someone, I think we should use the radio."

In the statements of **female participants**, it was observed that they focused on association and cooperation in terms of communication style. "I am also thinking that if unity and solidarity are important, let's say we took the gun with us, we ate, drank water, and at some point we got really angry. Someone would definitely disrupt the unity. I don't know, what is the purpose of the gun? Who would you bump into in space?"

In the statements of **male participants,** it was observed that there were more struggling and giving advice/recommendations in line with the communication style of men. As an example of this struggle, we can give the following statements: "okay, we would not use it inside, so let's not take it for outside too;" "let's put heat on number five, any ideas?;" "why would you use 'instead,' use it alternatively;" and "no, I say we don't need to argue that."

On the other hand, since establishing authority was in question in a sense, it was observed that the participants gave advice to each other. The examples in this context are as follows: "If we decided on the target area as our priority, then we have to do something for it; like we have the celestial map and the compass, we have located the ship, now what we need to do to reach the ship, ha?" and "We can also do this; like someone volunteers to go out, we warm him up with the heat unit and give him the rope."

Communication Behaviour

When the statements of female and male participants were analysed in terms of communication behaviour, it was observed that the statements of the female participants focused on sharing, relationships, cooperation, and harmony. On the contrary, the statements of the male participants focused on logic, reason, thought, and power. Besides, it was also observed that the statements of the female participants involved trust, ambiguity, and intimacy, while the statements of the male participants involved physiological needs, tangibility, and authority. It was observed that **female participants** did not like ambiguity, attached importance to trust, and focused way too much on their own feelings and opinions in the process of communication. Their emphasis on **ambiguity** was observed in the following statements: "How long should we tolerate hunger? There is no explanation on that;" "There is no exact information;" and "nothing is certain." Their emphasis on **trust** was observed in the following statements: "Why do you say we need guns? Will we shoot each other?;" "Am I not alone in space, should I have concerns about my safety?;" and "We should not disrupt unity and solidarity, and then there would not be any problems." Besides, it was observed that female participants gave prominence to **intimacy**. In other words, they expressed their **own opinions and feelings** in an egocentric way. The following examples may be given: "I don't buy milk because I don't like it;" "I think …;" "I think we should take the first aid kit;" and "Instead of risking someone, I think we should use the radio."

When the statements of female participants were analysed, it was observed that there were expressions of harmony and these generally focused on shared **decision-making, liaising, and keeping solidarity**. Some of the examples in this sense are: "First, we need to take something to show where we are, such as compass or rescue flare, shouldn't we?" and "Is this our shared decision?" Besides, it was observed in female participants that **sharing, cooperation, and relationships** remained at the forefront. The following examples may be given: "we might come across different types of people as in the movie she said. After all, we don't know his/her mood. I am thinking that we will need each other there, no one would want to be alone in that case;" "again it's a team work, do you understand? But parachute is something that we can use individually;" and "But how can we use the rope, we can't use the rope, it is true."

When the statements of the **male participants** were analysed, it was observed that they attached great importance to the **cause and effect relationship** and that they emphasised being **considerate and thinking clearly**. In this sense, male participants explained themselves by being clear-headed in general and by arranging the causes in order. The following statements can be given as examples: "What is the purpose of going into space? Why would we go there?;" "First, I would take the oxygen tubes to survive…;" and "That's why I made my move thinking all-or-nothing. First…."

When the statements of **male participants** were analysed, another remarkable point was that they were **power and authority-oriented**. Related statements are: "No need to argue, there are some certain things;" "mind the order of priority;" "any objections?;" "we need to make reasonable decisions, there is a spontaneous condition;" and "no, I say we don't need to argue that."

When the statements of **male participants** were analysed, physiological needs and authoritativeness were included in addition to the focus points determined by Tannen (1991) and Mohindra et al. (2013). In this context, the following statements show us that **physiological needs** come to the forefront in male participants: “I put food. Just in case, I don’t want to starve to death” and “I think we could endure thirst, food seems more important to me.” Besides, it was observed that the **male participants** tried to **establish authority**, especially when they reached a point of conflict, and the following statements indicate authority: “So our goal is to reach the ship, after putting oxygen tubes in the first place, then we should take the celestial map and the compass, any objections? None, right?;” and “Whoever manages to hold the rope to reach the ship he would be considered as successful. If we say let’s try it all together, we would lose, you can’t say that anyway.”

The reactions of participants regarding non-verbal communication were also observed in this study. In this context, it was observed that the female participants were talking with a soft voice and with their palms sticking outwards, they smiled more than males, and were joking around to receive others approval. It was also observed that female participants were frequently touching their hair and bodies. On the other hand, female participants faced the other participants in order to receive their approval after they finished their speech and they even finished their sentences with a question. When the male participants were analysed, it was observed that they were shaking their fingers when expressing their ideas and that they wanted to establish authority in this sense. Some male participants expressed their opinions by slamming their fists on the table and this may be interpreted as the expression of power. Some of the male participants made hand gestures to permit another participant and even to permit female participants to speak. It was observed that male participants nodded their heads to show their approval while listening. Female participants tried to make eye contact with almost all participants while expressing their ideas and even touched the participants near them. Male participants either preferred to make eye contact with a single person or spoke by focusing on the paper and pen in their hands.

Conclusion

At the end of the study, which was based on the study of Tannen (1991) and Mohindra et al. (2013), and which was performed based on the dimensions identified for the “rapport communication style” of women and the “report communication style” of men, it was observed that women and men showed different approaches in communication. In this context, it was determined that in terms of direct and indirect communication, female participants differed in focusing on relationships, unity, and cooperation, while male participants differed in struggle-competition and advice/recommendation. In addition, it was observed that there were also differences when gender differenceis assessed in terms of the focus points in communication. In this context, differences were observed in females in terms of sharing, relationships, cooperation, and harmony, while in males, differences were observed in terms of logic, reason, thought, and power. In this sense, this study supports the previous studies. Besides, it was observed that while the statements of female participants involved trust, ambiguity, and intimacy, the statements of male participants involved physiological needs and authority. Considering that these differences may also be influenced by culture, it may be suggested to research the effects of culture in future studies that will involve the communication differences between women and men.

References

Cinardo, J. (2011). *Male and Female Differences in Communicating Conflict*, Thesis Degree of Bachelor of Communication in the Honors Program at Coastal Carolina University, pp. 1–23.

Eunson, B. (2012). *Gender and Communication, C21 Communicating in the 21st Century*, 3rd Edition, Australia: John Wiley and Sons.

Gray, J. (1999). *Erkekler Mars'tan, Kadınlar Venüs'ten*, Çev: Gülden Şen, İstanbul: Altın Kitaplar.

Holley, S. R., Sturm, V. E. & Levenson, R. W. (2010). *Exploring the Basis for Gender Differences in the Demand- Withdraw Pattern*, Journal of Homosexuality, 57, pp. 666–684.

Holmstrom, A. J. (2009). *Sex and Gender Similarities and Differences in Communication Values in Same-Sex and Cross-Sex Friendship*, Communication Quarterly, Vol. 57, Issue.2, pp. 224–238.

McQuiston, D. H. & Morris, K. A. (2009). *Gender Differences in Communication: Implications For Salespeople*, Journal of Selling & Major Account Management, Vol. 9, No.1, pp. 54–64.

Mohindra, V. & Azhar, S. (2012). *Gender Communication: A Comparative Analysis of Communicational Approaches of Men and Women at Workplaces*, IOSR Journal of Humanities and Social Sciences (JHSS), Vol. 2, Issue.1, pp. 18–27.

Mohindra, V., Azhar, S. & Jaoolkar, V. (2013). *A Study of Communication with Reference to Male and Female Approaches and Perceptions*, An International Journal in English, Issue 12, pp. 1–6.

Nasa Exercise: Survival on the Moon, Retrieved from http://homepages.abdn.ac.uk/j.masthoff/pages/teaching/CS3021/practicals/MoonExercise.pdf.

Netshitangani, T. (2008). *Gender differences in communication styles: The impact on the managerial work for a woman school principal*, ANZCA 08 Conference, Power and Place, Wellington, pp. 1–19.

Newman, M. L., Groom, C. J., Handelman, L. D. & Pennebaker, J. W. (2008). *Gender Differences in Language Use: An Analysis of 14,000 Text Samples*, Discourse Processes, Vol. 45, pp. 211–236.

Stevens, K., Lehmann, N., Cooper, T. & Whitehouse, S. (2008). *Battle of the Sexes: Differences in Directness of Communication between Men and Women in a Group Situation*, Epistimi pp. 5–7.

Sullivan, P. (2004). *Communication Differences Between Male and Female Team Sport Athletes,* Communication Reports, Vol. 17, No.2, pp. 121–128.

Tannen, D. (1991), *How to Close the Communication Gap between Men and Women,* McCall's May, Vol. 118, N.8, pp. 97–100.

Betul Onay Dogan

Representation Forms of Cities in New Media: An Analysis of Websites Belonging to the First 10 Cities in the 2013 Mastercard Destination Cities Index

Introduction

The city emerged from the sheltering need of people and through the history by changing and aestheticizing its formal structure, it has become a value beyond sheltering. Just as people meet the protection need with clothes and in time clothes have had communicational meaning by changing, cities and indicators in cities have had the process of communication, too.

Cities came into existence by the systematic settlement of indicators. Every system has a meaning in itself. Thanks to this meaning, a sense related to finance occurs when London is said and a sense of romanticism comes when Paris is said. That a city is perceived as peaceful or that a city's historical identity affects its inner and outer target group's perception is always a result of the meaning the city has of itself.

In the global world, although it is emphasised that the meanings that the cities have are similar, the cities that people make an effort to go and see prove the fact that cities still have different identities despite their similarities.

Virtual extension is an important platform that offers identities to cities and enables them to be different. Representation in virtual extension differentiates from traditional communication tools. The most important point that is different is that the representation process occurs more freely. In traditional communication tools, the existence of a gatekeeper which should be passed in order to publish a news segment poses a huge obstacle for the institution most of the time. However, the design and the content of the website you create in a virtual extension are formed totally in accordance with your and your institution's requests.

City and Communication

The city does not have a stable form. Along with conserving essence, it changes. In the process of change, mutual interaction occurs. While cities change people, people change cities at the same time. Therefore, when you meet someone for the first time and ask "where" he or she is from, one of the things that you want to learn is the city that he or she belongs to. You make an inference about the person based on the city.

The city consists of a system of indicators. Along with the fact that the city is an object that can be perceived and even liked by millions of people who have various classes and characters, the city is also a product of creators who change the form according to personal reasons and develop it. Although the city remains stable in general terms, the details of it always change. Only a partial control can be established on its growth and form. A certain result cannot be achieved, but infinite stages can be mentioned (Lynch, 2010, p. 2). Elements like collective memory and symbols that make human communication possible give meaning to a city and constitute the city's image.

In a globalising world, the biggest problem about cities is the point that cities resemble each other. It is always emphasised that one of the biggest problems of new cities, which cannot preserve the old forms, do not have enough personality and lack identity (Shaukland, 1996, p. 24). However, preserving and constituting identity is also a must for the cities; this is an obligation for their maintainability. Every city tries to drive traffic and be known by emphasising its own difference. Society should not be thought only on tourist based. Along with the city being a study object, it has the feature of the place that is looked to understand what is happening in society (Aslanoğlu, 2000, p. 150).

Identity presentation of a city is based on its physical, moral, and executive features. While physical features are related to town planning and architectural features, moral features are shaped based on features like collective memory, urban legends, and culture which are constituted by social perception. Today, the executive form of the city is the most important fact that gives clues about both today and the future (Önay Doğan, 2012). Physical and moral features form a basis for the city's identity presentations and differentiation strategies. The executive form is the most important actor that affects city's identity and shapes its future.

City's Representation in Virtual Extension

Today, rather than as a tool, the use of the internet takes part in our lives as an element which shapes people, institutions, and establishments. Virtual extension is not a part of physical field; rather, it is a zoetic layer that has transitivity with a physical field. Therefore, positioning virtual extension apart and losing its touch with reality will result in the failure of communication.

Virtual extension provides the opportunity for cities to present their own identities to the extent that it does nowhere else. When we look at the representation of places in virtual extension, we see the cities first. In virtual extension, communication, information for tourists, trade, and executive elements which are conducted by cities' inner target groups can be assembled under the same roof for the global audience. In order to do this, the most suitable platform in virtual extension is websites. Websites exist as a common and easily accessible place for social sharers that is distinct from physical place (Grodach, 2009, p. 184). One of the important elements for websites is that they hold executive will and they are shaped according to executive will's requests. The lack of gatekeepers which exist in traditional communication tools is another reason for representation shaping freely.

City Websites

In a study on city websites, cities size, population densities, and economic situations are compared with the size of websites and the features the websites have (Urban, 2002). The most certain result gathered in this study is that big cities give more place to management services in their web pages and they update local news very often. Moreover, in big/world cities, tabs about tourists are less; a reason for this could be that they do not need this or that in the issues about tourism, special service suppliers are used. It is determined that cities' own representations expand like airports or shopping centres and in the same way, they have a lot of similarities with them. In another study which was conducted on the websites of city councils and which examined branding (Florek et al., 2006), it is stated that in the process of branding, slogans and logos take place in websites as the most diaristic feature and outer target group's awareness about the city occurs thanks to slogans and logos. Also, another result of the study is that while photographs about the city attract outer group's attention, news and planned projects attract the inner group's attention. It is highlighted that the links which are placed on websites and open to different pages are generally similar to museums, libraries, and amusement centres.

The websites belonging to cities show to what extent they can catch other cities in the global world and also force them to define their identities in a different way from others and present how they define their identities (Urban, 2002). When internet applications and traditional communication tools are compared in terms of advertising the city, it is seen that the internet has a more active form that is independent from the centre. On web pages, people have the opportunity to get the information about places. As a result, they have an idea about the city. The internet enables people to see all the information and to coordinate them (Florek et al., 2006).

A Study About the Representations of Cities on Web Pages Methods

There are lots of studies conducted on cities' web pages. Studies are generally shaped on a certain subject and they are engaged with whether or not the data about the subject exist on the web page. For example, while some studies concentrate on tourism, some others emphasise on the marketing aspect of the city. However, the studies are limited at the point of how it can be beneficial to use the features of the internet which is interpreted as a free platform; in other words, they are limited by how the cities present their identities.

Web pages are a place in which all social sharers are addressed at the same time, where the opportunity to communicate interactively exists, and where one can benefit from all application opportunities. How do the cities that are shaped by inner and outer target groups' perception benefit from the opportunities that web pages present and how do city communications affect web pages? From this question, by collecting study question titles that are taken from more than ten studies conducted on city web pages, the subjects that are accepted as determinants were retained. Within the frame of these subjects, we attempted to determine how the cities see themselves and how they want others to see them.

Table I: City Web Pages

Domain	
Bangkok	http://www.bangkoktourist.com/
London	http://www.visitlondon.com/
Paris	http://en.parisinfo.com/
Singapore	http://www.yoursingapore.com
New York	http://www1.nyc.gov/
Istanbul	http://english.istanbul.gov.tr/
Dubai	http://www.definitelydubai.com/
Kuala Lumpur	http://www.visitkl.gov.my/
Hong Kong	http://www.discoverhongkong.com/
Barcelona	http://www.bcn.cat/

City web addresses can be defined as the first stop where the places express themselves. Therefore, official websites should be different from other websites which have the city name and should be determinant. While this decisiveness is provided, at the same time, it is possible to also have a message within the websites name. When cities' web addresses are examined above, it is possible to see this situation especially in Dubai and Singapore. It can be stated that Singapore especially tries to be close to social sharers at the very first step. Bangkok, London, Paris, and Kuala Lumpur's web addresses are limited with implying the aim. There is not a determinant feature in New York, Istanbul, and Barcelona web addresses.

Table II. Tourism Web Pages of Well-known Cities

Logos and slogans	
Bangkok	Bangkok Smiles Bangkok Tourism Division
London	VISITLONDON.COM OFFICIAL VISITOR GUIDE
Paris	PARIS Official website of the Convention and Visitors Bureau PARISINFO
Singapore	YourSingapore
New York	NYC The Official Guide nycgo.com
Istanbul	ENGLISH.ISTANBUL.GOV.TR
Dubai	Not applicable
Kuala Lumpur	Visit KL
Hong Kong	Not applicable
Barcelona	Ajuntament de Barcelona

When the web pages of ten cities are examined, it can be seen that there are logos but no slogans. As it was mentioned in the studies before, slogans and logos are the most important determinant features for the target groups and they are the most important elements that shape social sharers' perception. Also, slogans and logos should take place on websites as the most apparent and the most easily perceivable element of representation. It can be said that the lack of slogans, which can encapsulate what is being told without any other explanation, weaken the web pages' power. Visitors are far away from canalising; they go into web pages only according to their own points of view. Although they are not defined as slogans, the word "smile" was added to Bangkok's logo and "YourSingapore" was added to Singapore's logo. In this way, the first communication with the people using the web page has started.

When logos are examined, it can be seen that the Dubai web page does not have a logo and a title that introduces the page. Among other websites, only the Istanbul web page was coloured with two different colours and its web address was used as the title. While blue, which symbolise the sea, peace, and calmness was used in half of the titles, grey was preferred in the other half. Bangkok, Paris, and Kuala Lumpur used city's signal elements in their logos. For example, the Eiffel Tower, which comes to mind when one says Paris, was symbolised with different colours. Singapore tried to represent the city's movement by putting the word "YourSingapore" onto geometrical figures with different colours. In New York's web page, the city's first letters were used. As city's first letters were also used in souvenir products, this application has identified with the city. London both emphasised the aim and made the website different from other sites belonging to London by using the word "visit" and stating that it is the official visitor web page in the title. It is possible to find web pages belonging to cities. Some of them were prepared by a private travel company. There are four sites that emphasise that they are official for people who search for an official website in a search engine. This emphasis increases the reliability of the websites. Only on Barcelona's web page, is there an arma belonging to and symbolising the city.

Video	
Bangkok	Content of the video: culture, river, food, shopping, and night (there are also 50 different videos under the gallery tab).
London	Non-existent
Paris	12 videos
Singapore	Non-existent
New York	Non-existent
Istanbul	Connection to 36 live cameras in the city and also two introductory videos of Istanbul.

Video	
Dubai	There is a 31 second introductory video (put on visitor page).
Kuala Lumpur	There is a video of 10:53 minutes prepared by Malaysian celebrities. Video content: economy, transportation, festivals, fairs, architecture, health, education, museums, art, parks, open air activities, night, shopping, and food.
Hong Kong	No video.
Barcelona	The video is an introductory video where different people talk about Bercelona and Barcelona's different images are shared; however, although the website is in English, the video is in Spanish.

Today's internet applications give the opportunity of communication via videos to people, institutions, and organisations apart from the visuals and literary language. In contradistinction to stable visuals, videos have the feature which enables them to put sounds and visuals together in a fiction. For this reason, videos are especially used in promotions. Promotion videos of the city generally touch on the city's salient features which is a summary of how the city looks at itself and how it represent itself in a virtual extension. With this aim, the videos that exist in the websites belonging to the cities being visited most in 2013 were examined and it was seen that there was no video on three cities' websites.

The Bangkok promotion video was separated into titles and each title was given almost equal time. Apart from the video on the main page, there are 50 different videos under the gallery tab. When the videos are examined, it is seen that they are more all-inclusive videos that include the subjects existing in the promotion video. The Paris website is one of the most decisive sites in terms of videos. Eleven of twelve videos on the website introduce historical places. The other video belongs to a contemporary art museum. As for Istanbul, it establishes connection to 36 different live cameras with its different applications. The importance of these cameras is that they exist in the places of Istanbul's historical and natural beauties. While the advantage of live cameras is that they show the city as is to people, it can be stated as a disadvantage that no information or guidance is possible. Moreover, two promotion videos of Istanbul exist on the website, too. Dubai put a short promotion video of 31 seconds onto the page which is prepared for visitors using the visuals of the sea and architecture.

The promotion video of Kuala Lumpur is the most all-inclusive website among the sites examined. The eleven minute video starts with a beginning by an artist and continues with different subjects about all of Kuala Lumpur's features told by Malaysian celebrities. The video's aim is to introduce the city to the people who both want to visit the city and who want to live in the city. The promotion video of Barcelona includes visuals of the city. However, it can be stated that this video cannot completely have an international feature because of the language used in the video.

Tabs on the Main Page: Tabs used generally have similarities. Therefore, we have attempted to find the differences by leaving introductory information, housing (excluding Istanbul), transportation in the city (excluding Istanbul and Dubai), and travel suggestions out of the study. Apart from the tabs mentioned above, the pages which are opened via representation tabs and different tabs taking place on the main page can be listed as:

Differently, Bangkok shows the price of the world's best city to the people who first open the page. Also, various news about the city takes place on the web page. Moreover, there are lots of videos and visuals under the gallery tab, but there is no guidance for people despite the number of visuals and videos. The most important lack of the site is that it is not clear when the site is updated.

Apart from the tabs mentioned above, on London's web page, afternoon tea and the places being preferred for afternoon tea, which makes London different from other cities, are put together under a tab. Also, there are activities which have the feature of suggestions for London trips in autumn and there is a video to promote London trips in autumn. Moreover, London's "cheap" part is detailed under the budget tab. And visually, afternoon tea, London in autumn, and the budget section cover a huge part of the page. With these tabs, while the values London has are emphasised, it is underlined that London is an active city at the same time. It also answers the criticisms about the expensiveness of the city with alternative suggestions.

The website of Paris resembles the website of London in terms of the content. The tabs in which autumn opportunities to trace the history and cheap travel suggestions exist are different from other websites. The most important difference of the page is that the ticket to travel to every place in the city can be bought from the site. This increases the use of the site and provides a huge easiness to the users.

When the Singapore website is opened, a little survey offer to develop the website comes to the screen. Besides this, the tab that has the futures like ways for easy travel to the visitors from other countries or the privilege of tax-free shopping cover a big place on the site. Apart from these, other tabs are similar to other web pages. It can be seen as a distinctive feature for New York that there is a place to search, see promotions for coming Broadway days, and links to buy tickets.

The only content that can be called distinctive about Istanbul's web page is that a historical or natural beauty with an informative note comes to the screen in every click to the page. This is an element that makes the user feel the difference in every entry.

Upon first opening the web page of Dubai, the site wants you to make a preference. It wants to know whether you want to continue to investigate as a visitor or about business life or as a place where you live or will live. When you enter the visitor page, you can see that different activities that can be done in Dubai and suggestions for accommodation are listed under other tabs. Like Dubai, a second page comes to the screen according to whether you enter the site as a visitor or a resident of the city on Barcelona's web page. Barcelona is different with its link about gastronomy. There is information about Spanish and Catalan cuisine and suggestions for restaurants in this gastronomy link.

Discussion

Like at the individual and institutional level, cities also feel the need to promote themselves and communicate social sharers. Today, the virtual extension in which communication is pursued most effectively is the most suitable platform for cities to make identity representations and for their communication. In virtual extension, websites are important because they give cities the opportunity to present all the features of them. It is important to ensure the effective use of websites for effective communication.

When the web pages of the first ten cities in the 2013 MasterCard Global Destination Cities Index were examined, it was seen that in the web pages, the definitions to "discover" the city, suggestions for accommodation and food during the visit, transportation ways, activities, and trip suggestions are the titles used most. The thing that is distinctive about websites is the design of the sites and the extent of the titles. For example, on the web pages of London it can be seen that the titles used most are put under the title "budget" again and that the suggestions for cheaper travel exists. On Singapore's web page, there is a special tab for activities and there are suggestions for activities on a full page.

As for the videos that create awareness, Paris could especially achieve a certain identity representation and especially underline the historical form of it. Kuala Lumpu tried to answer all the questions of the people who want to discover and underlined dissimilarities and modernity.

Among the web pages, Singapore is the city that has the most different presence with its logo design. YourSingapore tries to create both an invitation and a mutual point of view. Likewise, when we look at the domains of city web pages, while visitlondon.com, parisinfo.com, and similar domains explain the aim of the page, Singapore transfers the aim of catching a mutual point of view to the domain with yoursingapore.com.

Generally, the representation on web pages is far away from being distinctive, but at the same time, the identity representations of cities which can be called world cities and are arbiters in not only tourism but also other fields like the economy and policy can be defined as more professional compared to other cities. Virtual extension presents different alternatives but these alternatives are not used enough.

References

Aslanoğlu R. (2000) Kent, Kimlik Küreselleşme, Ezgi Kitapevi Yayınları. Bursa

Florek M. Insch A. Gnoth J. (2006) City Council Websites as a Means of Place Brand Identity Communication, *Place Branding*, vol. 2, 4, 276–296

Grodach C. (2009) Urban Branding: An Analysis of City Homepage Imagery, *Journal of Architectural and Planning Research*, 26:3, 181, 197

Lynch K. (2010) Kent İmgesi (çev. İrem Başaran), İş Bankası Yayınları: İstanbul

Onay Dogan B. (2012) Kentsel İletişim Stratejisi Oluşturmada Reklam Uygulamalarının Rolü ve Etkisi (unpublished doctoral thesis), İstanbul Üniversitesi, Sosyal Bilimler Enstitüsü

Shaukland G. (1996) Tarihi Değeri Olan Kentlere Neden El Atmalıyız?, *Cogito*, Yapı Kredi Yayınları: İstanbul

Urban F. (2002) Small Town, Big Web Site? Cities and their Representation on Internet, *Cities*, vol. 19, no. 49, 59

Bünyamin Ayhan & Selahattin Çavuş

Online Game Addiction Among High School Students

Introduction

The internet and the online world brought by the internet are considered to be an indispensable part of our everyday life. As each new technology develops, the internet brings many risks to an individual's life. Research studies concerned with new communication technologies and their products causing mental health problems and some of the psychological symptoms are increasing rapidly in scientific literature. For example, new types of addiction resulting from the online world began to be added into earlier types of dependencies. These studies focusing particularly on maladaptive use (a behaviour blocking ability in a particular context that is inappropriate or ineffective and harmful to an individual, group, or society), show that case will lead to more serious problems in future. Thus, the subject of dependencies began to be widely discussed in relation to the information and communication technologies and their content.

Playing games on computers or in the virtual world have an important place in the individuals' life and can be characterised as harmless. However, users being unable to stop playing regardless of a compelling urge and leading to negative consequences or demanding online activities of this type of game can turn into an addiction to online games. Thus, parents, teachers, and psychologists are concerned that young people will be unsuccessful in practical everyday life by reason of the game (Hollen, 2009: 272).

When considering the anatomy of game addiction, we can't say that an online game is a drug or it has an idealised structure, and its the results can be generalised. In particular, game addiction isn't a case that is always seen, it is a process that grows slowly. However, when game addiction is referred to as individual's spending more time than required (more than enough) and having a problem in taking care of business, denial and blaming cases related to time and knowledge are noteworthy (Clark, Scott, 2009: 91–114). In his studies about internet addiction in which he started to study at a clinic (2007: 673), Young (1998) reveals that individuals have problems in managing the centre areas of their life along with the addiction, they have begun to waste an important part of time at work and because of their lack of social relationships, they have started to compensate this gap with the internet. As a result, a life process began on which game and friendship relations have become online. This case is becoming problematic not only for individuals, but also for societies according to technology–society relations. For example, more than half of the population of South Korea are playing computer games and online gambling in particular causes abuse-dependency that affects social life. This situation is leaving deep scars on the country's culture (Chee, 2006: 226). Two to three million young people in South Korea are addicted and the health ministry is seeking remedies for it (Clark, Scott, 2009: 20). While the internet video games market was expecting $82 billion in 2017 (www.forbes.com), as it was $62 billion in 2012 (www.statistica.com).

Literature Review

When the literature related to this subject is examined, in the research conducted by Peker et al. on online game addiction conducted on 292 high school students in the 2008–2009 academic year in Sakarya, it was revealed that 7.9% participants were addicted to games. It was also determined that war and strategy games make people addicted, there weren't gender differences.

Griffiths, Davies, and Chappell (2004), studying teenager and adult computer game users, determined that game characteristics of adolescent and adult computer users differ significantly. The teenage users prefer violent games more than adults. Teenage users play more than adults. Teenage users are more likely to compromise their work and education.

A year later, Çağıltay and İnal (2005) investigated elementary school students' computer game playing habits in Turkey. According to the survey, men play games than more women. While girls prefer competition, questions and answers, general culture, and action-adventure games much more, men play action-adventure, war, and sports games. Having a computer has an impact on playing time.

In another study conducted in 2005 (Ko, Yen, Chen, Chen, & Yen), the level of online gaming addiction in college students was examined. Accordingly, men are more dependent than girls. Girls play games in order to spend time, while men play games to succeed and make many friends. In a survey by Ng and Hastings (2005) which included a group of high school students, online gaming habits were investigated. Accordingly, massively multiplayer online role-playing game (MMORPG) users are on the computer a large part of their time and prefer the enjoyable and satisfying atmosphere of a virtual world more so than the real world. MMORPG users, rather than real-life events, take pleasure in playing games; however, they are not expressed to be addicted. These users waste their energy and their social time on the game world. For the majority, MMORPGs are in the shape of an alternative form of social entertainment. The finding show that these users would prefer e-mail, chat rooms or instant messaging, and web-based social networks rather than social media (clubs, friends, environment) even if there wasn't MMORPGs.

In research conducted by Ko et al. (2009), the relationship between impulse and brain activity in online game addiction was studied. The study was conducted on ten participants who played the game and who didn't play the game. Game addiction and substance addition made up from definite sourced desire/drive in a similar manner. Therefore, online game addiction and substance addiction are considered to have the same neurobiological mechanisms.

In another study where the level of dependency of secondary school students that were online were examined, 3% of the students were revealed to have become addicted to online games. Users are discussed in two groups: the first group is heavily dependent online game users, while the second group is heavy but not dependent online game users. The gaming impact on children's psychosocial health is relatively less (Rooij, Schoenmakers, Vermulst, Eijnden, & Mheen, 2010).

In a research study where the levels of play of teenagers, young people, and adults were examined (Festl, Scharkow, & Quandt, 2012), men were determined to play more than women. There is a negative correlation by age. Young people mostly prefer digital games. Adolescents' level of playing of problematic gaming and addiction is higher compared to other groups.

The level of MMORPG addiction of Vietnamese youth was examined. People playing MMORPGs have more severe mental disorders compared to those who don't play. Due to the high addiction rates of the respondents, the likelihood of having a severe mental disorder is high (Son, Yasuoka, Poudel, Otsuka, & Jimba, 2012).

In the same year, in another survey conducted on high school students, the relationship between the level of internet and computer game addiction and shyness was investigated (Ayas, 2012). There is also a positive correlation between the level of internet and computer game addiction and shyness. Men play computer games at a higher level compared to girls.'

In the study conducted on 999 high school students by Kayri et al. in the province of Batman in 2012 (2014), men were more addicted than girls. Additionally, there was no differentiation between the level of parental education and addiction, while the existence of significant differentiation between income and addiction was observed. On the other hand, it is clear that as computer use increases, the level of addiction also increases.

Methods

While the population of the study is made up of high school students studying in Aksaray, the sample is comprised of 386 students selected by the randoml sampling method in four different high school located in the city of Aksaray. The scale used in the study was developed by Kimberly S. Young (www.net.addiction.com). The scale consists of 20 questions in total. Because the scale is a Likert-type scale, the responses were listed as "never (one)," "rarely" (two), "sometimes" (three), "often" (four), and "always" (five). Scores to be obtained from the full scale were evaluated out of a total of 100. The degree of addiction for each subject was determined according to the total score received as a subject. Accordingly, 20–49 points is a group where individual controls in spite of the fact that points spent a long time in the virtual world of online users. The degree of addiction to online world 50–79 points is a group of risk compared to other groups causing many problems to the individual's life is lower. 80–100 points is a dependent group that has serious problems in every day life. In order to look at the reliability of the scale, Cronbach's Alpha internal consistency coefficient, measuring the same construct as an interrelated scale item, was obtained. The reliability coefficient was found to be 0.879. The SPSS 20 software package was used in the analysis of the data made in the research study used in the study applications in June of the 2013–2014 academic year. The level of dependency of the subjects on the total score were measured in the data obtained primarily and the relationship between the data obtained and the other variables was analysed.

The frequency was analysed to determine the overall situation and to determine the socio-demographic characteristics of the subjects. However, the chi-square test was used in order to check whether there is a significant relationship between variables with two classes and the t-test was used to determine whether there is a significant difference between two groups. Furthermore, the one-way analysis of variance (ANOVA) was used in comparison groups In the evaluation results of the analysis, 0.05 was taken as the upper value of significance.

Findings

- 41.5% of respondents are male and 58.5% are female.
- According to the education class, 48.7% of respondents are in the ninth grade, 36.3% and in the tenth grade, 11.4% are in the eleventh grade, and 3.6% are in the twelfth grade.
- The distribution of family income is as follows: 11.9% of respondents have minimum wage, 25.9% have 811-1000TL, 18.1% have 1001-1500TL, 18.7%

have 1501-2000TL, 8.8% have 2001-2500TL, 7.8% have 2001-3000TL, and 8.8% have 3001TL.

- 80.8% of respondents say that they don't spend any money on games. 13% of them spend 10-30TL, 2.6% spend 31-50TL, and 3.6% spend 51TL or more.
- When the time spent at the beginning of the game is considered, the rate of respondents stating that they play at least an hour is 32.1% and it is at the significance level. In the same way, the rate of respondents stating that they play at least two hours is 26.9%, the rate of respondents stating that they play several days a week is 11.9%, and the rate of those playing three to four days a week is 10.9%. Those who state that they play the game several times a month make up 14.5% and those who never play have been identified to be 3.6%.

Table 1: Most played game types

		Number of respondents	Percent	Valid percent
Most Played Games	Action – adventure games	80	20.7	20.7
	Sport games	56	14.5	14.5
	Educational (intelligent puzzles, etc.) games	12	3.1	3.1
	Strategy games	30	7.8	7.8
	Facebook, etc. integrated games	62	16.1	16.1
	Mobile phone based games	146	37.8	37.8
	Total	**386**	**100.0**	**100.0**

Table 2: Participants' game playing habits

		Number of respondents	Percent	Valid percent	Total percent
Most popular sides of playing games	To create own game character and raise own level	160	41.5	41.5	41.5
	To feel superior to others	10	2.6	2.6	44.0
	To interact with other people	72	18.7	18.7	62.7
	To make money by selling level in games, etc.	38	9.8	9.8	72.5
	To kill time	106	27.5	27.5	100.0
	Total	**386**	**100.0**	**100.0**	

Table 3: Game addiction level

		Number of respondents	Percent	Valid percent	Total percent
Game addiction level	Those who don't have problems	272	70.5	70.5	70.5
	Risk group	110	28.5	28.5	99.0
	Addicted	4	1.0	1.0	100.0
	Total	386	100.0	100.0	

Relationships Between Variables

When monthly expenditure for the game and gender of the subjects, preferences of the type of game, favourite aspects of playing games, the average daily playing time, and relationship between the online time and number of players were considered, it was revealed that there is a significant difference (t=4.216; $p<0.05$) in terms of gender in monthly expenditures for games. The average and the standard deviation of men are higher than girls ($\bar{x}$ 1.46>1.16; sd 0.88>0.47). Accordingly, men spend much more time on games than girls.

Accordingly, gender is different in terms of selecting types of games (t=3.78; $p<0.05$). The average and the standard deviation of men are higher than girls ($\bar{x}$ 7.38>5.26; sd 5.49>5.37). When crosstab is considered in order to evaluate according to the content of the game, it is observed that while men concentrate more on war, adventure, and strategy games, girls prefer to play games including information agriculture and non-violent content (χ^2=197, df=21, p=0.00). There is significant difference between the most preferred aspects of playing games and gender (t=–0.296; $p>0.05$).

The average and standard deviation of men and girls are equal or very close to each other ($\bar{x}$ 2.76>2.81; sd 168=168). Accordingly, a significant difference between men and girls in terms of their favourite aspects of playing games isn't clear.

There isn't a significant difference between men and girls in terms of subjects wasting time playing games (t=1.6; $p>0.05$). The average and standard deviation of men and girls are equal or very close to each other ($\bar{x}$ 2.70>2.52; sd 1.64=1.48). There isn't a significant differentiation in terms of the time spent at the beginning of the game. Furthermore, it was determined that men and girls waste time on games in a similar way.

There is a significant difference in terms of the number of online players (t= 8.86; $p>0.05$). The average and standard deviation of men are higher than girls ($\bar{x}$ 8.51>2.57; sd 8.31>4.78). Accordingly, gender difference in terms of selected number of players in online game indicates significant difference.

Here, the main factor is the selected game type and the content of the played game. Especially, it can be observed that girl subjects prefer individual based games in the virtual world more than men who prefer multi-player systems such as war strategy and miscible.

There is a significant differentiation between total scores obtained as a result of subjects' sex and the addiction scale (t=6.07; p>0.05). The average and standard deviation of men are higher than girls ($\overline{x}$ 48.2>39.9; sd 14=74>12.01). Accordingly, it is clear that men are more addicted while achieving higher score than girls. When the category status of scale scores and the averages are considered, men are revealed to show significant deviation. When the relationship between their class and variables are considered, the existence of significant differentiation between classes and money spent for the game is seen (F=10.611; p<0.05;).

When the situation among classes is considered (Turkey Post Hoc), the fact that the average of ninth graders was higher and the average of other grades was lower and the fact that this situation got lower as class increased can be seen. Thus, lower form young people can be observed to be more inclined to spend money for games. When game preferences between classes are considered, a significant difference is clear (F=4.430; p>0.05;). If we look at situation between classes (Turkey Post Hoc), we can see difference between ninth, eleventh, and twelfth grades; however, the tenth grade didn't differ. There are significant differences between tenth and eleventh grades among their favourite aspects of playing games and their class (F=4.103; p>0.05;). There is not a difference among other classes, while there is a difference between tenth and eleventh grade classes in terms of the number of online players (F=3.846, p<0.05). While there is no difference among twelfth grade classes, there are differences between nine and eleven, eleven and nine, and ten and eleven classes.

When money spent monthly for the game and other variables are considered, it can be seen that there is differentiation among people whose family income is in the lower economic groups; however, there isn't differentiation among other groups (F=3.052; p<0.05). While there is differentiation of the average income level between types of games and monthly family income, there is no difference in terms of favourite games. When subjects whose family income is at the upper level are considered in terms of time playing games, in terms of lower and upper groups, it can be seen that the upper group wastes more time (F=3.377; p<0.05).

When the relationship between addiction level and variables are considered, the existence of significant differentiation between money spent monthly and dependency levels is observed (F=16.065; p<0.05). When the relationship between addiction level and money spent monthly is researched (Turkey Post Hoc), we can see three groups that differ in terms of spending. The group mostly wasting money is an addicted group. There isn't a significant difference between the level of addiction and the types of games and between the most favourite aspect and the time of games. However, significant differentiation among the number of online player is observed ($F=25.150$; $p<0.05$;).

Discussion

In the example of Aksaray, the research studying the case of high school students' addiction to online determines whether there are differences between gender, types of games, time of playing games, class, monthly expenditure, and level of addiction to games. It is observed that 1% of participants are addicted to online games. Meanwhile, 28.5% of subjects are in the risk group. It can be seen that gender is a significant variable in terms of online games; time of spending game, playing caused to differ accordingly to types of games and addiction. Men are more addicted than girls. A significant differentiation can be observed in terms of class. Accordingly, lower forms are more addicted. This case shows that this may turn into serious problems. In terms of money spent for games, subjects of the lower level income group are considered to be less problematic. The higher level income group was found to be more addicted. On the other hand, a strong relationship was observed to be present between addiction and the state of spending money.

References

Ayas, T. (2012). The Relationship between Internet and Computer Game Addiction Level and Shyness among High School Students. *Educational Sciences: Theory & Practice,* 12(2), 632–636.

Festl, R., Scharkow, M., & Quandt, T. (2012). Problematic Computer Game Use Among Adolescents, Younger and Older Adults. *Addiction* (108), 592–599.

Florence, C. (2006). The Games We Play Online and Offline: Making Wang-tta in Korea. *Popular Communication,* 4(3), 225–239.

Hollen, K. H. (2009). *Encyclopedia of Addictions.* United States of America: Greenwood Press.

İnal, Y., & Çağıltay, K. (2005). Turkish Elementary School Students' Computer Game Play Characteristics. *International Informatics Congress.* Eskişehir.

Kayri, M., Tanhan, F., & Tanrıverdi, S. (2014). Ortaöğretim Öğrencilerinde İnternet Bağımlılığı ile Algılanan Sosyal Destek Arasındaki İlişkinin İncelenmesi. *Online Journal of Technology Addiction & Cyberbullying* (1), 1–27.

Ko, C.H., Liu, G.C., Hsiao, S., Yen, J.Y., Yang, M.J., Lin, W.C., … Chen, C.S. (2009). Brain activities associated with gaming urge of online gaming addiction. *Journal of Psychiatric Research* (43), 739–747.

Ko, C.H., Yen, J.Y., Chen, C.C., Chen, S.H., & Yen, C.F. (2005). Gender Differences and Related Factors Affecting Online Gaming Addiction Among Taiwanese Adolescents. *The Journal of Nervous and Mental Disease,* 193(4), 273–277.

Neils, C., & Shavaun, S.P. (2009). *Game Addiction The Experience and the Effects.* United States of America.: Jefferson, N.C.: McFarland.

Ng, B.D., & Hastings, P.W. (2005). Addiction to the Internet and Online Gaming. *Cyberpsychology & Behavior,* 8(2), 110–114.

Peker, A., İskender, M., & Ada, Ş. (2010). Liselerdeki Öğrencilerin On-line Oyun Bağımlılıkları. *Journal of Kazım Karabekir Education Faculty* (20), 1–12.

Rooij, A.J., Schoenmakers, M., Vermulst, A.A., Eijnden, R.J., & Van de Mheen, D. (2010). Online Video Game Addiction: Identification of Addicted Adolescent Gamers. *Society for the Study of Addiction* (106), 205–212.

Son, D.T., Yasuoka, J., Poudel, K.C., Otsuka, K., & Jimba, M. (2012). Massively multiplayer online role-playing games (MMORPG): Association between its addiction, self-control and mental disorders among young people in Vietnam. *International Journal of Social Psychiatry,* 59(6), 570–577.

Young, K.S. (2007). Treatment Outcomes with Internet Addicts. *Cyber Psychology & Behavior,* 10(5), 671–679.

Http://www.forbes.com/sites/johngaudiosi/2012/07/18/new-reports-forecasts-global-video-game-industry-will-reach-82-billion-by-2017/.

Http://www.statista.com/statistics/270728/market-volume-of-online-gaming-worldwide/.

Cansu Aydemir

In the Context of Branding: Using Gender Roles, Creating Criteria, and Analysis of Advertisements Broadcasted in Turkey

Introduction

As it is widely known, world brands use mass media to the maximum benefit from every single channel to continue their existence. The marketing process developed out of this viewpoint usually makes the global economy a vivid mechanism, builds a high-level consumer society, and creates a setting from negative contents. Particularly in advertisements, presenting a fast/unstable utopia society and encouraging lives makes individuals act as unconscious consumers of society; global brands in this context create a reproducible mechanism for themselves on the basis of customers. Thanks to this vicious cycle, brands can completely build their marketing strategies on society. In other words, media creates a brand-based eclipse of reason environment on the audience through the advertisement channel. However, in branding, personal identities are attributed to the above mentioned audience. The existence of individuals living in society is valuable in terms of their outfit or the brands which they think that they belong to. At the same time, in social research, excluding social and cultural gender, the roles of gender in 21st century advertisements are discussed to show that an intensive influential and convincing object which results from global concerns is used.

Methods

As part of the research study, the following question has been discussed: "Which roles are portrayed particularly for genders in global-local advertisements broadcasted in Turkey?" On the other hand, we tried to specify which object in the content of the advertisement influenced the audience. The survey method through scales was used to measure how influential the advertisements broadcasted in Turkey were to the respondents. The survey was conducted to an audience of 50 people who have regular income and are actively working. Two open-ended questions were asked. Responses to these questions were analysed together with the evaluation of the advertisements. The reason for the open-ended questions in the survey was by no means to restrict the free will of the audience or to direct them. The reason for conducting a survey of people who are employeees is because the target audience of all advertisements is mostly active employees who have a standard income and status in society (target audience of public service advertising is excluded here). In this research study conducted using the open-ended survey method, a literature search, examination of legislations of the Supreme Board of Radio and Television (RTUK), and literature reviews were also included. As well as detailed resources and thesis reviews, advertisements that have been broadcasted/will be broadcasted were analysed over a branding and communication based platform. In the conclusion, Ümit Çelebi, Kadir Has University Advertising Department Lecturer, Chief Executive Officer of Brand Communication, and a member of the Turkey Advertisers Association delivered her professional opinions about the topic.

Findings

Within the scope of the research study, some particular criteria were set to find out which component of the advertisement influences the audience the most at the time of exposure to the ads. These components could be listed as place, montage, actor/actress, music, product, and slogan. Although readings conducted before the research proposed the "actor/actress" component, the conclusion at the end of the research study showed that the audience could evaluate the advertisement from a different component. Hereby, it is possible to say that we reached a different conclusion than we expected when the beginning and end of the research study are compared. When the audience was analysed based on which criteria made them watch the commercial till the end, the following conclusions were reached: in the 21st century advertisements, the digital age society reveals that advertisements which have rather attractive/different/fast/unstable and especially sexually explicit roles content make the audience watch the commercial until the end.

It is obvious that advertisements created using diverse perception management methods are somehow more influential on the customer. It is possible to explain the reasons why the audience watched commercials based on the views of two scholars. "According to Millard, advertisements are easy to understand by individuals. They are also influential because individuals have the chance to observe the characters and behaviors they are familiar with. In other words, advertisements include stereotyped social gender characters which audience is used to know; in return audience receives the messages without finding something odd." "According to Bonelli, when women see that women portrayed in advertisements are like themselves, they are more open to receive the messages of the ads and they also feel the sense of appreciation of their behaviors." When the views of Millard and Bonelli and the research topics are all taken into consideration, it can be argued that two types of advertisements are influential on the audience. These are: the ones where characters of the ads are similar to the target audience (more common in local advertisements with social and cultural content) or advertisements which offer utopia, imaginary lives, and a life of luxury (global advertisements).

In the survey, we asked the people who are actively working…

1-When you are watching a commercial, which one draws your attention the most?

Analyses of answers to the first question: The answers to the first question reveal that montage draws the attention of the audience the most and the last thing that the audience notices/perceives is the "place." We understand that fast/unstable/interesting and active advertisements are more permanent. The product, which is the main reason for the advertisement story, is penultimate in the list which shows that the audience does not focus on the product solely but instead focuses on the commercial as a whole. The second most popular answer, "music," demonstrates that consumer advertisements formed combining several different melodies are more remarkable. Especially considering the brands that you will see in the second question, advertisements with musical backgrounds are catchier.

Figure 1: Commercial Effectiveness

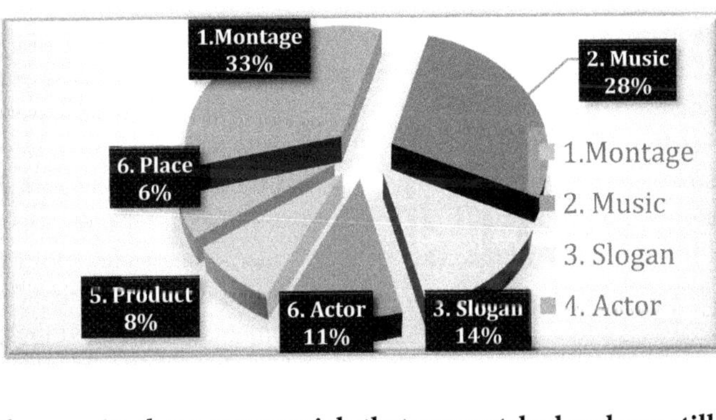

2-Could you write three commercials that you watched and you still remember?

The brands that the target audience stated that they watch the most in the advertisements are as follows: Is Bank, Familia, Dominos, Öncü Paper Paste, Kelebek Mobilya (Furniture), Algida, Kotex, Pınar Milk, Pepsi, Ace, Garanti Bank, Ulker Chocolate Wafer, Goodyear, Toyota, Vodafone, Akbank, Slazenger, Volvo, Citroen, Snickers, Vivident Extra, Mercedes, Cornetto, National Basketball Team, 118 80,

Lamborghini, Avon, Nike, P&G, Omoi Fiat, Teknosa, Panda, Tadelle, Sütaş Ayran (Yogurt Drink), Ford, THY, Avea, Lassa, Uludağ Gazoz, and Tadelle.

The answers which were given more than three times for question 2 are as follows: Is Bank, Toyota, Sütaş Ayran (Yogurt Drink), Snickers, and Ülker advertisements.

Analysis of the answers given to the second question: As we can clearly see from the answers given above, catchy advertisements for the audience are mostly the ones which contain cultural codes. For instance, in the commercials of Is Bank, there is continuity from past to present and future. Rather than the celebrities of the commercial, conveying the message together with the culture has been the most striking factor for the audience. In the advertisements of Toyota, the figure of "father" is referred to as part of a traditional Turkish family structure (patriarchal family structure). Concepts of fast and strong father and designing advertisements using infant-directed speech made the advertisements catchier and remembered more easily. Finally, when Sütaş Ayran (yogurt drink), which is in the third rank, is examined, it is found that it is a traditional drink for our culture and it is remembered easily thanks to its design on cultural facts. If we refer to Mc Luhan's "Global Village," it is apparent that through media, people everywhere in the world will watch commercials produced using the same techniques and with same concerns and people will in return have answers with the same background. It means that it will stick in our minds as an imposition of ideology, money economy, and globalisation. When rapidly changing media and consumer society are mentioned, it is not surprising to see society themed advertisements in the research conclusions about advertisements broadcasted in different time periods. Due to this reason, global advertisements aim to become localised to become globalised. Another surprising conclusion obtained from the answers of the survey is that the product is ranked second to last with a rate of 8%. It is also remarkable considering the main objective of the advertisement is to sell the product. In the conclusion of recent research studies, particularly in advertisements broadcasted in Turkey, it is aimed to use gender roles and culture in global advertisements to localise the advertisements. On the other hand, it is apparent that steps are taken to change the current gender perception. In relation to that, when we want to analyse it over two advertisements in Turkey, "Biscolata" and "Magnum," which bring the most distinct gender roles in play, would be the best choice. In these commercials, sex roles were reversed, advertising does not show men and women in all of their roles, and culture and traditions are emphasised but in an unfamiliar way. In the content of the commercials of Biscolata, we see that men are extraordinarily portrayed in the kitchen having a sexual image. It is another significant detail that the brand portrays skilful and sexy men in the kitchen. Similarly in commercials of Magnum, women are portrayed as picky and executive which is in contrast to the traditional role of women in the Turkish unity of family. The woman does not need anyone but herself to enjoy herself in the commercial. Dear Ümit Çelebi, Kadir Has University Advertising Department Lecturer, Chief Executive Officer of Brand Communication, and a member of the Turkey Advertisers Association delivered her professional opinions about the Biscolata and Magnum commercials among global advertisements. She stated the following: "Magnum and Biscolata advertisements pioneer big changes in this respect. Biscolata uses male body as an object instead of a female body. There is a French brand "Bonjour" and it is totally adapted to Biscolata brand. The muscle men you watch in the commercials do not symbolise strength or aesthetics. It directly appraises male body as a sex object. Chocolate is a product that appeals to women and sexy and attractive features of male body all together used as an object. The case is different for Magnum commercials. For a long time, this brand established a communication concentrating that women do not need anyone else to be satisfied. In fact starting from sexuality, this brand discussed self-sufficiency of women. Giving the brand Magnum name, matching it with the gun, the fact that general language of it is about sex, attributing the satisfaction of women to eating show us that the brand itself uses its product as a sex object. Differently from 60s and 70s, woman does not become an object rather she is the one who has the right for sexuality and satisfaction. In the last two years of Magnum commercials, design language is as the following: a confident woman dominates sexy and attractive men; man and woman are accepted to be equal in terms of sexuality and attractiveness; anytime she wants, woman can use sexual attractiveness to attract the interest of man. Sexuality of women is apparent in these advertisements although we cannot say that the woman is the object of the communication. All communication is based on the woman and she has the full control of the sexuality." If we view Magnum[1] and Biscolata[2] commercials, it will give us an opportunity to better analyse the problem defined in the beginning of the research study. As part of the research study, when we examine the broadcasting framework and the rights of broadcasting, law no: 6112 states that:

For the implementation of the second paragraph of the Article 9 of The Law No. 6112 on the Establishment of Radio and Television Enterprises and Their Media Services accepted in Grand National Assembly of Turkey (TBMM) on

---

1 http://www.youtube.com/watch?v=5w2R7i811Ec.
2 http://www.youtube.com/watch?v=C7X2NGVFHnA.

February 15th, 2011: "Subliminal techniques shall not be used in commercial communications."[3]

Article 11 of the Radio and Television Institutions Commercial Advertising Regulation states that: "Hidden advertisement is prohibited. Unless clearly indicated as an "advertisement," the products or services should not be presented in the programmes with the intention of advertising. No advertisement may include any technical device that, by using images of very brief duration or by any other means, exploits the possibility of conveying a message to, or otherwise influencing the minds of, members of an audience without their being aware, or fully aware, of what has been done.[4]

On the other hand, when the content of commercials and survey results are examined, the target audience is usually men and women (25–44 years old) that have a higher purchasing power (working).

Figure 2: Female and Male Population by the Age Groups

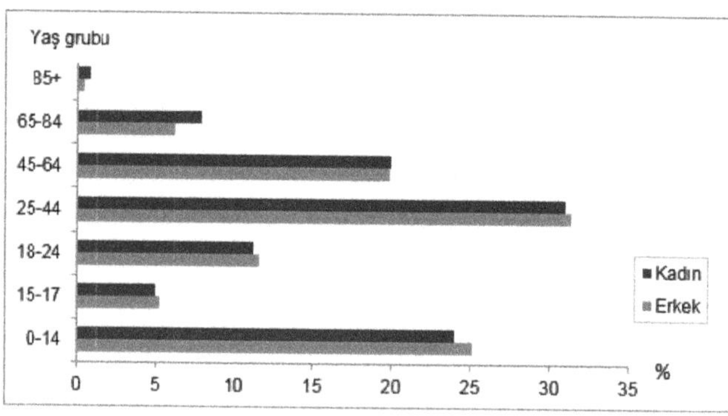

Source: TÜİK 2013 Reports-Female and Male Population / Turkish Statistical Institute (TUIK).[5]

As it can also be clearly seen from the graph, the child population as a target audience for advertisements is relatively high. It is extensively because the needs of children are met by their parents which could increase the advertisements which have kids as their target audience. By this way, do you think that we can state that branding and advertisements change the social gender roles? Or in other words, could we say that in the globalising world, different gender roles are not portrayed on cultural codes due to monetary policy and seeking profit but instead

3 http://www.rtuk.org.tr/#.
4 http://www.rtuk.org.tr/#.
5 http://www.tuik.gov.tr/PreHaberBultenleri.do?id=16056.

gender roles are reproduced through advertisements? Or in another perspective, could we say that subliminal techniques are not used in advertisements as it is implemented in the law?

Discussion

Within the scope of the research study, the influence of global and cultural advertisements has been measured on the audience based on specific criteria. Besides, analyses in this paper are based on relevant articles (no:6112) of legislations of the RTÜK the target audience of the advertisements (particularly the employed population as it is confirmed in the reports of the TUİK), and expert opinions about comparing and contrasting gender roles in Biscolata and Magnum commercials. Particular commercials were not chosen in the scope of this research study. This may be defined as a problem. However, the reason for this was to avoid canalising people towards one particular thing. The perception of advertisements has been analysed from various perspectives and it has been concluded that advertisements with cultural content are remembered more easily and advertisements with fast/unstable contents are viewed more than others.

References

Darıcı, S. (2012) Subliminal İşgal, DestekYayınevi.

Harris, L. T., Whalen, P. T. (2009) 21. Yüzyılda Pazarlama Profesyonelinin Halkla İlişkiler El Kitabı, Rota Yayınları.

Babür Tosun, N. (Ocak 2010), İletişim Temelli Marka Yönetimi, Beta Yayınları.

Cenk Ateş[1]

Historical Transformation of a Gift and Presentation on Television as Consumer Products in the Modern Era: Instance of Valentine's Day[2]

Introduction

The gift is a social phenomenon that has reached up to present society but has undergone a change over time in terms of its meaning. While it has a role in strengthening the social ties in the archaic societies based on the basis of mutual give-take-give-back, in modern societies, it has a change in meaning and in digressing its meaning, it started to serve to the capitalist system. As there has been no layout based on commodity in archaic societies, the gift has constituted the basis of the relationships. What is important is giving away a gift and the soul it has.

The given gift has been considered as a social phenomenon and has a role in reflecting the importance of social dialogue (Mauss, 2005 p. 160). The gift is an economic and social cultural pattern that has strengthened the social relations in the archaic period, passed from hand to hand in line with the requirements and given back far and away. Without separating subject and object, it constantly causes the sense of 'debtor' on oneself and it has a functional role underlying the social relations through these feelings (Godbout, 2003 p. 18).

A gift, which varies according to the intended use, has undergone a change with the emergence of capitalism. The separation of producers and consumers and the fact that they do not recognise each other has destroyed the gift system in terms of the economy and culture. Wealth, which has been achieved by spending as much as possible in the archaic period, is obtained by saving in the capitalist system.

As capitalism has been based on the profit concept, it designed gift as an object of profit and imposed this idea to society using mass media, especially television

---

1 Research Assistant at Radio – Television and Cinema Department of Faculty of Communication, Selcuk University.

2 This study is the summary of a master's thesis conducted in 2013, entitled "Historical Transformation Of Gift And Presentation On Television As Consumer Prodoctin Modern Era: Instance Of Valentine's Day."

(TV). In order to increase the consumption in this system, it has imposed special occasions to society such as Valentine's Day, Mother's and Father's Day, and Christmas and has made these a current issue through TV ads, serials, and news segments through which the gift system transformed into gift shopping (Arik, 2004 p. 81).

Methods

In this study, a literature review on the social function of the gift, the historical studies made concerning the subject, and the presentation of the gift phenomenon on TV is made.

Findings

Definition of Gift

In the archaic period, the gift is an object that is believed to have a soul that is presented dressily to a tribe to achieve a more peaceful way instead of fighting in order to obtain all sorts of the needed food and similar products that tribes do not have. Not only outside the tribe, also within the tribe, it is believed to carry the soul of the person who gives it away and is given to another person as a sign of generosity, dignity, and an expression of superiority (Sahlins, 2010 p. 187).

During this period, the gift and giving gifts is an economical system that creates a social bond which is based on the basis of consuming all the obtained or giving someone else, another tribe, or obliterating in case of excess during ceremonies regardless of pecuniary advantage.

Creating mutual reciprocal obligations, this cultural phenomenon triggers and maintains social and personal relations and is a complex whole that is an indicator of social status. It is possible to define the term gift, which lost its duty to create and maintain social bonds, as a cold tool that has turned into a benefit account and allows the sale of the manufactured and leads the individual to consumption in accordance with the benefits of dominant forces (Godbout, 2003 p. 18).

Social Function of Gift in the Archaic Period

The goods given as a gift in the archaic period have not been thought of as material objects. Unlike the concept of capitalism that sees people as objects, gifts are humanised. During this period, a gift given should be returned to its first original owner on the grounds that it carries the soul of its original owner. In this way, a gift is a totem that has a task to create and maintain social relations passing from hand to hand which accompanies festivals and demonstrations.

Helping each other is considered among the most important functions of the gift. This tradition, also known as Kula, enables communication between tribes and it is the dressily presentation of a gift to a tribe to achieve a more peaceful way instead of fighting in order to obtain all sorts of needed food and similar products that tribes do not have. The nature of Kula is a promise that the tribe who gives gifts obtained the needed goods in exchange for the given. Therefore, Kula is not a market that operates with the known market procedures and everyone exhibits their goods and an accepted value system is valid. Everyone gets their prize based on the gift claimed and the promise. The promise, which is already in the possession of the person, is considered as goods that are at home and will be given at the most appropriate time (Benedict, 2000 p. 169).

The gift, which enables social bonds between different tribes with a cooperation aspect, is also an indicator power and status in terms of generosity, dignity, and superiority. According to the Potlac tradition, which means 'Cherish' and 'Consume,' everything accompanied with the feast should be ceremonially given as a gift and the things that are more than needed should be obliterated. In these ceremonies, a chief presents the gift to his or her opponent in order to humiliate, to challenge, and to compel him or her, in other words, to establish superiority on him.

In Potlac ceremony, which is held to humiliate the opponent, the person receiving the gift should obliviate the humiliation and oppose the challenge. They should also respond by accepting the 'obligation' between them. But, this is only possible with another Potlac which is held after a while and is more generous. The modern day equivalent of this is the requirement of giving back with 'interest' by the person receiving the gift (Bataille, 2010: 83–84). On that sense, Potlac is an act of acquiring reputation and prestige based on spending (Malinowski, 1999 p. 22).

Potlac, similar to Kula, acts as the cooperation between close tribes and establishes not only personal bonds, but also social bonds between communities. With this aspect, the gift system constantly creates the sense of 'debtor' on oneself together with its functional role underlying the social relations; it also prevents the economical accumulation, private property, and socioeconomic inequalities by obliterating the surplus (Tezcan, 1989 p. 31).

Capitalism and the Gift

The gift system, which cannot produce anything and continues with only the goods released onto free circulation, has undergone a major change with the emergence of capitalism. The capitalist economic action, which is identical with gained effort, has saved the passage of goods from producer to consumer and emphasised the value of change rather than the value of use irrespective of direct community ties

(Weber, 2010 p. 10–11). Thus, the exchange became very distant to connecting people and the increase between the parties' number of gifts has been replaced with the interest between debtor and creditor (Hyde, 2008 p. 72). In other words, commodity production has caused a separation between producer and consumer and turned the gift object into a commodity. In this context, capitalism has transformed the giving concept in the archaic period into selling and taking into buying.

At the same time, the equivalence concept, which is not tolerated on the grounds that it may destroy the ties between people, has become ordinary with the usage of money as an exchange tool and exchanging has ended the ties between people (Sahlins, 2010 p. 217–218).

While the wealth in the archaic period gained with spending the possession, in the capitalist system, this situation is replaced with accumulation. Thus, sociability is degraded into individualism and through this, the dependence to another one is eliminated and addiction to things is provided. This system, which is based on the profit concept from every aspect, designed the gift as a profit object and imposed this to society through mass media. With the post-Fordist period, during which consumption is made in order to create identity, status started to be determined with the consumption products led by mass media and not with the profession. Thus, while selecting the consumption commodities, the individual decides based on exceptionalism and buys the goods by popular culture. Arousing artificial needs for consumers, the culture industry provokes the feelings and awareness of consumption using mass media (Atiker, 1998: 38, 52). Therefore, the goods determined by the capitalist system, which sees the feelings as a profit door, are considered as a gift and can be taken in return for a fee.

Presentation of Gifts on TV

Capitalism, which ignores the traditional values or capitalises on them, transformed the gift phenomenon, which has been a tool to strengthen human relations since the archaic period, into a consumption object through coding it apart from its actual meaning. Being easily accessible and given its visual power, TV is a mass communication tool that legitimises capitalism and contributes to the transformation of the gift.

Compared to other mass communication tools, TV has a more powerful effect and promotes consumption through broadcast programs. In this sense, capitalism codes the gift concept in accordance with its benefits and reaches to masses using TV as the most effective weapon. In other words, the gift concept is degraded to a tool that leads the masses to consume through advertisements, news, serials, and competition programs.

TV, which is under control of international or national companies, has caused the gift concept to lose its original meaning and standardised the other products of popular culture. In the capitalist system, the consumption products can be accessed over a certain price. In this sense, all kinds of commodities shown on TV as gifts have a price and the authenticity of the gift is lost. The gift in question has a price and is considered as an object to be purchased.

The advertisements, serials, competition programs, and cartoons for children on TV lay stress on the gift concept and create a role model for the masses about giving and taking gift behaviour. The presentation of gifts on TV is designed as a product that has a price. In order to create this perception, the products such as cars, jewellery, furniture, etc. are given to the winning competitor at a competition program and are considered as a gift. In this situation, the things given and the giving action are not the aim; they are a tool to gain profit. In such a case, these products cannot be seen as a gift (Özdemir, 2008 p. 475).

In the same way, the printed and visual media moves together for a common target. The gifts that will be given by newspapers in return for coupons are broadcasts on TV. The goods that are shown as a gift are presented as though they are needed and must be owned. In this context, the product that is presented as gift is the profit game of capitalism. The presentation of a gift on TV is not only for adults.

Capitalism, which is in search of new markets or in expanding the existing one, achieves to capitalise on every opportunity. Targeting on adapting not only adults but also the children, the culture industry presents gift advertisements for children through the TV. The products for school report gift, summer holiday gift and feast gift, popular cartoon characters, Barbie dolls, Rambo, Batman, and Spider Man, which are created to spread imperialism, are products of popular culture.

Popular culture and media create a culture of consumption unburdening all the cultural values and altering the games and tools tradition (Erdoğan and Alemdar, 2005 p. 169). The presentation of the gift on TV shows itself especially on special days.

The Presentation of Valentine's Day on TV

The capitalist system uses feelings for profit in order to increase consumption. In this context, each professional group has been declared a special day such as Mother's Day, Father's Day, and Valentine's Day. These days do not only accompany feelings and cause spending, but also cause changes in the minds of people (Ersoy, 2008 p. 150).

Turning every single point of life into a commercial language, capitalism has intervened the emotional ties between people through which it not only weakens the friendship and blunts the natural socialisation skills, but also becomes a service sector that created closeness, heartiness, and personal relations. It also market all these things. This aspects of capitalism recommends people to come over the feelings in order to create healthy communication and advice to periodically repeat these feelings (Çabuklu 2007, p. 98).

As a special day, Valentine's Day is emphasised on TV and is stressed as a mandatory traditional day, causing consumption to peak on this day. Valentine's Day, when feelings are used by the culture industry and consumption increases, influences society through media stressing on the day. The programs broadcasted on TV reflect the idea that people can show their feelings to their lovers or husbands/wives by buying presents. In this way, the thought that consumers can show their love only by buying presents and buying presents is the only way to show love is manifested (Bayuk, 2009 p. 189).

TV, which passes the idea that showing your love on Valentine's Day can be achieved only by buying expensive gifts, ignores the economic dimension of this scam offer. TV is creating a dense content to increase consumption. When news, advertisements, and the content of serials are considered, commercial orientation is self-evident. Where the couples will go on February 14th and the ads of restaurant, hotels, and resorts are introduced weeks prior to Valentine's Day (Arık 2004 p. 84).

Gift fairs are shown on news and advertisements, sometimes an interview is broadcast, and the audience is asked whether or not they decided on the present. The owner of the TV channel gets money for advertising from related sectors and any product belonging to any sector is shown as a present for Valentine's Day (Özdemir, 2008 p. 478).

The choice of gift is the most important element that revives today's consumption. TV shows which present can be bought for valentine, which present means what and which present makes the valentine happy. In this sense, buying presents on Valentine's Day has a parallelism with the fashion created by popular culture and the gifts are chosen in accordance with the ones that are presented by media. In other words, the gift that will be chosen for Valentine's Day is determined by the influence of TV.

February 14th is shown as an a important day to society on the news from the beginning of February. In the same way, it is seen that when Valentine's Day approaches, the intense and aggressive advertising campaigns directly affect even the rational consumers and turn these days into a consumer outbreak.

Knowing the effect of feelings on consumer behaviour, the companies focus on emotions and emphasise feelings such as love, longing, recalling, etc. They also encourage people to consume and it became easier to convert customers into a consumer society, making the consumption culture dominant (Bayuk, 2009 p. 188).

The advertisements for Valentine's Day do not only determine the gift selection, but also create brand loyalty, making people think that the most valuable present to give the valentine is a certain brand, causing people to evaluate the present according to its brand. TV helps ordinary products to turn into magical objects, giving them a new meaning and enabling them to be sold for more than their real value (Özdemir, 2008 p. 479). Advertisements attribute new meanings to ordinary products and present it to masses. They affect the community's gift choice, causing consumers to look for the products that are in the same quality and brand like in the ads.

Gift choice under the influence of brand ads also formats the individual's lifestyle. Except for the ads and news, the serials are among the most followed programs because of the frequency of their broadcast and follow up rates. Therefore, it is unavoidable not to have content related to giving gifts on TV serials where fictional messages are created and which cause certain changes in behaviour.

In series of 'Christmas special,' 'Valentine's Day special,' etc., serials it is common to see that the part includes all the elements of this special day. In this part, the scenes of purchasing gifts are shown a lot and there is mention of when the present will be given and who will receive it. The symbolic meaning that is being bought by the actor is legitimated through this way. The audience fondly following the serial is affected by the actor/actress and his or her behaviour so that they want to buy the same ring, car, lastest model mobile phone, etc.

Discussion

The gift is a social phenomenon that emerged in archaic societies. It has helped to create dialogues not only within tribes, but also between the tribes and designed the social relations.

In archaic societies, a gift is based on the basis of mutual give-take-give-back. The repayment of the person receiving the gift should be with 'interest.' This is the best possible way of accepting and maintaining gift relations. In archaic tribes, the gift system within the tribe is called 'Potlac' and the one between tribes is called 'Kula.' In order to gain supremacy within the tribe and among other tribes, all the possessed should be consumed until the end. So much so that this situation even leads to the killing of slaves in order to impose the superiority of one on the other.

Spending is a sign of wealth, superiority, and power. As it is seen, a gift is not only a tool to create dialogue within and between tribes, it is also concerned with social forces such as power, glory, honour, and supremacy. With this aspect, the gift, which is inserted as an object when needed, contributes to social solidarity and has a function based on consumption for prestige.

The gift has detached from its real meaning and has turned into a phenomenon which is reinterpreted by the dominant ideology. With the emergence of capitalism, the gift lost its function in the archaic period and has been replaced as a commodity. Society is degraded to the individual and the social function of the gift has disappeared.

The capital owners have turned every day into a special day and buying a gift under the influence of TV became a mandatory behaviour. After passing into the hands of capitalist powers, mass media has made the masses similar by creating a popular culture. A consumer society is created through advertisements, series, contests, etc. and the gift is turned into a commodity that should be bought in order to show love.

In this system, it has become possible to show love to another individual only with the consumer products that are legitimised by popular culture. This idea is spread to society via TV and the gift is degraded into a commodity that can be consumed through TV broadcast. TV ads, serials, competition programs, and cartoons for children directly or indirectly stress on the term gift and take an active role in guiding the masses about giving gifts.

References

Arık, B. (2004). Bir Kültür Endüstrisi Ürünü Olarak 14 Şubat Sevgililer Günü. *İstanbul Üniversitesi İletişim Fakültesi Hakemli Dergisi*, (20), http://www.journals.istanbul.edu.tr/tr/index.php/iletisim/article/view/12736/11963. Erişim Tarihi: 04.02.2013.

Atiker, E. (1998). *Modernizm ve Kitle Toplumu*. Ankara: Vadi Yayınları.

Bataille, G. (2010). *Lanetli Pay*. Ankara: Dost Kitabevi.

Benedict, R. (2000). *Kültür Örüntüleri*. Ankara: Öteki Yayınevi.

Bayuk, N. (2009). *Özel Gün ve Haftaların Tüketim Üzerindeki Etkileri*. www.kamuis.org.tr/pdf/1118. Erişim Tarihi: 02.10.2011.

Çabuklu, Y (2007). *Toplumsal Kurgular ve Cinsiyetçilik*. İstanbul: Everest Yayınları.

Erdoğan, İ & Alemdar, K. (2005). *Popüler Kültür ve İletişim*. Ankara: Erk Yayınları.

Ersoy, E. (2008), *Tarihsel Kapitalizmden Güncel Kapitalizme Küreselleşme*. Doğu Anadolu Bölgesi Araştırmaları.

Godbout, J. T. (2003). *Armağan Dünyası*. İstanbul: İletişim Yayınları.

Malinowski, B. (1999). *İlkel Toplum*. Ankara: Öteki Yayınevi.

Mauss, M. (2005). *Sosyoloji ve Antropoloji*. Ankara: Doğu-Batı Yayınları.

Özdemir, N. (2008). Türk Hediyeleşme Geleneği ve Medya. *Uluslararası Sosyal Araştırmalar Dergisi*. 1/4: 467–480.

Sahlins, M. (2010). *Taş Devri Ekonomisi*. İstanbul: Bgst Yayınları.

Tezcan, M. (1989). Folklorik ve Antropolojik Yönleriyle Hediye Geleneği ve Türk Kültüründeki Yeri. *Ankara Üniversitesi Eğitim Bilimleri Fakültesi Dergisi*, 22(1), 29–36.

Weber, M. (2010). *Protestan Ahlakı ve Kapitalizmin Ruhu*. Ankara: Alter Yayıncılık.

Ceyda Tetik[1]

Social Media and Identity Crisis of the Young

Introduction

With the development and expansion of communication technologies, the concept of social media has been the subject of study in many fields, especially in communication studies. Social media is an area in which social relations are established with different properties, such as interaction, bidirectional communication, being independent of time and space. Social media differs in a radical way from traditional mass media. Traditional mass media has a vertical structure. Post production is transmitted to heterogeneous social groups defined as the mass from a particular center in a linear way. The mass is not decisive in the production of the message and the technology offered by the tool is not enough for feedback. But social media has increased the probability of interference between production and reception of post (Timisi, 2003: 124). If we explain using the communication terminology, internet, as a communication "channel", includes all communication components. When a "source" that has the "messages" such as news, information and so on combines with social media as a "receiver" and "channel" that will receive these, conventional communication process is completed. Moreover, the response to the source of the receiver regarding the message, ie. "feedback" can easily be done in a short time in social media. While viewer / reader is extremely passive and feedback is indirect in the communication provided by the mass media such as radio, television and newspapers, feedback is much more direct in social media (Gönenli, 1996).

Social media environments are becoming a part of real life for its purposes. The users, who met through this media come together with old and new friends with either their real identities or by creating virtual identities. Researches show that social media tools are used widely and especially by the younger users. Very active and intensive use of social media by young people in the period that is the process of forming identity leads to the identification problems in them.

In this context, the concept of social media as a communication tool, its properties, and effects of social media on young people will be discussed in the framework of the identity formation and identity crisis issues in this study. Literature

1 Ins., Yalova University, Faculty of Art and Design, Department of Communication Arts.

scanning method based on secondary sources is used in this study. The evaluations on the studies investigating the effects of social media on the individual and society, especially young people, are carried out.

The Concept of Social Media and Its Features

Social media responding to people's desires such as socialization, escape, instruction, entertainment, communication, spending time with its interaction aspect has become a tool the most and fastest surrounding people today (Hazar, 2011: 153). Before defining the concept of social media, it is useful to explain the origin of the concept. Tom Truscott and Jim Ellis from Duke University have established Usenet that is a worldwide discussion system that allows users to send messages back in 1979. However, the Social Media Age as we understand it now, has began with the establishment of "Open Diary" that is the first social networking site established by Bruce and Susan Abelson that brings together online diary writers. The term Weblog has began to be used for the first time and this term has been changed to blog one year later. With the spread of high-speed internet connection, use of the term blog has increased and then has led to social networking sites like MySpace (2003) and Facebook (2004). Thus, the "Social Media" concept has put on the agenda and has taken its present form (Kaplan and Haenlein, 2010: 60).

Social media includes the projects based on joint works (eg. Wikipedia), blog and microblogs (eg. Twitter), social networking sites (Facebook, LinkedIn), sites where users create content (YouTube) and virtual social life (Second Life) (Boyd and Ellison, 2008).

Social media is a media system that allows double-sided and simultaneous information sharing, which is reached from one-way information sharing with the introduction of Web 2.0. In addition, social media is the sum of dialogue and sharings that people did with each other on the internet. Web 2.0 is not only a platform where the contents and applications created and published by people take place, but also all users can actively participate in and make changes to the messages (Kaplan and Haenlein, 2010: 60). Thanks to Web 2.0, and with the facilities granted to a certain extent, individuals create their identities as profiles or accounts and they communicate with other users of the platform (Hacıefendioğlu, 2010: 57).

Mayfield (2008) indicates common features of social media as follows. These are:

- Participation: Social media makes it possible to provide the participation or feedback of all concerned people.

- Clarity: Social media is open to feedback and participation. It makes possible to rating, evaluation, comment and sharing information. There is a few obstacle to access information and password-protected content is not preferred.
- Dialogue: While traditional media focuses on publishing, social media is considered as a two-way dialogue.
- Communities: Social media allows the formation of communities with common interests in a short time and allows to communicate effectively.
- Commitment: Social media is mostly based on the principle of commitment. Websites use the content created by other sites, resources and people.

Using Social Media In the World and Turkey

According to the report of We are Social (http://www.dijitalajanslar.com/internet-ve-sosyal-medya-kullanici-istatistikleri-2014/ Erişim Tarihi: 10.01.2015):

- 2.5 billion people use the internet on earth. 1.8 billion of these users have accounts on social media networks.
- The most popular social media platform is Facebook, according to the statistics of active users (1,184 billion).
- The Internet usage rate in Turkey is 45% compared to the entire population.
- There are over 35 million Internet users in Turkey and 36 million active Facebook accounts (Including fake accounts).
- We spend our average 4.9 hours via personal computers and 1.9 hours via mobil devices on the internet per day.
- We spend our average 2 hours 32 minutes a day on social media.

Young People's Use of Social Media

When we examine the user statistics on internet, the younger segment is highlighted. Adults met computer technologies later, they are unfamiliar with the internet technology (Kırık, 2011: 198). The Internet forms the infrastructure of social networkings and therefore it would not be wrong to say that young people will take part more actively in these networks. IAB, Turkey's Internet Measurement Research shows that young users use the internet extensively. While 12–16 age group creates 73% of users, 17–24 age group creates 78% of users. The Internet usage rate decreases with increasing age.

Figure 1: Internet User Statistics In Turkey

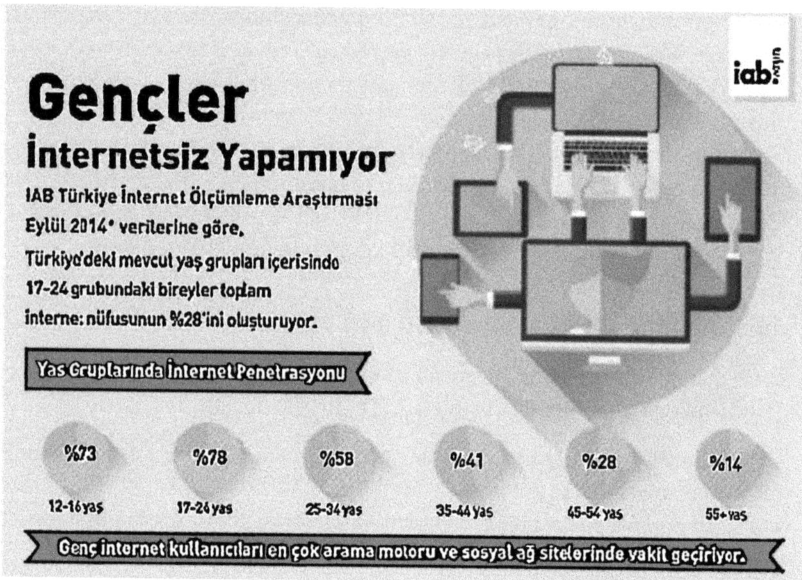

(http://www.iabturkiye.org/sites/default/files/infografik_eylul1.pdf Access Date:11.01.2015)

Youth and Sports Ministry carried out an investigation about social media usage behavior and attitudes of young people between July and September 2013. This research called as 'Youth and Social Media Research' included young people aged 15–29 and was conducted online using quantitative research methods. Interviews were conducted with a total of 2057 young people from 26 provinces for research. (http://gsb.gov.tr/HaberDetaylari/1/3816/genclik-ve-spor-bakanligi-turkiyenin-en-kapsamli-sosyal-medya-arastirmasini-yapti.aspx Access Date: 15.01.2015)

- 96% of young people, who are internet users and participated in the study, are social media users.
- 86% of young people connect to social media at least once a day and 72% of them connects several times each day. One of every three young people spends at least three hours in social media.
- 89% of young people follows the shares of people and institutions in the list of social media and 88% of them makes comments to the shares of friends according to the data obtained from this study.
- Facebook is the most used social network by young people among the other social media environments.

- When 76% of young people make a decision, they usually examine the person's profiles.

The users creating the sampling use social media in order to show themselves more successful and to compare themselves with peers according to the study carried out by B. Farber et al (2012) from Teachers College Columbia University over 300 internet users aged 25 and under. Adolescent and young adult users use social media in order to show their needs for acceptance, achievements, photos of physical images and good aspects and in order to satisfy their sense of social expenditures by these in a virtual environment (http://www.researchgate.net/publication/230826432_Children_technology_problems_and_preferences Erişim Tarihi: 15.01.2015).

As it is shown in studies, social networking sites are used widely, new social networks emerge everyday and the number of users increase. The holistic relationship between the concept of social grooming of Robin Dunbar and the concept of self-representation Erving Goffman has a descriptive nature about the popularity of social media (Toprak vd., 2014: 29).

Dunbar suggested that gossip and human curiosity is a human version of the social grooming in the Social Grooming theory. The gossip types create new areas of cultural interaction and these are seen as the tools towards socialization according to Dunbar (Toprak vd., 2014: 30).

Goffman says that when a new one comes to the environment, people usually try to obtain information about the person or they try to use the information they already have. The most curious things are general social and economic situation of that person, how s/he sees her/himself, attitude towards the environment, success in business and reliability (2014:15).

Identity and Identity Crisis

With the internet, socializing is not only meant to be together with people. Like Dunbar and Goffman said, people wonder other people's lives and want to tell the details of their own lives. Extremely widespread usage of social media and intensive use by young people, as shown by the research, lead to be transported their real life to social media and cause them to create their identities through the profiles in social media.

Before explaining the concept of identity, it is necessary to refer to the concept of self and personality that are the concepts confused with each other and to explain the similarities and differences between them. Personality includes properties, characteristics and trends that are very stable, have continuity and are hardly affected by social media. People move to these properties, characteristics and trends to different situations, contexts and interactions and this reveals differences between individuals. In contrast, the self is a structure resulting from social interactions and located in a social position. The answer to the question "who am i" asked to identify the self by person reveals the identity. Identity refers to the most stable, the most integrated and most constant factors of self-awareness. Our way of understanding and defining ourselves as integrated, consistent and stable individuality refers to identity (Hökelekli, 2013: 166).

According to Erikson's theory of psychosocial development identity formation begins in the adolescence period. Adolescents often think about how to establish a connection between ideal examples of daily life and skills and roles that s/he has in previous periods (Erikson, 1968).

Erikson (1968) indicates that individuals seek for answers to the questions "who am I and what will am I?" in the adolescence period. While he defines the age range 12–18 as adolescence period, he states that the adolescents are in the search for identity. Adolescents show extremely relevant, rebellious and responsive behaviors exhibiting sudden emotional changes and instability, trends towards the fellowship, in the search for identity, with physical and physical appearance according to Erikson. Adolescent tries to recognize and approve by society in the adolescence period (Arslan, 2008: 31).

The psychosocial crisis experienced in the adolescence period is called as identity crisis in the Theory of Psychosocial Development. Identity crisis experience may result in four ways according to Erikson (Bayraktar Süngü, 2013):

- Gaining a sense of identity.
- Suspending (Adolescent chooses a type of preparation and saving time period in the transition to adulthood responsibilities).
- Identity Confusion (Adolescent experiences confusion if s/he encounters with strong trauma and cannot find the social tolerance).
- Identity Clutter.
- Reverse Identity (The adolescent with intense identity confusion adopts the roles and ideals, which are the opposite of social expectations to get rid of this feeling of discomfort.).

An individual creates the identity through self-monitoring, making inference about her/himself by interpreting own behaviors, being impressed by opinions from the others, making inference about her/himself by interpreting others' behaviors, comparing her/himself with others (Hortaçsu, 2012: 258). Festinger suggested that social realities do not have the exact criteria such as physical realities, therefore the most important way for people to obtain information on their properties is to compare her/himself with others. Comparing oneself with other is not always done in order to obtain information about ownself. When people want to see themselves in a good condition, they compare themselves to those who are in poor condition or when they see others in good condition, they can query their status. Thus social comparisions can cause both positive and negative feelings and situations (Hortaçsu, 2012: 265).

One of the theories addressing the identity issue is impression management / creation theory of Goffman. The person is an asset forming its identity in continuous interaction with the environment, not passive according to this theory. Two regions of performance representing a total activities of the participants in a social situation are available according to Goffman: the stage (front side) and backstage. "The stage is the functioning part of the person's performance on a regular basis, in a general and steady way in order to describe the situation to the viewers". The backstage is the area where the player or actor moves relatively free / natural by taking off the stage role and viewers or observers can only see the watchful gaze or views. Goffman states that people use communication to spread the impression that they want to create (Yıldırım Becerikli, 2008: 119).

In this context, status, location notifications and photos shared in profiles created by users in social media contitute the stage. It is seen that the best and the most successful aspects of each user take place in the stage, in short, it is referred to positive features. Backstage remains as unknown. Young people who follow the stage constantly tend to compare themselves with their friends and they are affected by this condition negatively.

The Effect Of Social Media On Young People: Identity Crisis – Researches

Social networking sites such as Facebook and Twitter cause an 'identity crisis' among young people according to the research of Prof. Dr. Baroness Greenfield. Greenfield stated that the users sharing their photos or writing an opinion on these networking sites try to draw attention by saying "look, i'm here!" like a little child who wants to attract the attention of the mother and she added: "Life revolves around social networks for young people. They live an artifical, virtual life. A real person needs to hold, needs real support when s/he upsets. Anxiety and stress in the majority of people who are dependent on social networkings are extreme, self-confidence is very low." (http://articles.economictimes.indiatimes.com/2011-07-30/news/29833303_1_facebook-users-networking-sites-identity-crisis Access Date: 16.01.2015).

Larry Rosen from California University stated that children and adolescents using Facebook excessively experience communication difficulties. It was observed that general characteristics of those adolescents are extreme selfishness, arrogance, excessive impatience and aggression (http://www.apa.org/news/press/releases/2011/08/social-kids.aspx Access Date: 16.01.2015).

Facebook could unhappy users according to the study performed by H. Grace and N. Edge, Faculty Members in the Department of Sociology from Utah Valley University in the United States. The reason for this are photos/videos added by friends on Facebook. The person who sees only happy, enjoyable and fun photos of people on the social network is under the illusion that the others are much more happier than her/himself. According to the findings, there is a direct ratio between time spent on Facebook and believing that friends are happier. According to another finding, those who choose to socialize with friends in real life instead of socializing with friends in virtual environments feel happier than others. (http://edition.cnn.com/2013/08/15/tech/social-media/study-facebook-blues/ Access Date: 16.01.2015).

The research conducted by L. Denti et al (2012) under the leadership of the University of Gothenburg revealed that social media leads to identity crisis among young people by addressing the negative effects of social media on young people. 1,000 people were subjected to the survey in this research defined as the largest Facebook survey of Sweden. According to the survey, internet users following the lives of others via Facebook go into crisis after comparing them with her/his own life. Denti said that "people on Facebook share the most beautiful moments and the most beautiful images of life, these shares will confuse other people because you can not see the real life or unhappy moments of that person on Facebook, being jealous of the virtual life of the others became one of the problems affecting the people with social networking sites", by likening the situation to a false life. Continuous and long hours use of the social network and technology during pre-adolescence and adolescence period can lead to anxiety, depression and other psycho-pathologies. (https://gupea.ub.gu.se/bitstream/2077/28893/1/gupea_2077_28893_1.pdf).

Social media has negative effects on individuals according to Psychologist Professor Dr. Bengi Semerci (www.dhsturkey.com/presentations/bengi_semerci.pdf Access Date: 16.01.2015):

- Those who spend a lot of time on social media believe that other people have a better life than hers/his.
- Social media has increased the peeping and gossip culture.
- People have the need to be seen and heard more. Not sharing without an audience. As so followers increase, it is given more to be followed: As a result ego is fed. The feeling 'more the merrier' is fed and this leads to narcissism.

- It reduces face to face communication and increases the loneliness.
- Social media should be used when necessary, real communication should be preferred, because face-to-face communication and sharing are essential for personal development.

Time passing quickly in social media interrupts the effectiveness in social lives of young peoples according to psychologist Yegan Sasık. In addition to these, to make everything easy, makes young people lazy, impatient and encourages consumption rather than production. "I must have what s/he has! I must have it now! I don't even need to go to the store, I can order from the web! What if I fail? Then I am nothing!" These thoughts often occupy the minds of young people. (http://www.pudra.com/anne-cocuk/ergenlik-donemi/ergenlerin-sosyal-medyayi-kullanmasina-mudahale-etmeli-mi–15815.htm Access Date: 16.01.2015).

Conclusion

Generally the frequency of use of social media where the illusion of happiness and perfection reveal is directly proportional to effects on people. As it is seen from the results obtained from studies, young people spend too much time on social media environments and they devote themselves to the virtual world.

The effects on young people are very important, because young people gain their identity during this period. Young people using this environments too often remain between real life and virtual life. The photos, place notifications, state shares showing "the happiest" and "the most successful" affect negatively teenagers who are still in identity formation phase. They not only compare themselves with their family and close environment, but also compare themselves with virtual identities in a virtual environment. This comparison ends with identity crisis and leads to young people to break away from real life.

Social media causes to narcissistic tendencies, selfishness, lack of attention, unhappiness caused by constantly comparing her/himself with virtual identities, laziness, problems in establishing real social relationships, impatience, increased anxiety and depression in young people according to the results of the researches. It is not possible to stay completely away from social media surrounding our lives. However, when providing parental control especially in use of social media of adolescents and when it is used in a limited time intervals, it is possible to avoid the negative effects of social media.

References

Arslan, E. (2008). *Bağlanma Stilleri Açısından Ergenlerde Erikson'un Psikososyal Gelişim Dönemleri ve Ego Kimlik Süreçlerinin İncelenmesi.* (Yayımlanmış Doktora Tezi). Konya: Selçuk Üniversitesi Sosyal Bilimler Enstitüsü.

Bayraktar Süngü, E. (2013). *Kimlik ve Benlik.* Erişim Tarihi: 16.01.2015 http://www.tavsiyeediyorum.com/makale_11152.htm.

Boyd D., Ellison N. (2008). *Social Network Sites: Definition, History and Scholarship.* Journal of Computer-Mediated Communication, 13: 210–230. doi:10.1111/j.1083-6101.2007.00393.x.

Denti, L., Barbopoulos, I., Nilsson, I., Holmberg, L., Thulin, M., Wendeblad, M., Anden, L. & Davidsson E. (2012). *Sweden's Largest Facebook Study.* Gothenburg: Gothenburg Research Institute. Erişim Tarihi: 16.01.2015. https://gupea.ub.gu.se/bitstream/2077/28893/1/gupea_2077_28893_1.pdf.

Erikson, E. H. (1968). *Identity: Youth and Crisis.* NewYork: Norton.

Farber, A. B., Shafron, G., Hamadani, J., Wald, E. & Nitzburg, G. (2012). *Children, Technology, Problems and Preferences.* Teachers College, Columbia University: Journal of Clinical Psychology (Impact Factor: 2.12). 09/2012; 68(11): 1225-9. DOI: 10.1002/jclp.21922. Erişim Tarihi: 15.01.2015 http://www.researchgate.net/publication/230826432_Children_technology_problems_and_preferences.

Goffmann, E. (2014). *Günlük Yaşamda Benliğin Sunumu.* Ç. B. Cezar. İstanbul: Metis Yayınları.

Gönenli, H. (1996). *İnternet: Aydınlanmadan Sibertopluma Yeni Bir Kitle İletişim Aracı.* (Yayınlanmamış Yüksek Lisans Tezi). İstanbul: Marmara Üniversitesi Sosyal Bilimler Enstitüsü.

Hacıefendioğlu, Ş. (2010). *Sosyal Paylaşım Sitelerinde Üye Bağlılığı üzerine Bir Araştırma.* Kocaeli Üniversitesi Sosyal Bilimler Enstitüsü Dergisi, Vol. 20, No. 2, s. 56–71.

Hazar, M. (2011). *Sosyal Medya Bağımlılığı- Bir Alan Çalışması.* İletişim Kuram ve Araştırma Dergisi, Bahar 2011, Sayı 32.

Hortaçsu, N. (2012). *En Güzel Psikoloji Sosyal Psikoloji.* Ankara: İmge Kitabevi.

Hökelekli, H. (2013). *Psikolojiye Giriş.* Bursa: Düşünce Kitabevi.

Kaplan, A. M. ve M. Haenlein (2010). *Users of The World, Unite! The Challenges and Opportunities of Social Media.* Business Horizons, 53, 59–68.

Kırık, A. M. (2012). *Sosyal Medyada Gençlerin Dili Kullanımı ve Yozlaşma Problemi.* İzmir: 1st International Symposium On Language And Communication: Research Trends and Challenges.

Mayfield, A. (2008). *What is Social Media.* An e-book by Antony Mayfield from iCrossing. Erişim tarihi: http://www.icrossing.co.uk/fileadmin/uploads/eBooks/What_is_Social_Media_iCrossing_ebook.pdf.

Timisi, N. (2003). *Yeni İletişim Teknolojileri ve Demokrasi.* Ankara: Dost Yayınevi.

Toprak, A., Yıldırım., A., Aygül, A., Binark, M., Börekçi, S. & Çomu, T. (2014). *Toplumsal Paylaşım Ağı Facebook: Görülüyorum Öyleyse Varım.* İstanbul: Kalkedon Yayınları.

Yıldırım Becerikli, S. (2008). *Ve Halkla İlişkiler: Şeytanın Avukatlığından Arabuluculuğa; Bir Disiplinin Eleştirel Analizi.* Ankara: Karınca Yayınları.

http://www.dijitalajanslar.com/internet-ve-sosyal-medya-kullanici-istatistikleri-2014/Erişim Tarihi:10.01.2015.

http://www.iabturkiye.org/sites/default/files/infografik_eylul1.pdf Erişim Tarihi: 11.01.2015.

http://gsb.gov.tr/HaberDetaylari/1/3816/genclik-ve-spor-bakanligi-turkiyenin-en-kapsamli-sosyal-medya-arastirmasini-yapti.aspx Erişim Tarihi: 15.01.2015.

http://www.apa.org/news/press/releases/2011/08/social-kids.aspx. Erişim Tarihi: 16.01.2015.

http://edition.cnn.com/2013/08/15/tech/social-media/study-facebook-blues/ Erişim Tarihi: 16.01.2015.

http://articles.economictimes.indiatimes.com/2011-07-30/news/29833303_1_facebook-users-networking-sites-identity-crisis Erişim Tarihi: 16.01.2015.

https://gupea.ub.gu.se/bitstream/2077/28893/1/gupea_2077_28893_1.pdf Erişim Tarihi: 16.01.2015.

www.dhsturkey.com/presentations/bengi_semerci.pdf Erişim Tarihi: 16.01.2015.

http://www.pudra.com/anne-cocuk/ergenlik-donemi/ergenlerin-sosyal-medyayi-kullanmasina-mudahale-etmeli-mi–15815.htm Erişim Tarihi: 16.01.2015.

Ceyda Deneçli

Impact of Companies' Facebook Pages on Consumer Brand Preference

Introduction

As the internet has turned into a sizeable business platform, the emergence of many new communication tools has brought about certain changes to marketing activities as well. People who carry out marketing activities on the internet have been trying to find better ways of retaining their customers (King, 2008, p. 53). With the emergence of social networking sites such as MySpace, Facebook, Cyworld, and Bebo, and as millions of users have begun to use these sites in their daily lives (Boyd & Ellison, 2008, p. 210), the need has arisen for corporations to communicate with their customers through these social networks. Facebook, which is one of the social media networks that is suitable for individuals who look for new media to establish communications with other people, has become a popular medium for corporations that wish to create brands or expand their existing brands (Shen & Bissel, 2013, p. 630). Corporations try to keep customers faithful to their brands through social media. For this reason, they create fan pages on social media platforms and allow individuals to communicate with their brands at any time of day (Ang, 2011, p. 36). Corporations that have Facebook pages post updates or announcements about their brands through these pages and try to make their consumers prefer their brands.

Social Media and Facebook Brand Pages

Developments in communication technologies have provided a chance for individuals to express themselves and make comments. For instance, new media such as the internet offer an opportunity for selectivity and since the new media technologies are mobile, communication with users is on a tangible basis. A majority of communication technologies turn individuals into a source of communication, transforming them from being mere receivers through the interactive interfaces (Oliver & Krakowiak, 2009, p. 521). In this manner, individuals are no longer passive receivers in their communication with corporations or other individuals: They are able to express their own views and thoughts actively and to establish interactive communication with both corporations and other individuals. In particular, social media that allows individuals to share their ideas, thoughts, and content and establish communication in an online manner (Parker, 2010, p. 38) can be said to play a very effective role in individuals' assumption of an active role in communication.

According to Kaplan and Haenlein's (2010) definition, "Social Media is a group of Internet-based applications that build on the ideological and technological foundations of Web 2.0, and that allow the creation and exchange of User Generated Content" (Kaplan & Haenlein, 2010, p. 61). Social media, which is a product of internet-based applications built on Web 2.0 technology (Berthon et al., 2012, p. 263), offer participants interactive and changeable online communities. These communities give individuals an opportunity to produce, publish, control, criticise, and rate online content and to pass on interactive communication. In other words, social media is an umbrella term that includes social networking sites, virtual worlds and bookmarking sites, wikis, forums, and opinion sites (Tuten, 2008, p. 20).

Social media gives corporations a chance to establish communication with their customers, besides giving customers a chance to speak to one another. In the same manner, social media provides an opportunity for customers to express their views on corporations (Mangold & Faulds, 2009, p. 358–359). By this means, since the messages that corporations want to transmit via social media are easily circulated to their customers through this media, it may be said that they carry out various announcements about their products or brands and promotional activities, in addition to receiving consumers' views, suggestions, or feedback on the corporation in an interactive manner. As a result, it can be observed that brands have been taking more of a part in social media in terms of the advertising and marketing activities related to both their brands and their corporations.

When we talk about the concept of social media, social network services come to mind. The aim of a social network service is to create and strengthen social communication networks or social relationships between people who share common interests and activities (O'Leary et al., 2011, p. 3). Social networking, which is regarded as a component of social media, is a term used on sites such as Facebook, Twitter, LinkedIn, MySpace, and similar ones to express individuals' interaction with one another. Social networking takes place when individuals create personal profiles and when they interact with communities created by their friends and people with similar opinions in order to be a part of those communities and share information (Parker, 2010, p. 38). It can be seen that social networking sites have changed the social lifestyle, in terms of both interpersonal and social relationships. While social networking sites have been a part of the lives of numerous users in recent years, it can be stated that they grab the interest of other people in society who belong to different age groups and have other demographic characteristics.

People communicate speedily with each other through social networks and communities. When this speed merges with the development of social media platforms, this creates virtual environments/media on which people share similar tastes, ideas, and views. Real-time and social media platforms transmit information faster than traditional media such as television, radio, etc. (Macy & Thompson, 2010, p. 2). Two important online methods, asynchronous and synchronous, provide different technical characteristics and help individuals reach their communication purposes and results. Asynchronous online communication provides an opportunity for individuals to send each other direct messages through methods such as e-mail or to post messages for larger groups such as chat rooms or newsgroups. Meanwhile, synchronous online communication gives individuals a chance to send messages in real time, such as instant messages (Lin, 2009, p. 569).

The merging of real-time and social media has caused changes to take place in terms of marketing as well. Marketers are able to establish communication speedily between brands and consumers through platforms such as Facebook, Twitter, Flickr, and YouTube (Macy & Thompson, 2010, p. 2). Social networking sites help brands by including consumers in the processes of advertising, developing products, and acquiring information about the market, besides providing the opportunity for corporations to communicate with consumers (Richter et al., 2011, p. 98).

In recent years, it has been observed that a majority of corporations have been producing advertisements to be used in social media. They produce these advertisements with the purpose of encouraging users who spend time on social media platforms and socialise via online media to post them, for instance, on Facebook to be "liked" or "shared," or for them to be "retweeted" on Twitter, or "repinned" on Pinterest (Good, 2012, p. 8). In this manner, when brands' advertisements are liked, retweeted, or repinned by these users, this allows the brand to be recognised by numerous people who spend time on social media platforms. One of the social networking sites, Facebook, has also come face-to-face with developments such as the creation of new applications and new platforms. Corporations regard Facebook as a business networking site where they can market their products (King, 2008, p. 53). Since Facebook gives the opportunity for advertisers to advertise through different tools such as social ads and sponsored stories, Facebook pages, Facebook developers, etc., it has more strategic value in comparison to other social networks (Tuten, 2008, p. 38). One of the most popular tools for marketers is the Facebook pages that they create on the Facebook social networking site. Facebook pages are profiles created for corporations, products, services, and people. These pages allow corporations to demonstrate their existence on social networks and they are created in the same way as personal profiles.

Facebook pages are the equivalent of brands' user profiles. In other words, Facebook pages are a place/location where brands on the site create their brand identities. These pages can be developed through the corporation's own applications or the developer's widget applications (Tuten, 2008, p. 38). When the question is asked about why a corporation acquires a Facebook page although it has its own official website, the reason may be explained as the effort the corporation puts in to reach as many people as possible. Therefore, corporations create Facebook fan pages, which are one of the media on which numerous people spend time, in order to achieve the highest level of "reach" (Halligan & Shah, 2010, p. 89).

Companies that are able to advertise their brands on Facebook publish the most important news, videos, and images created for their brands and advertise their new products by displaying them on their page timelines. In this manner, brands influence their fans' choices and speedily spread information related to these new products (Makic & Duman, 2013, p. 2). As Macy and Thompson (2010, p. 31) explain, "as of April 2010, to 'like' something or someone became even more powerful because Facebook changed product and business 'fan' options and pages to 'like.'" The Facebook user may "like" a given brand's page and when the user does so, he or she becomes a fan who follows the brand. The moderators of Facebook brand pages have the authority to make updates and announce them. These updates do not only appear on the brand's Facebook page, but on their Facebook fans' timelines as well. Therefore, when an update is posted on the brand's page, it is not seen only by the brand's current consumers. Since Facebook timelines are semi-public web pages, the brand's potential consumers are able to see this update as well (Podobnik, 2013, p. 132).

The brand's fans communicate with the brand by either "liking" the posts that contain anecdotes, pictures, videos, etc. that are created through these pages or by commenting on these posts (Vries et al., 2012, p. 84). In order to express their interest in the current post, the brand's fans post content in accordance with the policy determined by the brand on the brand's wall, by commenting on the current post shared by the moderator of the page, by clicking on the "like" button, or by sharing the post on their own profile walls (Cvijikj & Michahelles, 2013, p. 846). The social, communal, and participative environment of brand pages allows advertisers to include consumers more closely and interactively in their advertising activities (Tsai & Men, 2013, p. 77).

In this context, it can be seen that when consumers "like" companies' Facebook pages, they actively establish communication with these companies' pages. In this manner, these people can continuously see the updates related to brands that have Facebook pages and they can comment on them whenever they like. This allows consumers to be constantly in communication with the corporation and to be aware of information related to it. In this manner, companies keep their brands and products in sight and spend effort on encouraging consumers to prefer their brands. This study aims at identifying the effects of companies' Facebook pages on the brand preferences of consumers. The study has been conducted on GSM operator brands which are among the brands that have the highest number of "likes" on Facebook. In Turkey, there are three different brands that are active as GSM operators. This study has been carried out on two brands which have the highest and lowest number of "likes."

Methods

Participants

The study was conducted on 306 university students. 56% of the participants were female and 71% were people in the 18–21 age group. 54% of study participants (166 people) said that they use Facebook "frequently" and "very frequently." In the analyses carried out within the scope of the study, the answers given by these 166 people, who said that they use Facebook frequently, have been taken as the basis for the analysis. All of the participants stated that they have purchased services within the last four years from the brands that are the subject of the study.

Measures

In the study, in order to evaluate the brand preferences of participants, the scale developed by Sirgy et al. (1997) was used. The scale includes a total of three statements arranged according to a five-point Likert scale (five: strongly agree; one: strongly disagree). The Cronbach's Alpha value calculated for the scale is 0.86.

In the study, the satisfaction shown for the brand and the status of making use of the brand's products and services, which are thought to be effective in influencing the participants' brand preferences, were used as control variables. Accordingly, the participants were asked which of the available two brands' products and services they make use of actively and to express their satisfaction concerning the brand's products and services by answering the "I am satisfied with this brand's products and services" statement which was put together in the five-point Likert scale.

In the study, in order to determine the effect of the brands' Facebook pages on brand preference, a scale was used to compile data on participants' use of Facebook and the participants were asked whether the brands included in the study have been among the Facebook pages they liked, at least in the last six months. In this light, in order to evaluate the frequency of participants' coming across the posts that the brands publish on Facebook and the rate at which they follow and share these, a scale including three expressions (for instance, "I regularly follow the posts published by the brand on Facebook") was prepared by the researcher. These expressions were put together in the five-point Likert scale (five:

strongly agree; one: strongly disagree). Factor analysis was carried out for the scale (with the Varimax rotation) and it was determined that the scale contains a single dimension (KMO=0.59; Barlett's Test p=0.00<0.01; Announced Total Variance=62.9%). The Cronbach's Alpha value calculated for the scale was 0.78.

Statistical Analyses

In the study, in order to identify the aspects that affect brand preference, hierarchical regression analysis was used. According to this, the status of satisfaction with the brand and using the brand actively, which are the control variables, were first included and then the values obtained from the scale measuring participants' frequency of following or sharing the brand's posts on Facebook and liking the brand's Facebook page, which are the independent variables, were added.

Findings

In the study, when the results of the hierarchical regression analysis that was conducted separately for the two brands are analysed (Table 1), it can be seen that satisfaction with the brand and actively using the brand, which were added to the analysis as control variables, have a significant impact on the preference for the brand that has the higher number of "likes." It is also seen that only satisfaction with the brand has a significant impact on brand preference for the brand with the lower number of "likes." In the second stage, when the status of liking the Facebook page and the frequency of following and sharing the brand's posts were added to the analysis, it can be seen that the status of liking the Facebook page does not have a significant impact on brand preference for either brand and that the frequency of following and sharing the brand's posts has only a significant impact on brand preference for the brand with the higher number of "likes."

It can be seen that the effect of adding the variables of liking the brand's page on Facebook and the frequency of following and sharing the brand's posts to the variables of satisfaction with the brand and usage of the brand is significant on brand preference, in particular for the brand with the higher number of "likes." However, it is noteworthy that the effect of this addition is a low rate such as 2% ($\Delta R=0.02$ $F=3.92$ $p=0.02<0.05$).

Conclusion

The results of the study show that if the number of "likes" is low for the brand's posts on its Facebook pages, this does not have a significant impact on brand preference. While the brand with the lower number of likes is positively affected by the satisfaction level with the products and services provided by the brand, for the brand with the higher number of likes, the additional variables of being an active user of the brand and the frequency of following and sharing the brand's Facebook posts become effective on brand preference. According to this, in order for the posts published by the brands on their Facebook pages to be effective on brand preference, it may be stated that the number of likes should be high. However, for both brands, it can be seen that the status of consumers liking the brand's Facebook page does not have a significant impact on brand preference. According to this, it may be stated that the posts that the brands share on their Facebook pages should be attractive enough for the target groups in particular to follow and share these posts. On the other hand, even if the brand achieves these conditions, the fact should not be ignored that the brand's having a Facebook page has a low effect on brand preference.

Table 1: The results of the hierarchical regression analysis

		Brand with High Number of Likes					Brand with Low Number of Likes				
		B	Std Error	Std B	t	p	B	Std. Error	Std B	t	P
Model 1	(Fixed)	1.15	0.18		6.28	0.00**	0.85	0.20		4.24	0.00**
	Satisfaction with the Brand	0.64	0.05	0.71	11.39	0.00**	0.72	0.08	0.75	8.64	0.00**
	Usage of the Brand	0.53	0.17	0.19	3.04	0.00**	0.05	0.25	0.01	0.20	0.83
Model 2	(Fixed)	0.88	0.20		4.34	0.00**	0.70	0.26		2.66	0.01*
	Satisfaction with the Brand	0.62	0.05	0.68	10.57	0.00**	0.67	0.09	0.70	7.31	0.00**
	Usage of the Brand	0.51	0.17	0.18	3.01	0.00**	0.02	0.25	0.01	0.09	0.92
	Following and Sharing Facebook Posts	0.19	0.07	0.17	2.77	0.01*	0.12	0.14	0.07	0.88	0.38
	Liking the Facebook Pages	-0.26	0.15	-0.11	-1.78	0.07	0.29	0.28	0.08	1.05	0.29

Dependent Variable: Brand preference
**$p<0.01$ *$p<0.05$

Brand 1:	Model 1: $R2=0.70$ $F=131.77$ $p=0.00<0.01$
	For Model 2: $\Delta R=0.02$ $F=3.92$ $p=0.02<0.05$
	Total $R^2=0.72$ $F=71.23$ $p=0.00<0.01$
Brand 2:	Model 1: $R2=0.59$ $F=55.79$ $p=0.00<0.01$
	For Model 2: $\Delta R=0.01$ $F=1.26$ $p=0.29>0.05$
	Total $R2=0.60$ $F=28.71$ $p=0.00<0.01$

References

Ang, L. (2011). Community relationship management and social media. *Journal of Database Marketing and Customer Strategy Management, 18*, 31–38.

Berthon, P. R., Pitt, L. F., Plangger, K., & Shapiro, D. (2012). Marketing meets Web 2.0, social media, and creative consumers: Implications for international marketing strategy. *Business Horizons, 55*, 261–271.

Boyd, D. M., & Ellison, N. B. (2008). Social network sites: Definition, history, and scholarship. *Journal of Computer-Mediated Communication, 13,* 210–230.

Cvijikj Pletikosa, I., & Michahelles, F. (2013). Online engagement factors on Facebook brand pages. *Social Network Analysis and Mining, 3*, 843–861.

Good, K. D. (2012). From scrapbook to Facebook: A history of personal media assemblage and archives. *New Media and Society. Sept.* 30, 1–17.

Halligan, B., & Shah, D. (2010). *Inbound Marketing: Get Found Using Google, Social Media and Blogs*. Hoboken, NJ: John Wiley & Sons.

Kaplan, A. M., & Haenlein, M. (2010). Users of the world, unite! The challenges and opportunities of social media. *Business Horizons, 53*, 59–68.

King, L. (2008). *Creating Facebook Applications: 100 Success Secrets to Creating Awesome Facebook Applications and Leverage Social Media*. Brisbane: Emereo Publishing.

Lin, C. A. (2009). Effects of the internet. In J. Bryant & M. B. Oliver (Eds.), *Media Effects: Advances in Theory and Research* (pp. 567–591). New York: Routledge.

Macy, B., & Thompson, T. (2010). *The Power of Real-Time Social Media Marketing.* New York: McGraw-Hill.

Makic, M. B., & Duman, T. (2013). Key motivational drivers for customer engagement on Facebook brand fan pages in Bosnia and Herzegovina. Paper presented at International Conference on Economic and Social Studies. 10–11 May, 2013. Sarajevo.

Mangold, G. M., & Faulds, D. J. (2009). Social media: The new hybrid element of the promotion mix. *Business Horizons, 52*, 357–365.

Oliver, M. B., & Krakowiak, M. K. (2009). Individual differences in media effects. In J. Bryant & M. B. Oliver (Eds.), *Media Effects: Advances in Theory and Research* (pp. 517–531). New York: Routledge.

O'Leary, S., Sheehan, K., & Lentz, S. (2011). *Small Business Smarts: Building Buzz with Social Media*. Santa Barbara, CA: Praeger.

Parker, C. (2010). *301 Ways to Use Social Media to Boost Your Marketing*. New York: McGraw-Hill.

Podobnik, V. (2013). An analysis of Facebook social media marketing key performance indicators: The case of premier league brands. 12th International Conference on Telecommunications, Zagreb, Croatia.

Richter, D., Riemer, K., & Brocke, J. V. (2011). Internet social networking research state of the art and implications for enterprise 2.0. *Business and Information Systems Engineering, 2*, 89–101.

Shen, B., & Bissell, K. (2013). Social media, social me: A content analysis of beauty companies' use of Facebook in marketing and branding. *Journal of Promotion Management, 19*, 629–651.

Sirgy, M. J., Grewal, D., Mangleburg, T. F., Park, J., Chon, K. S., Caliborne, C. B., Johar, J. S., & Berkman, H. (1997). Assessing the predictive validity of two methods of measuring self-image congruence, *JAMS, 25*, 229–241.

Tsai, W-H. S., & Men, L. R. (2013). Motivations and antecedents of consumer engagement with brand pages on social networking sites. *Journal of Interactive Advertising*, 13(2), 76–87.

Tuten, T. L. (2008). *Advertising 2.0: Social Media Marketing in a Web 2.0 World*. Westport, CT: Praeger Publishing.

Vries, L. D., Gensler, S., & Leeflang, P. S. H. (2012). Popularity of brand posts on brand fan pages: An investigation of the effects of social media marketing. *Journal of Interactive Marketing, 26*, 83–91.

Cüneyt Gök

Body: A Means of Expression

Introduction

The body, which is the backbone of all objective and subjective qualifications, is what attaches "Homo sapiens" to the emergence of modern humans anatomically 200,000 years ago in Africa, attaining modern behaviour almost 50,000 years ago. The idea is that the Homo sapiens have characteristics distinguishing humans from animals. Trying to understand their existence, human beings observed nature and tried to change some features found in nature, but not in themselves, by means of their strength of mind. The most basic activity of humans is to maintain their physical existence. Thus, they carry out various activities to meet their requirements. While humans constantly reproduce themselves by the virtue of these activities, they also shape their own history with their productive activities.

Considering "Maslow's hierarchy of needs" structure created in 1943 by American psychologist Abraham Maslow, by classifying human motives, we observe that physiological satisfactions of hunger, thirst, and sexuality take place on the bottom and at the most basic step of the pyramid. After the sub-steps are realised, the "self-actualisation needs" are attained and these are located at the very top of the pyramid.

Figure 1: Maslow's hierarchy of needs

The Human Being is a Creature of Action

Human beings attributed supernatural meanings to natural events with an abstract point of view since the very early era and along with the wide variety of powers to be feared and thus worshipped, they brought religion, totem, god, and ritual concepts. Dancing is the first creative action in which people combined body and rhythm. It was believed that dancing, bearing a religious and magical character, would help people to establish contact with supernatural powers and the gods.

A cult is the respect demonstrated to god, to the beings deemed as celestial. Performing a certain set of movements to show faith and loyalty and praying and worshipping to a cult figure or totem are all included in the cult. There is a sort of "bondage" (loyalty, slavery) in every culture and almost all of these rituals bring pain to body in their natures.

Figure 2: (a) The Caferis in Turkey no longer shed blood during these rituals, which are only applied in Iran, they donate blood; (b) The first dancers were the shaman; and (c) "Seppuku" Japan- samurai tradition

The Body is the Human Being's Place of Existence in Social Life: Body Sociology

Changing, transforming, and developing the historical, social, cultural, political, economic, and technological structure within the process where people create a "subject" also constantly changes the position of the body throughout life.

People have always struggled to «accomplish» themselves and have always sought to be «integrated» and «united» with something. Being forced to think and act in line with the demands of the community they created, beyond the activities for survival, people started to join the «artificial activities» produced by the community. The human body has become the subject of a great number of disciplines and fields, especially in diet, beauty, plastic surgery, the tabloid press, sports, body building, sexuality, punishment, health, education, and similar issues.

The body does not only consist of a biological process. The body is affected by our communal experiences as well as the principles, rules, and values of the group which we are members of.

Claiming in the 1960's that modern society could be defined as "the society of spectacle," Guy Debord stated that "the spectacle is not a collection of images;

rather, it is a social relationship between people that is mediated by images" (Debord, 2006:36).

In the 1970's, Michel Foucault argued that contemporary society was a society based on «following (or being followed)». Foucault carried out studies discussing how the bodies, which become the target and subject of power, are regulated and disciplined and on how the body is made to obey through various institutions.

"The body sociology, developed after the 1980s, basically examines the social nature of how the human body develops, the production of the body socially, the social representation and expression of body as well as the complicated relations among the body, society and culture" (Cirhinlioğlu, 2001: 93).

The Body and Identity

According to Fromm, the sane identity can only be established by means of the features of "self." Everything remaining other than a person's social and corporate identities, roles, occupation, religion, and national and ethnic identity is the "self" (Fromm, 1996: 23). Identity is a multi-dimensional and diverse notion. People may have more than one identity. The façade reflected outside, the social side oriented to society, and the face are all essential factors of the identity.

Giddens stresses that the changes brought by capitalism also change the characteristics of self-understanding, self-fulfilment, reaching personal satisfaction, privacy, and sexual relations at a personal level. The body is a significant channel, a means of outpouring of the relations.

The term social gender defines an individual's "social" or "psychological" gender as being distinct from biological gender. This term refers to the roles assigned to women and men, as well as to their responsibilities within society.

Figure 3: (a) Valeria Lukyanova and Justin Jedlica, who has had a considerable amount of plastic surgery to look like Barbie and Ken; (b) The woman side of a man's face; (c) «Androgen» model Andrej Pejic; and (d) 2014 Eurovision winner Conchita Wurst

Along with the globalisation process in the post-modern era, it adopts different notions such as sub-identity, supra-identity, or multiculturalism, instead of collective identities, and thus a "combination of differences" emerges. While lifestyles and identity structures are built on a consumption basis, the identities are shaped as being unstable, in a way to be internalised and abandoned in a flash. The basic elements of post-modern identity that are built are image and appearance.

Clothing and the Decoration of the Body

The basis of an individual's stance against the outer world is the way they use their body. By using movements and gestures, people have effectively developed their body language in a manner which includes the message within each and every movement that they make. People have started to read into life and thus discovered emotions just like the body and accordingly, people developed body language to convey these emotions. "Body language" holds a significant position in non-verbal communication. Our body language, tongue, stance of our body, mimics, and gestures, as well as our preferences of our hairstyle, the way we dress, and accessorises and make-up that we wear bear many messages.

"Clothing," "body," and "fashion" are intertwined concepts. "Clothing," beyond what we actually wear, reflects social standing, aesthetic values, religious beliefs, and practices as a notion encompassing everything from clothes to make-up and from accessorises to everything which is put on the feet and the head. While it is a factor of a financial culture, it also has a socio-cultural content.

Barnard lists the functions of fashion and clothing as the following: protection, modesty and concealment, immodesty and attraction, communication, individualistic expression, social worth or status, definition of social role, economic worth or status, political symbol, and social ritual recreation (Barnard, 2001: 47–68).

The type of clothing and dress is used as a symbol in social interaction and communication. These symbols provide meaning in social, cultural, political, and economic structure that the individuals are included in and play a significant role in the expression of identities.

In order to discover and determine the limits of the body, humankind always draws a line between itself and the "other;" they make preferences with the desire to be different and to look different and the essence of all body modifications is to be "completed" and "integrated."

In primitive societies where there was no clothing, the individuals painted their bodies and put shapes and garnishments on the skin with primitive tattoos covering the whole body in order to scare wild animals away, to establish power and dominance within tribes, and to obtain a higher share of the hunted animals.

Tattoos have features determining religious, magical, social, and sexual roles indicating the society that the individual belongs to. Warriors' jewellery made of animal fangs was used as a tool of communication to demonstrate their tribes, the number of animals they hunted, and to express the degree of their heroism against the enemy tribes.

While the first jewellery made of seashells and animal fangs carried religious and spell-related meaning, they have also been used to reflect class differences and economic levels throughout history.

«Tongue piercing» was a spiritual ritual in Mayan culture just like the piercings that the Egyptian pharaohs applied to their belly-buttons. Roman warriors applied piercings on their chests to show their masculinity and bravery and the aristocracy in the Victorian Era applied piercings on their nipples and sexual organs.

Limits of the Body - Extra Modifications

The social historian Bernard Rudofsky argues that there is no other species in the world other than humans which strive to change the shape of their body and which cannot settle with it.

In primitive societies where people try to express themselves through their body, the general principles of the tribes and societies were the determining factor instead of the personal pleasures. The tattoo, piercing, body painting, and similar body garnishments are the tools used by individuals to express themselves with cultural consumption products within the social structure which processes over today's consumption patterns. Individuals perform actions such as explaining, showing their existence, developing a sense of belonging, being aesthetic, complying or resisting, creating an identity, emphasising individuality, and highlighting the ego through these means. Enduring all body modifications is actually no different than "initiation" rituals, "rites of passage" seen in primitive societies. Rites of passage refer to "passing to a new phase" or from one social group to another. In primitive societies, the individuals often suffer, fast, or the body is tormented through physical tests.

Figure 4: *(a) Face scraping applications in South Ethiopia and Sudan; (b) Spiral bell metal necklaces placed around the neck in North Thailand; (c) The "pelele" stick into mouth in Mali Africa; (d) Ethiopia and Amazon, ear extension; (e) The "artificial cranial deformation" applied in Inca and by the Mayans in the Malay Archipelago and in central Africa; and (f) "foot binding" in China*

Figure 5: *Placing teflon or silicon prosthesis beneath the skin, excessive piercing and tattoo implementations, dividing the tongue into two; forming horns on the forehead; putting rings on the nose, lips and ears; scarring practices; organ amputations; operations performed on sexual organs (apadravya); and applying a metal mohawk head to give a "new shape" to body*

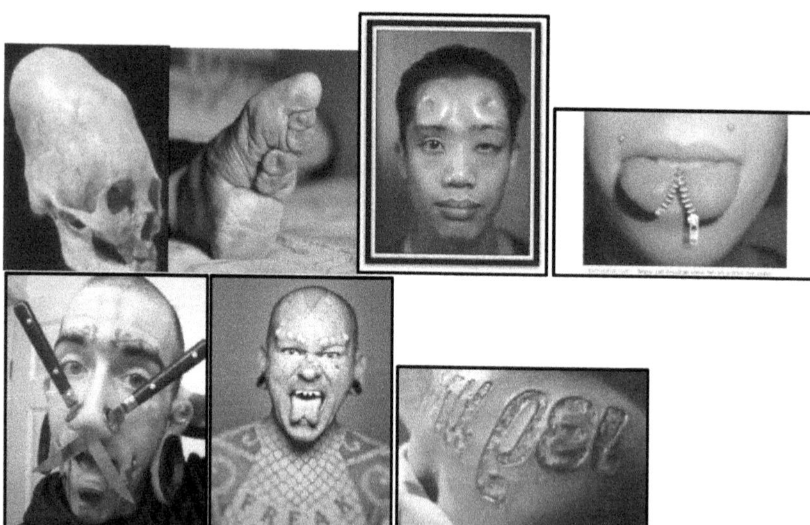

The Body and Performing Arts: Transformation of the Body

The human body, as an aesthetic value, is impacted by many factors such as the development of industrial capitalism, urbanisation, and an increase in new correspondence and communication tools. The "infinity perception" in 20th century art initiated the trend of literally using the human body as an "object of art." During this process, the artist uses his or her body directly as a material. Thus, usage of the body and the meanings attributed to the body gain different meanings.

The word "performance" covers the meaning of "completion" along with the words "showing" and "exhibit." "Completion" of a work of art refers to the completion by the audience. Performing art is a tension, a rebellion created with the body and the physical boundaries of the space, and something which is created between the boundaries. Thus, it is somewhat anarchistic and also slightly masochistic. Violent demonstrations of the artists tending towards the body through protest aim to re-establish the body which is established as other in front of the government. In this period, people started to put forth their reactions more through their bodies in social incidents.

Figure 6: (a) Animal rights protests in Barcelona; (b) Tunisian Amina and supporting Femen Group with the writing «My body belongs to me; it cannot be anyone's source of virtue»; (c) Woman standing in front of a water cannon vehicle in Taksim, Gezi Square Incidents; (d) Marina Abramovic's performance "The Lips of Thomas"; (e) Petr Pavlensky's performance called "stitch"

The Changing Sense of Aesthetics Based on the Body

Figure 7: The photography artists Sarah Jane Lynagh, Paul Rowland, and Pınar Yolaçan's works where entrails are used

Aesthetics tend towards beauty and deal with the relationship between sensual and beauty. Emerging as a philosophy of beauty, aesthetics deal with beautiful things that are made by people or are found in nature. In the history of art, the body represented ideal beauty, aristocracy, and sacred people in a way to give sexual pleasure in line with the desires of the aristocracy. The sense of beauty also changes depending on the developing, changing, and transforming world.

During and after modernism, the body started to be corrupted with the transformation of the body's expression. It degenerated apart from the ideal sense of beauty and it started to assume tainted and disgusting appearances.

Conclusion

In his book entitled "Frankfurt School," Phill Slater stated: *"Affirmative culture uses the soul as a protest against reification to be defeated against reification just at the end."*

While the human soul springs to life between sensuality and sensual pleasures and the mind, it also chases «beauty» and «supreme» oriented to sensual pleasure. Reaching carnal pleasure with the bourgeoisie era realised within the scope of «commodity order», it started to attain material pleasure with the pleasure objects in the form of «commodity».

Debord explains the dominance of commodity in daily life as follows: *"The spectacle is the moment when the commodity has attained the total occupation of social life. Not only is the relation to the commodity visible but it is all one sees: the world one sees is its world. The more an individual "accepts to find themself within dominant requirement images, the less they understand their existence and desires" (Debord, 2006: 52).*

Affirmative bourgeois culture creates «freedom allusion» by training and disciplining the human soul. In a consumption society, the body, which replaces the soul, is considered as a basic consumption object. Alienation is objectifying of the subjects. While the subjects turn into objects, the object, the capital, turns into the social subject.

The difference between the human-animal was eliminated with Darwin's theory of evolution in the 19th century. In today's world, the border between machinery and humanity has become indefinite. The body, which now has a «communal» state due to the limb and organ transplantations with both a plastic and bionic feature, goes beyond being our body. As a result of recent innovations in gene technology and applications such as cloning, it is now possible to consider the body as an engineering product.

While life continues within the bottom steps of Maslow's hierarchy of needs in the Amazon and in some regions of Africa and even in some rural areas, when it comes to developed societies and city life, life is sustained at the top level of the pyramid depending on the geographical and cultural features. Human beings who easily skip the bottom levels in today's world; who have nothing left to discover and fulfill in their bodies and the world; who are sentenced to hyper reality by being cut off from reality; who are alienated in their relations, social areas, and the business world; who live from one day to the next without concern for the future; who constantly consume without producing; or where self-straining evolves swiftly from the subject to object with the body become dysfunctional. The human becomes an object. Human returns to the days in which the body was defined as the "cloth of soul," just like other physical objects; but this time, with their soul taken off.

Now there is no other summit for new higher purposes in terms of humanity who take their place at the highest point of the pyramid. Deprived of new pleasures and searching or escaping with the aimless violence and within the scope of damaging the self physically, situations such as an inclination to suicide, interest in high risk bearing "extreme sports," over speeding, self-damaging, escaping behaviour, chronic alcoholism, excessive smoking, severe obesity, nervous breakdowns, tedium, and weariness become inevitable. Occupying themselves with artificial events of society, people experience pleasure by consuming it. The language of this society is the language of consumption and eventually it will consume itself just like it consumes all values and the world.

References

Barnard, Malcolm (2001). Fashion as Communication. London, New York: Routledge.

Cirhinlioğlu, Z. (2001) Sağlık Sosyolojisi [Health Sociology], Istanbul: Nobel Yayıncılık.

Debord, Guy (1996). The Society of Spectacle, Translated into Turkish by Ayşen Ekmekçi, Okşan Taşkent, Istanbul: Ayrıntı Yayınları.

Fromm, Erich (1996) The Sane Society, translated into Turkish by: Yurdanur Salman-Zeynep Tanrısever Istanbul: Payel Yayınları.

Demet Gürüz & Selma Didem Özşenler

Communicative Ecology and Digital Environment (Analyses on the Effects and Barriers of Interpersonal Communication)

Introduction

Ecology is known as a scientific discipline, which refers to the interactions and relations of the living based upon their extrinsic characteristics, and which is used to classify them. Communicative/communication ecology, a concept that emerged in the 1970s, refers to the frequency of preference of one communication instrument over another and to the relation established by an individual between these two communication instruments. The fact that an individual prefers a certain communication instrument over another gives us information about the lifestyle and communication behaviours of that individual. The relationship between communication ecology and the digital environment is a phenomenon that belongs to the new communication age. The rapid self-perpetuation of new communication technologies brings along ever-changing communication channels and new communication styles. The use of different communication channels, which emerged with new communication technologies, may create positive results in efficiency of interpersonal communication, but it may also cause negative results in terms of communication barriers.

Literature Review

Communication ecology appears as a result of the adaptation of the concept of ecology into communication. This term refers to giving a meaning to the distribution of various communication types and resources in a geographical region or in a society, which lives in a certain settlement on a macro scale, the communication channels, and the relationships among communication types. For example, the relationship between the time spent listening to the radio at home by a housewife and her frequency of going to a concert is a subject of communication ecology. While the relationship between the friendship of two individuals, who live away from each other in a town, and the means and conveniences of reaching each other through the telephone concerns macro communication ecology, while the concept of micro communication ecology makes us understand the influence of using a communication instrument over another (http://www.frmtr.com/felsefe-sosyoloji-psikoloji/987288-iletisim-ekolojisi.html).

In the digital environment, communicative ecology appears as a result of preferring one social media instrument, such as new information technologies like Facebook, Instagram, Twitter, Blogger, etc., over another. Various purposes come to the fore in these sharing activities. The preferences among social media instruments may be made for posting, sharing, chatting, making new friends, speaking, and sharing life and virtual life.

Efficiently used social media instruments are as follows: (1) **for posting** - Wordpress, Blogger, Wikipedia, Tumblr, and Soup; (2) **for sharing** - YouTube, Slideshare, Flickr, Last-fm, izlesene.com, dailymotion, and ideshot; (3) **for chatting** - Skype, Googletalk, MSN, and Yahootalk; (4) **for making new friends** - Facebook, LinkedIn, hi5, myspace.com, xing', and ning; (5) **for speaking** - Twitter, Twitpic, plurk (micro blog), and joikü; (6) **for sharing life** – Friendfeed and Foursquare; (7) **for watching** - uzman tv, tohumtv, televidyon, and geliştrend; (8) **for virtual life** - secondlife, yogurtistan, and sanalika, (9) **for playing games** – Farmville and mafia wars; and (10) **for playing major games** - World of Warcraft and metin2.

In the interpersonal communication process, it is necessary to overcome some obstacles in order to ensure that the source transmits its message completely and accurately and that the receiver accurately annotates the same message. When each individual manipulates his or her message by ignoring the perception, experiences, educational background, gender, etc. of the receiver, conflicts would be inevitable (Gürüz & Eğinli, 2011, p. 283).

When the social media instruments are analysed in the context of communication ecology, the frequency of preference of one digital media over another creates positive or negative outcomes. These barriers in the digital environment may reduce the efficiency of interpersonal communication. In a research study conducted for this purpose, the intended use of new communication technologies, media preferences, and usage frequencies were evaluated and the effects and barriers that emerge in interpersonal communication were discussed.

Methods

The participants of this study are juniors, seniors, and research assistants at Ege University, Faculty of Communication, Department of Public Relations and Advertising. Demographically, a total of 16 volunteer students, twelve of which were female and four of which were male students, between the ages of 21 and 31 years, have participated in this study. All of the students are closely associated with new media technologies and they spend at least one to two hours on social media. The data were collected from juniors, seniors, postgraduate, and doctorate students in the public relations and advertising department, who were following social media closely. A questionnaire was used which contained the following questions: (1) Which of the following social media instruments do you use?; (2) How many hours do you spend on social media (hours, minutes, etc.)?; and (3) Please set the social media instruments you use in order of priorities. Additionally, face-to-face in depth interviews were performed using the qualitative research method. Considering the psychological and mental states of the students and in order to receive the data under suitable conditions and at the right time, the questionnaire and interviews were conducted between December 15 and 30, 2014 (one to two weeks before the final exams). The interviews address the research question of this study because it gives the participants the opportunity to explain the cases that they encountered. Data were collected from 16 interviews; no other data search, collection, and analysis methods were used. The interviews were conducted in an environment, which was away from criticism, suggestions, and barriers of other people, and where the participants were able to disclose themselves and comfortably share their opinions. The interviews were conducted in a comfortable academic office in the Faculty of Communication, away from noise and distractions. The interviews took approximately 32 minutes (a minimum of 22 minutes and a maximum of 43 minutes) and the data were recorded on a tape recorder. The interview questions were grounded in order to reveal how the barriers of interpersonal communication, such as prejudice, stereotyping, silent enlightenment, attribution, default personality theory, stereotyped thinking, view from one side, etc., were changed and altered in social media with new information communication technologies. Data were analysed in accordance with commonly reiterated codes of recorded interviews. By focusing on communication barriers of new communication technologies in digital media and on manageable communication strategies, the codes generated by 16 participants were determined. In the next stage, both authors determined the codes and how one code was associated with another. As a result, we examined how the codes that emerged in this digital media revealed new communication barriers. In order to ensure the internal validity of the study and the reliability of analysis, the study went through a number of stages. First, a question, which was used to propound the same concept, was asked in a number of different ways. Second, the interviewer read each interview note to the participants in order to receive their approval. Finally, the findings were shared with other academicians, who were not involved in this study, but had other studies similar to this topic.

Results

As a result of the questions asked for communicative ecology, it was observed that the participants spend at least 1.5 hours in a day, mostly their time outside of sleeping hours, on social media. The participants' answers on their preferences of social media are shown in Table 1.

Table 1: Number of social media followers in terms of their purposes

For posting	Blogger		Wikipedia		Tumblr
	8		5		5
For sharing	Instagram	You Tube	Slideshare	Last-fm	dailymotion
	11	8	2	1	1
For chatting	Skype			Googletalk	
	11			2	
For making new friends	Facebook		LinkedIn		Xing
	16		10		1
For speaking	Twitter			Twitpicture	
	15			1	
For sharing life	Foursquare			Friendfeed	
	11			1	
For watching	Uzman Tv				
	6				
For virtual life	Secondlife				
	2				

When the participants were asked to set the social media instruments they use in order of priorities, the following scores were obtained: Blogger (five), Wordpress (six), Instagram (eight), YouTube (nine), Skype (five), Googletalk (ten), Facebook (three), LinkedIn (seven), Twitter (3), foursquare (7), and the remaining social media instruments received a total of ten points and were ranked as the least significant media instruments. When the data was analysed in a teleological context in consideration of these data, Instagram, YouTube, Slideshare, and Flickr are preferred over Last-fm for sharing; Skype is preferred over Googletalk or Yahootalk for chatting; Facebook is preferred over LinkedIn and Hi5 for making new friends; Twitter, Twitpic, and Plurk (micro blog) are preferred over joikü for speaking; Foursquare is preferred over Friendfeed for sharing life; and Secondlife is preferred over Yoğurtistan and Sanalika for watching. In consideration of these findings, social media is mostly preferred for making new friends and to tell something; these are followed by speaking, posting, sharing life, watching, and virtual life.

At this point, this study analyses how the interpersonal communication problems experienced by participants, who frequently use and closely follow social media, reflect on social media, and how they contribute to or inhibit communication. These barriers, which cause communication to begin and continue improperly, are evaluated as prejudice, silent enlightenment, aspect loyalty, attribution, and prophecy theory within the context of this study. Besides, it is observed that new communication technologies propounded by social media instruments create different communication barriers, problems resulting from Whatsapp usage, icons, message codification and opening those codes, and usage of time and space.

Prejudice/Stereotyping

Prejudice means learned, adopted, and rooted perceptions about a person or a group, which are also referred to as stereotypical judgments, and it is considered as one of the fundamental communication barriers of the interpersonal communication process. In this research study, the participants were asked the following question to reveal the ways that prejudices emerge in the digital environment: "***Would you accept a friend request on Facebook from someone you don't know and how do you decide on whether to accept or decline a friend request?***" The codes from reiterated answers were counted and all 16 participants stated that they never accept a friend request from someone they did not know. The codes are as follows:

Mutual friend, message, common life intersection, pragmatism (social exchange), physical attraction, being at the same place, photograph, purpose, and association

According to a research study performed in this context, the number of mutual friends is the most important criteria when adding someone as a friend. Besides, notifying the reason for adding in a message, overlapping lifestyles, social benefit, thinking that you might need the other persons help, physical attraction, having been in the same place before, having even a few ideas about that person, photographs, and association emerge as findings, which are suitable for eliminating prejudice barrier regarding that person.

Icons

Even though the icons were considered as a communication barrier when used by themselves, they substitute for non-verbal communication in daily life. The question regarding the icons was asked as follows: "***How does using de facto icons affect your communication?***" The reiterated codes are as follows:

Humour, attitude when it is used alone or when it is never used, despondency, strengthening verbal communication, emotional substitution, circumlocution, communicational obliqueness, sympathy and sweetness, facilitating communication, closeness, and ending conversation

When humour is used alone, it bears the meaning of attitude and despondency. It is useful for strengthening verbal communication. Emotion substitution, slide over, by the time icons are not used, it can have a meaning to assume a pose and when it is used, it can have a meaning of sympathy. It is useful for personalisation. Even a simple smiley icon may have various meanings. Cuteness might bear the meaning of mocking, and when used, it might cause incompleteness and resentment. It supports face-to-face communication. In consideration of these data, it is observed that the icons mostly clarify written communication and they make the emotions.

Unverbal Enlightenment

Unverbal enlightenment is evaluating the information obtained about a person in a certain order. Generally, appearance and physical characteristics of the person are effective at the beginning of the cognitive process that forms silent enlightenment. The question asked to reveal silent enlightenment in this study was: "***What is the degree of relationship between your communication with a person that you have added and his or her profile picture?***" The codes reiterated by 16 participants are as follows:

Virtual personality, categorisation, internal consistency, and self-control

When the comments were reviewed depending upon these codes, it was observed that the people shared their ideas in line with their beliefs and values and evaluated others in the same manner. However, it is suggested that it is beneficial in terms of meeting and chatting with different people on social media. It is observed that this is sometimes viewed as the inability to communicate with people with different opinions and value judgments, openness/closeness to communication, separation of common grounds, and differentiation of tastes and ideas, and thus, it created a virtual personality. In this sense, it is important to introduce the right personality, to transmit consistent information, and to not create a different identity.

View From One Aspect

View from one aspect is the state when a person believes that only his or her own ideas and behaviours are accurate and does not accept other ideas and behaviours. The people with this mentality expect others to approve themselves and accept their beliefs. The question, which was asked to get information about the equivalent of this communication barrier in digital media, was: "***Are your profiles in digital media, such as Twitter, Facebook, Instagram, etc. important in terms of making you feel important and in terms of uniqueness of your feelings and ideas?***" The reiterated words in the answers given within the frame of this question are as follows:

Being of great value, being considered important, popularity, ideal self, feeling special, being admired, being recognised, feeling special, and association

The individuals present themselves in social media as they picture themselves in their ideal selves. The individuals prefer to fake their own identities in social media. The individuals want to feel special and be appreciated by others. Since social media differentiates the individual, and since everyone tries to be unique through the same way, non-uniqueness also becomes a standard. However, association must be emphasised more than uniqueness and social media should not dissociate people, it should rather unify them. In consideration of these data, social media creates a gap between the ideal self and the existing and possessed self.

Using Whatsapp

The following question was asked in order to study the contributions and barriers of a new communication technology product: "***How does the fact that there is one or two blue ticks on Whatsapp influence your communicative expectations?***" The codes and comments are as follows:

Privacy and restriction on freedom

In line with the findings, it is anticipated that Whatsapp creates major problems, is perceived as a violation of privacy, creates communication barriers, and restricts freedom.

Status

The question on status was asked to support and crosscheck the question regarding attribution and the answers verify each other. As in their daily lives, the individuals tend to pattern individuals on a certain scheme and shape their other behaviours accordingly. The question asked was as follows: "***Let's say someone added you as a friend on Facebook and the person has a profile picture that involves a lawyers' gown or doctors' apron and a stethoscope. Would you accept his or her friend request? Why?***" The answers and codes are as follows:

Pragmatism, superiority, repulsive, and showoff

People stand out with their personalities, rather than their social status. The people, who are trying to stand out with their social status, might be trying to propound their superiorities. Since Twitter is an idiosyncratic and a special social media channel, it mostly addresses to feelings and emotions. Decent education does not mean that the person would also have successful social relations. Emphasis on identity brings repulsion.

Attribution

Attribution is similar to unverbal enlightenment and default personality theory. Attribution involves listing of qualifications known by the evaluator based on certain visible characteristics and behaviours of the person in tandem and it involves prediction of other characteristics and behaviours. In this sense, the following question was asked to the participants in order to measure the attribution barrier in social media: "***Would you attribute any personal characteristics to a person that you met online?***" The answers are reiterated and the following codes were propounded:

Common traits, sincerity, physical attraction, cool, and self-righteous

In accordance with the findings, it is observed that the similarities are considered first when adding someone as a friend. If all pictures are nothing but sunglasses and leaning poses, some characteristics, such as cool, perky, self-righteous, etc. may be attributed. Since pictures, liked movies and common traits, provide information about the personality of a person, they give an opportunity to get to know that person better. The prejudices in face-to-face communication are also prevalent in social media. The pictures and real life may not coincide. A person might add someone as a friend by going through his or her pictures and comments, sincerity, chitchat, and physical attraction. Sense of fashion, music, lifestyle, and graciousness are also important factors.

Referential Communication

The following question was asked regarding whether social media provides referential communication: "***Does social media provide referential communication? How?***" The codes and comments in this context are as follows:

To look rich, to look like he or she is living a luxurious life, suffering the pangs of love, inability to build up trust, and not believing that the person is living in delusion

When these codes are disclosed, there may be some problems in sharing accurate and real information by the communicating parties. Open and comprehensible communication, which is a significant factor in interpersonal communication, might give way to referential communication in social media. In this case, it is stated in aforementioned codes that the truth is hidden and referential statements and images are reflected. In line with these data, it is propounded that a communication style exists, where indirect communication style and implicit meanings are dominant, and thus, referential communication becomes a barrier.

Use of Distance

People try to protect themselves with various reactions in places with different spaces/distances (at home, work, outing, entertainment, in transportation vehicles, etc.), which has boundaries that are not seen but are felt in interpersonal communication, and the existence of this space is constantly reminded to other people. The boundaries of this space or the distance vary among cultures and societies. The behaviours of people and the characteristics and level of their interpersonal relations are associated with the use of this space. The boundaries of this area are classified as private space, personal space, social space, and general space. A study on this subject tries to measure the reflections of use of space in interpersonal communication in the context of social media and new communication technologies. We asked the following question: "***What do you think of the use of distance in the virtual environment as the factors affecting interpersonal communication? What do you think about the lack of space and time unity?***" The codes and comments regarding communication are as follows:

Accelerating communication, continuous communication, restriction of private life, self-control, the experiences in internal and external environment, the ability to go back in time, and differentiation of the boundaries of space

In line with these codes, the distances are shortened, the communication is accelerated, and it is possible for individuals to reach each other. In a case where the general space will be used, it is observed that the boundaries of the space are narrowed and personal/private space is used. As a result, the concept of being close or distant may create some problems in defining distances, and in this sense, individuals may be disturbed by violation of their own spaces and may feel the need of defining their own boundaries. Various reactions may be developed to show the boundaries of personal space (turning off the screen, putting on silent, etc.).

Besides, it is set forth with these data that it disturbs people in terms of social communication norms and values or communication ethics, since continuous communication ensures accessibility, and ensures that the individuals straighten their affairs easily, but it also affects the biological clocks of the individuals.

Prophecy Theory

Prophecy theory is based on the fact that an individual creates a belief in line with his/her characteristics, desires, expectations, and purposes, and starts to become attached to this belief as if it is real and behaves accordingly (Devito, 1995, p. 57). The following question was asked to the participants for research in social media: "***Do the beliefs of a person reflected on social media coincide with their real life beliefs?***" The codes generated by the words reiterated in answers of the participants are as follows:

Congruency of situations, of beliefs, and the existence of fudge factor in social media

In line with these findings, the followings answers were given by the participants regarding prophecy theory on social media: "I have had many friends, whom I thought were swanky, but they became more sincere and sweet when we chatted in real life;" "It reflects the real life in general. The social media reflects the reality because what he/she posts/shares on Twitter is his/her own idea. The way he/she takes a picture is already his/her own point of view. Even though some incorrect attributions are made sometimes, the great majority of the predictions come out right;" "Anyone can make mistakes. What you try to put on that person may look so different;" and "Sometimes I attribute a different meaning to a picture, but later on, I can understand that my first impression was not right after all."

The fact that the beliefs created by people's own characteristics, desires, expectations, and purposes are directed towards lifelike behaviours, causes some predictions at the heart of the prophecy theory. In accordance with the answers given in this study, the behaviours developed by a person's own perceptions and predictions, whether they exist in real life or not, may have negative effects on the communication process and this verifies the accuracy of the prophecy theory barrier.

Discussion

In this study, which was conducted with juniors and seniors of the Public Relations and Advertising Department to determine the factors and barriers that affect interpersonal communication in the context of communication ecology and digital media, the reflections on new communication technologies were discussed by emphasising communication barriers. It is observed that the barriers, which are known as prejudice, attribution, prophecy theory, aspect loyalty, and silent enlightenment, also exist in social media channels. It is also observed that apart from these barriers, there are also other interactions, which may prevent initiation, continuation, and conclusion of interpersonal communication in digital media. These include: the use of verbal and non-verbal communication styles, the use of space and time, culture, perception, manners, values, personality, feelings, self, norms, personal characteristics, etc. As a result of measurement of communicative ecology, it is determined that digital media channels are mostly preferred to make new friends and to share feelings and opinions instantly. In addition, it is also observed that these preferences and usage frequencies create correct and functionally positive results; however, in the contrary case, they may create negative results in terms of communication norms and ethics. The purpose of this study is to reveal how the communication barriers realised in interpersonal communication in daily life change in social media. It is observed that the social media preferences are determinative factors in reflection of feelings, thoughts and behaviours, and communication styles of individuals. The interpretations reveal significant evaluations in positive or negative conclusion of interactions.

References

Gürüz D., Eğinli A. (2011). Kişilerarası İletişim, Second Edition, Nobel Yayınları.

Devito, Joseph A.(1995). The Interpersonal Communication Book, Seventh Edition, New York: Harper Collins College Publishers.

–, iletişim ekolojisi, retrieved 12 January 2015, http://www.frmtr.com/felsefe-sosyoloji-psikoloji/987288-iletisim-ekolojisi.html.

Figen Algül

Greek Community Radio in Turkey: İHO TİS POLİS

Introduction

It might be said that community radios are the media which are used by society or people who have common ideas, characteristics, interests, or ownership (Possi, 2003, p. 167–169). Community radios are the kind of media which ensure media plurality, freedom of speech, diversity of content, and representation of distinct groups and interests of society; they encourage public and gender balanced access, support for cultural diversity, self governance and media literacy, open dialogue at the local level, transparency, and voice the sound of the voiceless, becoming the voice of the people (Milan, 2009, p. 600). Community radios are used for mobilisation, sensitisation, and education for holistic development. Community radios are small-scale and they are non-profit seeking, open, or accountable to the community which they serve. They are essentially run by volunteers, are open to the participation of community members in terms of programme making and governance, enable participation and access in terms of integrating the non-professional media producers in the work, and contribute to social change. Community radios can serve communities of interest, geographical communities, and cultural communities. The key role of community radio is to green tolerance and pluralism in society. Community radios provide a public broadcasting service and present accessibility for all. On the other hand, they serve reproduction and representation of common, shared interests. In this sense, community radios present a tool of empowerment for the marginalised communities. Under the framework of all these features, community radios constitute a separate subgroup within the media sector (European Parliament, 2007, p. 3).

An Alternative Type of Media: Community Radios

This subgroup is an alternative for the established processes and conditions of media production; it is free from state intervention, market actors, and multilateral institutions; it is produced by local communities in their own languages about issues, which they assume significance with regard to their own needs, and for their own consumption. Thus, it is also an alternative for the dominant media content (Saeed, 2009, p. 470). Community radios present news and information appropriate for the needs of the community members; they integrate their members in public debates and contribute to their empowerment in social and political aspects. In general, the ownership and control of community radios is shared by the local residents, local administrations, and community based organisations. The content is considered and produced at the local level (Jankowski, 2003, p. 8). Community radios establish counterbalances against the concentration of media power in the hands of few people and the homogenisation of the cultural content. Community broadcasts present alternatives for endogenous development. They make programmes over the basis of specific needs such as health, education, employment, gender, peace, and the environment. Community radios use the language (languages) of the community members. They accept the positive, moral, and cultural values of the community to which they serve. They are expected to not broadcast sexist or biased programmes against handicapped and minority groups. Community media may be an important tool for the disadvantaged members of the community for becoming active participants in society and to participate in debates that are important to them. The sector in general has also been an educational basis for its volunteers to become future media professionals (European Parliament, 2007, p. 23). The distribution of the content may be by cable television infrastructure or by electronic networks like the internet (Jankowski, 2003, p. 8). Funding for community radios is not essentially commercial, though the total budget may include company sponsorship, advertisements with limited numbers and types, and governmental subsidies (Jankowski, 2003, p. 8) In some examples, both due to editorial preferences and as they do not constitute an attractive target for the advertisers, they do not broadcast advertisements. However, the lack of stable financing resources, like subsidies governed by the state, endangers their existence (Milan, 2009, p. 600). In some cases, some of them are against receiving advertisements and state support on an ideological or pragmatic basis. In administrative terms, they have a broadcasting board or board or administrators. In other words, community radios are people's media made by the people for the people. They are services which influence the public opinion, create consensus, and enhance democracy.

The European Union and Community Radios

Within the framework of the research study, by taking the membership process of Turkey into the European Union into consideration, legal legislation and implementations about community radios in the European Union are examined. The Committee of Ministers of the European Council, on 11 February 2009, accepted the "Declaration on the role of the community media in promoting social cohesion and intercultural dialogue." According to the Declaration, community radios which have activities in more than 115 countries also including various European Council member states, provide an opportunity to express one-self and for the interchange of opinions for such groups in society, including cultural, linguistic, ethnic, religious, or other minorities. Community radios, thanks to this, contribute to the promotion of public debates, political pluralism, and awareness about distinct opinions. According to the Declaration, community radios play a significant role in the participation of the community at the local and regional level and they are an extension of democratic participation by promoting social cohesion, intercultural dialogue, and tolerance. In this context, The Committee of Ministers of the European Council accepts community radios as another media sector alongside with public service media and private commercial media; they also recommend giving priority to community radios in frequency allocations (Council of Europe, 2009, p. 1–3).

As it is shown in Table 1, there are more than 2000 community radio stations in the European Union. The countries in the European Union where a large community radio sector exist are in general those countries which have a firm legal and regulatory framework, clear public policy commitments about the promotion of the sector, and financial support measures. In the European Union countries, community radios have a mixed financial model which contains public and private grants, advertisement and programme sponsorships, and subscriptions. And in some countries, in order to provide help to the sector, public financing measures exist. Among them, the largest and longest living is the French-FSER. Also in Denmark, Germany, and Netherlands, considerable public financing measures exist. In Belgium, Hungary, Ireland, and England, smaller financing programmes are in effect (Buckley; Duer; O'Siochru & Mendel, 2008, p. 4.)

Table 1: List of community radios in the European Union

Country	Number of Services	Legal status	Public Finance
Austria	12	**No special provision**	No
Belgium	11	**Well established**	Yes
Bulgaria	3	**No special provision**	No
Czech Republic	3	**No special provision**	No
Cyprus	0	**No special provision**	No
Denmark	175	**Well established**	Yes
Estonia	0	**No special provision**	No

Country	Number of Services	Legal status	Public Finance
Finland	5	No special provision	No
France	683	Well established	Yes
Germany	304	Changes according to the region	Yes
Greece	10	Basically without license	No
Hungary	100	Well established	Yes
Ireland	21	Well established	No
Italy	100	Well established	No
Latvia	0	No special provision	No
Lithuania	0	No special provision	No
Luxemburg	1	No special provision	No
Malta	38	Well established	No
Netherlands	264	Well established	Yes
Poland	30	No special provision	No
Portugal	30	Basically without license	No
Romania	10	No special provision	No
Slovakia	2	No special provision	No
Slovenia	3	No special provision	No
Spain	130	Basically without license	No
Sweden	165	Well established	No
England	159	Recently accepted	Yes

Source: Steve Buckley, Third Pillar of Media Pluralism; Community Broadcasting in UK and Europe, **Meccsa Conference Presentation,** 2009.

Community Radios in Turkey

Community radios represent a vital input in the development processes by playing important roles in democratisation, construction of citizenship, social struggles, and promotion of awareness. However, despite this, community radios are still confronted with difficulties stemming from restrictions caused by national media legislation. Turkey is one of the countries where such difficulties related with community radios are experienced. It is not possible to state that the same environment of freedom experienced in Western Europe is available in Turkey. The Law of the Radio and Television Supreme Board (RTSB) puts the local radio definition under the "private radio and television broadcasting" section and does not recognise the identity of community radios in legal terms. Thus, the radios which try broadcast as community radios are also expected to comply with the same conditions in issues such as broadcasting permission and licencing with commercial radios/televisions (Timisi, 2003, p. 70–71). On the other hand, as the financial conditions for establishing radios in Turkey are very severe, community broadcasters founded their solution by establishing internet radios.

The first practical example of community radio in Turkey is Nor Radio, founded in 2009 as an internet radio. Nor Radio started its road with the slogan "voices of the whole world, unite" and broadcasts from the internet address www.norrradyo.com. The radio is now broadcasted in nine languages including Turkish, Armenian, Syriac, Homshetsi, Adygean, Chechen, Pomak, Lazuri, and Kurdish languages (www.norradyo.com). The programmes broadcasted in Nor Radio until today included workers, animal rights, women's movement, LGBT, gender, and the green movement (Algül, 2013.).

The First and the Single Radio of the Greek Community in Turkey: İHO TİS POLİS

Together with the Lausanne Exchange of Populations among the State of the Turkish Republic and State of Greece implemented in between 1922–24, 1942 Property Tax practice, 6–7th September, 1955 events, 1964 exile (more than 12,000 Greeks were deported), and 1974 Cyprus events, according to various resources, an average of 1.2 million Greeks from the Aegean, Trace, and Black Sea regions migrated from the lands to which they belong. Nowadays, the number of individuals who constitute the Greek community in Turkey is about 2,500 (Akın, 2014).

The Greek community's press in Turkey goes back to the 1800's, simultaneously with the Turkish press history. In this time span, nearly 150 newspapers and 80 magazines were published in Turkey in the Greek language. At times, ten publications made in the Greek language co-existed. At the moment, only two newspapers of the Greek community in Turkey survive. One is Apoyevmatini, which has been published for 89 years, and the other is the IHO newspaper, which has been published for 37 years.

With İho Tis Polis, which was established in April 2012, the Greek community in Turkey had a radio broadcast. The subject matter of this research study is İho Tis Polis, the first and the single radio broadcast of the Greek community in Turkey.

Methods

In this research study, the first and only radio broadcast of the Greek community in Turkey, İho Tis Polis, is examined in terms of the characteristics of community radios; first, by making a literature survey where the characteristics of community radios are stated theoretically and by taking the membership process of Turkey into the European Union into consideration, by assessing the legal legislation and practices are about the community radios in the European Union. In the field study, an in-depth interview with Andrea Rombopulos, one of the founders of the radio broadcast, was conducted on 29 August 2014. Furthermore, content analysis was conducted over www.radio.ihotispolis.com, which is the internet web site of the radio. Also, the information received from the servers to which the radio is attached was analysed.

The hypothesis (H) of the research study is:

H1: "İho Tis Polis radio of the Greek community in Turkey is a practical example of a community radio."

The objective is to prove that even though there is no legal legislation and legal recognition about community radios in Turkey which exist in Western European countries, there are practical examples of them.

Findings

According to the results which are found in the in-depth interview and content analysis, when İho Tis Polis radio, which is broadcasting from the internet is examined, the below findings are reached:

Year of Foundation: April 2012

Founders: Andrea Rombopulos and Hristos Vasiliadis

The meaning of the radio's name: Echo of the City

Internet website: www.radio.ihotispolis.com

Internet website language: Turkish and Greek languages

Kind of music: Every kind of Greek music (rembetiko, zeybekiko, layka, and pop-old and new)

Content: Culture, news, art, journey observations, news about the Rum community. On the other hand, on Sundays and religious days, the religious rituals are broadcasted live from the Patriarchate. These religious rituals reach the Orthodox Christian world by live broadcasts. We see an approach of broadcasting that provides communication for the Greeks in Turkey and that is related with their problems.

News bulletin: There are four news bulletins daily. These are at 17:00, 19:00, 21:00, and 00:00 o'clock.

Audience: The radio is listened especially by three generations of Greeks who migrated from Istanbul into four different continents and nearly 70 countries. The first ten countries among them are Turkey, Greek, Germany, Australia, the United

States of America (USA), Russia, Cyprus, Canada, France, England, and Belgium. The radio has a daily audience between 10,000 and 22,000.

Broadcasting time span: During the foundational era, it started with a test stage with two hours of daily broadcasting and then twenty four hours broadcasting started.

Number of volunteers: 17

Broadcasting language: Greek language but when the guests talk in Turkish, interpretation is provided.

Organisational structure: The decisions are taken in meetings made every 15 days together with the participation of all volunteers. In these meetings, new ideas, broadcasting policy, technical problems, etc. are discussed.

Open door policy: The radio is open to the ideas coming from the audience and the audience may become programmers.

Disadvantages of being an internet radio: The radio cannot be listened to while traveling by car, but in the latest introduced cars in the USA there is 3G technology. Hence, this problem has been overcome. This technology still does not exist in the cars in Europe and Turkey. On the other hand, the radio can be listened to on mobile phones by the Tune-in programmes.

Technical infrastructure: The SAM Broadcaster programme and analogue-digital mix microphones are used.

Communication with the audience: It is maintained by Facebook, Skype, e-mail, and telephone.

Social media usage: Facebook page: https://www.facebook.com/ihotispolis. By 1 September 2014, 4,991 people liked their Facebook page. Also, each programme has its own Facebook page. Instant communication is possible with the audience through these pages.

Twitter page: https://twitter.com/ihotispolis By 1 September 2014, it has 262 followers.

Promotion: It is made mainly by Facebook and media (Turkish and Greek media). Links are also provided by various internet sites to the radio.

Installation cost: 3,000 Euros

Monthly expenditures: As the radio station is at the IHO newspaper office, the costs (rent, invoice etc.) are afforded over the newspaper. On the other hand, there is nearly 300 dollars in monthly expenditure for stationary costs, server fee, internet fee, etc. When advertisements are received, the invoices are arranged over the newspaper.

Financing: It is provided by the IHO newspaper and the advertisements delivered by the community firms during the Christmas and Easter periods. They emphasise that İho Tis Polis is not a profit oriented institution and that they need money to maintain their basic needs.

Problems: There is a problem in finding people who will conduct broadcasting in the mother tongue.

Demand: For the next ten years (after which they believe that radio broadcasting will be carried on entirely over the internet), there is provision of frequency allocation under legal guarantee.

Discussion

Community media is seen as a natural part of contemporary democracies in general and it is considered as a field of variety and values to which the market and state cannot reach. Community media has been created by the belief that civil society is in need of communication platforms. Thus, community media and civil society are interdependent in this sense. The pirate broadcasts, which do not have commercial characteristics, especially caused community media to appear. As it is observed in the European context, community broadcasting, in many examples, was established as a result of the continuous pressures coming from community groups rather than directives inspired by the state. Community media can present alternatives for the communication agenda which is established by the dominant social-political or even cultural order by contributing to the political emancipation and democratisation processes and by creating a change in life conditions of the poor, marginalised, deprived, or oppressed communities. Community media makes contributions to the social and cultural dimensions of development by presenting channels for development, for social and political empowerment, and for the realisation of citizen's rights (Milan, 2009, p. 601).

It is seen that there is overlap when the characteristics that were given in the first part of the study under the theoretical framework about community radios are matched with the characteristics of the İho Tis Polis internet radio in the findings. Thus, the first and the single radio of the Greek community in Turkey, İho Tis Polis, is at the same time a practical example of community radio from Turkey. Hence, although the identity of community radio is not legally recognised in Turkey as in Western European countries, we can see examples of it in practice. On the other hand, because of the severe financial conditions in Turkey, the community broadcasters found their road of exit in founding internet radios.

For a more democratic society, the area should be opened for the identities in society which are oppressed and marginalised by the dominant discourse. Community radios have such a function. Also, in terms of a more democratic media environment and media pluralism, it is necessary to support community radios in Turkey, which are independent both from the commercial interests and from the state, which are small scaled, and which give alternative public service broadcasting. The İho Tis Polis model should be encouraged in our countries for developing democracy.

On the other hand, in future studies, İho Tis Polis may be compared with examples abroad or research may be done over the İho Tis Polis audience in terms of reception.

References

Akın, K. (2014). Ermeni Soykırımının Provası: 1913–14'de Rum "Tehciri". *www.bianet.org.*

Algül, F. (2013). An Internet Radio from Turkey as an Example of Community Radio: Nor Radyo. *AJIT-e: Online Academic Journal of Information Technology,* Vol: 4, Num: 12., pp. 75–103.

Buckley, S., Duer, K., O'Siochru, S. & Mendel, T. (2008). *Broadcasting, Voice and Accountability: A Public Interest Approach to Policy, Law and Regulation,* Washington: World Bank/Ann Arbor: University of Michigan Press.

Council of Europe. (2009). *Declaration of the Committee of Ministers on the Role of Community Media in Promoting Social Cohesion and Intercultural Dialogue,* Strasbourg.

European Parliament. (2007). *The State of Community Media in the European Union Report by KEA for the Committee on Culture and Education,* Brussels: European Parliament.

Jankowski, N. W. (2003). Community Media Research: A Quest for Theoretically-Grounded Models. *The Public,* Volume 10, 1, pp. 5–14.

Milan, S. (2009). Four Steps to Community Media as a Development Tool. *Development in Practice,* Volume: 19, Numbers: 4–5, pp. 598–609.

Possi, M. (2003). Community Media Defined in Nasanga, G. In The East Africa Media and Globalization: *Defining the Public Interest* (pp. 167–169). Kampala: Industrial Graphic System.

Saeed, S. (2009). Negotiating Power: Community Media, Democracy and the Public Sphere, *Development in Practice,* Volume 19, Numbers 4–5, pp. 466–478.

Timisi, N. (2003). Küresel İletişim Ortamı ve Yerel Radyolar. *Radyo ve Radyoculuk,* Alankuş, S. (ed.), İstanbul: BİA, pp. 55–77.

www.norradyo.com.

www.radio.ihotispolis.com.

Öykü Ezgi Yıldız

The Role of Advertising Music in Brand Memorability

Introduction

It would not be possible to think that music, which has the ability to bring all societies together on a common ground, would not be in cooperation with the area of communication. Music, which has an important place in human communication, has influenced all societies throughout the centuries, as an artistic area that is unique to humans that is used to transmit emotions. Music, which embodies cultural and local characteristics, is a universal language that allows societies with different tongues, beliefs, and lifestyles to seize on the same language and common emotions. Due to these characteristics, it is quite natural for there to be ties between music that can find a place in the global market and the advertising sector.

It is possible to associate the connection between music, which attempts to reach people from different cultural areas and different contexts, and advertising to a period when it did not exist as a professional area of expertise. The point at which the exchange occurred between the history of music and that of the advertising sector can be predicted to have occurred during a former period, but in our world where the spatial boundaries to the process of communication have been removed, the importance of music to advertising has strengthened even more. As one of the persuasive elements of advertising, the influence of music in guiding individuals' choices has given rise to numerous studies being conducted in this field. The current study will deliberate the relationship between music and advertising and its role in the memorability of the brand being advertised. The process of making advertising music memorable in the minds of the target audience and allowing it to become associated with the brand will be dealt with by making use of focus group discussions.

Interaction Between Advertising and Music

Music is effective for people to transmit their thoughts to each other, share common ideas, and develop some sort of joint approach to specific events. While music makes memory effective in terms of specific concepts, it activates basic emotions as well. Therefore, music takes a large role in the area of advertising too (Zaltman, 2003, p. 195).

The emotions that music awakens in individuals are numerous, including: passion, compassion, self-sacrifice, patriotism, aggressiveness, anger, serenity, nostalgia, pride, hope, happiness, sadness, fear, sincerity, and many other similar emotions (Fowles, 1996, p. 120). Sound, which is an effective aspect of memory in the same way as visuality, can create differences in individuals' moods (Küçükerdoğan, 2000, p. 89).

Music has been an important aspect since sound recordings started to be featured in advertising. Jingles, popular melodies, and musical arrangements are used to grab attention, to convey a message, or to create an emotional effect in the advertisement (Shimp, 2007, p. 320). The emotional and communicative effects created by the use of music in advertising have been studied since the 1950s. However, it is possible to locate the cooperation of advertising and music to much older periods. At the end of the 19th century, the singing of street vendors to advertise their goods can be regarded as an indication that communication between advertising and music goes a long way back (Wang, 2012, p. 22). Types of popular music belonging especially to the post World War II period in America and Britain have been effective in the development of this area of music which can exceed the boundaries of written and spoken language and reach audiences of global dimensions (Giddens, 2008, pp. 666–667). In the 20th century, the communication tools that are beginning to be effective in all areas of life have caused the music industry, which comes to the fore with its cultural and economic dimensions, to communicate closely with the area of advertising.

After the invention of recording systems, the most important development observed in terms of the music industry was achieved with the advent of radio broadcasting in the 1920s (Argan, 2006, p. 220). When we look back to the 1930s, a decade in which radio gained a serious degree of importance in America, it can be seen that advertisers guided radio programs that were followed by large numbers of people, as well as determining the context of music. After World War II, the music industry, as a tool by which public communication is transmitted through the media throughout the world, as well as in the United States of America (USA), was shaped by advertising (Wang, 2012, p. 22). The advertising sector, which has powerful effects on the music industry and on music as a whole, also makes use of music's effects on consumers' emotions.

Music produces an atmosphere behind the dialogue in advertisements, but its primary use is in jingles. Through attractive phrases and short bursts of music, memorable messages are created in the consumer's mind. Jingles enable consumers to remember the advertising message (Moriarty et al., 2012, p. 304). Music, which has an important place in television commercials as well as radio advertisements, prevents the message of the advertisement from being lost among a multitude of other advertising and also forms an attention-grabbing aspect of advertisements that can also contribute to the imaginative narrative of the message (Belch & Belch, 2001, p. 293).

Jingles are not only in song or background format; they embody all kinds of sounds and sound effects and play a role in shaping consumers' perceptions (Kubacki & Croft, 2010, p. 581). While music often remains only in the background of an advertisement, it sometimes has a central position. However, under all conditions, the role of music in advertisements is quite effective (Moriarty et al., 2012, p. 308).

The importance of music in advertising brings with it the fact that many organisations invest in this area and transform popular songs into jingles (Belch & Belch, 2001, p. 294). In general, no matter how positive the reactions are to the popular music used in advertising, the music may not always be effective in increasing awareness of the brand. Therefore, marketing experts should primarily focus on forming connections between brands and jingles (Kubacki & Croft, 2010, p. 581).

When music acts together with the other persuasive aspects of advertisements in order to realise a common goal, it allows viewers to keep their interest alive throughout the advertisement and remember the brands.

The Place of Music in Brand Memorability in the Area of Advertising

Beyond giving pleasure to listeners under suitable conditions, music, the universal language of emotions, has a more powerful effect than words in the transmission of brand information in advertisements (Zander, 2006, p. 478). In addition, despite the tendency towards visuality that has a large place in human life, photographs and visual images may not be as effective in the cognitive process as certain melodies in certain contexts. Therefore, the widespread musical technique of jingles helps make products more memorable (Huron, 1989, p. 562).

Different types of music have the ability to change consumers' impressions of products and their thoughts in relation to brands. In accordance with the type of music used, the meanings conveyed by the brands can vary, from docility and serenity to violence and vitality. Different types of music are able to change individuals' focus of perception without preventing positive reactions when the appropriate musical match-up is achieved (Zander, 2006, p. 476).

Music creates a powerful impact on the products that individuals buy. While prices or other aspects can have an equal influence, the brand, which has a triggering effect in the subconscious mind, is distinctive in an individual's decision-making process in terms of choosing to buy a particular product. Therefore, even if a product or service basically has the same characteristics as its rivals, the use of music can be effective in creating a positive perception towards it (Woodward, 1982, pp. 14–15). Music, which plays a role in matching brands or products with positive concepts, is also effective in the creation of associations in an individual's mind in terms of brands as an attractive aspect of advertisements.

Brand associations, which play a role in the transmission of information quickly and accurately to consumers and in the recall of information related to the brand (Tosun, 2014, p. 210), "can be anything 'related' to brands in the memory" (Aaker, 2007, p. 130). Associations allow consumers to have a certain foresight on the basis of the tangible characteristics of products and the communication aspects of brands and help them remember information related to brands (Uztuğ, 2008, p. 31). The use of music in advertisements is an attempt to allow consumers to remember the advertising message.

Through words sung to a certain melody, jingles created with the purpose of making products, services, or brand names that remain in the consumer's memory do not consist of a single mnemonic aspect. There are four different aspects to structures of a jingle that allow remembrance, which are: melody, rhythm, rhyme, and repetition. Each song or jingle makes use of these aspects and helps listeners remember the message. These aspects work together and increase potential remembrance level by level (Woodward, 1982, p. 13).

Music additionally helps in the formation of a connection between successive visual images and product attractiveness and brings these aspects together. Music acts as a mediator in the association of different images and can play a role as a background that produces continuity in advertisements. In addition, music as an aspect that increases the rate of remembrance of products and brands provides information for consumers about product benefits. In this way, it allows brand recognition and a feeling of familiarity towards products (Huron, 1989, pp. 560–561).

Study

Purpose of the Study

This study attempts to understand the role of different types of music used in television advertisements, in terms of the associations they create and the remembrance of brands, using the focus group research method. In accordance with this purpose, university students in the 20–25 year age group, who reside in Istanbul, were selected as samples for the study. These participants were asked to listen to advertising music belonging to six different brands from different sectors, three of which were created directly for the brand advertisements and published between the 1960s and the 1990s; the other three were adaptations of pop songs or film music which had been performed by known artists and were published in 2014. An attempt was made to determine how the participants interpret the relationship between these pieces of advertising music and the brands concerned.

Compilation of Data

In the focus group study, data were obtained as a result of interviews conducted on 18 June 2014 with three male and three female graduate students who study advertising. In the interview, the participants made evaluations without actually watching the television advertisements for the brands (they only listened to them) and without knowing which brands were involved. The interviews were tape-recorded.

Data Analysis Method

In the study, data obtained as a result of the interviews were analysed through the qualitative analysis technique. The participants in the focus group were named P1, P2, P3, P4, P5, and P6. The advertisements in question were named A1, A2, A3, A4, A5, and A6. The brands that these advertisements represent are as follows: A1 – Ülker, A2 – Eti, A3 – Kent's 'Bonibon,' A4 – Uludağ Lemonade, A5 – Bellona, and A6 – Yapı Kredi playing cards.

Findings of the Study

Determining Which Advertising Music Belongs to Which Brands

In this part of the study, in which participants were asked to state their ideas about the brands without watching the advertisement but only by listening to the music, the answers were as follows. While P1, P2, P3, and P4 did not have a clue about brand A1, which was the first music clip that they listened to, P5 and P6 accurately stated the name of the brand. As for advertising films A2, A3, and A4, all participants guessed the brands without error. For advertisement A5, all participants, with the exception of P1, correctly stated the name of the brand from only the music. For advertisement A6, while P1, P5, and P6 correctly guessed the name of the brand, P2, P3, and P4 matched the advertising music to different brands.

Noteworthy Aspects of Advertising Music

Among the noteworthy aspects of advertising music, its melody, lyrics, rhythm, the popularity of the song, its familiarity, sound effects, and similar aspects were determined by the participants. For advertisement A1, while P1 and P4 stated "its melody," P3, P5, and P6 stated "its melody and rhythm," and only P2 stated "its rhythm." For advertisement A2, while P1, P2, P4, and P6 stated "its melody, lyrics, and repetitions," P3 stated "its melody," and P5 stated "its rhythmical structure, enjoyable tone, lyrics, and melody" as its noteworthy aspects. For advertisement A3, while P2 and P3 stated "its lyrics," P1 and P6 made an evaluation of "its lyrics and rhythm." Participants P4 and P5 found "its lyrics, rhythm, and sound effects" noteworthy. For advertisement A4, while all participants focused on "its familiar and popular music," P3 and P6 stated "its rhythm" as an additional noteworthy aspect. For advertisement A5, all participants stated "its melody, rhythm, familiarity, popularity, and being old" as noteworthy aspects. For advertisement A6, "its rhythm and the dynamic structure of the music" were determined as the noteworthy aspects by the participants.

The Associations and Emotions Created by Advertising Music

The participants in general likened the music for advertisement A1 to a "children's song" and expressed that they found it "cheerful and nostalgic." For the music for advertisement A2, the participants used concepts such as "cheerful," "sincere," "real," "fun," "past," and "happiness." For the music for advertisement A3, while participants P2, P4, and P6 gave the answer "does not create a clear association," P1 and P3 expressed that it evokes the "past," and P5 found the music "cheerful." For the music for advertisement A4, the associations that the participants formed were related to the movie *Hababam Sınıfı* ("The Dunce Class"). In addition, the participants found it "cheerful, familiar, and sincere." When the participants evaluated the music for advertisement A5, they used expressions such as "cheerful," "nostalgic," "belonging to the past," and "fun." For the music for advertisement A6, while the participant with code P1 stated "does not create a clear association," participants P2, P4, and P6 likened it to "festival music." In general, the participants found this advertising music "cheerful," "lively," and "fun."

The Associations Created by Advertising Music and Its Place/Role in the Memorability of Brands

For advertisement A1, all participants gave similar answers. They found that this advertisement does not create a clear association to the brand. However, the melody and lyrics of the advertising music create the idea that it may be a sort of food product that children consume. For advertisement A2, all participants expressed that the association of the advertising music with the brand makes it easier to remember the brand. Participants evaluated advertisement A3 in the same way. They found that the sound effect related to the product used in the advertisement allows the product to be remembered. In addition, participants found that this product's sound effect was much more effective than its music. For advertisements A4, A5, and A6, participants considered that the music for these advertisements was not helpful for them to remember the brands. The music evoked different feelings and thoughts that do not relate to the brands. For example, for advertisement A6, participants could not associate the music with the brand.

General Evaluation of Popular Old Songs and Music Composed for Advertisements as Advertising Music

Table 1: Participants' Evaluation on Popular Old Songs and Music

Participants	Participants' General Evaluation
P1	"If the advertising music created by the brands themselves is admired, I believe that they will be remembered years after. The use of adaptations of music may vary. It sometimes contributes to the memorability of certain brands, but may harm others. I think that especially the use of popular old songs by different brands may confuse the target audience."
P2	"Nostalgic songs do not have any effect on adaptations. In addition, I do not see them as a mnemonic aspect either. I think that advertising jingles such as the one used by Eti are catchier."
P3	"In recent years, retro music in advertisements has been used by many brands and brands imitate each other. This may prevent the target audience from remembering the brands."
P4	"I do not find the use of old music with the purpose of creating associations in terms of new brands very successful. This does not facilitate the memorability of brands. It is not long-lasting, because I think that these brands will create new jingles some time later."
P5	"The use of old music can be effective in brand association. However, I think using special advertising music unique to the brand is stronger in terms of memorability."
P6	"I do not like the use of old music in new advertisements. I find this method ordinary. I think that new and different music can be more permanent in terms of memorability. These kinds of music grab my attention more."

Conclusion

This study has attempted to understand whether music creates associations with brands and whether such associations are effective in the memorability of these brands, primarily taking into consideration the popularity of the advertising music selected.

The common characteristic of the chosen advertising music is its tie with the past. While a number of the advertisements sampled involve music that was directly created for advertisements in the past, the others consist of film music and pop song adaptations, with are part of the structure of popular culture and are defined as "nostalgic." Through the focus group study that was carried out, an attempt was made to understand participants' "likes," "associations," and "emotions" in relation to these pieces of music; the role of advertising music in forming a connection with a brand was also examined.

In the study, while the participants interpreted the relationships between advertising music, brands, and products in general, they did not find the adaptation of these types of music, which has been a part of our cultural lives and has the characteristic of nostalgia, to be successful in every case. The primary reason they pointed out for this is the use of music in a manner that does not harmonise with the brands or the general context and structure of the products. In the same manner, advertising and music professionals, who were asked for their views, also underlined that utilising music in this way should be done with great care; they found the application of advertising jingles that "define all the characteristics of brands" more successful than the adaptations of old popular songs that have become "fashionable" in recent years.

The experts who stated the importance of "melody, rhythm, and lyrics" in advertising music emphasised the relationship between the adaptation of advertising music to brands, the characteristics of products, and advertising texts and visuality. Furthermore, they found advertising music that mainly consists of traditional Turkish melodies insufficient in terms of "tone," "lyrics," and "emphasising brands/products," just like the focus group participants. The experts, who agree with the participants about the weak relationship between brands and music that has been imprinted on people's minds for years and known through generations, defined this method used in the advertising sector to foster the memorability of brands as "confusing."

As a result of both the interviews conducted with the experts in this area and the group participants, it has been observed that the tie of these kinds of adaptation music, used for different brands and products in various areas and with different concepts, has negative effects on the memorability of brands. In the minds of consumers, the matching up of this music, which exists within a certain context, with new brands and products can remain weak. Therefore, as the participants have also commented, it is not possible for these popular types of music, which are used for a certain period, to be identified with brands and be "lasting." However, successful examples of these kinds of applications can also be observed. Advertising music adaptations, if they are able to form a strong tie with the brand and other aspects of the advertisement and strongly emphasise the brand in musical terms, can contribute to the memorability of a brand.

References

Aaker, D. A. (2007). *Marka Değer Yönetimi*. İstanbul: Mediacat.

Argan, M. (2006). *Eğlence Pazarlaması*. Ankara: Detay.

Belch, G. E., & Belch, M. A. (2001). *Advertising and Promotion: An Integrated Marketing Communications Perspective*. New York: Irwin/McGraw-Hill.

Fowles, J. (1996). *Advertising and Popular Culture*. Berkeley, CA: Sage.

Giddens, A. (2008). *Sociology*. İstanbul: Kırmızı.

Huron, D. (1989). Music in advertising: An analytic paradigm. *Musical Quarterly*, 73(4), 557–574.

Kubacki, K., & Croft, R. (2010). Mass marketing, music, and morality. *Journal of Marketing Management*, 20(5–6), 577–590.

Küçükerdoğan, R. (2000). *Reklam Nasıl Çözümlenir?* İstanbul: Beta.

Moriarty, S., Mitchell, N., & Wells, W. (2012). *Advertising and IMC Principles and Practice*. Edinburgh: Pearson Education.

Shimp, T. A. (2007). *Advertising, Promotion, and Other Aspects of Intergrated Marketing Communication*. Stamford, CT: Thomson.

Tosun, N. B. (2014). *Marka Yönetimi*. İstanbul: Beta Yayınları.

Uztuğ, F. (2008). *Markan Kadar Konuş*. İstanbul: Mediacat.

Wang, P. (2012). Music and advertising: The influence of advertising and the media on development of the music industry in the USA. *International Journal of Music Business Research*, 1(1), 21–43.

Woodward, W. (1982). *An Insider's Guide to Advertising Music*. New York: Art Direction Book Company.

Zaltman, G. (2003). *Memory, Metaphor, and Stories, How Customers Think*. Boston, MA: Harvard Business School Press.

Zander, M. F. (2006). Musical influences in advertising: How music modifies first impressions of product endorsers and brands. *Psychology of Music*, 34(4), 465–480.

Emel Karagöz & Güiden Özkan

Presidency as a New Political Field of Power: The Reflections of Field-Habitus Relations on Twitter

Introduction

Political election processes can be, in a sense, defined as processes of active struggle for power in various social fields. Considering Pierre Bourdieu's basic approaches to sociological analysis, we can say that this struggle takes the actual place between the ones who dominate the field and who have the power and the capital to dominate. In this regard, people who have the opportunity to dominate are the visible actors who put up an active struggle in the political field. However, the struggle in question is between the ones who have the ability to dominate, as well as the capital kinds which give the "dominant ones" the opportunity to dominate the field. In this respect, the main factor determining the direction, severity, and greatness of the struggle are the capacity, size, and richness of the symbolic capital that are held by the dominant ones who struggle in the field. When considered from this point of view, the struggle of the power domain is a field of conflict and rivalry in which fierce battles are experienced from time to time.

Other actors in the field of political power struggle are the people who take an actual place in the field, under dominance. The dominant ones who have the ability to dominate want to turn the dominated ones or the ones they intend to dominate into the actors of the play they fictionalised. They construct and apply the required strategies to involve these people into the rules of the play they created.

Here, it is important to state that the ground on which the dominants struggle with each other corresponds to the concept of "field" which is the theoretical basis of our study defined in terms of the terminology of Bourdieu's sociology. The electoral body, however, whom the dominants (that we defined in terms of political power struggle) aim to keep or take under dominance, finds it equivalent under the concept of "habitus." In this regard, the expressions of "field" and "elector habitus," which are used throughout the study, should be evaluated within the framework of meaning that is assigned above.

In this study, it is aimed to analyse the process of the August 2014 presidential election, one of the important fields of political power struggle, differently from previous processes. By drawing inspiration from the perspective stated above, and regarding the election process as a complement of strategies constructed towards the ones who took place in the field (the ones who were tried to be dominated) by the candidates to dominate, we tried to study the process from a framework, the limits of which are narrowed.

Within this context, we aimed to display the narrowed dimensions of the shaping in question by analysing the Twitter posts of candidates on their official Twitter accounts, a micro-blog that enables candidates to shape both the field of political power struggle and the target group in it, namely the elector habitus.

Surely, it is not possible to read and analyse a campaign regarding a political election process by only one channel like Twitter. Such a study could only shed light on the holistic aspect of the campaign. Therefore, this study asserts no claim such as carrying out a holistic analysis regarding the process of the August 2014 political campaign.

Before analysing the tweets sent to the elector habitus by the candidates from their official Twitter accounts in the election process, a conceptual-theoretical basis was formed by mentioning the essentials of Bourdieu's concepts which help to analyse the relationship between the social field and the individual act. Next, the Twitter posts that were sent by the candidates from their official Twitter accounts in the process of the August 2014 presidential election, the analysis object of the study, were analysed using quantitative and qualitative content analysis. The data obtained were evaluated in light of the theoretical-conceptual basis.

Basic Concepts of Bourdieu's Sociology

Bourdieu employed the game metaphor in order to explain his cluster of various concepts that he used to pass on his own understanding of social mechanism and aimed to make his practical theory more understandable with the operation of a game.

According to Bourdieu, social life resembles a game with its wins and losses, namely bets. Continuous competition, struggle in the field of play, and improvisation which perpetuate the game among the players, are the principals.

Players (*actuators*) participate in the game only to the extent that they believe (*doxa*) in the game and their bets. They also sometimes confront one another head-to-head. By only participating in the game, players accept that it is worth playing. They have the trump (*capital*), namely basic cards, the power of which changes from game to game. In other words, there are different cards (*kinds of capital*) that are valid in each game (*field*). For example, using Greek or the knowledge of integral calculus depend on recognising this knowledge as valuable capital in the game, that is in the field (Bourdieu & Wacquant, 2003: 82).

As it can be seen, Bourdieu's basic concepts of field and capital are dependent on each other. A capital or sort of capital is a thing that is both a struggle instrument and what is fought for in a specific field.

For this reason, there is a *habitus*, the capacity for each player to sense the next move, the next play, and hit (Coulhan, 2007: 79), namely a sum of inclinations which a player (actuator) acquires by all of the objective structures and opportunities he or she encounters and the connections between these and himself or herself.

Field – Habitus Connectivity

As it can be seen in the game metaphor, being one of the basic concepts of P. Bourdieu, the field also occupies a central position in his analyses. The field is the place where the game is played. Fields can be defined as the objective connections among positions (Bourdieu & Wacquant, 2003: 81).

A field is also the place of conflict and competition. This is a war analogy and those who engage in this war compete with each other to attain the power of establishing a monopoly on the specific capital kind that is effective in this field (cultural capital, scientific capital, religious capital, etc.) and to decide on the "rate of conversion" among different authority forms and hierarchy in the field of power (Bourdieu & Wacquant, 2003:25–26).

Therefore, each field has its own capital, investment, dominants, and the ones under dominance. Each field is both a field of power, since it has an unequal source-capital distribution, and thus an oppressor and oppressed, and a field of struggle. The actuators in this field struggle to either change the balance of dominant powers or even the limits of the field or maintain them (Aydın, 2005: 124).

As each field has its own internal logic and value potential, there are some "game rules" that are sociologically determinative in their operation. The existence of a field begins when a sufficient number of people participate in a social game. This social game is not the one which has settled rules and becomes operative with a prize which is the result of players' competition (Tatlıcan & Çeğin, 2007: 318).

The actuator/group in the field tries to make himself or herself/itself different all the time so as to decrease rivalry (and therefore to establish a monopoly in a specific sub-segment of the field). They also cast out some of the people who participated or would participate in the field by creating a description of belonging (Bourdieu & Wacquant, 2003: 84). Witnessing this kind of rivalry in the political field is quite easy. It was seen that, especially during the time during which the election campaigns were carried out, political parties placed the electors they represented in a privileged position in the field and promised this position to the ones who would elect them.

One of the sets of principles that the dominant group determines and tries to protect with respect to the limits of the field is what Bourdieu describes as "the right to enter the field." This means having "certain characteristics configuration" (Bourdieu & Wacquant, 2003: 93), namely an appropriate habitus.

At this point, it is significant to state that habitus and society are not in opposition, but rather interact eachother. To put it in Bourdieu's words, becoming a socialised body is one of the ways that a society exists" (Bourdieu, quoted from 1980 by Swartz, 2013: 139).

Besides being a result of our social experiences on certain grounds and conditions, habitus also tells us about the set of our constant inclinations (class, language, ethnicity, and gender) that we bear in our minds (Tatlıcan & Çeğin, 2007: 315). Experiences that are gained through various ways of socialisation affect the actuator's view of life and determine the set and pattern of behaviour practices based on this view.

However, it should be stated that although habitus forms the basic social motives of individual's actions, it shouldn't be reduced to a mechanic operation state since the individual has a creative side.

In this sense, habitus contributes to the homogeneity in terms of class and society while it doesn't destroy the original identity of the individuals.

Capital

For Bourdieu, capital is an effective source in a specific social arena that enables a person to participate in a specific field and reach special gains brought by the rivalry within it (Wacquant, 2007: 62). The habitus of individuals depends on the position they have in the social field, namely the capital kind they have and the quantity of it.

Bourdieu defines three capital kinds which are economic, social, and cultural, and adds symbolic capital as the fourth, a form that these basic capital kinds take when they are understood by the categories of perception.

Clearly, it can be seen that capital (Bourdieu & Wacquant, 2003: 82), the only thing that is both a struggle instrument and what is fought for, which enables its owner a certain power to dominate and exist in a specific field, has a relational connection with the field and habitus. According to this information, the actuators try to save the maximum amount of this capital, which is highly important in the related field, and strengthen their position by using the amount they have.

The actuators participate in the struggle in proportion to the amount of the capital they possess, while the unequal distribution of the capital causes the field to be divided into two parts as the dominants of the field and the dependent ones respectively. Each field, as an extension of the capital that is "the thing" which is struggled for in the field and which needs to be reproduced after being obtained, is split between the rich and the poor in terms of the capital that has valid reserve in it (Yüce, 2007: 52).

It is useful here to state Bourdieu's emphasis that the capital as a gain which stimulates the actuator cannot only be economic, but also social, cultural, religious, and political.

Social capital, which is defined as the "sum of real or potential resources related to a durable network that is established with somewhat institutionalised friendships and acquaintance relations" (Bourdieu, 1986: 249), was developed to explain the connections among the gains the individuals make by their social environments in the field. The actuators get some privileges, favours, and responsibilities as a result of the families, circle of friends, the group memberships they have, and this network of relations.

With *cultural capital,* which Bourdieu keeps in a more central position compared to other capital kinds in the capital theory, Bourdieu expresses all of his experiences that he has gained since his birth and that have strengthened with the socialisation process starting with the basic institution of family at first and school life later on. The cultural capital under analysis can take many forms like "religious capital," "bureaucratic capital," "political capital," and "educational capital" depending on the structure of social space (Göker, 2007: 282). The fact that these capital kinds can be regarded as the sub-types of cultural capital should be taken into consideration.

According to Bourdieu, who argues against the view that economic capital is the only creator of dominance relations, cultural capital undertakes two functions. These are namely, a metaphor mentioning that wealth in the forms of knowledge or ideas or the material wealth of a society's culture are not equally distributed and that culture, as well as material wealth, encourages class differences and depicts itself as natural which in turn legitimates the continuity of status and power (Mutlu, 1995: 238).

Cultural capital, like social and economic capital, forms the material basis of symbolic capital. As for symbolic capital, it is defined as "a legitimate form of accumulation by which dominant groups obtain a credibility capital" (Bourdieu, quoted from 1977 by Swartz, 2013:132). The unequal distribution regarding other capital kinds between the dominant and dependent ones in the field shows itself with the status of social respectability of the dependent group and the faith and confidence they have in the dominant one when symbolic capital is in question. The privileged position and the legitimacy given take its root from the opinion of the dependent group that it is for their own profit.

Symbolic capital, by being perceived by the actuators who have the perception and evaluation categories that enable them to see, know, and accept it, is any characteristic like physical power, wealth, and militancy power values that become active in a symbolical sense like a real *magical power* (Bourdieu, 1995: 187).

Therefore, symbolic capital functions as the legitimiser of other capital kinds and is obtained by the usage of other capital kinds in a successful way.

Symbolic Violence

According to Bourdieu, symbolic violence is imposing the means which helps us to understand and adapt the social world by representing under the forms which are taken for granted and of which economic and political power has been disguised.

The concept which is used to explain the symbolic dimension of the power that the dominants have over the dependent ones is described as "complicity" by Bourdieu (Bourdieu & Wacquant, 2003:166). Since the actuators take the ascribed conditions of the social life naturally, reproduction of the process is possible.

Symbolic violence is based on the harmony between the structures that form the habitus of the ones under dominance and the structure of the dominance relation by which these are implemented: The one under dominance perceive the dominant one by means of the categories that are produced by the dominance relation, hence by the categories which are compatible with the dominant person's interest (Bourdieu, 1995:210).

It is possible to find the most transparent examples of symbolic violence and dominance relations, the final points on which field, habitus, and capital connectivity rest on, in language and communication which are symbolic forms. Bourdieu states that symbolic systems carry out three different functions at the same time, as follows: recognition, transfer, and differentiation (Bourdieu, quoted from 1977 by Swartz, 2013:121).

Symbolic systems function as a means of dominance by integrating dominant groups, while separating the dependent ones. Therefore, they ensure the recognition of the hierarchy which is in favour of the dominant groups and makes the social stratification legitimate.

Having treated the main concepts of Bourdieu's sociology in general, at this stage, we can move to the analysis part of our study.

Description of the Research Study

Presidency, involved in the political field by general elections, is accepted as the main determinant of political power field in terms of our study. There are three candidates competing in the field as social actors. How candidates drew the lines around their competitive environment and what struggle strategies they used for the dominance of the field were analysed using qualitative and quantitative content analysis of their tweets which they sent from their official Twitter accounts between July 1 and August 10, 2014.

At this point, the exposition was conducted around two main questions:

1. What kind of struggle strategies did candidates prefer to involve or stay in the field through the tweets on their official Twitter accounts as a process of the campaign conducted for the position of presidency whose definition has broadened as an actual field of political field?
2. How did candidates describe the elector habitus and how did they wish to shape it by means of the tweets which are a part of the struggle strategy developed to take part or to stay in the field by the candidates throughout the election campaign of presidency?

The method to answer the research questions was determined by making use of Bourdieuian approach. We attempted to answer the first research question using the three strategies that Bourdieu (Swartz, 2013:179) defined regarding field struggle, as follows: conservation, succession, and subversion.

The strategy of conservation is a strategy which dominant groups follow to maintain their dominance and protect their status. A possible change can cause them to lose their dominance concerning the introduction, distribution, and reproduction of capital. Therefore, the present condition must continue. They want change, if necessary, to take place only under their control. They are cautious against surprises and radical outbursts.

Another strategy which is adopted by the newly involved ones is *succession*. They wait for an opportunity to get dominant positions. Being fascinated by the dominant field, the succession strategy is an indicator of how newly involved ones can shift to orthodoxy expressions (conscious or unconscious) with heterodoxy fever.

The *subversion strategy* belongs to a marginal group who has the least desire to get the capital of the dominant groups and questions the legitimacy of the field in the most proper way compared to others.

The second question of the research study concerns the elector habitus. We attempted to reveal how each candidate describes his electoral body in terms of the strategy they follow and the position they have/wish to have in the field. Presidency candidates, notable members (according to the political view they represent), and those who have power and dominance take place in the field that semantically comprises an actual political power struggle, while the electoral body is the population which is under dominance or that is wished to be taken. In this sense, they use symbolic violence to have an effect on the habitus of the electoral body in the intended way and make their presences felt in the field by symbolic forms.

Each of the tweets between July 1 and August 10, 2014, forming our sample units, were accepted as recording units. Selahattin Demirtaş, one of the candidates, started using his Twitter account on July 10, 2014 for the presidential election. Therefore, his tweets were recorded as of that date. Retweets were not included within the scope of evaluation.

Analysing each of the recording units within the sample of the research study by pre-reading, the tweets candidates posted were categorised and the coding scale was formed accordingly. All of the tweets analysed were encoded by three researchers.

Twitter Accounts of the Candidates and Quantitative-Qualitative Findings

In this section of the study, the quantitative results of the content analysis, which was done in accordance with the aims of the study, are included. The election campaign carried out by the candidates on Twitter was compared quantitatively.

Table 1: Twitter accounts of the candidates and the number of followers

Candidates	Address	Number of Followers
Recep Tayyip Erdoğan	https://twitter.com/RT_Erdogan	5.06 million
Ekmeleddin İhsanoğlu	https://twitter.com/profdrihsanoglu	282 thousand
Selahattin Demirtaş	https://twitter.com/hdpdemirtas	455 thousand

Table 1, in which information on the follower number of candidates' is shared, shows that Ekmeleddin İhsanoğlu has the least number of followers, while Recep Tayyip Erdoğan has the most. It is seen that introducing İhsanoğlu to the electoral body at the very beginning of the election process and the fact that he did not have a political background as the two other candidates are the determinants of this situation. It can be said that İhsanoğlu has a lower accumulation of political and social capital compared to the other candidates.

Table 2: Rate of popularity of tweets – retweets in July

Candidates	Tweet Frequency	Tweet Percentage	Retweet Frequency	Retweet Percentage	Popularity Frequency	Popularity Percentage
Recep Tayyip Erdoğan	114	31.31%	164,441	48.56%	220,004	60.38%
Ekmeleddin İhsanoğlu	242	66.48%	162,765	48.07%	132,699	36.42%
Selahattin Demirtaş	21	5.76%	11,393	3.36%	11,606	3.18%
Total	364	100%	338,599	100%	364,309	100%

Table 3: Rate of popularity of tweets – retweets in August

Candidates	Tweet Frequency	Tweet Percentage	Retweet Frequency	Retweet Percentage	Popularity Frequency	Popularity Percentage
Recep Tayyip Erdoğan	56	36.84%	75,544	33.26%	124,212	45.60%
Ekmeleddin İhsanoğlu	85	55.92%	134,044	59.03%	122,933	45.13%
Selahattin Demirtaş	11	7.23%	17,488	7.70%	25,222	9.26%
Total	152	100%	227,076	100%	272,367	100%

Table 2 and Table 3 show the rates of tweets, retweets, frequency of popularity, and the rate of these to the grand total. As it can be seen in the tables, the highest number of tweets was posted by İhsanoğlu, yet Erdoğan caught up with him in terms of the popularity number, although he posted approximately half the number of tweets compared to İhsanoğlu.

As it is known, Twitter is a social networking site which allows short posts of 140 characters. A retweet means to re-share a post to enable the followers to see the post of the person they follow. A tweet shared in this way reaches many others in large numbers. In this regard, since 114 tweets posted by Erdoğan were retweeted 164,441 times, his one tweet was shared 1,442 times on average, while one tweet by İhsanoğlu, who has 242 tweets, was shared 672 times. Under these circumstances, it is not wrong to say that the spread of Erdoğan's tweets are wider and he reached more electors by means of this channel compared to other candidates.

In the next part of the study, evaluations were carried out in terms of Recep Tayyip Erdoğan and Ekmeleddin İhsanoğlu's tweets, who are the two main actors of the struggle in the field. Interpretations of the tweets regarding Selahattin Demirtaş will be treated under a separate heading.

The Analysis of Tweets

In the next part of the study, the tweets sent by candidates were first analysed according to the "subjects." Afterwards, they were analysed under the headings of "the messages taking aim at the electors" and "the messages taking aim at the rivals" with respect to the elector habitus. The definitions adopted concerning the categories formed during content analysis are stated below.

The Messages Taking Aim at the Electors: The messages which are intended to affect and manipulate the elector habitus.

The Messages Taking Aim at the Rivals: The messages to dismiss all of the actuators out of the field except for himself.

Information About Campaign Activities: The messages giving information about the television or radio programs the candidates attended, the cities they visited, non-governmental organisations by which they came together with, etc. throughout the election campaigns.

The Messages of Thanks/Greetings/Praises: The messages of thanks, greetings, and praises that show courtesy.

Other: The messages including campaign funding, campaign videos, and various links.

Religion: The messages emphasising the bond of religion which includes words such as Muslim, Middle East, Palestine, Gaza, Israel, Srebrenica, Bosnian, etc.

National Values: The messages including values like flag, homeland, anthem, solidarity, independence, liberty, etc. which were transferred by being communed with the "nation."

Rights and Freedoms: The messages referring to human rights, law, and freedoms in particular.

Universal Values: The messages that draw attention to universal values like love, respect, tolerance, peace, inner peace, peaceful coexistence, politeness, etc.

Opinion Leaders: The messages that recall the opinion and acts of important people as a guide in literature, science, politics, religion, and opinion fields.

Practices: The messages that mention the works done in the previous period.

Past Experiences: The messages that remind us of difficulties or good times by referring to history.

The Definition of President: The messages of promises that emphasise the acts regarding the works to be done in the future when the position is reached, which are stated as "I believe," "when I take up the position," "I will take in charge," "I will follow," etc.

National Will: The messages which emphasise social wills.

Socially Integrative Language: The language that is generally passive and has a null subject which creates a perception of togetherness and wholeness without emphasising any kind of competition.

Socially Discriminatory Language: The language in which "us" and "them" subjects are used to define the person through the habitus of the rival, the other, and the others.

Despising/Trivialising: The messages intended to disgrace the rival in the eye of the elector habitus.

Nicknaming: The messages in which the rival is addressed with other names or titles rather than his own to be discredited.

Irony: The messages in which the rival is made fun of by implications.

Criticising/Blaming: The messages which disparage the rival and/or his actions directly.

Unity/Solidarity: The messages which mainly emphasise social integration in the context of universal values.

Social Peace: The messages that refer to social and political peace as a whole society.

Table 4: Messages according to their subjects

	Subjects of the Tweets										
	The Messages Taking Aim at the Electors		The Messages Taking Aim at the Rivals		Information About Campaign Activities		The Messages of Thanks/ Greetings/ Praises		Other		Total
Recep Tayyip Erdoğan	88	51.76%	38	22.35%	28	16.47%	14	8.23%	2	1.17%	170
Ekmeleddin İhsanoğlu	182	55.65%	21	6.42%	59	18.04%	58	17.73%	7	2.14%	327
Selahattin Demirtaş	8	25%	3	9.37%	5	15.62%	6	18.75%	10	31.25%	32

When the tweets were classified according to their purposes of use, it was seen that candidates shared posts which can be evaluated under the topic titles in the table above in terms of their content. According to Table 4, Erdoğan and İhsanoğlu posted tweets mostly taking aim at the electors, while Demirtaş's tweets can be evaluated under the title of other. Secondarily, İhsanoğlu focused on information about the campaign activities, while Erdoğan concentrated on the messages taking aim at his rivals.

Bourdieu states that those who struggle to dominate the field draw a strategy that approximates similar habituses and excludes others in the configuration of each field. They continuously try to differentiate themselves from their closest rivals in order to establish a monopoly on a special part of the field (Bourdieu & Wacquant, 2003:84). In this sense, the categories of "messages taking aim at the electors," which aim to homogenise and bring the electoral body closer to each other, and "messages taking aim at the rivals," which intend to exclude others, were analysed within themselves. Table 5 shows the results of this analysis.

Table 5: The categories of messages taking aim at the electors

The Categories of Messages Taking Aim at the Electors		Recep Tayyip Erdoğa					Ekmeleddin İhsanoğl				Selahattin Demişt			
		Socially Integrative Language		Socially Discriminatory Language		Total	Socially Integrative Language		Socially Discriminatory Language	Total	Socially Integrative Language		Socially Discriminatory Language	Total
Values and Sensitivities	Religion	11	26.82%	21	44.68%	32	17	9.34%	–	17	–		–	
	National Values	6	14.63%	5	10.63%	11	32	17.58%	–	32	–		–	
	Rights and Freedoms	1	2.43%	–	–	1	16	8.79%	–	16	–		–	
	Universal Values	1	2.43%	–	–	1	29	15.93%	–	29	1	12.50%	–	1
Social Memory	Opinion Leaders	–	–	–	–	–	14	7.69%	–	14	–		–	
	Practices	8	19.51%	7	14.89%	15	2	1.09%	–	2	–		–	
	Past Experiences	3	7.31%	3	6.38%	6	3	1.64%	–	3	1	12.50%	–	1
Representation	The Definition of President	4	9.75%	4	8.51%	8	53	29.12%	–	53	5	62.50%	–	5
	The Definition of Presidency	2	4.87%	2	4.25%	4	15	8.24%	–	15	–		–	
NATIONAL WILL		5	12.19%	5	10.63%	10	–		–	–	–		–	
OTHER							1	0.54%			1	12.50%		1
TOTAL		41	100%	47	100%	88	182	100%		182	8			8

Values and Sensitivities

Religion, national values, rights and freedoms, and universal values were determined as sub-categories within the values and sensitivities category. As it can be seen from Table 5, Recep Tayyip Erdoğan posted tweets most of which had emphasis on "religion" in the category of values and sensitivities, while Ekmeleddin İhsanoğlu, his closest rival, referred to "national values."

The fact that Erdoğan's tweets mainly had an emphasis on religion can be understood as the endeavour of creating integration in his own elector habitus while trying to create disintegration in the rival habitus, especially by the happenings in neighbour countries.

İhsanoğlu shared posts in the category of religion as well. However, it is one of the conclusions derived that İhsanoğlu did this by an integrating language rather than a confrontational one. On the other hand, according to the election results, it can be seen that the message strategy of İhsanoğlu towards the electors, who follow Erdoğan very closely, has a focus on national values in the category of values.

Another noteworthy conclusion is that Erdoğan shared one post in the same category under the topics of "rights and freedoms" and "universal values," while this number is 45 in total for İhsanoğlu.

Social Memory

In this study, we tried to explain in what ways social memory affects positional homogeneity and differentiation. In the tweets, which were analysed for this purpose, three main categories came out.

While Recep Tayyip Erdoğan often made use of the performances he gave throughout his twelve-year-term of government, Ekmeleddin İhsanaoğlu put opinion leaders to work.

Erdoğan is in a struggle for transferring the perception of execution in the election habitus to the presidential field by reminding the performances and services he gave throughout his prime ministry period.

As it can be seen, İhsanoğlu tried to arouse interest in each part of society by referring to important people in the history of the country in fields like literature, politics, religion, etc., while Erdoğan tried to enliven the works done before in the social memory.

The fact that Ekmeleddin İhsanoğlu mentioned about the works he performed previously, though not many in number, is seen as one of the conclusions which must be interpreted. As was expressed before, İhsanoğlu is poor in terms of the political field and he does not have as much experience as the other candidates with regard to social capital since he is not well known by the electors. Therefore,

İhsanoğlu tried to bring the only kind of capital, cultural capital, to the forefront, and he mentioned his education, knowledge, academic life, and mediation services. However, in order for the cultural capital to be a valid reserve in the field, it has to have a legitimate place in the elector habitus and İhsanoğlu doesn't seem to have this symbolic capital, either.

National Will

When the tweets that emphasised the national will were analysed, it was seen that only Erdoğan shared posts in this category. This situation is compatible with Erdoğan's sensitivity regarding the change by which the president was decided to be chosen by through public votes in 2007.

Representation

It can be seen that the prominent name in the category of representation is İhsanoğlu. He shared 68 posts in total regarding the president as an actuator and presidency as a position. He used a socially integrating language in all of his posts and shared his ideas that the presidential position should be beyond politics and political parties.

Messages Aiming the Rival

In this section of the study, the messages taking aim at the rival were analysed categorically. First, the posts were classified according to their content as having marginalisation purposes and reconciliation purposes. Then, they were arranged in sub-headings.

Table 6: The category of messages taking aim at the rival

The Category of Messages Taking Aim at the Rival		Recep Tayyip Erdoğan	Ekmeleddin İhsanoğlu	Selahattin Demirş
Marginalisation	Despising/Trivialising	21	2	–
	Nicknaming	6	–	–
	Irony	–	5	**2**
	Criticising/Blaming	11	10	**1**
Reconciliation	Unity/Solidarity	–	**2**	–
	Social Peace	–	**2**	–
TOTAL		38	21	3

Table 6 was presented in light of this analysis. The most remarkable fact at this point of analysis is that none of the posts written by Erdoğan for his rivals have a conciliatory characteristic, while İhsanoğlu adopted conciliating language.

As it can be seen from the examples, Erdoğan tried to exclude the opposition parties from the field through İhsanoğlu and tried to create homogeneity in his own elector habitus via them.

Selahattin Demirtaş as a Subversing Actor in the Field

Selahattin Demirtaş, as the third candidate of the August 2014 presidential election process, should be treated in quite a different manner considering his place in the field of election struggle. Unlike the two other candidates, he had never been directly within the struggle for the presidential position; however, he created a distinct field of political struggle to exist in a wider social sphere and gain legitimacy. In this regard, it won't be wrong to say that he instrumentalised the process of the presidential election to address and reach a wider social sphere beyond the presidential field.

When we look at the tweets that form the sample of the research study, it is possible to see that he preferred an implied criticism strategy regarding the present political system and its operation through the tweets which he covered with humorous and even sarcastic language.

In this respect, he gives quite a marginal impression in the presidential election process when compared with the two other candidates. Therefore, he occupied a subversing position in terms of the struggle for the presidential field.

Conclusion

Up to this part of our study, we have tried to analyse the August 2014 presidential election campaign within a limited frame.

As a result of the referendum held in 2007, a legal arrangement was made by which the president could be chosen by a direct public referendum. Consequently, the process of the August 2014 presidential election became a real test and the breaking point for the problems regarding political, legal, and social fields. The perception, which has a classical usage basis, related to the definition of presidency and the profile of presidential position and its quality, began to change which in turn led to some arguments about new and alternative discourses and definitions in the public realm.

The arguments mentioned and the struggle of the election were formed and shaped by the political, social, and cultural knowledge of presidential candidates. To put it in Bourdieu's terminology, the political, social, and cultural capital of candidates determined the direction, manner, focus, and purpose of this argument.

The struggle at issue was among Recep Tayyip Erdoğan, an active politician who was actively carrying out his duty as the prime minister of that period, Ekmeleddin İhsanoğlu, who was not a politician and is not well-known in the social field, but defined himself by his academic knowledge, and Selahattin Demirtaş, who is mostly known as one of the important representatives of the Kurdish movement and is a well-known person because of his position in active political life. In other words, the struggle of the presidential election in 2014 took place among candidates, two of whom had powerful political capital and a certain type of social capital and three of whom had capital especially in education and the cultural subfield, but were quite weak in terms of social and political capital.

The ground on which the election struggle took place is a political field in the Bourdieuian sense for our study. The candidates competing in this field are the rivals and actors that struggle according to the capital power they have. The field in question has specific capital distribution, too. Thus, each candidate tried to structure a specific field that is suitable for his own purposes and a selector habitus that is suitable for this field.

In this regard, every candidate aimed to structure their elector habitus throughout the election campaign process they carried out in order to enter the field, exist in the field, and/or dominate it by means of different strategies that were suitable for their purposes.

As an active field of political power struggle, the presidential position was redefined and the field of struggle was broadened by Recep Tayyip Erdoğan. This definition, the scope and political power of which have been broadened, became the main focus of struggle that determined the direction of the presidential election process. Ekmeleddin İhsanoğlu, who used the exact opposite of this definition and determined his election strategy according to that, became Recep Tayyip Erdoğan's rival directly with the status quoits attitude he adopted. To put it more explicitly, Recep Tayyip Erdoğan, who was the head of execution at that time, showed that he wanted to carry his active political power to a higher authority. It is also possible to say that he used the strategy of integrating dominant groups and separating dependent ones by the religious messages he mainly posted. A preference in this direction, in Bourdieuian sense, can be understood as a strategy to protect his political, and thus his social capital power, which he accumulated on the field, and his elector habitus by widening and strengthening his political capital. It was seen that Ekmeleddin İhsanoğlu, by following old presidents and their sense of duty, adopted an attitude which was beyond parties and politics and defined presidency as representative rather than active. İhsanoğlu, by preferring to be the supporter of the status quo, which continues regarding the perception of presidential position and its definition, settled in the field as a follower, in Bourdieuian sense, regarding the presidential position. Not only did Selahattin Demirtaş give a different point of view to this adversary struggle, but he also tried to carry his struggle into the field and preferred a strategy to open a new political domain while pushing the limits of the field in the meantime.

References

Aydın, U. U. (2005). "Bourdieu'de Habitus, Alan ve Eylem Sosyolojisi". Sosyalist Demokrasi İçin Yeni Yol, Haziran- Temmuz, Sayı: 16–17. 121–128.

Bourdieu, P. (1995). Pratik Nedenler. İstanbul: Hil Yayınları.

Bourdieu, P. (1998). Outline of a Theory of Practice, Çev. Richard Nice, Cambridge: Cambridge University Press.

Bourdieu, P. & Wacquant, L. (2003). Düşünümsel Bir Antropoloji İçin Cevaplar. İstanbul: İletişim Yayınları.

Calhoun, C. (2007). "Bourdieu Sosyolojisinin Ana Hatları" (içinde) Ocak ve Zanaat: Pierre Bourdieu Derlemesi Der: Güney Çeğin-Emrah Göker- Alim Arlı-Ümit Tatlıcan. İstanbul: İletişim Yayınları.

Göker, E. (2007). "Ekonomik İndirgeme mi Dediniz?" (içinde) Ocak ve Zanaat: Pierre Bourdieu Derlemesi Der: Güney Çeğin-Emrah Göker- Alim Arlı-Ümit Tatlıcan. İstanbul: İletişim Yayınları.

Mutlu E. (1995). İletişim Sözlüğü. Ankara: Ark Yayınları.

Swartz, D. (2013). Kültür ve İktidar Pierre Bourdieu'nün Sosyolojisi. İstanbul: İletişim Yayınları.

Tatlıcan, Ü. & Çeğin, G. (2007). "Bourdieu ve Giddens: Habitus veya Yapının İkiliği" (içinde) Ocak ve Zanaat:Pierre Bourdieu Derlemesi Der: Güney Çeğin-Emrah Göker- Alim Arlı-Ümit Tatlıcan. İstanbul: İletişim Yayınları.

Wacquant, C. (2007). "Pierre Bourdieu: Hayatı, Eserleri ve Entelektüel Gelişimi" (içinde) Ocak ve Zanaat: Pierre Bourdieu Derlemesi Der: Güney Çeğin-Emrah Göker- Alim Arlı-Ümit Tatlıcan. İstanbul: İletişim Yayınları.

Yüce, E. (2007). "Simgesel seçkinler ve Habitus: Hürriyet Gazetesi'nde Köşe Yazarlığı". Sosyal Bilimler Enstitüsü, Yayınlanmamış Doktora Tezi, Ankara Üniversitesi: Ankara.

Emel Baştürk Akca & İdil Sayimer

Secondary School Students' Attitudes to and Awareness of Cyberbullying in Turkey: A Scaling Method Case Study in Ankara

Introduction

New information and communication technologies have brought new risks as well as new opportunities for children. With the popularity of electronic communication among adolescents, traditional bullying has taken on a new form and the phenomenon of cyberbullying has emerged as a new threat for children and teens.

Cyberbullying has its roots in traditional bullying but differs in distinct ways. Cyberbullying describes the repeated, deliberate, and hostile behaviours of an individual or a group toward another individual, which includes insulting, defamation, rumour, teasing, flaming, threatening, outing, exclusion, and denigration in an electronic environment such as e-mail, instant messaging, chat rooms, blogs, and social networks (Patchin & Hinduja, 2006). Repetition is among the criteria of traditional bullying. However, repetition is not a necessary criterion of indirect cyberbullying, as the repetition occurs by the constant and spreading nature of the ICT (Vandebosch & Van Cleemput, 2009; Langos, 2012; Slonje, Smith & Frisen, 2013). Unlike traditional bullying, cyberbullying cannot be easily observed, allowing the offenders to hide their identity. The power of the bullies is not based on physical strength but on their superior technological knowledge. According to the European Union (EU) Kids Online Project report, Turkey belongs to the "lower use, some risk" group in terms of children's online use and risk (Haddon & Livingstone, 2012). However, in line with technological developments, internet access has risen and the starting age of internet users in Turkey has fallen to six years of age (TÜİK, 2013). In April 2013, the percentage of households with internet access was 49.1% and this rate has risen to 60.2% in April 2014 (TÜİK, 2014). This increase in internet use is reflected in the increasing rate of cyber-bullying, as well as increased benefits. In Turkey, the subject of cyberbullying began to be addressed in the early 2000s, with attention focused on cyberbullying among high school students and risk factors associated with cyberbullying (Erdur-Baker & Kavşut, 2007; Topçu, 2008; Çifçi, 2010; Çivilidağ & Cooper, 2013; Peker, 2014). The number of studies on secondary school students is still relatively limited (Arıcak et al., 2008; Manap, 2012; Serin, 2012). The results of these independent studies are difficult to compare because of divergent survey questions and sampling methods. Therefore, it seems obvious that more inclusive and integrated research is needed.

This study aims to examine the experiences of secondary school students in Ankara with cyberbullying by looking at gender differences, as well as their awareness and attitudes towards it. The research is part of a broader field study conducted in seven different provinces in Turkey.

Methods

Participants included 200 students (100 boys and 100 girls) in seventh (n=100) and eighth (n=100) grade from the most crowded secondary schools in the six districts of Ankara in the 2013–2014 academic year. Students' participation was voluntary. 60 minute surveys were conducted in classrooms to evaluate the students' awareness of cyberbullying, their feelings when witnessing it, and their coping strategies for dealing with it, as well as their usage of the internet and social media.

After reviewing previous research, The Cyber Bully/Victim Scale was used to measure the students' level of experiences with cyberbullying. Using a five-point Likert scale with 22 items, students were asked to indicate how often they experienced (as a victim or perpetrator) each of the 22 potentially harrassing situations. The definition of cyberbullying was given in a separate section and students were asked to choose responses to the question "How would you feel if this was happening to you?" Along with descriptive statistics, the statistical package SPSS 20 was used to conduct t-test and correlation analysis.

Findings

The first part of the survey is concerned with the internet and social media usage of the students. 87% of students have computers with internet connections at home. The most common internet access device is a home computer (70%), followed by a mobile phone (25%). The students use the internet mainly for social networking (21%) and only 1% of the students use it for online education. Male students use the internet mostly for playing games (29%) and for social networking (20%), while female students use the internet mostly for research (29%) and chatting (25%). Students stated that the benefits of internet use were easily getting information (48%), communicating with friends (33%), having fun (12%), culturally improving themselves (5%), and sharing events about their own lives (2%). On the other hand, students also stated that due to internet use, they spent less time studying (40%), their family activities were reduced (30%), and they spent less time outside of the home (21%). Online harrassment from strangers was reported by 7% of the students. Facebook is the main social networking site of 95% of the students and 80% of the students reported visiting social networks at least once a day. Students use social networking sites for chatting with their friends (62%), looking at posts from pages they follow (15%), sharing content (6%), following their friends (6%), and for meeting new people (4%). Of the students, 31% reported that they have more than one profile on social networking sites. In order to avoid abuse, the "report this profile" link on social networking has been used by 60% of students. The submitted reports were mainly related to "verbal abuse" (44%), "advertising" (20%), and "insult" (18%). A large proportion of students (87%) stated that they rejected some of the online friendship requests they received. The main reasons for Facebook friend refusal were "don't know this person" (78%) and "don't like this person" (52%). The data reveal no significant gender difference in the friend refusal and reporting ratios and reasons. Of the students, 28% reported that they are members of hate groups on Facebook. Male students are significantly more involved in online hate groups than female students ($p=0.027$). More than half of the students (60%) reported making new friends online. Students reported that they communicated anonymously with people they don't know (33%) and even with people they already know (42%). The data reveal no significant gender difference in the online friend making and anonymous online communication with strangers and nonstrangers ($p=0.389$, $p=0.765$, and $p=0.569$ respectively). After the questions related to internet and social media usage were asked, students were asked about their awareness and attitudes towards cyberbullying. Students were asked to indicate whether or not they approve of some behaviour associated with cyberbullying. Behaviours not approved by more than half the students are "sharing sexual images" (96%), "sharing the private lives of friends and acquaintances" (93%), "repeatedly sending friend requests" (91%), "writing provocative messages" (90%), "writing negative things about teachers" (90%), "opening fake profiles with photos of other people" (88%), "saving others' photos and sharing them on other sites" (87%), "writing insulting messages to websites holding opposite views" (86%), "sharing photos and videos that are insulting to individuals, groups, or football clubs" (80%), "communicating anonymously in a virtual environment" (73%), "declaring love to someone" (68%), and "expressing anger to friends in an online environment" (66%). The figures also show that a higher proportion of girls than boys do not approve of these behaviours, while there is a significiant gender difference regarding "sharing photos and videos that are insulting to individuals, groups, or football clubs," "writing insulting messages to websites holding opposite views," "saving others' photos and sharing them on other sites," and "declaring love to someone" ($p=0.013$, $p=0.042$, p=0.036, and p=0.006 respectively). The only behaviour approved by more than half the students is "sending a friend request" (52%). However, there is a significant gender difference in attitudes toward this behaviour (p=0.004). Most of the female students (n=58) do not approve of "sending a friend request," while most of the male students (n=68) approve of it. The majority of students (90%) agree that it is necessary to follow some rules of morality on the internet. The data reveal a significant gender difference in attitudes toward rules of morality on the internet (p=0.011). Female students (n=95) cared more about the ethical rules than the male students (n=84). The majority of both female (n=68) and male students (n=72) reported that "raising user awareness" (71%) is crucial to ensure ethical behaviour. Students also reported other preventative measures such as "internet filtering" (16%), "reporting unethical users" (8%), and "blocking the internet access of some users" (6%) can be taken.

After students were given the definition of cyberbullying, they were asked how they would feel if this was happening to them. It is found that cyberbullying can cause many problems such as "anger" (84%), "anxiety" (61%), "sadness" (49%), "frustration" (45%), "feeling physically sick" (34%), "behaving differently to friends" (31%), "behaving differently at home" (29%), "loneliness" (25%), "loss of appetite" (21%), "loss of concentration in school" (20%), "refusal to attend school" (18%), and "disturbed sleep" (18%). "Loss of concentration in school" was more common in male students, while female students experienced all other effects more than the male students. However, the data reveal no significant gender difference in total influence scores (Mann-Whitney U Test, p=0.112) and in each effect (all p>0.05).

To evaluate their experience with cyberbullying, students were asked to state how often they had committed or experienced the described acts. The lowest and highest possible scores a student can earn on the "Cyber Bully/Victim Scale" are 22 and 110, respectively. The average "Cyber Bully Subscale" score (M=32, SD=15) was lower than the average "Cyber Victim Subscale" score (M=40, SD=20). Students who scored one standard deviation above the mean on the "Cyber Bully Subscale" are identified as cyberbullies, those who scored one standard deviation above the mean on the "Cyber Victim Subscale" are identified as cyber victims, and those who scored one standard deviation above the mean on both of the scales are identified as cyberbullies/victims. Accordingly, 17% of students (n= 34) are included in the group of cyber victims and 14.5% of students (n= 29) are included in the group of cyberbullies. When the 7.5% of students (n=15) who are both cyberbullies and cyber victims are excluded, 9.5% of students (n=19) are cyber victims only, 7% of students (n=14) are cyberbullies only, and 24% of all students (n=48) are included in cyberbullying in one way or the other (see Table 1).

Table 1: Involvement in cyberbullying and cyber-victimisation

Involvement	Number of Female Students	Number of Male Students	Number of Total Students	Total Students % (N=200)
Cyberbullies Only	4	10	14	**7**
Cyber Victims Only	8	11	19	**9.5**
Cyberbully/Victims	10	5	15	**7.5**
Total Involved	22	26	48	**24**

Examination of gender differences on the "Cyber Bully/Victim Scale" shows that male students are more likely than female students to be cyberbullies (Mann-Whitney U Test, p=0.038). But the data reveal no significant difference regarding the cyber victim scores (Mann-Whitney U Test, p=0.155). Examination of each item on the "Cyber Victim Subscale" shows that the most commonly reported victimisation experiences are "sending insulting messages" (55%), "teasing" (54%), and "name calling" (51%) (see Table 2). The independent *t*-test was used to examine whether there was a statistically significant gender difference in each of these victimisation experiences. Male students were more likely to be victims of "making fun of shared content" and "using humiliating expressions" (p=0.001 and p=0.043, respectively). Examination of each items on the "Cyber Bully Subscale" shows that the most commonly reported cyberbullying perpetration experiences are "teasing" (41%), "making fun of shared content" (34.5%), and "sending insulting messages" (34.5%) (see Table 2). Male students were more likely to be perpetrators of "hacking" compared to female students (p=0.05).

Table 2: Rates of students involved in cyberbullying at least once in their lifetime

I have been exposed to			Cyber Acts	I have done		
Number of Female Students	Number of Male Students	Total (%) (N=200)		Number of Female Students	Number of Male Students	Total (%) (N=200)
43	47	45	Spreading rumours	18	19	18.5
49	53	51	Name calling	27	33	30
38	44	41	Using insulting symbols	17	24	20.5
48	60	54	Teasing	36	46	41
35	56	45.5	Making fun of shared content	28	41	34.5
38	46	42	Making rude comments about news	11	24	17.5
37	53	45	Using humiliating expressions	20	30	25
32	32	32	Using others' identity	23	23	23
41	45	43	Concealing identity	32	31	31.5
37	38	37.5	Accessing others' pages without permission	21	31	26
43	40	41.5	Hacking	23	31	27
42	42	42	Sending virus-infected files	14	21	17.5
24	31	27.5	Showing videos without permission	8	10	9
29	38	33.5	Posting photographs without permission	16	24	20
28	29	28.5	Altering photos to humiliate	17	21	19
24	33	28.5	Forcing sexual chatting	8	15	11.5
21	33	27	Using sexual symbols while chatting	7	15	11
21	31	26	Sharing sexual images	9	10	9.5
48	62	55	Sending insulting messages	33	36	34.5
28	31	29.5	Defaming someone	16	14	15
30	34	32	Using internet for propaganda purposes	12	13	12.5
25	29	27	Using internet for fraudulent purposes	8	8	8

Students were asked to describe their response to the experience of cyberbullying. Students reported solutions such as "telling the person to stop harassing" (74%), "blocking online content" (57%), "seeming to be offline" (54%), "telling their school friends" (44%), "laughing it off" (38%), "getting away" (36%), "telling their families" (33%), "telling an online friend" (30%), "deleting offensive content" (24%), "reporting internet service provider" (24%), "doing nothing" (18%), "retaliating in the same way" (17%), "reporting to the police" (16%), "changing their online names" (16%), "telling their teachers" (14%), and "printing out the proof and showing other people" (13%). The independent *t*-test was used to examine whether there was a statistically significant gender difference in each of these responses. Female students were more likely to "tell the person to stop harassing," while male students were more likely to "retaliate in the same way" ($p=0.001$ and $p=0.043$, respectively).

Finally, students were asked whether it is possible for cybervictims to eliminate the negative effects of victimisation. Of the students, 41% think that the negative effects of cyber-victimisation can be eliminated, 38% think that they can be partly eliminated, and 21% think that they cannot be eliminated.

Discussion

The present survey results reveal that secondary school students' internet usage was very high and that they used the internet mainly for social networking. The finding that more than half of the students reported making new friends online indicates that for teenagers, the internet is an important interaction platform and public sphere. Students stated that they can easily access information and communicate with friends through the internet, but they also mentioned having some problems related to internet use. One of those problems is the exposure to online harassment. More than half of the students stated that they had reported another user for reasons of verbal abuse, personal insults, and advertising and that they had rejected some online friend requests. The data reveal no significant gender differences in the friend refusal and reporting ratios and reasons. It is worthy of note, however, that male students are significantly more involved in online hate groups than female students. Male students are also more likely to approve of cyberbullying-related behaviours compared to female students. Significantly more female students than male students do not approve of "sharing photos and videos that are insulting to individuals, groups, or football clubs," "writing insulting messages to websites holding opposite views," "saving others' photos and sharing them on other sites," and "declaring love to someone." Most of the female students do not approve of "sending a friend request," while most of the male students approve of it. These results reveal that traditional gender stereotypes in Turkey have been transferred to cyberspace. Male students are more likely to behave bravely, recklessly, and even aggressively in their social relations, whereas female students are more likely to report being withdrawn, cautious, and careful not to violate the rights of others. Students are most likely to have negative feelings such as anger, anxiety, and sadness when faced with cyberbullying. The number of female students who had emotional effects exceeded the number of male students, whereas the majority of male students reported having "loss of concentration in school." This result can also be explained by the gender stereotype that shows males as being more reluctant to admit emotional weakness compared to girls. The cognitive problem of "loss of concentration in school" is also more about the public sphere than the private sphere. However, the data reveal no significant gender difference in total influence scores of students.

The present study revealed that 9.5% of students are cyber victims only, 7% of students are cyberbullies only, and 7.5% of students are both cyberbullies and cyber victims. Of the whole sample, 24% are found to be involved either as a cyberbully, cybervictim, or both. Examination of gender differences regarding cyberbullying experiences shows that male students are significantly more likely to be perpetrators than female students. It is noteworthy that male students were more likely to state that they respond to cyberbullying with an aggressive reaction such as "retaliating in the same way." On the contrary, female students are more likely to prefer telling the person to stop harrasing instead of retaliating. These findings are consistent with other research studies on cyberbullying which have found that boys are more likely to self-report as cyberbullies compared to girls (Bayar, 2010; Karlıer Soydaş, 2011; Türkileri, 2012; Serin, 2012; Manap, 2012). But the data reveal no significant gender difference regarding cyber-victimisation. The majority of students agree that it is necessary to follow some rules of morality on the internet, while female students care more about the ethical rules than the male students.

The majority of both female and male students reported that "raising user awareness" is crucial to ensure ethical behaviour on the internet, whereas only a small number of students stated that "blocking the internet access of some users" is necessary. These findings support the idea that, in the fight against cyber threats faced by adolescents, it will be more efficacious to conduct awareness and consciousness raising initiatives instead of prohibitive measures. Students' emphasis on the need to raise awareness shows that they do not feel themselves to be sufficiently informed on this issue. In this context, it is necessary to conduct awareness raising initiatives through formal education courses, such as media literacy, and through mass media and non-governmental organisations. When adolescents are informed about internet ethics and become more concerned about morality, they will be able to reduce their aggressive behaviour, while acquiring skills for keeping themselves safe in cyberspace.

References

Arıcak, T., Siyahhan, S., Uzunhasanoğlu, A., Saribeyoğlu, S., Çıplak, S., Yılmaz, N., & Memmedov, C. (2008). Cyberbullying among Turkish adolescents. *Cyber Psychology & Behavior*, 11(3), 253–261.

Bayar, Y. (2010). Okul sosyal iklimi ile geleneksel ve sanal zorbalık arasındaki ilişkiler: Genellenmiş akran algısının aracı rolü. Unpublished masters' thesis. Hacettepe University, Ankara.

Çifçi, S. (2010). Dokuzuncu sınıf öğrencilerinin sanal zorbalık düzeyleri ile empatik eğilim düzeyleri arasındaki ilişki. Unpublished masters' thesis. Gaziosmanpaşa Üniversitesi, Tokat.

Çivilidağ, A., & Cooper, H. T. (2013). Ergenlerde siber zorba ve öfkenin incelenmesi üzerine bir araştırma: Niğde ili örneği. *International Journal of Social Science*, 6(1), 497–511.

Erdur-Baker. Ö., & Kavşut, F. (2007). Akran zorbalığının yeni yüzü: Siber zorbalık. *Eurasian Journal of Educational Research, 27,* 31–42.

Haddon, L., & Livingstone, S. (2012). *EU Kids Online: national perspectives.* EU Kids Online, The London School of Economics and Political Science, London: UK.

Karlıer Soydaş, D. (2011). Ergenlerde ebeveyn izlemesi, sanal zorbalık ve yaşam doyumu arasındaki ilişkilerin cinsiyete göre incelenmesi. Unpublished masters' thesis. Hacettepe University, Ankara.

Langos, C. (2012). Cyberbullying: The challenge to define. *Cyberpsychology, Behavior and Social Networking*, 15(6), 285–289.

Manap, A. (2012). İlköğretim ikinci kademe öğrencileri ve siber zorbalık: Samsun ili örneği. Unpublished masters' thesis. On Dokuz Mayıs University, Samsun.

Patchin, J., & Hinduja, S. (2006). Bullies move beyond the schoolyard: A preliminary look at cyber bullying. *Youth Violence and Juvenile Justice*, 4(2), 148–169.

Peker, A. (2014). Ergenlerin siber zorbalıkla başa çıkma davranışlarının cinsiyet ve sınıf düzeyi açısından incelenmesi. *Online Journal of Technology Addiction & Cyberbullying*, 1(1).

Serin, H. (2012). Ergenlerde siber zorbalık / siber mağduriyet yaşantıları ve bu davranışlara ilişkin öğretmen ve eğitim yöneticilerinin görüşleri. Unpublished doctoral dissertation. İstanbul University, İstanbul.

Slonje, R., Smith, P. K., & Frisen, A. (2013). The nature of cyberbullying and strategies for prevention. *Computers in Human Behavior*, 29(1), 26–32.

Topçu, Ç. (2008). The relationship of cyber bullying to empathy, gender, traditional bullying, internet use and adult monitoring. Unpublished masters' thesis. Middle East Technical University, Ankara.

TÜİK (2013). Use of Information and Communication Technologies and Media by Children aged 06–15. No: 15866, 22 August 2013.

TÜİK (2014). Information and Communication Technology (ICT) Usage Survey on Households and Individuals, No: 16198, 22 August 2014.

Türkileri, N. (2012). Ergenlerde sanal zorbalık: Nedenlerine ilişkin algılar, duygusal tepkiler ve baş etme yöntemleri ile zorbalık statüleri arasındaki ilişkiler. Unpublished masters' thesis. Hacettepe University, Ankara.

Vandebosch, H., & Van Cleemput, K. (2009). Cyberbullying among youngsters: Profiles of bullies and victims. *New Media and Society, 11*, 1349–1371.

Emre Osman Olkun

Change in the Structure of Media Ownership in Turkey: Example of Milliyet and Vatan Newspapers[1]

Introduction

Milliyet and Vatan, which are important newspapers for Turkish readers, were taken in hand in the content of this study and their ownership structures have changed several times from the beginning. The change in ownership of Milliyet is especially interesting because of its history and circumstances of time. Ali Naci from a journalist family established Milliyet in 1950 and it became one of the most effective newspapers of Turkey in a short time. However, until the year 1979, the newspaper reached an important place in Turkish press by organisation of Abdi İpekçi who was the managing editor but was killed in the same year. Following this, Ercüment Karacan, who was son of Ali Naci Karacan, sold Milliyet to Aydın Doğan because of some economic and family problems. This is so important because after this time, capital from other sectors started to make investments in the press. Aydın Doğan has become one of the most important actors in Turkish press in a short time after buying Milliyet. Because of economic problems in 2009, Aydın Doğan had to sell Milliyet and Vatan to Demirören-Karacan consortium. In this study, ownership structures of Milliyet, which are so important for Turkish press history, and Vatan, which has got an important place in Turkish press in a short time with its writers and owners, will be taken in hand in terms of the economy-politic approach.

Turkish Press History and Its Ownership Structure From the First Years of the Republic of Turkey to the Present Economy-Politic Approach

Political economy as a science was born at the end of 17th century and it obtained the feature to become real science with supports of the studies of Adam Smith and physiocrats in the 18th century. After then, it was developed to explain the welfare of societies as a result of capitalism and the Industrial Revolution (Yaylagül, 2008: 125).

---

1 This study is a summary of a master's thesis which was accepted by Selcuk University Institute of Social Sciences in 2013.

All approaches taken in hand under the title of Economy-Politic are about understanding the basic purpose of Economy-Politic, social, and historical transformations. It also focuses on the interaction among "economic structure, political, social, and cultural life" by refusing the existence of separate fields such as economy, politics, or communication. The capitalist economic system and its political structure are criticised by the Economy-Politic approach and it is generally accepted that the roots of the Economy-Politic approach resulted from Marxism like other critical approaches (Tekinalp and Uzun, 1991: 140). In this context, Karl Marx focuses on the idea of dominant classes which are always dominant in his studies about Economy-Politic (Shoemaker and Reese, 1991: 140).

Today, media industries have turned into the centre of powers which have relations with financial institutions, military organisations, and political elites. The specific problem for this subject is that today, media organisation producing news and information have been transformed as parts of huge industrial companies (Hamelink, 1994: 175). According to Doyle (2002: 171–172), the most important thing that must be taken in hand carefully is the risk of dominance of a minority on the democratic and political system after the density in media ownership. Consequently, one of the most important necessities for continuing political and cultural pluralism in a democratic society is to form diversity in the media ownership structure.

Finally, subjects such as how production is realised in media, how audiences or readers can reach media content, the conscious and behaviours of audiences, and the effects of media content on audiences' daily practices consist of the field which is studied by the Economy-Politic approach. The Economy-Politic structure of American mass media is controlled by opinion leaders who manage big media companies and have close relationships with governments and financial institutions. This powerful organisation produces news and media content that is suitable with the demands of elites and it does not give permission to produce pluralist media content (Herman, 1995: 92). This organisation is similar in Turkey. Media companies and groups who control huge parts of the media sector can determine the agenda of the country and they can form the content of media according to their political or economic interests.

Ownership Structure of Turkish Press from 1923 to Present

With its national struggle in 1923, Turkey started its first democratic experience and since then, many fundamental transformations have been realised in social, political, economic, and cultural fields. In this process, republican politicians, knowing the importance of the press very well, tried to benefit from the power of the press and they also wanted to control the press (Eraslan, 2010: 151).

Until the end of 1945, the press was always controlled by CHP and elites; writings about religion and socialism were banned from being published. Beside this, the Anadolu Agency and radio broadcasts, which were main news sources of Turkey in that time, were used unilaterally by CHP. Moreover, almost all newspaper owners were members of parliament and they used this priority to get support from the government for the paper, official ads, and importing publication vehicles. That is why these newspapers continued their supportive editorial policies in favour of the one-party government (Girgin, 2001: 121–122).

The establishment of the Democrat Party (DP) in 1946 and beginning of the multi-party system increased demands and expectations of society for democracy and freedom. The struggle of the DP for democracy encouraged the Turkish press to support democratic policies and the democratic system. The establishment of the Istanbul Journalists Association was another important event in favour of the Turkish press (Tutar, 1993: 11). It can be said that the Turkish press was not pluralist in the period of the one-party government. With the beginning of the multi-party system, the Turkish press started to change itself in terms of pluralism. Under these circumstances, some newspapers like Hürriyet and Milliyet started their publication life in Istanbul and after this time, they have affected the history of Turkish press in terms of so many aspects (Tokgöz, 2003: 39). Until 1948, newspaper owners generally came from families who learned journalism from elder family members and they were also editorial writers. However, this situation has started to change since 1948 (Bulut, 2009: 67).

The DP, which won the elections in 1950, started its political life and the press expected so many things from the DP at the beginning. In a short time, the DP turned into a party to which the press depended on. Journalists started to believe that the DP would solve every problem of the Turkish press in a short time. Even some journalists working for newspapers supporting CHP willingly supported the Democrat Party in this process. Positive relations among the press and the Prime Minister were developed in this period (Topuz, 2003: 192–193). The DP winning the elections with the huge support of society changed the way and method of politics in Turkey. In the same years, capital started to let the press know about its power (E. Kaya, 2010: 55). After 1954, these positive situations started to deteriorate and the positive relations were turned into negative ones in a short time (Tutar, 1993: 21). The Turkish press was a unique example compared with other press organisations in the world in the last years of the DP (Topuz, 2003: 207).

The time interval from 27 May 1960 to 12 September 1980 is the period that Turkish society experienced a rapid development process in terms of the economy and industrialisation. Beside this, this time interval is the period of military coups and political crisis and five different attempts were conducted to organise military coups and two of them were achieved (Koloğlu, 2006: 132–133). At the ends of 1960s, the press started to develop close relations with private capitals more than governments and the ownership structure of the press also experienced a new period of time. The private sector took the place of the state for incomes of advertisements and announcements and this played an important role in the transformation of the ownership structure of the Turkish press.

Capital started to create pressure over the press by using advantages of distributing advertisements and announcements. The best example of this situation was the attempt of some businessmen in 1971. These capital owners established an association and declared that they will not give publication of their advertisements to newspapers which were opponents to the interests of capital owners. Some newspapers were negatively affected by this declaration and changed their editorial policies or got rid of some journalists working for these newspapers (Bulut, 2009: 70–71). Although the selling rates of newspapers and interests to different publications increased, technological developments increased the expenses and this caused economic problems for the Turkish press. These economic problems played an important role in the change of the structure of the press (Bulut, 2009: 69–70). Except Cumhuriyet, so many newspapers tried to become monopolies in Turkey by using the method of horizontal and vertical monopolisation (Tokgöz, 2003: 40). Similar to other newspapers, changes in the ownership structures of Hürriyet and Milliyet in the 1970s were again associated with the features of that time. Beside this, the attractiveness of journalism was not important for second and third generations of families interested in journalism for a long time (Adaklı, 2006: 135). At the end of 1970s, capital owners like Aydın Doğan from other sectors started to make investments in the press (Sönmez, 2010: 20).

Besides the economic measures taken before January 1980, the military coup realised in September 1980 caused people to remember this year as the most important year of Turkey's history (Kejanlıoğlu, 2004: 28). According to Kaya (2009a: 233), the Turkish press overcame the military coup with so many important events in a short time. Turkey has started to turn its press organisation into a reach media structure since 1980. State monopoly in radio and television broadcasts ended and the ownership relations of capital in the media has changed steadily. In this process, both the legal framework and linked situation of media-state relations were constructed again and within a different concept.

The 1980s are the turning point of the press into media monopolies in Turkey. The control of Turkish media was in the hands "big bosses" instead of families originally coming from journalism (Tokgöz, 2003: 40–41). In these years, the phenomenon of monopolisation started and this caused media not to realise its main functions. Journalists could not explain their ideas and opinions freely. Beside this, two or three big consortium for television investments could be organised by only big capital owners and banks; they had also become dominant on the media sector and used media as a vehicle for their commercial purposes and interests (Demir, 2006: 186).

The dominance of the boss from journalism or journalist families lost their importance in Turkish press in the middle of the 1990s. Capital owners in the press have also made some investments in the fields of radio and giant consortiums have controlled television and media after this transformation process (Adaklı, 2006: 136). Rapid developments of media organisations in 1990 encouraged media owners (bosses) to intervene in the political situations of governments and they became so effective for the determination of politicians who were candidates for governing the country.

The most important event in Turkey in the 2000s was the election victory of the AK Party in 2002 as a one-party government and the events realised after this political situation. The fact that the AK Party won all the elections conducted after 2002 as a one-party government caused so many changes and transformation in media organisations and similarly in other fields. The AK Party governments changed the balances in the media sector and groups with good relations with the AK Party governments have increased their investments in the media sector and became dominant. Opponent media groups have experienced economic and politic problems in this process and they have lost a large amount of their power in the media sector since 2002. Even some opponent media groups in Turkey stopped their investments in the media sector and sold their newspapers and channels. For example, Doğan Holding sold Milliyet and Vatan to the consortium of Demirören-Karacan in 2011 because the Turkish government fined Doğan Holding with a huge tax penalty. This selling was not enough to pay this huge tax penalty and Doğan Holding sold other media institutions to pay the tax penalty.

Milliyet and Vatan Newspapers and Changes in Their Ownership Structure

Milliyet

Milliyet was founded by Ali Naci Karacan on the 3rd of May in 1950 to support the DP which supported the newspaper economically and politically. In a short time, Milliyet became one of the most important and effective newspapers of the Turkish press. The assignation of Abdi İpekçi as editor especially affected Milliyet positivelly and it became an important newspaper. In this process, Ali Naci Karacan died in 1955 and Ercüment Karacan became the owner of Milliyet. Milliyet continued its effectiveness in the Turkish press until 1979 when Abdi İpekçi was killed. After this tragic death, Ercüment Karacan sold the newspaper to Aydın Doğan who was the only a businessman in that period of time. At first, Aydın Doğan bought a huge part of the newspaper and then he bought the newspaper completely. Aydın Doğan directed Milliyet for approximately 32 years and after the big tax penalty which Aydın Doğan had to pay, he had to sell the newspaper to Erdoğan Demirören and the grandsons of Ali Naci Karacan whose names are Ali and Ömer Karacan. To sum it up, Milliyet, which was owned by a journalist family for a long time, had to be sold to a businessman for political and economical reasons.

After his big investments in media, Aydın Doğan became an effective person in the economic and politic structure of Turkey in a short time and he also became one of the most powerful businessmen in business life. Moreover, he became the spokesman of TÜSİAD, which is the most important association of Turkey for businessman, and he also assigned Ertuğrul Özkök, who was the responsible person for all of Aydın Doğan's media institutions, as a member of TÜSİAD. Using the power of TÜSİAD, Aydın Doğan has become an effective person in the political and economic situation of Turkey and his daughter Arzuhan Doğan Yalçındağ became a member of TÜSİAD's directory board in 2003 (Sönmez, 2003: 121). She was also assigned as president of TÜSİAD in 2007 and continued her position in TÜSİAD as president until 2010.

Except for media, the Doğan Group has so many investments in different sectors such as energy, trade, tourism, insurance, etc. The income of the Doğan Group in 2006 was approximately 8.5 billion dollars and they have had more than 11,000 workers since 2007 (Akyol, 2008: 14). Milliyet, providing an avenue for Aydın Doğan to become a powerful businessman in Turkey, is one of the most important newspapers of Turkey. The sale of Milliyet to Aydın Doğan in 1979 has changed the fate of the Turkish press completely.

In 2011, Milliyet was sold to the consortium constituted by Erdoğan Demirören and Ali/Ömer Karacan 32 years later. Milliyet sold the DK Journalism and Publication Incorporated Company with its 48 million dollar value and the Aydın Doğan era ended with this sale in Milliyet. Because Ali and Ömer Karacan's are grandsons of Ali Naci Karacan, Milliyet again returned to its original owners. The consortium constituted by Karacan and Demirören families has started to experience some disagreements in terms of controlling newspapers Milliyet and Vatan and also economic problems since 2011. After long discussions, newspapers were controlled by the caretaker. These problems were solved by the Demirören Group who bought two newspapers in the same year.

Demirören Group, which did not make investments in media before, stepped into the media sector by buying Milliyet and Vatan. This group was established to distribute liquid gas in Turkey 53 years ago and today it has had investments in four main fields. These are Demirören Petrol and Gas Group, Milangaz, Likid Gas, Mutfak Gas, Demirören Gas I.C, and M Oil. Demirören Group has made so many big investments in Azerbaijan and it continues its investments in this country. They are also the owner of Azpetrol, the biggest petrol company of Azerbaijan. Demirören Group is also the owner of Azerelektroterm which is a big industry in Azerbaijan. According to the Birgün newspaper, Demirören Group has started to increase its capacity and investments after the AK Party governments and this group has won so many big awards in the period of the AK Party governments. Today, the Demirören Family has taken its place on the top of the list of the richest families in Turkey (Birgün, 25 April 2011).

Vatan

Vatan started its publication life in 2002 by the important names of Sabah such as Zafer Mutlu (Director of Media Group), Güngör Mengi, Tayfun Devicioğlu (chief editor of Sabah), Selahattin Duman, Zülfü Livaneli, Salih Memecan, Bilal Çetin, and Ercan Arıklı. These names were supported by Aydın Doğan during the preparation process of Vatan. Vatan, among the most important newspapers released in the last decade, has reached a suitable circulation rate of 180,000 (Toruk, 2008: 129). The economic support of Aydın Doğan to Vatan organised by Zafer Mutlu was the most spoken event of that year in Turkish media. It means that Vatan was perceived as an illegal vehicle of Aydın Doğan. However, Vatan started its publication life under the name of "independent journalists" but it was sold to Aydın Doğan in 2007 and he started to control newspaper directly. Vatan was sold to the same consortium constituted by Demirören and Karacan in 2011. By paying 26 million dollars to Doğan Groups, Demirören and Karacan Group became the new owners of the newspaper. Although circulation rates of the newspaper decreased to 80,000 in 2012, at the beginning of 2013, this rate increased up to 130,000 for a day.

Sales of Vatan and Milliyet to the consortium of Demirören and Karacan Groups resulted in some economic problems which caused some disagreements. With applying of Karacan Group, control of these newspapers was given to the caretaker. Mustafa Mutlu and Güngör Mengi, who are important names of Vatan, charged Karacan Group with being responsible for these disagreements and they said that Karacan Group should end its mutuality in the consortium. They wrote some columns defending their proposal in Vatan. Beside these journalists, so many journalists from Milliyet and Vatan stated their reactions to Karacan's in this process. Journalists from Milliyet and Vatan supported Demirören Group and they continued their reactions to Karacan Group for a long time. After controls of the caretaker, Demirören and Karacan Groups started a law struggle against each other and pressure on the Karacan Group persuaded the group to sell their portions in Milliyet and Vatan to Demirören Group. This problematic situation was solved by the purchase of Demirören Group and after that, Vatan started to return to its former potential. Today, it has become one of the most important newspapers, having valuable and famous writers and journalists in its board.

In Conclusion

The findings obtained in this study display that the Turkish press was shaped according to economic and politic conditions which change historically. When it is examined from this point of view, the Turkish press could not escape from the adaptation of the liberal economy because it was affected by Economy-Politic processes, especially after the 1980s. The economic life of Turkey in the liberal economy caused so many transformations in the structure of Turkish media ownership, such as collecting different institutions in one structure.

The social and economic structure in Turkey especially changed after the 1980s, affecting the Turkish press. Additionally, capital from different sectors started to take the place of the press from journalist families. These big media companies took control of the Turkish press which was showed as "fourth estate" and then big media companies became effective over political powers, government awarding, and political processes.

In this study, changes in the ownership structure of Milliyet and Vatan and their relations with political powers were taken in hand and factors determining these relations and changes were defined according to the conditions of that time. According to the results of this study, the ownership structures and contents of the Turkish press are generally shaped and determined by economic and politic conditions of the country and this situation actually started after the 1980s; however, today it has become so rapid and effective in determining the contents and ownership structure of the Turkish press.

References

Adaklı, Gülseren (2006). Türkiye'de Medya Endüstrisi: Neoliberalizm Çağında Mülkiyet ve Kontrol İlişkileri. Ankara: Ütopya Yayınevi.

Aykol, Hüseyin (2008). Haber Basınından İslamcı Medyaya. İstanbul: Agora Kitaplığı.

Bulut, Selda (2009). Osmanlı'dan 1980'li Yıllara Basının Mülkiyet Yapısı. (Editör: Selda Bulut). Sermayenin Medyası Medyanın Sermayesi: Ekonomi Politik Yaklaşımlar. Ankara: Ütopya Yayınevi, 61–74.

Demir, Vedat (2006). Medya Etiği. İstanbul: Beta Basım Yayım Dağıtım.

Doyle, Gillian (2002). Media Ownership. London: Sage Publication.

Eraslan, Hülya (2010). İlk Basın Kongresi (1935). (Editör: Nazife Güngör). Cumhuriyet Döneminde İletişim Kurumlar, Politikalar. Ankara: Siyasal Kitabevi, 151–158.

Girgin, Atilla (2001). Türk Basın Tarihi'nde Yerel Gazetecilik. İstanbul: İnkılap Kitabevi.

Golding, Peter and Murdock, Graham (1991). "Culture, Communication and Political Economy", (Edited by: James Curran and Michael Gurevitch). Mass Media and Society. London: Edward Arnold, 15–32.

Hamelink, Cees J. (1994), The Politics of World Communication. London: Sage Publications.

Herman, E. (1995). Media in the U.S. Political Economy, (Eds. Jhon Downing, Ali Mohammadi, Annabelle Sreberny-Mohammadi) Questioning the Media. London: Sage Publication, pp. 77–93. http://www.birgun.net/actuels_index.php?news_code=1303732695&day=25&month=04&year=2011.

Kaya, A. Elif Emre (2010). Cumhuriyet'in Gazetesi: Cumhuriyet. (Editör: Nazife Güngör). Cumhuriyet Döneminde İletişim Kurumlar, Politikalar. Ankara: Siyasal Kitabevi, 51–63.

Kaya, A. Raşit (2009). İktidar Yumağı Medya-Sermaye-Devlet. Ankara: İmge Kitabevi.

Kejanlıoğlu, D. Beybin (2004). Türkiye'de Medyanın Dönüşümü. Ankara: İmge Kitabevi.

Koloğlu, Orhan (2006). Osmanlı'dan 21. Yüzyıla Basın Tarihi. İstanbul: Pozitif Yayınları.

Shoemaker, P. ve Reese, S. (1991). "İdeolojinin Medya İçeriği Üzerinde Etkisi", Medya Kültür Siyaset. (Derleyen: Süleyman İrvan). Ankara: Alp Yayınevi.

Sönmez, Mustafa (2003). Türkiye Medyasında Yeni Sahiplik Yapısı, Cepheler ve Profiller. (Editör: L. Doğan Tılıç). Türkiye'de Gazetecilik: Eleştirel Bir Yaklaşım. Ankara: ÇGD Yayınları, 107–131.

Sönmez, Mustafa (2010). Medya, Kültür, Para ve İstanbul İktidarı. İstanbul: Yordam Kitap.

Tekinalp, Şermin ve Uzun, Ruhdan (2004). İletişim Araştırmaları ve Kuramları. İstanbul: Derin Yayınları.

Tokgöz, Oya (2003). Temel Gazetecilik. Ankara: İmge Kitabevi.

Topuz, Hıfzı (2003). II. Mahmut'tan Holdinglere Türk Basın Tarihi. İstanbul: Remzi Kitabevi.

Toruk, İbrahim (2008). Gutenberg'den Dijital Çağa Gazetecilik: Türkiye'de Haber Siteleri. İstanbul: Litaratürk.

Tutar, Hilmi (1993). 21. Yüzyıl'da Türk Basını: Tiraj, Promosyon ve Değişim Gerçeği. Ankara.

Yaylagül, Levent (2008). Kitle İletişim Kuramları: Egemen ve Eleştirel Yaklaşımlar. Ankara: Dipnot Yayınları.

Eylin Babacan & Özge Mutlu

The Effect of Corporate Personality and Credibility on Organisational Commitment: Rotary and Rotaract Clubs*

Introduction

The high organisational commitment level provided in Rotary and Rotaract clubs in which the voluntary works form the base allows for the effective operation and progress of these clubs. The voluntary organisational commitment levels of individuals to Rotary clubs maintains the continuance of the club as well as the ability for these clubs to continue their operations effectively and increase the attraction of these clubs for new members.

The purpose of this study is to analyse the effect of perceptions of Rotary's corporate personality and corporate credibility on the organisational commitment to Rotaract clubs. In this respect, organisational commitment and its three components are first explained. After that, corporate personality and credibility concepts are discussed.

The **organisational commitment** of the employees of the organisation constitutes the basis for them to effectively maintain the assets of these organisations. Organisational commitment levels of employees to the organisation ensure their desire to maintain their works within the body of the organisation, including making it long lasting. Considering the main components of an organisation, we get "human" as the most influential and effective factor because the organisation can only continue its activities by the efforts of these employees. The concept of commitment that we encounter at that point, points to profitability of the relationship between the organisation and the employee and the organisation's continuity. Commitment means showing likeness, respect, and feelings, as well as showing intimacy and loyalty (Access Date: 15.09.14, http://www.tdk.gov.tr/index.php?option=com_gts&arama=gts&guid=TDK.GTS.54169f830f19a0.90894147). Commitment makes employees realise the importance of long-term relations instead of short-term relations by establishing an ongoing relationship with partners (Bowen & Shoemaker, 1998, p. 15). Commitment to Helm and Tolsdorf

---

* Acknowledgement: This study has been supported with the project no. 2389 by the Pamukkale University, Scientific Research Projects Coordination Unit.

(2013, p. 145) has an important potential to reduce the risks of the organisation, to accelerate the growth of the organisation, and to increase customer profitability. Thus, the behaviour of organisational commitment has great importance in the success of organisations as a dependent variable (Helm & Tolsdorf, 2013, p. 145). Mayer and Allen (2004, p. 2) stated that employees who remain loyal to their organisation have more desire to work and will sacrifice more for the achievement of organisational goals. On the other hand, organisational commitment is an important factor for employees because it maintains the organisation's continuity and that fact affects the performance of the organisation (Rahmani, 2014, p. 111). In general, it has been observed that employees with a high level of commitment to their organisation work much more when compared to others, do more work than expected, and exert more effort (Meyer & Allen, 2004, p. 2). Buchanan (1974), described commitment as a "partisan, affective attachment to the goals and values, and to the organisation for its own sake, apart from its purely instrumental worth" (p. 533).

Considering organisational commitment, Meyer and Allen (1984) conducted a study in 1984 and recommended the conceptualisation of the organisational commitment in two components as "affective commitment" and "continuance commitment." Then in 1990, they added a third component by the name of "normative commitment" (Allen & Meyer, 1990, p. 63). Employees with a strong **affective commitment** stay because they want to, those with strong **normative commitment** stay because they feel they ought to, and those with strong **continuance commitment** stay because they have to do so (Meyer & Allen, 2004, p. 2).

Affective commitment includes extraordinary efforts of employees for the benefit of an organisation by adopting its goals and values (McGee & Ford, 1987, p. 638–642). Affective commitment refers to emotional affiliation with the organisation, employees' desire to be identified with the organisation, and the sense of unity with the organisation (Allen & Meyer, 1984, p. 374). Affective commitment results from the conciliation between personal and organisational values that attach employees to the organisation and make them feel happy to be part of the organisation (Wiener, 1982, p. 423–424). In their 1990 research study on the three-component model and factors affecting components of this model, Allen and Meyer (1990, p. 63) defined the factors influencing affective commitment as job challenge, role clarity, goal clarity, goal difficulty, openness to ideas, reliance on the organisation, equity, importance of individuals for the organisation, and feedback.

Continuance commitment is shaped by the economic interests of employees of the organisation. It reflects employees' perception that staying in the organisation is a must for not losing the earned investments and costs (Bergman, 2006,

p. 646). Continuance commitment refers to employees' dedication themselves to the continuity of the organisation. It's hard and costly for employees with continuance commitment to leave the organisation since they have made personal investments to it. They have to stay in the organisation for their self-sacrifice for the organisation (Kanter, 1968, p. 499–517). Therefore, continuance commitment shows itself if the employee very highly esteems his or her investments in the organisation such as seniority, career, and other facilities (Ince & Gul, 2005, p. 40). If the employees consider that the number of job alternatives is low, then the commitment to their current organisation becomes higher (Allen & Meyer, 1990, p. 4). That's why the employees may continue to work in their current organisation despite their unwillingness; this situation is identified with continuance commitment.

Normative commitment is related to employees' feeling that they ought to stay in the organisation (Erdheim, Wang & Zickar, 2006, p. 961). The employees believe they have a responsibility towards the organisation and they continue to work with the idea that the organisation deserves their loyalty thanks to organisational implementations, socialisation efforts, or personal conditions (Meyer et al., 1993, p. 539). Social pressures have an important place in the development of normative commitment (Powell & Meyer, 2003, p. 159). Allen and Meyer (1990, p. 18) listed factors affecting normative commitment as employees' personality, personal and family life, and cultural and socialisation processes. While affective and continuance commitments are affected by certain moral and material instruments gained from the organisation, normative commitment is mostly influenced by pre-organisation values (Ince & Gul, 2005, p. 43).

Corporate personality is a concept which is to personify the character of the corporation. It is a useful strategy for corporate branding and differentiation (Shamma, 2012) and also building strong corporate image. Davies et al. (2001) developed the corporate personality scale which is a scale that would measure both internal (employee) and external (customer) perspectives about corporations. The corporate personality scale is a scale that could be used to characterise the personality of an organisation. It is used as a way to "personify" the characteristic of an organisation (Shamma, 2012, p. 155).

According to Kim, Lee, and Prideaux (2014), **corporate credibility** is "the extent to which consumers perceive that the company has the capability to implement management activities based on its knowledge, expertise, and trustworthiness (p. 132). Corporate credibility is one dimension of corporate reputation and represents the degree to which consumers, investors, and other constituents believe in the company's trustworthiness and expertise (Fombrun, 1996). The focus of corporate credibility is being reliable and trustworthy. Newell and Goldsmith

(2001) developed a corporate credibility scale that measures corporate credibility in two dimensions, expertise and trust.

Methods

This study aims to examine and investigate the Rotary club members' effect of perceptions of corporate personality and corporate credibility on their organisational commitment to Rotaract clubs. The hypotheses (H) of this study in accordance with this purpose are as follows:

H1: There is a significant positive relationship between the Rotary club members' perception of corporate personality and the organisational commitment to the Rotaract club.

H1a: There is a significant positive relationship between the Rotary club members' perception of corporate personality and the affective commitment to the Rotaract club.

H1b: There is a significant positive relationship between the Rotary club members' perception of corporate personality and the continuance commitment to the Rotaract club.

H1c: There is a significant positive relationship between the Rotary club members' perception of corporate personality and the normative commitment to the Rotaract club.

H2: There is a significant positive relationship between the Rotary club members' perception of corporate credibility and the organisational commitment to the Rotaract club.

H2a: There is a significant positive relationship between the Rotary club members' perception of corporate credibility and the affective commitment to the Rotaract club.

H2b: There is a significant positive relationship between the Rotary club members' perception of corporate credibility and the continuance commitment to the Rotaract club.

H2c: There is a significant positive relationship between the Rotary club members' perception of corporate credibility and the normative commitment to the Rotaract club.

The research process designed in order to test the above-listed hypotheses can be defined as an empirical research study. This research study can be included in screening survey research in nature. The study population for the survey administered within the context of this research study is rotaractors. It has been studied on only one sample group because it was impossible to reach the whole group in terms of time and financial requirements. Decisional (purposive) sampling out of non-random sampling techniques was used in determining the sample group. In this regard, the survey was administered to 174 people in the Aegean Region, to 49 people in the Central Anatolia Region, and to 54 people among the foreign members of the Rotaract club. In total, 277 participants answered the survey questions.

The survey technique was used in the collection of the primary data of the research study conducted within the context of the study. The survey questions were prepared by taking the language and meaning structure into account. Since it had been thought that questions should be understood by the participants, terms and concepts were chosen to be appropriate for the daily language used by them. The data collection process took four months and the data had been collected through the internet. Facebook, Twitter, and LinkedIn, the elements of social media, were especially used in the process of data collection. In particular, e-mails had been sent to foreign citizen Rotaractors to get data. In addition, face-to-face survey interviews had been made during the joint meetings that had been held in some clubs in the Aegean Region.

Considering the data collection tool, it benefited from the scales in the literature used in this field in order to measure organisational commitment, corporate personality, and corporate credibility. Meyer and Allen's (1991) three-component model of organisational commitment in order to measure organisational commitment, Davies et al., (2001)'s corporate personality scale in order to measure corporate personality perception, and the scale developed by Newel and Goldsmith (2001) for corporate credibility were used in this regard. Questions about both corporate positions and demographic characteristics of rotaractors were included in the survey form. The survey forms were administered to rotaractors carrying out activities in Turkey and to foreign citizen rotaractors in the English language. An expert group examined questions in the survey form in order to evaluate the relationship of them with the subject and whether or not these questions serve in this research.

Cronbach's Alpha coefficient was used to test the reliability of the scales and the components in these scales. In this respect, the results with regard to these scales and components are shown in Table 1.

Table 1: Reliability of the scales

	Cronbach's Alpha (α)	**Number of items**
Corporate Personality	0.895	50
Organisational Commitment	0.712	18
Corporate Credibility	0.840	8

As is shown in Table 1, alpha coefficient values for all components exceed the value of 0.70 recommended by Hair et al. (1995:118). It can be said that the measurement power of these scales used to measure these values are sufficient to conduct this study.

Findings

In the findings section, we first determined the demographic features of the sample group. This is followed by their regional distribution in terms of Rotaract clubs, the time they spent in the club, and their duties in the club. It's likely to say that the majority of the sample group is in the 23–27 year age range (51.5%). Considering the distribution of the sample group in terms of gender, it's seen that there are 141 male and 136 female participants. It is also seen that the large part of the sample group is single (246 people, 88.8%).

Considering the regional distribution of the sample group, it is seen that a great part of the participants are active in the Rotaract clubs in the Aegean Region (176 people, 63.3%). The Aegean Region is followed by foreign citizen Rotaractors (53 people, 19.1%) and clubs in the Central Anatolia Region (48 people, 17.3%).

A major part of the sample group (239 people, 86.3%) has been serving in Rotaract clubs for one to five years. The rate of participants who have been serving in Rotaract clubs for five to ten years is 13.7% (38 people). This finding is important as it reveals that the individuals in the sample group haven't served in Rotaract clubs for a long period of time.

The sample group was also examined in terms of duties in the Rotaract clubs. In this regard, 23.6% of the respondents (65 people) are serving as members, 12.7% (35 people) as Previous Period President, 12% (33 people) as President, 7.2% (20 people) as Applicant Member, and 7.6% (21 people) as Vice President. The other members are Secretary (5.8%), International Services Committee Chairman (5.4%), Guest Member (5.1%), Club Services Committee Chairman (4.7%), Social Functions Committee Chairman (4.3%), Information Services Committee Chairman (4.0%), Professional Services Committee Chairman (4.0%), and Accountant (3.6%).

The research hypotheses were tested based on the descriptive findings about the sample group. SPSS 17.0 package software was used to test the research hypotheses and the collected data were examined by linear regression analysis. The relationships between the corporate personality and corporate credibility independent variables were measured for each dependent variable (organisational commitment, affective commitment, continuance commitment, and normative commitment) (See Table 2).

Table 2: Hypothesis tests

Organisational Commitment						
	Model R	Unstandardised Coefficients		Standardised Coefficients	T	Sig.
		B	Std. Error	Beta		
Corporate Personality	0.456	0.399	0.084	0.315	4.733	0.000*
Corporate Credibility		0.164	0.057	0.193	2.901	0.004**
Affective Commitment						
Corporate Personality	0.430	0.323	0.077	0.285	4.217	0.000*
Corporate Credibility		0.330	0.114	0.195	2.885	0.004**
Continuance Commitment						
Corporate Personality	0.228	0.392	0.102	0.228	3.861	0.000*
Corporate Credibility		-0.021[a]	-0.295	0.768	-0.018	0.658
Normative Commitment						
Corporate Personality	0.409	0.450	0.112	0.275	4.022	0.000*
Corporate Credibility		0.200	0.075	0.182	2.669	0.008**

Note: *Significant at 0.001 level. ** Significant at 0.05 level **Sig.**: Significance

Considering Table 2, positive significant relationships were found between the corporate personality and corporate credibility independent variables and the organisational commitment, affective commitment, and normative commitment dependent variables. In this line, H1, H2, H1a, H2a, H1c, and H2c were admitted at $p<0.05$. On the other hand, a positive significant relationship was found between corporate personality and continuance commitment, while no relationship was found between corporate credibility and continuance commitment. In this regard, H1b was admitted at $p<0.05$ and H1b was not admitted at $p>0.05$.

Discussion

This study has been designed and administered in order to measure how the perceptions of Rotaractors with regard to corporate personality and corporate credibility of the Rotary club affect the organisational commitment of Rotaractors to their club. In this respect, it was examined and investigated how the perception of sub-organisations reflects their corporate structure to top institutions. Organisational commitment (affective commitment, continuance commitment, and normative commitment), corporate personality, and corporate credibility have been examined within the study.

In line with these findings, Rotaractors' perceptions of corporate personality and corporate credibility to the Rotary club have been found to have a positive impact on their commitment to their club. However, the results especially showed that the component of continuance commitment remained weak when compared to the other components which requires a more detailed examination. Besides, a relationship could not be found between corporate credibility and continuance commitment. In this regard, including this commitment component in future studies for the development of the component will be useful and beneficial for the strengthening of organisational commitment.

To mention the limitations of the research study, decisional (purposive) sampling method was used. A random sampling method may be used in further studies in interviewing the Rotaract club members. This is likely to allow the sample group to represent the study population in a more effective way. Since the research study was carried out on social media, it's not possible to reach all Rotaractors using social media. On the other hand, it also wasn't possible to find the e-mail or regions of the foreign citizen Rotaractors. Therefore, it would be more useful to establish direct connections with Rotaract clubs for using data in further studies. For foreign citizen Rotaractors, surveys were prepared only in English. The ones who don't speak English did not answer the survey. The survey form might be translated into different languages for further studies.

References

Allen, N. J., & Meyer, J. P. (1990). Organizational commitment: Evidence of career stage effects. *Journal of Business Research*, 26(1), 46–91.

Bergman, M. E. (2006). The relationship between affective and normative commitment: Review and research agenda. *Journal of Organizational Behavior, 27*, 645–663.

Bowen, J. T., & Shoemaker, S. (1998). Loyalty: A strategic commitment. *Cornell Hotel and Restaurant Administration Quarterly*, 39(1), 12–25.

Buchanan, B. (1974). Building organizational commitment: The socialization of managers in work organizations. *Administrative Science Quarterly, 19*, 533–546.

Davies, G., Chun, R., Silva, R. V. D., & Roper, S. (2001). The personification metaphor as a measurement approach for corporate reputation. *Corporate Reputation Review*, 4(2), 113–127.

Erdheim, J., Wang, M., & Zickar, M. (2006). Linking the big five personality constructs to organizational commitment. *Personality and Individual Differences, 41*, 959–970.

Fombrun, C. J. (1996). *Reputation*. Boston, MA: Harvard Business School Press.

Hair, J. F. Jr., Anderson, R. E., Tahtam, R. L., & Black, W. C. (1995). *Multivariate data analysis with readings*. New Jersey: Prentice Hall Inc.

Helm, S., & Tolsdorf, J. (2013). How does corporate reputation affect customer loyalty in a corporate crisis?. *Journal of Contingencies and Crisis Management*, 21(3), 144–152.

Ince, M., & Gul, H. (2005). *Yönetimde yeni bir paradigma: Örgütsel bağlılık*. Ankara: İleri Giden Ofset.

Kanter, R. M. (1968). Commitment and social organization: A study of commitment mechanisms in utopian communities. *American Sociological Review*, 33(4), 499–517.

Kim, S. S., Lee, J., & Prideaux, B. (2014). Effect of celebrity endorsement on tourists' perception of corporate credibility and corporate loyalty. *International Journal of Hospitality Management, 37*, 131–145.

McGee, G. W., & Ford, R. C. (1987). Two (or more?) dimensions of organizational commitment: Reexamination of the affective and continuance commitment scales. *Journal of Applied Psychology*, 72(4), 638–642.

Meyer, J. P., & Allen, N. J. (2004). *TCM employee commitment survey academic users guide*, Canada: The University of Western Ontario.

Meyer, J. P, Allen, N. J., & Smith, C. A. (1993). Commitment to organizations and occupations: Extension and test of a three-component conceptualization. *Journal of Applied Psychology*, 78(4), 538–551.

Meyer, J. P., & Allen, N. J. (1991). A three-component conceptualization of organizational commitment. *Human Resource Management Review*, 1(1), 61–89.

Meyer, J. P., & Allen, N. J. (1984). Testing the side – bet theory of organizational commitment: Some methodological considerations. *Journal of Applied Psychology, 69*, 372–378.

Newell, S. J., & Goldsmith, R. E. (2001). The development of a scale to measure perceived corporate credibility. *Journal of Business Research, 52*. 235–247.

Powell, D.M., & Meyer, J.P. (2004). Side-bet theory and the three-component model of organizational commitment. *Journal of Vocational Behavior*, 65(1), 157–177.

Rahmani, N. (2014). Cultural differences in organizational commitment Gadjah Mada University. *American Journal of Management*, 14(1–2), 111–125.

Shamma, H.M. (2012). Toward a comprehensive understanding of corporate reputation: Concept, measurement and implications. *International Journal of Business and Management*, 7(16), 151–169.

Turkish Dictionary (2014). http://www.tdk.gov.tr/index.php?option=com_gts&arama=gts&guid=TDK.GTS.54169f830f19a0.90894147, (15.09.2014).

Wiener, Y. (1982). Commitment in organization a normative view. *Academy of Management Review*, 7(3), 418–428.

F. Betul Aydın & Sukru Balcı

Political Effect and Ideology in the News Discourse: An Example of the 2014 Local Elections

Introduction

The relationship between media and politics has always been one of the important discussion fields. The need for politics to public opinion and power of the media in terms of affecting the public turns the media into an important and indispensible power in the sight of rulers. Media is a power whose importance is undeniable with the aim of gaining public support or governing the public in the desired way, not only in democratic countries, but also in management types other than the democracy (Demir, 2007, p. 1).

In a democratic constitutional state that is governed with a political regime, both authority of the political power and media organs are accepted as legitimate and "liable" by the public conscious as required by their structure. Therefore, both of these institutions have arguments in the way that they carry out their actions on behalf of the public and sharpening functions. Instinctively, both of these institutions are in a dialectic relation. These two institutional systems can be examined with their relation and interactions in the communal system and their point of views to each other and communal outputs (Damlapınar, 2007, p. 117).

Within the context of media-politics relations, media gains a different importance, especially in the electoral periods. This is because political parties, nominees, and actors of the political system are in the effort of understanding the citizens and electors and transmitting themselves to them (Balcı and Damlapınar, 2014, p. 23); therefore, media plays a key role in these efforts of the parties.

Therefore, when the studies concerning the media are examined, ideology within the context of political communication becomes an issue at which critical approaches are problematised. Marx, who saw culture and ideology as the aspects of upper structure in the basis/upper structure formulation, has been the most important course that critical approaches are fed into.

While Adorno, among the leading names of the Frankfurt School, who initiated critical media studies and critically approached the capitalist system, stated that ideology is a comprehensive and indispensible domination system (Canpolat,

2012, p. 59); Herbert Marcuse set forth that products direct the minds of people and indoctrinate a wrong conscious to them (Yaylagül, 2010, p. 105).

The ideology aspect of Gramsci, who studies ideology as one of his main interest fields (and the hegemoia that he put forth within this frame), carried importance in his media studies. According to Gramsci, ideology is not only a strategy, but it is also one of the explanation practices that put the values of a communal group into words (Maigret, 2013, p. 190). According to Althusser, ideology is the imaginary relationship between the individuals and their own existence conditions. Althusser' conceptualising ideology as a dynamic and communal process brought different initiatives in the approaching media as well as the Marxist ideology aspect (Dursun, 2001, p. 30). According to that, the media finds people at every turn and injects its ideology by giving a bang rather than a pain. People voluntarily accept the mentality and culture of the dominant class and as a result, they dictate many things as their mentality and cultures and they consent to their hegemony and think that this system processes to their benefit (Çoban, 2013, p. 159).

Stuart Hall, who was one of the leading names of British Cultural Studies, stated that media pretends to reflect the truth, although it constructs the truth (Yaylagül, 2010, p. 129). According to Hall, the ideological area is restructured and reshaped within the economical relations along with the communal, political, and technological relations that are not a part in the analytic perspective (Hall, 2002). The economical politic view that analyses historical developments and communal transforms takes the relationships between economy, politics, culture, and ideology into hand with a holistic approach and asserts that it is first necessary to look at the economical structures of the institution, such as the media that produce culture and ideology.

Using media in technical terms has not only caused the changing of the message producing and expression styles of the people, but it has also transformed life conditions of the people who have received these messages as a routine part of their daily life. It has only been possible with the development of mass communication that ideological aspects have become mass aspects; in other words, the aspects that have capacity about affecting so many people who are at various and separated frames (Thompson, 2013, p. 28–31). The wideness of the media in the spatial size has importance in the mediation of dominant ideology, especially for the ones who possess the political power.

The everyday changing agenda, and accordingly, the ideological reaction and assessments that should be given to the public by stereotyping them to the desired pattern without allowing "wrong" interpretations and opinions, should enter into the desired shape and the reactions should be in this direction (Coban, 2013, p. 151). Within this process, language is a very important in the discursive reproduction of media. But language and discourse does not completely coincide with the ideology. Such that language is articulated with the ideology and processes by ideological practice, it does not completely disappear in itself (Işık, 2010, p. 37). Discourse is the primary tool at which dominance relations are established and represented and ideology contextualised discourse and dominance relations and functions with meditative capacity (Mumby, 2004, p. 137). While discourse communally and institutionally reveals the ideology coded through the language, it describes and limits the one that is possible to say or the one that is impossible to say.

Media ideologically becomes integrated and reproduces dominant ideology. At the same time, the one that is ideological carries plainness along it within the context of news. But while ideological production is stable in terms of media institutions, the size, type, and appearance of this production can change for each media group (Ozer, 2011, p. 61). Thus, the news source, the institution at which the news is produced, the economical policy of the community, the news professionals, and the editorial processes play a crucial role in the constitution of news discursion that are the texts at which media products and discursions are represented. While media uses the language that people use in their daily life, a unique language that every newspaper or television uses comes in sight. Therefore, every media type reaches its reader/audiences through the language. When a newspaper is examined, photos and writings of this newspaper, the way it places these on the page, the point size, headings, subheadings and interim writings, explanation writings, and harmonisation way of the photos over the page make a contribution to the constitution of dominant discursion. On the television and in newspaper news, the dominant ideology can be constituted with the help of professional practices and dominant codes within the industrial structure that these institutions belong to (Bulut and Yaylagül, 2004, p. 124). The journalist places his or her opinion and ideology inside the news through his or her discursion. When the people that he or she support do positive actions, the journalist gives more places to them and when they do a negative action, his or her sentences are passively structured and the actor is ignored or given limited place in the news. On the other hand, not giving enough places to positive actions of the people that he or she disagrees with in the news reflects his or her negative actions to the public even by taking the actors precedence over the news. Van Dijk calls this situation the "ideological frame" and summarises these with the following four items: (a) emphasising our good characteristics and behaviours, (b) emphasising bad characteristics and behaviours of the others/alternates, (c) facilitating and not belabouring his or her own bad characteristics and behaviours, and (d) despising good characteristics and behaviours of others and nosing about them too much (van Dijk, 1998, p. 33).

By setting off from this ideological frame statement of Van Dijk, the statement of "*news does not reflect the real life as is and it is a text that establish/construct the trueness, Dursun, 2004, p. 40*" is the most known statement of critical frame in criticising the news and journalism and the statement that is mostly used in the news analysis. However, news plays a role in the establishment of communal domination within the context of statement and ideology. In terms of operation of the ideology, media comes true as the process at which benefits of specific parts are masked out with specific types and become legal within the natural flow.

In this study, we aim to show the ideological point of view in the election news that took place during the first pages of national newspapers during the 2014 local elections. But before the news analysis, mentioning the political and communal environment available before the 2014 local elections is necessary for the integrity of the study.

Even if the 30 March 2014 local elections were a local election, they were carried out in a general election atmosphere. Bribery and corruption claims that occurred after the 17 December and 25 December operations and Fethullah Gulen and his community named as "parallel structures" constituted the main theme of competence and opposing parties during the 2014 local elections.

Methods

The critical statement, a method that tends towards power/information, political, and ideological relations and shows how these relations have gone through changes and transformations around this statement, will be used in this study as the method. According to the "critical statement analysis" that Dutch linguistic scientist Teun van Dijk developed, the news is constituted from two parts known as the "macro" and "micro" parts. In macrostructure analysis, aspects such as headings, news entries (sports if available), main events, news sources, background and context information, and event parties' assessing the events (interpretation) are taken into hand (van Dijk, 1983, p. 34). In microstructure analysis, van Dijk examines whether sentence structures called "syntactic analysis" are active or passive or whether they are simple-complicated sentence structures. Van Dijk takes regional harmony and the relation of subsequent sentences and their relations in itself. Causality, functionality, and referential relations constitute the main parts of the harmony between these sentences. In causal relations, causal relations are searched for in the sentence and whether or not the opening of a general expressive sentence takes place in the next sentence is controlled for (Ozer, 2011, p. 84).

In this study, the election news that took place in the *first pages* of Hürriyet, Sabah, Sözcü, Star, and Zaman newspaper issues that cover the process two weeks before the 2014 local elections were examined. The Star and Sabah newspapers were selected because they make pro-government news. The Hürriyet newspaper was selected because it is the main flow newspaper. The Sözcü newspaper was included in the study because it is the opposing media organ. The Radikal newspaper was included because it represents the left part and the Zaman newspaper was included in the study because it makes news opposite to the government. The analysis of the newspapers' news was alphabetised.

Findings

Three news articles concerning the government and opposing parties were given place in the first page of the ***Hürriyet*** newspaper dated 17 March 2014. Izmir-Manisa public meeting of Justice and Development Party AKP leader and Prime Minister Erdoğan were given under the title of "Pennsylvania Neo-Ergenekon." Furthermore, a wide place was given to the news in the inner page of the newspaper. Even if the Prime Minister criticising Pennsylvania was given as the heading, photographs took place above this heading (the photo at which crowds took place) with Tencere-Tava and Berkin-Misket in writing. It was schematically brought into the forefront in the status part that Izmir publicly protested Prime Minister Erdoğan by pots and pans, holding Berkin Elvan posters, and throwing taws.

The newspaper gave Antalya public meeting of CHP under the title of *"Everything will be revealed on 19 March"* in the same dated newspaper. Interim headings were used at the continuance of the news in the inner page and sentences were effectively given place syntactically. The newspaper gave a wide place to the CHP leader Kılıçdaroğlu coming to the meeting area with his grandchild and richened the rhetoric of the news with photos from the meeting area.

In the Hürriyet newspaper dated 23 March 2014, published under the title of *"Last week,"* the Ankara public meeting of Justice and Development Party AKP and Izmir public meeting of the main opposing party CHP leader Kemal Kılıçdaroğlu were given place. Firstly, the photo of Kemal Kılıçdaroğlu, at which he greeted a big crowd, was drawn attraction in the CHP news. When the news is examined in a macro perspective, it was given from spot that CHP leader was not able to enter into the meeting area for a long time due to crowd. Interim headings were used on both the first and inner pages of the newspaper and a wide place was given to the news in the inner page. The speech of CHP leader was given directly in terms of sentence structures. The Ankara public meeting of Prime Minister Tayyip Erdoğan was given a limited place compared to the CHP public meeting in terms of both its footprint in the page and its details in the same dated newspaper. The newspaper that gave the criticisms done by Prime Minister

Erdoğan to the leader of the community Fethullah Gülen as interim headings, directly transmitted sentences of Erdoğan. As the agenda of the news was issues such as parallel structure claims, background and contextual information was not given a place. The newspaper that gave the Erzurun public meeting of MHP leader Devlet Bahçeli a small place under the title of "*You are a dangerous poison*" widely detailed the news in the inner page. In the news at which interim headings were thematically used, the words of Bahçeli were also directly transmitted in terms of syntactic.

In the news that was given under the title of "*Their real targets are huge projects*" in the 18 March 2014 dated issue of the ***Sabah*** newspaper, the public meetings of Prime Minister Erdoğan in Aydın and Kahramanmaraş were given place. Visuals of the Prime Minister Erdoğan showing that he greeted the crowds were used rhetorically and major details of the news were given place in the inner page. From a thematic perspective, the speech of the Prime Minister was given in the shape of interim headings. From a syntactic perspective, statements of Prime Minister Erdoğan were transmitted directly.

In the newspaper of Sabah dated 24 March 2014, a wide place was given to the big public meeting of the Justice and Development Party. In the news that was given under the title of "*Here is Istanbul,*" Erdoğan statement, "*We will give a lesson not only to the voters in Istanbul but also to Pennsylvania on 30 March,*" was given from spot. The news stated that more than two million citizens attended the public meeting and that the crowd was supported using a very big photo. In the news that continued in the inner page under the title of "*You are making the biggest backstabbing to this country,*" spots and interim headings were used from a thematic perspective and statements of the Justice and Development Party Leader Mr. Erdoğan were transmitted directly. In continuance of the news in the inner page, as on the first page, the rhetoric of the news was strengthened using a photo belonging to the public meeting area. In the Sabah newspaper, the news of opposing parties CHP and MHP public meetings were not given a place on the first page; rather, they were presented as small news in the inner pages.

In the first page of the ***Sözcü*** newspaper dated 16 March 2014, election news of CHP and MHP were given place side to side under the title of "*Opposing parties resounded the meeting areas.*" In the inner page, in continuance of the news, the statement of CHP leader Kemal Kılıçdaroğlu, "*Rest on your laurels with Dollar,*" was given as the heading. From a macro perspective, interim headings were used and background information was not given. From a micro perspective, the speech of Kılıçdaroğlu was transmitted directly and rhetoric of the news was increased with a photo taken in the crowded public meeting area. In the same page under this news, the speech of MHP leader Devlet Bahçeli, "*Protect your ballot boxes,* *these are robbers,"* was given as the heading; additionally, upper headings and interim headings were thematically used. While only criticisms of Bahçeli to the government among his meeting statements were given place in the news, the words of Devlet Bahçeli were syntactically transmitted directly. Also in the news, words such as "you," "government," "Turkey," and "council" were emphasised by writing them in dark letters. Even if the public meeting news of CHP and MHP were taken from the same news agency, a photo for the MHP public meeting was not used. While a place was not given to the public meeting news of the Justice and Development Party in the first page, criticisms of Erdoğan to Fethullah Gülen and spraying water to the ones who were protesting Tayyip Erdoğan from the water cannon vehicles in Adana public meeting were given place in the inner page under the news of CHP and MHP.

In the news given the heading of *"Tayyip and Apo Show"* in the ***Sözcü*** newspaper dated 24 March 2014, the big Istanbul public meeting of the Justice and Development Party dated 23 March Sunday was shown by comparing it with the BDP public meeting that was organised two kilometres away from it. In the news that was given under the title of *"Government vehicles transported AKP supporters"* for the Justice and Development Party AKP public meeting, the speech of Erdoğan, who criticised CHP, was given with the comments of the correspondent. In the continuance of the news in the inner page, upper heading and interim headings were syntactically used and the speech of Erdoğan was transmitted directly. In the rhetorical context of the newspaper, the usage of basil, the veiled, bearded, and turbaned participants present a different coding for the readers. While the newspaper gave a wide place to the public meeting of CHP, words of Kılıçdaroğlu were transmitted directly and the details concerning the public meeting atmosphere such as how Kılıçdaroğlu was welcomed and how he got on the stage were given under a separate subheading.

In the ***Star*** newspaper dated 16 March 2014, the speech of Erdoğan, *"Parallel structure manages the new Ergenekon,"* that he gave both in Adana and during the Antalya public meetings were given above the fold. A crowded photo of the meeting area that was taken from above the public meeting area was used in the news at which effective sentences were syntactically used. The news was given a full page in its continuance in the inner page and interim headings were rhetorically used.

The Star newspaper gave the words of Prime Minister Erdoğan, 'Sordidness, *rascality,'* as the heading on 28 March 2014, two days before the election. In the continuance of the news in the inner page, where photos from Tayyip Erdoğan and the meeting area were presented, interim headings were thematically used and statements of Erdoğan were syntactically transmitted directly. In the Star newspaper, no place was given to election news concerning the opposing parties CHP and MHP.

In the ***Zaman*** newspaper dated 21 March 2014, the *"we'll dig up Twitter – all of them – from the roots"* statement of Prime Minister Erdoğan was given above the fold. In the news at which spot was also used thematically, while statements of Prime Minister Erdoğan were syntactically given with effective sentence patterns, they were given by commenting these as "made astounding statements" and this time Erdoğan who continued his invectives for Fethullah Gülen Hoca effendi used assassin metaphor that he formerly used for service movement for CHP. A news article was given under this news with the title of *"Eleven slanders in two hours"* in the first page and the statements that Prime Minister Erdoğan made for Fethullah Gülen and his community in the common broadcasting with TRT were interpreted as "slander" by the newspaper. These two news concerning to Tayyip Erdoğan were detailed in the same inner page. In the continuance of the news in the inner page, it was continued under the title of "Eleven slanders from *Erdoğan in 120 minutes*" and while statements of Prime Minister Erdoğan concerning Twitter in his Bursa public meeting were placed in the page as small news, the responses of service movement to the statements of Erdoğan that were assumed as slander were given a wide place.

The Zaman newspaper gave a minute amount to election news in the first page of the election term. On 23 March 2014, a news article concerning the Erzurum public meeting of MHP leader Devlet Bahçeli was given a place on the first page. In the news, the statements of Bahçeli, *"You raise Cain by playing off against God believer,"* were given as the title and the newspaper thematically used interim headings and syntactically transmitted sentences of Devlet Bahçeli directly. In the news that continued under the same heading in the inner page, photos from the public meeting at which a wide community mass can be seen were rhetorically given place.

Discussion

As stated in the institutional part of the study, there is a dialectic relationship between media and politics. When media organs construct their political news, they construct their news in the line of ideological or economical-political vision. This situation has become one of the areas that media research studies are problematised with. In this study, we attempted to reveal how the newspapers from the national press saw politicians and the political atmosphere within the context of ideology and how they coded these aspects to the readers.

The *Sözcü* newspaper was among the newspapers included in the study that made news opposing the government and represented the radical left party that carried out a multi-sided broadcasting policy. The newspaper that named Prime

Minister Erdoğan as "Tayyip" in all headlines was one of the newspapers that best reflected the determination of van Dijk stated at institutional part of the study and names as *"ideological frame."* As it can be remembered, van Dijk describes this ideological frame as *"While emphasizing our good characteristics/behaviors, emphasizing bad characteristics/behaviors of others; while facilitating and not putting emphasis on his/her bed characteristics and behaviors, ignoring and not mentioning too much about good characteristics and behaviors of others/alternates"* (1998, p. 33). While the news devoted to CHP were emphasised by affirming them in the Sözcü newspaper, the news belonging to AKP leader Tayyip Erdoğan were given by minimising and sublating them.

The *Zaman* newspaper, which makes opposing news to the government and which is a media organ of the Fethullah Gülen community, adopted an apolitical manner to the election news in the election term. The newspaper had not given any place to the political campaigns of either government or opposing parties with a few exceptions. Among these exceptions, two news sources were analysed and one of these was the rejection of Devlet Bahçeli to community criticisms of Prime Minister Erdoğan. The other one was the accusation of what the Prime Minister did as his devotion to the community and the defences that the newspaper did for these.

The Hürriyet newspaper that was included in the study as the main flow media organ gave place to the political activities of both governor party AKP and opposing parties. When the ownership of the Hürriyet newspaper and the relationship of its ownership with the government were taken into hand, it was detected that they made more positive news for CHP. For example, while small positive details from the public meetings of CHP leader Kılıçdaroğlu were given, the ones that showed negative behaviours concerning AKP were given place.

The *Sabah* and *Star* newspapers, which make pro-government news, gave the news of the AKP from the first page. In particular, the community that fell out with the government after the 17 and 25 December operations had become a target. It was detected that the criticism that Prime Minister Erdoğan did for the community, called "parallel structure," was in the line with the broadcasting policies of the Sabah and Star newspapers.

Consequently, 2014 local elections took place anxiously. While the Sözcü and Zaman newspapers portrayed the government as its target, pro-government newspapers portrayed the community rather than CHP as their targets. The readers of their parties also accepted this ideological point of view that the newspapers detected in their opinions.

References

Balcı, Ş. ve Damlapınar, Z. (2014). *Siyasal İletişim Sürecinde Seçimler, Adaylar, İmajlar,* Konya: Literatürk Yayınları.

Bulut, S. ve Yaylagül L. (2004). "Türkiye'deki Yazılı Basında Yargıtay ve Mafya İlişkisine Yönelik Haberler", *İletişim: Gazi Üniversitesi İletişim Fakültesi İletişim Dergisi,* 19: 119–142.

Canpolat, N. (2012). *Geçmişten Günümüze Örneklerle Türkiye'de Halkla İlişkilerin Gelişimi,* Ankara: Seçkin Yayıncılık.

Çoban, S. (2013). *Hegemonya Aracı ve İdeolojik Aygıt Olarak Medya,* İstanbul: Parşömen Yayıncılık.

Damlapınar, Z. (2007). *Medya Okuryazarlığı Dersi Öğretmen El Kitabı,* Ankara: RTÜK Araştırma Geliştirme Daire Başkanlığı, s.117–128.

Demir, V. (2007). *Türkiye'de Medya Siyaset İlişkisi,* İstanbul: Beta Yayınları.

Dursun, Ç. (2001). *TV Haberlerinde İdeoloji,* Ankara: İmge Kitabevi.

Dursun, Ç. (2004). "Haberde 'Gerçekliğin İnşa Edilmesi' Ne Demektir?", Çiler Dursun (Ed.), *Haber Hakikat ve İktidar İlişkisi,* Ankara: Elips Yayınları, ss. 37–65.

Hall, S. (2002). "İdeoloji ve İdeoloji Kuramı", Süleyman İrvan (Ed.), *Medya Kültür Siyaset,* 2. Baskı, Ankara: Ark Bilim ve Sanat Yayınları, p. 101–126.

Işık, G. (2010). "Medyada 'Yeniden Üretilen' Cumhuriyet Mitingleri", *İletişim: Kuram ve Araştırma Dergisi,* 31: 29–57.

Lippmann, W. (1945). *Public Opinion.* New York: The Macmillan Company.

Maigret, E. (2013). *Medya ve İletişim Sosyolojisi,* Halime Yücel (Çev.), İstanbul: İletişim Yayınları.

Mumby, D. K. (2004). "İdeoloji ve Anlamın Toplumsal İnşası: Bir İletişim Bakış Açısı", Çiler Dursun (Çev), *Doğu Batı İdeolojiler-3,* Sayı:30, Ankara, ss.123–141.

Özer, Ö. (2011). *Haber Söylem İdeoloji,* Konya: Literatürk Yayınları.

Thompson, J. (2013). *İdeoloji ve Modern Kültür Kitle İletişim Çağında Eleştirel Toplum Kuramı,* İdil Çetin (çev.), İstanbul: Dipnot Yayınları.

Van Dijk, Teun (1998b). "Opinion and Ideologies in the Press", *Approachesto Media Discourse,* Allan Bell ve Peter Garrett (Eds.), London: Blackwell Publishers.

Yaylagül, L. (2010). *Kitle İletişim Kuramları: Egemen ve Eleştirel Yaklaşımlar,* 3. Baskı, Ankara: Dipnot Yayınları.

Feride Akim

Academicians' Use of Social Media Tools for Education: An Assessment of Communication Faculties in Turkey and in Baltic Countries[1]

Introduction

Social media, which enters our lives as an evolution of Web 2.0, is a medium which expands with social interaction through the use of the internet and web based technologies and which has a high rate of accessibility of content and sharing. In other words, they are platforms like social networks, blogs, microblogs, forums, etc. where users share the content that they produce (Tiryakioğlu & Erzurum, 2011, p. 1034). Through these platforms, users have the chance to share the content that they produce or that they follow as their areas of interest.

Social media tools are a powerful communication channel that enables individuals to convey their knowledge, feelings and thoughts, and areas of interest through texts, video, music, pictures, photographs, etc. to a wide mass of receivers on the platform of virtual reality, while receiving instant feedback. It provides users with the realisation of communication independent of time and space on an intercontinental level and enables images and texts to cover every place of the virtual world and interconnects them. In this new world where the real world comes through in the virtual world, individuals try to gratify their needs for obtainment of news, information, and entertainment along with their real life social and psychological needs of belonging, honouring, favouring, etc. With this aspect, social media tools prove to work smoothly with the "Uses and Gratifications Approach."

The "Uses and Gratifications Approach" starts from the understanding that individuals have social and psychological needs and in order to satisfy these needs, they are in a constant search for media contents. This approach emphasises that individuals' consciously and voluntarily look for, find, and use media contents for their own needs and inclinations. As a result, by using these media contents, individuals reach gratification (Yaylagül, 2008, p. 62–63).

1 This study was presented at the V. European Conference on Social and Behavioral Science. The research part has been conducted in cooperation with Akademetre Research & Strategic Planning Corporation.

Today, social media tools are also used for educational and training purposes. Via these tools, academicians can move educational action from the traditional faculty and classroom to the digital environment. They can create digital course content and share them; they can exchange ideas with students on papers and projects. At the same time, academicians make use of social media tools in order to contact their students, to share course material, to exchange thoughts about papers, to establish book clubs, to suggest new books, to make discussions with students and with other academicians on books and articles, to prepare visual presentations and videos for educational purposes, and to share their opinions on public issues and politics. They can also use e-portfolios in order to monitor and evaluate the developmental process of students. So, they have the chance to keep track of students' performance in a particular time of their courses.

The utilisation of social media as an educational tool individualises learning by enabling course content to be archived in the digital environment so that it helps students to instantly access information independent of time and space and repeat the course content as much as they want. At the same time, it introduces a pleasant and creative learning platform by allowing educational materials to be enriched by visual, audible, and graphical elements. It encourages students to study voluntarily and to access and question the information. By meeting educators and students on a platform of teamwork, it leads to learning that is based on collaboration.

Social Media Tools That Are Used for Educational Purposes

Social networks, which hold many possibilities in the field of education, have numerous user features and facilities; help educators to support an active, creative, and collaborative education-training processes; increase student-student, student-content, and instructor-student interaction; and sustain and develop students' utilisation of research, inquiry, and problem solving skills (Özmen et al., 2011, p. 46). Along with social media, the aided education environment, an alternative education and learning platform, can be implemented by gathering audio and video and text and audio-video together just like video chats on the internet (http://ab.org.tr/ab13/bildiri/302.pdf). Major social media tools that academicians would use for educational purposes can be explained as follows (http://www.scoop.it/t/sosyal-medya-araclar):

Symbaloo is a conceptually different and a beneficial social network that helps educators to organise their favourite websites or mobile applications, to share them, and to also gain access to worldwide favourite applications. Educators can collect and share websites and mobile applications that they think might interest their circle of students and colleagues. They may also benefit from other practices in the world. Edcanvas is a social network to create and share digital course content. With this platform that has the feature of adding students or courses, educators can obtain a digital content archive and can also access various course content created worldwide. Scoop.it is a social network application that allows users to create and share their own digital bulletins on various subjects. With this application, educators can follow other bulletins created worldwide, comment on them, and share them with their followers. Edmondo is a very safe social network application designed entirely for educational purposes. Its web-based or mobile use and administration is very easy. The Edmodo platform is the most assertive social network that is active in the digital learning field. Educators can share any educational content for their students and their parents, can create online quizzes, and can organise activities via this platform. Pinterest is a coinage of two English words, pin and interest. Educators can pin down content (videos, articles, course activities, etc.) that they find interesting onto their own boards and publish them under different categories in their profiles. Vialogues is a social network that introduces spectacular services to educators. Educators may initiate meaningful discussions around a video or comment on content created worldwide. Educators may also share their own content with their students and encourage them to participate in a video-course. Google-Plus is a social media platform associated with Gmail accounts where you can share content socially. Users may share anything on this platform, they may add more than one person to their circles and follow them, make people follow him or her, and even conduct a live stream. Educators may share content, plan various organisations, etc. with this platform that introduces many important advantages for educational purposes. Twitter is a social networking and a microblogging site where users share their opinions on current events and facts, exchange ideas, follow opinion leaders and specialists, develop their language skills, offer books and articles, and announce course content or date changes within only 140 characters of text. Facebook is a social networking site that allows people to communicate with each other and exchange ideas and thoughts. Educators may use Facebook to announce activities like conferences, congresses, seminars, competitions, etc., to establish book clubs, to share books or articles, to share thoughts on books with academicians and with students, to share course content (PowerPoint presentations), to announce changes to course content and dates, to announce and give recommendations on projects, to share educational visual presentations and videos, to make online quizzes, and to collect data by surveys. YouTube is the leader in online video and is the premier destination to watch and share original videos worldwide with the web. YouTube allows people to easily upload and share video clips across the Internet through websites, mobile devices, blogs, and e-mail (http://www.fullerton.edu/ technologyservices/_resources/pdfs/social-media-in-higher-education.pdf). Blogs are websites where individuals share their thoughts, hobbies, interest areas, and journeys; in short, they are a place where individuals can share everything that belongs to their life (Kahraman, 2010, p. 27). Academicians may use blogs to inform students about their courses and course content; to introduce books; to recommend books; to collect data by surveys; to announce activities like conferences, congresses, seminars, competitions, etc. relating to the university; and to share their articles in news sites and/or periodical publications.

Purpose of the Study

The aim of this study is to demonstrate how academicians use social media tools and to reveal academicians' thoughts on the benefits of social media for educational purposes. During this study, academicians were sent a survey via web links and the websites of the relevant higher education institutions that have public relations departments were examined to determine whether or not they have social media courses among their undergraduate and graduate courses.

Methods

Participants

In order to reach the participants in Turkey, a total of 175 universities, 104 state and 71 private universities, were sought for the active departments of public relations, public relations and publicity, public relations and advertising, or public relations and relationship management departments. Related departments are active in 22 out of 104 state universities and 14 out of 71 private universities. There are a total of 262 instructors in office, 192 instructors in 22 state universities and 70 instructors in 14 private universities. In Latvia, there are 17 state colleges, 15 institutions that offer higher education which are established by juridical people, 13 state institutions that offer higher education, eight colleges that are established by juridical people, and six universities. Public relations, communication and public relations, and public relations and advertising departments are found in three of the institutions that offer higher education which are established by juridical people, in two state universities, two of the colleges that are established by juridical people, and one of the state institutions that offers higher education. There are a total of 55 instructors in office, 24 of them are at the three institutions that offer higher education which are established by juridical people, 16 of them are at the two state universities, nine of them are at the two colleges that are established by juridical people, and six of them are at the one state institution that offers higher education. There are twelve public universities in Estonia (all universities are public in Estonia) and eight special institutions. Among these universities, there is only one department called communication and public relations. There are eight instructors that are in the office in that department.

107 out of 262 instructors that are in office in public relations departments in Turkey responsed to the survey. 26 out of 55 instructors that are in office in public relations departments in Latvia responsed to the survey. Six of the Turkish instructors pointed out that they do not use social media because they thought that social media is a waste of time and that they prefer face-to-face communication, while one of the Latvian instructors noted that he does not use social media because it is unnecessary in education. There was no return back from eight Estonian instructors that are in office in public relations departments. Accordingly, 40.8% of the Turkish instructors and 47.3% of the Latvian instructors participated in the survey sent via web link.

Data Collection Technique

The research study was conducted in an online environment. In the scope of this survey, the online survey technique was applied. In the interviews, Webropol, worldwide online survey software, was utilised and a link was generated and sent to the e-mail addresses of the participants for quick access to the survey. The completed surveys were instantly transmitted to the Akademetre database and were made ready for analysis.

Findings

Among all participants in Turkey, 61.7% were women and 38.3% were men. Latvian academicians that participated in the survey were distributed as 61.5% women and 38.5% men. The mean age of the participants from Turkey was predominantly between the ages of 37–41 years with a rate of 29.9%. The mean age of the participants from Latvia was mainly between the ages of 32 to 36 years with a rate of 30.8%.

The most commonly used social media tools were Facebook (86.1%), YouTube (67.3%), Twitter (61.4%), WhatsApp (57.4%), LinkedIn (48.5%), and Instagram (40.6%) respectively for Turkish academicians. For Latvian academicians, the most commonly used social media tools were Facebook (92%), Twitter (72%), LinkedIn (56%), YouTube (52%), WhatsApp (44%), and Instagram (36%). The most commonly used social media tool is Facebook for both Turkish and Latvian academicians that participated in the survey. 73.6% of the participants from

Turkey and 78.3% of the participants from Latvia use Facebook everyday. 65.5% of the participants from Turkey use WhatsApp and 64.5% use Twitter on a daily basis; 61.1% of the Latvian participants use Twitter and 36.4% use WhatsApp on a daily basis.

While Turkish academicians use Facebook to follow the agenda (78.2%), to announce activities relating to the faculty and university (74.7%), to correspond with colleagues, and to maintain communication (66.7%), Latvian academicians use Facebook to share photographs and videos (78.3%), to share their opinions on public matters and politics (78.3%), and to announce activities relating to the faculty and university (73.9%). When we look at the use of Facebook, Latvian academicians depart from their Turkish colleagues on the issue of "sharing their opinions on public matters and politics." Facebook is more actively used by the Turkish academicians "to follow the agenda" and "to correspond with colleagues."

While YouTube is used by Turkish academicians for sharing visual presentations and videos for educational purposes (23.5%), for following the agenda (22.1%), and for sharing photographs and videos (19.1%), Latvian counterparts use it for sharing photographs and videos (30.8%), for following the agenda (23.1%), and for sharing visual presentations and videos for educational purposes (15.4%). Turkish and Latvian academicians' YouTube use seems to be similar.

The use of Twitter shows similarities for both countries and it has a political and social dimension. Academicians from Turkey use Twitter for following the agenda (87.1%), following the opinion leaders and specialists (83.9%), and sharing their views on public problems and on politics (74.2%), while academicians from Latvia use Twitter equally for following the opinion leaders and specialists and sharing their views on public problems and on politics (77.8%) and for following the agenda (72.2%).

When we look at the usage area of the WhatsApp application, besides sharing photographs and videos, Turkish academicians use it for corresponding with colleagues and maintaining communication (29.3%) and for announcing projects and giving advice relating to them (12.1%), while Latvian academicians use it equally for collecting data for surveys and announcing activities relating to the faculty and university (18.2%). It is seen that in both countries, WhatsApp is used in the professional field apart from its use for sharing photographs and videos.

Turkish academicians use LinkedIn for corresponding with colleagues and maintaining communication, while Latvian counterparts use it in different areas. While the primary interest of Turkish academicians to use LinkedIn is to correspond with colleagues and to maintain communication (57.1%), Latvian academicians' primary use is to correspond with colleagues and to maintain communication (64.3%), to follow opinion leaders and specialists (42.9%), and to announce activities relating to the faculty and university (35.7%).

There are also other social media tools that are used less frequently by the academicians including Instagram and blogs and it is possible to point out their primary concern for using them: Academicians from both countries use Instagram for sharing photographs and videos. Turkish academicians utilise blogs for sharing books or articles, while Latvian academicians use blogs for announcing course content and information relating to the dates of courses.

According to the academicians from both countries, the most important advantage of social media tools for educational purposes is that they "allow for the sharing of information anytime and anywhere." 43.6% of the Turkish academicians were concentrated on this remark, while 40% of the Latvian academicians agree on this remark. Obtaining bidirectional communication, accessing information, increasing the skills of use and assessment of information, and rapid feedback are among the other advantages of the use of social media tools for educational purposes.

Assessments relating to the use of social media for educational purposes are similar for the academicians working in both countries. When we look at the statements that gain importance in terms of positive values, 85.1% of Turkish academicians and 72% of the Latvian participants agree that social media tools for educational purposes are beneficial. 75.2% of the Turkish and 72% of the Latvian participants are of the same opinion that students should be encouraged to use social media tools during the education process. When we look at the criteria relating to the use of social media tools for educational purposes, the biggest clash is in the ease to learn how to use them. 87.1% of the Turkish academicians think that social media tools are easy to learn compared to 48% of Latvian academicians. Academicians from both countries are indecisive about the use of social media tools' influence on students' grades.

The findings that are obtained from the examination of the websites of the relevant higher education institutions that have public relations departments to determine whether or not they have social media courses among their undergraduate and graduate courses can be expressed as follows: In Turkey, 22 out of 104 state universities have actively operating communication faculties and 14 of them have courses on social media in their undergraduate courses. These courses are taught mainly in third and fourth year respectively. In Turkey, 14 out of 71 private universities have actively operating communication faculties and ten of them have courses on social media in their undergraduate courses. These courses are taught mainly in fourth and second year respectively. 13 out of 22 state universities that have actively operating communication faculties have masters programs and eight of them have PhD programs in public relations. Seven out of 13 state universities that have masters programs and four out of 8 state universities that have PhD programs offer courses on social media. Eleven out of 14 private universities have masters programs and two of them have PhD programs on public relations. Five out of eleven private universities offer courses on social media, whereas there are no courses on social media in the PhD programs of the two private universities.

In Latvia, there are courses on social media in two of the institutions that offer higher education which are established by juridical people and in one of the colleges which is established by juridical people. Only one out of six higher education institutions that have masters program offer courses on social media. There are two higher education institutions that have PhD programs but none of them offer courses on social media. In Estonia, there is only one public university that has a communication management and public relations department; the course plan cannot be reached in the website of the related university.

Conclusions and Discussion

Facebook is the most frequently used social media tool among the academicians that participated in the survey both from Turkey and Latvia: It is proven that they use social media tools for "correspondence and exchange of information" and for "socialisation." For the academicians from both countries, the use of social media tools for educational purposes has a number of advantages: "allows for the sharing of information anytime and anywhere," "provides users with a bidirectional communication," "rapid feedback," "allows individual learning," "increases the skills of use and assessment of knowledge," and "allows course content to be archived digitally." The use of social media tools for educational purposes are found to be beneficial in general; however, Turkish academicians find them more beneficial than their Latvian counterparts. Even though academicians claim that social media tools for educational purposes are beneficial, it is found that they do not use social media tools like Symbaloo, Edcanvas, Scoop.it, Edmodo, Vialogues, etc.

When course plans are considered, it is found that Turkish higher education institutions offer more intense courses on social media compared to Latvian higher education institutions. However, academicians are of the same opinion on the encouragement of students to use social media tools. When taken into consideration, it becomes a necessity to increase the courses on social media in Latvian higher education institutions. The majority of academicians that participate in the survey from Turkey think that it is easy to learn to use social media tools for educational purposes; this proportion is below 50% for the academicians from Latvia who participated in the survey. When this factor is considered, the courses on social media should transmit both theoretical information on the educational use of social media and practical information on how to use these tools. When it is considered that academicians are of the same opinion that students should be encouraged to use social media tools during the educational process, the treatment of courses in a like manner should also prompt both academicians and students to use social media for educational purposes. It is a strong possibility for students that use social media with a conscious mind would increase their potentials of thinking, questioning, and criticising. Sharing of the educational material by educators via social media would help to increase the students' activity in lessons. At the same time, it allows both academicians and students to improve their communication skills and gives way to collaborative learning. The internalisation of the shared educational materials may have a positive influence on students' grades. Academicians' sharing of the educational materials in foreign languages may be encouraging on students' development of language skills.

As a result, the utilisation of social media for educational purposes by both students and academicians may make for more productive and higher quality education and learning activities and may take them to higher standards.

References

Kahraman, M. (2010). Sosyal Medya 101 2.0. İstanbul: MediaCat Kitapları.

Özmen, F., Aküzüm, C., Sünkür, M., & Baysal, N. (2011). Sosyal Ağ Sitelerinin Eğitsel Ortamlardaki İşlevselliği. 6th International Advanced Technologies Symposium, Elazığ, Turkiye, 16–18 Mayıs, 42–47.

Reuben, R. The Use of Social Media in Higher Education for Marketing and Communications: A Guide for Professionals in Higher Education from http://www.fullerton.edu/technologyservices/_resources/pdfs/social-media-in-higher-education.pdf.

Tiryakioğlu, F. & Erzurum, F. (2011). Bir Eğitim Aracı Olarak Ağların Kullanımı. 2nd International Conference on New Trends in Education and Their Implications, Antalya, Türkiye, 27–29 Nisan, 1031–1047.

Toğay, A., Akdur, T. E., Yetişken, İ. C. & Bilici, A. Eğitim Süreçlerinde Sosyal Ağların Kullanımı: Bir MYO Deneyimi from http://ab.org.tr/ab13/bildiri/302.pdf.

Yaylagül, L. (2008). Kitle İletişim Kuramları. 2. bs. Ankara: Dipnot Yayınları. http://www.scoop.it/t/sosyal-medya-araclar.

Gül Coşkun Değirmen

The Representation of Public Relations as a Profession in Turkish Cinema after 2000

Introduction

The profession of public relations in today's Turkey develops gradually. The departments of public relations, human relations, and advertisement agencies in the area of advertisement and public relations consultancy services are preferred by the organisations, and therefore, are the areas of application expanding day by day.

When the theories regarding the public relations profession are examined from past to present, it is possible to state that the profession shifted from certain applications which could cause adverse images to the ones which are positive and attaches importance to balanced communication. Of course, the image of the profession is very important for the public in terms of the perception of the profession. It is possible to put forward that the public is not knowledgeable enough regarding the profession in Turkey. The public gets informed about the profession by getting an idea when confronted with the representatives of the profession and news regarding the profession or reflections of the profession in the media. Therefore, it is very important to represent the profession in the manner, both in the application areas of the public relations profession and the media, for the development of the profession.

The Concept of Public Relations

Public relations is the endeavours exerted as a whole by an organisation to integrate with the public (Işık, 2012:3). Public relations is also certain policy, agenda, and programme implementation in a planned manner by an administrator to strengthen the public trust and increase the interest rate of the public to the organisation. Public relations is a management function covering different activities to protect and reinforce the reputation of the organisation acting as a bridge between all the target groups and the organisation for effective communication to convey the image of the organisation to all the target groups (Yurdakul & Coskun, 2008:10).

According to the best definition by IPRA, "public relations is an original management function which helps developing mutual understanding between the organisation and the target groups and establishing and sustaining cooperation and communication; related to management of problems and issues; which informs the management about the public opinion continuously, helps management be sensitive about the public; defines and highlights the responsibility of the management to serve the public; acting as a early warning system to define the tendencies to ensure management could keep up with and benefit from the changes; primarily making use of research techniques and communication techniques appropriate to healthy and ethical principals"(Sjöberg, 1998:53–54).

Public relations not only covers organisation's and institution's relations with the public, but also their relations with other organisations and communities.

Historical Development of Public Relations and the Present

The history of public relations dates back to very early times. The foundation of the states could be taken as the historical beginning of public relations in organisational times. In kingdoms, the fact that kings got together with the public, the techniques and activities the kings used for explaining themselves to the public, and the fora and conferences organised by the philosophers and thinkers and their face to face communication with the public in order to inform the public and receive their support regarding different subjects could be addressed within public relations (Uluğ, 1989:7). It is observed that public relations applications have been conducted for centuries but regarding the very area as a discipline took place in the 19th century.

The appearance of public relations in today's terms occurred in the 1960's in the United States of America (USA) and disseminated to the rest of the world from the USA. When we examine the development of public relations within the scope of public relations models, there is the publicity model, the informing the public model, the two-way asymmetrical model, the model of excellence in public relations, and the communication model recently put forward by James Grunig.

The publicity model is the model for making use of each and every kind of possible application and the implementation of the technique is called manipulation which is named after press agencies. The representative of this period is P. T. Barnum. Barnum ensured that the publication of many make-up news articles appeared in the press and published the news of his clients free of charge. According to this model, the reality itself is not important; it is for propaganda purposes and the content is only for addressing the large masses and for persuasion. Environmental dominance is on the upfront, is one-way, and represents a kind of communication in which research is not important at all (Göksel, Yurdakul, 2010: 14–5). In his studies, Barnum conducted his applications with the principle of "there is no such thing as bad publicity" (Tarhan, 2008:16–17).

The basis of informing the public model is "the public has to be enlightened."

The fact that enterprises were only interested in making profit by ignoring the health and social security problems of workers and by not taking any action about the occupational injuries brought about certain criticisms. The representative of this period, Ivy Lee, highlights that the realities should not be kept from the public and that the foundation policies should be formed in a way to reflect the realities. Communication in this period was for disseminating information, environmental adaptation and cooperation were the priorities, communication was one-way, and the flow of information was important. Research was not very important back then (Peltekoğlu, 2014: 100).

In the informing the public model, the person in charge of public relations acts like a journalist and gives information about organisation to the public (Grunig, 1984:6). Until 1900–1920, when the two-way asymmetrical model was developed, the informing the public model was used extensively.

After the 1920s, the two-way asymmetrical model started to be applied; however, it was based on an imbalanced communication process. Edvard Bernay was the representative of the model; however, it was very close to the informing the public model. Messages were conveyed for persuasion purposes and that is where the difference lied. The model has a structure for persuasion purposes, gave importance to environmental control in organisational terms, made two-way communication from the source to the receiver possible, and again gave importance to communication-formative research. It is possible to state that with this model, the understanding that "the public should be understood and its needs should be understood" was achieved (Tarhan, 2008:135).

The two-way symmetrical model concept was brought forward by Scot M. Cutlip. The model signifies a two-way and balanced communication between the resource and the receiver-public. The model objects at creating mutual understanding and environmental adaptation, is affected by feedbacks of management policies and applications, and feedback from the public is taken into account by management (Göksel, Yurdakul, 2010:19).

Grunig, examining the development of public relations models, in his book "Public Relations and Excellence in Communication Management" (2005), puts forward the characteristics of excellent public relations management based on the symmetrical model (Grunig 2005:IV). The criteria of excellence in management defined as a result of the research of Grunig et al., 2005 are as follows: human resources, organic structures, organisational entrepreneurship, symmetrical communication systems, leadership, strong and participatory cultures, strategic planning, social responsibility, quality, effective operation systems, and cooperative public culture. When these criteria are examined in general, it is observed that the relations between the public, both inside and outside the organisation, are highlighted profoundly based on the balanced two-way communication model; therefore, the symmetrical communication system is kept upfront.

When the development process of public relations are analysed, public relations were used for retouching, making things beautiful, and as a manipulation tool for the purpose of surreptitious advertising in the early stages. Then, public relations were a one-way communication process used by the organisations for creating a positive image. However, as time went by, public relations was shaped as a profession covering a two-way communication process. In the beginning, public relations was more interested in conflict resolution; however, today, it is a profession covering relations established with various target groups.

Public Relations as a Profession and Turkey

The historic development of public relations shows the perception of the public relations profession by the public. Developments within the scope of models change the perspective of public relations in time. Even though the perception of the profession is not yet ensured in Turkey, it is possible to state that there is a positive change by the big enterprises, especially in sectoral terms.

When we analyse research regarding the development of public relations, the planned and informed organisation of public relations activities started for the first time in the 1960s in the public sector. The Press and Consultancy Department of Public Relations was established for the first time in 1984 with a decree. Informed and systematic public relations activities started in the 1970s in the private sector. In the 1980s-1990s, there was a shift to more contemporary structuring in the profession in Turkey (Yamanoğlu, Hızal, 2013:24–25).

In the research carried out regarding the perception of the profession of public relations in the world as well, it is possible to state that a change in the perception took place in parallel to the models defined in the chapter of public relations development. However, the publicity agency, informing the public, and two-way asymmetric model effects went on in the 1990s and the public relations perception had certain image related problems.

Spicer, in his research in 1993, divided the profession of public relations into seven categories and explained the perception of public relations accordingly (Spicer, 1993: conveyed by Gürkan from 57, 2012:138–139).

Public relations is a tool of attention: The specialist of public relations is the one who tries to and does distract the journalist, drawing attention as a news source, and therefore, directing the attention of the public in any direction he or she wants to through the media.

Public relations is a tool of destruction: By using the practices of the profession, public relations could cause disasters in the public when desired. The public relations specialist could uplift or destruct any company/firm/organisation he or she wants to through a message or a mass communication tool.

Public relations is challenging tool: The professionals of this very profession hold power and could uplift or harshly criticise the company they work with. Therefore, the profession of public relations is accepted as a challenging tool.

Public relations is a tool of exaggeration: In the profession of public relations, messages with the elements of exaggeration could always be used as the work done could be presented differently than it is in order to draw attention and arouse interest.

Public relations is a tool of distortion: Organisations and institutions prefer different applications instead of expressing the essential subject thanks to the applications of public relations. Therefore, they could convey their desired messages to the target group when they want to.

Public relations is a tool of war: Public relations is in continuous war for being affirmed by the public.

Public relations is a stereotype: It is attractive woman and man able to talk properly. Under the light of this information, the profession of public relations was not perceived as a profession in the 1990s and the specialists were not perceived as professionals. However, until the 2000s, the profession of public relations started to exercise according to its definition. Since the 2000s, the perception of the profession of public relations changed and a leap of faith took place regarding the necessity of public relations and publicity activities for strengthening the organisational image and reputation. In today's world, many organisations need public relations specialists who could take strategic decisions and use initiative.

The defining, evaluating, interpreting, and communicative role of public relations has required greater skills and delicacy with the increase of groups and organisations representing different interests in the world. The development of specialism has also increased the need for more extensive understanding and requires more specialism and general competence (Black, 1998: 17). Grunig, Crable, and Vibbert et al. point out that public relations is evolving towards to the role of a communication manager focused on establishing and sustaining relations with the main groups from the role of communication technician focused on producing and disseminating information (Aydede, 2002:41). Asna, who contributed a lot to the area of public relations' academic and application field in Turkey, categorises the characteristics of a public relations specialist in the 2000s as follows: could establish effective use of language equipped with general knowledge who has gone through education in terms of social and economic matters; is educated;

knowledgeable regarding the profession of journalism, careful with the outlook; full of love towards humans, cheerful, patient, flexible with common sense, imaginative, researcher, and self-confident; who knows the code of conduct and manner; understands the realities fast, evaluates himself or herself and events honestly, and knows how to criticise; knows how to organise people; and knows different languages (Asna, 1997:256–258).

Research

This research studies the representation of the professionals working in public relations and related professions in the sector in Turkish movies in the 2000s.

Methods

The seven features of public relations put forward by Spicer, which Hasan Gürkan previously benefited in his studies "Representation of Public Relations Sector in Cinema: Profession of Public Relations and Representation of Public Relations Specialist in Movies "Again You?," "Sex And The City," and "Thank You For Smoking" are addressed within the scope of the study. The features of public relations specialists by Aleaddin Asna are also addressed. "Public relations" is the key word for the study and the movies after 2000 in which there is public relations, and as the number of movies in this regard is very limited, the ones related to "advertising" in relation to public relations, were examined. Qualitative content analysis was used as the research technique in this study.

Limitations of the Research Study

Limitations of the research study could be expressed as follows:

- The fact that only in one of the Turkish movies, there is direct concept of public relations used, and in the others, there is the advertising concept which is another form of promotion and addressing both of the concepts in the research;
- There is not any previous study regarding the perception and representation of public relations in the media and public;
- The scales regarding the perception of the public relations profession are for foreign countries, were prepared before 2000, and there is an absence of a scale for Turkey.

Findings

Post-year-2000 Turkish movies, in which stereotypes regarding public relations and advertising, directly giving information about the profession, are taken into account within the scope of the study. These movies are: Pek Yakında - Coming Soon (2014), Romantik Komedi - Romantic Comedy (2009), and Mustafa Hakkında Herşey - Everything About Mustafa (2003).

Subject of the Movies

Pek Yakında (Director: Cem Yılmaz, 2014/Comedy)

Pirated DVD seller Zafer, who is formerly an extra in movies, swore to give up illegal works because his wife wanted to get a divorce. To win his family and his life back, he and his old-fashioned crew decided to make a movie called "Summit - The End Of Evil" which is a fantastic science fiction movie and couldn't be shot since 1977. Arzu wants to get a divorce and Zafer wants to win her back, claiming that he is going to pull his life together and promising that they will be very happy. Zafer decided to involve the old crew into the project and is struggling with the challenges of shooting a movie and his previous life. The pirated DVD seller and undercover producer of the movie, Zafer, decided to give a role to his wife Arzu and international television (TV) show star Boğaç Boray. Zafer's plan is to realise his wife's dream, present her a movie showing that he is very qualified, and show her that he is done with illegal work. A funny, entertaining, and emotional journey awaits Zafer.

Romantic Comedy (Director: Ketche-2009/Romantic-Comedy)

Different love stories of three very close friends, Esra, Didem, and Zeynep, are addressed in the movie which starts with Zeynep's wedding resulting in surprises. Esra discovers problems with her boyfriend in the wedding and quits her job, which she doesn't like or want, and ends her relationship with the boyfriend. She works in a fictional advertisement agency as a copywriter. One day, Esra goes to a big agency and walks into the wrong room where there is an ongoing presentation to a client and says something about the job post which makes the client give a second chance to the agency about working with them. Esra is hired. Esra starts to work in the advertisement agency and gets closer with the creative director of the agency Mert and Didem gets impressed by Cem Sezgin, a friend of Mert. Deniz does not want to have kids, but has to make a decision. The three friends' decisions change their lives.

This movie is evaluated within the scope of the study because the Esra and Mert characters are working in the advertisement sector and there are parts regarding the advertisement profession in the movie.

Everything About Mustafa (Çağan Irmak-2003/Action-Suspense Thriller)

The lead actor, Mustafa, has a seemingly great life as he is very successful in working life in the advertisement sector. This very successful career is accompanied with a happy marriage with a very cute child. Therefore, Mustafa leads a life which everybody is green with envy. However, the flaws of this excellent life start to unfold following an accident his wife gets involved in. When his wife loses her life in the accident, she is not alone; she is with some stranger Mustafa has not seen before whose name is Fikret. Mustafa wants to learn why and kidnaps Fikret. They confront each other in a deserted place and have tantrums. The truths Fikret states will unveil the mysteries of both Mustafa's and his wife's lives.

Assessment of the Characters Regarding Public Relations and Advertisement in the Movies

Table 1: Spicer's Definition of the Profession

	Coming Soon (Zafer)	Romantic Comedy (Mert and Esra)	Everything About Mustafa (Mustafa)
Genre			
Tool of attention	+	+	
Tool of destruction	+		
Tool of challenging		+	+
Tool of exaggeration	+	+	
Tool of distortion	+		
Tool of war		+	+
Stereotype		+	+

In the movie Coming Soon, the concept of "public relations" is used directly. In the movie, "the concept of public relations" is applied with the fact that the crew wants the famous actor of the time, Boğaç Boray, to play the lead role in the movie "Summit - the End of Evil" which character Zafer wants to shoot. The idea is based on the fact that Boğaç Boray would never play in the movie with this short budget; so by taking his fame, the crew thinks that they would convince Boğaç Boray to take part in the movie. The character Zeki is with the character Ayben right from the start and he states that public relations is his area of specialisation in the 1990s and creates many scenarios to disrupt the fame of Boğaç Boray. In the show, Boğaç Boray is made to get angry on a floweriest boy and slaps him; he is also approached in the street and is made to curse. So with such things, his fame came to an end. All these instances are called public relations.

The scenes in the movie according to Spicer's definition are as follows:

- Public relations is the news source as a person drawing attention and draws public attention to the direction he wants; it is used as a tool of attention,
- The specialist of public relations when desired could have the ability to destruct an organisation or a person, it is used as a tool of destruction,
- Public relations deliver the work done in a more exaggerated manner than it really is; it is used as a tool of exaggeration,
- The events which are not in the movie to be shot or which do not take place as they did are reflected; it is used as a tool of distortion.

In the movie Romantic Comedy, the profession of "advertisement" is addressed and not the "public relations" concept. There are two characters, Esra and Mert, who work in the advertisement sector, that are attracting attention on the area of advertising. The character Esra quits her job where she previously worked and takes steps towards the advertisement profession she has been dreaming of. She goes to a job interview and enters a room that she is not supposed to enter as the interview is going to take place in another room. Without realising it, this contributes to the fact that the clients give the job to the company. The company is hired for the job, so they hire Esra to the company. The main theme is actually a love story, where the high rank manager Mert and Esra like each other in the movie. The two characters working in the advertisement sector address their achievement in the advertisement sector separately. The character Esra creates an advertisement about a jewellery company full of attractive slogans and visuals. The job post from the client is granted with this campaign. However, Esra quits her job when she presents an advertisement at the end of the project presentation because of certain problems with Mert.

The scenes in the movie according to Spicer's definition are as follows:

- The advertiser is the one that attracts the attention and draws the attention of the public and the client; it is used as a tool of attention,
- The advertiser holds the power and could glorify an idea with his or her work; it is used as a tool of challenging,
- The advertiser could deliver the work done in a more exaggerated manner than it really is, it is used as tool of exaggeration,

- The work of the advertisement is presented as a continuous war for the approval of the public,
- Both characters, Esra and Mert, have effective use of language and are attractive as a man and a woman; the advertisement is used as a tool of stereotype.

In the movie Everything About Mustafa, the lead actor Mustafa has a successful business life in the area of advertising. There are scenes where the character Mustafa represents an advertisement; however, the movie then becomes more focused on Mustafa's life with his wife. Mustafa has an advertisement agency called the Art House. Information regarding the advertiser identity of Mustafa is gathered from the scenes and agency images from the beginning of the movie where he held a meeting.

The scenes in the movie according to Spicer's definition are as follows:

- The advertiser holds the power and could glorify an idea with his work; it is used as a tool of challenging,
- The work of the advertisement is presented as a continuous war for the approval of the public,
- The character, Mustafa, uses effective language and is attractive as man; the advertisement is used as a tool of stereotype.

Table 2: Alaeddin Asna's definition of the profession

	Coming Soon (Zafer)	Romantic Comedy (Mert and Esra)	Everything About Mustafa (Mustafa)
Genre			
Could establish effective use of language		+	+
Equipped with general knowledge as someone who has gone through education in terms of social and economic matters and is educated		+	+
Knowledgeable regarding the profession of journalism	+		
Careful with the outlook		+	+
Full of love towards humans			
Cheerful		+	
Patient		+	
Knows the code of conduct and manner		+	
Quickly understands the realities		+	
Evaluates himself or herself and events honestly		+	
Knows how to criticise		+	+
Knows how to organise people	+	+	
Flexible			
Has common sense			
Imaginative	+	+	+
Researcher	+	+	+
Self-confident	+	+	+
Knows different languages			

When the characters in the movie are examined based on the definition of Alaeddin Asna, it is possible to state that certain messages are conveyed to show how the characters give the following features:

- The character Zafer in Coming Soon is knowledgeable about the journalism profession, knows how to organise people, and is imaginative, a researcher, and self-confident.

- The characters Esra and Mert in Romantic Comedy could establish effective use of language equipped with general knowledge as someone who has gone through education in terms of social and economic matters and is educated, is knowledgeable regarding the profession, careful with the outlook, full of love towards humans, cheerful, patient, flexible with common sense, imaginative, a researcher, and self-confident. They are also both someone who knows the code of conduct and manner, who quickly understands the realities, who evaluates himself or herself and events honestly, who knows how to criticise; and who knows how to organise people.
- The character Mustafa in Everything About Mustafa could establish effective use of language equipped with general knowledge as someone who has gone through education in terms of social and economic matters and is educated, is careful with the outlook, knows how to criticise, and is imaginative, a researcher, and self-confident.

Conclusion

The public relations and advertisement professions are taken into account together within the scope of the study. It is seen that both professions have developed and changed to a large extent with the growth and increase in employment. It is possible to say the professions of public relations and advertisement are recognised in Turkey as very professional activities that are especially conducted by large-scale companies. The presence of such activities is observed in small and medium enterprises and family companies.

Many different factors could be cited in the formation of a perception regarding a profession. Some of factors for creating perception of the profession in the public are as follows: success rate of the parishioners of the profession in realising their role, ensuring that the profession is exercised by establishing certain standards by the professional organisations and promotion of the profession to the public, news about the profession in the media, success and functionality of the vocational education, and the accurate representation of the profession in various TV shows, movies, radio programmes, etc.

The representation of public relations and advertising in post-year-2000 Turkish movies are taken into account within the scope of the study. It is possible to say that negative features of the profession are more represented in Coming Soon when compared to other movies. In addition to that, according to Spicer, the profession is qualified as a tool of attention, exaggeration, and war in Romantic Comedy and Everything About Mustafa. The commonality in both movies is the stereotype used for the profession. The movie Coming Soon highlights the press agency model, while the scenes in Romantic Comedy serve more for a two-way asymmetrical model.

When Aladdin Asna's definition is closely examined, in the movie Coming Soon, which represents the profession, the character has limited specialist features; however, this is observed more clearly and a more positive image is formed especially for the professional perception of advertisements in the other two movies.

In terms of creating professional perception, cinema movies are important points of representativeness. It would be more accurate to present both the negative and positive features together in the movies. The fact that the professional definitions in the movies are made taking into account the current situation of the profession will vitally contribute to the development of the perception of the profession.

References

Işık, M (2012). Halkla İlişkilere Giriş, Konya: Eğitim Yayınevi.

Yurdakul, N. B., Coşkun, G. (2008). Teoriden Pratiğe Halkla İlişkiler Projeleri: Ödüllü Örnek Uygulamalar, Ankara: Nobel Yayın Dağıtım.

Sjöberg, G. (1998). Mesleki Uygulama için Bir Halkla İlişkiler Eğitim Modeli, Çev. Nur Nirven, Altın Kitap, Sayı:4, İstanbul: Rota Yayınları.

Uluğ, F. (1989). Türk Kamu Yönetiminde Halkla İlişkiler ve Enformasyon, Ankara: Todaire Yayını.

Göksel, A. B., Yurdakul, N. (2010). Temel Halkla İlişkiler Bilgileri, İzmir: Ege Üniversitesi Basımevi.

Tarhan, A. (2008). "Halkla İlişkiler Modelleri", Halkla İlişkiler, Ahmet Kalender (Editör), Mehmet Fidan, Konya: Tablet Yayınları.

Peltekoğlu, F. B. (2014). Halkla İlişkiler Nedir, İstanbul: Beta Basım Yayım Dağıtım A. Ş.

Grunig, J. E., Hunt, T. (1984). Managing Public Relations, Holt, Rinehart & Winston.

Grunig, J. E. (2005). Halkla İlişkiler ve İletişim Yönetiminde Mükemmellik, Çev: Elif Özsayar, İstanbul: Rota Yayınları.

Yamanoğlu, M. A., Hızal, G. S. G, Özdemir, B. P. (2013). Türkiye'de Halkla İlişkiler Tarihi: Kurumsallaşma Yılları 1960–1980, Ankara: De Ki Basım Yayım Dağıtım Ltd. Sti.

SPICER, C. (1993), "Images of public relations in the print media", Journal of Public Relations Research. Vol: 5.

Gürkan, H. (2012). "Halkla İlişkiler Sektörünün Sinemada Temsili: "Again You?", "Sex And The City" Ve "Thank You For Smoking" Filmlerinde Halkla İlişkiler

Mesleği ve Halkla İlişkiler Uzmanının Temsili, Gümüşhane Üniversitesi İletişim Fakültesi Elektronik Dergisi, Sayı:3, Mart 2012.

Black, S. (1998). Halkla İlişkiler Eğitimi, Çev: İbrahim Çamlı, IPRA Altın Kitap Sayı:7, İstanbul: Rota Yayınları.

AYDEDE, C. (2002). Teorik ve Uygulamalı Halkla İlişkiler Kampanyaları, 2. Baskı, İstanbul: MediaCat Yayınları.

Asna, A. (1997). Halkla İlişkiler, Public Relations, PR, İstanbul: Sabah Kitapları.

Prof. Dr Gülseren Yücel

Beykent Üniversitesi, İstanbul, 34396, Türkiye
gulserenyucel@beykent.edu.tr

From "the Golden City" to "the City of Darkness": the Changing Image of Istanbul in the Turkish Cinema

Introduction

Istanbul is a city with a history of thousands of years. It has been a bridge between Eastern and Western cultures as well as between Asia and Europe, was the capital city of three great empires, and has experienced their glorious times. Ankara became the capital city upon the foundation of the Republic of Turkey in 1923. Istanbul, however, has never lost its significance in the economic and cultural life of the country, as in had in the past. On the contrary, it has turned into the most crowded megacity of Turkey with its ongoing population increase that has approached 20 million people as a result of the immigration from the provinces to the city. The problems about the city have also multiplied and diversified with the population increase. The number of people living in Istanbul slightly exceeded one million in the 1950s. We can see the changes and transformations in Istanbul since then and the spaces, lifestyles, and human relationships, most of which are now extinct, in many movies of the Turkish cinema. Istanbul is the heart of both Turkey and the Turkish Cinema. The majority of movies had been shot in Istanbul from the initial years of cinema until recently. As a "model," Istanbul constituted the focus of Turkish modernisation and of the cinema (Narlı, Kotaman, 2008, p. 204). In the stories told, Istanbul is not only the place where the story takes place but also the founding element of the story and one of the characters in the movie. It even has the leading role. Everybody is familiar with the following scenes of black and white Turkish movies: mansions with their beautiful gardens, gardeners, and private drivers; very green hills where lovers meet; tea gardens; ferries; seagulls; attached timber houses at historical districts; the neighbourhoods where warm neighbourly relationships are experienced; mosques; minarets; sparkling storefronts; avenues, etc. With all its beauties, the historical fabric that bears the traces of its noble past, and urbanites as "gentlemen" and "ladies," the image of "Istanbul as a place to live in" got established in the memory of the audience. Having changed very little throughout the 1950s and the 1960s, this image was very strong and no other description of Istanbul came to mind. The image of Istanbul in cinema has changed since the 1950s and this change is closely associated with the changes in the social, cultural, economic, and political structures of the city, as well as of Turkey. On the one hand, the movies reveal the urban change in Istanbul physically and spatially, but on the other hand, they display the changes in the perspective of society on Istanbul and in its perception of the city.

Keywords: Turkish Cinema, Istanbul, gecekondu (squat), varoş (the suburbs), internal migration, urbanisation, identity, and belonging.

Methods

In this study, the changing image of Istanbul in the Turkish Cinema since the 1950s will be analysed by employing the methods of sociological and historical criticism. The changes in the image of Istanbul were divided into subtitles which referred to this change and connections were made between the movies representing the period and the changes in the social structure. In the study, the quality of movies as social/cultural documents was utilised, inferences were made regarding the social, cultural, and spatial changes in Istanbul, and the changes in the perspective of society on Istanbul and in its perception of the city were studied thoroughly by means of the movies.

Black and White "Lost Istanbul"

Many authors and poets were inspired by the natural beauties and historical past of Istanbul. Songs were composed and poems and novels were written for it. Nedim (the 17th century), the famous poet of our Divan literature and one of the poets influenced by its magic and mystery and speaking admiringly of Istanbul like the love felt for a darling, addresses Istanbul with the following lines: "*Bu İstanbul Şehri ki Biçilmez Bir Pahadır/Bir Taşına Bütün Acem (İran) Ülkesi Fedadır*" *(This city of Istanbul is priceless/it's worth sacrificing the whole Persian (Iranian) country for a stone of It).* In addition, *Yahya Kemal* talks to Istanbul with his following famous lines: "*Sana Dün Bir Tepeden Baktım Aziz İstanbul.../Ömrüm Oldukça Gönül tahtıma Kurul/Sade bir Semtini Sevmek Bile Bir Ömre Değer.*" "*Yesterday I looked at you from a hill, dear Istanbul.../Get established on the throne of my heart as long as I live/only loving a district of yours is even worth a lifetime*" (Birkiye, 1999, p. 13–19).

A literary image of Istanbul created by many artists such as Nedim and Yahya Kemal had existed before cinema. A description of Istanbul, full of admiration felt for it and praise, continued to be told for centuries. The literary image of Istanbul in the imagination of such authors as Abdülhak Şinasi Hisar, Ahmet Hamdi Tanpınar, Yahya Kemal, Reşat Ekrem Koçu, and Orhan Pamuk equals to the image of Istanbul in the black and white movies of the Turkish Cinema in the 1950s and the 1960s. To describe this image briefly, it is "the lost city" of remembering, sorrow, and melancholy. These authors become sorrowful by looking at the remains of an empire which passed away and of the civilisations of thousands of years. The melancholic narration of loss also includes the construction of the new national identity and the abstention/hesitation about modernisation besides the sorrow over the desolation of abandoned and ruined large houses and waterside mansions, as well as over the fact that the days when the beauties of the Bosphorus shores were experienced with pleasure remained in the past. *Üç Arkadaş (Three Friends) (Memduh ÜN, 1956)* and *Ah Güzel İstanbul (Oh! Beautiful Istanbul) (Atıf Yılmaz, 1966)* are movies which provide one with the feeling of sorrow over lost Istanbul and which present the black and white memory image of Istanbul (Arslan, 2010, p. 171).

The dominant role of Istanbul as the founding element of the story/plot of movies begins with the opening scene; the camera tours over Istanbul and we enter Istanbul together with Haliç (the Golden Horn), the Galata Bridge, the sea, ferries, boats, rowing boats, mosques, waterside mansions, the Sultan Ahmet Square, streetcars with their ringing sounds, Beyoğlu, Eminönü, pigeons, seagulls, and the sounds of seagulls and of the azan (the call to prayer). Not only this movie, but also many movies began with the same opening scene; similar scenes were shown repeatedly and Istanbul got established in the minds of the audience as a cinematic image. With these movies, which make one watch Istanbul with its wonderful scenery, the spectators from the lower-income group watch what they lack and reach catharsis by regarding the city where the movie takes place as their own city and their own space and the actor/actress in the leading role as themselves (Narlı, Kotaman, p. 206). The moviemakers, the actors/actresses, and the audience all meet at the same perspective and this perspective was "an endogenous perspective on Istanbul from the eyes of Istanbulites," as Suner (2006) also stated, and continued throughout the 1950s and the 1960s (p. 219).

In *Üç Arkadaş*, the camera is turned to a ruinous large timber house after these scenes. The abandoned old and large house houses three poor friends. *Murat* is a man who tours around streets with his pigeons which pick the fortune papers and makes a living in this way. *Mösyö (Monsieur) Artin* is a street photographer, whereas *Mıstık* is a mobile shoe painter. *Gül*, who is blind and lives on streets, joins them. The three friends do not tell her that they are poor. They make her believe that they are rich and noble and establish an imaginary world. They tell *Gül* about their noble relatives, their grandfathers who were pashas, and the past magnificent days. Meanwhile, we tour the interior of the large house together with them and see the interior of the large house with a few broken belongings, collapsed stairs, and broken windows. The poor friends have no relation with the magnificent past they mention. Likewise, the large house bears no traces which remind one of those days either. With this state of the large house, it makes us feel a rather sorrowful gap which is experienced after the loss of things. Large timber houses are one of the most obvious representatives of the feeling of sorrow in the city. Having been evacuated and having burnt up and collapsed due to lack of good care, these large houses are as if they were identified with the loss of vitality, and disintegration, of the Ottoman State in our minds and always remind us of the loss of civilisation and of change (Pamuk, 2003, p. 15). The remains of the collapsed city walls seen in the movie also intensify this feeling.

In many scenes of the movie, we see Istanbul with its Bosphorus shores, rowing boats, mosques, the pigeons in front of the mosques, the sea, and seagulls. The heroes of the movie mention these beauties with praise. Their poverty is not an obstacle to seeing them and they do not indeed complain about their condition either. They are happy in the traditional/old Istanbul, where they live. This badly-established "imaginary" life, which has leaned against the past, will collapse one day like the large house that stands with difficulty. They are confronted with another face of the city when they have to find the money for the operation which is necessary for *Gül* to see. With the houses inhabited by wealthy families and with its crowded avenues, modern Istanbul takes them out of the imaginary world in which they live. The money is found after great struggles; *Gül* begins to see, they first lose her and find her again in the end, and the movie has a happy ending. The heroes of the movie are people who live with love, friendship, solidarity, and optimism and who are satisfied with what they have. The movie places these people in traditional Istanbul, the old and large timber house, and confines the framework of this happy life but considers new Istanbul and the modern life with abstention/hesitation. The quality of the city which encourages individualism is not appreciated in this "idealistic" movie, where it is shown that the feeling of "we" has not been lost yet and where the importance of being able to make a collective effort for the sake of their goal is represented (Narlı, Kotaman, p. 208).

In *Ah Güzel İstanbul*, we see Istanbul with the eyes of *Haşmet*, a worldly-wise old gentleman of Istanbul. *Haşmet*, whose grandfathers were members of the Ottoman palace and who was born in a waterside mansion in Beylerbeyi, consumed his wealth as he failed to adapt to the time, goes on living with a few belongings remaining from the good days of the past in a small hut next to the waterside mansion he sold, knows of poetry and music, knows how to speak well, and makes a living as a mobile photographer on streets. Street photographers used to tour around streets and take the photographs of those who sat in front of a piece of cloth on which the "Memory of Istanbul" was written by means of their old hooded cameras. Having taken the memory photograph of Istanbul, these photographers no longer exist today. With their images remaining in movies only, they also now constitute part of the memory image of lost Istanbul.

The movie starts with the most beautiful views of Istanbul; the camera tours over the waterside mansions by the sea and *Haşmet* talks about the noble past of Istanbul with praise and sorrow while watching the Bosphorus by saying "Oh! Beautiful Istanbul. O! My Dear Bosphorus." Throughout the movie, Istanbul is like a friend whom *Haşmet* will want to talk to whenever he grieves and responds to him with the sounds of waves and seagulls. In this movie, Istanbul is a space in which the sorrow of its hero, who is committed to the lost past with melancholy, is reflected (Arslan, p. 181).

The Istanbul of *Ayşe*, who arrived in Istanbul with a desire to become an artist as well as to become rich and famous after she had escaped from her family and whose path crossed *Haşmet*'s path, is very different from that of *Haşmet*. She is ready to do anything to live in another Istanbul with its sparkling avenues, storefronts, and nightclubs. She experiences many things owing to her desires concerned. *Ayşe* has no relation to the previous Istanbul which *Haşmet* is trying to describe. This is the fundamental clash in the movie. Tired, melancholic, and sorrowful, *Haşmet* is the past of Istanbul, whereas immigrant *Ayşe* with no relation to the past of Istanbul is the new face of Istanbul which is full of traps. Change and modernisation are considered with abstention/hesitation in this movie too. Istanbul is full of traps for the immigrants who do not know Istanbul or how to perceive being an Istanbulite. *Ayşe* is rescued thanks to *Haşmet*, abandons her desires, and takes refuge in *Haşmet*. In the last scene, we see *Ayşe* and *Haşmet* on the Bosphorus ferry; they watch the sea and embrace each other and *Haşmet* says "Look at this beauty. There is no such beauty anywhere in the world." *Haşmet* has been able to protect *Ayşe*. The movie ends with some optimism which implies that the identity of Istanbul can still be protected by true Istanbulites.

A Poor but Proud Slum: "Traditional Istanbul"

The neighbourhoods, which reflected economic difference and the distinction between statuses, involved populations with different qualities and did not constitute any integrity with each other were also available in Istanbul, as in many cities of the world. The dual structure which had existed as the traditional city and the westernised modern city for a long period of time changed qualities upon internal migrations. A ternary structure formed with the squats (gecekondu) that immigrants built overnight as a solution to their housing problems (Güçhan, 1992, p. 44). If we include the satellite towns, created on the fringes of the city by middle and upper middle class families to escape from the crowds of the city, in this ternary structure today, four different structures must be mentioned. The traditional neighbourhoods composed of timber houses which were left alone, which decreased in number, and some of which disappeared completely upon the move of their owners to modern sections, although they had once been important in the social life of the city, in time they turned into slums. Having fallen into disfavour even though they are located in the centre of the city, these neighbourhoods house immigrants and low-income people today. The lifestyle and culture in these neighbourhoods constituted the former culture of Istanbul and were very different from those of the present. Dağbağyan (2006) mentions the lifestyle in these neighbourhoods, which continued throughout the 1950s and the traces of which disappeared slowly as of the 1960s, as follows: "Individual, familial and massive solidarity was the fundamental component of the former people of Istanbul… The poor families at the neighborhood were not deprived of anything thanks to neighborhood and solidarity. That's why we were happy notwithstanding any condition" (p. 78). Tanpınar (2000) defines a slum as "it was in ruins, poor, and destitute but had a life and style in its own way," puts emphasis on its traditional and unspoiled side which has not been influenced by the West, and praises its beautiful, sorrowful, and national view (153).

The image of a slum was repeated in many movies of the Turkish Cinema, thereby almost constituting its spirit. This image created an Istanbul where all tensions were soothed with some "we" atmosphere, where poor but proud people and crowded families coexisted with a community feeling, where poverty was shared, which we could love, and which belonged to us (Arslan, p. 176, 377).

Avare Mustafa (Idle Mustafa) (Memduh Ün, 1961) tells the story of a poor family that lives in a slum with its attached timber houses, streets with cobblestones on which children run, and gossip at the fountain. The fate of these innocuous people that live with peddlers selling yoghurt and simit, a coffee house, a bar-like restaurant, reliable, honest, and idle "külhanbeyler (hoodlums)," and their yells that make the inhabitants of the neighbourhood shiver while they are returning from their entertainment at the bar-like restaurant at night changes with the rich man who comes to the neighbourhood in order to construct a new apartment building. *Mustafa* is one of the unemployed young men of the neighbourhood. The daughter of the rich man falls in love with him. Although *Mustafa* loves his neighbour's daughter, he marries the rich girl upon his family's insistence. Even though they obtain money and a good house, the marriage does not last long and

Mustafa leaves everything and returns to his neighbourhood, the girl he loves, and his former life notwithstanding its poverty. The tension between the westernised city and the neighbourhood always culminates in a return to the neighbourhood, to us, in this movie and in many movies. This is a stance on gravitating towards the attractiveness of the city, as well as on metamorphosis and change, and the slum which is ours is exalted in spite of its poverty.

In *Mahalleye Gelen Gelin (The Bride Came to the Quarter)* (Osman Seden, 1961), *Belgin*, a rich girl who is interested in literature, wants to collect information for her novel. She starts to live in a slum with her nursemaid by trying to resemble them. *Belgin* is engaged to someone from her own circle. She falls in love with the young driver in the neighbourhood. The rich paternal uncle wants to prevent this relationship. At the end of the movie, the factory-owning paternal uncle comes to the coffee house in the neighbourhood and apologises to the inhabitants of the neighbourhood for his lies and everything is settled.

With the behaviour of peeping at newcomers from windows, the typical view of newcomers by the people in the neighbourhood, having a chat with each other, gossip, the coffee house and the bar-like restaurant, the tradesmen in the neighbourhood, the watchman of the neighbourhood, the street quarrels which are settled, and the ranking police officer who ends the quarrels in a fatherly manner, the slum is described, in this movie too, as a place where kind, reliable, and honest people who are happy despite any condition live. On the other hand, the factory-owning paternal uncle of *Belgin*, her fiancé, and the people around them are greedy and snobbish. The description of the difference between classes in favour of the inhabitants of the neighbourhood and the fact that the rich always take a step backward before the virtue of the poor are ordinary things for the Turkish Cinema. These movies, stating that the inequality between classes could be eliminated so, also facilitated bearing the inequalities in real life.

"Beautiful Istanbul" to Live In

The audience of the Turkish Cinema is very familiar with the following scenes as much as with the scenes of traditional Istanbul or slums: modern flats; mansions or villas with a garden and a pool; the scenery of the Strait which enters as far as the interior of houses; the parties on the shore; scenes of going swimming from the waterside mansions; and the trouble-free and comfortable lives of rich people with maids, private drivers, cooks, and gardeners. Having told their stories via the melodramatic patterns of factory-owning fathers and the spoiled beautiful daughter or the irresponsible handsome son of the house, these movies were produced in large numbers and watched throughout the 1960s, the golden age of the Turkish Cinema. Istanbul was described as an attraction and a place "to live in" with its nightclubs, restaurants, trips in the Strait, luxurious cars, sparkling avenues, storefronts, and the urbanites with chic clothes. In these movies, human relationships, spatial arrangements, and the urban culture as a lifestyle make one feel their existence and weight. While the immigrants coming from the provinces are watching these views admiringly and in a confused manner, the urbanites look down on their presence. The condition for the assimilation, by the city, of provincials who come to the city from outside, for their adaptation, and for their becoming of urbanites is their acclimatisation to the urban culture. Many movies were made which stated that only the urbanites could train them and which used the provinces and provincials as an element of comedy.

In *Hep O Şarkı (Always That Song) (*Atıf Yılmaz, 1965), *Mine*, a rich urban girl, bets 10,000 liras on turning *Ali*, a sweet-voiced villager whom she found on the farm of her maternal uncle, into an "urban, urbane, well-mannered, and famous" person in three months. The solution to becoming an urban, urbane, and well-mannered person is to receive "lessons about good manners." For example, to learn how to walk, dance, sit at a dining table, eat, drink wine, and speak properly. The provincial learns them comically. This formula of the transformation of the provincial into an urbanite also states that the differences between classes are things which are easy to overcome. The setting of the movie is a well-kept mansion by the sea in Tarabya. Istanbul accompanies the process of transformation of the provincial into an urbanite and watches him. When urbanites look down on the provincial hero, he looks at the sparkling waters of the Strait in order to eliminate his oppression and to relieve himself. The beautiful waters of the sea say that becoming an Istanbulite will be worth these efforts and that the city can allow the incoming person to enter. In the following years, the struggle of the provincial with the city will no longer be a cultural problem and there will not be many urbanites who state that the transformation will take place in this way. At the end of the movie, *Ali* learns all lessons and is introduced to high society. Mine confesses that she started this deed for a bet and the new urbanite *Ali* breaks down and leaves the mansion; however, he returns as a person who has succeeded in transformation and become famous and gives the urban spoiled girl a lesson by enabling her to feel ashamed. The representation of the provincial as an honest and virtuous person who is equipped with positive values and the urbanite as an unreliable and arrogant person who has departed from traditional values appears in this movie and in other movies many times. It is possible to read this representation, which states that having Western values will cause us to degenerate and that departing from traditional and moral values will be bad, as the hesitations of the society which is stuck between traditionalism and modernism.

The first movie, *Küçük Hanımefendi (the Little Lady)* (Nejat Saydam, 1961), was followed by the series produced by the same director, namely *Küçük Hanım Avrupa'da (the Little Lady in Europe)* (1962) and *Küçük Hanımın Şöförü (Driving Little Missy)* (1962). With the formula of the factory-owning rich father, the spoiled beautiful girl, and the poor handsome young man, all the movies of the series told stories which stated that two people from different classes who were first looked down on and were rejected, but later loved, could merge and that it was possible for the rich upper classes to have close relationships with those who belonged to the lower class. Offering the possibility of a transition between classes, love, and all beauties, Istanbul became an object of desire even for those who had never seen it. The movies presented the representation of Istanbul from the eyes of Istanbulites (i.e. from an endogenous perspective) and this perspective was a close and endogenous one.

"Golden City Istanbul" from the Perspective of Immigrants

Created by the endogenous perspective of Istanbulites on Istanbul, this perspective was replaced by a foreign perspective with *Gurbet Kuşları (Birds of Exile)* (Halit Refiğ, 1964) (Suner, p. 219). *Gurbet Kuşları* is the first movie of the Turkish Cinema which is about immigration to the city and which discusses it as a problem. With this movie, the problem of internal migration, dating back to the 1950s in Turkey, was first addressed in the cinema. The immigrants who came to Istanbul from their villages or the provinces were available in many movies; however, they were in other stories. *Gurbet Kuşları* is the first movie to consider internal migration with its dimensions via the reasons for immigration, the difficulties encountered in the city, and the problems of finding a job and accommodation (Güçhan, p. 11).

In this movie and in many other movies, Haydarpaşa Railway Station is the first space where immigrants meet the city and is the gateway and the threshold of the city (Çiçekoğlu, 2007, p. 84). In the movie, the family, which has immigrated to Istanbul from Maraş, gets off the train. They stop on the stairs at Haydarpaşa Railway Station and look at the sea, ferries, and the passers-by admiringly, in a confused matter, and delightedly. Elucidating how great their hopes and expectations are, the following words get out of their mouths: "We will become a chief to this Istanbul, God willing!..." The poor villager who has got off the same train with his patched clothes says: "We've come to become a king to you, perfidious city. Protect yourself!..." We also often hear the following public statement from the heroes: "Istanbul is paved with gold, but you shall know how to earn!.." From an immigrant's perspective, Istanbul is a place to conquer and is "the golden city" of dreams and desires.

The image of Istanbul in movies undergoes a transformation with this exogenous perspective. The relationship of immigrants with the city is not an intimate relationship, like those in the slum or that of the urbanites, but a rather hostile relationship (Suner, 220). For them, Istanbul is a place to fight for and win and they also believe that they will be able to succeed in this. This belief in the fact that Istanbul is paved with gold has changed substantially since the years of commencement of immigration. The immigrants are aware of how hard it is to find a change in Istanbul, let alone gold. Nevertheless, immigration to Istanbul from all around Turkey is going on. It is clear that immigration will not cease unless the problems causing immigration, such causes as, unemployment, financial difficulty, and the scarcity of educational possibilities, change (Güçhan, p. 32). In *Gurbet Kuşları*, we see the long-standing dual structure of Istanbul as traditional and westernised Istanbul. The family settles in an old timber house in Süleymaniye, one of the old districts of traditional Istanbul. There is no obvious difference between them and the inhabitants of this neighbourhood, one of the good neighbourhoods then. The perspectives of the men and the girl in the family are the places where upper classes live. The dominant scenes in the movie are not the slum where their house is located, but such districts as Nişantaşı and Maçka which particularly show the city as an attraction with its entertainment and consumption possibilities. In *Gurbet Kuşları*, the difficulties regarding the class-related positions of immigrants stand out among the problems they are confronted with in the city. Even though this is not a problem for the parents in the family from Maraş, this is a problem for the children. They feel oppressed because they are provincials and long to resemble urbanites. For *Fatoş*, the daughter of the family, the longing to resemble urbanites tragically results in death upon her escape from the family and her falling into the trap of men. The male siblings also disregard their work and earning money, the main reason for their immigration, and fall into the trap of urban women. The family loses everything they had and returns to Maraş. *Kemal*, one of the children, goes to the university and succeeds in staying in the city. The reason for the failure of the family in the city is their perception of the events with provincial values and their failure to change their attitudes and behaviour. That's why they are deceived and fall into traps. Even though internal migrations continued intensively in the 1960s, when the movie was produced, the urban fabric of Istanbul had not undergone any profound change yet. The traces of cultural duality, which was created by immigrants and would further deepen and completely separate later, had not yet occurred. The urban culture preserved its dominant quality. Immigrants are different in terms of their clothes and behaviour. The urbanites look down on their presence. *Ayla*, *Kemal*'s girlfriend, is the daughter of an old bureaucrat from Istanbul. One day, they come across a beggar. According to *Ayla*, the beggar is "one of those who have arrived from the provinces and intend to rob Istanbulites." "Have all the people who have come from outside come to rob Istanbulites?" *Kemal* asks. "Are you also one of those people?" *Ayla* asks. *Kemal* cannot dare tell his real identity and replies: "Oh, come on! God forbid!"

The poor villagers of *Bitmeyen Yol (the Unending Road)* (Duygu Sağıroğlu, 1965) also get off the train at Haydarpaşa Railway Station. With their patched clothes, caps, rubber shoes, and the beds they carry on their backs, their eyes have grown because of bewilderment. When they arrive at the main avenue, they are afraid of the traffic and of losing each other and walk hand in hand. They rather draw attention with this appearance of theirs. They find a job at a sand job site. Although they live in a shelter they have been shown, they are delighted very much when they get their first money and say "We're so glad that we didn't stay in the village. We've become capital owners. We have no obstacles, God willing! Even Vehbi Koç started as a grocer. Now it's our turn!..." This hopeful optimism of the immigrants about Istanbul will be replaced in the immigration movies of the following years by more realistic longings. In *Bitmeyen Yol*, we see single-room gecekondus with a tinplate roof which are constructed with briquette, dusty and earthen roads, the poor interiors of houses, and the people who share a single room. Still, what is mainly intended to be emphasised in the movie through the more dominant urban scenes is not the problems of gecekondus, but the attractiveness of the city. The immigrants tour Beyoğlu and parks and secretly watch those who dance at nightclubs. They enter the archaeology museum and they are bewildered by the sculptures they see for the first time; the city gives immigrants hope by means of its attractive features which justify immigration.

In the 1970s, the population rate increased and Istanbul turned into a sea of people with its increased population. The stories of immigrants in movies became more bitter. The scenes which showed Istanbul as an attraction change in *Gelin (Bride)* (1973), *Düğün (Wedding)* (1974), and *Diyet (Ransom)* (1975), the best immigration trilogy by Lütfü Akad that has gone down in the history of the Turkish Cinema, and we cannot see the entertainment spaces and promenades of the city or the beautiful views of Istanbul in these movies. Now, the scenes which show the city as an attraction are crowded squares like Eminönü with their shoe painters, peddlers who sell any kind of goods on stands, and porters. The dreams of immigrants to become the king of the city have turned into the struggle to feed themselves in this representation of Istanbul which shows its employment structure that allows marginal jobs. Istanbul is no longer a place to conquer, but a place in which one tries to hold on to.

Gecekondus and Varoşs: "Istanbul Under Siege"

The year of construction of the early gecekondus was 1948 and the word 'gecekondu' first entered Turkish in this year. The gecekondus that immigrants built on the lands on the margins of cities as a solution to their housing problems were initially perceived as a village on the margins of cities and were considered temporary. However, the elapsed time made these houses permanent. These houses with no infrastructure, roads, or electricity gradually turned into neighbourhoods and districts. The gecekondulu people (squatters), who were considered as potential votes during election periods, obtained the title deeds of the houses and the lands that they laid claim to became a source of rent for them. Together with the people who resembled them and who migrated from the same regions, they set up a place in Istanbul which was similar to the place from which they had come, thereby creating a culture which was somewhere between a village and a city and which was called "the arabesque culture." Having set up their own provinces in Istanbul with their lifestyle, clothes, behaviour, and value judgments, these people had no cultural ties with the city either. Large cities have urban societies in which human relationships become anonymous. In Turkey, however, immigration has created a special difference as it has taken place in an Islamic society and the structure of large cities like Istanbul has been segregated by the communities that have adopted a community-type lifestyle resulting from Islam. These communities can live differently from the modernised section of the city (Güçhan, p. 37).

In *Bitmeyen Yol*, we see the gecekondus built on one of the hills of the Strait with a steep slope only with their states at the foundation stage of these regions. The houses are scattered and have spread over an extensive land. The single-story buildings with a tinplate roof, which are constructed with briquette, resemble each other. The primary spatial feature of gecekondus is their resemblance to a village. Neither the settlement forms of squats conform to city planning, nor do they comply their use as a space with urban values. They are like a copy of the village life.

In *Düğün* (1973), the siblings who have migrated from Urfa try to live by acting with solidarity. Their squat is not a place of poverty or a primitive shelter like the gecekondus in *Bitmeyen Yol*. It is located in a region which benefits from municipal services, which has roads linked with the city centre, and which has become a neighbourhood. Although the elapsed time has changed these regions, the movie contains no spatial arrangement to show that the house inhabited by the family is in Istanbul. On the contrary, it is not different from a village house as it is surrounded by a hoarding, has a fireplace at one corner where they cook dishes, and contains a courtyard, floor beds, chests, and kilims. We only see the family in the urban spaces of Istanbul while making sales with their mobile pushcart.

Apart from this, they have no ties with the city. The immigrants who considerably struggle to earn money are not in a condition to realise the beauty of the Strait, on the shore of which they sell meatball sandwiches.

The words ‘gecekondu’ and ‘varoş (the suburbs)’ represent different phenomena. The use of the word ‘varoş’ became widespread as of the 1990s. *Varoş*, a word of Hungarian origin, reminds us of the concepts of exception, being makeshift, and poverty; it represents what is at the periphery and on the border (*peripherie*) of the real area of the city (i.e. the centre); and involves any phenomena which are “other” for the centre in a social, economic, political, or functional sense (Perouse, 2008, p. 306).

Büyük Adam Küçük Aşk/Hejar (Big Man, Little Love/Hejar) (Handan İpekçi, 2001) tells the story of a retired judge who is an old Istanbulite and *Hejar*, the little Kurdish girl who lost her family and took refuge in him as a result of a coincidence. *Hejar* does not know Turkish, whereas the judge is sensitive to the issue of speaking Turkish and reacts to speaking Kurdish in his house. The other character of the movie is the maid of Kurdish origin and she cannot speak her own language either. In the movie, we go to two faces of Istanbul which contradict each other from Ulus, where the wealthy sections live, to the varoş towards Ayazma in Istanbul.

As Perouse (2008) states, gecekondus have by no means been considered in the context of the suburbs at the periphery of, or outside, the city in the Turkish Cinema and are almost like an unreal decor, …with no political or social grounds,… and are like the staging of the neighbourhood. With the concept of varoş, the optimistic and light-hearted perspective on the gecekondu has been destroyed and a tragic scene that ends hopes for the future has been created (p. 306).

Büyük Adam Küçük Aşk obviously defines the varoşs of Istanbul. The judge decides to take the little girl staying in his house to Ayazma, where her relatives live. This journey from the inside of Istanbul to the outside, to the varoşs, by the judge takes us away from the splendid view of the image of “the beautiful Istanbul to live in” in the cinema and enables us to approach true Istanbul. The silhouette of Istanbul has also begun to change with the globalising economy. When viewed from the Strait, Istanbul had had a magnificent silhouette which had made one feel its geographical and historical structures until the 1980s. Later on, the Maslak line began to be “Manhattanised.” Those who objected to this were accused of reactionism. However, the hurrying of huge Istanbul to become Manhattanised was an incomprehensible preference. When we now watch the city from the Strait, the most striking fabric is unfortunately the Manhattanised fabric (Atlar, 2014, p. 86). The gigantic skyscrapers ascending to the sky, the imposing buildings of multinational companies and holdings, and the shopping centres are the symbolic spaces of the newly globalising Turkish economy. Ulus, where the judge lives, is a place which also takes this view as the background and where one can live properly and comfortably thanks to its detached houses and green areas for sporting activities. In the movie, Istanbul is also seen with its shores on the Strait where people fish, as well as its ferries, and the promenades on the islands. The retired judge will be disturbed by, get bored of, and be bewildered by what he sees during his journey from these protected and comfortable living spaces to the varoş of the city. The scene which is visible during his journey between Ulus and Ayazma, first by the suburban train, later by a dolmuş (minibus) in which one sits by squashing, and then inevitably on foot includes peddlers, beggars, workers, those who speak Kurdish, a muddy road on which he will have to walk with difficulty after he has got off the dolmuş, streets full of garbage, jerry-built gecekondus, children with curious looks, and people who have become disconnected from their roots and live in extreme poverty.

The movie not only reveals the touching and contradictory relationship between the two different cultural worlds which are foreign to each other, but also describes the social breaks and gap that have left their mark on the present in Istanbul and are creating worries about the future (Perouse, p. 314).

"Istanbul of the Lonely and of the Other"

The familiar image of Istanbul in the cinema, with which the audience was acquainted as of the 1950s, changed and almost completely disappeared as of the 1990s. Neither the endogenous sorrowful and possessive perspective of Istanbulites on Istanbul, nor the exogenous perspective on Istanbul by the immigrants who were determined to fight and achieve, existed. The overwhelming majority of the events take place in claustrophobic indoor spaces, in the poor flats furnished with the provincial aesthetic, and at unkempt and dark workplaces. The outdoor shots are generally comprised of avenues which are filled with the urban crowd and which have no identity with the people who resemble each other. The city no longer appears the addressee of either a close relationship or a hostile struggle (Suner, 224). The heroes whose stories were told became as ordinary as Istanbul. *Üçüncü Sayfa (The Third Page)* (Zeki Demirkubuz, 1999) tells the story of "those at the very bottom," those who struggle to survive, in Istanbul. *Meryem* is a woman who works as a superintendent together with her husband at an apartment building. The rise of superintendents and their families as an important element of the urban life in Turkey took place with the enactment of the law which encouraged the construction of apartment buildings instead of detached houses. This new housing system created a field of employment which was filled by the first-generation male immigrants and which developed upon the arrival of more villagers in time (Özyeğin, 2012, p. 60). *İsa*, the neighbour of *Meryem* who lives on the basement floor of the same apartment building, is a poor and solitary young man who tries to make a living out of acting walk-on roles in movies. As many similar people in Istanbul, *İsa* also lives by worrying about finding a job and earning money without expecting many things. He is sick and tired of being unable to pay his rent and of being treated badly. One day, he is badly beaten in the workplace by his boss merely owing to the loss of some 50 dollars. *Meryem* is also fed up with being beaten by her husband and she plans to get rid of him. The majority of superintendents live on the damp basement floors which do not receive much light and air and about which they complain by saying "we've been jammed underground" in their own words. Living under such conditions leads to the continuous feelings of discomfort and alienation and the house is defined as a jail by its inhabitants (Özyeğin, p. 63). *Meryem*'s superintendent flat, where the pipes of the central heating system pass, where they sleep on the floor beds, and in which they eat on the floor, is dark and untidy. In fact, it is a temporary place for *Meryem*. In order to ascend to upper floors and to move up the social ladder, she has plans which also involve murder. On the day when he is beaten, *İsa* shoots his landlord after the insistent behaviour of his landlord on asking for the rent and faints, although he had actually intended to kill himself. When he comes to himself, he finds *Meryem* next to him. *Meryem* helps him; however, her intention is to use *İsa*. The movie takes its name from the third page of newspapers which contains the news about the inhabitants of the varoş and the outskirts with a bloody ending. The new cinematic image of Istanbul has changed into an insecure and unsafe city with the stories of those people who are merciless towards each other and who tend to use violence in any way.

The walls of the single-room house of *İsa* opposite the superintendent's flat on the basement floor of a lower middle class apartment building in which any type of violence is experienced are full of the posters of famous people whom he imitates. According to *İsa*, they are people "who have succeeded." He wants to resemble them but knows that this will not happen. He is lonely, weak, and oppressed. *İsa*'s room and the corridors of the apartment building are dark and boring. The description of poverty with claustrophobic spaces, which are not tranquil, is considerably far from the description of the slum which states that one can also be happy while being poor. The neighbourhoods where warm and sincere relationships were experienced and where the ties were strong provided their inhabitants with a feeling of belonging. The heroes of *Üçüncü Sayfa* are lonely. When they go out of the apartment building, they only go to a children's park.

As of the 1980s, the Turkish Cinema abandoned describing the social problems and directed itself to individuals and their problems. Depoliticised with the September 12th military intervention, the characteristic of the period, and then having undergone change upon the transition to a liberal economy in a wide variety of aspects such as human relationships, lifestyles, multiplication of consumption possibilities, and the changes in value judgments, the structure of Turkish society was undergoing a radical transformation. The identities which had been known and had been identified as either cultural or ideological until then also began to be reviewed and questioned and then a deep identity crisis began to be experienced. The Turkish Cinema was also affected by this transformation. Many movies describing the identity crises of movie heroes were produced in this period. The stories of different ethnic or sexual identities, which had previously taken place in movies as elements of comedy, began to be told too. Marginal people and anti-heroes were like the emergence of what had been suppressed until then. Discussions and searches regarding the problem of identity continued in the 1990s from time to time by turning into a crisis. From this crisis arose two identities in an identified and segregated form, which were the political Islamic identity and the Kurdish identity.

The problem of identity always exists with a problem of "the other": "we" and "others." Our social existence is defined according to this contrast and is located within power relations. *Güneşe Yolculuk (Journey to the Sun)* (Yeşim Ustaoğlu, 1999) tells the story of ethnic "others." Before this movie, the Turkish Cinema contained no movie which was about being a Kurd or which would remind us of this. Neither any emphasis on the ethnic roots of the immigrants who arrived in Istanbul, nor any problem originating from the roots of immigrants, was contained in the movies. The most important of the problems that the immigrants were confronted with in Istanbul in the 1960s was cultural problems, including: the problems of adaptation to the city, of assimilation by the city, and of becoming an urbanite. The 1970s and the 1980s demonstrated that those who had come failed to become urbanites, whereas Istanbul gradually turned into a village or a province.

Ethnic identity, language, accent, and even the skin colour first occur as a problem for the immigrants in Istanbul in *Güneşe Yolculuk*. The movie opens with a scene in which the camera tours over Istanbul, as in the movies describing "the beautiful Istanbul to live in." Nevertheless, this time, the camera tours over the peddlers who are making preparations at Eminönü Square in Istanbul which has just woken up, has been solitary, and will later attract many vendors and marginal jobs. The camera stops at the stand of a peddler and we also slowly begin to hear a Kurdish song and see many cassette players containing Kurdish names on the stand and the Kurdish young man who owns the stand. *Mehmet*, the hero of the movie, is a young man who immigrated to Istanbul from Tire, a town in the Aegean Region. He has found a job and has been working. He lives in a large ward-like shelter with the immigrants like him and maintains his life without complaining. In the movie, Istanbul is present with its crowded main avenues and dense traffic including people who resemble each other. In this crowd, it is hard to clearly distinguish between immigrants and Istanbulites. We once see the sea at a distance in the background when *Mehmet* meets his girlfriend. The movie heroes talking to, having a heart-to-heart with, and praising Istanbul remained in the old movies.

What *Mehmet* worries about is very different. While he does not feel different or other, he is likened to a terrorist Kurd due to his dark skin, is accused, is excluded, and loses his job. Even though he dyes his hair blonde, he can never explain that he is not a Kurd. In the former immigrant stories, the heroes looked at the city admiringly and turned their eyes to the centre, the city, with the expectation of the things they failed to reach. In this movie, the place in which the immigrants are happy is their shelter, where they sing the songs belonging to their own culture and dance the halay. *Güneşe Yolculuk* tries to eliminate the problem of identity, as well as the damaged feeling of belonging, through the description of the place and culture of origin. The movie created considerable arguments in the period when it was displayed.

Sır Çocukları (Children of Secret) (Aydın Sayman, 2002) describes those at the very bottom of society or the "others" who have hit rock-bottom owing to neither ethnic nor cultural difference. The heroes of the movie are the street children who run towards cars whenever the traffic stops at the main avenues of Istanbul, who disturb the conscience with their dirty faces and hungry looks, who are sent away sometimes by dressing down or sometimes with some change, and who have come to Istanbul from somewhere in Anatolia mostly by escaping from intra-family violence and poverty. They do not resemble the street children in the old black and white Turkish movies who lived on the streets, worked as shoe painters, and collected money by singing songs. They used to reach a happy ending upon such blessings and coincidences as the finding of a lost mother and the occurrence of a rich paternal uncle. The stories of the street children in the movies of the 2000s have no such happy endings. One of the impacts of the liberalisation policies in Turkey since the 1980s has been to stimulate an unprecedented process of division and polarisation. While the people queue up to buy bread that is a little cheaper at some neighbourhoods, richness is displayed with ostentatious methods in some districts. On the one hand, the number of homeless street children increases every day, but on the other hand, luxurious jeeps mushroom (Kandiyoti, 2012,

p. 15–19). From the perspective of homeless and unemployed street children who are addicted to substances like thinner and stay together in a damp and dingy place, Istanbul has become a place where no one pays attention to anyone and everybody is indifferent apart from the merciful people who appear few and far between. This time the camera tours the storefronts and the restaurants that the street children look at but cannot reach and they will satisfy their hunger if there is anyone who is merciful towards them. With disappointment and anger, the children return to the shelters in which they take refuge, try to console themselves with the substances that they are addicted to like thinner, and get established in the new representation of Istanbul.

In *Uzak (Distant)* (Nuri Bilge Ceylan, 2003), *Yusuf* comes to Istanbul by hoping to work at the vessels by which he could go to distant countries from his town in which he could see no future for himself. He has to stay with *Mahmut*, his relative. *Mahmut* is a lonely man that has put his life in order in Istanbul, failed while intending to "make movies like Tarkovsky," departed from his ideals, and makes a living out of taking advertising photographs. He does not want to put anybody at the centre of his life. He has become selfish and alienated. He badly treats his relative *Yusuf*, whom he has accepted unwillingly, cannot stand his naïve and good manners, and does everything for his departure.

The two different characters of the movie represent social segregation and the contradiction between urbanites and provincials that we were previously used to seeing in the movies. This contradiction has always existed in every period. Nevertheless, the identity of an urbanite lording it over the provincial is different from that in the past. *Mahmut* also comes from the same origin as his guest, whom he does not like, but he seems to have forgotten this. A new "urban intellectual" type emerged in the 1980s. With their intellectual accumulation, these people worked in rising occupations such as media, advertising, and public relations. *Mahmut* is also one of them. He has become selfish and alienated as he has departed from his ideals and humanistic values and is unhappy. On the contrary, *Yusuf* is someone who is naïve and has not lost his humanistic emotions. Those who have found a place for themselves and succeeded in holding on in the city are now looking down on the newcomers.

Yusuf tours to find a job on vessels. The only vessel he could find is a vessel which has tilted to one side in the sea. Always appearing in the background of *Yusuf*, Istanbul lies like an imaginary city under a pure white blanket of snow. First, *Yusuf* looks at everything he sees admiringly, but this face will gradually become bitter towards the end of the story. He walks by the sea and in parks, follows young girls, but he cannot succeed in talking to anyone. The views of Istanbul in some deep silence give much deeper sorrow than the sorrow created by lost Istanbul in black and white movies. The old movies implied that the gap created by loss could be overcome with love. *Uzak* says that no such probability remained. At the end of the movie, *Mahmut* drives away *Yusuf* from the house. In the last scene, we see *Mahmut* while sitting on a bench alone by the sea and he looks at the sea with some insignificant emptiness and a nihilistic feeling. The cost of becoming an Istanbulite is loneliness, indifference, and unhappiness.

Anger, Rebellion, and Chaos: "The Dark City" Istanbul

The children and grandchildren of the first generations that had immigrated to Istanbul were born and grew up in Istanbul. Being an "urbanite" was a cultural problem in the 1960s in the early periods of the immigration process. The assimilation of immigrants by the city was regarded as something which could take place provided that they obeyed the rules of the city. The elapsed time did not produce cultural harmony but rather cultural duality. A culture qualifying neither as a village culture, nor as an urban culture, but as a mixture of both, created by the immigrants who had disconnected ties with the places from which they had come and with their traditions in the 1970s but who failed to become urbanites completely, was called "the arabesque culture." The arabesque culture carried the taste of this mass with its music, clothing, and lifestyles. This culture flourished as the number of immigrants increased in the city. The arabesque culture underwent a transformation in time. The lyrics which were full of grief and which described the fight of immigrants with the city, their oppression, and their rebellion were replaced by more joyful lyrics in the 1980s. The symbol of the 1970s was Orhan Gencebay, whereas the symbol of the 1980s was İbrahim Tatlıses. Gencebay symbolised the desperate and those who endured pain in the city. On the other hand, Tatlıses, who was also an immigrant from Urfa, became the symbol of the new urbanites who insisted by saying "I also want everything" through more energetic melodies (Gürbilek, 2012, p. 16). It has become hard to make definitions of culture regarding Istanbul since the years when definitions of the arabesque culture were made and discussed. We can only speak of the cultures of unlike communities and religious communities at very different layers and in various statuses and positions. This multipartite structure catches one's eyes in many places of Istanbul in the spatial dimension first, including: the skyscrapers and the gecekondus located side by side or the gated communities of the upper-income group with pools and gardens and, immediately next to them, the houses of the rather middle class that have been converted from gecekondus into apartment buildings. With a large number of projects which destroy the fringes and forest basins of Istanbul by promising a different and privileged life intertwined with nature, the appearance of Istanbul in recent years has rather resembled a "ragbag." The historical silhouette of Istanbul composed of mosques, minarets, and palaces, which is part of its urban symbol, is also endangered. We can make this "ragbag" definition in the spatial appearance for culture too. The identity created by the varoş youth by defining themselves with a name and by distinguishing themselves from their parents and the youth of the upper-income group in the city is striking within this multipartite structure, in which it does not seem so possible for them to integrate with each other. "Apaçis" have formed a subculture with their own jargon, clothing, and hairstyle as an expression of their disappointment and rebellion regarding the city. The regions which are full of teenagers who fail to benefit from the job, educational, entertainment, and cultural possibilities of the city, who search for ways to earn money, who feel that they belong nowhere, who belong to neither the culture of their parents nor the city, who are desperate, and who are angry at the system always involve tension. Their lack of belonging turns into the emotion of anger at the city, which becomes evident, and the rates of crime gradually increase (Barış, 2010, p. 281).

In the Turkish Cinema, the movies describing the youth in the varoşs began to be produced towards the late 2000s. *Başka Semtin Çocukları (Children of the Other Side)* (Aydın Bulut, 2008) tells the story of the teenagers who live in the Gazi Neighbourhood in Istanbul, formed as a result of immigration and that is also known with its political actions.

In *Gurbet Kuşları* and *Bitmeyen Yol*, the immigrant teenagers did not lift up their voice and hoped to be able to move up the social ladder even though they felt oppressed and excluded against Istanbul. In *Başka Semtin Çocukları*, the teenagers are full of anger. The reason for their anger is not the failure to move up the social ladder, but the failure to become something. For them, there is neither any promise, nor any solution, to exiting their district. *Veysel* and *Simo*, the two main characters of the movie, are close friends. The movie contains no scene of the historical or natural beauty or the city centre of Istanbul. The visible spaces are a textile workshop, an unkempt folk song (türkü) bar, poor houses, women sitting in front of doors, and children wandering around. *Veysel* and *Simo* meet on the roof of their houses where they feed pigeons and tell each other their dreams, anger, and hopelessness, state that they do not belong to this poor district, and desire a life in which they will be considered human beings and will not be disregarded. Istanbul is seen as a silhouette under a blanket of fog at a distance close to the horison line. In the old movies, lovers used to meet on the hills of Çamlıca. The scenery of the Bosphorus that is visible from the hills used to accompany the emotions of lovers. The place where *Veysel* meets his girlfriend is a junkyard for cars. They try to beautify an old junk car by placing pot flowers in it.

The leftist teenagers of the neighbourhood perform political actions and distribute leaflets. *Veysel* and his friend do not join them. They are not conscious in the political sense. They cannot perceive the reason why they are stuck in this neighbourhood, the source of inequality, and the meaning of a political struggle. For them, the solution is to go away from here but how? The only job they can find in the end is to work as a bodyguard at the door of a bar. *Simo* wants to be the bodyguard who stands at the door, but he is not considered physically eligible for this job and is told to stand at the bar counter. *Simo* is jealous of *Veysel*; they argue and he shoots him with a gun, kills him, and throws his corpse in the garbage. Nobody suspects him. *Simo* becomes the bodyguard who will stand at the door of the bar instead of *Veysel*. He wears a black suit and white shirt, wears an imposing ring on his finger, combs his hair backwards by using hair gel, the indicators of *Simo*'s new identity, and goes to the bar. On the first night in his job, he is also given his first slap by his boss because of a wrong act. In the last scene of the movie, we see *Simo* while standing at the door of the bar and teenagers pass from the same place with posters in their hands and by chanting slogans. For *Başka Semtin Çocukları (Children of the Other Side)*, there is no alternative other than getting mixed up in illegal affairs or becoming potential terrorists.

The heroes of *Kara Köpekler Havlarken (Black Dogs Barking)* (Mehmet Bahadır Er, Maryna Gorbach, 2009) are also two teenagers who try to hold on in Istanbul. *Selim* and *Çaça* live in Çeliktepe immediately behind Mecidiyeköy, one of the most central places of Istanbul. The lack of harmony between the large and imposing buildings and the small quiet houses stuck among them is very clear. *Selim* and *Çaça* never have a chance to get a good education, a good occupation, and a good position. Their hope to earn money and "move up" in a short way will cause them to get mixed up in illegal affairs and crime. Istanbul does not offer immigrants any employment structure which will enable them to work in jobs that will provide them with a regular income. Therefore, the fields of work the immigrants can find are marginal jobs with no guarantee such as constructions, being a superintendent, and being a peddler. Besides, the structure of the city which allows marginal jobs has been under the control of organised criminal gangs or "the Mafia," with its known name. Finding a place here is possible through either joining them or giving them money. Events resulting in guns, acts of injuring, and killings are often experienced between these criminal gangs. Operating parking lots and the security tender of shopping centres are also under the control of these gangs. The two teenagers who dream of becoming rich in the movie come across *Sait*, who immigrated to the city before them and became rich through illegal affairs. *Sait* is a man who can do anything and take others' lives to set up a business and survive in Istanbul. *Sait* kills *Selim* and *Çaça* by siccing his wild dogs on them.

Anlat İstanbul (Istanbul Tales) (Ü. Ünal, K. Sabancı, Y. Yolcu, S. Demirdelen, and Ö. Atay, 2004) starts with the story of a clarinetist and adapts five different fairy tales to Istanbul. The fairy tales end happily; however, the heroes of all fairy tales in the movie, such as "the Little Red Riding Hood" and "the Pied Piper of Hamelin," are unhappy and there is no good ending for anyone. With the people who are deceived, who escape and are chased, who are injured, who are threatened, and who are intended to be killed, as well as with the dark streets and sewage pipes of Istanbul and the strange apartment buildings where transsexuals live, Istanbul has turned into the city of chaos and darkness. With crimes such as theft and extortion, as well as acts of injuring, the problem of security of life and property has become the primary problem. Everybody escapes from something in the movie. Haydarpaşa Railway Station, the gateway of the city, is now the gate of escape from the city. They want to exit through this gate, leave Istanbul, escape, and survive. *Anlat İstanbul* intends to close the gates of Istanbul. In *Ah Güzel İstanbul*, *Haşmet* looked at Istanbul and addressed it as "Oh! Beautiful Istanbul. O! My Dear City." In the last scene of *Anlat İstanbul*, clarinetist *Hilmi* addresses Istanbul on the Galata Bridge while the early light of the morning was appearing and walks away by playing his clarinet, as follows: "These are lies. All are fairy tales./Your love, your house and your blue all are lies./You sleep. They deceive you./Come on! Let's go/Istanbul is over. Let's go somewhere else./You stay alone, totally empty, Istanbul. I'm taking everybody./Wake up Perfidious Istanbul./We were deceived by your fairy tales and consumed our lives!/Wake up. Everybody wake up. The fairy tale is over."

Conclusion

The image of Istanbul in the movies and, by means of movies, the perspective of society on the city and the way it perceives the city, have changed and transformed in the Turkish Cinema from the 1950s to the 2000s. In the movies of the 1950s and the 1960s, Istanbul was "the golden city" of opportunities, the fantasies of becoming the king of the city, dreams, and desires, and the movies had a happy ending. In the Turkish Cinema of the 2000s, "the golden city to live in" and the happy endings of movies no longer exist. Desires and dreams have been replaced by disappointments. The stories of the losers struggling to feed themselves no longer contain the fantasies of becoming the king of the city. The sparkling avenues and streets have turned into insecure spaces which are full of violence and crime and the image in the memories has turned into "the city of darkness." The movie camera now shoots the ruined Istanbul that has become considerably ugly with its people and spaces but not the Istanbul that poet *Nedim* "*sacrifices the Whole Persian (Iranian) Country for a Stone of it*" or the "*Dear*" Istanbul that *Yahya Kemal* addresses by saying "*Only Loving a District of Yours is Even Worth a Lifetime*" and looks at from a hill. The unique natural beauty, Bosphorus shores, and historical spaces of Istanbul, which still exist no matter how much they have been plundered, have not been lost indeed. The movies do not present this Istanbul, but the Istanbul that darkens as one goes deeper and that lost its spirit a long time ago (i.e. a view of "the new Istanbul").

References

Arslan, U. T. (2010). Mazi Kabrinin Hortlakları, Türklük, Melankoli ve Sinema: Metis, İstanbul.

Atlar, A. B. (2014). *Yedi Kule İstanbul.* Kentleri Savunmak Mekan Toplum ve Siyaset Üzerine: Editör, Aysun Koca, Çare Olgun Çalışkan, Esra Kaya, Gürkan Akgün, Notabene, İstanbul.

Barış, J. (2010). *Kentin Taşralaşmasıyla İç İçe Geçen Haller,* Taşrada Var Bir Zaman: Derleyen, Zeynep Tül Akbay, Aslı Güneş, Çitlembik, İstanbul.

Birkiye, A. (1999). Aşk ve Hüzündür İstanbul: Özgür, İstanbul.

Çiçekoğlu, F. (2007). Vesikalı Şehir: Metis, İstanbul.

Dağbağyan, L. P. (2006). Zaman Tünelinde Şehr-i İstanbul'un Seyir Defteri: Karadağ, İstanbul.

Gürbilek, N. (2012). Kötü Çocuk Türk: Metis, İstanbul.

Güçhan, (Yücel) G. (1992). Toplumsal Değişme ve Türk Sineması Kente Göç Eden İnsanın Türk Sinemasında Değişen Profili: İmge, Ankara.

Kandiyoti, D. (2012). *Parçaları Yorumlamak,* Kültür Fragmanları: Editör, Deniz Kandiyoti Ayşe Saktanber, Metis.

Narlı, N., Kotaman, A. (2008). *Modernleşmeden Küraselleşmeye İstanbul Modeli,* Sinematografik Kentler, Mekanlar, Hatıralar, Arzular: Derleyen, Mehmet Öztürk, Agora Kitaplığı, İstanbul.

Özyeğin, G. (2012). *Kapıcılar Gündelikçiler ve Ev Sahipleri,* Kültür Fragmanları: Editör, Deniz Kandiyoti Ayşe Saktanber, Metis.

Pamuk, O. (2003). İstanbul. Hatıralar ve Şehir, İstanbul: İletişim, İstanbul.

Perouse, J. F. (2008) *İstanbul Varoşları,* Sinematografik Kentler, Mekanlar, Hatıralar, Arzular: Derleyen, Mehmet Öztürk, Agora Kitaplığı, İstanbul.

Suner, A. (2006). Hayalet Ev Yeni Türk Sinemasında Aidiyet, Kimlik ve Bellek: Metis.

Tanpınar, A. H. (2000) *İstanbul* Beş Şehir: YKY, İstanbul.

İlknur Doğu Öztürk

The Effects of Culture on Marketing Communication in Positioning: An Examination Regarding Yandex Positioning in the Turkish Market

Introduction

In today's world, expectations and purchasing habits of the consumer differ from one group to another and even from one person to another. As a result, a brand should approach a country market and the different groups of the very country with different strategies. In the competitive environment arouse from the factors like changing structures of the society, technological innovations, developments, a concept, brand comes into prominence as the element provides preference of the products.

Creating a qualified product and a positive brand evaluation is the first step of the brand construction. The place of the concepts of quality and perception of quality is the consumer's mind (Can cited from Riesand Ries Can, 2007: 229). The name, the package, the product, and the emotion it awakes in consumer are the properties that help products differ from competitors and branding.

If we look at the old definitions of the term brand, we observe a link to the term "to burn." In fact, the word brand derives from the ancient Scandinavian word brandr (to burn). In that age, farmers used to sear the animals which is the first use of "branding." The aim is to define a product and provide a way to distinguish it. Today, in definitions of brand, we read in dictionaries that the aim is to distinguish. This is described as "the registered trademark" (Borça, 2013:4). Pointing to the brand as a concept that has a distinguishable part makes the emotional response about the product possible.

Brands undertake not only distinguishing features but also different strategies. Jim Blyth (2001) lists these strategical functions as posessive sign, differentiation, functional tool, symbolic, risk reducer, shortcut tool, legal tool, and strategical approach (Can cited from Blyth, 2007:227–228). It affects the positioning process by the visual differentiation from the competitors and makes a connection to the target group via cultural communication applications.

Marx defines culture as "against the ones nature has created, the ones human has done" (Güvenç cited from Marx, 1999:100). As a combination of the human made value system, morality, art, symbol, belief, custom, and tradition, culture is one of the main factors that determines wishes and behaviours. Within a culture, people are in constant interaction with their families and the other social foundations; therefore, they develop values, preferences, and perceptions accordingly (Peltekoğlu cited from Tek, 2010, 132). Culture, differing from one society to another, among groups and even in sub-cultures, is the fact that determines demands and wishes.

With technological innovations and massification of communication, the effect of culture on brand positioning increases for brands. Culture gets a higher importance in communication applications within the scope of affecting the customer's purchasing preferences and positioning the brand's differentiating features. Based on the way that a brand is percepted, the concept of positioning comes forward as the leading concept in communication studies.

As Horald and Gilson (1987:170–171) state, positioning "places brand into target group's rerefential frame" indicates that the main theme of positioning is to differentiate the brand from its competitors. On the other hand, Kotler (2006:309) argues that positioning means customers' defining of a brand according to its important and exclusive features, that is, in the customer's mind, the criteria of the position of a brand among its competitors is important. Furthermore, Kotler states that in today's competitive environment, management has to decide the target market departments and then find different positioning for each market department (Tosun cited from Harold and Gilson and Kotler, 2010, 33). The answers to the questions of who are the competitors and what are the differences and similarities between them should be considered in the brand positioning process.

Brand positioning aims to place the brand in a position that has a competitive superiority in the mind of the target group (Uztuğ, 2002:72). Positioning is important as it provides the determination of the brand's status in the market and the desired place for the brand by differentiating the brand from its competitors. In this process of communication, applications like advertisements are operative with their effect on the target group.

In an environment of intensive competition and with the pressure of this competition, similar "new" products are put into market and management sends various messages to their customers and consumers via various channels (Odabaşı and Oyman, 2001: 61). An advertisement, one of the communication applications used in brand positioning in the competitive environment, is "the announcement of the description of a business or a commodity or a service in general broadcast media" (Kocabaş and Elden, 1997: 12).

In an advertisement, one of the elements of brand communication, the message in the form of a word, picture, sound, image, and symbol, is transmitted in order to generate the aimed effect on the target group. The most significant communicative feature of the advertisement is that the objective effects are designed in order to set the target group in motion in relation to a brand (Tosun, 2010:271). According to Tosun, advertisements are capable of not only charging a product or a brand, but also a way of life and a point of view (Tosun, 2010:273).

Constructing a message with cultural and social codes such as humour, sexuality, fear, or emotional attraction serves as brand positioning. Creating advertisement attraction by using these emotions is used to create a distinctive and objective change which is the desire to access the physical, psychological, and social demands of the target group.

According to Berger, advertisements reflect the dominant ways of thinking, points of view, and trends and advertising is the process of producing attraction (Berger, 1990:131). Advertisement applications using cultural codes creating objective advertising attraction are inevitably the efficient responses to the question of how the brand positions itself.

Advertisements consist of cultural codes and a part of the brand positioning aims to place the product brand in people's mind in a desired way. For this purpose, using cultural codes in advertisement is inevitable. In the phase of interpretation of these codes, we confront semiotics.

Semiotics begin with Sweden philologist Ferdinand de Saussure (1857–1913) and American thinker Charles Saunders Pierce (1839–1914) who help to explore the meanings beyond the visible image (Fiske, 1996:61–62). One of the most important contributors of semiotics, Barthes, defines sign as the rose is only a flower. But if a young man presents himself to his girlfriend, it becomes a sign. The rose refers to the young man's romantic passion and this meaning is accepted by the girlfriend (Mutlu, 2004:113). Semiotics aim to expose the syntax of signs in a text and review the meanings of signs and especially the generation ways of these signs and the meanings they produce.

Saussure mentions two ways of arranging the codes. The first one is paradigmatic and the second one is syntogmatic (Fiske, 1996:62). Saussure argues about the arbitrary relationship between the signifier and signified that plays a huge role in the development of semiotics. Pierce is concentrated on the three images of sign (icon, index, and symbol). A movement derives from this starting point and semiological decoding spreads the world (Berger, 1996:12). Semiotics are used in all communication applications, transferring meaning to advertisements, television (TV), newspapers, and magazines. Advertising is definitely at the top of the list of using signs. By examining what a sign is, how they form, and the connotations they produce, semiotics contributes to understanding the advertising language as a communication syntax and searches the buried meanings under the surface.

The main problem of semiotics is sign. There are three basic fields it studies in, which are: the sign itself, the code that signs are arranged in, or systems and codes and the culture the signs are treated by (Fiske, 1996:62). Codes and signs are transferred between generations and cultures. People born into the culture get these codes and signs via the transferring process.

Advertisement movies construct the narrative structure fictionally and include a lot of images. Looking from the beginning of the constructing process of coding the images, it is evident that they contain the values and elements of the cultural structure they are born in.

Methods

Yandex, with 64% market share and being the biggest search engine in Russia, is the fifth biggest internet based product and service providing firm in the world. It reaches more than 56 million people all around the world. It offers service in Russia, Belarus, Kazakhstan, Ukraine, the United States of America, and Turkey (http://tr.wikipedia.org/wiki/Yandex, 05.06.2014). Yandex broke into the Turkish market in 2011 after it opened a branch office in Istanbul (http://kliknete.com/yandex-turkiye-pazarinda.html, 10.07.2014).

In this study, cultural effects on advertising and using visual and linguistic codes reflecting culture as a marketing communication application in the process of brand positioning are emphasised.

The objective of this study is to put forward the importance of culture in the brand positioning process. With this objective, theoretic information observation on practice was run on the Yandex brand. Explanations on brand and positioning were made and with the help of Pierce's Semiotic approach (icon, index, and symbol), language, slogan, colours, and narration of advertisement movies from the advertisement studies with the slogan "answers of all life questions" run in 2011 of Russian orginated search engine brand Yandex. The chosen advertisement movies belong to the campaign during the year that Yandex broke into the Turkish market. These advertisements were downloaded to a computer from the fourth popular site in Turkey, the video sharing channel YouTube (http://www.alexa.com/topsites/countries/TR01.09.2014).

The overall objective of the study is to reach the conclusion that with the aim of breaking into a market and brand positioning, universal cultural signs and local cultural signs must be included together in communicative applications like advertisements. The effects of Turkish culture in advertisement applications are questioned. Information about the communicative studies of the brand in the Turkish market is given generally, while semiotic analyses are restricted to the TV advertisements in Turkey on air in 2011.

Findings

Advertisements are formed of two parts, image and text. In the advertisement movie, an image of a black frame on a computer screen is in the shape of a search engine. In advertisement movies, there is a Yandex text, a search bar, and a find button on the background and the film goes on with the changing text.

Image 1: A shot from the movie

In the advertisement movies, sound, images, and music are used integrally. In the movies there was a voice over saying the slogan at the end, along with the music of the advertisement campaign. At the end of the advertisement, the brand name, the slogan, and a voice over saying the slogan "Find all the answers of all life questions" came onto the screen. Following this, the phrase "Yandex, New search engine," the brand, and the slogan of the campaign are put into words.

One of the signs in advertisements is music. Music is an important element of the advertisement that strengthens the emotional content and provides a dramatic effect. The music in advertisements can be used both as primary and supportive elements. With music, it is possible to call attention to the advertisement, as well as to provide retention of the message in mind. Searches indicate that people find the arguments of the advertisements with music more convincing than the ones without music (Elden and Bakır, 2010:96–97).

Duck Sauce's disco-house song "Barbara Streisand" is used in the advertisement movie to boost the impressiveness as an audial element.

Screen changes like blurriness or contrast or techniques like shotting moves aren't used in the movies. A constant contrast setting is used all over the advertisement to emphasise only the product.

Like music, colours have a language and every colour is communication. According to Ünsal, using colour as an element in the advertisement occurs for five reasons (cited by Yaman, 2014:46), as follows:

- To call attention,
- To represent the scene and object as faithful to the origin,
- To indicate a part of the product or the message,
- To create some imaginations in customer's, and
- To create a strong impression.

Vivid colour signs are preferred to support the cultural signs in order to preserve the youth and energy and the humour in the local culture, so as to support the integrity of the campaign in the advertisement. By using bright and vivid colours, positive feelings like happiness are attempted to be created. The Turkish advertisement movie is framed with black, the colour that is explained as power and prestige in the local culture. By this way, boundries are drawn to the advertisement.

At the end of the advertisement, the Yandex logo on the white background and the advertisement logo appear. Black and white colours are used well and are balanced together. White colour is mainly provide to be noticed of other colours. Therefore, it affects the recognition of the logo and the brand.

The logo, the emblem, and the slogan call the target group to use the new search engine. Perception of the colours varies according to factors like age, sex, environment, habits, and culture. Colour and music strengthen the convincing feature of the advertisement.

Table 1: First advertisement movie with the slogan "answers of all the life questions"

Image	Text	Analyse
Dancing robot	Dancing schools	Universal sign, access to the young target group, assertion of possessing the newest technology, emphasis on local entertainment culture
Ducklings and mother duck	Child names	Assertion of being capable of presenting multiple choice, emphasis on family as a universal value, using of universal and local cultural signs
Cucumber	Can we be cacik?	Emphasis on food culture as a local sign
Hippopotamus	Waterproof mascara	Completing the text with the universal visual sign connotation
Donkey	Compete recipe	Local cultural sign, traditional public cultural sign
The Earth and satellite	How will I go home?	Assertion of being capable of showing the way to the furthest places, assertion of possessing the newest technology, assertion of navigation service

Table 2: Second advertisement movie with the slogan "answers of all life questions."

Image	Text	Analyse
Running ostrich	Running shoes	Using universal code
Watermelon	White cheese	Emphasis on Turkish food and using local cultural sign
Cat	Funny person video	Using universal linguistic and visual sign
Undershirt and pyjamas on the clothes line	Picnic sites	While picnic is a universal cultural code, pyjamas belong to Turkish entertainment culture
Backgammon, dice	Mars travelling	A universality with a universal code in text and emphasis on locality with local code
Shark	Public beaches	Textual content meaningful in local culture on an image reflecting universal culture

In the Yandex advertisement with short words on a screen designed as it is being searched on and images contributing the textual content are used to benefit from humorous attraction. It is found that the images or text called the signs are well known and recognised by the audience and are used in a a way that complete each other.

As Yandex represented by an advertisement, it is the signified in Pierce's semiotics triangle. Signifieds are the side of the part representing Yandex. To direct this process, images and content, especially by humour and addressing feelings like joy and entertainment, are chosen in order to convince the target group in the advertisement. The exertion of creating a younger, more cheerful, and energetic image is reflected by the word "new" in the slogan "new search engine" and significations can be made like innovation, humour, and assertion. It is observed that qualities like speed, multiple choices, and multiculturalism are transferred to the target group by the visual and textual signs.

Advertisements show that they care about the culture of the target group by using signs like brand name, slogan, colour, and language of the textual message. For example, as a universal brand, Yandex presents a universal sign like family and a sign reflecting local culture as it can exceed to interpret the proverb, what a donkey knows about compete, together. It is aimed to position the brand in people's minds as a search engine that is finding all kind of answers of the audience's possible questions and that is fast, young, equipped with the latest technology, and facetious. Especially, there are connotions in linguistic content in which advertisements humorous attraction is applied.

Discussion

Being a brand in order to earn the dependence and loyalty of the target group is based on being different. Communicative applications like advertisements influence positioning as a profession which has effects on the brand. Culture in the competitive environment transforms into stylistic, linguistic, and visual signs in the form of universal-local cultural codes.

It is seen that every linguistic and visual sign like the brand name, logo, slogan, and colours in an advertisement movie can be interpreted by the target group and consist of universal and cultural codes. By universal codes, its universality is emphasised and by cultural codes, its locality is emphasised.

As a part of society, an individual interprets the things he or she sees in the advertisments by the leading of the knowledge he or she gets after a while in that very culture. Using signs formed of images and texts to strengthen the signification in all of the advertisement movies, the cultural effect of the target group to interpret the process of the signifers encountered before is communicated to the signified. Culture is reflected in the advertisements by using signs to access the desired positioning in the mind of the target group. Visual and linguistic signs like sound, image, music, and text in the advertisements are interpreted by the audience equipped with the culture.

Yandex has developed a positioning strategy, having a peculiar benefit and function.

References

Asa Berger, A. (1996). Kitle İletişiminde Çözümleme Yöntemleri. Eskişehir: Anadolu Üniversitesi Yayınları

Berger, J. (1990). GörmeBiçimleri. İstanbul:Metis Yayınları

Borça,G.(2013). Marka ve Yönetimi. Eskişehir: Anadolu Üniversitesi Yayınları http://eogrenme.anadolu.edu.tr/eKitap/mai102u.pdfBorça Erişim T.07.06.2014

Can, E. (2007). Marka ve Marka Yapılandırma. Marmara Üniversitesi İ.İ. B.F. Dergisi, cilt 22, No: 1. http://dosya.marmara.edu.tr/ikf/iib-dergi/2007-1/225-237-MARKA-YAPILANDIRMA.pdf Erişim T: 7.02.2014

Fiske, J. (1996). İletişim Çalışmalarına Giriş. Ankara: Bilim ve Sanat

Güvenç, B. (1999). İnsan ve Kültür. İstanbul: Remzi Kitabevi.

Kocabaş, F. ve Elden M. (1997). **Reklamcılık.** İstanbul: İletişim Yayıncılık.

Mutlu E. (2004). İletişim Sözlüğü. Ankara: Bilim ve Sanat

Odabaşı, Y., Oyman, M. (2002). Pazarlama İletişimi Yönetimi. İstanbul: Mediacat Yayınları.

Olgundeniz, S. S., Parsa, A. F (2014) Reklam dünyasinda imgenin gücü "Arçelik ve Vestel reklamlarinda robot karakterlerle yaratılan evren" -Journal of New World Sciences Academy April 2014 http://www.newwsa.com/download/gecici_makale_dosyalari/NWSA-7201-3375-4.pdf Erişim T. 5. 06.2014

Peltekoğlu, F. B. (2010). Kavram ve Kuramlarıyla Reklam. İstanbul: Beta Yayınları

Tosun, N. B. (2010). İletişim Temelli Marka Yönetimi. İstanbul: Beta Yayınları

Yaman, F. (2014) Reklamlarda Kullanılan Renkler ve Gazete Reklamlarının Nitel Analizi İletişim Kuram ve Araştırma Dergisi - Sayı 38/ Bahar 2014 Gazi Üniversitesi İletişim Fakültesi

http://www.iletisimdergisi.gazi.edu.tr/busayi/3.pdf

http://www.alexa.com/topsites/countries/TR

http://tr.wikipedia.org/wiki/Yandex

http://kliknete.com/yandex-turkiye-pazarinda.html

Mehmet Ali Gazi[1]

Reflections of Gatekeeping on Social Media

Introduction

Communication and media have been subjected to great change since the period when the Persian Empire brought the first mailing services into being in 550 B.C. 2600 years later, it has become so important for people to access information (Büyükşener, 2009, p. 19). In particular, the printing press paved the way for conveying information to larger masses and enabled more people to use that information. On the other hand, this process has brought along the challenge of the accession of reliable information (Burke, 2005, p. 25–75).

The most prominent change that came about in the 20th century is that the internet has made it possible to form a social group and maintain communication at the same time. While the telephone has provided a "one-to-one" type of communication, other means such as the television, radio, magazines, and books have managed to build a "one-to-many" type of communication. Nevertheless, the internet presents a "many-to-many" type of communication. As media becomes more digital, the internet grows into a conveying element for all the other media forms. That is to say, telephone calls, magazines, movies, and many other media forms have moved onto the internet. In this way, a new type of media has come to the forefront whose content is created by the users themselves. On these new media platforms, such as on Facebook, Twitter, and YouTube, we could easily share our ideas and opinions, articles, videos, and photos. Additionally, people could broadcast them to millions of people depending on the broadness of their social network.

As conventional media casts a unilateral and passive role for the target masses, social media has given the chance to users to create and share their own content (Chin-Fook, Simmonds, 2011, p. 9–10). With the use of social media, the unidirectional flow of information on conventional media has come to an end. Instead of it, a new type of flow of information has been used that could be created and shared by multiple users at the same time. By this means, each individual has been granted the equal right with other users to intervene in the flow of information on social media (Chin-Fook, Simmonds, 2011, p. 22). Such change in intervening in

1 Research Assistant, Gazi University, Faculty of Communication, Department of Public Relations, mehmetaligazi@hotmail.com.

the flow of information has made it essential to discuss the functions and definition of gatekeeping on conventional media once more.

The objective of this study, on which the literature review and content analysis methods are used, is to examine how the gatekeeping functions of conventional media have changed on the social media means.

Role of the Gatekeeping on Conventional Media

As for conventional media that is mostly regarded with concepts such as "industrial," "mass," or "broadcast," the printed, visual, and audial media organs such as radio, television, and newspapers first come to mind (Yurdigül & Zinderen, 2012, p. 84).

Media is directly related to social, economic, and political organisations. It is fed and shaped by these organisations. Within this context, while the changes happening in social, economic, and political areas feed the developments of communication, they are also fed and affected by the new formations in communication (Işık, 2002: 3). Therefore, it is highly necessary to support and feed the intellectual basis that the communication systems are based on with the common values and traditions, while building the normative theories (Kaya, 1985, p. 38). As media reflects the social control systems regulating the relations of the individuals and institutions, the social, political, and economic perspectives of society should be well understood in the analysis of the communicative tools.

Noam Chomsky and Edward Herman claim that there are certain structural "filters" on media. After putting the news, comments, and analyses through these structural filters, they are purified from the "harmful materials" to a large extent and transformed into what coincides with the agenda and interests of distinguished people (2008, p. 43–73) These "structural filters" determine what is worthy to be made news or what kind of priorities the comments will have. The journalists, commenters, and professionals working within the system may perform their job in compliance with the objective criteria; however, it will not be effective enough to amend the system by itself. Such filters work so well that they seize the journalists, commenters, and analysts on their own circle and serve the interests of the aforementioned distinguished people.

The elements that Chomsky called structural filters include: size and monopolistic structure of the media companies and their tendency for interest; the fact that advertisements are the main source of revenue and as to the sources of the news, they are generally the rulership's structures or the "specialists" serving for these rulership's structures; and the periodical prominent ideologies taking the media on their own discipline and regarding it as a "creation of reaction" or a national inspection tool.

Chomsky and Herman call the system consisting of these five structural systems as the "propaganda model." The first two media filters (property and advertisement) have gained much more importance. The downfall of public radio and television broadcasting, the accession of the companies to all around the world, and the unification and centralisation of media companies have made the turnover requirements much more significant. The completion of who may better serve the advertisers has become intensified. The process of attaching the news centres to multi-national companies has moved to further dimensions. Now fewer places are allocated to investigative journalism and the managers have already lost their willingness to support such kind of journalism.

The third and fourth filters (sources of news and the reaction) have become more powerful within recent years as mechanisms reinforcing the effects of distinguished people. Reducing financial sources allocated for the journalism profession means to increase the power of the people and minimising the cost of the media by providing the news. Moreover, it is observed more densely how public relations companies guide the media and intervene in the contents of the news during this process. The number of public relations specialists intervening in the news has exceeded the number of journalists writing the news. As for the fifth filter (ideologies), although it is said that the power of ideology has been weakened by the collapse of the Soviet Union, such weakening has been compensated easily with the "miracle of the market" possessing much more ideological power.

It is not possible to expect that all and any of the news materials received by mass communication tools will enter into the news. For this reason, some news could not reach the community. The news that is decided to be presented into the community after being selected and re-edited from these materials are conveyed to the community within the information and inspection of gatekeepers (Tekinalp & Uzun, 2004, p. 98).

Gatekeepers play an important role during the process of shaping and rebuilding the truths. This concept was first used by Kurt Lewin (1947) in one of his studies where he was searching for the decision-making mechanism in food expenses of the family. It was used later on by M. White (1950) who made good use of this concept by analysing the relations and procedures in selecting the news to be published in newspapers (Mutlu, 2008: 99). The concept of gatekeeping is the act of communication professionals choosing or rejecting a topic for publishing and broadcasting. Being a prominent institution in understanding media communication, the gatekeepers are the ones who select, edit, or refuse the posts and accordingly disable the flow of information to a receiver or a group of receivers (Alemdar & Erdoğan, 1996, p. 114). In the classic theory of gatekeeping, it is not possible that all the news materials received by mass communication tools will be entered into the news. Therefore, some news does not get the chance to reach the community. The news that is decided to be presented into the community after being selected and re-edited from these materials are conveyed to the community within the information and inspection of gatekeepers (Tekinalp & Uzun, 2004: 98).

The concept of gatekeeping stands for the act of communication professionals choosing or rejecting a topic for publishing and broadcasting. Being a prominent institution in understanding media communication, the gatekeepers are the ones who select, edit, or refuse the posts and accordingly disable the flow of information to a receiver or a group of receivers (Alemdar & Erdoğan, 1996, p. 114). Gatekeepers in conventional media act as an important part in creating new truths and rebuilding the existing truths after forming them. Highlighted with their choices in information, there are various main factors that affect the gatekeepers while selecting information. These factors are individual, professional, corporate, non-media environment, and social environment (Çebi, 2002, p. 85).

The gatekeeper stands for the authority selecting and framing all kinds of information to be conveyed to the audience. "Gatekeeping" studies regarded within the liberal studies have concentrated on the causes for the choices of the news and changes in news texts. Many social scientists have claimed that various effects are influential in the definition and classification of gatekeeping. White has highlighted the personal effects in gatekeeping while McNelly has brought the role of intermediaries into the forefront and argued that the gatekeeping process is done before the information is conveyed to mass communication tools.

Shoemaker, making a composition of the models developed by the aforementioned theorists, has proposed an integrative theory of gatekeeping. This model is defined as the modern model of gatekeeping. The fundamental assumptions of this model are studied under five headings, as follows (Shoemaker, 2009, p. 30):

1. Individual Level: The ways of thinking, cognitive foresights, decision-making strategies, and understandings of profession of the journalists have an influence on the gatekeeping activity in this level.
2. Professional Experience Level: Hierarchical structure, understanding of the information value, and impartiality form the content of the conveyed information.
3. Corporate Level: Some changeable elements such as the characteristics of the institutions, in-house rolls, and corporate socialisation affect the gatekeeping activity.
4. Non-corporate Level: It affects the gatekeeping activity through variables such as target audience, competitors, advertisers, pressure groups, public relations activities, and other mass communication vehicles.

5. Social Level: In this area, the influences of variables such as the ideology and culture are on the gatekeeping activity.

Shoemaker's (1991, p. 70–77) gatekeeping theory is based on a mould that examines the gatekeeping activity on the large, medium, and small scales. In reference to this mould, inter-corporate gatekeeping activities performed on the large scale are studied within the ideological and cultural structure of society. The elements guiding and shaping inter-corporate gatekeeping activities are channels and sources of information, news, advertising clients, media market, pressure groups, public relations activities, government, and other social institutions. On the medium scale, the elements guiding gatekeeping activities in the media institutions are professional and corporate conventions, communication activities, and the characteristics of the media institutions. As for individual gatekeeping activities performed on the small scale, they are affected by some certain psychological processes and personality characteristics such as corporate socialisation, secondary assessment procedures, values, approaches, moral principles, decision-making strategies, models of thinking, understanding of the journalist's role, foresights, and professional types of journalism.

Structure of Social Media and Gatekeeping

Castells describes social media as a network architecture which could not be controlled by any centres and that is made up of thousands of autonomous computer networks passing through electronic barriers and making numerous connections with each other (Castells, 2013: 8).

Just as real life does, social media has become established on the talks, relations, exchanges, shared ideas, and matters drawing general attention. At the present time, social media presents an environment in which a large mass consisting of managers, consultants, internet leaders, blog writers, and journalists perform an exchange of views. Social media is very simply the platform providing an interpersonal dialogue and communication through Internet. This new type of media enables people to publish their own opinions, knowledge, and experiences on a global platform. In most cases, these people's voices may be as effective as the well-known journalists, famous people, and specialists (Breakenridge, 2009:15). Human beings today live in a network community ignoring organisational knowledge, personal creativity, learning capacity, and as being sources of values, capital and workmanship (Taatila et al., 2006: 312). It is highly possible that this network community is mainly created by new communication technologies. On the other hand, human beings also make new communication effort in this virtual environment. Such effort is quite visible particularly in social networks and these social networks are defined as web-based services enabling people to share their profile which is obligatory to make a connection with the masses.

The most prominent feature of social media is that individuals may express themselves in a manner of being open to other people via the internet.

Gürsakal (2009, p. 23–24) gathers the main features of social media under five headings, as follows:

1. Participation: Social media makes it easy for the connecting people to give feedback and make the necessary contribution. It makes the line between the media and the audience grey and the users are granted with the patronage.
2. Openness: It provides the accession of usage of the content together with disabling the obstacles. It has made the usage quite easy and open.
3. Dialogue: Conventional media mostly includes unidirectional communication. It is difficult and takes time to receive feedback from the classic mass communication vehicles. Nevertheless, social media grants the individuals with two-way communication and comfortable and timely feedback.
4. Community: Social media enables communities to be formed on relevant matters or people rapidly and accordingly to build an effective communication.
5. Connectivity: Most of the social media organs are connective. They give links to other sites, sources, and people on the grounds of being user friendly, an advertisement, or any other objective.

Social media has eliminated the restrictions of time and space and has hereby created a platform where sharing, discussing, and being active are highly important. People in social media platforms meet and set a communication. Social media is a combination of technology, telecommunication, and a structure that social communication is built through words, images, and audial files. It is circled with a framework that people may share their stories and experiences in this context. Social media, at the same time, has brought about the concept of "user production content" (Kaplan 2009, p. 59–68).

In another sense, the change of news content has gained a real-time manner (Chin-Fook, Simmonds, 2011, p. 13) and being the first to create information has also become more important. Self-confidence gained by hiding behind a virtual identity has granted individuals with the freedom of expression. Thus, people have found the chance to easily express their thoughts and emotions stuck in the depths of the subconsciousness. Having an opinion and being sincere have become important instead of having a reality and being objective. With the entry of social media in our lives, the means of accession to the news and consuming the news have been dramatically transformed. In addition, the experienced journalists have integrated social media with both their channels of collecting news and their channels of distributing and promoting their works. They have also adapted their methods of news writing, sourcing, and spreading to these changes.

What will distinguish the internet portals, websites of the newspapers, and sources of information on the virtual world from each other in the new media age is the content. The reliability, quality, and content of the news and information produced by everyone at the same speed and with the same sources will gain much more prominence. Besides the role of gatekeeping in controlling the flow of information, activities such as coding, selecting, editing, screening, timing, restricting, and adding have again become more significant (Barzilai-Nahon, 2008: 1496).

The flow of information is maintained through all possible channels and means. Further to that, the larger scale of information is waiting in the greatest information storages to be used once more. The tie between human and information has been torn off and information has been transformed into something that develops randomly at great scales and speed together with various theories separately from a guidance of any other information or a meaning and objective (Postman, 2013, p. 70–71)

Gatekeeping Differences in Conventional and Social Media

Table 1: Gatekeeping differences in conventional and social media

	Conventional Media	**Social Media**
Gate (Transit Point)	A sole gatekeeper for many news types/sources.	Many gatekeepers for many news types/sources.
Gatekeeping Mechanism	Manually done by the editorial mechanism.	Automatically done with software.
Gatekeeper's Identity	On the name of institutions.	On the name of individuals.
Relation (Sender-Receiver)	Sender-gatekeeper	A continuous exchange between sender-receiver.
Information Production	Only the gatekeepers may produce information.	Anyone may produce information.
Political Power	Political power is dominant.	Political power is not requested.
Level of Authority	Editors (specialist's view)	Users (active) (user's view)
Infrastructure Provider	Employer	Network founders determine the flow of information and speed.
Gate Value	Circulation	User and Follow
Flow of Information	Unidirectional	Bilateral

	Conventional Media	Social Media
Information of Identity	Gatekeeper's identity is open.	Gatekeeper may hide its identity.
Cultural Background	Only the elites.	Everyone is equal.
Inspection	National Inspection	Global Inspection

Conclusion

As media is the "the fourth power" and inspecting the rulership on behalf of citizens has been removed due to the changes in mass communication tools, the editorial director of the Le Monde Diplomatique, Ignacio Ramonet has described social media as "the fifth power" with respect to its functions of auditing "the fourth power" media and revealing the distorted news and imperfect information (Ramonet, 2004, p. 3–7). The monopolism of media over the flow of information during the 1970s has been destroyed and converted into a new system thanks to the strengthening of the internet and social media later on.

The main feature of this system is that the information is not distributed from a single centre but is shared by multiple users simultaneously. Changes in the structure of the gatekeepers have transformed the media's function of giving information. Gatekeeping in social media is performed digitally by computer software. While the information is disabled prior to entering into social media, it is disabled on social media after entering into the platform. By this way, citizens may see and even intervene the information that is hidden and disabled from them as they wish. Thus, they may access the information unchanged by the gatekeepers providing the formation of their agenda. However, owing to the effects of social media, media has not only been a source of information, but it has been becoming a centre of coordination as well. The groups who once were solely watching and listening to, for the time being, may gather and talk to each other. Users are not solely consumers anymore but are also producers. Furthermore, whenever a new consumer participates in the platform, a new producer automatically comes along at the same time because the same equipment, telephone, or computer enables people to both consume and produce simultaneously.

Gatekeepers are not so determining on the distribution of information as they were in the past. Everyone has accession to the information regarding what is worthy to be news or not and accordingly, the users may freely make choices on the media within the framework of their wishes and likes. Developments in communication technologies continue at a head spinning speed. Social media, one of these developments that we have recently met, has brought about a new situation during the transmission process of information. As Fournier (1996) states, the end user is one of the most effective gatekeepers and builds a social identity within a community though consumption.

References

Barzilai Nahon, K. (2008). Toward a Theory of Network Gatekeeping: A Framework for Exploring Information Control. *Journal of the American Society for Information Science and Technology.*

Breakenrıdge, D. (2009), PR2.0 New Media, New Tools, New Audiences, New Jersey: FT Press.

Burke, P. (2001). Bilginin Toplumsal Tarihi. İstanbul: Tarih Vakfı Yurt Yayınları, İstanbul.

Büyükşener, Ercüment Türkiye'de Sosyal Ağların Yeri ve Sosyal Medyaya Bakış inet-tr'2009 - XIV. *Türkiye'de İnternet Konferansı Bildirileri* 12–13 Aralık 2009 Bilgi Üniversitesi, İstanbul.

Castells, M. (2013). Enformasyon Çağı: Ekonomi, Toplum ve Kültür, Ağ Toplumunun Yükselişi. Çev: Ebru Kılıç, İstanbul Bilgi Üniversitesi Yayınları, cilt-1, İstanbul.

Chın-Fook, L., Sımmonds H. (2011). "Redefining Gatekeeping Theory for a Digital Generation", *McMaster Journal of Communication* 8:

Çebi, Sadullah, (2002) Haberi Anlamak, Ankara: Gazi Kitabevi.

Herman, Edward S., and Noam Chomsky. Manufacturing Consent: The Political Economy of the Mass Media. Random House, 2008.

Gürsakal, N. (2009) Sosyal Ağ Analizi, Bursa: Dora Yayıncılık. Innovation Networks, European Journal of Innovation Management, Vol. 9, No. 3.

Işık, M. (2002), *Kitle İletişim Sistemleri*, Konya, Eğitim Kitabevi.

Kaplan, Andreas M.; Michael Haenlein (2010) "Users of fhe World, Unite! The Challenges and Opportunities of Social Media". Business Horizons.

Kaya, A. Rasit (1985) Kitle İletisim Sistemleri, Teori yay., Ankara.

Mutlu, Erol: (2008) İletişim Sözlüğü.

Postman, Neil. (2006), Teknopoli-Yeni Dünya Düzeni (Çev. Mustafa Emre Yilmaz). *İstanbul: Paradigma Yayincilik.*

Ramonet, "Beşinci Kuvvet", çev. Y. İnceoğlu, N. Akıner, U. Aydın, (2004) Varlık Dergisi.

Shoemaker, P. J., & Vos, T. (2009). *Gatekeeping theory*. Routledge.

Shoemaker, Pamela J. (1991) Communication Concepts 3: Gatekeeping. 1. baskı, Newbury Park.

Taatıla P. Vesa- Suomala, Jyrki, Sıltala, Reijo- Keskınen, Soili (2006), Framework to Study the Social.

Tekinalp & Uzun, (2008); İletişim Araştırmaları ve Kuramları Beta, İstanbul.

Yurdigül, Yusuf & Zinderen, İ. Etem. (2012) "Yeni Medyada Haber Dili." The Turkish Online Journal of Design, Art and Communication - TOJDAC Volume 2 Issue 3.

Mehmet Oğulcan Turan

The Use of the Images of MOBESE Cameras in Television news: A New Type or Source?*

Introduction

Surveillance, at the simplest level, works as 'surveillance of someone by another one.' Also, according to the broad and comprehensive definition of Clarke (1988), "surveillance is action of observing/monitoring of communication or actions of one person or more people in a systematic way." The main purpose is gathering information about specific individuals and their environment. The secondary purpose is ensuring that people refrain from certain actions and to dissuade them. In order to understand surveillance completely, its relationship with social supervision shouldn't be overlooked. In this regard, as symbolic materials that will be retained by an organisation or community, surveillance that is indicative of supervision of knowledge and activities of ones in lower positions by ones in upper positions is inseparably intertwined with rulership and power relations (Dolgun, 2008, p. 39).

Changes and transformations that surveillance underwent have been shaped through operation logic of rulership mechanisms and techniques used since the period when surveillance occurred. Surveillance activities were based on the fact that tribes, empires, and monarchies showed their powers on population ruled directly and they did this through intense violence and pressure in the first centuries (Dolgun, 2008, p. 37).

Systematic, rational, and relieved violence and pressure tools began to be used in surveillance with the emergence of the modern nations states (Dolgun, 2008, p. 37). The dominance of the capitalist mode of production and the birth of the modern nation state strengthened the central position of rulership and increased spatial abilities of surveillance. In this period, distinction between surveillant and surveilled was sharpened in places such as prisons, hospitals, madhouses, and schools starting from the factory through rulership, mandatory closure, and expert surveillants. These places were fictionalised as places in which social problems would be solved and they became concrete examples of social conditions

* This study is a summary of the master's thesis titled '*The Use of the Images of MOBESE in Television News: A New Type or Source?*'.

undergoing a significant change and restructuring of rulership in centrality of the state (Bauman, 2003, p. 58).

Also, in postmodernism information society, a new era was entered together with improved communication and the use of computer technologies (Dolgun, 2008, p. 37). A person living in this new society leaves electronic traces in his or her business life, shopping, trips, and in many other daily activities and his or her life is stored systematically under recording mechanisms of computer and communication systems (Lyon, 1997, p. 16–17). In this respect, what a person does in a day is recorded independently of his or her own desire and it is kept ready to use "when necessary." This situation shows that surveillance indicates far beyond the definition "monitoring a person who is criminal or suspect." at this point. Therefore, today, spreading and intensification of surveillance brings concerns about going towards a totalitarian surveillance society.

Developments in computer and communication technologies enabled the integration of visual recording technologies with surveillance. As a result, cameras that are used in cinema and television media as recorders turned into devices that are used for providing 'security' of the government such as surveillance systems.

In today's sense, the first camera surveillance application was carried out in the Queen's parade using four security cameras in England in 1956 (Çoban, 2005). Camera surveillance systems that have been used by security forces since the end of the 1960s have shown a significant increase in the last ten years. Imaging in shopping centres, parking spaces, and any kind of public field has turned into part of routine of life in many places of the world from Europe to the United States of America (Ryberg, 2007, p. 127).

The main criticism made about camera surveillance systems is the concern about the violation of surveilled people's privacy (Ryberg, 2007, p. 128). The 'being everywhere at the same time' situation of the cameras is far from being surprising today and in addition to security cameras which are used commonly and became a routine surveillance tool, expansion in monitoring and surveillance activities in electronic communication and internet activities is at a noticeable level (Wacks, 2010, p. 1).

The system that started to be used in England entered into literature as 'Closed-Circuit Television' (CCTV) which is basically "a special video system that is used to monitor an area for the purpose of security or another purpose" (Çapar, 2011, p. 13). These systems generally consist of the following components: "camera, time shift recorder, and control unit" (Çapar, 2011, p. 13).

Although the Mobile Electronic System Integration (MOBESE) system corresponding to CCTV in Turkey began to be used late when it is compared to many other countries, it is seen that it has developed both qualitatively and quantitatively in a very short period of time (Çapar, 2011, p. 1). The 'security' concept creates a legitimacy basis for MOBESE applications in Turkey in the same way as states that have advanced surveillance networks (Çoban, 2008, p. 127).

MOBESE began to be used in the Diyarbakır Provincial Directorate of Security under the administration of the General Directorate of Security, Information Processing Branch Office on 10th of April 2001 and it was not put into service in Mersin, Ankara, and İstanbul until 2005 (Çoban, 2005). It is seen that the system was put into practice quickly after 2005 and it has spread to all provinces as of 2010 (http://www.polisbulteni.com/haber_detay.asp?haberID=478).

One of the prominent features of MOBESE is that it is a mobile application and has the capacity of gathering information of offenses taking place in different times and places together and sharing them in one centre (Çoban, 2005). This feature shows that surveillance technology in Turkey has begun to be used in following data intensively and effectively.

Basically, the MOBESE application is based on monitoring places that are crowded or that people use as transit routes by cameras and recording these images and immediately transferring them to a centre. One of the most important issues to be considered at the operation of this system is the risk of violation of security of personal data and the limits of privacy due to arbitrariness or lack of legal regulations (Eralp, 2006, p. 41). One of the main criticisms related to camera surveillance made in the context of the MOBESE application that is a security concept is 'whether deficiencies in legal regulations are really affective in prevention of crime and violation of privacy and personal liberty rights or not.'

Television channels that have a high level of dependency on images have begun using MOBESE images recorded by security units of the state in the last period. This is a new phenomenon and this is a clear indication of the intersection of surveillance and reporting areas and a change in the field of reporting. In this regard, the use of MOBESE images in television news pointing out a new resource usage requires us to ask this question: "Is it an indicative of a recent news type that can be defined as MOBESE reporting?" In this study, we attempted to reveal basic features of news in which MOBESE images are used starting from the use of MOBESE images recorded for the purpose of "prevention and detection of crime" in television news within the knowledge and permission of the Directorate of Security.

Methods

This study consists of a compilation of significant findings as a summary of a master's thesis bearing the same title. While selection has being made among national television channels that broadcast news bulletins in Turkey, the viewing ratio of news bulletins broadcasted has been determined as a criterion to generalise the sample to the universe. In this respect, according to rating measurements made by independent measurement companies, TNS and SBT (http://www.medyafaresi.com) and three television channels (Show TV, Kanal D, and Fox TV) that have the highest viewing rates have been taken as samples. News in which MOBESE images are used has been determined as an appropriate unit of analysis for the purpose of the study. Study categories have been created by obtaining data from news containing MOBESE camera images that were broadcasted in the main news bulletins of Show TV, Kanal D, and Fox TV between the dates of 01 August 2013 and 31 August 2013. Because the main news bulletins of Show TV dated August 10th and Kanal D dated August 3rd couldn't be reached, 324 news clips under a total of 91 main news bulletins have been reviewed under the created categories. News has been analysed using the content analysis method.

Table 1: Distribution of MOBESE news according to their duration

	Minimum	Maximum	Mean	Standard deviation
Duration of the News	31	302	84.18	35.923

When examining the distribution of news according to their durations, it has been understood that the shortest news segment lasts 31 seconds (sec) and the longest news segment lasts 302 sec. The average duration of a news segment is 84.18 sec. It can be inferred from the average duration of news that most of the news reviewed isn't research-oriented special news that is rich in terms of resources of the incidents because the 84.18 sec. duration is quite a short time for such news.

Table 2: Distribution of MOBESE news according to their subjects

Subject of the News	Number	Percent
Public Peace	228	70.4
Life	28	8.6
Terror-Conflict	27	8.3
Others	41	12.7
Total	324	100.0

When examining the distribution of news according to their subjects, it is seen that public peace themed news is in first place with 70.4%. It is followed by life with 8.6% and terrorism-conflict with 8.3%. The prominence of public peace can be interpreted as news in which MOBESE is used as an image resource based on action. The fact that MOBESE records the moment in which incidents in the news occurs supports this assertion.

Table 3: Distribution of MOBESE news according to newsworthy factors

	Answers		**% Events**
Newsworthy Factors	**Number**	**Percent**	
Consequence	318	29.5	98.5
Human Interest	281	26.1	87.0
Proximity	210	19.5	65.0
Prominence	166	15.4	51.4
Timeliness	102	9.5	31.6
Total	1077	100.0	333.4

According to Table 3 showing the distribution of newsworthy factors, the consequence factor is found in 98.5% of MOBESE news segments, the human interest factor is found in 87% of them, the proximity factor in 65% of them, the prominence factor in 51.4% of them, and the timeliness factor in 31.6% of them. It is normal for the consequence factor to be so high because at the end of the incident, a clip is shown which shows what happens in almost all news. The human interest factor that is in second place as a ratio shows that the interesting aspects of the examined news are highlighted. This result is important for today's understanding of reporting in terms of seeing human interest as a main factor. The fact that the prominence factor that should be primary for news doesn't take place in about half of the news segments shows that this factor is ignored in topic selection and treating and points out that the emphasisis of the importance of issues discussed aren't emphasised. Timeliness, falling furthest behind among newsworthy factors, can be interpreted as the majority of news examined doesn't contain suddenness and freshness breaking news.

Table 4: Distribution of MOBESE news according to number of image repeats

	Answers	
Repetition	**Number**	**Percent**
1	226	30.5
2	150	20.3
3	109	14.7
4	96	13.0
5	64	8.6
6	39	5.3
7	24	3.2
8	12	1.6
9	14	1.9
10	2	0.3
11	2	0.3
12	1	0.1
16	1	0.1
Total	740	100.0

When Table 4 showing how many times images are repeated in the news is reviewed, it is seen that images are displayed more than once at a rate of 69.5%. What is striking is that the number of repetitions reaches up to 16. In general terms, it can be said that the number of repetitions is high. The main reason for this is the fact that MOBESE images are so short that they can't fill the coverage of news.

Table 5: Distribution of visual effects that are used in image resources

	Answers		%
Visual Effects	**Number**	**Percent**	**Events**
Zoom	174	35.7	70.4
Focus	171	35.1	69.2
Deceleration	78	16.0	31.6
Others	64	13.2	26.0
Total	487	100.0	197.2

When the effects that are used in image resources is examined based on intensity, zoom with 70.4% and focus with 692% are in first and second place. These effects have similar effects. Both of them are effects that are used by reporters in order to call the audience's attention to a certain object in the image. It can be said that the attention is attempted to be directed unnaturally in the news reviewed and this situation occurs because the raw incident image is insufficient to explain issues. Apart from these, deceleration is in third place with 31.6%. Deceleration is one of the effects that disturb reality of the incident the most because it fiddles with images' time.

Table 6: Distribution of sound use in MOBESE news

	Answers		% Events
Sound	**Number**	**Percent**	
Perforation	320	48.9	98.8
Natural Sound	268	40.9	82.7
Volume Raising	41	6.3	12.7
Music	7	1.1	2.2
Others	19	2.8	5.8
Total	655	100.0	202.2

When the sound use in the primary video source is examined, it is seen that perforation is used in almost all of the news segments. This is perfectly normal in terms of narration because the images need explanation and background knowledge. Natural sound with 82.7% and volume raising with 12.7% come after it. Even if it doesn't have a very high rate, the fact that volume raising is used in 41 news segments shows that intensity is desired to be brought into the forefront in order for images to gain a sensational nature.

Findings

As a result of this analysis, it is possible to make the following inferences related to news in which MOBESE images are used from the findings obtained:

- Analysed MOBESE news is intensively public peace oriented news such as accidents or crimes. Human interest, one of the newsworthy factors, is fundamental in making news.
- News, of which the majority is public peace themed, has negative contents as long as the elements containing violence such as crimes and accidents are presented repeatedly: The audience is abstracted from the integrity and meaning of the incident.
- While mobility owned by almost all of the MOBESE images and strikingness factors in terms of showing the time of incident became the main factors for the preference of these images in terms of television reporting, it can be said that the fact that the images get all balled up aesthetically is ignored.

- This is the only thing remaining in the hands of reporters in news. It makes news compliant with other news in news bulletins. In this regard, television reporters add visual effects that are disruptive for reality on raw moving incident images that are quite attractive for them. Preferences in use of sound show compatibility with this approach. Temporally and spatially altered images with the use of focus, zoom, and deceleration techniques are transformed into a completely different reality after the addition of the effect of raising sound. All of these techniques remove distance between the audience and the incidents and create an obstacle to make logical inferences focusing on causalities of incidents and cause the audience to enter into the incident and activate their emotions. And consequently, while the audience is being pulled into the accident and violent crime that is unlikely to be experienced exactly by them, the impression that is left on them by the incidents watched is a sort of relief consisting of catharsis based on only pity and being thankful that this hasn't happened to them.
- Consequently, it is not possible to say that MOBESE reporting exists as a type of reporting. However, this can be said that news in which MOBESE images are used is distinguished from other types of news, particularly in terms of resource use.

Discussion

MOBESE reporting stands in a very different point than other reporting styles in terms of the acquisition of intelligence of an issue/incident. In MOBESE news consisting of images that are served by the local unit of the Directorate of Security, the main source of information is the Directorate of Security. In this context, production of MOBESE news makes the reporter dependent on the Directorate of Security as both a news and source of image. This type of news that is so dependent to source causes a decline in the quality of news in addition to reducing the cost of news production. It is not possible to make news without receiving images and permission from this organisation that monopolises images. While this situation is an indicator of resource dependence on the one hand, it lays the problematic aspect of MOBESE reporting bare as the bearer of the state's official discourse on the other hand. Moreover, one of the major problems caused by resource dependency is the difficulty of discussing information and images coming from the state and putting it into a different context that looks after public benefits. As an extension of the passive reporting style that is reduced to the status of the transmitter of information coming from the source of news, incidents in images are presented in the shadow of the official discourse and boundaries are drawn by unites of the state before information and images are served.

Presentment of MOBESE images by the Directorate of Security to reporters holds legislative and legal problems. Statements of authorities from the Department of Security contradict each other and temporary regulations and permissions received from the Chief Public Prosecutor's Offices have a role in presenting to the media. However, as a result, it can be said that there aren't any legal regulations and state institutions that keep its citizens under surveillance for the purpose of "providing security" serves images that they obtain for "raising the awareness of public" arbitrarily. Therefore, the use of MOBESE images without relying on any law is attempted to be legalised with regulations made by the Department of Security.

In consideration of its subject matter, this study that has the distinction of being the first in its field is expected to promote other studies to be made about MOBESE reporting. Making audience oriented reception analysis that lies beyond the scope of the study will mean addressing a different aspect of the subject and will enable the enrichment of literature by revealing different aspects of the subject.

References

Bauman, Z. (2003). *Yasa Koyucular ile Yorumcular.* (Translated by Kemal Atakay). İstanbul: Metis.

Clarke, R. (1988). *Information Technology and Dataveillance.* http://www.rogerclarke.com/DV/CACM88.html, 20.12.2012.

Çapar, S. (2011). *Caddelerde Güvenlik Nöbetindeki Kameralar.* Ankara: Turhan.

Çoban, B. (2008). "Gözün İktidarı" Üzerine. In B. Çoban & Z. Özarslan (Eds.), *Panoptikon: Gözün İktidarı* (pp. 111–137). İstanbul: Su.

Çoban, E. (2005). Ülkemizin Modern Bilgi ve Güvenlik Konsepti Mobese. http://www.caginpolisi.com.tr/47/36-37-38.htm, 28.12.2012.

Dolgun, U. (2008). *Şeffaf Hapishane Yahut Gözetim Toplumu.* İstanbul: Ötüken.

Eralp, Ö. (2006). Şu Mobese Dedikleri, *Bilişim ve Hukuk Dergisi,* 1, 40–41.

Lyon, D. (1997). *Elektronik Göz.* (Translated by Dilek Hattatoğlu). İstanbul: Sarmal.

Ryberg, J. (2007). Privacy Rights, Crime Prevention, CCTV, and the Life of Mrs. Aremac, *Res Publica,* 13, 127–143.

Wacks, R. (2010). *Privacy: A Very Short Introduction.* New York: Oxford University.

Http://www.medyafaresi.com, 02.09.2013.

Http://www.polisbulteni.com/haber_detay.asp?haberID=478, 07.05.2013.

Metin Kasim & Özlem Güleç Kinali

A Study for Measuring Effects of Children Oriented Food Advertisements Broadcasted on Television on Primary School Freshmen

Introduction

The effects of mass media, especially the effects of television on children, are subjects that are constantly discussed. Children are acquainted with television when they are born and this technology becomes an inevitable source of information. Small children might see exaggerated and biased messages in advertisements as accurate and reliable and they might easily believe the information provided. Children are in a vulnerable position in this colourful, sparkly, musical, and animated world.

The people supporting the opinion claiming that children are manipulated by advertisements suggest that children don't have mental structure which will protect them from the effects of messages from advertisements because they don't have the ability to fulfil some mental functions up to age of eight years old.

Children who have learned the purpose of advertisements know that advertisements don't always reflect the truth. However, this situation doesn't completely eliminate their belief to messages of advertisements.

The purpose of this study is to reveal the degree of belief to messages of food and beverage advertisements broadcasted on television, the brand awareness, and the levels of perceiving the harms of foods and beverages of children that are six, seven, and eight years old.

Through this study, the connection between behaviours that children display with the impact of television advertisements will be determined and parents will be allowed to display more consistent behaviours against their children's requests.

As well as children being valuable members of families, they represent the future of the world. A world without children can't be thought of in terms of the future of the world just as a world without advertisements can't be thought of by manufacturers and advertisers. The thing to be done here is to learn how advertisements affect children and what perceiving status children depend on. In this way, children can be protected against the harmful effects of advertisements and we can determine what can be done in this direction.

Methods

A questionnaire was conducted on a total of 200 people consisting of 100 students studying in the first grade at the Şükriye Onsun Elementary School in Selçuklu district of Konya province and 100 people who are the students' parents. The questionnaire was conducted on 100 students consisting of 51 female and 49 male students in the first two weeks of May 2013. Simple random sampling was preferred in the selection of subjects. In the study, the connection between food and beverage advertisements and student's consumption habits has been investigated.

Subjects related to the effects of food and beverage advertisements on children have been examined by reviewing the literature. A three-point Likert-type questionnaire has been found as appropriate to ensure that children can respond more comfortably and that the answers of children and parents can be compared in a correct, valid, and reliable manner. Answers are arranged as follows: one-no, two-sometimes, and three-yes. Questionnaire data were analysed using the SPSS statistics program 17. We attempted to determine the frequency distribution of responses to questions and general tendency with the help of graphics. The harmony between answers of students and parents has been analysed using the chi-square test and the structure of relations has been revealed. In statistical tests, the alpha meaning level has been regarded as 5% and established hypotheses have been tested at the 95% confidence level.

Findings

Positive effects of children have been used through food and beverage advertisements broadcasted on television:

Music, rapid image changes, and repetition in advertisements contribute to children's development exiting them and sticking in their minds. Again, children's knowledge about the object of consumption increases with the help of brand image related to a product or service strengthening colour, names, and shape memories with a commercial message (Ertunç, 2011:38).

Under favour of some advertisements, children remember that they should brush their teeth, wash their hands before leaving the bathroom, and drink milk and eat yogurt because they are healthy once again: Advertisements are educational and and a reminder with this aspect (Karaca et al., 2007:239). Furthermore, advertisements where numbers and colours take part in and have educational aspects are also seen. For example, Vodafone and the colour red. Advertisements in which religious and national holidays take part in strengthen children's knowledge about these important days.

Traditional images belonging to Turks like Rumi of Konya can be transferred to children through television advertisements (Şimşek, 2006:175). Sultans of Turks who they are proud of and Atatürk who is the hero of war of independence might be included in these images.

As well as advertisements being used as tools to transfer cultural values to children, they can also transfer values that are strange for that community or are accepted by a small part of the target audience at the same time. For example, while a child of a house is learning to say "god bless your hands" or "enjoy your meal," besides this, it transfers a new value by the way of receiving a product from older people and giving it to younger people and it contributes to being accepted by society in time. Another factor that is transferred to the children in advertisements is gender role. Children can learn a number of gender roles that will be expected from them and they will have to play in these roles in the future. Advertisements transfer information about family relationships and role models to children (Asena, 2009:5).

Negative effects of children have been used through food and beverage advertisements broadcasted on television:

Because of the reason that eight-year-old children and children under the age of eight years are not able to evaluate critically, they see exaggerated and biased messages as accurate and reliable and they tend to believe them. This situation may cause drawbacks for children in terms of development being influenced by advertisements such as falling into an unhealthy nutritional habit, conflicting with their parents developing unreasonable demands about certain products, and leaving their parents in a difficult economic situation (istanbulparentingclass.com).

Concerns of parents about the effects of children oriented advertisements have increased within the last ten years. For children, having advertised products being influenced by advertisements became the focus of discussions. In many countries including ours, there are many laws and regulations about the effects of advertisements on children. Advertisements in Turkey are inspected by the Advertising Board of the Ministry of Industry and Trade, the Radio and Television Supreme Council, and the Advertising Self-Regulatory Board: These organisations attempt to protect children from the negative effects of advertisements (Bilim and Teknik, Mayıs 2011: 69).

Television advertisements may lead to deterioration in language. For example, çilak (strawbarry) instead of çilek (strawberry), portıkal (orınge) instead of saying (orange), and yiyin artık (eat now) instead of saying yiyin gari (eat meow) might be used by children modeling what they have seen in advertisements. In addition to this, the use of children in advertisements may mislead children. Advertisements in which children who open and close the refrigerator constantly contribute to children becoming rebellious: Examples include children saying things like "I can't do that, I don't have hands" in helping their mother, violating school rules, and objecting to their teachers (Karaca et al., 2007: 239) Advertisements served with the slogan "It is nice to be contaminated with Omo" are a bad example for children.

Problems such as inactivity, fatigue, lack of concentration, and marginalisation of the reading habit appear in children who spend too much time in front of the screen. In addition, child who memorise messages offered by television programs without questioning repeat discourses and movements that they like, then they accept them, and finally they practice them (Çetin, 2005: 461). Said preferences may lead to parent-child conflicts that develop in association with socio-economic background (Ertunç, 2011: 38).

Today's sociologists and communication scientists settle on opinion about the fact that standing in a circle of advertisements starting from a very young age may affect children negatively. Moreover, children who develop consumer identity meetings with television advertisements at early ages will not be able to gain accurate and beneficial eating and drinking habits. The misleading nature and non-necessity of products that children consume will harm the economic interests of family and children's health. Besides this, they will turn into materialistic, selfish people who ignore social values and can't be restricted (Pembecioğlu, 2006: 327).

Discussion

The roles and efficiency of children in both the family economy and the national economy increase day by day. Children become targets of advertisers and manufacturers place advertisements with these aspects. Depending on these cases, advertisers increase their spending in the promotion of products for children and provide infrastructure for effective advertising techniques. Together with diversification of products and services, as a natural result of the increase of advertising for children, legal regulations, restrictions, and measures taken are inevitable (Ertunç, 2011: 75).

To the question "Is everything said in television advertisement true?," 17.6% of eight-year-old children, 29.2% of seven-year-old children, and 36.4% of six-year-old children said yes. According to these rates, as long as age increases, the level of consciousness increases and the rate of believing the accuracy of advertisement messages decreases.

To the question of whether or not advertisements are challenging, 29% of children said no, 19% of children said sometimes, and 52% of children said yes. Therefore, more than half of the children find advertisements challenging.

To the question of whether or not they want foods and beverages that they see in advertisements, 25% of children said no, 27% of children said sometimes, and 48% of children said yes. When the yes and sometimes options are combined, it shows that 75% of children want to try foods and beverages that they see in advertisements. This indicates how advertisements are effective for children.

When children are asked whether they want to have foods and beverages that they see on advertisement, while 14% of them said no, 9% of them said sometimes, and an overwhelming majority (77%) said yes. In this case, parents have difficulty in making a selection among child's requests, their own budgets, and their logic.

With the influence of food television advertisements, the most demanded products by children to be purchased are chocolate, chips, biscuits, candy, wafers, chewing gum, cornflakes, milk and dairy products, yoghurt, pudding, ice cream, delicatessen products, juice, and fizzy drinks (Çetin, 2005: 461). However, due to additives that these products contain, many diseases such as cancer threaten our children.

To the question "Do you insist and want to purchase the advertised product that you want to have if it is a product that your parents don't allow?," 79% of children said no, 5% said sometimes, and 16% said yes. Unfortunately, in practice, these rates can be reversed and children might be more insistent to make their parents purchase what they want.

Television advertisements may unnecessarily increase children's desire of consumption and the objection of parents may result in family-child conflicts. On the other hand, 24% of children said no, 3% said sometimes, and 73% said yes to the question "Do you love your parents more if they purchase advertised foods and beverages that you want?" The fact that a significant value like loving parents is indexed to chocolate, wafers, chewing gum, or fruit juice is another indicator of advertisement's power of influencing children.

51% of children said no, 6% said sometimes, and 43% said yes to the question "Do you want the same brand of foods and beverages that you see in advertisements while shopping?" When we look at the status of recognising brands of products according to ages of children, it has been determined that 47.7% of eight-year-old children, 44.4% of seven-year-old children, and 27.3% of six-year-old children recognised brands. As we understood from here, the ability to recognise brands increases proportionally with age.

4% of children said no, 4% said sometimes, and 92% said yes to the question "May some of the advertised foods and beverages be harmful?" Even if this high rate makes us think that children are very conscious, their desire to eat and drink these products despite everything shows that they can't make logical decisions.

33% of children said no, 10% said sometimes, and 57% said yes to the question "Would you like to be in the shoes of children who act in a commercial film and behave like them?" 33% of children said no, 14% said sometimes, and 53% said yes to question "Do you want to purchase foods and beverages in advertisements where cartoon characters take part in more than other foods and beverages?" According to results from here, advertisements that are made through cartoon or game characters are quite effective in directing children.

17.6% of eight-year-old children, 4.2% of seven-year-old children, and 0% of six-year-old children said yes to the question "Do you purchase food or beverage that you see in advertisements that you like without getting permission from your family?" As it is understood from here, as long as age increases, children tend to purchase what they want more comfortably. Of course, it is important to know how much money is given to children at which age and how shopping freedom is granted to them.

It is important for adults to know how children who are exposed to psychological, social, and cultural effects of television advertisements give meaning to advertisements and how they position them in their world. Children who create the most important mass of advertisements recognise advertisement jingles, watch advertisements that they know cheeringly, and dance before they start talking. It is a known fact that children who are open to harmful messages of advertisement before completing their mental development have an effect on directing their parents towards consumption. Because of this reason, children's value judgments, presentation of elements related to feelings, and behaviours should be considered while advertisements are being fictionalised. In addition, the regulations about television advertisements are unquestionably gaining importance. There are a lot of parents who don't have a lot of knowledge about this subject and whose consumer awareness has not developed enough. Legal regulations should be introduced to these parents, children, and teens. A media literacy lesson should be included in the education curriculum with certain topics from the first grade of primary school.

References

Asena, Melike Başak (2009). Gıda Reklamlarının Okul Öncesi Çocuklar Üzerindeki Etkilerinin Anneler Tarafından Değerlendirilmesi, (Yayınlanmış Yüksek Lisans Tezi), Bahçeşehir Üniversitesi, Sosyal Bilimler Enstitüsü, İstanbul.

Badur, Fadime (2007). Televizyon Reklamlarının Çocukların Marka Farkındalığı Üzerindeki Etkisi: Yiyecek ve İcecek Reklamları Üzerine Bir Uygulama,

(Yayınlanmış Yüksek Lisans Tezi), Atatürk Üniversitesi, Sosyal Bilimler Enstitüsü, Erzurum.

Bilim ve Teknik Dergisi, Mayıs 2011.

Çetin, Cem (2005). Televizyon Reklamlarının Çocuklar Üzerindeki Etkisi ve Ortaya Çıkan Sorunlar: Obezite ve Hareketsizlik Televizyon Çocukları Hareketsizleştiriyor Mu, 2. Uluslararası Çocuk ve İletişim Kongresi, İstanbul Üniversitesi İletişim Fakültesi Yayını.

Elden Müge ve Ulukök Özkan (2006). Çocuklara Yönelik Reklamlarda Denetim ve Etik, Ege Üniversitesi, İletişim Fakültesi, Küresel İletişim Dergisi, sayı 2.

Ertunç, Filiz (2011). Çocuk Dünyasında Reklamın Rolü: Televizyon Reklamlarında Çocuklara Yönelik Düzenlemeler, (Uzmanlık Tezi), Radyo ve Televizyon Üst Kurulu, Ankara.

Gökbulut, Hasret (2006). Televizyon Reklamlarının Toplumsal Roller Pekiştirmesi, (Yayınlanmış Yüksek Lisans Tezi), Gazi Üniversitesi, Sosyal Bilimler Enstitüsü, Ankara.

Gültekin Bilgehan ve Yıldız Elif (2009). İletişimde Çocuk Figürü, Yıldız Nobel Yayıncılık, Ankara. http://www.istanbulparentingclass.com/makaleler.php?id=31.

Işık Metin, Erdem Ayhan, Güllüoğlu Özlem ve Akbaba Ebru (2007). Televizyon ve Çocuk, Eğitim Kitabevi Yayınları, Konya.

İşcibaşı, Yaprak. (2001), Televizyondaki Şiddetin Çocuklar Üzerindeki.

Kapferer, Jean Noel (1991). Reklam Ve Çocuk, Afa Yayınları, İstanbul. Onur Bekir (1999). Cumhuriyet ve Çocuk, II.Ulusal Çocuk Kültürü Kongresi, Çocuk Kültürü Araştırma ve Uygulama Merkezi Yayınları No: 2.

Karaca Yusuf, Pekyaman Asuman ve Güney Hatice (2007). Ebeveynlerin.

Oktay, Ayla (1990). Ana Baba Okulu, Remzi Kitabevi, İstanbul.

Pembecioğlu, Nilüfer (2006). İletişim ve Çocuk, Ebabil Yayıncılık, Ankara.

Saldırganlık Etkisi (Amerikan Örneği), Anadolu Üniversitesi, İletişim Bilimleri, Kurgu Dergisi, Sayı: 18.

Sönmez, Sezin (2006). 7–12 Yaş Arasındaki Çocukların Aile Satın Alma Kararına Etkisi Üzerine Bir Araştırma, (Yayınlanmış Yüksek Lisans Tezi), Sakarya Üniversitesi Sosyal Bilimler Enstitüsü, Sakarya.

Şimşek, Sedat (2006). Reklam ve Geleneksel İmgeler, Nüve Kültür Merkezi Yayınları, İstanbul.

Taşkıran. Nurdan (2005) Büyülü Reklamlar, Çocuklara Mesajlar; Yetişkin Reklamlarına Çocuk Gözü İle Bakış, 2. Uluslararası Çocuk ve İletişim Kongresi "İletişimin Çocuğa Etkisi", İstanbul Üniversitesi İletişim Fakültesi Yayını.

Tokgöz, Oya (1979). Televizyon Reklamları ve Çocuklar, Ankara Üniversitesi, Siyasal Bilgiler Fakültesi Dergisi Yayınları, Cilt: XXXIV.

Tosun, Nurhan Zeynep (1991). Çocuklara Yönelik Reklamların Etkileri ve Bir Araştırma, (Yayınlanmamış Doktora Tezi), Marmara Üniversitesi, Sosyal Bilimler Enstitüsü, İstanbul.

Murat Kocyigit & M. Nejat Ozupek

Personality Factors that Affect the Use of Facebook: A Research Study on University Students

Introduction

Personality Factors and the Use of Facebook

When we look at the studies examining the relationship between personality traits and social media, we can see a continuous increase of studies on the interaction between Facebook usage habits and individuals' personality. In this study, we primarily focused on personality factors and social media concepts. Furthermore, we then aimed to examine the relationship between personality traits and the use of Facebook. In the last part of research study, findings and conclusions are given.

Personality Factors

Personality is the unique factors that affect a person's feelings, thinking, and behaviour. Constantly, under the influence of internal and external stimuli, personality includes the individual's biological, psychological, genetic, and all acquired abilities; motives; feelings; desires; habits; and all behaviours.

Briefly, it is possible to see the formation of innate properties and environmental impact in human personality. Here, by taking into account environmental effects, not only in people's individual-specific features, but a certain extent in human society, it can be concluded that it reflects some common features of humans in a certain extent (Tınar, 1999).

Personality is a name that is loaded by time to people a biological and social characteristics, also within a certain time it continuity protects the psychological behaviour in the (thoughts, feelings, and actions in the) differences and partnerships all of the defining trends and character.

In this definition, there is an approach to personality theory as a general behaviour theory, instead of some similar characteristics of humans even having common; it is also noted that there are differences in other parts and as time goes by, personality traits change (Hellriegel et al., 1989).

Many studies have been conducted to determine the size of personality traits. In these analyses, it has been observed that the factor model of personality number varies between three and seven (Salgado et al., 2001). In his study based on the five-strong factor adjectives in the dictionary, Goldberg (1981) suggested that many personality traits could be theoretically organised within the framework's five factors.

Costa and McCrae (1985) developed a scale under the five-factor personality traits based on specific attributes. Somer et al. (2002) have developed an inventory to measure normal personality traits under the five-factor model of personality that has sub-dimensions. The five-factor model of personality that is the basis for our study and has been developed by McCrae and John (1992) can be briefly summarised as follows:

Factor I - Extraversion: This factor's features are lively, exciting, cheerful, talkative, and sociable and includes being social. Extraversion is related to relations and more people are associated with the amount of social stimuli. In addition, sociability and loving being with people, entertainment, love, leadership, power, and friendliness features such as willingness represent this factor.

Factor II - Docility-Conciliation (Agreeableness): On the positive side of this factor, gentle, subtle, respectful, safe, flexible, openhearted, and compassionate are included features. Accommodating in size is a key factor in interpersonal relations. This affects a person's self-perception and the development of social attitudes, as well as his or her ability to develop a philosophy of life (Costa, McCrae, and Dye, 1991). Researchers define this factor with honesty, helpfulness, compliance/obedience, humility, and compassion.

Factor III - Integrity-Self Control (Conscientiousness): Costa, McCrae, and Dye (1991) have indicated that this factor has both promoter and supportive aspects. They have also mentioned that prior to defining this factor, they thought of the direction concept. While the progressive side of the factor can be seen with the need for achievement and commitment to work, the supportive side of the factor can be seen with prudence moral and providence. To represent this factor, competence, order, rigor, work-addict, achievement striving, self-discipline, and prudence properties are expressed.

Factor IV - Emotional Imbalance-Neuroticism (Neuroticism): This factor, as described in various studies, includes traits such as anxious, insecure, dealing with it, self-pitying, anger, anxious, nervous, irritable, unstable, helpless, vulnerable, and fragile. Costa and McCrae (1985) pointed out that many research studies have the same idea on the basis of emotional instability, anxiety, depression, anger, anxiety, and other negative emotions.

In some other research studies, emotional instability, irrational thoughts, and the illustration of the lack of coping mechanisms are explained. People who have a high score on the emotional instability factor are often forced to deal with complex emotions, such as delusional thoughts and hostile reactions which can be applied to inappropriate coping mechanisms (Amirkhan, Rising and Swickert, 1995; Matthews, Derryberry and Siegle, 2000).

Factor V - Clearance (Openness): Researchers have reached the least consensus on the fifth factor in the model. This factor has been called intelligence by some researchers, culture by others, and openness to experience by some. The defining characteristics of the factor are traits such as analytical, complex, curious, independent, creative, liberal, non-traditional, original, imaginative, broad interests, brave, change-loving, artistic, and open-minded.

Social Network Platform: Facebook

Individuals within the limits specified in a system ring a semi/open profile to create the connection as in other users' list explicitly grant to that other users on the system listed links to see, and among them a ride to allow web-based services are called social networks (Ellison, 2007). As in the rest of the world, Facebook, which is a social networking platform, has the most users in Turkey. Within the social networking site Facebook, which has a very different place, the best of online communication opportunities are offered to the user. As in the rest of the world, when we look at Facebook, which has become a craze in Turkey, Turkey has 30 million users and is the third country after the United States of America (USA) and the United Kingdom (UK) with the most Facebook users.

According to a study conducted in Turkey, the use of Facebook can change according to age, gender, and socio-economic status. Facebook has been observed as a part of users' everyday practices and a place that they visit whenever they want, spend their leisure time, expand rather than control existing friendships to continue as an instrument, and use their own information on the check thought; therefore, it limits itself on the frame of publicness and sharing with friends, rather than experiencing the forefront of surveillance (Sener, 2009).

Another factor that affects the use of Facebook is user personality. Individuals' personalities that reveal an active social life can be similar with personalities in the online environment.

The Relationship Between Personality Traits and Facebook Use

According to the theoretical model developed by Ross et al. (2003), the relationship between personality traits with the use of Facebook is required to explain situational variables that have an effect on personality traits. According to this theoretical model, it has been proposed that Facebook usage patterns significantly differ from each other only in individuals that have certain personality traits.

One of the theoretical assumptions of the model is determined by two mechanisms that interact with each other, the relationship between personality and the Facebook user. The first of these "computer-based communication" tendencies, personality traits associated with situational stimuli and certain personality traits, reflect the more intensive use by the users of Facebook. The person that has the neurotic personality (neuroticism) that is included in the five factors has been found to have more intense desires for online social support. Besides, they also do not share personally identifiable information on Facebook and they spend too much time on Facebook.

The other online social networking trend is observed more intensely in some personality traits. In the research model, outbound (extraversion) individuals who have personality traits are more susceptible to socialise. The study revealed that there is not a significant relationship between conciliation, honesty factors, and Facebook use habits.

Methods

In this study that examines the relationship between personality traits with the use of Facebook, working groups, data collection tools, and data analysis was used.

Working Group and Application

The samples of the research study are from 488 university students from the following universities: Gümüshane Public Relations, Publicity Konya Selcuk, Necmettin Erbakan, and Kayseri Erciyes. As a measurement tool, questionnaires were used.

Data Collection Tools

In this study, to measure personality traits that affect the use of Facebook, the NEO five-factor inventory developed by Costa and McCrae (1985) was used. This inventory consists of 34 items and is intended to measure "extraversion," "emotional instability (neuroticism)," and "openness" personality dimensions located in the five-factor model of personality. Conciliation and integrity factors located in the five-factor Inventory are not valid and reliable measurement tools so they are not included in this study related variables with these personality traits. Responses of the inventory to the statements in the articles range from "strongly disagree" to "totally agree" on a five-point scale.

Research Questions

Investigations underlying the study questions are as follows:

1) With respect to extraversion (extraversion), how is the use of individual's Facebook habits affected?
2) With respect to neurotic (neuroticism), how is the use of individual's Facebook habits affected?
3) Wit respect to openness (openness), how is the use of individual's Facebook habits affected?

Data Analysis and Interpretation

The above measurement tools for the analysis of the data collected through data collection have been entered into the data processing program. Upon completion of data entries for the purposes of the study, data were analysed using statistical techniques. In this study, the personality factors and variables that affect the relationship between Facebook usage were analysed using Pearson's correlation coefficient.

Findings

In the study, descriptive analysis of the variables, the correlation between variables, and the results are shown in Tables 1–3.

Table 1: Results related to demographic characteristics (N=488)

	Size	Value	Number	Percent
Gender	Female	207	42.4	
	Male	281	57.6	
	Total	488	100.0	
Age	16–20	120	24.6	
	21–25	359	73.6	
	26–30	7	1.4	
	30+	2	0.4	
	Total	488	100.0	
Income	500 TL	250	51.2	
	501–1000	180	36.9	
	1001–1500	36	7.4	
	1501–2000	12	2.5	
	2000+	10	2.0	
	Total	488	100.0	
University	SÜ	201	41.2	
	ERÜ	123	25.2	
	GÜ	139	28.5	
	NEÜ	25	5.1	
	Total	488	100.0	

The demographic characteristics of the respondents are given in Table 1. 207 of the respondents are women (42.4%) and 281 are men (57.6%). The distribution of respondents by age and income level, considering the 73.6% in the 21–25 age range, income distribution is taken into consideration, 51.2% in the range of $ 500 and six are abundant. Research study participants analysed according to their universities are as follows: Selcuk University with 201 participants (41.2%), Erciyes University with 123 participants (25.2%), Gümüshane University with 139 participants (28.5%), and Necmettin Erbakan University with 25 participants (5.1%).

Table 2: Results related with Facebook account

Do you have a Facebook Account?	Number	Percent
Yes	447	91.6
No	41	8.4
Total	488	100.0

When we look at the survey results, 447 participants (91.6%) currently have a Facebook account and 41 participants (8.4%) do not. This shows that Facebook has a very intensive use of among students as a social media tool.

Table 3: Correlation analysis between personality traits and Facebook use

	Extraversion	1	2	3	4
Pearson Correlation		0.295**	131**	0.227**	0.259**
Sig (2-tailed)		0.000	0.006	0.000	0.000
N	447	447	447	447	447
	Openness	**1**	**2**	**3**	**4**
Pearson Correlation		0.357	186**	0.332**	0.307**
Sig (2-tailed)		0.000	0.000	0.000	0.000
N	447	447	447	447	447
	Neuroticism	**1**	**2**	**3**	**4**
Pearson Correlation		0.246**	0.234**	0.174**	218**
Sig (2-tailed)		0.000	0.000	0.000	0.000
N	447	447	447	447	447

When "correlation" analysis between personality traits variables and Facebook usage variables are considered, the variables that measure the use of Facebook among the variables of personality traits and outward positive and significant ($p < 0.01$) relationships were identified. The highest relationship in the correlation analysis is for "commenting on other people's photos" with 0.295 ($p < 0.01$) and the lowest relationship on the other hand is for "between sending a message to other people's walls and outward personality trait" with 0.131 ($p < 0.01$). In other words, people who have outward personality traits intensively use commenting on other people's photographs (1), sending a message to their walls (2), checking their walls (3), and sharing photo (4).

Positive and significant relationships between variables that measure the use of Facebook and the variables of personality traits were identified ($p < 0.01$). The highest relationship in the correlation analysis is for "commenting on other people's photos" with 0.357 ($p < 0.01$) and the lowest relationship on the other hand is for "sending a message to other people's walls" and the personality trait of openness with 186 ($p < 0.01$). In correlation analysis, people who have the personality trait of openness intensively use commenting on other people's photos on Facebook, sending messages on the walls, checking their walls, and sharing photo.

Between neuroticism and the use of Facebook, a positive and significant (p <0.01) relationship was determined. The highest correlation in the correlation analysis is for "commenting on other peoples' photos" with 0.246 (p <0.01) and the lowest relationship on the other hand is for "checking their walls with" with 174 (p <0.01) personality trait was observed between Outward. As a result of correlation analysis, individuals who have neurotic personality traits use Facebook intensively to comment on other people's photos, send messages on walls, check their walls, and share photos. It has been proclaimed that individuals who have neurotic personality traits tend to spend too much time on Facebook; however, they share very little. In this study, it has been identified that individuals with neurotic personality traits spend too much time on Facebook, but they do not share as well as other people.

Discussion

One of the most important findings obtained in this study, with the use of Facebook in personality traits interact with each other. Research indicates the results of correlation analysis of these results.

The results of this research study are similar with research that was applied previously to explain the relationship between personality traits and Facebook use and it is obvious that when valid and reliable measurement tools are used, personality traits greatly affect Facebook usage (Ross et al. 2009). However, in previous studies revealed that the five personality factors included in the other personality factors Conciliation and Integrity factors of individuals online socialising and Facebook usage patterns to measure valid and reliable measurement tools available for this research, these personality traits related to variables not included.

According to the results of the analysis, individuals who have extroverted personality traits use Facebook intensively for sharing photos. Commenting on other people's photos is the least common feature that is used.

Individuals who have the openness personality trait use the commenting application more intensively. People with this personality trait write messages on other peoples' walls the least. Individuals that have neurotic personality features intensively comment on other people's photos. The lowest one is to control their own walls. The interesting point here is that individuals who have the openness personality trait use commenting other people's photos than others.

While individuals who have neurotic personality traits write messages application on other people's walls more frequently compared to other personality traits, very few are controlling their wall. At the same time, they use the sharing application the least.

This also shows that individuals who have neurotic personality traits are more eager to follow than share. In other words, individuals with neurotic personality traits, disguising themselves more than others, prefer to follow what others do.

According to the results of the analysis, individuals who have extroverted personality traits use Facebook intensively for sharing photos. Commenting on other people's photos is the least common feature that is used.

Individuals that have neurotic personality features intensively comment on other people's photos. The lowest used feature is to control their own walls. The interesting point here is that individuals who have the openness personality trait comment on other people's photos more frequently than others. While individuals who have neurotic personality traits write messages on other people's walls more frequently compared to other personality traits, very few are controlling their wall. At the same time, they use the sharing application the least.

References

Amirkhan, J. H., Risinger, R. T., & Swickert, R. J. (1995). Extraversion: A Hidden Personality Factor in Coping, *Journal of Personality*, (63) 2, 188–212.

Costa, P. T. & McCrae, R. R. (1985). *The NEO Personality Inventory Manual*. Odessa, FL: Psychological Assessment Resources.

Costa, P. T., McCrae, R. R., & Dye, D. A. (1991). Facet Scales for Agreeableness and Conscientiousness; A Revision of the NEO Personality Inventory. *Personality and Individual Differences*, (12) 9, 887–898.

Ellison, N. B. (2007). Social network sites: Definition, history, and scholarship. *Journal of Computer-Mediated Communication*, 13(1), 210–230.

Goldberg, L. R. (1981). Language and Individual Differences: The Search for Universals in Personality Lexicons. In L. Wheeler (Ed.) *Review of Personality and Social Psychology* (Vol.2, pp. 141–165). Beverly Hills, CA: Sage.

Hellriegel D., Slocum J. W., Woodman R. W. (1989). *Organizational Behaviour*. Fifth Edition, West Publishing Company.

Matthews, G., Derryberry, D., & Siegle, G. J. (2000). Personality and Emotion: Cognitive Science Perspectives. *Advances in Personality Psychology*. (Ed.) S. E., Hampson, Psychology Press Ltd., East Sussex.

McCrae, R. R., & John, O. P. (1992). An Introduction to the Five-Factor Model and Its Applications. *Journal of Personality*, Vol. 60 Issue 2, 175–215.

Ross, C., Orr, E. S., Sisic, M., Arseneault, J. M., Simmering, M. G., & Orr, R. R. (2009). Personality and motivations associated with Facebook use. *Computers in Human Behavior*, 25(2), 578–586.

Salgado, J. F., Viswesvaran, C. & Ones, D. S. (2001). Predictors Used for Personnel Selection: An Overwiev of Constructs, Methods and Techniques. In N. Anderson, D. S. Ones, H. K. Sinangil & C. Viswesvaran (Ed.), *Handbook of Industrial Work and Organziational Psychology* (Vol. 1; p. 165–199). London, SAGE Publication.

Somer, O., Korkmaz, M. ve Tatar, A. (2002). Beşli Faktör Kişilik Envanteri'nin Geliştirilmesi-I: Ölçek ve Alt Ölçeklerin Oluşturulması. *Türk Psikoloji Dergisi*, 17(49), 21–33.

Şener, G. (2009). Türkiye'de Facebook Kullanımı Araştırması. inet-tr'09 - XIV. *Türkiye'de İnternet Konferansı Bildirileri*, 12–13 Aralık 2009 Bilgi Üniversitesi, İstanbul. 33–41.

Tınar, M. Y. (1999). *Çalışma Yaşamı ve Kişilik*. MESS Mercek Dergisi, Yıl:4, Sayı:14, 92–97.

Murat Yetkin & Yaşar Yiğit Kaçmaz

Do We Need Mobile Applications in Tourism: Case of Alanya

Introduction

Humankind is a being who needs to continuously gather information. Tourism, as a set of activities, is one of the leading areas where information collecting reaches its utmost level. Traveller's information search process, especially those who travel internationally for their holiday to a destination which they have not previously visited, commences in the pre-trip phase as a form of destination choice, purchasing the holiday, and finding out more about the benefits offered by the chosen destination. It continues during the trip to explore the place efficiently. After the travel is completed, by another saying, in the post-trip phase, the role of travellers changes direction and they become information providers rather than searchers. While word of mouth, defined as the recommendation of friends-relatives, and tour operators were the main information sources before the internet era, online travel search has replaced them. The traveller of the present time reaches an almost unlimited amount of information about the destinations and communicates with peers at all stages of the trip through travel 2.0 tools. Nowadays, mobile appliances like smart mobile phones and tablets are used more and more by travellers, particularly during the trip phase; this coincides with the recent advances in ubiquitous computing and wireless networking technologies that facilitate the efficient delivery of rich multimedia content to mobile devices (Biuk-Aghai et al., 2008, p. 1).

In the literature review, it is noted that there is no unanimous definition of mobile tourism. According to Rodriguez-Sanchez et al. (2013, p. 4154), it contains mobile applications developed to provide information to tourists. Brown & Chalmers defined mobile tourism as a field that compounds the information search of a tourist with the services offered through mobile appliances (2003, from Kenteris et al., 2010, p. 840). Schwinger et al. (2005, p. 1) draws attention to the role of mobile applications as an extended information source that is especially beneficial during the trip stage. Mobile applications, as the main part of mobile tourism, allows mobile users to re-plan their itineraries and retrieve revised recommendations during their trips. "*Such capability is crucial since a traveler may wish to obtain a new recommendation depending on the latest situation/availability of the tourist spots*" (Biuk-Aghai et al., 2008, p. 1). M-tourism tools also play an important role to enrich the holiday by providing deeper information on the physical environment through augmented reality applications (Yovcheva et al., 2012, p. 63).

According to E-marketer data, the number of mobile phone users will reach 4.55 billion by the end of 2014. The share of smart phones are 38% of the total. It is predicted that half of the mobile phones will be smart phones by the end of 2017 (emarketer.com).

According to Max Starkov's report, there is a massive shift from desktop to mobile devices and in the first six months of 2014, nearly 16% of bookings and 19% of room nights came from tablets and mobile phones (hebsdigital.com). Another research study, as a confirmation of the former, reveals that 20% of the total purchase of two major tourism product component, transportation and accommodation, were realised through mobile devices. Furthermore, 37% of travellers globally access the internet via their smart phones during their trip (mdgadvertising.com).

Methods

This exploratory research study aims to reveal the mobile device usage habits of tourists who visit Alanya, a major Turkish mass tourism destination. The research study also aims to define intensified areas of needed information by tourists in the destination during their holiday. The data were collected from tourists, regardless of nationality, at nine all-inclusive hotels in Alanya during August 2014 through a self-administered questionnaire. A total of 400 questionnaire were distributed, using the convenience sampling technique. A total of 159 usable surveys were collected, giving a response rate of 39.75%. 46 respondents stated that they do not use a smart phone so only 113 questionnaires were analysed.

Findings

Table 1 provides the profie of the respondents. Among 113 survey respondents, there were slightly more males than females. 67.9% of the respondents are highly educated (university or master's degree) and 32.1% have high school degrees. The majority of participants are in the 18–32 year age group, representing almost 68% of the total. The respondents are mainly from Europe. The results of the number of visits to Alanya reconfirm the maturity of Alanya as a touristic destination. Almost 40% of the respondents have visited the destination four times or more. 96% of the respondents access the internet via their mobile devices during holiday and 78% use mobile applications. This result is higher than the generally indicated numbers in reports but might be explained by the age group of the respondents.

Table 1: Demographic variables

Gender	**n**	**%**	**Number of Visits**	**n**	**%**
Female	54	49.5	1 time	34	30.1
Male	55	50.5	2–3 times	34	30.1
Education	n	%	4–6 times	20	17.7
High School	36	32.1	7 +	25	22.1
University and Master	76	67.9	**Accessing the Internet via Mobile Device**	n	%
Age	n	%	Yes	112	99.1
18–25 age	48	42.5	No	1	0.9
26–32 age	29	25.7	**Using Mobile Phone During Holiday**	n	%
33–40 age	20	17.7	Yes	110	97.3
41 +	16	14.2	No	3	2.7
Nationality	n	%	**Accessing the Internet During Holiday**	34	16.7
Germany	23	20.4	Yes	108	95.6
Holland	23	20.4	No	5	4.4
Sweden	27	23.9	**Using Mobile Applications**		
Others*	40	35.4	Everyday	88	77.9
			Frequently	17	15.0
			From time to time	8	7.1
* Russia, Finland, Denmark, England, Belgium, America, Philippines					

The four statements indicated in Table 2 provide information on participants' general attitudes towards the use of technology. Half of the respondents are satisfied with the information supplied by the tour operator, although they stated that some additional information might be needed. The majority of the respondents (60%) also stated that they use mobile applications during their holiday as an information source. 63% of the participants trust the information supplied by these applications.

Table 2: Use of technology

Statements		I Totally Disagree	I Disagree	I Neither Agree Nor Disagree	I Agree	I Totally Agree
The tour operator provides all the information that I need during my holiday.	n	6	4	43	44	10
	%	5.6	3.7	40.2	41.1	9.3
I need additional information sources apart from the tour operator during my holiday.	n	4	14	42	35	12
	%	3.7	13.1	39.3	32.7	11.2
I use mobile applications as an information source during my holiday.	n	6	15	23	53	13
	%	5.5	13.6	20.9	48.2	11.8
I trust the information provided by mobile applications during my holiday.	n	3	5	32	57	12
	%	2.8	4.6	29.4	52.3	11.0

Table 3 shows the scores of 21 statements divided in seven information categories, as follows: shopping, historical places, food & beverage, entertainment, public places, destination facilities, and daily excursions. Each category has been divided into three sub-categories as general information, location information, and consumer reviews about the place or activity. The highly scored statements are on the food & beverage places and entertainment in a row. Information on shopping facilities are the least scored. The results of the sub-categories indicate that general and location information are more valued that consumer reviews for the respondents. According to the results, the importance level attributed and usage frequency of each statement are in accord.

Table 3: Importance level and usage frequency of mobile applications

Not Important At All n %	**Not Important** n %	**Neither Important nor Unimportant** n %	**Important** n %	**Very Important** n %	**Statements**	**I Never Use** n %	**I Rarely Use** n %	**I Sometimes Use** n %	**I Often Use** n %	**I Always Use** n %
40 35.4	27 23.9	16 14.2	18 15.9	12 10.6	General information about shopping facilities via mobile applications	43 38.1	30 26.5	15 13.3	16 14.2	9 8.0
31 27.7	35 31.2	17 15.2	24 21.4	5 4.5	Location information about shopping facilities via mobile applications	40 35.7	34 30.4	13 11.6	16 14.3	9 8.0
31 27.4	26 23.0	31 27.4	15 13.3	10 8.8	Customer reviews about shopping facilities via mobile applications	39 34.5	30 26.5	20 17.7	17 15.0	7 6.2
19 16.8	24 21.2	35 31.0	27 23.9	8 7.1	General information about historical places via mobile applications	21 18.8	33 29.5	30 26.8	21 18.8	7 6.2
18 15.9	21 18.6	36 31.9	24 21.2	14 12.4	Location information about historical places via mobile applications	21 18.9	30 27.0	33 29.7	19 17.1	8 7.2
22 19.6	23 20.5	32 28.6	25 22.3	10 8.9	Customer reviews about historical places via mobile applications	27 24.1	31 27.7	26 23.2	19 17.0	9 8.0
9 8.0	14 12.5	30 26.8	40 35.7	19 17.0	General information about food & drink facilities (restaurants, cafes, etc.) via mobile applications	12 10.7	21 18.8	33 29.5	30 26.8	16 14.3

Not Important At All	Not Important	Neither Important nor Unimportant	Important	Very Important	Statements	I Never Use	I Rarely Use	I Sometimes Use	I Often Use	I Always Use
n %	n %	n %	n %	n %		n %	n %	n %	n %	n %
5 4.5	18 16.1	34 30.4	39 34.8	16 14.3	Location information about food & drink facilities via mobile applications	8 7.1	24 21.4	38 33.9	28 25.0	14 12.5
12 10.8	14 12.6	27 24.3	39 35.1	19 17.1	Customer reviews about food & drink facilities via mobile applications	16 14.3	23 20.5	34 30.4	26 23.2	13 11.6
12 10.7	14 12.5	39 34.8	27 24.1	20 17.9	General information about entertainment facilities (discos, bars, etc.) via mobile applications	14 12.5	30 26.8	31 27.7	19 17.0	18 16.1
14 12.5	16 14.3	32 28.6	31 27.7	19 17.0	Location information about entertainment facilities via mobile applications	14 12.6	31 27.9	36 32.4	15 13.5	15 13.5
14 12.5	21 18.8	29 25.9	29 25.9	19 17.0	Customer reviews about entertainment facilities via mobile applications	21 18.9	28 25.2	32 28.8	14 12.6	16 14.4
20 17.9	30 26.8	30 26.8	21 18.8	11 9.8	General information about public places (beach, park, etc.) via mobile applications	26 23.2	40 35.7	26 23.2	11 9.8	9 8.0
22 19.5	30 26.5	33 29.2	14 12.4	14 12.4	Location information about public places via mobile applications	25 22.1	37 32.7	30 26.5	12 10.6	9 8.0
20 17.7	39 34.5	26 23.0	15 13.3	13 11.5	Customer reviews about public places via mobile applications	29 25.9	39 34.8	24 21.4	9 8.0	11 9.8

Not Important At All	Not Important	Neither Important nor Unimportant	Important	Very Important	Statements	I Never Use	I Rarely Use	I Sometimes Use	I Often Use	I Always Use
n %	n %	n %	n %	n %		n %	n %	n %	n %	n %
18 16.1	27 24.1	34 30.4	20 17.9	13 11.6	General information about destination facilities (transportation, hospitals, etc.) via mobile applications	26 23.0	39 34.5	26 23.0	10 8.8	12 10.6
18 15.9	29 25.7	33 29.2	21 18.6	12 10.6	Location information about destination facilities via mobile applications	33 29.5	34 30.4	19 17.0	19 17.0	7 6.2
20 17.9	29 25.9	33 29.5	18 16.1	12 10.7	Customer reviews about destination facilities via mobile applications	35 31.2	32 28.6	21 18.8	16 14.3	8 7.1
16 14.2	36 32.1	29 25.9	14 12.5	12 10.7	General information about daily excursions (safari tours, boat tours, aqua parks, etc.) via mobile applications	35 31.0	35 31.0	24 21.2	12 10.6	7 6.2
21 18.8	36 32.1	29 25.9	14 12.5	12 10.7	Location information about daily excursions via mobile applications	37 33.3	35 31.5	22 19.8	11 9.9	6 5.4
23 20.4	37 32.7	22 19.5	17 15.0	14 12.4	Customer reviews about daily excursions via mobile applications	42 37.2	31 27.4	15 13.3	18 15.9	7 6.2

Conclusion

This research study has been conducted to reveal the attitudes of tourists towards mobile tourism applications who visit mass tourism destinations like Alanya where 2.88 billion USD in tourism revenue is generated from 3,617,884 tourist arrivals (Altso, 2013, 99–100). The results of the survey have academic and managerial implications. First of all, tourists use mobile devices during their holiday and they are very familiar with mobile applications. The results also show that extended information on food & beverage like restaurants, bars, and entertainment facilities like discos are important for tourists. Although they stay at all inclusive hotels, which means that they already paid in advance for their meals and drinks, they still desire to explore these spots of the destination. Destination managers shall invest on these applications in order to increase the satisfaction level of visitors and also to create added value through this hedonistic approach. Managers of the cafes, bars, and discos shall be aware that reputation on bad or good service quality is spread rapidly through customer reviews. Information on historic places is less important for the respondents. The reason for this result might be twofold. Either because mass tourists are only interested in core tourism products, which are the 3'S in our case, or the 5's by including sex and sangria, and leave out the other benefits offered by the destination, or because historical sites are well advertised through different media contexts, information has already been gathered during the pre-trip stage. Further studies shall be conducted to reveal this gap. Mobile applications providing information on public places, destination facilities, and daily excursions do not draw the attention of tourists. Related information about these areas may be easily reachable for them, taking into consideration that respondents have purchased package tours and have a real-time guide within the place they stay.

References

ALTSO. (2013). *Alanya Ekonomik Rapor 2012*, Alanya: Alara Matbaası.

Brown, B. & Chalmers, M. (2003). Tourism and Mobile Technology. Proceedings of European Conference on Computer Suported Collaborative Work.

Buik-Aghai, R. P., Fong, S. & Si Y. (2008). Design of a Recommender System for Mobile Tourism Multimedia Selection. Paper Presented in 2nd International Conference on Internet Multimedia Services Architecture and Applications.

Emarketer. (2014). Smartphone Users Worldwide Will Total 1.75 Billion in 2014. Retrieved from http://www.emarketer.com/Article/Smartphone-Users-Worldwide-Will-Total-175-Billion-2014/1010536.

Hebsdigital. (2014). Mid-Year Review: The Rising Tide of Mobile Bookings – How Hoteliers Can Stay Afloat. Retrieved from http://www.hebsdigital.com/blog/mid-year-review-the-rising-tide-of-mobile-bookings-how-hoteliers-can-stay-afloat/.

Kenteris, M., avalas, D. & Mpitziopoulos, A. (2010). A Mobile Recommender System. Proceedings of the 15th IEEE Symposium on Computers and Communications.

Mdgadvertising. (2014). The Year of The Mocal Traveler. Retrieved from http://www.mdgadvertising.com/e-books/Year-Of-The-Mocal-Traveler/.

Rodriguez-Sanchez, M. C., Martinez-Romo, J., Borromeo, S. & Hernandez-Tamames, J. A. (2013). GAT: Platform for Automatic Context-Aware Mobile Services for m-Tourism. *Expert Systems with Applications.* 40, 4154–4163.

Schwinger, W., Grün, C., Pröll, B., Retschitzegger, W. & Schauerhuber, A. (2005). Context-awareness in Mobile Tourism Guides - A Comprehensive Survey. Retrieved from http://www.wit.at/people/schauerhuber/publications/contextAwareMobileTourismGuides_TechRep0507.pdf.

Yovcheva, Z., Buhalis, D. & Gatzidis, C. (2012). Overview of Smartphone Augmented Reality Applications for Tourism. *e-Review of Tourism Research.*10(2), 63–66.

Nurettin Güz*, Hayrullah Yanik** & Ozan Kocabaş***

Gatekeeping and Online Journalism

Introduction

The term gatekeeping has been one of the most discussed subjects in traditional media since 1950, whereas in new media, this term has been discussed for the last 15 years. The term was first brought into communication in 1947 by the social psychologist Kurt Lewin in his unfinished manuscript. On the other hand, he had previously written about gatekeeping and "channel theory" in a government research report in 1943. In his gatekeeping model, Lewin showed how food passed through channels on its way from the store or garden to the dining table. In these channels, there are gates and decision-makers. The entrance to a channel or to each section is a "gate" and movements of the food within the channels are controlled by one or two "gatekeepers" or by some rules. The job done by gatekeepers is called the gatekeeping process. As a result, he emphasised the changes that an event or news story undergoes while it is going through different processes (Lewin, 1948: 144; Shoemaker, 2009: 12; Mutlu, 1998: 122). It has been emphasised that information is generally always passing through some channels, which are called gates, and at these gates, decisions are made based on unbiased rules or personal information which gatekeepers have. As Lewin also explained, studies have shown that information or content is always transmitted by gatekeepers who function as a gate. Moreover, gatekeepers undertake the functions of controlling and mediation of information or content. Within the framework of subjective and objective rules, the decisions and the implementations made by gatekeepers either provide the passing of information through the channels-gates or cause the rejection of information (McQuail & Windahl, 2010: 209; Barzilai, 2008: 1506). On the other hand, a gatekeeper needs some criteria to decide what information will pass through channels or gates (Schudson, 1997: 310). Especially in White and McNelly's studies, it has been found that the gatekeeper or gatekeepers' personality structures, worldview, attitudes, beliefs, preferences, trends, interests, prejudices, and values are reflected on the content of the news starting from the phase of news gathering until the phase of news forming and delivering it to the target

* Prof. Dr., Gazi University, Communication Faculty.
** Research Assistant, Gazi University, Communication Faculty.
*** Research Assistant, Gazi University, Communication Faculty.

audience at different stages (White, 1997: 66–70; McQuail & Windahl, 2010: 212; MacGregor, 1997: 51). Furthermore, Gieber's study (1956) showed that organisational factors such as policy of media organisations, professional concerns, organisational structure of media organisation, the organisation's relations with political power, economic status, reactions of target audiences, and pressures groups played key roles in gatekeeping (McQuail & Windahl, 2010: 220). In Galtung and Ruge's study, time interval, intensity or gate value, the absence of uncertainty, the validity of cultural affinity, harmony, expectation, continuity, composition, and socio-cultural values are applied to gatekeeping (McQuail & Windahl, 2010: 220). The most detailed study on gatekeeping was made by Shoemaker (Shoemaker, 1997: 57–62). In the study, gatekeeping processes were examined in three categories: large-scale, medium-scale, and small-scale. In large-scale gatekeeping, there are ideological structure of society, cultural codes, news and information sources, advertisers, pressure and interest groups, governments, and other social institutions. In medium-scale gatekeeping, there are professional principles and practices, the position of media organisation, organisation structure, and organisational principles. Finally, in small-scale gatekeeping, there are more individual factors. In this context, there are ideologies, prejudices, individual attitudes and principles, political, social and cultural trends, and personal considerations. When it comes to new media, one of the detailed research studies was done by Barzilai in 2008. In her study, she has shown the gates and application of gatekeeping by gatekeepers in the news production process in new media.

Being parallel with the advances in technology, especially the advances in communication technology, in media organisations, the number of organisations that are interested in the subject of news content and news itself has decreased. The conveniences provided in reaching the subject (which is the basis of the news), reaching the news sources, compiling the news, preparing the news in broadcasting form, and realising the delivery of the news to the target audiences with less employees turned out new approaches in the concept of gatekeeping. Thanks to the increasing number of news sources, it is possible to rapidly see the interventions of gatekeepers in the news text by target audiences who may know the subject well in detail, which is basis of the news. With the rapid spread of internet-based news organisations, which are mostly the result of the last quarter century, how the position of the concept of gatekeeping has been changed is wondered.

Methods and Findings

In the framework of structure and organisation of news sites in new media, a field study was conducted on three online news websites (internet based), which do not have printed version, in order to identify what kind of controlling and gatekeeping are applied in the news of these media organisations. In determining the three most visited news sites in Turkey, alexa.com was used, a sub-institution of amazon.com, which determines the daily number of visitors of news sites all over the world. On July 1st and 2nd, by using the in-depth interview method, this study was conducted with four people. Three of them were editors in chief and one of them was an expert editor. Later on, data obtained in the study were analysed. Considering data from the study, three online news sites use largely similar methods in terms of news sources and news making processes. They avoid having correspondents and they only have traditional reporters for the assembly. Furthermore, almost all news sources largely consisted of national agencies. Three media organisations subscribe to all widespread national news agencies, but only one of them subscribes to one of the international news agencies. Competitors, other media companies, traditional media and their extensions on the web, and news organisations are in the position of the secondary news sources. Furthermore, each media organisation has editors to follow the rival media organisations. Primarily Twitter and Facebook, as well as other social media networks, hold a special place among sources of three media organisations. Editors who are working for these three media organisations are particularly following and monitoring social media according to their concerns and they also select subjects which have newsworthiness according to their preferences and reproduce these subjects as news. From news sources on a daily basis, 3,000 news stories flow into those media organisations; however, only 200 of 3,000 news stories are covered in the home pages. Despite the fact that these three media organisations are technologically able to broadcast the news directly to their target audiences, they are opposed to carry out this method because they worry that their position may be affected adversely considering their target audiences' interests, desires, and expectations. Therefore, they must select or reproduce the news that their audience will be interested in, that is to say, they must select or reproduce the news according to target audiences needs and wants.

Advertisements are the main source of income in new media. Jobs for getting advertisements can be carried out either directly by the broadcasting organisation or through advertisement agencies. To get advertisements to the broadcasting organisation, in other words, to increase the number of visitors to news sites of media organisations, is a key factor in the success in new media. Each media organisation has visitors who regularly visit and follow their news site every day, but visitors who are reaching the news sites by search engines, especially Google, constitute a significant proportion as well. In order to increase the number of visitors to a news site through search engines, a new news making process, called "**hooking journalism**," is being carried out. In this method, news sites learn the most searched words or phrases in search engines by visitors who do not visit news sites regularly and they highlight these words in their news and sometimes these words are more weighted than other words. Consequently, in this way, they direct visitors to their news sites. Another point worth mentioning is that prominent words or phrases which are learned from search engines are often attempted to be repeated in the generated content. Furthermore, they do not only use the keywords or phrases, but they also add key questions to the news which may be written by visitors in search engines. A major cause of "hooking journalism" is the sharing of the most searched words in a particular geography at certain periods by search engines, mainly Google, with the media organisations that are doing journalism in new media. Data coming from search engines are evaluated by making some changes on the news information. Target audiences and internet users simply bite the hook of news sites in new media. Additionally, this kind of news does not have a news format; they are only a way of leading target audiences and internet users to the news sites.

Another method related to "hooking journalism," but not considered ethical, is producing "**junk news**" (Işık & Koz, 2014, 27–43). In this method, target audiences obtain the news through search engines owing to the keywords in which the news contain. However, these news stories are not covered in news sites, that's to say, these news stories are connected the news websites by given links. As a result, target audiences can get the news through these links. These kinds of news stories do not often have newsworthiness because their contents are different.

Unlike traditional media, news headlines and the spotlights come into prominence much more in new media. Drawing the attention of the target audience, thus extending the length of staying on the news sites by reading the page, is one of the main objectives of new media. Consequently, headlines are particularly made of interest, and as a new method, headlines are formatted as a question. As a result, the curiosity evoked by using questions directs the target audiences to the content of the news. In traditional media, criticisms about the responses and comments of target audiences, which are not sufficiently considered, are always a matter of discussion and criticism. On the contrary, reactions and responses of target audiences quickly reach the new media. Moreover, the content of the responses and comments can be seen and read by both newsmakers and target audiences. News and its content are instantly prepared and broadcasted to the target audiences in new media. Changing contents of the news is always possible depending on the situation even after it is broadcasted. In terms of the news, being interesting or attractive, which is the essential element in the selection of the news in traditional media, also comes into prominence much more in new media

(Güz, 2005:60–61). This is because it stems from the desire of capturing the target audiences and internet users and the desire of drawing the attention of target audiences and internet users to the news sites who are trying to find information especially through search engines. Nevertheless, this approach trivialises the field of the news which the news belongs to such as politics, culture, magazine, sports, science, technology, and so on. The type of news broadcasting and type of news making can be changed according to the interest of these categories. Each broadcasting organisation categorises the news according to the target audiences' situation under the main topics such as politics, sports, science, magazine, economy, culture, and so on; therefore, new media organisations have created a space different from the main page where target audiences will collectively find the news which are categorised according to main topics. At this point, search engines make a contribution to media managers and editors about which subject or subjects draw the attention of the target audiences and internet users because the number of target audiences is almost single handedly the basic factor which is a determiner of the importance of the news. The news, which will be covered primarily on the main page, varies depending on the time of the day. In this context, a day is divided into time periods and the time period that target audiences tend to get the news is determined. Consequently, the news density is changed depending on the time periods. To give an example, in morning hours during weekdays, at the beginning of the shift, news stories which are much more interesting for workers or clerks are largely weighted more than other kinds of news stories on the news site because it is already known that news related to workers and clerks are read, listened, and viewed by this kind of target audiences in the mornings more than during other periods of the day. Approximately 3,000 news stories come to each media organisation from news sources. The news first reaches an editor who is an expert and more experienced in news selection. At this point, sometimes the number of editors may increase up to three editors who are called "selecting editors and expert editors." These editors may also constitute categorised units under some main topics such as politics, sports, magazine, and so on according to their interests. Other than those editors at the first step of the news selection, there may be other editors who are the leaders or managers of the categorised units, so they can use their authority within the category they are in charge of. They may decide whether or not data are newsworthy. Therefore, the editor who is in charge of news selection is not alone in the first gate. It is impossible that the editor who selects 200 news stories in order to be broadcasted knows everything well in detail about the contents of the news and subjects. Editors who are in charge of processing and transforming data into news are authorised to decide whether or not selected subjects or data have news value in terms of media organisation and target audiences. When they decide that subjects or data do not have news value, subjects and data cannot be transformed as news. For this reason, **at the first gate**, both the editor who selects the news and data and editors who process data and transform data into news appear together. After it has been decided that the data is newsworthy, the news making process begins. Editors who are in charge of selecting news are also in a position of processing news and changing its title or spots even if the data comes as news from news agencies. Rarely, there are situations where news flows through gates unchanged because of the time limit, the density of news, and the increase in the number of news stories. In these situations, news is directly put on the news web page. As I have mentioned at the first gate, there are editors who are categorised and work in their expert field depending on their interests under various and categorised units such as sports, politics, magazine, social media, and so on. In these categorised units, they have a leader editor who coordinates, supervises, and leads the units. As editors, they are authorised to intervene and control the news making process and news content, so they constitute **the second gate** and we may call them as lead editors. Besides this, it is probable that editors in working conditions can always interact with each other. The lay out in traditional media has been involved in different forms in new media and the lay out in new media is at least as important as the lay out in traditional media. Each media organisation in new media tries to design each page and especially the main page to draw the attention of target audiences. In addition to this, each page and the elements of the news are prepared in a style that can be seen easily for the target audiences. On main page of every media organisation, the news is prepared to be more attentive. This news is replaced in the top of the main page as a headline. When the target audience visits the news websites, they first see the headline news. In a sense, the headline news is a kind of news that the media organisations primarily want the target audience to see. The main page and headline news are essential in terms of position of the third gatekeeping in new media. There are editors in chief in the position of top managers in media organisations. Monitoring and evaluation tasks of the main page are under the editor in chief's responsibility. In case of need, the editor in chief directly intervenes in all parts of the news including the content, location, and style of the news. Moreover, the editor in chief directly affects the determination of headline news, content creation, and determination of location and broadcasting or publication format of the news. In new media, editors in chief stand as the **third gate** and they have some tasks different from the editors in chief that are working in traditional media. In traditional media, editors in chief and managers control and monitor the news content before the news are not replicated in numbers and reach the target audiences. On the other hand, in new media, news content are seen and controlled after the news content is opened to the use of target audiences. When editors in chief and managers determine that there are deficiencies and inaccuracies related to news or topics that do not conform to the editorial policy, they have the opportunity to decide on the publication or broadcasting of the news after the news content are corrected and completed. Furthermore, in these situations, they may decide to discontinue broadcasting and publication. In new media, comments, criticisms, and complaints related to news are quite intensive in the home page or in extensions of media organisations such as in Twitter and Facebook. This structure is quite an important method in terms of content monitoring and feedback. Different from traditional media, hundreds or thousands of comments and criticism are republished to the target audiences below the news. However, depending on the degree of reaction and the degree of intensity of their righteousness, the news may be changed or discarded. Each media organisation in the context of the study has to authorise some editors to see and control the comments and criticisms before they are published. They have an authority to filter the comments and criticism which are not appropriate for their policy, out of law, and exceed the red lines of the media organisation. Apart from this, after filtering and evaluating the comments and criticism, they republish the comments and criticism to the target audiences. On the other hand, in social media networks, as well as on Twitter and Facebook, the comments and criticisms could be controlled after they are published. As a result, the filtering process and other duties of comment controlling editors constitute **the fourth gate**. On the other hand, editors in chief are seen at all the gates in new media. As a result, in new media, news making processes and control mechanisms differ in comparison to traditional media. The model concerning the news making process, control mechanisms, and gatekeepers in new media (Figure 1) may be helpful for future studies.

Figure 1: Proposed gatekeeping model in new media

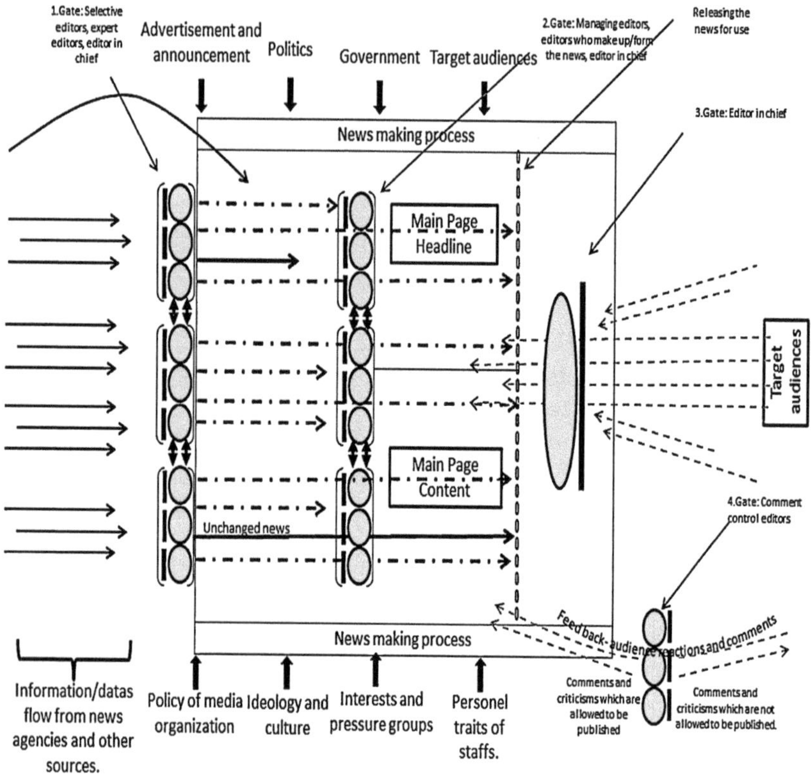

Conclusion and Discussion

It is clearly seen that the long debates on the concept of gatekeeping in traditional media takes its place in the structure and organisation of new media. Both traditional and new media news selection processes are exposed to similar factors, but in news selection in new media, editors have mainly taken the positions of reporters and the people who are in different managing positions in traditional media. The findings of the study reveal that in new media organisations, the news making process is not only limited to delivering the news to the target audiences, but comments and criticisms also involved in the same process are seen as new news. It is clearly understood from the literature and field research that with the increase of news and information sources in new media, the news is categorised much more than in traditional media. Rivalry in news and the desire in making top stories are reasons for generating a special journalism method called "hooking journalism" in new media. Whereas news agencies constitute the news sources mostly in new media, in special news, social media make an impression as an important part of news sources. Unlike traditional media, it has been clearly shown from the research data that the positions of reporters and other workers who process the news in traditional media are replaced with the editors in new media who are using more authority to process the news. And these editors in new media function as gatekeepers. In traditional media, all the produced news is controlled by a lot of gates before the news is broadcasted or published. On the contrary, in new media, it is an important determination of this study that news is controlled by more authorised editors and then delivered to the target audiences. In addition to this, in new media, the news can both be controlled by editors before it is published or broadcasted and after it is published or broadcasted. While comments and criticism are included in the news making process, they are loaded news worthiness, and therefore constitute a new gate that are important features of the new system. When examining the news making process and the delivery process as a whole, as a result of this study, it has been determined that the news are delivered to the target audiences in Internet-based news organisations after passing through only two gates. In the context of new media, the news making process and concept of gatekeeping and its practices have changed as well. From this aspect, it has been thought that the news making process needs to be modeled. Thus, we have generated a model in new media. It is clearly seen in the proposed model that the most important result of this study is that the system in new media basically processes through four stepped gates.

References

Barzilai-Nahon, Karine (2008) "Toward a Theory of Network Gatekeeping: A Framework for Exploring Information Control", *Journal of the American Society for Information Science and Technology*, 59(9), DOI: 10, 1002, 1493–1512.

Güz, Nurettin (2005) *Haberde Yönlendirme ve Kamuoyu Araştırmaları*, Nobel Yayınevi, Ankara.

Hicks, Wynford (2004) "Writing News", *Writing for Journalists*, (Ed. Hicks Wynford), Routledge Taylor & Francis Group, London and New York.

Işık, Umur, Konuralp Koz (2014) "Çöp Yığınlarında Haber Aramak: İnternet Gazeteciliği Üzerine Bir Çalışma", *E-Journal of New World Sciences Academy*, C.9, S. 2, Seri: 4/C, DOI: 10.12739/ NWSA. 2014.9.2.4C0178, 27–43.

Lewin, Kurt (1948) "Action Research and Minority Problems" Resolving Social Conflicts: Selected Papers on Group Dynamics, (ed. G. W. Lewin, Harper & Row Publishers, New York, London.

Lewin, Kurt (1951) *Field Theory in Social Science.* New York: Harper and Row.

Mcquail, Denis (1994). *Kitle İletişim Kuramı*, (Çev. A. H. Yüksel), Anadolu Üniversitesi Yayınları, Eskişehir.

Mcquail, Dennis, Sven Windahl (1986) Communications Models, 3rd Impression, Longman, New York; For Turkish Translation. (2010) *İletişim Modelleri*, (Çev. G. Yumlu), 2. Volume, İmge Yayınları, Ankara.

Mutlu, Erol (1994). *İletişim Sözlüğü,* Ark Yayınları, Ankara.

Schudson, Michael (1994) *Haber Üretiminin Sosyolojisi*, (Çev. Abdülrezak Altun & Meltem Ağduk-Gevrek), Ankara Üniversitesi, İLEF Yıllık, 307–325.

Shoemaker, P. J. (1997) "A New Gatekeeping Model", *Social Meanings of News: A Text-Reade.* (Ed. D. A. Berkowitz), Sage Publication, London. 57–62.

Shoemaker, P. J., P. Tim (2009) *Gatekeeping Theory*, Routledge. New York and London: Taylor & Francis Group.

White, D. M. (1997). *The Gate Keper: A Case Study In The Selection Of News, Social Meanings of News: A Text-Reader.* (Der) Dan Berkowitz, London: Sage Publication.

Nükhet Eltut Kalender

A Review of the Nonverbal and Written Communication in the Work of Boris Pasternak Named as "Doctor Zhivago"

Introduction

Types of communication are classified in two ways which are including verbal and nonverbal communication, but at this point it should be noted that the type of communication carried out by correspondence. When classifying or written description communication is mentioned under the name of a different species. However, researchers have evaluated this type of verbal communication in the beyond language group.

1. Written Communication

In fact, such as verbal communication, written communication of the exact date is also unknown, but drawing pictures on the walls of caves can be traced to the first ages. According to Zıllıoğlu also accumulate knowledge and experience in remote communication in a way which is more reliable than oral communication in writing transmission is one of the origins of cave paintings (1993: 174)

1.1 Examples of Written Communication in Dr. Zhivago

Pasha, who voluntarily joined the army, sends a letter from Siberia to his wife Lara and her daughter Katya. In the letters are expressed news on the front, what their health status and longing to his families. He expects to get permission, because he misses his family and wants to see them by succeeded or slightly wounded. Lara has not worried about Pasha, until he started to not to send letter, but after some time Lara increasingly concerned about Pasha. In order to investigate her husband Pasha in Moscow, Lara gets permission from where she worked, at the end of six months from the military hospital's nursing courses and leaves her daughter Katya to Lipa. His wife goes to Meso-Laborch in the Hungarian border, where the latest letter came from. Although, there are instances where an open letter Pasha and Lara's correspondence is a communication between them, the letters indicate that the means of communication. This situation represents for us an example of written communication (Pasternak, …Chapter 4/7, p. 73).

Yurii Andreievich mentions to his wife Tonya in the letter, that his life in Melyuzevo, staying with Lara Antipova, working as a nurse, in the same house, but he does not interest with her, he could not go to Moscow, because he could not find any vehicles, but after a week he intends to departure and he has possibility to be in front of the family. (Pasternak, … Chapter 5/2, pp. 85, 86)

Yurii Andreievich wrote to his wife:

> *"The disintegration and anarchy in the army continue. Measures are being taken to improve discipline and morale. I have toured units stationed in the neighborhood."*
>
> *"By way of a postscript, though I might have mentioned it much earlier, I must tell that I do a lot of my work with a certain Antipova, a nurse from Moscow who was born in the Urals… You remember the girl student who shot at the public prosecutor on that terrible night of your mother's death? I believe she was tried later. I remember telling you that Misha and I had once seen her, when she was still a schoolgirl, at some sordid hotel where your father took us. I can't remember why we went, only that it was a bitterly cold night. I think it was at the time of the Presnia uprising. Well, that girl was Antipova…So I may turn up any day out of the blue, though I'll try to send a telegram."*

Yurii gets an answer from his wife, before departing. Tonya's letters is transmitted from the narrator's speech to the reader. In the narrator's expressions can be seen such informations as Tonya's jealous about husband from Lara, for this reason her letter stays wet with tears, there is no reason for husband to worry about Sasha and to come to Moscow, reproachfully writes him to go to the Ural with that wonderful nurse Antipova (Pasternak,….Chapter 5/2, p. 86)

> *"Don't worry about Sasha's future," she wrote. "You will never need to be ashamed of him. I promise you to bring him up in those principles which as a child you saw practiced in our house."*

Yurii immediately replied to apologize to his wife Tonya for misunderstandings. Also in the letter despite Yurii stays with Lara at the same home, even he does not know that in which room she stays, moreover, he did not wonder, as soon as she returns from where she was, as servant of the surrounding villages outgoing nurse, he can apology for that situation, Tonya has mistaken in her thoughts, and even he takes his power from Tonya. (Pasternak, …Chapter 5/2, p. 86)

> *"You must be out of your mind, Tonia! How could you imagine such a thing? Don't you know, don't you know well enough, that if it were not for you, if it were not for my constant, faithful thoughts of you and of our home, I would never have survived these two terrible, devastating years of war? But why am I writing this—soon we'll be together, our life will begin again, everything will be cleared up."*
>
> *"What frightens me about your letter is something else. If I really gave you cause to write in such a way, my behavior must have been ambiguous and I am at fault not only before you*

but before that other woman whom I am misleading. I'll apologize to her as soon as she is back. She is away in the country. Local councils, which formerly existed only in provincial capitals and county seats, are being set up in the villages, and she has gone to help a friend of hers who is acting as instructor in connection with these legislative changes."

"It may interest you to know that although we live in the same house I don't know to this day which is Antipova's room. I've never bothered to find out."

Whites withdrew from Yuriatin, replaced the city to reds. Yurii sees four declarations posted on the figured house walls, where previously lived Lara in Yuriatin.

In the first declaration some informations are located about where will be provided the work report from, and those, who will be punished, who have not work report and for giving wrong information and so on. (Pasternak,...Chapter 13/1, p. 241)

"Workbooks are obtainable by those qualified at the cost of 50 rubles each, at the Food Office, Yuriatin Soviet, 5 October Street (formerly Governor Street), Room 137.

"Anyone without a workbook, or filling it in incorrectly, or (still worse) fraudulently, will be prosecuted with the utmost rigor of the wartime regulations. Detailed instructions for the correct use of workbooks are printed in I.Y.I.K. No. 86 (1013) for the current year and are posted at the Yuriatin Food Office, Room 137."

The second declaration is about the foods in the city, some stocks are in the hands of the bourgeois and they keep, if the stocks are determined that they will be punished as a warning. (Pasternak,...Chapter 13/1, p. 241)

"Anyone found hoarding food will be shot on the spot."

The third declaration is about the exploitation of people who will unite in consumer unions. (Pasternak,...Chapter 13/1, p. 241)

"Those who do not belong to the exploiting class are admitted to membership in Consumer Associations. Details are obtainable at the Food Office, Yuriatin Soviet, 5 October Street (formerly Governor Street), Room 137."

The fourth declaration is about the troops. This declaration contains information that without a license who carry weapons would be punished, where and how the new licenses will be provided. (Pasternak, ... Chapter 13/1, p. 241)

"Anyone who fails to surrender his arms or who continues carrying them without having the appropriate new permit will be prosecuted with the utmost severity of the law. New permits are obtainable at the Office of the Yuriatin Revolutionary-Military Committee, 6 October Street, Room 63."

Yurii understood that Lara and her daughter Katya were not at home, hoping to find any trace of them, Yurii wants to look in the hole that Lara had left the keys and finds the keys in the hole with a written note covered with bricks. This note is by Lara. Lara thinks that Yurii will go to Varykino, she went there with his daughter, and coached him to wait her. Yurii did not release the notice from the excitement of the back of the note. (Pasternak, … Chapter 13/2, p. 243)

> *"Lord, what happiness! They say you are alive and have turned up. Someone saw you near the town and rushed over to tell me. I take it you'll go straight to Varykino, so I'm going there with Katenka. But just in case, I'm leaving the key in the usual place. Wait for me, don't move. You'll see I am using the front rooms now. The flat is rather empty, I've had to sell some of the furniture. I've left a little food, boiled potatoes mostly. Put the lid back on the saucepan with a weight on it, to keep the rats out. I'm mad with joy."*

And the last declaration of the back of page is about food shortages, the black market and corruption. (Pasternak,…Chapter 13/3, p. 244)

> *"The reports on the famine disclose the unbelievable inactivity of the local organizations. There are glaring abuses, there is speculation on a gigantic scale, but what are our regional and municipal factory committees doing? Only mass searches in the commercial districts of Yuriatin and Razvilie, only terror applied in all its harshness, down to the shooting of speculators on the spot, can deliver us from famine."*

Yurii initially failed to notice that the notes on the back, Lara mentions when they meet with Tonya and her children, they will talk everything face to face, she wants to provide a horse, but it would be very difficult with Katya.(Pasternak,… Chapter 13/7, p. 251)

> *"You surely know what's happened to your family. They are in Moscow. Tonia has had a little girl." After that several lines were crossed out, then: "I've crossed it out because it's silly to write about it. We'll talk our fill when we meet. I'm rushing out, I must get hold of a horse. I don't know what I'll do if I can't. It's so difficult with Katenka…." The rest of the sentence was smudged and illegible.*

When Tonya's letter reached after months to Yurii, he was in Lara's home. In this letter, she writes that borned the second child, during the maternity nurse Lara Antipova helped her, love of her husband, awaring about her husband loveless-ness, news about their children, and mentions that they are removed from Russia, and they will never meet again with Yurii, by this way she says goodbye to him with the good wishes. (Pasternak,…Chapter 13/18, pp. 265, 266, 267)

> *"Yura," Antonina Alexandrovna wrote, "do you know that we have a daughter? We have christened her Masha in memory of your mother, Maria Nikolaievna….The whole trouble is that I love you and that you don't love me. ….Before we left the Urals—what a terrible and fateful place it turned out to be for us—I got to know Larisa Feodorovna fairly well. I am thankful to her for being constantly at my side at a difficult time and for helping me through my confinement. I must honestly admit that she is a good person, but I don't want to be a hypocrite—she is my exact opposite. I was born to make life simple and to look for*

sensible solutions; she, to complicate it and create confusion…Farewell, I must stop. They have come for the letter, and it's time I packed. Oh, Yura, Yura, my dear, my darling, my husband, the father of my children, what is happening to us? Do you realize that we'll never, never see each other again? Now I've written it down, do you realize what it means? Do you understand, do you understand? They are hurrying me and it's as if they had come to take me to my death. Yura! Yura!"

Yurii and Marina are not married legally, they live together and have two children. However, Yurii suddenly disappears one day, Marina and her friends Dudorov and Gordon seek on Yurii, but they do not find him anywhere. The third day of departure Yurii sent letter to Marina, Gordon and Dudorov individually. But there is no any details in this letters. According to the narrator's expressions, Yurii wrote that not to worry about him generally, not to seek on him, he wants to be alone for a while, as soon as he gets a job, he will go back to Marina. Yurii wants from Gordon to provide a job for Marina and by asking about finding the nanny to his children, also refers that he will send money to Gordon and asks him to give to Marina. (Pasternak,…Chapter 15/8, pp. 309, 310)

2. Nonverbal Communication

The second way of the interpersonal communication is to use hands, face and the other body motions. (Eltut Kalender, 2012: 2,3)

"Our body language shows itself with different gestures, mimics and postures. In interpersonal communication these movements are called as "nonverbal messages". And also this type of communication is called as "nonverbal communication." (Ergin and Birol, 2000: 123)

Haiyan Wang, writes John C. Condon's classification of nonverbal communication with these sentences:

"Condon summarizes twenty-four types of nonverbal behaviors, which already drew scholars' attention; including: gestures, facial expressions, posture, costume and hair style, walking posture, proxemics, touching behavior, eye gaze and contact, architectural design and home decoration, signs and symbols, body odor, paralanguage, color, make-up, conception about time, silence, etc." (Wang, …)

Expressing the importance of nonverbal communication, Isac Florin Lucian says:

'The nonverbal communication is important because the individuals use this system of messages to express attitudes and emotions, consequently, inner states. The nonverbal communication is a strong means of communicating the relational or emotional feelings towards another person. More than that, the nonverbal communication is important in the human interaction because it is partially responsable for creating the impressions. In most of the cases, the nonverbal messages appear before the verbal ones and influence the course of the interactions.' (Lucian, …: 1003, 1004)

Nonverbal communication is classified in two groups in itself, which are called as "sign languge" and "body language". (Eltut Kalender, 2012: 26). The sign language is used by deaf people to transmit own ideas or to have a communication with the other people, but they do not use the voice or speech while using the sign language. But in the body language parts of the body can be used with the voice and / or speech, and these body messages may be expressed consciously or unconsciously. (Eltut Kalender, 2012: 41).

Because of this reason, it is important that the signs of the sign language and the body language are different and they do not have the same meaning.

> *"A means of unconscious non-verbal communication is what is termed body language, or kinesics. Our bodies sometimes express our feelings and emotions better than words can. The body uses reflexive and non-reflexive movement, postures and positions to convey its message to anyone who would care to receive it. Our pupils dilate when we are excited. Our eyes narrow when we are concentrating. We slump when we are tired."* (Khan, 2001)

2.1 Examples of Nonverbal Communication in Dr. Zhivago

Below are the sentences from this literary work which are identified as examples of nonverbal communication, and events and situations which caused nonverbal communication:

1- *He raised his head and from his vantage point absently glanced about the bare autumn landscape and the domes of the monastery. His snub-nosed face became contorted and he stretched out his neck. If a wolf cub had done this, everyone would have thought that it was about to howl. The boy covered his face with his hands and burst into sobs. The wind bearing down on him lashed his hands and face with cold gusts of rain.* (Pasternak,…Chapter 1/1, p. 10)

From the sentence above it can be understood that with his body language and by sitting cross-legged in the coach box and hunching his back Pavel reinforces or confirms that he was not a coach man, which he previously said as a reply to Nikolai Nikolaievich.

2- *There was a faint stench from the lavatories, not quite dispelled by eau de cologne, and a smell of fried chicken, a little high and wrapped in dirty wax paper. As though nothing had happened, graying Petersburg ladies with creaking chesty voices, turned into gypsies by the combination of soot and cosmetics, powdered their faces and wiped their fingers on their handkerchiefs. When they passed the door of the Gordons' compartment, adjusting their shawls and anxious about their appearance even while squeezing themselves through the narrow corridor, their pursed lips seemed to*

Misha to hiss: "Aren't we sensitive! We're something special. We're intellectuals. It's too much for us." (Pasternak,...Chapter 1/7, p. 13)

Misha thinks that the grey haired women who got on the train in Petersburg were self-conceit and derogative because they sneered while they were passing in front of Gordon's compartment. The message between the resource and the receiver is transmitted to its destination.

3- *What Antipov was saying came in one ear and went out the other. Fuflygin had his own thoughts; he kept taking out his watch and looking at it; he was in a hurry to be off.* (Pasternak,...Chapter 2/5, p. 21)

Fufligin was not only deaf to Antipov's words, but also had different things in his mind. Constantly taking the watch out of his pocket and checking the time is an indication that he is in a hurry.

4- *A blow from a nagaika had fallen on her back, and though she had hardly felt it through her thickly quilted coat she swore and shook her fist at the retreating horsemen, indignant that they had dared to strike an old woman like herself, and in public at that.* (Pasternak,...Chapter 2/8, p. 27)

Marfa Gavrilovna's behavior of clenching her fists in anger and showing it to the soldiers as a response to the Kazak soldier who whimped her back is a sign of challenging in nonverbal communication.

5- *Ruffina Onissimovna took a dislike to her sick lodger the moment she saw her. She considered Lara a malingerer. The girl's feverish ravings seemed to her nothing but play-acting. She was ready to swear that Lara was impersonating Gretchen gone mad in her dungeon. She expressed her contempt for Lara by being brisker than usual. She banged doors, sang in a loud voice, tore through her part of the apartment like a hurricane, and kept the windows open all day long.* (Pasternak,...Chapter 4/2, p. 62)

Komarovskiy rents a room to help Lara. The housekeeper has regarded Lara with disfavour from the very first moment and she displays her disapproval through her behaviors.

6- *"Here's Daddy, here's your Daddy, wave your hand like a good boy," Antonina Alexandrovna was saying. She lowered the net of the crib to make it easier for the father to kiss the boy and pick him up. Sashenka, though doubtless frightened and repelled, let the unshaven stranger get quite close and bend over him, then he jerked himself upright, clutching the front of his mother's dress with one hand, and angrily swung the other arm and slapped him in the face. Terrified by his own daring, he* *then threw himself into his mother's arms and burst into bitter tears.* (Pasternak,... Chapter 6/3, p. 112)

Tonya delivers Sasha into his father's arms, who is back home, but the little child draws back in horror from this ungroomed stranger.

7- *A little girl of about eight came in, her hair done up in finely braided pigtails. Her narrow eyes had a sly, mischievous look and went up at the corners when she laughed. She knew her mother had a visitor, having heard his voice outside the door, but she thought it necessary to put on an air of surprise. She curtsied and looked at the doctor with the fearless, unblinking stare of a lonely child who had begun to think early in life.*

"My daughter, Katenka. I hope you'll be friends!"

"You showed me her photograph in Meliuzeievo. How she's grown and changed since then!"

"I thought you were out. I didn't hear you come in."

"I took the key out of the crack and there was an enormous rat in it—as big as this! You should have seen me jump! I nearly died of fright."

She made an absurd face, opening her eyes wide and rounding her mouth like a fish out of water. (Pasternak,...Chapter 9/15, p. 190)

Lara invites Yurii to her house, her daughter Katya enters the room and in her glance at Yurii, by the help of her mimics, she displays the fear she felt at the moment she wanted to take keys.

8- *Yurii Andreievich had no rifle; he lay on the grass watching the course of the engagement. All his sympathies were on the side of these heroically dying children. With all his heart he wished them success. They belonged to families who were probably akin to him in spirit, in education, in moral discipline and values.*

It occurred to him to run out into the field and give himself up, thus obtaining his release. But that was dangerous, too dangerous. While he was running with his arms raised above his head he could be shot down from both sides, struck in the breast and in the back—by the partisans in punishment for his betrayal and by the Whites in misunderstanding of his motives. He knew this kind of situation, he had been in it before, he had considered all the possibilities of such escape plans and had rejected them as unfeasible. So resigning himself to his divided feelings, he lay on his belly on the grass, his face toward the clearing, and watched, unarmed, the course of the battle. (Pasternak,...Chapter 11/4, p. 214)

While Yurii is laying on the grass and watching the fight between the whites and the gangs, he thinks he can survive from the fight if he takes sides against the whites, however he also knows that it won't be possible to survive from both sides if he tries to go away just putting his hands up.

9- *It was again damp and dark in the rooms, this time because the weather was overcast. It was less cold, and judging from the look of the dark, low clouds it would snow any moment. Yurii Andreievich was exhausted by the physical and mental strain of too many sleepless nights. His legs were weak and his thoughts were in a tangle; shivering with cold and rubbing his hands, he walked about from room to room, waiting to see what Lara would decide and what he would have to do in consequence.*

She did not know herself. Just then she would have given anything to exchange their chaotic freedom for a daily round, however strenuous, but laid down once and for all, for work and obligations, so that they could live a decent, honest, sensible life. (Pasternak,…Chapter 14/10, p. 282)

Yurii is wringing his hands while waiting Lara decide to return to the city or stay in Varykino.

10- *Now she felt a wave of pride and relief, as always at the thought of Yurii and as in the short intervals of her life that she had spent beside him. Now, too, she was enveloped in the air of that freedom and unconcern that he had always emanated. She got up impatiently from her chair. Something incomprehensible was happening to her. She wanted, if only for a few moments, to break free with Yurii's help into the open, out of the sorrows that imprisoned her, to feel again the joy of liberation. Such a joy, it seemed to her, would be the joy of taking leave of him, of using the right and the occasion to weep her fill over him unhindered. With a passionate haste, she looked around her at the crowd, with eyes as smarting, unseeing, and tearful as if an oculist had put caustic eye-drops into them, and all the people began to move, shuffle, and walk out of the room, leaving her at last alone, behind half-closed doors. She went up to the table with the coffin on it, quickly crossing herself, got up on the footstool Evgraf had brought, made three sweeping signs of the cross over the body, and pressed her lips to the cold forehead and hands.* (Pasternak,…Chapter 15/14, pp. 318–319)

Lara's crossing three times, after standing on the chair next to Yurii's coffin and kissing him indicate a last farewell and that she wants her beloved to be forgiven by the God.

Findings

In Dr. Zhivago, the primary literal resource of our research, totally ten written communication instruments have been identified: four letters, five declaration texts which are put up to notify and warn the people of Yuriatin and a written note. Some letters written by Pasha to his wife have been mentioned but the number of letters are not specified.

In Dr. Zhivago totally seventy six examples of nonverbal communication components are identified which consist of head, each organ of the face, hands, arms and all the body postures. However, in order to follow the declaration spelling rules and keep the page number this study includes the examples containing nonverbal statements rather than verbal statements and expressing different feelings, which are collected from different chapters and subchapters.

References

AKİŞİNA, A. A, KANO, HİROKO. (2010). **Slovar' russkih jestov i mimiki**, Russkiy yazık, Moskva.

ELTUT KALENDER, N. (2012). **Türk ve Rus Toplumlarında Kullanılan Beden Dillerinin Karşılaştırılması.** (Yayımlanmamış Doktora Tezi). Ankara.

ERGİN, A., BİROL, C. (2000). **Eğitimde İletişim**, Ankara, Anı Yayıncılık.

KHAN, A. A. (2001). **Nonverbal Communication: Fact and Fiction,** http://www.strangehorizons.com/2001/20010226/nonverbal.shtml (Erişim Tarihi: 28.04.2011).

LUCIAN, I. F. **The Role of the Cultural Factors in the Verbal and Nonverbal Communication.**

PASTERNAK, B. (….). **Doctor Zhivago**, Trans. Max Hayward and Manya Harari, 21.printing, Pantheon Books, New York.

SERGEEVA, O., (2001). **Yazık jestov, kak çitat' mısli bez slov?**, Glava 6 Kak ispolzavat' znaniye neverbal'nogo yazıka na praktike?, Moskva, Eksmo.

WANG, H., **Nonverbal Communication and the Effect on Interpersonal Communication**, Asian Social Science, Vol. 5, No:11, China http://www.ccsenet.org/journal/index.php/ass/article/view/4196/3633 (Erişim Tarihi: 18.04.2011).

ZILLIOĞLU, M. (1993). **İletişim Nedir?**, I. Basım, İstanbul, Cem Yayınevi.

Selin Türkel & Ebru Uzunoğlu

Fostering Social Networks for Corporate Social Responsibility Communication: An Exploratory Study on Twitter

Introduction

Changes in the 21st century business environment are forcing organisations to adapt new mind-setting and management strategies in order to achieve a competitive edge. These changes can generally be observed both in the corporate world and in society. Particularly, emerging advanced communication technologies enable easier access to information, resulting in more sophisticated, info savvy, and conscious individuals. As Kitchen and Uzunoglu (2014: 1) highlighted, "the vital essence of any business – *customers* - are not only more demanding, but more discerning of what businesses and brands are and what they stand for." Moreover, from the perspective of *Stakeholder Theory* (Freeman, 1984), rather than regarding solely customer expectations, it is essential for organisations to consider each stakeholder group, including suppliers, investors, employers, and so on. Defining the stakeholder as (1984: 25) "any group or individual who can affect or is affected by the achievement of the firm's objectives," Freeman underlines the necessity of "integrated approaches for dealing with multiple stakeholders on multiple issues" (26). Therefore, building a strong relationship with each stakeholder group is vital to gain their respect (Puncheva, 2008; Zhao, 2014), to enhance loyalty (Finch, 2008; Roberts, 2009) and trust (Bregoli & Del Chiappa, 2013; Dervitsiotis, 2003), and to meet their expectations. In order to achieve/secure all these necessary requirements for survival in this intensely competitive environment, it is inevitable for organisations to build/develop and sustain new strategies, one of which can be identified as *corporate social responsibility* (CSR) initiatives (Türkel, Uzunoğlu, Kaplan & Vural 2015).

CSR, which involves varying aspects such as social welfare, environmental sensitiveness, and ethical concerns, is considered as a crucial factor due to its influential role on corporate image and reputation (Etter, 2013). According to Werther and Chandler (2010: 5), CSR refers to "a view of the corporation and its role in society that assumes a responsibility among firms to pursue goals in addition to profit maximization and a responsibility among a firm's stakeholders to hold the firm accountable for its actions." This definition reveals that CSR not only includes organisations' economic and social roles, but also, in particular, it emphasises their operational and ethical obligations towards their own stakeholder groups. Thus, it can be said that a stakeholder approach provides an extensive theoretical framework for organisations' responsibility considerations. Moreover, since achieving stakeholder involvement and participation would enhance the effectiveness of CSR initiatives, it is crucial to provide a platform in which interactive and dialogical features are an integral part of communication. With this consideration in mind, for this study, Capriotti's definition of CSR communication is adapted:

> "… a tool to facilitate and promote the collaborative building of CSR: establishing dialogic communication channels among the organisation and its stakeholders to ask about the stakeholders' needs and what the corporate responsible behavior should be, at the same time stimulating participation and collaborative decision-making about CSR issues" (2011: 373).

Gaining currency of dialogical CSR communication calls for strategic approaches that are more refined in terms of attaining CSR involvement among varying stakeholders. Social media can therefore be utilised to provide an interactive communication environment. The interactive nature of social media (Grover & Stewart, 2010; Sashi, 2012; Whelan, Moon and Grant, 2013) is attracting the attention of a growing number of companies due its capability to build dialogical communication (Bortree & Seltzer, 2009; Briones, Kuch, Liu & Jin, 2011; Rybalko & Seltzer, 2010).

In particular, Twitter, with its accelerating number of users, is now considered as an important tool for establishing communication among organisations and stakeholders. Consequently, Twitter, the focus of this study, has also gained popularity as a communication tool for CSR message dissemination (Colleoni, 2013; Etter, 2013; Lee, Oh & Kim, 2013).

An extensive amount of research exists with regard to CSR (Aguinis and Glavas, 2012; Dhaliwal, Tsang and Yang, 2011; Servaes and Tamayo, 2013) and CSR communication (Bortree, 2014; Ingenhoff and Sommer, 2011; Wong, Leung and Law, 2015); however, there is still lack of studies examining the content of CSR communication on social media, particularly in the case of Twitter, both a social network and news outlet. In this respect, this study provides a new understanding of social media CSR communication in organisations and specifically represents an attempt to identify the topics and nature of tweets of corporate messages.

Literature Review

'Communication' as the key driver for the reception of CSR initiatives

No one can deny the current critical strategic role of CSR initiatives. However, it is also extremely important to consider the process of creating awareness about these initiatives, in order to strengthen stakeholders' admiration and advocacy (Tench and Sun, 2014). Consequently, the significance of CSR message dissemination has also highlighted the key role of communication. According to Morsing and Schultz (2006: 323), "messages about corporate ethical and socially responsible initiatives are likely to evoke strong and often positive reactions among stakeholders." There is lots of evidence stating that a well-designed and maintained CSR communication effort would result in public acceptance and engagement (De Bakker & Den Hond, 2008; Wang and Chaudhri, 2009).

CSR communication refers to "communication that is designed and distributed by the company itself about its CSR efforts" (Morsing, 2006: 171). From a stakeholder perspective, CSR communication refers to "a process of reciprocal influence between organisations and their audiences" (Brennan, Merkl-Davies and Beelitz, 2013: 665) to convey collaborative CSR messages. The need to engage with stakeholders through CSR initiatives necessitates more precise and continuing stakeholder awareness which can be derived from carefully considered CSR communication strategies (Morsing and Schultz, 2006). O'Riordan and Fairbrass (2014: 136) address the vital role of communication, naming it a key priority, and acknowledge it as "an additional critical step for identifying sustainable management solutions in the CSR stakeholder engagement process."

CSR related messages can be disseminated through either publicity, advertising (Skard and Thorbjørnsen, 2014), or by the usage of annual reports, newspapers, television, radio, and corporate websites. However, these channels, most of which represent traditional media, are effective but not sufficient since they provide organisations with only a didactic, one-way form of communication (Liu and Shrum, 2002). Yet, in order to engage with today's sophisticated stakeholders, it is important to establish/constitute dialogue based on mutual understanding, a process which necessitates interactivity. According to Johnson-Cramer, Berman, and Post (2003: 149), "the essence of stakeholder dialogue is the co-creation of shared understanding by company and stakeholder." The rising importance of building dialogue-based stakeholder relationships forces organisations to find new channels enabling them to achieve interactivity. At this point, an alternative, which allows the attainment of interaction between stakeholders and organisations, is social media, which is characterised as an enabler of user-generated content and a facilitator of individual expression through a provided dialogical platform (Lovejoy and Saxton, 2012). Thus, it is valuable to focus on Twitter, a particular form of social media, and its role on CSR communication in order to gain a deeper understanding of how organisations utilise this platform to achieve dialogic stakeholder communication.

Twitter: An evolving platform for disseminating CSR messages

There has been an explosion in the use of Twitter, a multi-faceted social networking site, which is "an intersection between professional and personal, formal and informal, and resource and conversation" (Weller, 2011: 73). Organisations have started to utilise this tool for building stakeholder relationships and enabling interactivity between a company and its target groups. According to Whelan, Moon, and Grant (2013: 779), "the decentralising and interactive possibilities of social media are potentially significant for CSR." It is clear that various networking sites such as Facebook, Linkedin, and Tumblr can also provide a conversational platform. However, Twitter's characteristics, such as being real-time, fast, direct, and concise (Parmelee and Bichard, 2012), make it unique in terms of its reach and engagement. Thus, Twitter represents an appropriate channel for organisations to convey CSR messages. Due to its user-generated nature (Hannon, Bennett and Smyth, 2010; Phelan, McCarthy, Bennett and Smyth, 2011; Smith, Fischer and Yongjian, 2012), rather than being simply a platform where CSR activities and policies are announced in a one-way format from organisation to stakeholders, Twitter is an environment that encourages peers to talk on CSR related issues.

Twitter is beneficial for companies since it enables them to establish relationships and dialogues with their stakeholders, especially consumers (Saffer, Sommerfeldt and Taylor, 2013). However, it carries a certain amount of risk, as adverse publicity on Twitter might result in companies becoming the target of activist groups (Timothy Coombs and Holladay, 2013). Therefore, it is important for companies to prevent any communication gaps. For example, they should be sufficiently well represented in this highly effective medium. Rather than manipulating their audiences, they should aim to involve them in ongoing conversations. However, there is still some evidence that organisations fail to fully exploit this communication channel, either consciously or unconsciously. According to research conducted by Inauen and Schoeneborn (2014), the majority of organisations use Twitter as a form of one-way communication for informative purposes rather than establishing a dialogue to encourage interactivity. Another recent study has revealed that companies on Twitter avoid interacting with stakeholders in the context of CSR. The author considers that there is reputational risk arising from such reluctance and the criticism it brings (Etter, 2013).

In this epoch of communication and information technology, silence and withholding communication can be considered as an ineffective and naive approach. As Werther and Chandler (2010) state in terms of CSR, free flow of information is significant in a globalised world and companies need to employ open communication channels in order to reach their stakeholders. It is important to remember that non-presence in Twitter has many drawbacks, as mentioned above. Thus, it is vital for organisations to integrate Twitter into their CSR communication strategies with well-planned proactive programs that follow appropriate implementations. In order to realise such strategies and to achieve such implementations, it is necessary for organisations to gain a more detailed understanding and a deeper knowledge of CSR communication, which this study aims to provide.

This study aims to advance the prevailing literature on CSR communication and to shed light on the usage of Twitter as a CSR communication channel. Thus, the main objectives of this study are defined as below:

- to engage in a comprehensive analysis of the CSR activities of an organisation with the most highly-rated CSR reputation made public through its Twitter account, and
- to provide insights into consumer expectations towards the organisation's CSR activities.

To this aim, we focus on the following research questions (RQs):

RQ1. How do consumers perceive an organisation's CSR activities?
RQ2. What social responsibility domains are most presented on the Twitter account?
RQ3. What social responsibility categories within domains are mostly presented on the Twitter account?

Methods

In this study, RQs on Twitter as a CSR communication tool for organisations were examined through content analysis. The sample was drawn from the 10 Companies with the Best CSR Reputations list (2013). A pilot study, top of mind awareness test, was conducted on a sample size of 80 which was large enough to include a corporate brand from each category. The sample was further narrowed to four as the most recalled companies.

A study on five focus groups with a total of 40 participants was held in İzmir, Turkey. The purpose of the focus group study was twofold: (a) to identify the organisations to undertake content analysis on, and (b) to bring about comments and insights pertaining to the CSR domains' knowledge level of the four identified companies in a natural but well-planned conversation style. The focus group methodology was chosen because it encourages new thinking and ideas and also promotes interaction through debate (Hennink, 2007; Mooi and Sarstedt, 2011;

Stopher, 2012) on CSR-related activities of companies. A convenience sample was selected from a university community. In addition, there was an equal representation of males and females participating in the focus groups to ensure more balanced research results. Although this sample clearly does not reflect the whole population, its profile corresponds well with consumers of companies in the research sample. Focus groups were conducted between November 2 and November 17, 2014 and lasted for about 1.5 to two hours, depending on the degree of discussion. All the sessions were recorded to enable verbatim transcription. Focus group transcripts were independently analysed by two researchers and the results were compared to ensure inter-rater agreement. The intercoder-reliability (93.3%) was calculated with the following formula:

(Number of agreements) / (Number of agreements + Number of disagreements) * 100 (Branson, Farr, Peksoz, Nam and Cao, 2005: 43)

In order to identify the organisation on which to undertake content analysis, the focus groups made use of a moderation technique (Demant, 2012). In this technique, respondents were asked to place the names of companies on circle diagrams with regard to the domains of CSR. The closer to the centre, the better the company's perceived CSR perception. Google was given the leading position in all six domains by the majority of participants (22 out of 30) and was therefore chosen as the subject of the research study.

In the second part of research study, content analysis was employed to examine the Twitter account of Google. Content analysis is "a research tool used to determine the presence of certain concepts within texts" (Klenke, 2008: 89). All tweets sent between 20th of November, 2014 and June 26, 2014 were extracted, resulting in a total of 400 tweets. Each tweet was coded manually by two coders to indicate the presence or absence of the CSR-related domains (product, community support, diversity, overseas operations, employee support, and environment) identified by KLD Company (2003) and the three categories (ethical, legal, and economic) defined by Schwartz and Carroll (2003). With an intercoder-reliability coefficient of 0.91, the results are considered sufficiently reliable. Disagreements were resolved by discussion.

Findings Related to the RQs

The first RQ examined the perceptions of an organisation's CSR activities. Focus group discussions on CSR domains reflect a very positive attitude towards Google, the company with the CSR reputation. As highlighted previously, the company outperformed the other three in the focus group moderation technique. Accordingly, in this section, general attitudes towards domains of CSR and CSR perceptions of Google are investigated.

Product Domain

The focus group findings suggest that innovation and quality are key determinants in the evaluation of social responsibility. These were among the few themes mentioned in all focus groups. Product safety (three times) and experimentation on animals (two times) were also referred to in the discussion. Google, perceived as innovative and of high quality, was considered the most responsible brand. With regard to the themes of innovation and quality, participants in focus group one and three stated:

> *"Google has its own department and is conducting Research and Development (R&D) activities, working on synthetic meat, and showing interest in different subjects. They dedicate quite a significant budget to these areas."*
>
> *"Google provides a lot of convenience, ...is of supreme quality."*

Respondents have also discussed personal privacy and consent marketing in one of the group (group four) discussions. Both for and against arguments are presented, as revealed by the following contrasting opinions:

> *"Google is recording all websites that you enter and shows you advertisements based on your web page visits. That's great! Ads are readily available without entering the site- for instance, Trendyol (fashion and private shopping websites)- itself"* (Participant A).
>
> *"...showing advertisements based on web page visits, I think, it is unethical. This is violation of privacy"* (Participant B).

Community Support

The participants identified a wide variety of factors which make up the community support domain. They are listed as follows, with frequencies in brackets: cause marketing opportunities (three), philanthropic approach of leader of a company (three), social sponsorships (three), alliances with non-governmental organisations (NGOs) (two), provision of necessities for the disadvantaged (two), aid during natural disasters (one), and internships for youngsters (one).

Although the majority recognised the company as a leader of this domain, the participants were unaware of the company's specific philanthropic activities and stance, with one exception ("*...Google currently supports health programs, helps prevent the spread of AIDS*").

One participant said:

> *"...informing us in all aspects of our lives, is the greatest support ever given to the community."*

This statement corresponds to the raison d'etre of the company as an economic entity, which exists, to provide information services.

Another respondent drew attention to the Google Doodle (i.e. changes to the Google logo) to commemorate special days, people, and events, mentioning that:

> *"...takes into account the sensitivities of many societies. In particular, Google changes its background on national days."*

Employee Support

The findings reveal that conversations surrounding this issue are generally related to the ideal working conditions for young people. In four of the focus groups, the importance of an enjoyable work environment was emphasised. The other themes were training opportunities (two) and safety precautions (two).

The Google work environment resonated well with all participants. According to a respondent:

> *"There are photos of Google's offices on the web. There are slides and special places for entertainment. They do their best to make employees feel comfortable."*

Many commented positively about Google's responsibility towards its employees. Most believed that there was a supportive environment in which employees were valued and recognised for their contributions. Two direct quotes illustrate this:

> *"I know that Google values its employees enormously."*

> *"If there is a business success story about Google's employees, Google will definitely announce it on Twitter."*

Environment

The environmental impact of companies has recently become significant to many. This view is supported by focus group findings which highlight general environmental issues such as global warming (two) and pollution problems (two). In terms of the environmental responsibility of companies, the focus was on producing green products (four) and recycling materials (three). Moreover, while participants were largely unaware of the environmental stance of Google, the lack of knowledge on the topic did not seem to impact their CSR perception. As one of the respondents stated:

> *"If there were an environmental problem, we would have heard it anyway."*

Overseas Operations

In this domain, all participants pointed to a particular theme, the exploitation of workers. Similar to the environmental domain, participants uninformed about human rights policies of Google expressed positive perceptions. For instance, one respondent made the following remark:

> *"Google does not employ cheap labour."*

Diversity

For the diversity domain, two themes were expressed on single occasions, namely employment of LGBTT individuals and racial minorities. Only one participant said:

> *"...by diversity if we can mean nations, I know there are Turkish employees of Google. Employees of all regions are hired as well."*

To answer RQ2 and 3 RQ3 of the study, frequencies were conducted. RQ2 asked which social responsibility domains were present in the tweets of the company rated most highly for CSR reputation, namely Google. Each analysed tweet was placed in one of the following six domains: product, community support, environment, overseas operations, employee support, and diversity.

The two most frequently occurring domains portrayed on the Twitter profile were product (292 tweets, 73%) and community support (71 tweets, 18%). The least common domains observed in the tweet posts were environment and overseas operations, with no tweets available for either. Moreover, the rest of the domains were underrepresented to the point where they were almost non-existent in the Twitter profile, including employee support (8 tweets, 2%) and diversity (3 tweets, 1%). Out of 401 tweets, only 27 (7%) did not fall into any of the categories measured.

The third RQ examined the types of CSR categories within domains employed on the Twitter account. In terms of product domain, purely economic was the most frequent category across CSR responsibility types, appearing in 199 tweets (52.4%), followed by economic and ethical categories (93 tweets, 24.5%). For the community support domain, the majority of the tweets were of the purely ethical type (54 tweets, 14.2%). In addition, the second recurrent category was economical and ethical with 4.5% (17 tweets). Furthermore, in comparison to the most frequent categories, occurrences in the other categories within domains are relatively low, including employee support (economic and ethical, six tweets; purely ethical, two tweets) and diversity (purely ethical, two tweets; economic ethical, one tweet).

Discussion

For many years, businesses have almost exclusively focused on satisfying shareholders and maximising profits. However, in today's global competitive marketplace, in which consumers have become more conscious about business practices, organisations are expected to behave with greater sensitivity toward social and environmental issues and to make a greater effort to contribute to the well-being of society. Therefore, CSR has become a practice which can no longer be ignored. However, from a strategic point of view, not all CSR activities contribute significant value to companies' image and reputation (Porter and Kramer, 2006). Within this context, the measurement of corporate social performance (Carroll, 1979; Wood, 2010; Font, Walmsley, Cogotti, McCombes, and Häusler, 2012) has become a corporate priority in order to convince stakeholders of the impact of business on society. However, despite its importance, the assessment of social performance is coming to be seen as a necessary, but not in itself a sufficient, condition for social acceptance. A further significant requirement in order to be approved by society is communication. As revealed in the findings, corporations need to communicate their CSR initiatives to create greater levels of awareness of their activities in this area. In order to increase the audience for their messages, it is important to utilise every type of communication tool, among which Twitter has a vital role in terms of building and maintaining relationships. As discussed in the literature, Twitter's characteristics enable organisations to not only disseminate messages, but to also develop interaction and allow messages to be disseminated among peers gathered around common interests and concerns. Moreover, the gained support of stakeholder engagement would also be beneficial for organisations in terms of achieving goodwill and delivering widespread CSR related messages.

The focus group results show that Google is the brand that the majority of participants associate with CSR initiatives. Even though the other brands are also well-known global brands, this clear numerical superiority can be explained by the participant age profile (i.e. university students). This result is not surprising since the young generation is colloquially known as the "Google Generation" (Nicholas, Rowlands, Clark, & Williams, 2011). Google permeates many practices into their daily life which makes this search engine a highly familiar brand. The results demonstrate that the greater the brand familiarity, the greater the associations with CSR initiatives observed.

Although focusing on a single case, identified as Google, in this study, is a limitation which prevents generalisations, the findings of Google's Twitter account's content analysis still provides insightful knowledge for both practitioners and scholars who are interested in carrying out further research.

Global brands utilise Twitter for communication purposes (Kwon and Sung, 2011). From the analysis of the Twitter account, it is observed that Google prefers to use this form of media intensively for CSR communication manner. However, when tweets are examined, the majority belong to product and community support domains. An unexpected result is the absence of tweets related to environmental issues, even though this has become a priority for today's nature conscious individuals, many of whom are more concerned about corporations' environmental values than their products (Estes, 2009; Ottman, 2011).

Another interesting finding is related to the non-existence of tweets with regard to the overseas domain. The company, highly criticised for its entry into China with regard to censorship, was even questioned by the Congressional Committee (Dann and Haddow, 2008). As one of the well-known global companies, Google would be expected to address human rights issues. Even with their known involvement with related NGOs, communication of such efforts would be beneficial in creating awareness and interest on these issues within society.

Scholars have pointed out the significance of localisation for global companies that are aiming to obtain a social license to operate (Bianchi and Arnold, 2004; Reimann, Ehrgott, Kaufmann, and Carter, 2012). It is important to bear in mind that local values have an essential impact on the evaluation of global brands (De Mooij, 2013). Thus, it is unexpected that Google has no Turkish Twitter account to reach the 11,337,505 users in the country (Turkish State Institute of Statistics, 2013). This would be understandable if Google had a single account in a manner of centralised policy. A the search reveals, however, Google has local accounts in Germany and Latin America. Consequently, for the sake of global consistency (Begley and Boyd, 2003; Quirke, 2007; Yeung, Xin, Pfoertsch and Liu, 2011), Google having a coherent policy for each country/culture in which it operates would seem to be a more an appropriate strategic approach.

Additionally, the addressed domains on Twitter are very representational and limited. However, this is an acceptable approach when the need to adopt CSR strategies in line with companies' own corporate identity and mission/vision is considered. Nevertheless, a brand that has a wide range of users all over the world and touches almost all the areas of everyday life could be expected to display greater variety in terms of social performance.

The detailed examination of the two most frequent domains, namely product and community support, has shown that for the product category, the economic dimension is the most obvious aspect. A for-profit organisation is obliged to provide quality products and services (Ghosh, 2005). As a fundamental assumption of the market economy, this is also acceptable. However, the economic emphasis on Twitter communication demonstrates that Google mostly utilises the medium for informative ends. This is not likely to be the most suitable approach, considering the highly interactive nature of Twitter, which sets it apart from its traditional competitors. Unlike the product domain, the community support one generally emphasises the ethical dimension. This is also expected when the ethical connotations of the community support domain are taken into consideration.

References

Aguinis, H., & Glavas, A. (2012). What we know and don't know about corporate social responsibility a review and research agenda. *Journal of Management*, 38(4), 932–968.

Begley, T. M., & Boyd, D. P. (2003). The need for a corporate global mind-set. MIT Sloan Management Review, 44(2), 25–32.

Bianchi, C. C., & Arnold, S. J. (2004). An institutional perspective on retail internationalization success: Home Depot in Chile. *The International Review of Retail, Distribution and Consumer Research*, 14(2), 149–169.

Bortree, D. S. (2014). The State of CSR Communication Research: A Summary and Future Direction. *Public Relations Journal*, 8(3), 2.

Bortree, D. S., & Seltzer, T. (2009). Dialogic strategies and outcomes: An analysis of environmental advocacy groups' Facebook profiles. *Public Relations Review*, 35(3), 317–319.

Branson, D., Farr, C., Peksoz, S., Nam, J., & Cao, H. (2005). Development of a prototype personal cooling system for first responders: user feedback. *Journal of ASTM International* 2(2), 40–51.

Bregoli, I., & Del Chiappa, G. (2013). Coordinating relationships among destination stakeholders: evidence from Edinburgh (UK). *Tourism Analysis*, 18(2), 145–155.

Brennan, N. M., Merkl-Davies, D. M., & Beelitz, A. (2013). Dialogism in corporate social responsibility communications: Conceptualising verbal interaction between organisations and their audiences. *Journal of Business Ethics*, 115(4), 665–679.

Briones, R. L., Kuch, B., Liu, B. F., & Jin, Y. (2011). Keeping up with the digital age: How the American Red Cross uses social media to build relationships. *Public Relations Review*, 37(1), 37–43.

Capriotti, P. (2011). Communicating corporate social responsibility through the internet and social media. In Ø. Ihlen, J. Bartlett, & S. May (Eds.),

The handbook of communication and corporate social responsibility (pp. 358–378). Oxford: Wiley-Blackwell.

Carroll, A. B. (1979). A three-dimensional conceptual model of corporate performance. *Academy of Management Review*, 4(4), 497–505.

Colleoni, E. (2013). CSR communication strategies for organizational legitimacy in social media. *Corporate Communications: an international journal*, 18(2), 228–248.

Dann, G. E., & Haddow, N. (2008). Just doing business or doing just business: Google, Microsoft, Yahoo! and the business of censoring China's Internet. *Journal of Business Ethics*, 79(3), 219–234.

De Bakker, F. G., & Den Hond, F. (2008). Activists' Influence Tactics and Corporate Policies. *Business Communication Quarterly*, 71(1), 107–111.

Demant, J. (2012). *Natural interactions in artificial situations: Focus groups as an active social experiment*. INTECH Open Access Publisher.

De Mooij, M. (2013). *Global marketing and advertising: Understanding cultural paradoxes*. California: Sage Publications.

Dervitsiotis, K. N. (2003). Beyond stakeholder satisfaction: aiming for a new frontier of sustainable stakeholder trust. *Total Quality Management and Business Excellence*, 14(5), 515–528.

Dhaliwal, D. S., Li, O. Z., Tsang, A., & Yang, Y. G. (2011). Voluntary nonfinancial disclosure and the cost of equity capital: The initiation of corporate social responsibility reporting. *The Accounting Review*, 86(1), 59–100.

Estes, J. (2009). *Smart green: How to implement sustainable business practices in any industry and make money*. Hoboken, NJ: John Wiley & Sons.

Etter, M. (2013). Reasons for low levels of interactivity: (Non-) interactive CSR communication in twitter. *Public Relations Review*, 39(5), 606–608.

Finch, D. J. (2008). Performance through relationships: A case for the integration of strategic stakeholder management and community investment. *Journal of Sponsorship*, 1(4), 338–349.

Font, X., Walmsley, A., Cogotti, S., McCombes, L., & Häusler, N. (2012). Corporate social responsibility: The disclosure–performance gap. *Tourism Management*, 33(6), 1544–1553.

Freeman, R. E. (1984). *Strategic management: A stakeholder approach*. Boston: Pitman.

Ghosh, B. (2005). *Ethics in management and Indian ethos*. New Delhi: Vikas Publishing House.

Grover, A., & Stewart, D. W. (2010). Defining interactive social media in an educational context. In C. Wankel, M. Marovich, & J. Stanaityte (Eds.), *Cutting edge social media approaches to business education: Teaching with LinkedIn, Facebook, Twitter, Second Life, and Blogs* (pp. 7–38). Charlotte, N. C: Information Age Pub.

Hannon, J., Bennett, M., & Smyth, B. (2010, September). Recommending twitter users to follow using content and collaborative filtering approaches. In *Proceedings of the Fourth ACM Conference on Recommender Systems* (pp. 199–206). ACM.

Hennink, M. M. (2007). *International focus group research: A handbook for the health and social sciences.* Leiden: Cambridge University Press.

Inauen, S., & Schoeneborn, D. (2014). Twitter and its usage for dialogic stakeholder communication by MNCs and NGOs. *Communicating Corporate Social Responsibility: Perspectives and Practice (Critical Studies on Corporate Responsibility, Governance and Sustainability, Volume 6) Emerald Group Publishing Limited*, 6, 283–310.

Ingenhoff, D., & Sommer, K. (2011). Corporate social responsibility communication. *Journal of Corporate Citizenship, 2011* (42), 73–91.

Johnson-Cramer, M. E., Berman, S. L. and Post, J. E. (2003). Re-examining the concept of "stakeholder management". In Andriof, J., Waddock, S., Husted, B. and Rahman, S. S. (Eds.), *Unfolding stakeholder thinking: relationships, communication, reporting and performance* (pp. 145–161). Sheffield: Greenleaf.

Kitchen, P. J., & Uzunoglu, E. (2014). Introduction: Integrated Communications in the Postmodern Age. In P. J. Kitchen, & E. Uzunoglu (Eds.), *Integrated Communications in the Postmodern Era*, (pp. 1–18). London: Palgrave Macmillan.

KLD Research and Analytics, Inc. (KLD). (2003). KLD Ratings Data: Inclusive Social Rating Criteria.

Klenke, K. (2008). *Qualitative research in the study of leadership.* Bingley: Emerald Group Publishing.

Kwon, E. S., & Sung, Y. (2011). Follow me! Global marketers' twitter use. *Journal of Interactive Advertising*, 12(1), 4–16.

Lee, K., Oh, W. Y., & Kim, N. (2013). Social media for socially responsible firms: Analysis of fortune 500's twitter profiles and their CSR/CSIR ratings. *Journal of Business Ethics*, 118(4), 791–806.

Liu, Y., & Shrum, L. J. (2002). What is interactivity and is it always such a good thing? Implications of definition, person, and situation for the influence of interactivity on advertising effectiveness. *Journal of Advertising*, 31(4), 53–64.

Lovejoy, K., & Saxton, G. D. (2012). Information, community, and action: how nonprofit organizations use social media. *Journal of Computer Mediated Communication*, 17(3), 337–353.

Mooi, E., & Sarstedt, M. (2011). *A concise guide to market research: The process, data, and methods using IBM SPSS statistics.* Berlin Heidelberg: Springer.

Morsing, M. (2006). Corporate social responsibility as strategic auto communication: on the role of external stakeholders for member identification. *Business Ethics: A European Review*, 15(2), 171–182.

Morsing, M., & Schultz, M. (2006). Corporate social responsibility communication: stakeholder information, response and involvement strategies. *Business Ethics: A European Review*, 15(4), 323–338.

Nicholas, D., Rowlands, I., Clark, D., & Williams, P. (2011). Google Generation II: web behaviour experiments with the BBC. *Aslib Proceedings*.

O'Riordan, L., & Fairbrass, J. (2014). Managing CSR stakeholder engagement: A new conceptual framework. *Journal of Business Ethics*, 125(1), 121–145.

Ottman, J. (2011). *The new rules of green marketing: Strategies, tools, and inspiration for sustainable branding*. California: Berrett-Koehler Publishers.

Parmelee, J.H., & Bichard, S.L. (2012). *Politics and the Twitter revolution: How tweets influence the relationship between political leaders and the public*. Lanham, Md: Lexington Books.

Phelan, O., McCarthy, K., Bennett, M., & Smyth, B. (2011). Terms of a feather: Content-based news recommendation and discovery using twitter. In *Advances in Information Retrieval* (pp. 448–459). Berlin Heidelberg: Springer.

Porter, M.E., & Kramer, M.R. (2006). The link between competitive advantage and corporate social responsibility. *Harvard Business Review*, 84(12), 78–92.

Puncheva, P. (2008). The role of corporate reputation in the stakeholder decision-making process. *Business & Society*, 47(3), 272–290.

Quirke, B. (2007). *Making the connections: Using internal communication to turn strategy into action*. Aldershot: Gower Publishing.

Reimann, F., Ehrgott, M., Kaufmann, L., & Carter, C.R. (2012). Local stakeholders and local legitimacy: MNEs' social strategies in emerging economies. *Journal of International Management*, 18(1), 1–17.

Roberts, C. (2009). An experimental investigation into the impact of crisis response strategies and relationship history on relationship quality and corporate credibility.

Rybalko, S., & Seltzer, T. (2010). Dialogic communication in 140 characters or less: How Fortune 500 companies engage stakeholders using Twitter. *Public Relations Review*, 36(4), 336–341.

Saffer, A.J., Sommerfeldt, E.J., & Taylor, M. (2013). The effects of organizational Twitter interactivity on organization–public relationships. *Public Relations Review*, 39(3), 213–215.

Sashi, C.M. (2012). Customer engagement, buyer-seller relationships, and social media. *Management Decision*, 50(2), 253–272.

Schwartz, M.S., & Carroll, A.B. (2003). Corporate social responsibility: A three-domain approach. *Business Ethics Quarterly*, 13(4), 503–530.

Servaes, H., & Tamayo, A. (2013). The impact of corporate social responsibility on firm value: The role of customer awareness. *Management Science*, 59(5), 1045–1061.

Skard, S., & Thorbjørnsen, H. (2014). Is Publicity Always Better than Advertising? The Role of Brand Reputation in Communicating Corporate Social Responsibility. *Journal of Business Ethics*, 124(1), 149–160.

Smith, A. N., Fischer, E., & Yongjian, C. (2012). How does brand-related user-generated content differ across YouTube, Facebook, and Twitter? *Journal of Interactive Marketing*, 26(2), 102–113.

Stopher, P. (2012). *Collecting, managing, and assessing data using sample surveys*. Cambridge: Cambridge University Press.

Tench, R., & Sun, W. (2014). *Communicating Corporate Social Responsibility: Perspectives and Practice* (Vol. 6). Bingley: Emerald Group Publishing.

Timothy Coombs, W. & Holladay, S. J. (2013) The pseudo panopticon: the illusion created by CSR related transparency and the internet. *Corporate Communications: An International Journal*, 18(2), 212–227.

Turkish State Institute of Statistics (2013). Retrieved on 15 December, 2014, from: http://www.tuik.gov.tr.

Türkel, S., Uzunoğlu, E., Kaplan, M. D., & Vural, B. A. (forthcoming, 2015). A strategic approach to corporate social responsibility communication: examining the impact of brand familiarity on consumer responses. *Corporate Social Responsibility and Environmental Management*.

Werther Jr, W. B., & Chandler, D. (2010). *Strategic corporate social responsibility: Stakeholders in a global environment*. California: Sage Publications.

Wong, E., Leung, R., & Law, R. (2015). How effective are Asian hotels in communicating CSR efforts through the property websites? The case of Hong Kong. In *Information and communication technologies in tourism* (pp. 651–663). Lugano: Springer International Publishing.

Wood, D. J. (2010). Measuring corporate social performance: a review. *International Journal of Management Reviews*, 12(1), 50–84.

Wang, J., & Chaudhri, V. (2009). Corporate social responsibility engagement and communication by Chinese companies. *Public Relations Review*, 35(3), 247–250.

Weller, M. (2011). *The digital scholar: How technology is transforming scholarly practice*. London: Bloomsbury.

Whelan, G., Moon, J., & Grant, B. (2013). Corporations and citizenship arenas in the age of social media. *Journal of Business Ethics*, 118(4), 777–790.

Yeung, A., Xin, K., Pfoertsch, W., & Liu, S. (2011). *The globalization of Chinese companies: strategies for conquering international markets*. Singapore: John Wiley & Sons.

Zhao, H. (2014, August). On corporate social responsibility and enterprise responsibility culture in new period. In *2014 2nd International Conference on Education Technology and Information System (ICETIS 2014)*. Atlantis Press.

Senem Gungor

Baskent University, Turkey

Advancement of the Awareness of Social Responsibility at Universities: A Research Study on a Lesson of "Social Responsibility Campaigns" at Baskent University

Introduction

This article describes how a corporate social responsibility (CSR) course will be beneficial for communication students. First, as a result of increasing demands from society that corporations act responsibly, they have come to realise that they are responsible not only to capital shareholders, but also to a broad base of stakeholders, including consumers, customers, employees, governments, and local communities (Ballou, Heitger, & Landes, 2006). Businesses worldwide are now starting to evaluate the way that their products, production processes, operations, and reporting affect society and these stakeholders. Society expects the organisations to not only produce goods and services, but also to make contributions to social, cultural, educational, and political development of society; deal with their problems; and create solutions. Social organisations are evaluated in accordance with the things they do for society. In this regard, it is especially seen after the year 2000 in Turkey that the number of social responsibility projects carried out in such fields as the environment, education, sports, arts, and culture has increased. In fact, the associations related with social responsibilities (Social Responsibility and Training Association, Corporate Social Responsibility Association of Turkey) or websites (sosyalsorumluluk.org, kssrehberi.com, and kurumsalsosyal.com) are established and further importance is attached to the issue.

Therefore, it is essential to sensitise undergraduate communication students to CSR so that they could become the socially responsible business leaders of tomorrow. In this sense, social responsibility studies are now more important to educational institutions as well because previous experience in social responsibility projects is now one of the conditions for employment. The institutions prefer candidates with an improved individual and social sense of responsibility that have served on social responsibility projects or have designed one. As a result, educational institutions started to give courses related with social responsibilities in their educational programs. While many educational institutions include social responsibility courses into compulsory courses, some others require that students work on at least one project before their graduation through the clubs that are established (such as Bahçesehir, Bilkent, Bogaziçi, Gazi, Işık, Koç, Kültür, Sabancı, Yaşar, Yeditepe, and Yıldız Teknik University).

Second, students are interested in environmental and social responsibility issues (Persons, 2012). The learning by serving process in the universities' curriculum efforts are exerted to create awareness about social problems through the active participation of students (Anderson, 1998). In other words, the activities aimed at learning by serving cover the studies aimed at combining social service activities and academic skills (Karayan and Gathercoal, 2005). Students started to engage in recycling, saving energy, protecting the environment, helping local communities, and donating to local charities by projects which are designed at universities. Consequently, it is the responsibility of university level communication educators to further enhance students' interest in and understanding of CSR.

Third, the duties of the institutions of higher education are designated under the Turkish Higher Education Law. One of the duties of how universities should take an important role in social responsibility is clarified as follows:

> *Duties of the Institutions of Higher Education to carry out research and educational activities pertaining to the country's scientific, cultural, social and economic progress and development, and through cooperation with other organisations to encourage public organisations to contribute to such activities; to make research results available to the public, to carry out studies requested by public institutions, and to offer relevant proposals, Cuhadar, 2008.*

As also indicated by Çuhadar (2008:10), this situation will be highly useful in the education of young people. Furthermore, considering that the individuals with a high degree of social sensitivity are necessary in order to establish a society with a high degree of social sensitivity (Yılmaz, 2011:105), it will be practical to use the action learning approach in order to ensure that important role values are internalised in individuals' behaviours. As a result, it could be suggested that the social projects should be spread and practiced both in society and educational institutions. The pre-school and primary school-age students could be provided with the opportunity of being involved in such social projects, as they start to especially gain values in those ages.

This article makes significant contributions to the very scant literature on CSR education because there are no studies about how to incorporate CSR issues into undergraduate communication courses. There are some studies published which discuss CSR courses at Education Faculties; however, they are not enough to discuss the course's design. The closest article to the present article in terms of subject matter is the article "Improving the Consciousness of Social Responsibility at Universities: A Research on Lesson of Social Service Practice at Ege University" (Saran, Coskun, Zorel & Aksoy, 2011), in which the authors describe the coordination and application of social service lessons in Ege University and the challenges in designing such a course. However, most communication faculties do not have such a track and a standalone CSR course at either the undergraduate or graduate levels. The CSR Association of Turkey's (CSR Turkey) second CSR Report in 2010[1] shows that a study has been done in 30 universities by sampling from 141 universities in Turkey according to their allocation in different cities. The study analysed how CSR is performed at the undergraduate level. The findings highlight CSR as an area which is analysed under different topics such as business ethics marketing, public relations, and social entrepreneurship. While few universities have CSR academies, most of the universities have social responsibility units or student clubs and lessons for undergraduates. Social responsibility lessons are mostly electives and credited, in which students develop projects by working together with non-governmental organisations (NGOs) and doing several philanthropic activities. Social responsibility lessons, which focus on the individual responsibilities of students, developed rapidly after the year 2000, while the CSR topic is still in a developing stage. However, the study also shows that there is no direct information about CSR on the websites of the universities; as a result, it was hard to access information. For this reason, this article may be applicable to the undergraduate communication curriculum at most universities.

In the present study, this article attempts to address fulfilling the literature gap by sharing the experience of and materials for CSR issues into undergraduate communication courses. The remainder of this article is presented in four major sections. The first section provides background information about CSR. In the second section, the importance of integrating these issues across the communication curriculum is discussed. In the third section, there is a discussion about sophomore level course design at Baskent University. In the fourth section, student evaluation of the CSR learning experience were held.

Background of CSR

Since Bowen's "Social Responsibilities of the Businessman" book in 1953, a long debate on social responsibility has been taking place. This concept has grown significantly and since then, there has been a shift in terminology from the social

1 CSR Turkey Baseline Report, April 2010. Retrieved from http://csrturkey.org/wp-content/uploads/2013/06/csrbaselinereport.pdf.

responsibility of business to CSR. It has become increasingly important worldwide in the last few decades as society demands that a corporation be accountable for its environmental and social impact. According to Salmones, Crespo, and Bosque (2005: 369), CSR is defined as "the moral obligations that maximise the positive impact of the firm on its social environment and minimise the negative impact." The European Union defines CSR[2] as "a concept whereby companies integrate social and environmental concerns in their business operations and in their interaction with their stakeholders on a voluntary basis." It includes a wide variety of issues ranging from ethical financial reporting to environmental protection, relations with local communities, working conditions, and donations to charities. Therefore, CSR stakeholders are not only limited to shareholders of a corporation, but also to consumers, customers, employees, suppliers, potential investors, local communities, governments, and NGOs. Consumers are asking for green products, employees and local communities are concerned with the health and safety aspects of production, governments have imposed more environmental regulations, and NGOs are running campaigns for the environment and sustainability. In other words, CSR is more of an umbrella term which covers principles and responsibilities related to business ethics, accountability, transparency, human and worker rights, occupational health and safety, gender equality, corruption, environmental awareness, social dialogue, etc. With this comprehensiveness, CSR as a term can be used in all social dimensions.

Although some may think that meeting these emerging CSR challenges means additional costs of conducting business, there is indeed supporting evidence for the benefits of CSR including greater efficiency and cost reduction. Recent studies have shown that CSR actions have a positive influence on the preferences of a) consumers (i.e. Brown & Dacin, 1997; del Mar Garcia de los Salmones et al., 2005; Madrigal, 2000), b) investors (i.e. Orlitzky, Schmidt, & Rynes, 2003), and c) job applicants (i.e. Backhaus, Stone, & Heiner, 2002; Greening & Turban, 2000). Zairi and Peters (2002) also documented links between CSR, return on equity, business image, and performance. Therefore, when CSR issues are successfully incorporated into corporate strategy, they can be transformed into competitive advantages. In Boran's (2000) "Institutional Social Responsibility with Turkish Samples", Korkmaz's (2009) "Social Responsibilities of Cooperationsand Ozgen's (2006) "Projects of Institutional Social Responsibility" books, the CSR projects which Turkish leading companies apply and how the number of projects is increasing each year are discussed.

---

2 Commission Green Paper 2001 "Promoting a European Framework for Corporate Social Responsibility". COM (2001) 366 Final.

As organisations are increasingly involved in CSR, scholars have an important opportunity to engage in CSR research. For example, Peloza (2009) focused on how to measure the impact of CSR on financial performance, Carroll (1999) and Waddock (2004) explored the operationalisation of CSR as well as differences and sometimes confusing overlaps between CSR and similar constructs, Wood (2010) reviewed the literature on how to measure CSR, and Peloza and Shang (2011) conducted a review of how CSR can create value for stakeholders. In addition, other reviews of the CSR literature have focused on specific disciplines such as marketing (Enderle & Murphy, 2009; Maignan & Ferrell, 2004); organisational behaviour, human resource management, and industrial and organisational psychology (Aguinis, 2011); and operations (Brammer, Hoejmose, & Millington, 2011). In the fields of communication, Du, Bhattacharya, & Sen (2010) highlight a need for companies to communicate CSR more effectively to stakeholders. Furthermore, Morsing and Schultz (2006) argue that companies need to communicate through carefully crafted and increasingly sophisticated processes through 'informing' and 'responding' to 'involving' stakeholders in CSR communication itself. In the debate of public relations (PR) and CSR, Kima and Reber (2008) argue about the relationship between PR and CSR through the 173 PR practitioners lenses by analysing their roles and contribution to CSR; Clark (2000) compares CSR and PR by reviewing their origins, theories, processes, and primary responsibilities and found them to be quite similar in these respects; and Masuku and Moyo (2013) discuss how CSR, which is modern PR, is guided by reciprocity between the corporations and their public in an effort to create mutual understanding and goodwill between corporations and their public.

In spite of the reviews published thus far, the CSR literature remains highly fragmented. As noted by Waddock (2004: 5), "parallel and sometimes confusing universes exist." One reason for this fragmentation is that scholars study CSR through different disciplinary and conceptual lenses (Carroll, 1999; Garriga & Melé, 2004; Waddock, 2004). Moreover, the CSR literature is fragmented regarding levels of analysis. First, CSR is usually studied from one level of analysis at a time. Second, CSR is primarily studied at the macro level (i.e. institutional or organisational level) compared to the micro level (i.e. individual level). Accord ingly, there is a need for a multilevel and multidisciplinary review in which the vast and diverse extant literature can be integrated and synthesised in a coherent and comprehensive manner. As Mele´ and Garriga (2004: 65–66) address, most of the current CSR theories are focused on four main angles: "(1) meeting objectives that produce long-term profits, (2) using business power in a responsible way, (3) integrating social demands and (4) contributing to a good society by doing what is ethically correct." This modality helps scholars to classify the most relevant theories on CSR and related concepts into four groups, which are called instrumental, political, integrative, and value theories.

Importance of CSR in Communication Curriculum

The scandals at Enron and WorldCom, as well as the largest United States (US) offshore oil spill at BP's Deepwater Horizon, have definitely propelled the issues of CSR onto the world stage. Meyer and Kirby (2010: 41) stated that "the key to becoming a contemporary corporate leader is to take on responsibility for externalities—what economists call the impacts you have on the world (like pollution) for which you are not called to account." Communication education at universities has a crucial role in training future corporate communication leaders and equipping them with socially conscious thinking and community values that are needed in the turbulence of the changing requirements concerning CSR issues, as these demands about CSR are expected to rapidly increase in the future (Pesonen, 2003). Because CSR cover practically all functions of a corporation, including product development, production management, marketing, human resources, and public relations, management of CSR issues should not be confined to a small expert group in a corporation, but rather integrated throughout a corporate enterprise. Likewise, effective education about CSR should be integrated throughout the curriculum (Brammer, 2005). This practice is known as the mainstreaming of CSR education. The European Academy of Business in Society, created by six European business schools that are leaders in CSR teaching, has also recommended this approach of teaching CSR (Anderson, 2002). Such ranking on the basis of CSR highlights the importance of integrating CSR into communication curriculum which could provide competitive advantages for attracting star students. It is crucial to help undergraduate students understand and appreciate the significance of CSR because this issue will likely define business strategy and performance globally in the next decade.

Design of Social Responsibility Campaigns

As understood from the content, the *Social Responsibility Campaigns* course is conducted under the guidance of a lecturer and is composed of theoretical and practical studies. In this course, students are in the foreground, playing an active role. The lecturer is responsible for guiding, directing, leading, and observing the studies. The course is practiced mostly in society rather than the classroom. The implementation of these projects by the students, and not the preparation of various projects, is important. The failure to practice the projects that are developed would hinder the realisation of the course objective. However, the important thing related with this course is to enable students to deal with social problems, offer solutions to problems, and implement various applications. These applications to be implemented will enable students to realise social problems and develop very important values in social life such as helping each other, cooperation, collaboration, equality, and social justice as well. Furthermore, they will learn how to conduct and realise the campaigns that they will jointly develop. The students will be able to improve their communication skills and also develop other skills such as taking responsibility, conducting single market research, marketing, fundraising, and self-confidence thanks to these projects.

Although the *Social Responsibility Campaigns* course objectives are considerably comprehensive, they are basically capable of creating social sensitivity in a student and thus, bring him or her to the level of playing the role of a social leader, creating an atmosphere necessary for providing him or her with entrepreneurship skills, and enabling him or her to become integrated with society (Coşkun, 2009). The students should be trained and equipped to a degree capable of fulfilling these goals. In this regard, social responsibility campaigns are becoming more important.

A great number of studies could be conducted with regard to the *Social Responsibility Campaigns* course. The education, environment, and aid that could be delivered to children, elders, and the handicapped could be headings of these various studies. As part of the alternatives offered by the course lecturer in the classroom at the beginning of each academic year on the basis of this course, the aid for pre-schools classes at primary schools has been preferred among the alternatives each year and the projects involved in the course have been selected under this heading.

The research study has ensured that the students, as the architecture and individuals of society in the future, prepared social projects in order to be able to turn their values into behaviours through the action learning approach. The changes that are likely to occur in student's values through these social projects are important in terms of becoming a good example in the business atmosphere in which they will work in the future, in case they are turned into behaviours. The prospective leaders of the business world, who bring the social projects that they participate in to their pupils into their business atmosphere, will become the social citizens with an awareness of serving the public and social responsibility. Within this framework, the answers to following sub-problems were sought in order to direct the study:

I. Which values were reflected on students through the social projects that they have implemented?
II. What sort of impacts were created on students through this course?

Working Group and Process

The working group of the research study covers 30 students who attended the Faculty of Communication, Başkent University, in the 2013–2014 academic year. As part of the course, it was decided that the project was implemented as a result of classroom discussions related with social problems under the title of education like the past years. As a result of this decision, the school that was in need around Ankara started to be sought because of students' requests to deliver the aid by hand, as well as the transportation facilities to be provided by the university to immediate surroundings. The project, which emerged from municipalities and also resulted from social media research studies, is indicated in the table below.

Table 1: Projects designated to be implemented

	Project Name to be Implemented	Designated Problems	Selected Solution Offer
2013–2014 Academic Year	Aid campaign for Kütahya/ Altıntaş Yalnızsaray Primary School	As a result of contacts with teachers at the primary school, the coal bunker in the garden will be turned into a nursery school. Also, there are lack of toys, books, stationery equipment, and computers that are necessary for educating the children, as well as a lack of physical needs and limited possibilities. Furthermore, the primary school students are in need of clothes and their classrooms need brand new stoves.	Collecting money and purchasing the needs through the aid campaign to be organised until the end of the academic year. Afterwards, delivery of aid by hand.

After the project was determined, the student teams who are supposed to implement the project consisted of the students taking the course. The groups consisting of a total of five people opened a stand on the campus where they sold home-made food and beverages, thus earning money in a designated day in line with permission obtained from the rectorate with the aid provided by the department of health, culture, and sports by using the strategies and tactics that they learned throughout the course in order to implement the project. The students who are responsible for the implementation of the project also involved their volunteer friends from other faculties into the planning related with their projects. They supplied all of the needs by themselves with the money they earned in line with their market research. Furthermore, the charity to be provided for those both from inside and outside the campus at the Faculty of Communication was collected in the office of the teacher of the course. In the course of the lesson, information was shared with regard to the plans and operation of projects in weekly theoretical classes. The information related with the process of implementing the projects are shown in Table 2.

Table 2: Process of implementing social projects

Project Name	Process of Implementing the Projects
Are you in or out to build their future?	The team conducting the aid campaign for the pre-school firstly established contact with the deputy head of Yalnızsaray primary school and received the list of requirements from him. The school's needs were further clarified with the pictures. Welcoming the requests from students who implemented the project, the dean of the Faculty of Communication and the rector of the Baskent University gave permission so that the stand could be opened for two days. Besides, the Department of Health, Culture, and Sports supplied required physical conditions for the stand, including the process of printing the posters and the leaflets. A poster was printed for the activity which was designed by the students at the university and hung at various places in the campus. Approximately 40 people delivered the aid to the designated school by hand with a vehicle provided by the university on June 5, 2014. The project activity was covered by local press, as well as the university activity bulletin.

Student Evaluation of the Course

The research study was prepared using the qualitative research pattern. The qualitative research methods are important, as they consist of an integrated approach, ensure that the perceptions are revealed, consist of flexibility in the research pattern, as well as an inductive analysis, and enable the research to be conducted in its natural atmosphere. At the end of the course, a semi-structured interview form consisting of ten questions was applied. The forms were evaluated in accordance with the content analysis method.

The data used in the research study have been obtained with the content analysis method, namely, one of the qualitative research methods. As part of the research study, the content analysis was used, as it brings systematicity to the forefront, ensures that a significant number of written texts are analysed, and exerts efforts to obtain the unknown on the basis of a known situation. The values that are emphasised were determined in the answers.

Table 3 emerged as an answer to the following question which is one of the previously mentioned sub-problems in order to direct the study: "Which values were reflected on students through the social projects that they have implemented?"

Table 3: Values reflected on students' statements

Values	Number of Students	%
Being helpful for society	30	100
Togetherness	29	96.67
Enjoying the feeling of success	30	100
Helpfulness	30	100
Responsibility	30	100
Establishing communication	30	100
Social sensitivity	29	96.67
Self-improvement	30	100
Entrepreneurship	28	93.33
Being planned, creating awareness in people	27	90
Self-confidence	30	100
Being capable of problem solving	30	100

Table 4 emerged as an answer to the following question which is one of the previously mentioned sub-problems in order to direct the study: "What sorts of impacts were created on students through this course?"

Table 4:

Impacts	Number of Students	%
Positive impact	30	100
Improve creativeness	29	96.67
Enhanced communication skills	30	100
Understanding CSR	30	100
Intensify the concept of social responsibility	30	100
Leverage his or her experience in the face of competition	30	100
Tactics and promotional ideas to influence the national & regional media	27	90
Tactics and promotional ideas to influence the customers	28	93.3

As is understood from the student's expressions of value and also what is indicated by Brynildssen (2002:2–3), it should be ensured that the students are provided with practice in the classroom, as well the opportunity to participate in social service practices. As a result, their positive characters are developed in the course of value teaching. One of the most attention-grabbing issues among research findings is that the students are capable of noticing social problems through social projects; furthermore, values such as social sensitivity, togetherness and unity, responsibility, and helpfulness were brought into the forefront. These values, which correspond to the course objective, were also shown in other studies conducted by other researchers. In a study carried out by Akkocaoğlu, Albayrak, and Kaptan (narrated by Arkun and Seferoğlu, 2010:4), the prospective teachers' awareness about social problems were increased as a result of social projects that were implemented within the scope of the Community Service Practices course. Similarly, positive changes were observed in their attitudes and behaviours. A study carried out by Elma et al. (2010:246) within the scope of the Community Service Practices course also found that the prospective teachers were provided with such values as communication, solidarity, responsibility, ability to create solutions to problems, sensitivity about social problems, leadership, self-confidence, empathy, and the ability to gain a different point of view.

Conclusion

This study discusses the importance of CSR in communication education and describes the design of the "Social Responsibility Campaigns" course at Baskent University, Faculty of Communication. In sum, this study argues how CSR theories and real life projects positively impact students. With their communication education, the senior year students' action is to use learning approach and experience to integrate CSR strategies to their communication plans effectively. Students' ratings and feedbacks indicate that most of them consider the social responsibility project that they are involved in to be very valuable to their education journey. This is consistent with society's rising demand for corporations to be more environmentally and socially responsible. Consequently, communication faculties should try to incorporate CSR across the undergraduate curriculum because this will likely add value to their communication programs and can serve as an important mechanism for recruiting star students. Educating students about CSR would also make students become more marketable in the job market because an ability to incorporate sustainable processes into a business model can indeed make the business more efficient and reduce costs. Because across-curriculum changes endorsed by the school administration may take some time to materialise, this study's aim is to encourage all communication educators to start incorporating CSR into their courses now. The design of the course, assignments, and the final real life project that are discussed in this study should be useful for accomplishing this objective.

Such academics as Adler, Bigge, Blumer, Dewey, Horney, Lewin, and Sullivan advise that the action learning approach should be practiced at schools. According to this approach, which takes examples of values in people's behaviours, the factor on the basis of an individual's thoughts and behaviours is important. As a result, the action learning approach focuses on allowing a student to turn his or her values into behaviours. As a result, the action learning deals with social studies that have an impact on society rather than a classroom environment based on learning with experiments and lecturing.

Accordingly, the aim of this study is to evaluate the "social responsibilities" course within the scope of social responsibility at faculties of communication. Firstly, the concept of social responsibility was clarified and then evaluated in terms of educational organisations. Afterwards, student feedback on this class and insightful information provide a reference on the enhancement of students' research skills. The project that they design requires them to conduct a research study on CSR policies and actions of an assigned company. This experience sharpens students' critical thinking ability. Students also appreciate an opportunity to learn about their school's sustainability policy because they likely had not been aware of its existence prior to the assignment. Moreover, this course requires students to think critically about how to improve their university's sustainability which is highly relevant to them because they are its stakeholders. Given the limited class time in a semester, most instructors may not have much time to cover CSR issues in addition to required course topics. An answer to this concern would be to use a less intensive approach. For example, instructors may want to use the short class notes and then link the remaining course content to the project that they design.

References

Akkocaoglu, N., Albayrak, A. & Kaptan, F. (2010). "Topluma Hizmet Uygulamaları Dersini Alan Ögretmen Adaylarının Toplumsal Duyarlılık Düzeyleri Üzerine Nitel Bir Çalısma (HÜ Ilkögretim Bölümü Örnegi)", II. Uluslararası Ögretmen Yetistirme Politikaları ve Sorunları Sempozyumu'nda sunulmus bildiri. Ankara: Hacettepe Üniversitesi Egitim Fakültesi. 16–18 Mayıs 2010.

Anderson, L. (2002). CSR on the agenda. *The Banker*, 152(919), 190.

Anderson, J. (1998). "Service learning and teacher education", ERIC Clearinghouse on Teaching and Teacher Education (Report No. ED421481). Washington, DC.

Aguinis, H. (2011). Organizational responsibility: Doing good and doing well. In S. Zedeck (Ed.), *APA handbook of industrial and organizational psychology* (Vol. 3): 855–879. Washington, DC: American Psychological Association.

Backhaus, K. B., Stone, B. A., & Heiner, K. (2002). Exploring the relationship between corporate social performance and employer attractiveness. *Business & Society, 41*, 292–318.

Ballou, B., Heitger, D. L., & Landes, C. E. (2006). The future of corporate sustainability reporting. *Journal of Accountancy*, 202(6), 65–74.

Boran, T. G. (2000). Kurumsal Sosyal Sorumluluk (Türkiye'den Uygulama Örnekleriyle). Beta Yayınları: İstanbul.

Brammer, S. (2005). Teaching corporate responsibility in education. *Corporate Responsibility Management*, 2(2), 4–5.

Brown, T. J., & Dacin, P. A. (1997). The company and the product: Corporate associations and consumer product responses. *Journal of Marketing*, 61(1), 68–84.

Brynildssen, S. (2002). "Character Education though Children's Literature". *ERIC Clearinghouse on Reading English and Communication*. ED469929. http://www.ericdigests.org/2003-3/character.htm.

Carroll, A. B. 1999. Corporate social responsibility. *Business & Society*, 38: 268–295.

Clark, C. E. (2000). Differences Between Public Relations and Corporate Social Responsibility: An Analysis, *Public Relations Review*, 26(3): 363–380.

Çuhadar, A. (2008). "Topluma hizmet uygulamaları dersi aracılıgı ile yurttas-ögretmen yaratmak", VII. Ulusal Sınıf Ögretmenligi Egitimi Sempozyumu'nda sunulmus bildiri. Çanakkale: Çanakkale Onsekiz Mart Üniversitesi Egitim Fakültesi. 2–4 Mayıs 2008.

Coskun, H. (2009). Toplum Hizmet Uygulamaları. Ankara: Anı Yayıncılık.

Del Mar Garcia de los Salmones, M., Herrero Crespo, A., & Rodriguez del Bosque, I. (2005). Influence of corporate social responsibility on loyalty and valuation of services. *Journal of Business Ethics, 61*, 369–385.

Du, S., Bhattacharya, C. B. & Sen, S. (2010). Maximizing Business Returns to Corporate Social Responsibility (CSR): The Role of CSR Communication, *International Journal of Management Reviews,* 12(1): 8–19.

Elma, C., Kesten, A., Kıroglu, K., Uzun, E. M., Dicle, A. M., Palavan, Ö. (2010). "Öğretmen Adaylarının Topluma Hizmet Uygulamaları Dersine İlişkin Algıları", *Kuram ve Uygulamada Eğitim Yönetimi,* Cilt 16, Sayı 2, s.231–252.

Enderle, G., & Murphy, P. E. (2009). Ethics and corporate social responsibility for marketing in the global marketplace. In M. Kotabee & K. Helsen (Eds.), *The Sage handbook of international marketing:* 504–531. Thousand Oaks, CA: Sage.

Garriga, E., & Melé, D. (2004). Corporate social responsibility theories: Mapping the territory. *Journal of Business Ethics,* 53: 51–71.

Greening, D. W., & Turban, D. B. (2000). Corporate social performance as a competitive advantage in attracting a quality workforce. *Business & Society, 39,* 254–280.

Karayan, S. & Gathercoal, P. (2005). "Assessing service-learning in teacher education", Teacher Education Quarterly, 32, 79–85.

Kima, S. Y. and Reber, B. H. (2008). Public relations' place in corporate social responsibility: Practitioners define their role, Public Relations Review 34 (2008) 337–342.

Korkmaz, S. (2009). İşletmelerin Sosyal Sorumlulukları. Umuttepe: İstanbul.

Madrigal, R. (2000). The role of corporate association in new product evaluation. *Advances in Consumer Research,* 27(1), 80–86.

Maignan, I., & Ferrell, O. C. (2004). Corporate social responsibility and marketing: An integrative framework. *Journal of Academy of Marketing Science,* 32: 3–19.

Masuku, C. and Moyo, P. (2013). Corporate social responsibility as an invention of public relation: A case of Econet and National Railways of Zimbabwe (NRZ), *Journal of Media and Communication Studies,* Vol. 5(8), pp. 113–122.

Meyer, C., & Kirby, J. (2010). The big idea: Leadership in the age of transparency. *Harvard Business Review,* 88(4), 38–46.

Morsing, M. and Schultz, M. (2006). Corporate social responsibility communication: stakeholder information, response and involvement strategies, Business *Ethics: A European Review,* 15(4): 323–338,

Orlitzky, M., Schmidt, F. L., & Rynes, S. L. (2003). Corporate social and financial performance. *Organization Studies, 24,* 403–441.

Özgen, E. (2006). Kurumsal Sosyal Sorumluluk Projeleri. Mavi Ağaç: İstanbul.

Peloza, J. (2009). The challenge of measuring financial impacts from investments in corporate social performance. *Journal of Management,* 35: 1518–1541.

Peloza, J., & Shang, J. (2011). How can corporate social responsibility activities create value for stakeholders? A systematic review. *Journal of the Academy of Marketing Science,* 39: 117–135.

Persons, O. (2012). Incorporating Corporate Social Responsibility, *Journal of Education for Business.* Vol. 87 Issue 2, p. 63–72.

Pesonen, H. L. (2003). Challenges of integrating environmental sustainability issues into business school curriculum: A case study from the University of Jyvaskyla, Finland. *Journal of Management Education, 27,* 158–171.

Salmones, M., Crespo, A. H. and Bosque, I. R. (2005). Influence of Corporate Social Responsibility on Loyalty and Valuation of Services, *Journal of Business Ethics*, Volume 61, Issue 4, pp. 369–385.

Saran, Coskun, Zorel & Aksoy, (2011). "Improving the Consciousness of Social Responsibility at Universities: A Research on Lesson of Social Service Practice at Ege University", Journal of Yasar University 2011 22(6) 3732–3747.

Yılmaz, K. (2011). "Eğitim Fakültelerinin Sosyal Sorumluluğu Ve Topluma Hizmet Uygulamaları Dersi: Nitel Bir Araştırma", *Kuramsal Egitimbilim*, 4(2), 86–108.

Waddock, S. A. (2004). Parallel universes: Companies, academics, and the progress of corporate citizenship. *Business and Society Review*, 109: 5–42.

Wood, D. J. (2010). Measuring corporate social performance: A review. *International Journal of Management Reviews*, 12: 50–84.

Zairi, M., & Peters, J. (2002). The impact of social responsibility on business performance. *Management Auditing Journal*, *17*, 172–178.

Sevda Deneçli

Impact of Viral Marketing through Social Media on Corporate Image

Introduction

Technology is a part of our lives and its development each day affects us in many ways. Technological progress, which began when people started using the internet, has been continuously increasing. The internet began as a technology that allows for one-way communication through which information could be obtained and thus, individuals were passive in this process. However, Web 2.0 technology made two-way communication possible and has provided individuals with the opportunity to participate in the internet and, thus, to pass into an active state.

Through Web 2.0 technology, where two-way communication is possible, a period of social media has begun in which all kinds of information can be shared, comments can be made on desired issues, and individuals can interact with each other or with organisations through social networks. Individuals' sharing, liking, posting, and tweeting information, etc. allows that information to reach other individuals in their network. When the individuals in their network do the same, that information can be spread to many people within a very short period of time, thus allowing viral communication to be possible.

Marketers' use of social media as a marketing tool on the basis of this aspect of viral communication has become widespread today. In addition to the viral marketing efforts initiated by marketers, a comment written by ordinary individuals on an organisation, a post they share or tag, and so on may also constitute a viral marketing process. In viral marketing, the difficulty of supervising the context of the message brings the question of affecting the corporation's image to the fore.

Social Media and Viral Marketing

Today, the fact that social media is frequently said to have become an indispensable concept has caused traditional marketing activities to become less efficient. Traditional marketing concepts have transformed into an understanding of marketing based on social media and marketing activities have become more complicated (Kirby & Marsden, 2006, p. xviii). It has been observed that people obtain the information they require prior to purchasing products to meet their needs not from the corporation itself, but from the internet. Therefore, when the situation is taken into consideration from a marketing point of view, the consumer has started to have a more important status in comparison to the organisation (Larson, 2009, p. 6).

In the social media world, not only a certain category of people, but everyone changes the views of others and has a say. When social media is regarded in this context, people are given the chance with a single tick to achieve a power that they have never had before. This constitutes the core of a great revolution in communication through this innate characteristic (Lincoln, 2009, p. 10–11). In addition, by giving people who are separated due to their geographic locations a chance to come together (Weinberg, 2009, p. 1), social media causes the world to turn into a global village, as Marshall McLuhan states. In this village where boundaries have disappeared, people from all over the world can interact with each other on any subject they desire, at any time they wish.

The concept of social media is a technological whole which embodies communication, context, individuals, friends of the individuals, and their social networks. The social network in turn expresses groups of people who have common interest areas, similar points of view, and similar pasts. People who are a part of social networks have a social graph. The social graph contains information related to the individual's past, such as with which corporations the individual has a relationship, in which schools the individual has been educated, what the individual likes, and with whom the individual is friends with (Treadaway & Smith, 2010, p. 24–25). When the issue is considered within the framework of these concepts and when the social networks of individuals within social media are analysed, it can be seen that these individuals have individuals with the same social graphs in their social networks. This is because individuals generally add those who have the same tastes, those whose points of views overlap with theirs, and those whose ideas are similar to theirs to their networks.

Social media marketing serves as a tool for creating brand awareness, identifying the opinion leaders in research on the opinions of the consumers and the masses, spreading certain messages virally, developing consumer databases, creating trust and prestige for the brand, and increasing the image of the brand (Tuten, 2008, p. 26). The power held by corporations, which in traditional media have the competence to create a context and transmit that context to individuals, has turned into a position in which everyone can create a context and transmit and share their messages and ideas through social media (Lincoln, 2009, p. 21).

It can be observed that Web 2.0 technologies have transferred communication activities from the desktop to the web. The focus of creating production value has shifted to consumers rather than companies and control has been transferred from companies to consumers. In technological terms, when Web 2.0 and Web 1.0 are compared, it can be seen that the focus has been redirected from companies to consumers, from individuals to groups, and to an environment in which individuals participate rather than a single source (Berthon et al., 2012, p. 262). Web 1.0, which made it possible to publish context, has ceded its place to blogs, wikis, and other media in which the user can also participate with the emergence of Web 2.0 technology (Kaplan & Haenlein, 2010, p. 61). In Web 2.0, which is defined as the 'participatory web' (Lincoln, 2009, p. 8), it may be stated that through social networks, individuals achieve viral marketing due to them posting or sharing their information and areas of interest with other individuals (Solomon et al., 2013, p. 435). In line with the development of social media, the democratisation of communication activities has transferred the power held by marketing and public relations to individuals and communities who write blogs, tweet, and share movies, pictures, etc. in social media circles such as Facebook and create and share content (Kietzmann et al., 2011, p. 242).

In this context, in cases where a corporation/brand takes part in an individual's network, the interaction of the corporation/brand with the individual means that this person is seen by the other people within his or her own network. This communication that the corporation establishes with the individual initiates a chat chain in that person's social group or network and creates positive word-of-mouth communication (O'Leary et al., 2011, p. 3).

The concept of viral marketing functions based on the social network. Internet users first assume a role as the receiver, then as the transmitter of the message. The presentation of pre-prepared viral information to individuals who have social networks and the person who receives the information transmitting it to other people constitutes the viral marketing process. In viral marketing, since information is transmitted by other individuals whom the individuals knows, it is spread speedily, as it is perceived as reliable and the individuals do not see any harm in sharing a message that they find reliable (Skrob, 2005, p. 5). Evans (2008, p. 20) comments: "The value of 'trust' between friends and colleagues gained in its role in purchase decisions. It is exactly this sentiment that drives word-of-mouth, and now social media. The dynamics of trust have long been part of the marketing conversation."

The speed of the spread of the virus through distribution channels such as e mails, chats, blogs, and video services on the internet is just as fast as the spread of viruses known in medicine. The internet virus develops in three stages: contamination (acceptance of the information), development (becoming used to the information), and spreading (transferring of the information to other users; Kwiatkowska, 2009, p. 1049). Viral communication is carried out when a person within the network shares his or her message with the other people in his or her network. When an individual shares a message in his or her network, the message reaches the individuals in his or her network. The individuals who receive this message and share the same message in their own networks causes them to reach the people in their own networks and viral communication thus takes place (Deckers & Lacy, 2012, p. 130).

It can be observed that the context of the posts that have a tendency to spread virally in social media is entertaining, gives unique information about a subject besides giving examples from real life, involves beneficial sources or tools for readers, or can be a competition giving away a prize or a subject that is on the current agenda (Parker, 2010, p. 21). Besides the positive aspects of viral marketing such as being cost-free, reaching a great number within a short period of time, spreading speedily, increasing incrementally, transmitting the message voluntarily, and creating more powerful targets, there are negative aspects such as not being able to provide control over the context and the rate at which it spreads, spamming, attacking the privacy of the consumer, the possibility of consumers feeling cheated, negative comments made on the message, the complications these negative comments may create, and negative brand perception (Woerndl et al., 2008, p. 36).

In viral marketing, a message that is only about a brand, product, or service is expressed only by a word-of-mouth communication process. In addition, it affects the preferences of consumers and their attitudes prior to using goods and services, as well as shaping their perception after usage. Through social media tools, consumers, who have the chance to reflect their point of view on corporations and brands, influence the image that the corporation wishes to create with what they share on the web (Palka et al., 2009, p. 172; Larson, 2009, p. 6).

It may be stated that, due to not being able to control social media contexts and posts, negative contexts and comments threaten the image of corporations (Kuvykaite & Piligrimiene, 2013, p. 306), while positive posts and comments may have a positive effect on the image of these corporations.

This study aims at identifying the effect of viral marketing in social media on corporations' images. With this purpose in mind, participants who stated that they had read a post by any friend about an experience related to a brand they know in the last three months on Facebook were taken into consideration and an attempt was made to identify how and in what manner the viral kind of posts influence consumers' image of a company.

Methods

Participants

The study was conducted among 286 university students. 58% of the participants were female and 73% were in the 18–21 age group. 45% of the participants in the study (128 people) stated that they had read a friend's post on Facebook about an experience with a brand with which they are familiar with in the last three months. In the analysis carried out in the study, the answers given by the 128 people in question were taken as the basis for the analysis. In terms of identifying whether the posts were viral or not, the participants were asked if they had heard about the post in question from other people and if they had shared it with other people. 44.5% of the participants (57 people) stated that they had heard about the post from others and shared it with others.

Measures

In the study, a survey was conducted in order to compile the data. The survey consisted of various questions about the subject and a scale. In the study, the participants were asked whether they had heard about the context in relation to a given brand and whether they had shared it with other people with the purpose of identifying whether they had been subjected to a viral context (yes/no). In addition, the participants were asked to make an evaluation of the context of the post (five: very positive, one: very negative). In the study, in order to determine how the participants were affected by the perception of the corporate image, they were asked what kind of changes took place in their views about the brand after the post (five: very positive, one: very negative). Furthermore, the participants were asked about their attitude to the brand prior to the post, which is thought to be effective on their views of the brand (five: very positive, one: very negative) and whether they had had any experience of the brand (yes/no). In the study, a scale consisting of four expressions (for instance, "I write comments to my friends' posts on Facebook") was designed in order to determine the participants' level of active use of Facebook (following posts, liking posts, commenting on posts, and sharing posts). These expressions were organised as a five-point Likert scale (five: strongly agree, one: strongly disagree). Factor analysis (with Varimax rotation) was carried out and the scale was determined to have one dimension (KMO=0.80; Barlett's Test $p=0.00<0.01$; Declared Total Variances–74.3%). The Cronbach's Alpha value calculated for the scale was 0.88. Prior to the survey, the survey form was completed by the research group consisting of twelve people and the survey was repeated ten days later to carry out the reliability analysis. According to this analysis, the test-repeat-test coefficients calculated for the questions on the survey (these changed between 0.88 and 0.96) showed that the survey form was reliable.

Statistical Analysis

In the study, multiple regression analysis was used to determine the aspects that affect the change in corporate image perception. Two separate analyses were conducted for posts that were viral and not viral. In the analysis, the dependent variable was the change in corporate image perception, while the independent variables were the context of the post, the participant's active usage level of Facebook, the participant's attitude towards the brand prior to the post, and having experience with the brand.

Findings

According to the regression analysis carried out to determine the effects of posts that are not viral on the change of perception of corporate image (Table 1), a significant model has not been achieved ($R2=0.11$ $F=2.00$ $p=0.10>0.05$). However, it has been observed that among all the variables, the context of the post variable has a significant impact (Standard Beta=0.33 $p=0.02<0.05$). According to the regression analysis carried out to determine the effects of posts that are viral on the change of perception of corporate image (Table 2), a significant model has been achieved ($R2=0.39$ $F=7.53$ $p=0.00<0.01$). According to the model, among the variables it can be seen that the context of the post (Standard Beta=0.53 $p=0.00<0.01$) and the participants' level of active use of Facebook (Standard Beta=0.30 $p=0.01<0.05$) have a significant impact on the change of perception of corporate image. Although the explanatory power of the model, which explains the effect of posts that are not viral on the change of perception of corporate image, is not significant, the explanatory power of the model, which explains the viral posts on the change of perception of corporate image when 0.11 is 0.39. According to this, it is possible to state that posts that are viral are more effective on the change of perception of corporate image.

Table 1: Regression analysis results of the effect of posts that are not viral on the change of perception of corporate image

	B	**Standard Error**	**Standard Beta**	**t**	**p**
(Fixed)	1.97	0.27		7.11	0.00**
Post context	0.18	0.07	0.33	2.44	0.02*
Active use of Facebook	0.01	0.07	0.03	0.21	0.83
Attitude towards the brand prior to the post	-0.08	0.07	-0.15	-1.12	0.26
Having experience with the brand prior to the post	-0.26	0.16	-0.19	-1.57	0.12

Dependent Variable: Change in the perception of corporate image
$R2=0.11$ $F=2.00$ $p=0.10>0.05$
**$p<0.01$

Table 2: Regression analysis results on the effect of viral posts on the change of perception of corporate image

	B	Standard Error	Standard Beta	t	p
(Fixed)	0.89	0.42		2.12	0.04*
Post context	0.31	0.07	0.53	4.30	0.00**
Active use of Facebook	0.21	0.08	0.30	2.57	0.01*
Attitude towards the brand prior to the post	−0.12	0.09	−0.16	−1.24	0.22
Having experience with the brand prior to the post	0.16	0.23	0.08	0.69	0.49

Dependent Variable: Change in the perception of corporate image
$R2=0.39$ $F=7.53$ $p=0.00<0.01$
$^{**}p<0.01$ $^{*}p<0.05$

Conclusion

The study results show that a viral post on a given brand posted on Facebook is effective on the brand's corporate image. The positive effect of viral posts on the consumer's image of the company takes place in accordance with the context of the posts' level of positivity, the consumer actively following the posts on Facebook, and a high frequency of sharing these with others. On the other hand, if a post on a given brand is not viral (at least, in the eyes of the consumer who is subject to that post), then it is not possible for the consumer to affect the corporate image related to the brand. In both models, the contexts of the posts affecting a change in corporate image to a positive and significant level underline the fact that the contexts of posts about brands in social media are important.

References

Berthon, P. R., Pitt, L. F., Plangger, K., & Shapiro, D. (2012) Marketing meets Web 2.0, social media, and creative consumers: Implications for international marketing strategy. *Business Horizons, 55*, 261–271.

Deckers, E., & Lacy, K. (2012) *Branding Yourself: How to Use Social Media to Invent or Reinvent Yourself.* 2nd Ed. Upper Saddle River, NJ: Pearson.

Evans, D. (2008) *Social Media Marketing.* Toronto: Wiley.

Kaplan, A. M., & Haenlein, M. (2010) Users of the world, unite! The challenges and opportunities of social media. *Business Horizons, 53*, 59–68.

Kietzmann, J. H., Hermkens, K., McCarthy, I. P., & Silvestre, B. S. (2011). Social media? Get serious! Understanding the functional building blocks of social media. *Business Horizons, 54*, 241–251.

Kirby, J., & Marsden, P. (2006) *Connected Marketing: The Viral, Buzz and Word of Mouth Revolution*. London: Elsevier.

Kuvykaite, R., & Piligrimiene, Z. (2013). Communication in social media for company's image formation. *Economics and Management*, 18(2), 305–317.

Kwiatkowska, J. A. (2009) Viral marketing in the Internet. Characteristics of an effective virus. *Annales Universitatis Apulensis Series Oeconomica*, 11(2). pp. 1047–1054.

Larson, R. J. (2009) The rise of viral marketing through the new media of social media: An analysis and implications for consumer behavior. R 1 MKT7001-11. Faculty Publications and Presentations, Lynchburg, VA: Liberty University.

Lincoln, S. R. (2009). *Mastering Web 2.0: Transform Your Business Using Key Website and Social Media Tools*. London: Kogan Page.

O'Leary, S., Sheehan, K., & Lentz, S. (2011). *Small Business Smarts: Building Buzz with Social Media*. Santa Barbara, CA: Praeger.

Palka, W., Pousttchi, K., & Wiedemann, D. G. (2009). Mobile word-of-mouth: A grounded theory of mobile viral marketing. *Journal of Information Technology, 24*, 172–185.

Parker, C. (2010). *301 Ways to Use Social Media to Boost Your Marketing*. New York: McGraw-Hill.

Skrob, J. R. (2005). Open source and viral marketing: The viral marketing concept as a model for open source to reach the critical mass for global brand awareness based on the example of TYPO3. Kufstein: University of Applied Science Kufstein, http://www.tuga.at/fileadmin/tuga/downloads/tyon3_2005/paper50.pdf.

Solomon, M. R., Bamossy, G. J., Askegaard, S. T., & Hogg, M. K. (2013). *Consumer Behaviour: A European Perspective*. 5th Ed. London: Pearson.

Treadaway, C., & Smith, M. (2010) *Facebook Marketing*. Toronto: Wiley.

Tuten, T. L. (2008). *Advertising 2.0 Social Media Marketing in a Web 2.0 World*. Santa Barbara, CA: Praeger.

Weinberg, T. (2009). *The New Community Rules: Marketing on the Social Web*. Newton, MA: O'Reilly Media.

Woerndl, M., Papagiannidis, S., Bourlakis, M., & Li, F. (2008) Internet-induced marketing techniques: Critical factors in viral marketing campaigns. *International Journal of Business Science and Applied Management*, 3(1). pp. 33–45.

Şifa Elcil*

Strategic Role of Leadership Approach in Corporate Communication

Abstract Competition and constant change intensifying with globalisation have rendered activities of corporations even more complex. Corporations have to adapt themselves to any environmental factors and make a difference in a competition atmosphere threatening their existence. Corporate communication is for a corporation to strategically plan and implement communication measures oriented to all target audiences of that corporation. Corporate communication, at the same time, is to create awareness about products and services offered by the enterprises and to improve the commitment and trust to the target audience. The most important value of a corporation to create a difference and gain a competitive advantage is their employees. Customer satisfaction is closely related to employee satisfaction for corporations. Therefore, one cannot achieve customer satisfaction without first improving human capital. Employees that are communicated with and managed well results in qualified products/services and customer satisfaction. Carrying out corporate communication in a healthy way is about first incorporating relevant values into the corporate vision and mission and then reflecting this understanding to all work processes of the corporation. The aim of this study is to determine the role of leadership approaches for the activation of employees in corporate communication. The research study is important in terms of determining manners and behaviours of managers on this issue.

In the first section of the research study, corporate communication, leadership approaches, and its strategic importance are discussed. Survey questions consisting of research questions were applied to senior executives at companies in the second section. The sample and scope of research consist of senior executives at 50 companies registered to the Istanbul Chamber of Trade. The random sampling method was used for the selection of companies and companies on the first, fifth, tenth, fifteenth, etc. sequences were chosen. The research study was conducted through phone interviews.

Keywords: Corporate communication, leadership, leadership approaches.

1. Introduction

Competition and constant change intensifying with globalisation have made activities of corporations even more difficult. Corporations have to adapt themselves to any environmental factors and make a difference in a competitive atmosphere

* İstanbul Aydın University, Faculty of Communication, Lecturer at Public Relations and Promotion Major.

threatening their existence. Corporate communication is for a corporation to plan and implement communication measures strategically oriented to any target audience. Corporate communication is also the act of raising awareness about products and services offered by enterprises and improving the trust and commitment to the target audience.

The most important value of corporations to make a difference and gain an advantage in competition is their employees. Customer satisfaction is closely related to employee satisfaction for corporations. Therefore, one cannot achieve customer satisfaction without first improving human capital. Employees that are communicated with and managed well results in qualified products/services and customer satisfaction. Carrying out corporate communication in a healthy way is about first incorporating relevant values into the corporate vision and mission and then reflecting this understanding to all work processes of the corporation.

Those who will implement corporate communication understanding are senior managers and corporate employees leading in line with an understanding of quality and excellence. Therefore, leaders are expected to have a high awareness about the role of employees in corporate communication and development. In this respect, it is highly important whether leaders in corporations adopt an understanding of central management or participative management and whether or not the importance of employees are stated in strategic development plans. It is also important for managers to train employees and encourage them to improve their skills, to encourage team spirit, to authorise and strengthen employees, and to improve communication skills and the creativeness of employees.

The strategic importance of leadership in corporate communication is first manifested in this work and then it is aimed to determine whether or not senior executives having a significant role in corporate communication include the following in their plans: the importance given to employees, training, improving, encouraging employees, encouraging team spirit, improving communication skills, and creativeness of employees.

2. Corporate Value of Corporate Communication

Communication is a complicated concept as a senior discipline related to many elements. It becomes even more complicated. A number of factors affect forms of perception and evaluation on an individual and social basis and structure the formation of reality, including: corporations created by mankind, rules, values, social needs, and expectations managing the operation of corporations; quality of relations among people; and other such factors. Furthermore, public relations contribute to the formation of reality with all of its functions. The concept of communication as a senior discipline is a guiding compass in both corporate and social terms. Society, corporations, and communication contribute to social reality interacting with each other as concepts related to each other (Mumby and Stohl, 1996; Ellis and Maoz, 2003).

Various elements such as the competitive environment, changing social sensitivities, technological developments, decrease of product and service differences, increase of customer expectations, and the crisis gaining speed with rapid replacement of information directs companies to different quests. Upon understanding strategic importance of public relations, it became obligatory for corporations to offer quality products and services making a difference, to create their social reputation, and sustain it with the understanding of strategic management and strategic communication and a certain approach of social responsibility. In this respect, strategic communication and strategic management functions of public relations stand out in the agenda of corporations.

The concept of strategy is used in the meaning of way, line or manoeuvre, position, pattern, and perspective. Strategy in public relations means politics on the corporate and industrial level to be followed for achieving targets and aims (Botan, 224–225; 2006). Strategy, in this context, is communication and decisions of a corporation conducted with all partners.

Employees in a corporation become more effective through their in-house development activities (Pfeffer, 143; 1995). Public relations aim to create a change of attitude and behaviour in the target audience with its own areas of activity. Corporate communication has a privileged place among other corporate strategies and politics in terms of motivation of employees and their commitment to the corporation and the development of the corporation. This is because individuals commit to a corporation thanks to communication, resulting in corporate structure being formed through communication. Corporate pattern is a reality created by communication.

The sense of corporate communication is about the vision and mission of corporations (Reilly and Diangelo, 1990: 129–140). In other words, communication is a summary of information about humans and the environment with meanings, values, symbols (Reilly and DiAngelo, 1990), and ideologies. In this respect, it first contributes in corporate structuring to the production of goods and services by providing collaboration, harmony, and synergy among employees of the corporation and increases organisational effectiveness. The operation of corporate communication is directly proportional to effective leadership approaches because managerial understanding in a corporation reflects on all work processes and methods of working in a corporation.

3. Strategic Role of Leadership in the Development of Corporate Communication

The sense of management is as old as the history of humanity. The sense of management has always existed in environments where people come together and cooperate for various purposes. In this respect, considering management is a process, four important elements attract attention, as follows (Ülgen and Mirze, 2014: 23–24):

- For corporations achieving their aim,
- Producing work through others,
- Planning, organising, executing, and controlling functions,
- Effectiveness and productivity in all these processes.

The text mentions the difference between leader and leadership in corporation activity; furthermore, while a leader is defined as the person motivating and leading others, leadership is defined as the process of influencing others' activities to realise their targets (Koçel, 729; 2010). Managers of the company take required decisions in light of feedback and information in line with the corporation's philosophy, vision, and mission and provide corporate effectiveness. Managerial effectiveness and productivity especially gain importance at this point. Managers are responsible people to provide a corporation with the ability to achieve their goals effectively and productively through their planning, organising, executing, and controlling functions.

Strategic management means a lot for skilled leaders and supports them in their activities (Theodore and Streib, 324; 1999). Strategic management process is for corporations all information collection, analysis, election, decision and application activities oriented to carry on their long term existence and provide sustainable competitive advantage. n this respect, the strategic management process is about understanding subjects such as:

- Application of strategies is leaded,
- Corporations and competitors produce and apply various strategies,
- How such strategies will be improved more effectively,
- How it will benefit from environmental opportunities and threats regarding change,
- Flexibility,
- Effective leading of human resources,
- Winning employees' trust. (Ülgen and Mirze, 33: 2014; Thompson, 4: 1990).

Managers make decisions in a corporation for corporate effectiveness and productivity in light of feedback received. A scientific and systematic communication process oriented to multidirectional and environmental relations of corporations is recommended in a sense of modern management. Therefore, managers have to benefit from communication and adopt a modern management philosophy in order to create a positive change of manners and behaviours in people and corporations they communicate with in both an individual and corporate sense. High solidarity and communication in the operation of corporate processes depends on good relations and harmony with employees. Harmony with employees in corporate communication will increase production and service quality and contribute to corporate effectiveness.

Communication is an administrative behaviour. Moreover, another important matter is the employees of a corporation. The most important value of corporation to create a difference and gain a competitive advantage is their employees. The reason is that customer satisfaction is closely related to employee satisfaction in corporations. Therefore, one cannot reach customer satisfaction before first improving human capital. Employees that are communicated with and managed well results in qualified products/services and customer satisfaction. Carrying out corporate communication in a healthy way is about first incorporating relevant values into the corporate vision and mission and then reflecting this understanding to all work processes of the corporation; both managers and employees will be the people to provide this. In other words, those who will apply corporate communication understanding are senior managers and corporation employees leading in line with a sense of quality and excellence. Leaders are expected to have a high awareness regarding the role of employees in corporate communication and development. In this respect, it is highly important whether leaders in corporations adopt an understanding of central management or participative management and whether or not the importance of employees are stated in strategic development plans. It is also important for managers to train employees and encourage them to improve their skills, to encourage team spirit, to authorise and strengthen employees, and to improve communication skills and the creativeness of employees.

4. Purpose and Importance of the Research Study

The reason for the research study is to determine the role of leadership approaches in enabling employees in corporate communication. The research study is important to determine manners and behaviours of managers on this subject.

4.1 Methods and Means of the Research Study

Corporate communication, leadership approaches, and its strategic importance are discussed in the first section of the research study. Survey questions consisting of research questions were asked to senior executives at companies in the second section.

The sample and scope of the research consist of senior executives at 50 companies registered to the Istanbul Chamber of Trade. The random sampling method was used for the selection of companies and companies on the first, fifth, tenth, fifteenth, etc. sequences were chosen. The phone interview method was used for the research study.

The textile industry was chosen as it is a rapidly developing industry and that has many employees.

There are more than 500 textile companies registered to the chamber. 50 companies were chosen as the first, fifth, and tenth among them using the random sampling method. 30 out of 50 companies were reached and interviewed on the phone.

4.2 Hypothesis (H) of the Research Study

H1: Corporation's corporate vision and mission is related to all work processes to achieve its strategic goals.

H2: The strategic goals and targets of the corporation include importance given to employees.

H3: Leaders of the corporation adopt a leader role supporting the improvement of employees.

H4: Supporting the improvement of employees and the improvement of corporate communication are directly proportional.

4.3 Findings of the Research Study

Twelve questions were asked to senior executives. Answers to questions and findings are detailed below.

Question 1. Are vision, mission, purpose, and strategies of the corporation clear?

30 managers out of 30 answered yes to this question. The proportion of this result is 100%.

Question 2. Is the importance given to employees of a corporation stated in its vision and mission?

22 out of 30 managers answered yes to this question, while eight answered no. According to this result, 73% of managers replied in the affirmative.

Question 3. Is the importance given to employees of a corporation stated in its strategic aims and goals of the corporation?
25 out of 30 managers answered yes to this question, while five answered no. According to this result, 83% of managers replied in the affirmative.

Question 4. Are vision and mission of your corporation in compliance with its aims and goals?
26 out of 30 managers answered yes to this question, while four answered no. According to this result, 87% of managers replied in the affirmative and 13% replied unfavourably.

Question 5. Are vision and mission of your corporation associated with all work processes?
Twelve out of 30 managers answered yes to this question, while 18 answered no. According to this result, 40% of managers replied in the affirmative and 60% replied unfavourably.

Question 6. Do leaders care about corporate communication and its role in the corporate development of employees?
27 out of 30 managers answered yes to this question, while three answered no. According to this result, 90% of managers replied in the affirmative and 10% replied unfavourably.

Question 7. Is a central sense of management or a participatory sense of culture adopted in the corporation?
18 managers answered that a participatory sense of culture is adopted, while twelve managers answered that a central sense of management is adopted. This result indicates that 60% participatory and 40% central sense of management is dominant.

Question 8. Are employees encouraged to receive training and improve their skills by the managers in your corporation?
26 managers answered yes to this question, while four managers answered no. According to this result, 87% of managers answered positively and 13% answered negatively.

Question 9. Is it encouraged in your corporation to authorise and strengthen employees?
17 managers answered yes to this question, while 13 managers answered no. According to this result, 57% of managers answered positively and 43% answered negatively.

Question 10. Is teamwork and team spirit encouraged in your corporation?
23 managers answered yes to this question, while seven managers answered no. According to this result, 77% of managers replied in the affirmative and 23% replied unfavourably.

Question 11. Is there a corporate culture in your corporation where employees can improve their creativity?
15 managers answered yes to this question, while 15 managers answered no. This rate equals 50% for both answers.

Question 12. Are activities carried out in your corporation to improve the communication skills of employees?
16 managers answered yes to this question, while 14 managers answered no. According to this result, 53% of managers replied in the affirmative and 47% replied unfavourably.

Result and Evaluation

Corporate communication means the visions and missions of corporations, values shared in a corporation, and the meanings and symbols creating corporate culture. It is information spread to all partners starting inside the corporation. In this respect, it first contributes in corporate structuring to the production of goods and services by providing collaboration, harmony, and synergy among employees of the corporation and increases organisational effectiveness. Operation of corporate communication is directly proportional to effective leadership approaches. In other words, those who will apply corporate communication understanding are senior managers and corporation employees leading in line with a sense of quality and excellence; this is because managerial understanding in a corporation reflects on all work processes and methods of working in a corporation. Thus, leaders are expected to have a high awareness regarding the role of employees in corporate communication and development. In this respect, it is highly important whether leaders in corporations adopt an understanding of central management or participative management and whether or not the importance of employees are stated in strategic development plans. It is also important for managers to train employees and encourage them to improve their skills, to encourage team spirit, to authorise and strengthen employees, and to improve communication skills and the creativeness of employees.

When the results of the research study are examined, questions one, four, and five are related to H1. Accordingly, all participants gave affirmative answers to the question of whether the vision, mission, purpose, and strategies of the corporation are clear. Our second question, whether strategic aims and goals of your company comply with its vision and mission, was affirmed at a rate of 87%. The fifth question, whether corporation's vision and mission are associated with all work processes, was answered positively by 40% of respondents and negatively by 60% of respondents. According to this result, our assertion that corporation's vision and mission are associated with all work processes to achieve the corporation's strategic goals, H1, was confirmed. Accordingly, 73% of managers answered positively to the question of whether the importance given to corporation employees is stated in the vision and mission of the corporation. The question of whether the importance given to employees is stated among strategic aims and goals of the corporation was answered positively by 83% of respondents. Based on this result, the hypothesis that strategic aims and goals of a corporation include the importance placed on its employees is confirmed. Questions six to twelve are about H3. Accordingly, 90% of respondents answered positively to the question of whether the role of corporation's employees in corporate communication and corporate development is cared about by the leaders. The question of whether a central sense of management or a participatory sense of culture is adopted in the corporation was answered with the participatory sense of culture by 60% of respondents. The question of whether employees' training and improving their skills are encouraged by managers was answered positively by 87% of respondents. The question of whether employees in the corporation are encouraged to be authorised and strengthened was answered positively by 57% of respondents. The question of whether teamwork and team spirit is encouraged in the corporation was answered positively by 77% of respondents. The question of whether there is a corporate culture in the corporation where employees can improve their creativity was replied in the affirmative by 53% of respondents. According to this result, H3, stating that corporate leaders support the improvement of employees, is verified. H4, which states that supporting employees' improvement and the improvement of corporate communication are directly proportional, is largely confirmed by corporations; however, it was concluded that there are still some deficiencies about associating this understanding with all processes of corporate operation. Evaluating the results in general, strategic aims and goals of corporations include the importance placed on its employees and corporation leaders supporting the improvement of employees. The idea that supporting development of employees is directly proportional to the development of corporate communication is common among corporations and it was concluded that values in the vision and mission of corporations are not sufficiently reflected on all work processes. Strategy is about visions and missions of corporations. The matter to take into consideration is associating the strategic decisions and aims emphasised on the vision and mission with all work processes and applying them. Effective strategic leaders can practice strategic decisions and plans. Today, as the competition grows bigger, it is becoming more important for corporations to obtain high efficiency from their employees which are the most important value of corporations. Successful leaders and corporate development are possible through effectiveness in corporate communication and through benefitting from information and skills of human resources.

References

Aktan, C. C. (1999). Strateji ve Stratejik Yönetim Kavramları, 2000'li Yıllarda Yeni Yönetim Teknikleri, İstanbul: Tügiad.

Botan, C. (2006). "Grand Strategy, Strategy and Tactics in Public Relations", Carl H. Botan and Vincent Hazleton (Eds), Public Relations Theory II, New Jersey: Lawrence Erlbaum Associates, 224–225.

Ellis, D. G. and Maoz, I. (2003). A Communication and Cultural Codes Approach to Ethnonational Conflict. The International Journal of Conflict Management, 14, 255–272.

Mumby, D. K. & Stohl, C. (1996). Diciplining Organizational Communication Studies Management Communication Quarterly, 10, 50–72.

Oliver, S. (2001). Public Relations Strategy, London: Kogan Page Ltd., 2.

Reilly, B. J. and DiAngelo, J. A. (1990). Communication: A Cultural System of Meaning and Value, Human Relations, 43(2), 129–140.

Ülgen, H. & Mirza, S. K. (2014). İşletmelerde Stratejik Yönetim, 7. Baskı, İstanbul: Beta.

Koçel, T. (2010). İşletme Yöneticiliği, 12. Baskı, İstanbul: Beta.

Thompson, J. L. (1990). Strategic Management: Awareness and Change, Chapman and Hall, 1st Edition.

Theodore, P. H. & Gregory, D. S. (1999). Strategic Management In The Public Sector. Public Productivity & Management Review, 22, 308–324.

Pfeffer, J. (1995). Rekabette Üstünlüğün Sırrı: İnsan, (Çev: Sinem Gül), Birleşik Basın Dağıtım, İstanbul.

Songül Omur*

Television Watching Habits of Turks Living in Germany**

Introduction

Without a doubt, television (TV) is one of the most remarkable inventions in human history and has become an important activity for human kind. TV channels or the programs that people prefer to watch can be regarded as a reflection of their socio-economical life and culture. Furthermore, TV has an important role in the distribution of culture to the people both at the national and international level. In addition, TV is an important resource that people often make use of in meeting their various social needs in society. While the individuals utilise this resource to get information, for entertainment, and hearing current news, TV performs its responsibility to society and individuals by providing correct and unbiased information, educating, entertaining, and socialising people (Kocadaş, www.insanbilimleri.com, 13 Şubat 2011, p. 1). Without a doubt, the aforementioned functions of TV weigh more importance for the people of a nation who emigrated to another country. Especially for the immigrants who fail to adapt themselves to the new culture and isolate themselves from the society they live in, and for those concentrate in certain regions, TV becomes more important. The Turks who live in Germany watch Turkish and German channels both for the sake of protecting their own culture and for adapting themselves to the local community. However, this situation becomes more complicated for Turks who live in Germany. The reason is that those people experience a different culture and lifestyle and do not want to distance themselves from their local community and also the Turkish culture.

* Research Assistant, Gazi Univeristy, Faculty of Communication, Cinema, Radio, Television Department, songul2591@hotmail.com.

** This study has been composed on the basis of the postgraduate thesis titled "TV Watching Habits of Turks living in Germany" (İstanbul-2013), prepared by the author at the Department of Radio and Television of the Institute of Social Sciences of Marmara University.

Migration from Turkey to Germany

Migration is an event related with many areas of society like social, political, cultural, and economical ones and has direct influences to society. The migration from Turkey to Germany began with the signing of "Turkish - Federal Germany Labor Agreement" on 30 October 1961 (Perşembe, 2005: 62–63). The accepted workers have been regarded as "guest workers" since they had only planned to stay in Germany for a limited amount of time of one year before returning to their own country. Over time, the Turks that were supposed to stay for only one year have started to live in Germany permanently. The first wave of Turkish immigrants who went to Europe and especially Germany were composed of people from rural areas of Anatolia who have departed their villages and moved to bigger cities in search of jobs (Peköz, 2002, p. 30).

Development of the Communication Medium and Adaptation Process during the Post Migration Period into Germany

The communication medium concept involves all of the elements of the individual such as his or her family structure, personal state of belonging, the cultural activities, and especially all the verbal and behavioural events within the group that the individual feels attached to. In this respect, many social preferences such as reading, listening to music, and other media activities should be evaluated within this context. On the other hand, it is quite possible to say that the communication medium is closely related to environmental factors and can both positively and negatively affect the individuals social adaptation process to the community that he or she lives in (Yağbasan, 2008, p. 315). It is possible to say that the adaptation problems stem from the differences between the environment that the individual has left and the one he or she migrated to. The cultural and environmental differences not only create adaptation problems for individual, but also lengthen the period of adaptation. The Governor of Bayern Region, Gunther Becstein, defines adaptation as the acceptance of the German pioneer culture (i.e. the Christian tradition, humanism, and enlightenment), German constitution, and cultural identity as a whole without denying its origins (Gaste, 2008, p. 2). With migration, the Turks have brought along their language, religion, and culture as a part of their accustomed lifestyle besides other social habits. For this reason, the Turks who share a common language, origin, beliefs, and customs in Germany have been conglomerating in certain areas (Turan, 1997, p. 101). On the other hand, the majority of Turks who migrated in Germany have started to slowly adapt to the culture and social structure of Germany while trying to protect their own cultural values. Without a doubt, the adaptation process of the second and third generation of immigrants is in a far different dimension than the first generation. As is indicated by many research outcomes, many young Turks in Germany do not strictly hold on to the Turkish culture and lifestyle. Young Turks have in way immensely integrated with German society. Yet, the young generation of Turks in Germany watch far more German TV channels than their families. This passive activity can be regarded as a passive way of integration with German society (Buckingham, 2002, p. 17).

Objective, Methods, and Context of the Research Study

The reasons for watching TV differs from person to person. Some people watch TV mainly for obtaining information, getting social benefit, for entertainment, or as a distraction. However, besides these reasons, people also watch TV for purposes of protecting and developing their culture or obtaining a personal identity. In this sense, this research study aims to manifest the TV watching habits of Turks living in Germany.

The data in this research study has been collected through the survey method. With prior permission from the Turkish Embassy, the survey has been applied to 1,055 test subjects passing by the area around the Turkish Consulate who are assumed to be living in Stuttgart and other cities in Baden-Württemberg State. After pre-screening, 1,012 survey results have been used in the analyses.

We have been inspired by the prior research study by Ahmet Atilla Dogan and the Turkish Radio and Television Supreme Council (RTUK) in preparing the questionnaire in accordance with this specific objective. The survey used in the research study is composed of four sections. These are socio-demographic traits, TV watching habits, the affects of TV on the individual, and the most viewed Turkish TV channels and the expectations and thoughts towards these channels.

The data gathered through this survey has been computerised using the SPSS package program and then statistical analyses has been accomplished. During the analyses, the chi-square test has been used for all questions in order to determine if there is any correlation between frequency analyses and some other variables.

Findings and Interpretation

Average Daily TV Watching Time of Subjects

The survey indicates that half of the subjects watch between three to six hours of TV every day. According to the results of the Departments of Public Opinion and Broadcast Research and Measurement in RTÜK in 2007, it was determined that the daily duration of watching TV was 3.58 hours on average.

Most Preferred TV Channels of Subjects

Indicates that 40.6% of Turks in Germany prefer to watch mostly Turkish TV channels. This is followed by 35.9% watching both German and Turkish TV channels. While 10.5% prefer mostly German TV channels, only 7.2% prefer only German TV and 6.3% prefer only Turkish TV channels.

Motivation of Subjects in choosing to watch German Channels (more than one answer has been accepted). This question has not been answered by 64 subjects who reported "I only watch Turkish TV channels," so the number of participants (n) = 948).

The majority of the subjects (31.6%) have responded to the question "Why do you prefer German channels?" with "because there are too many commercials in Turkish TV" (29.8%). This is followed by responses such as "since other family members prefer," "because I live in Germany and will stay here," "since I know German better than Turkish," and "since movies and other programs are better" to a certain degree.

Program Types that the Subjects Prefer the Most in German TV (This question has not been answered by 64 subjects who reported "I only watch Turkish TV channels," so the number of participants (n) = 948).

The table consists of the responses given regarding the mostly preferred programs in German TV. According to the table, the most preferred programs are news programs (58.1%), movies (35.1%), and sports programs (32.2%). Besides these, series, educational, and info programs are also among the preferred programs in German TV.

Motivation of Subjects in Preferring Turkish TV Channels (More than one answer has been accepted n=939. This question has not been answered by 73 people who report "I only watch German TV channels.")

The Turkish TV channels are mostly preferred in order to learn about news concerning Turkey. Also, other news programs have been a determining motivation for Turks to prefer Turkish TV channels. The research conducted until today indicates that the immigrants are very much interested in news and information concerning their homeland. This situation is also evident in the studies made by both German and Turkish researchers concerning Turks in Germany.

Subjects' Most Preferred Program Types on Turkish TV Channels. (More than one answer has been accepted (n= 939). This question has not been answered by 73 people who report "I only watch German TV channels.")This was constructed to find out the most preferred program types in Turkish TV channels which Turks choose to watch. According to the table, the news programs (73.4%) are mostly preferred in Turkish TV channels. On the other hand, there is a large interest towards series programs (63.9%) as the second most preferred program type. In addition, sports programs, music, and entertainment programs reside in the mostly preferred categories by the subjects. The least preferred program type is talk shows with a ratio of 14.8%.

Effect of TV on Social Integration During the Post Migration Period
In this sense, while 29.6% of subjects responded to the "effect of TV on social integration post migration period" question with "effective," only 10% responded with "not effective." Considering the given responses of the subjects, we can clearly see the effectiveness of TV on social integration for the immigrants who have become part of a different society.

All Data on the following are answered by subjects who responded with watching "only Turkish channels," "mostly Turkish channels," and "mostly German channels" (n=939).

Most Preferred Turkish TV Channels by Subjects (more than one answer has been accepted).
Lately, there has been an increase in the number of Turkish channels broadcasted in Germany via cable networks and satellites. The Turks who live in Germany have gotten the chance to watch more alternative Turkish TV channels. The question of "which TV channel you prefer the most" has been asked to find out the preferences with the new increase in the number of channels. The findings indicate that the three most preferred TV channels are Kanal D (51.2%), ATV (44.1%), and Show TV (40.9%) respectively.

Determining Factors in Subjects' TV Channel Preference (More than one answer has been accepted).
When we analyse the data, we can see that with a ratio of 63.9%, the "quality of series programs and the presence of favoured actors in the series" has been the determining factor. "Better news" and "being better informed" can be regarded as the other determining factors. The development of communicative media, especially the wide spreading of TV during the last 40 years, has made it easier for people to be more entertained than educated. People no longer need to attend groups in order to be entertained (T. C. Milli Eğitim Bakanlığı Eğitimi Araştırma and Geliştirme Dairesi Başkanlığı, 2008, 20).

The Benefits that Turkish TV Channels Provide to Subjects (More than one answer has been accepted).

The subjects participating in the survey have been asked "the benefits that Turkish TV channels provide to the subjects" and the majority (82.4%) have replied with the "informs us about the developments in Turkey" answer. Moreover, subjects who think about "not forgetting the mother language" (34.8%) and "preserving the culture" (32.6%) as a motivation are not negligible at all.

What the Subjects Feel in Case Any Turkish TV Channel is Not in Service Any Longer

The question "How do you feel about the fact that Turkish channels broadcasting in Germany have been cancelled for a reason?" was formed in order to confirm what Turkish channels mean to Turks living in Germany. It has been answered by the subjects with answers such as "I feel the deficiency a lot" (52.4%), "I feel it less" (36.4%), and "I never feel the deficiency" (11.2%).

Correlation Analysis of Chi-Square Test

In the study, many chi-square test correlation analyses have been conducted. Yet, only the ones that have statistically significant correlations have been evaluated. According to the chi-square analyses, variables with a level of significance (p) less than 0.05 between each other have statistical correlation, while those with p greater than 0.05 are not statistically correlated.

Bilateral and Chi-Square Analyses Results between TV Watching Time and Gender, Age, and Education Level ($n=1012$ $p<0.05$)

When we evaluate the gender and TV watching time data within the range of "the longest watching period" and "shortest watching period," the daily seven hour or more TV watching time is 29.4% in women, while it is 22.6% in men. The smallest amount of time which is regarded to be zero to two hours is observed in 22.6% of women, while this rises to 37.3% in men. One can draw from these results that women tend to spend more time in front of TV compared to men. When we evaluate the TV watching time against age, we see that the average period is between three to six hours for all ages. When we correlate the TV watching time and the education level, we observe that 43.6% of primary school graduates watch three to six hours of TV. When we collectively evaluate the three to six, seven to nine, and above ten hours TV time data collectively, it can be seen that 74.8% of secondary school graduates, 66.5% of high school graduates, 62% of university graduates, and 61.1% of masters graduates have a TV time of more than three hours.

Mutual Relationship and Chi-square Analyses Results Between the Preferred TV Channels and Gender, Age, Birth Place, and Length of Residence

When we study the mutual relationship between the preferred channel and gender, we observe that 43.8% of women prefer mostly Turkish channels and 34.9% prefer Turkish and German TV equally, while 36.9% of men prefer mostly Turkish channels and 36.7% prefer Turkish and German channels equally. According to these results, we can conclude that women have a greater tendency to watch Turkish TV channels compared to men. However, the majority of both men and women prefer to watch mostly Turkish TV channels. When we correlate the TV channels with age, we observe that subjects in the age group 15–24 years and 25–34 years have a greater tendency to watch only German TV channels compared to other age groups. In addition, subjects in the age groups of 35–44 years and 45–54 years tend to watch both Turkish and German TV channels. The results indicate a rising tendency to watch Turkish TV with age. However, from a broad perspective, we observe that the Turkish TV channels are preferred by all age groups. If we take look at the birth place and TV channel preference, we observe that subjects who were born in Turkey prefer only and mostly to watch Turkish channels, while those who were born in Germany tend to watch German and Turkish TV equally. If we compare the length of residence in Germany and TV channel selection, we observe that the longer the subjects live in Germany, the greater the tendency they have in preferring German TV. However, despite these results, the majority of the Turkish viewers have a tendency to watch Turkish TV.

Mutual Relationship and Chi-square Analyses Results Between the Preferred TV Channels and Location of Residence in Germany ($n=1012$ $p<0.05$)

The Turks who reside in areas mostly inhabited by Turkish people tend to prefer mostly Turkish channels with a 33.3% ratio and only Turkish TV with a 21.9% ratio, while subjects who live in areas where there are mostly Germans prefer mostly German TV with a 47.9% ratio and only German TV with a ratio of 47.2%. In areas populated equally by Germans and Turks, the subjects tend to watch mostly Turkish channels and both Turkish and German channels. Additionally, Turks who live in multinationally inhabited areas tend to watch only German TV and both Turkish and German TV. With these findings, we can conclude that the location of residence has a strong influence on the TV channel preference.

Mutual Relationship and Chi-Square Analyses Results Between German TV Preference Motivations and Gender ($n=948$ $p<0.05$)

18.5% of women and 27.0% of men prefer to watch German TV because they find the movies, series, and other programs better. Those who report that they choose this option because "a family member prefers a certain channel" is 36.4% in women and 25.8% in men. The news channels have played a role in the preference of 30.4% of women and 36.6% of men for German TV. In addition, 23.6% of women and 19.0% of men prefer German TV in order to learn better German.

Mutual Relationships and Chi-Square Analyses Results Between the Preferred German Programs, Gender, and Age (n=948 P<0.05)

The percentage of subjects who prefer series in German TV channels is 27.9% in women and 20.7% in men. Women tend to prefer series more than men. The news programs in German TV are mostly preferred by mid-aged and older subjects. The news and documentary programs are the most favoured programs broadcast in German TV which are preferred by all majorities of all age groups. Moreover, while the series, movie, magazine, music, and entertainment programs in German TV are preferred by younger subjects, new and documentary type informative programs are preferred by mid-aged and older subjects.

Mutual Relationship and Chi-Square Analyses between Motivations for Choosing Turkish TV Channels and Gender

When we analyse the relationship between those preferring Turkish TV and gender, we observe that 47.9% of women and 30% of men prefer Turkish TV because they find the movie, series, and the programs better in Turkish TV. Those who report that they prefer Turkish TV because they are not interested in German TV are 13.0% in women and 8.9% in men. The presence of themes towards customs and traditions has played a role for 20.7% of women and 14.6% of men. Furthermore, while 9.7% of women and 5.9% of men prefer Turkish TV since they don't speak German, 18.4% of women and 10.3% of men prefer to state that they prefer Turkish TV in order to not forget their mother language and develop it further.

The Mutual Relationship and Chi-square Analyses Results Between the Preferred Turkish TV Channels, Gender, and Age

The most preferred programs preferred by both women and men in Turkish TV channels are news and series. However, from a broad perspective, men tend to prefer news, sports, and documentaries in Turkish TV channels more than women to a certain degree. On the other hand, the women prefer talk shows, magazines, entertainment, and music programs more so compared to men. According to the findings, the most preferred programs in Turkish TV channels across all age groups are news and series. In addition, news, documentaries, sports, informative, and education programs are mostly preferred by middle aged and older people.

The series, magazine, music, and other programs which are used for entertainment are mostly preferred by young people.

The Mutual Relationship Between the Effect of TV on the Social Integration Process and Age and Chi-square Analyses Results

The majority of Turks in Germany have the opinion that TV had a big impact on their social integration process. This impact has been found effective across all age groups. On the other hand, this impact has been found to be more pronounced over the first generation of immigrants.

Conclusion

It is an significant finding that Turkish TV channels, which increased in number over the years in Germany, impact the TV watching habits of Turks living in Germany who have an average TV watching period of 4.5 hours. Women and people described as middle aged and older tend to prefer Turkish TV channels. The ratio of German TV preference tends to increase from the first generation to the third generation of immigrants. The main determining factor in choosing Turkish TV channels is being informed about events in Turkey. The news programs are the secondary factors, while the better quality of movies, series, and other programs in Turkish TV channels is in third place. The elements which tend to protect and develop cultural values such as the presence of broadcast that reflect customs and traditions, not forgetting the mother tongue, protecting ties with the homeland, and children's motivation to learn better Turkish have a certain influence in the preference of Turkish TV channels. The main motivation for Turks living in Germany in choosing to watch German TV channels is news programs. On the other hand, the presence of too many commercials in Turkish TV channels comes across as another important factor in the preference of German TV channels. In the first place, people prefer to watch news programs in Turkish TV. This is followed by series with a little margin. On the other hand, sports, entertainment, and music programs are also among the most preferred programs in Turkish TV channels respectively. The news programs are viewed by the majority of both women and men. The series are viewed by nearly all women and half of men. Those who prefer German TV mostly watch the news, documentaries, films, and sports programs. The results obtained show us that besides entertainment, education, and informative functions, TV is a tool for immigrant Turks in social integration and protecting and developing cultural values. As a result of the study, TV watching habits of Turks living in Germany vary in accordance with sociodemographic and cultural elements and TV has an influencing factor in the lives of Turks living in Germany.

References

Buckingham, D. (2002). *Children and Media*, Centre for the Study of Children Youth and Media Institute of Education, University of London, April.

Doğan, A. A. (1994). *"Almanya'daki Türk Toplumunun Radyo ve Televizyon İzleme Eğilimi"*, Anadolu Üniversitesi Yayınları, Yayın No. 834, Eskişehir.

Gaste, D. (2008). *Almanya'da Entegrasyon ve Asimilasyon Tartışmaları*, Sayı:1/ Mayıs.

Kocadaş, B. (13 Şubat 2011). *"Medya ve Kültür"*, http://www.insanbilimleri.com/ojs/index.php/uib/article/view/86/84.

Peköz, M. (2002). *Avrupa Birliği"nde Göçmenler Almanya'da Türkler Kürtler*, Gün Yayıncılık, İstanbul.

Perşembe, E. (2005). *Almanya'da Türk Kimliği Din ve Entegrasyon*, Birinci Basım, Araştırma Yayınları, Ankara.

Radyo Televizyon Üst Kurulu. (2007). *"Almanya'da Yaşayan Türklerin Televizyon İzleme Eğilimleri Kamuoyu Araştırması"*, Kamuoyu, Yayın Araştırmaları ve Ölçme Dairesi Başkanlığı, Kasım, Ankara.

T. C. Milli Eğitim Bakanlığı Eğitimi Araştırma ve Geliştirme Dairesi Başkanlığı. (2008). *"Öğrencilerin Televizyon İzleme Alışkanlıkları"*, Ankara.

Tekin, U. (2007). "Avrupa"ya Göç ve Türkiye", *İstanbul Üniversitesi Siyasal Bilgiler Fakültesi Dergisi*, No: 17, Ekim.

Turan, K. (1997). *Almanya"da Türk Olmak,* T. C. Başbakanlık Aile Araştırma Kurumu Başkanlığı Yayınları, Ankara.

Yağbasan, M. (2008). *"Kültürlerarası İletişim Bağlamında Almanya'daki Türklerin İletişimsel Ortamlarının Belirlenmesine Yönelik Bir Alan Araştırması"*, Fırat Üniversitesi Sosyal Bilimler Dergisi, Cilt: 18, Sayı:2, Elazığ.

Sultan Başaran

ergunsultan@hotmail.com

Differences Between Male and Female Brains and Their Influences on Effective Behaviours in Organisations

Abstract Human interaction is present in all parts of life. Every communication has its purpose which is formed with communication and interaction in organisations and society. Human beings form the foundation of organisations. By forming and providing the continuity of an organisation, humans form the basics of all institutions. The success in organisations is achieved by managers and workers. It has been confirmed that there is an increase in workers' performance and their respect towards their superiors as the care and interest towards the workers by the administration increases. It's indicated that successful communication skills play a big role in organisational achievements. The key to organisational achievement lies in effective and positive communication. Our personality, behaviour, emotions, and thoughts are directly controlled by our brains. One must keep in mind that cultural, historical, and biological structures form unity. Althouh female and male brains are different, we mustn't ignore the fact that female brains can imbody some male characteristics and vice versa.

Keywords: Organisations, effective communication, behaviours, male and female brains.

1. Introduction

We spend most of our time at work. In my opinion, to be able to work efficiently, we should be aware of two facts. Firstly, we should follow eight basic disciplines to have healthy communication at work. Secondly, the differences are between male and female brain structures. In organisations that have both male and female personnel, there is a kind of richness which is a path to success.

2. Basic Disciplines for Effective Communication in Organisations

Human beings are the most important aspects of organisations and society. It is accepted that there are eight basic disciplines that play a key role in organisations and society, which are as follows:

1. **Caring for people**
   It is stated that being loved, cared for, and respected are all profound feelings. The most severe punishment that can be given to a person is to ignore him or her. It is known that there are numerous ways of showing that we care for a person in organisations and society. Those who are interacting must make eye contact and call each other using their names, as well as show concern for their needs. One should hear a person's sorrow and joy as long as they are permitted. Women are more sensitive to smell, sound, and touch. Women are better at perceiving what they have seen and can remember more details (Aytürk, 2010, 10). As a result, they are better and give more importance to human relations. Women are more capable of showing their interest in human relations using body laguage. Women smile more often than men. Women are more polite even to people they dislike. Having deep and meaningful relationships is more important for women. **Corpus callosum is stronger in women which makes them better performers in communication** (Moir & Jessel, 2002, 61). In the world of business, praising is not common. However, women need to be praised and men need to be rewarded with extra pay (Moir & Jessel, 2002).

2. **To trust and to reassure**
   If there is no trust in organisations and society, it is replaced with fear, lies, and betrayal. The feeling of trust is mutual. Trust consists of love, respect, dependence, belief, friendship, and sincerity. It is said that human relations are emphasised in companies set up by women. In these companies, it is possible to see trust instead of fear and cooperation instead of competition. There is trust among the workers. They are free to speak their mind. Women can sense the troubles of their workers beforehand. On the other hand, men are more aware of objectives at work. Women can see details better, have a good memory, organise efficiently, and are more thrustworthy (Aytürk, 2010, 10). Hippocampus is the centre which never lets women to forget details and memories (Brizendine, 2014, 13).

3. **Being Honest**
   Honesty is a great virtue in working life. Being honest means being consistent and fair. According to the British researcher Corinn Hut, status at work is important; however, for women, it is self development, fairness, and honesty (Moir & Jessel 2002, 185). Women are more law abiding and sensitive to human relations. Women accept that to have a society, there must be laws and regulations. If there is a disagreement between laws and individuals, women always take the individual's side. According to Corinn, women have never had the opportunity to change the "male principles" compelled by governments (Moir & Jessel, 2002, 186). This is because those women who have become

members of parliment act accordingly to "male principles." Today, we can see more and more sucessful women. The thing that matters is that they can be successful in their own companies, make up their own rules, and change these rules when necessary. Wise company management quickly adapt to the potential for success found in "female" management (Moir & Jessel, 2002). Ventromedial and orbitofrontal areas manage moral behaviours. Also, being emotional and rational are closely related to this part (Carter, 2013, 138).

4. **Giving importance to clothing and appearance**
   It is a well-known fact that looking tidy and neat plays a significant role in a person's professional life. The fact that our first impression of a person is found in the first four seconds clearly shows how important physical appearance is (Aytürk, 2010, 11). Primer vısual korteks is highly appreciated (Carter, 2013, 138).

5. **Paying attention to the words and behaviour**
   In human relations, showing good will and being sincere and respectful rather than being impolite is essential (Aytürk, 2010, 11). Men feel good while developing strategies to go up the ladders of success. However, friendship is important for women. As men are not skillful at noticing how much women are affected by work related problems. As a consequence, an emotional gap can be seen between men and women. In contrary to women, men prefer to hide their emotions at work. However, a woman sees no reason not to cry at work. Unlike men, women are easily affected by criticism. Deciding is not a simple process for women as the female brain stores more information and details than the male brain. For women, personal and moral values are really significant in decision-making. Women use a much more complex way of thinking while deciding (Moir & Jessel, 2002). The anterior cingulate cortex, which is responsible for evaluating options, noticing problems, and clarifying decisions, is larger in women's brains (Brizendine, 2014, 13). As this centre is also responsible for anxiety, women can not easily take risks, unlike men. Men know that taking big risks can sometimes be profitable. Men have an advantage over women in that they have the ability to use all possible alternatives to solve the problems as they imbody the temporal parietal centre (Brizendine, 2014, 13). A decrease in their income is a sign of weakness for men. Women do not interpret the fall in their income in the same way. Women become more depressed at work since they can't cope with the pressure of work as well as men. The only reason for this is that women take their work seriously. Men are affected by the pressure of the work when they are obliged to do the task. Women are better at lowering the level of tensity and solving problems thanks

to their ability to interpret a person's attitude, mimics, gestures, and intonation. Men are one step ahead in sensing threats, danger, and fear as their amygdala covers a larger area (Brizendine, 2014, 14).

6. **Using body language efficiently**
   Our body language is actually the reflection of our thoughts. Effective communication can be achieved with correct body language accompanied with carefully chosen words and an appropriate attitude (Aytürk, 2010, 11). As women are more sensitive to sounds, smells, and physical contact, they can distiguish the variety in sound and they can easily comprehend the sub-meaning in communication. The sharing of space in communication is different between men and women. While men are more protective of their personal space, women are more than willing to sit closely. Women use their body language more effectively because their self-control mechanism is more advaanced. While speaking, having eye contact isn't as important for men as it is for women. Research studies show that having eye contact meets the need for being admired, approved, and accepted. On the other hand, men do this as a show of power (Moir & Jessel, 2002). The superiot temporal girus records body movements, gestures, and mimics. The amygdala records the emotional sides of these and they are also analysed by the orbitofrontal cortex (Carter, 2013, 142).

7. **Communicating in a positive and effective way**
   Having positive and effective communication among people allows for healthy communication. Calling workers with their first name, smiling, treating them respectfully, and appreciating them will allow you to have success in organisational and social life (Aytürk, 2010, 12). The thalamus, ventral striatum, amygdala, and sub anterior cingulate cortex are responsible for the emotions which have great influence on healthy communication. *(Carter, R., 2013, 126)*

8. **Empathy**
   Empathy is being able to understand the emotional world of the person whom we are interacting with. In short, it is the action of putting yourself in his or her place. Empathy can assist us in having the right relations at work (Gürüz & Eğinli, 2013. The mirror neuron system, which controls and assesses gestures, mimics, intonation, and emotional signs, covers a larger area in a female brain (Brizendine, 2014, 15). The centre called the insula, which is in charge of intuition, covers a larger area in a female brain which allows them to have a high level of empathy (Brizendine, 2014, 13). The ventral tegmental is the motivation centre in a male brain; additionally, the male brain is superior to the female brain in initiating motivaton (Brizendine, 2014, 14).

2.1 Methods

This study is carried out with a survey technique called the qualitative research method. Data in the study were collected via answering semi-structured open-ended questions by colleagues working at Nine Eylül University School of Foreign Languages regarding "**differences between male and female brains and their influences on effective behaviour in organisations**." The answers were analysed by examining the documents obtained from these questions. In a qualitative research method, the common opinions of individuals participating in the study are evaluated by forming themes and codes after they are examined using specific criteria (Yıldırım and Şimşek, 2000).

2.1.1 Data Collection Process

The data were collected from colleagues by asking them to do the "sex of the brain" test distributed as a questionnaire. Additionally, one-on-one interviews, which took about 20 minutes, were done with the participants via voice recording.

2.1.1.1 Data Analysis

In data analysis, the "content analysis technique" was used. The analysis was conducted by two researchers and one field expert. Firstly, the researchers created themes independently from each other. The reliability of the research study was determined by comparing the two results by the two researchers. To increase the correspondence rates, experts and researchers came together, compared the forms, and evaluated them by examining and discussing different situations and overlooking details again and again. In this way, the reliability of the study and open-ended questions were provided. The frequency and percentage of descriptive values were analysed by Assistant Professor Suat Türkoğuz.

3. Tables & Acknowledgements

*Table 1: The views and descriptive values of the people working in the organisations according to the criteria of "**caring for people**"*

	WOMEN					MEN				
Code	**Feminine**	**Common Area**	**Different Brain Type**	**Total**	**Opinions**	**Masculine**	**Common Area**	**Feminine**	**Total**	**Opinions**
Social relations of proximity	5(45%)	2(18%)	4(36%)	11(100%)	Fp1 (75pts) "Having social relations of proximity, sharing ideas cooperation make me think like this."	3(30%)	3(30%)	0(0%)	6(60%)	Mp5 (50pts) "The way my colleagues greet me is by heart."
Sharing	4(36%)	1(9%)	5(45%)	10(91%)	Fp3 (95pts) "Sharing our happiness or sadness is important."	0(0%)	3(30%)	1(10%)	4(40%)	Mp10 (70pts) "My colleagues who share their happiness & sadness."

	WOMEN					MEN				
Code	Feminine	Common Area	Different Brain Type	Total	Opinions	Masculine	Common Area	Feminine	Total	Opinions
Cooperation	3(27%)	0(0%)	2(18%)	5(45%)	Fp10 (110pts) "Sharing and helping each other at work is important."	3(30%)	4(40%)	0(0%)	7(70%)	Mp6 (40pts) "I enjoy taking part at the projects."
Geniality	2(18%)	1(9%)	4(36%)	7(64%)	Fp8 (110pts) "Sincerity in speech and smiling is essential."	1(10%)	0(0%)	0(0%)	1(10%)	Mp3 (40pts) "Geniality is essential."
Respect	2(18%)	3(27%)	3(27%)	8(73%)	Fp3 (95pts) "They show respect to my experience."	5(50%)	4(40%)	1(10%)	10(100%)	Mp5 (50pts) "I show my respect using my words and body language."
Love	3(27%)	2(18%)	5(45%)	10(%91)	Fp9 (110pts) "Sharing shows love and respect."	5(50%)	1(10%)	0(0%)	6(60%)	Mp4 (5pts) "I feel happy when we work together."

	WOMEN					MEN				
Code	Feminine	Common Area	Different Brain Type	Total	Opinions	Masculine	Common Area	Feminine	Total	Opinions
Interest	4(36%)	2(18%)	3(27%)	9(82%)	Fp4 (50pts) "When I ask a question, they listen to me."	0(0%)	0(0%)	0(0%)	0(0%)	Mp7 (55pts) "When necessary I do favours individually."
Verbal Communication	1(9%)	1(9%)	2(18%)	4(36%)	Fp10 (110pts) "I express my feelings honestly."	6(60%)	2(20%)	0(0%)	8(80%)	Mp1 (45pts) "My colleagues express their feelings using verbal cm. & body lg."
Body Language	0(0%)	1(9%)	4(36%)	5(45%)	Fp8 (110pts) "I try to be sincere."	6(60%)	4(40%)	0(0%)	10(100%)	Mp2 (15pts) "Body language is important."
Sharing ideas about profession	4(36%)	1(9%)	0(0%)	5(45%)	Fp2 (80p) "They are willing to hear my job experience."	2(20%)	3(30%)	1(10%)	6(60%)	Mp6 (40pts) "They are willing to hear my experience on my job."

Semi-structured interview questions were directed to the participants according to the criteria for the content of "***caring for people.***" As a result of the content analysis, the thematic codes, descriptions, and opinions in Table 1 have been obtained. The frequency and percentage of descriptive values given in the table correspond to each code. According to the criteria of "***caring for people,***" the following thematic codes have been obtained from the participants: social relations of proximity, sharing, cooperation, geniality, respect, love, interest, verbal communication, body language, and sharing ideas about profession. The thematic codes that **women** concentrate on are mostly love, interest, sharing, sharing ideas about profession, and social relations of proximity. The thematic codes that **men** concentrate on are mostly love, verbal communication, body language, and respect. While men and women have a common attitude in the concept of cooperation, they seem to think differently on the other thematic codes. When the common area of men and women are compared, it is seen that women concentrate on respect, social relations of proximity, love, and interest. However, men concentrate on respect, cooperation, and body language. It is also seen that women who have different brain types concentrate on social relations of proximity, sharing, love, geniality, and body language. It is also seen that feminine men concentrate on sharing, respect, and sharing ideas about profession. In general, while the thematic codes which women concentrate on are social relations of proximity, sharing, respect, and love, men concentarate on body language, respect, and verbal communication according to the criteria for the content of "***caring for people.***"

*Table 2: The views and descriptive values of the people working in the organisations according to the criteria of "**to trust and reassure**"*

		WOMEN					MEN				
		Feminine	Common	Different Brain Type	Total		Masculine	Common	Feminine	Total	Opinions
	Code		Area			Opinions		Area			
1	Male colleagues	2(18%)	1(9%)	0(0%)	3(27%)	Fp6 (60pts) "Men are more objective."	2(20%)	0(0%)	0(0%)	2(20%)	Mp2 (15pts) "Men understand me better/"
	Female colleagues	3(27%)	0(0%)	2(18%)	5(45%)	Fp2 (80pts) "I trust women more."	3(30%)	0(0%)	1(10%)	4(40%)	Mp1 (45pts) "Women are more sincere."
	Gender doesn't matter	2(18%)	1(9%)	3(27%)	6(55%)	Fp9 (110pts) "If the person gives confidence, there is no problem."	3(30%)	3(30%)	0(0%)	6(60%)	Mp3 (40pts) "No matter for me."
	Personality	2(18%)	1(9%)	3(27%)	6(55%)	Fp11 (110pts) "Personality is more important than gender."	2(20%)	4(40%)	0(0%)	6(60%)	Mp5 (50pts) "Personality is more important than gender."

		WOMEN					MEN				
		Feminine	Common	Different Brain Type	Total		Masculine	Common	Feminine	Total	Opinions
	Code		Area			Opinions		Area			
2	Familiarity	2(18%)	0(0%)	1(9%)	3(27%)	Fp8 (110) "If I feel close, gender doesn't matter."	1(10%)	2(20%)	0(0%)	3(30%)	Mp4 (5pts) "They clearly express their feelings."
	Sharing	4(36%)	2(18%)	1(9%)	7(64%)	Fp3 (95pts) "I feel good when they share their feelings."	2(20%)	2(20%)	1(10%)	5(50%)	Mp4 (5pts) "They share their top secrets."
	Sharing ideas about profession	3(27%)	1(9%)	1(9%)	5(45%)	Fp10 (110pts) "They share their ideas about profession and want help."	0(0%)	1(10%)	0(0%)	1(10%)	Mp5 (50pts) "While trying to find a solution, they consult me."
	Verbal communication	4(36%)	2(18%)	4(36%)	10(91%)	Fp7 (110pts) "I got from their words"	3(30%)	2(20%)	0(0%)	5(50%)	Mp7 (55pts) I got this feeling from their words."
	Body language	0(0%)	2(18%)	2(18%)	4(36%)	Fp6 (60pts) "From their behaviours."	3(30%)	2(20%)	1(10%)	6(60%)	Mp2 (15pts) "Their body language."

Semi-Structured interview questions were directed to the participants according to the criteria for the content of "***to trust and reassure***." As a result of the content analysis, the thematic codes, descriptions, and opinions in Table 2 have been obtained. The frequency and percentage of descriptive values given in the table correspond to each code. According to the criteria of "***to trust and reassure***," the following thematic codes have been obtained from the participants: male colleagues, female colleagues, gender doesn't matter, personality, familiarity, sharing, sharing ideas about profession, verbal communication, and body language. The thematic codes that **women** concentrate on are mostly female colleagues, sharing, verbal communication, and sharing ideas about profession. The thematic codes that **men** concentrate on are mostly female colleagues, gender doesn't matter, verbal communication, and body language. While men and women have a common attitude in the concept of female colleagues, they seem to think differently on the other thematic codes. When the common area of men and women are compared, it is seen that women concentrate on sharing, body language, and verbal communication. However, men concentrate on personality and gender doesn't matter. It is also seen that women who have different brain types concentrate on verbal communication, personality, and gender doesn't matter. It is also seen that feminine men concentrate on body language, sharing, and female colleagues. In general, while the thematic codes which women concentrate on are verbal communication and sharing, men concentarate on gender doesn't matter, personality, and body language according to the criteria for the content of "***to trust and reassure***."

Table 3: The views and descriptive values of the people working in the organisations according to the criteria of ***"giving importance to clothing and appearance"***

	WOMEN					MEN				
Code	**Female**	**Common**	**Different Brain Type**	**Total**	**Opinions**	**Masculine**	**Common**	**Feminine**	**Total**	**Opinions**
		Area					**Area**			
Self -care	3(27%)	2(18%)	3(27%)	8(73%)	Fp1 (75pts) "It's important."	5(50%)	3(30%)	1(10%)	9(90%)	Mp1 (45pts) "It's important."
Self- respect	3(27%)	2(18%)	3(27%)	8(73%)	Fp2(80pts) "It's a sign of self-respect."	5(50%)	3(30%)	1(10%)	9(90%)	Mp7 (55pts) "It is a sign of caring for yourself"
No matter	2(18%)	0(0%)	1(9%)	3(27%)	Fp3(95pts) "I don't care."	0(0%)	0(0%)	0(0%)	0(0%)	x
Style icon	1(9%)	0(0%)	1(9%)	2(18%)	Fp5 (90pts) "It's a sign of style."	0(0%)	0(0%)	0(0%)	0(0%)	x

Semi-Structured interview questions were directed to the participants according to the criteria for the content of "***giving importance to clothing and appearance.***" As a result of the content analysis, the thematic codes, descriptions, and opinions in Table 3 have been obtained. The frequency and percentage of descriptive values given in the table correspond to each code. According to the criteria of "***giving importance to clothing and appearance,***" the following thematic codes have been obtained from the participants: self-care, self-respect, no matter, style icon. Thematic codes that **women** concentrate on are mostly self-care and self-respect. Thematic codes that **men** concentrate on are mostly self-care and self-respect, too. Men and women seem to think differently on the thematic codes such as, doesn't matter and style icon. When the common area of men and women are compared, it is seen that women concentrate on self-care and self-respect. Similarly, men concentrate on self-care and self-respect. It is also seen that women who have different brain types concentrate on self-care and self-respect. It is also seen that feminine men concentrate on self-care and self-respect. In general, both men and women focus on self-care and self respect according to the criteria for the content of "***giving importance to clothing and appearance.***"

Table 4: The views and descriptive values of the people working in the organisations according to the criteria of ***"being honest."***

	WOMEN					MEN				
Code	Female	Common	Different Brain Type	Total	Opinions	Masculine	Common	Feminine	Total	Opinions
		Area					Area			
Honest men	2(18%)	0(0%)	1(9%)	3(27%)	Fp2 (80pts) "Men are honest."	2(20%)	1(10%)	0(0%)	3(30%)	Mp9 (60pts) "Men are honest."
Honest women	1(9%)	0(0%)	3(27%)	4(36%)	Fp10 (110pts) "Women are better."	2(20%)	0(0%)	1(10%)	3(30%)	Mp10 (70pts) "Women are honest."
Women legal	3(27%)	0(0%)	3(27%)	6(55%)	Fp1 (75pts) "Women."	4(40%)	3(30%)	0(0%)	7(70%)	Mp5 (50pts) "Women are legal."
Men legal	3(27%)	0(0%)	2(18%)	5(45%)	Fp2 (80pts) "Men care about legal matters."	2(20%)	2(20%)	1(10%)	5(50%)	Mp10 (70pts) "Men care about being legal."
Personality	1(9%)	2(18%)	1(9%)	4(36%)	Fp4 (50pts) "Personality is important."	2(20%)	2(20%)	1(10%)	5(50%)	Mp4 (5pts) "Personality is important."
Emotional women	3(27%)	2(18%)	0(0%)	5(45%)	Fp2 (80pts) "Women may interfere with feelings."	3(30%)	2(20%)	0(0%)	5(50%)	Mp7 (55pts) "Women are emotional."
Rational men	2(18%)	2(18%)	1(9%)	5(45%)	Fp5 (90pts) "Men are rational."	3(30%)	0(0%)	0(0%)	3(30%)	Mp1 (45pts) "Men consider being rational more."

	WOMEN					MEN				
Code	**Female**	**Common**	**Different Brain Type**	**Total**	**Opinions**	**Masculine**	**Common**	**Feminine**	**Total**	**Opinions**
		Area					**Area**			
Prestigious women	2(18%)	2(18%)	2(18%)	6(55%)	Fp9 (110) "Women mind prestige more."	3(30%)	3(30%)	0(0%)	6(60%)	Mp2 (15pts) "It's clear that women are more prestigious."
Prestigious men	2(18%)	2(18%)	3(27%)	7(64%)	Fp11 (110pts) "Men care for prestige."	3(30%)	2(20%)	1(10%)	6(60%)	Mp3 (40pts) "Men are one step further."
Women equality	2(18%)	2(18%)	2(18%)	6(55%)	Fp10 (110pts) "Equality is important for women."	3(30%)	1(10%)	1(10%)	5(50%)	Mp9 (60pts) "Women."
Men equality	3(27%)	2(18%)	1(9%)	6(55%)	Fp2 (80pts) "Men are more equal as they don't interfere with feelings."	2(20%)	1(10%)	0(0%)	3(30%)	Mp3 (40pts)" "Men."
Information Sharing women	3(27%)	2(18%)	3(27%)	8(73%)	Fp8 (110pts) "They are always better."	3(30%)	2(20%)	1(10%)	6(60%)	Mp9 (60pts) "Women share more."
Information Sharing men	3(27%)	2(18%)	1(9%)	6(55%)	Fp1 (75pts) "Men are more relaxed."	4(40%)	2(20%)	0(0%)	6(60%)	Mp3 (40pts) "Men share information more."

Semi-Structured interview questions were directed to the participants according to the criteria for the content of "***being hones***t." As a result of the content analysis, the thematic codes, descriptions, and opinions in Table 4 have been obtained. The frequency and percentage of descriptive values given in the table correspond to each code. According to the criteria of "***being honest***," the following thematic codes have been obtained from the participants: honest men, honest women, women legal, men legal, personality, emotional women, rational men, prestigious women, prestigious men, women equality, men equality, information sharing women, and information sharing men. The thematic codes that **women** concentrate on are mostly women legal, men legal, emotional women, men equality, information sharing men, and women. The thematic codes that **men** concentrate on are mostly women legal and information sharing men. While men and women have a common attitude in the concept of women legal, information sharing men, and women, they seem to think differently on the other thematic codes. When the common area of men and women are compared, it is seen that women don't concentrate on being honest and legal for both men and women. However, men concentrate on women legal and prestigious women. It is also seen that women who have different brain types concentrate on honest women, women legal, prestigious men, and information sharing women. It is also seen that feminine men concentrate on honest women, men legal, personality, information sharing women, prestigious men, and women equality. In general, both men and women focus on women legal, emotional women, prestigious women, and men equality according to the criteria for the content of "***being honest***."

*Table 5: The views and descriptive values of the people working in the organisations according to the criteria of "**paying attention to the words and behaviour.**"*

	Women					Men				
Code	**Feminine**	**Common**	**Different brain type**	**Total**	**Opinions**	**Masculine**	**Common**	**Feminine**	**Total**	**Opinions**
		Area					**Area**			
Affected (sadness)	4(36%)	2(18%)	5(45%)	11(100%)	Fp2 (80pts) "Deeply affected."	5(50%)	4(40%)	1(10%)	10(100%)	Mp5 (50pts) "Of course."
Expressing thoughts	2(18%)	2(18%)	2(18%)	6(55%)	Fp1 (75pts) "Surely."	2(20%)	2(20%)	1(10%)	5(50%)	Mp1 (45pts) "I talk to him or her.
Reducing Communication	2(18%)	1(9%)	1(9%)	4(36%)	Fp3 (95pts) "Communicate at a certain level."	0(0%)	0(0%)	0(0%)	0(0%)	x
Ending Communication	1(9%)	0(0%)	0(0%)	1(9%)	Fp1 (75pts) "Possibly end it."	1(10%)	0(0%)	0(0%)	1(10%)	Mp4 (5pts) "End it."
Acting professionally	2(18%)	2(18%)	0(0%)	4(36%)	Fp 6 (60pts) "I act professionally."	0(0%)	2(20%)	0(0%)	2(20%)	Mp7(55pts) "I'd reduce the relation."
Strong response	1(9%)	1(9%)	1(9%)	3(27%)	Fp9 (110pts) "Certainly I show it."	3(30%)	1(10%)	0(0%)	4(40%)	Mp2 (15pts) "My response would be harsh."

	Women					Men				
Code	Feminine	Common	Different brain type	Total	Opinions	Masculine	Common	Feminine	Total	Opinions
		Area					Area			
Observation	2(18%)	1(9%)	0(0%)	3(27%)	Fp5 (90pts) "Keep silence and wait for a while.	3(30%)	0(0%)	0(0%)	3(30%)	Mp3 (40pts) "I'd think it over."
Quick Decision	2(18%)	2(18%)	0(0%)	4(36%)	Fp4 (50pts) "I can decide quickly."	5(50%)	3(30%)	1(10%)	9(90%)	Mp1 (45pts) "Very quickly."
Taking Risks	1(9%)	0(0%)	1(9%)	2(18%)	Fp1(75pts) "I can take risks."	3(30%)	3(30%)	1(10%)	7(70%)	Mp2(15pts) "I like risks."
Deliberation	3(27%)	1(9%)	4(36%)	8(73%)	Fp3 (95pts) "I think twice."	3(30%)	4(40%)	1(10%)	8(80%)	Mp3 (8(55pts) "I prefer consulting."
Emotions	0(0%)	0(0%)	2(18%)	2(18%)	Fp9 (110pts) "I follow my emotions."	0(0%)	0(0%)	0(0%)	0(0%)	x
Solution Oriented	1(9%)	1(9%)	1(9%)	3(27%)	Fp 2 (80pts) "I'm impatient in solving problems."	3(30%)	4(40%)	1(10%)	8(80%)	Mp7 (55pts) "I look for solutions."
Zero risk	2(18%)	1(9%)	1(9%)	4(36%)	Fp5 (90pts) "No risk."	1(10%)	1(10%)	1(10%)	3(30%)	Mp5 (50pts) "I don't take risks."

	Women					Men				
Code	**Feminine**	**Common**	**Different brain type**	**Total**	**Opinions**	**Masculine**	**Common**	**Feminine**	**Total**	**Opinions**
		Area					**Area**			
Sharing	3(27%)	0(0%)	1(9%)	4(36%)	Fp10 (110pts) "I'd consult my colleagues."	3(30%)	0(0%)	1(10%)	4(40%)	Mp2 (15pts) "I like getting different points of view."
High Awareness	4(36%)	2(18%)	5(45%)	11(100%)	Fp1 (75pts) "I'd notice it quickly."	4(40%)	4(40%)	1(10%)	9(90%)	Fp1 (45pts) "Very quickly."
Observation	2(18%)	1(9%)	0(0%)	3(27%)	Fp3 (95pts) "I'd be calm and watch people."	1(10%)	1(10%)	1(10%)	3(30%)	Fp5 (50pts) "I'd wait for a while"
Sharing (response)	2(18%)	0(0%)	2(18%)	4(36%)	Fp11 (110pts) "As soos as I notice, I share it."	4(40%)	2(20%)	1(10%)	7(70%)	Fp2 (15pts) "I'd response at the right time"

Semi-Structured interview questions were directed for question onr to the participants according to the criteria for the content of "***paying attention to the words and behaviour***." As a result of the content analysis, the thematic codes, descriptions, and opinions in Table 5 have been obtained. The frequency and percentage of descriptive values given in the table correspond to each code. According to the criteria of "***paying attention to the words and behaviour***." the following thematic codes have been obtained from the participants: affected(sadness), expressing thoughts, reducing communication, ending communication, acting professionally, strong response, and observation. The thematic code that **women** concentrate on is mostly affected(sadness). The thematic code that **men** concentrate on is mostly affected(sadness). While men and women have a common attitude in the concept of affected(sadness), they seem to think differently on the other thematic codes. When the common area of men and women are compared, it is seen that women concentrate on affected(sadness), expressing thoughts, and acting professionally. However, men concentrate on expressing thoughts, strong response, and observation. It is also seen that women who have different brain types concentrate on affected(sadness). It is also seen that feminine men concentrate on affected(sadness) and expressing thoughts. In general, both men and women focus on affected(sadness) and expressing thoughts according to the criteria for the content of "***paying attention to the words and behaviour***."

Semi-Structured interview questions were directed for question two to the participants according to the criteria for the content of "***paying attention to the words and behaviour***." As a result of the content analysis, the thematic codes, descriptions, and opinions in Table 5 have been obtained. The frequency and percentage of descriptive values given in the table correspond to each code. According to the criteria of "***paying attention to the words and behaviour***," the following thematic codes have been obtained from the participants: quick decisions, taking risks, deliberation, emotions, solution oriented, zero risk, and sharing. The thematic codes that **women** concentrate on are mostly deliberation and sharing. The thematic codes that **men** concentrate on are mostly quick decisions, taking risks, deliberation, solution oriented, and sharing. While men and women have a common attitude in the concept of deliberation and sharing, they seem to think differently on the other thematic codes. When the common area of men and women are compared, it is seen that women concentrate on quick decisions. However, men concentrate on deliberation and solution oriented. It is also seen that women who have different brain types concentrate on deliberation. It is also seen that feminine men don't concentrate on emotions, but rather concentrate on the others. In general, both men and women focus on deliberation and sharing according to the criteria for the content of "***paying attention to the words and behaviour***."

Semi-Structured interview questions were directed for question three to the participants according to the criteria for the content of "***paying attention to the words and behaviour.***" As a result of the content analysis, the thematic codes, descriptions, and opinions in Table 5 have been obtained. The frequency and percentage of descriptive values given in the table correspond to each code. According to the criteria of "***paying attention to the words and behaviour.***" the following thematic codes have been obtained from the participants: high awareness, observation, and sharing. The thematic code that **women** concentrate on is high awareness. The thematic code that **men** concentrate on is mostly high awareness, too. While men and women have a common attitude in the concept of high awareness, they seem to think differently on the other thematic codes. When the common area of men and women are compared, it is seen that women concentrate on high awareness. Likewise, men concentrate on high awareness. It is also seen that women who have different brain types concentrate on high awareness. It is also seen that feminine men concentrate on all the thematic codes, which include: high awareness, observation, and sharing(response). In general, both men and women focus on high awareness according to the criteria for the content of "***paying attention to the words and behaviour.***"

*Table 6: The views and descriptive values of the people working in the organisations according to the criteria of "**communicating in a positive and effective way**"*

		WOMEN					MEN				
	Code	**Female**	**Common Area**	**Different Brain type**	**Total**	**Opinions**	**Masculine**	**Common Area**	**Feminine**	**Total**	**Opinions**
1	Competition	0(0%)	0(0%)	0(0%)	0(0%)	x	4(40%)	3(30%)	1(10%)	8(80%)	Mp2 (15pts) "If necessary, why not?"
	Achieving The goal	4(36%)	2(18%)	4(36%)	10(91%)	Fp2 (80pts) "I do my best."	5(50%)	4(40%)	1(10%)	10(100%)	Mp4 (5pts) "It should be reasonable."
	Taking risks	1(9%)	1(9%)	2(18%)	4(36%)	Fp7 (110pts) "Without disturbing the others I do anything."	4(40%)	4(40%)	1(10%)	9(90%)	Mp3 (40pts) "It's important to take risks."
	Dominating	0(0%)	0(0%)	0(0%)	0(0%)	x	3(30%)	4(40%)	1(10%)	8(80%)	Mp4 (40pts) "It should be done properly."
	Achieving victory	0(0%)	1(9%)	2(18%)	3(27%)	Fp9 (110pts) "It is important."	5(50%)	4(40%)	1(10%)	10(100%)	Mp10 (70pts) "It's necessary."
	Responsibility	4(36%)	2(18%)	5(45%)	11(100%)	Fp11 (110pts) "Responsibility is important."	5(50%)	4(40%)	1(10%)	10(100%)	Mp7 (55pts) "All is essential."
	Personal development	1(9%)	0(0%)	0(0%)	1(9%)	Fp1 (75pts) "I'm always ambitious./"	5(50%)	4(40%)	1(10%)	10(100%)	Mp1 (45pts) "I want to be the best."

	Code	WOMEN					MEN				
		Female	Common	Different Brain type	Total	Opinions	Masculine	Common	Feminine	Total	Opinions
			Area					Area			
2	Superiors Subordinates	4(36%)	2(18%)	5(45%)	11(100%)	Fp1 (75pts) “It's necessary.”	5(50%)	4(40%)	1(10%)	10(100%)	Mp5 (50pts) “It must be.”
	Respect	3(27%)	1(18%)	5(45%)	9(82%)	Fp2 (80pts) “It should be witout losing respect.”	5(50%)	4(40%)	1(10%)	10(100%)	Mp1 (45pts) “Respect is inevitable.”
	Justice Equality	4(36%)	2(18%)	5(45%)	11(100%)	Fp10 (110pts) “It must appear with these terms.”	5(50%)	4(40%)	1(10%)	10(100%)	Mp9 (60pts) “Surely.”
3	Feminine approach	4(36%)	1(9%)	4(36%)	9(82%)	Fp1 (75pts) “Women are more willing to cooperate.”	4(40%)	4(40%)	1(10%)	9(90%)	Mp2 (15pts) “Women are better at following the rules.”
	Masculine approach	3(27%)	2(18%)	5(45%)	10(91%)	Fp5 (90pts) “Men are more reasonable.”	3(30%)	3(30%)	1(10%)	7(70%)	Mp8 (55pts) “Men are more successful.”
	Personality	1(9%)	1(9%)	1(9%)	3(27%)	Fp11 (110pts) “Personality is important.”	1(10%)	1(10%)	1(10%)	3(30%)	Mp3 (40pts) “It's important.”

		WOMEN					MEN				
	Code	Female	Common	Different Brain type	Total	Opinions	Masculine	Common	Feminine	Total	Opinions
			Area					Area			
4	Theory	1(9%)	1(9%)	2(18%)	4(36%)	Fp10 (110pts) "Theory."	4(40%)	3(30%)	0(0%)	7(70%)	Mp1 (45pts) "Theory."
	Aesthetic	2(18%)	2(18%)	2(18%)	6(55%)	Fp4 (50pts) "Aesthetics."	2(20%)	3(30%)	1(10%)	6(60%)	Mp7 (55pts) "Aesthetics."
	Intellectual methods	4(36%)	2(18%)	5(45%)	11(100%)	Fp8 (110pts) "Intellectual methods."	5(50%)	3(30%)	1(10%)	9(90%)	Mp4 (5pts) "Intellectual methods."
	Social relations	4(36%)	1(9%)	5(4%5)	10(91%)	Fp1 (75pts) "Social relations."	5(50%)	4(40%)	1(10%)	10(100%)	Mp6 (40pts) "Social relations."
	Dominating	1(9%)	0(0%)	1(9%)	2(18%)	Fp7 (110pts) "Dominating."	0(0%)	0(0%)	0(0%)	0(0%)	X
	Ethics	4(36%)	2(18%)	5(45%)	11(100%)	Fp 5 (90pts) "Ethics."	5(50%)	3(30%)	1(10%)	9(90%)	Mp10 (70pts) "Ethics."

Semi-Structured interview questions were directed for question one to the participants according to the criteria for the content of "***communicating in a positive and effective way***." As a result of the content analysis, the thematic codes, descriptions, and opinions in Table 6 have been obtained. The frequency and percentage of descriptive values given in the table correspond to each code. According to the criteria of "***communicating in a positive and effective way***," the following thematic codes have been obtained from the participants: competition, achieving the goal, taking risks, dominating, achieving victory, responsibility, and personal development. The thematic code that **woen** concentrate on is mostly achieving the goal. The thematic codes that **men** concentrate on are mostly personal development, responsibility, achieving victory, and the goal. While men and women have a common attitude in the concept of achieving the goal, they seem to think differently on the other thematic codes. When the common area of men and women are compared, it is seen that women concentrate on achieving the goal and responsibility. However, men concentrate on nearly all the thematic codes. It is also seen that women who have different brain types concentrate on responsibility and achieving the goal. It is also seen that feminine men concentrate on all the thematic codes. In general, both men and women focus on responsibility and achieving the goal according to the criteria for the content of "***communicating in a positive and effective way***."

Semi-Structured interview questions were directed for question two to the participants according to the criteria for the content of "***communicating in a positive and effective way***." As a result of the content analysis, thethematic codes, descriptions, and opinions in Table 6 have been obtained. The frequency and percentage of descriptive values given in the table correspond to each code. According to the criteria of "***communicating in a positive and effective way***." the following thematic codes have been obtained from the participants: superiors-subordinates, respect, and justice-equality. The thematic codes that **women** concentrate on are the three codes mentioned. Likewise, the thematic codes that **men** concentrate on are the three codes. While men and women have a common attitude in the concept of superiors-subordinates, respect, and justice-equality, they seem to think differently on the other thematic codes… When the common area of men and women are compared, it is seen that both women and men concentrate on nearly all the thematic codes given in advance. It is also seen that women who have different brain types and feminine men concentrate on the same three thematic codes.

Semi-Structured interview questions were directed for question three to the participants according to the criteria for the content of "***communicating in a positive and effective way***." As a result of the content analysis, the thematic codes, descriptions, and opinions in Table 6 have been obtained. The frequency and percentage of descriptive values given in the table correspond to each code. According to the criteria of "***communicating in a positive and effective way,***" the following thematic codes have been obtained from the participants: feminine approach, masculine approach, and personality. The thematic code that **women** concentrate on is feminine approach. Likewise, the thematic code that **men** concentrate on is feminine approach. Men and women have a common attitude in the concept of feminine approach. When the common area of men and women are compared, it is seen that women concentrate on masculine approach. Yet, men concentrate on both feminine and masculine approach. It is also seen that women who have different brain types concentrate on masculne approach. But, feminine men concentrate on all three thematic codes.

Semi-Structured interview questions were directed for question four to the participants according to the criteria for the content of "***communicating in a positive and effective way.***" As a result of the content analysis, the thematic codes, descriptions, and opinions in Table 6 have been obtained. The frequency and percentage of descriptive values given in the table correspond to each code. According to the criteria of "***communicating in a positive and effective way,***" the following thematic codes have been obtained from the participants: theory, aesthetics, intellectual methods, social relations, dominating, and ethics. The thematic codes that **women** concentrate on are mostly intellectual methods, social relations, and ethics. The thematic codes that **men** concentrate on are mostly intellectual methods, social relations, theory, and ethics. Men and women have a common attitude in the concept of intellectual methods, social relations, and ethics. When the common area of men and women are compared, it is seen women concentrate on aesthetics, intellectual methods, and ethics. Yet, men concentrate on social relations. It is also seen that women who have different brain types concentrate on intellectual methods, social relations, and ethics. But, feminine men concentrate on all the thematic codes except for theory and dominating. Both men and women focus on intellectual methods, social relations, and ethics according to the criteria for the content of "***communicating in a positive and effective way.***"

*Table 7: The views and descriptive values of the people working in the organisations according to the criteria of "**emphathy.**"*

		WOMEN					MEN				
	Code	Female	Common Area	Masculine	Total	Opinions	Masculine	Common Area	Feminine	Total	Opinion
1	Success	3(27%)	2(18%)	2(18%)	7(64%)	Fp2 (80pts) "Success."	4(40%)	1(10%)	1(10%)	6(60%)	Mp1 (45pts) "Success."
	Motivation	4(36%%)	1(9%)	4(36%)	9(82%)	Fp1 (75pts) "Motivation."	4(40%)	4(40%)	1(10%)	9(90%)	Mp3 (40pts) "Motivation."
	Competition	0(0%)	0(0%)	0(0%)	0(0%)	X	0(0%)	1(10%)	0(0%)	1(10%)	Mp9 (60pts) "Competition."
	Cooperation	2(18%)	0(0%)	4(36%)	6(55%)	Fp5 (90pts) "Cooperation."	2(20%)	3(30%)	1(10%)	6(60%)	Mp5 (50pts) "Cooperation."
	Money	1(19%)	1(9%)	1(9%)	3(27%)	Fp4 (50pts) "Money."	2(20%)	0(0%)	0(0%)	2(20%)	Mp4 (5pts) "Money."
	Confidence	2(18%)	2(18%)	4(36%)	8(73%)	Fp10 (110pts) "Confidence."	4(40%)	4(40%)	0(0%)	8(80%)	Mp8 (55pts) "Confidence."
2	Healthy Communication	4(36%)	2(18%)	5(45%)	11(100%)	Fp1 (75pts) "It is essential."	5(50%)	4(40%)	1(10%)	10(100%)	Mp1 (45pts)" It has great influence."
	Positive impact	4(36%)	2(18%)	5(45%)	11(100%)	Fp2 (80pts) "Absolutely."	5(50%)	4(40%)	1(10%)	10(100%)	Mp5 (50pts) "Surely."

Semi-Structured interview questions were directed for question one to the participants according to the criteria for the content of "***emphathy***." As a result of the content analysis, the thematic codes, descriptions, and opinions in Table 7 have been obtained. The frequency and percentage of descriptive values given in the table correspond to each code. According to the criteria of "***emphathy***," the following thematic codes have been obtained from the participants: success, motivation, competition, cooperation, money, and confidence. The the matic codes that **women** concentrate on are mostly motivation and success. The thematic codes that **men** concentrate on are mostly success, motivation, and confidence. Men and women have a common attitude in the concept of motivation. When the common area of men and women are compared, it is seen women concentrate on success. Yet, men concentrate on motivation and confidence. It is also seen that women who have different brain types concentrate on motivation, cooperation, and confidence. But, feminine men concentrate on all the thematic codes, such as: success, cooperation, and confidence. Both men and women focus on motivation, cooperation, and confidence according to the criteria for the content of "***emphathy***."

Semi-Structured interview questions were directed for question two to the participants according to the criteria for the content of "***emphathy***." As a result of the content analysis, thematic codes, descriptions and opinions in Table 7 have been obtained. The frequency and percentage of descriptive values given in the table correspond to each code. According to the criteria of "***emphathy***" the following thematic codes have been obtained from the participants: healthy communication and positive impact. Thematic codes that **women and men** concentrate on are healthy communication and positive impact. When the common area of men and women are compared, it is seen that women and men concentrate on both??? sentence incomplete. It is also seen that women who have different brain types and feminine men concentrate on healthy communication and positive impact. Both men and women focus on healthy communication and positive impact according to the criteria for the content of "***emphathy***."

*Table 8: The views and descriptive values of the people working in the organisations according to the criteria of "**using body language efficiently**"*

	WOMEN					MEN				
Code	**Female**	**Common Area**	**Masculine**	**Total**	**Opinions**	**Masculine**	**Common Area**	**Female**	**Total**	**Opinions**
Intensive use	4(36%)	2(18%)	5(45%)	11(100%)	Fp1 (75pts) "Very often."	0(0%)	0(0%)	0(0%)	0(0%)	X
Proper usage	4(36%)	2(18%)	5(45%)	11(100%)	Fp3 (95pts) "It prevents misunderstandings."	2(20%)	0(0%)	2(20%)	4(40%)	Mp1 (45pts) "Generally try it."
Eye contact	4(36%)	2(18%)	5(45%)	11(100%)	Fp4 (50pts) "Definetely use it."	5(50%)	3(30%)	1(10%)	9(90%)	Mp2 (15pts) "I do my best."
Gestures-mimics	4(36%)	2(18%)	5(45%)	11(100%)	Fp5 (90pts) "Definetely use it."	1(10%)	2(20%)	1(10%)	4(40%)	Mp4 (5pts) "I'm not good at it."
Level of voice	3(27%)	2(18%)	5(45%)	10(100%)	Fp6 (60pts) "Efficiently use it."	3(30%)	2(20%)	1(10%)	6(60%)	Mp1 (45pts) "I try using it."
Personal space	4(36%)	2(18%)	5(45%)	11(100%)	Fp7 (110pts) "Surely use it."	2(20%)	2(20%)	1(10%)	5(50%)	Mp6 (40pts) "I care about it."

Semi-Structured interview questions were directed to the participants according to the criteria for the content of "***using body language efficiently***." As a result of the content analysis, the thematic codes, descriptions, and opinions in Table 8 have been obtained. The frequency and percentage of descriptive values given in the table correspond to each code. According to the criteria of "***using body language efficiently***," the following thematic codes have been obtained from the participants: intensive use, proper usage, eye contact, gestures and mimics, level of voice, and personal space. The the matic codes that **women** concentrate on are mostly all the thematic codes mentioned. The the matic codes that **men** concentrate on are mostly eye contact and level of voice. Men and women have a common attitude in the concept of eye contact. When the common area of men and women are compared, it is seen women concentrate on all the thematic codes. Yet, men concentrate on eye contact. It is also seen that women who have different brain types concentrate on all of them. But, feminine men concentrate on nearly all the thematic codes. Both men and women focus on eye contact according to the criteria for the content of "***using body language efficiently***."

4. The Sex of the Brain Test & Questions

THE SEX OF THE BRAIN TEST

1) You hear a cat meowing. Could you determine where it is coming from?
   a) I'd listen for a while then determine its location.
   b) I'd locate it right away.
   c) I might not be able to locate it for sure.
2) How well can you remember a piece of music which you have heard just now?
   a) I could easily remeber it and sing a part of the song without making a mistake.
   b) I coul remember it if it had a rhythmic melody.
   c) I would have difficulty remembering it.
3) A person you have only seen a few times has phoned. Could you recognise this person if he or she didn't introduce himself or herself?
   a) I could almost recognise everyone.
   b) I could recognise only half of the people in such a situation.
   c) I could recognise less than half of them.
4) You're in a large group of married couples. Could you sense the love affair between the couple?
   a) I would most definetely sense it.
   b) I would only sense it in the later stages of the affair.
   c) I would hardly ever sense it.

5) You meet five people at a party. If you heard their names the following day, could you remember their faces?
   a) I could remember most of them.
   b) I could remember some of them
   c) I could remember only one at most.
6) Were you good at essay writing and punctuation in primary school?
   a) I was good at both.
   b) One of them was good
   c) Neither of them was good.
7) You see a space to park while you are driving; however, you need to do reverse park and it is quite a tight space. What do you do?
   a) I'd try to find somehere else to park.
   b) I'd carefully park it.
   c) I'd easily park it.
8) You are a stranger in a city and you arived only three days ago. Someone in the street asks you which way north is.
   a) I don't think I could show him or her the right direction.
   b) I could direct him or her the right way if I thought for a few minutes.
   c) I could show him or her right away.
9) You're at the dentist. There are five or six people with the same sex. How close could you sit without feeling any discomfort?
   a) Closer than 15cm
   b) Between 15 to 60cm
   c) Further than 60cm
10) You are in your new neighbour's house having a chat and you hear a tap dripping.
   a) I'd notice the dripping right away, but I'd try not to focus on it.
   b) If I were to notice it, I'd probably mention it.
   c) The dripping wouldn't bother me.

Scoring:

men:	a) 10 points	b) 5 points	c) -5 points
women:	a) 15 points	b) 5 points	c) -5 points

unanswered questions: 5 points

Evaluation:
Most men score between 0–60
Most women score between 50–100
Men with a score higher than 60 have a female brain

Women with a score lower than 50 have male brain
Women with a score over 100 have a different kind of brain

But not all men and women show this pattern. These are all avarage scores. However, there is always an exception (Moir & Jessel, 2002, 64–67).

QUESTIONS

1) **Caring for people**
   1. Do you think that your colleagues care about, respect, and honour you? How do your colleagues express these feelings?
   2. Do you think that you care about, respect, and honour your colleagues? How do you express these feelings?
2) **To trust and to be trusted**
   1. Who do you think you can trust and express your feelings to without feeling anxiety more at work, the men or the women?
   2. How do you know if a colleague trusts, cares, and honours you?
3) **Being Honest**
   1. How would you comment on your male and female colleagues understanding of equality, honesty, obeying rules and regulatioms, sharing information, being consistent, and perceiving the concept of prestige?
4) **The importance of dress code and appearance**
   1. How important is a person's physical appearance and what he or she is wearing?
5) **Being careful in speaking and behaviour**
   1. How are you affected by malicios intentions, insincerity, and disrespect at work? How do you react to people that do these things?
   2. How do you determine the process and speed of deciding, the risk factors, and problem solving faces?
   3. How quickly do you sense and react to threats, danger, and anxiety?
6) **Using body language effectively**
   1. How well do you integrate your body language (mimics, gestures, intonation, personal space) into your interactions at work?
7) **Communicating in a positive and effective way**
   1. How do you express the importance of rivalry, reaching your goal, taking risks, and being dominant at work?
   2. How do you see superior-subordinate relations and status at work?
   3. Please choose the first four terms which you value the most from the following: theory, esthetic, thinking strategies, social relations, being dominant, and morality.

8) **Emphathy**
   1. Please choose the first three terms which you value the most from the following: success, motivation, rivalry, cooperation, money, and trust.
   2. How does emphathy influence the power of communication at work?

6. References

Brizendine, L., (2014)., *Erkek Beyni*, (4th ed.), Say Yayınları, İstanbul

Winston, R., (2014), *İnsan Beyni*, (2nd ed.), Say Yayınları, İstanbul

Carter, R., (2013), *Beyin Kitabı*, Alfa

Aytürk, N., (2010), *Örgütsel ve Yönetsel Davranış*, Detay Yayıncılık, İstanbul

Yıldırım, A. & Şimşek H., (2013), *Sosyal Bilimlerde Nitel Araştırma Yöntemleri*, (9th ed.), Seçkin, Ankara

Moir, A. & Jessel, D., (2002), *Beyin ve Cinsiyet*, PencereYayınları, İstanbul

Gürüz, D., & Eğinli A. T, (2013), *Anlamak, Anlatmak, Anlaşmak*, (4th ed.), Nobel Yayınları, Ankara

Brizendine, L., (2014), *Kadın Beyni*, (12th ed.), Say Yayınları, İstanbul

Güney., S., (2004), *Açıklamalı Yönetim-Organizasyon ve Örgütsel Davranış Terimler Sözlüğü*, Siyasal Kitabevi, Ankara

Fatma Kamiloğlu[1] & Özge U. Yurttaş[2]

A Field Research Study on the Brand Equity of Internet and Social Media Applications

Summery To create a brand and brand equity has turned into an extremely significant competition among foundations. The brand equity that is analysed both on the financial gounds and the consumer basis consists of the total values identified with the brand itself. Today, social media, under the usage of a significant number of users, is becoming one of the root elements for marketing strategies of brands. A lot of brands carry out operations tending to create long-term trends through social media which has the overwhelming power of global communication. The purpose of this work is to put forth the place of social media being a brand within itself and social media applications over the perception of young people. Among the service brands, with billions of users, social media and its applications have become "a brand" within itself as well.

In this research study prepared to determine the brand equity of social media, the brand equity has been evaluated cognitively following a field survey applied on high school students in Istanbul/Turkey (n:1498), which was evaluated putting its basis on root ingredients such as how well known the brand is, how liked it is, how dependable it is found to be, how pleased its users are, and how much it is recommended. Brand equity models of Aaker, Keller, Milward Brown Research Company, GfK Research Company, and Xsight Research Company have been taken as the basis for brand equity determination for creating a model of the brand value/equity.

Keywords: Social media, branding, brand equity, brand value, high school students.

1. Introduction

Along with the marketing conditions enjoying brand battlefields, not every brand would get the targeted success resulting in not creating the desired effect in the consumers' eyes. A powerful brand has high brand equity. Brand equity is the positive differential effect that knowing the brand name has on customer response to the product or service (Amstrong & Kotler, 2009: 211). Creating a powerful brand and making that brand valuable both financially and customer wise is one

---

1 Ass. Prof. Dr. Fatma Kamiloğlu, İstanbul Aydın University, Faculty of Communications, Department of Advertising, İstanbul-Turkey.

2 Ass. Prof. Dr. Özge U. Yurttaş, İstanbul Arel University, Faculty of Communications, Department of Public Relations and Advertisement, İstanbul-Turkey.

of the upper most values that foundations might get in today's world of cracking competition. What lies beneath these careful brand planning management strategies is but a mere target to create a valuable brand. The thing that makes a brand valuable for customers is a brand that is bought by customers, a mixture that creates satisfaction and a sentimental relationship as well as physical characteristics, and that has a personality, which is to say, it is a brand that's built (Borça, Karpat, Aktuğlu, 2004:39). In order to shape brand equity, the communication between the customer and the brand should be focused on observingly. One of the most significant contemporary communication tools is the internet and its current social structure; social media has a tremendous effect on customers in order to create a powerful relationship between the brand and customers. Another very significant point to be focused on is to analyse the brand equity of these applications. In this study, the main approach depends on analysing the brand equity of these applications that contribute to increasing the brand equity of foundations.

2. Brand Equity and Brand Value Approaches

Brand is a term that expresses qualitative peculiarities that differentiate and separate a product or service from others. It is also defined as names, symbols, designs, and their various combinations that those who offer their products or services to the market use in order to show their difference from others in the market (American Marketing Association, http://www.marketingpower.com/_layouts/Dictionary.aspx?dLetter=B Research date: 09.10.2013). Taking it from this point of view, the basic point of having/using a brand is to avoid being simple or ordinary. Similarly, Aaker (2009:25) defines a brand as a name and/or symbol that differentiates or determines some goods or services of either one or a group of vendors from their competitors.

Baudrillard, states that brands lead consumers to a group of more complicated choices (Boudrillard, 2008:18). However, as Baudrillard also mentions in his definition, brands not only create a limited relationship in meeting the consumers' needs for the usage of products/services, but they also shape with a structure that meets the expectation, addresses the personal specifications and pleasures, and makes individuals have different experiences as well. Taking the definitions above into consideration, we can express that there is an effort to build up relationships in various dimensions between brands and customers. In marketing literature, the attempt to define the relationship between brand and customer created the concept of brand value (Wood, 2000:662). Brand equity is "a set of assets and liabilities linked to a brand, its name and symbol that adds to or subtracts from the value provided by a product or service to a firm and/or to that firm's customers" (Aaker, 1991). According to Kotler and Armstrong (2004: 291), the value of a strong brand refers to how strong it is to meet the customers' needs along with the customers' loyalty. In general meaning, when the studies concerning brand value are analysed, one can see different approaches on the way to define its concept and conceptual meaning. Comprehending the brand value can be approached in various ways according to the businesses' different functions and it also varies according to targets (Keller, 1993:4). This difference in general, as Lassar et al. (1995:12) mention, is based on two different perspectives: It is analysed financially and based on the consumer base. Kim et al. (2003:337), on the other hand, mention that a third (a mixture of both approaches) approach might also be observed. While the financial approach emphasises the monetary value of a brand, according to Pelsmacker et al. (2001:45), the real value of a brand also involves the financial market value of the brand's identity value, the profit it is likely to make in a particular period of time, and, in case it enjoys, the financial credibility of its instruments that exist in the stock and shares range. While it is possible to determine the measurements and/or methods to clearly evaluate the financial value of a brand, the second approach, which is called the consumer based or customer focusing approach, exhibits an ambiguous and unclear structure when compared with the financial approach.

However, when the basics are analysed, the brand equity that the consumer based approach concerns is also a precession point as in financial profits. When one examines the studies concerning the consumer based brand value determining approach, he or she will definitely find out that consumer based brand value consists of four elements (brand awareness/popularity, brand loyalty, brand association, and the quality perception) (Toksarı and Inal, 2013:1427). Aaker (2009:46–48) mentions that the brand value can be determined through brand loyalty, brand credibility, perceived quality of the brand, brand associations, and connections with other brands. These objects obtain various profits and value as well (Leone, Keller et al. 2006:126).

Keller defines the brand value as a different effect, which is totally different form the brand information, and in which the consumer originated brand value is based on the reactions of consumers toward a brand's marketing activities and programs. Accordingly, the brand information depends on all the thoughts, feelings, perceptions, and experiences; however, it is not necessarily the reality of that particular brand (Leone, Keller et al. 2006:126). Therefore, it is essential that a serial attempt be made to improve and protect the ingredients of the brand (Karpat Aktuğlu, 2004:40). Keller also mentions that consumer based brand value can be created by planning these differences and taking brand strategies and differences of consumer's attitudes into consideration (Keller, 2003:694). Consumer based brand value is realised when the consumer approaches the brand and forms a unique and strong brand perception (Keller, 1993:2).

Ad agency Young & Rubicam's Brand Asset Valuator measures brand strength along four consumer perception dimensions, as follows: differentiation (what makes the brand stand out), relevance (how consumers feel it meets their needs), knowledge (how much consumers know about the brand), and esteem (how highly consumers regard and respect the brand). Brands with strong brand equity rate high on all of these dimensions (Amstrong & Kotler, 2009: 211).

Figure 1: Customer based brand equity pyramid

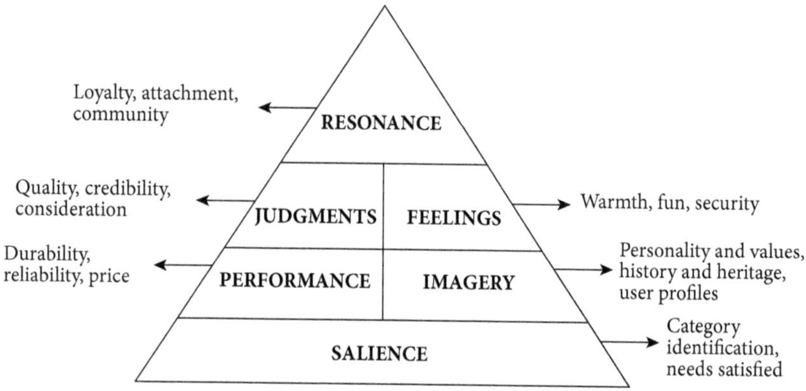

Source: Keller (2001) Model Customer-Based Brand Equity (CBBE) Pyramid

Brand salience relates to how often and easily the brand is thought about under various purchase or consumption situations. **Brand performance** relates to how the product or service meets customers' functional needs. **Brand imagery** deals with extrinsic properties of the product/service including the ways in which the brand attempts to meet customers psychological and or social needs. **Brand judgments** focus on customers' own personal opinions and evaluations. **Brand feelings** focus on customers emotional responses and reactions with respect to the brand. **Brand resonance** focuses on the nature of the relationship that customers have with the brand and the extent to which customers feel that they are 'in sync' with the brand (https://avaremy.wordpress.com/2013/11/09/brand-equity).

On the way to measure the perceived value of brands, various methods are utilised. In this field, the most effective measurements are compiled by Millward Brown Research Company, GfK Research Company, and XSights Research Company. These three research companies, while measuring the perceived value of brands on customer basis worldwide, regularly make use of various criteria, as well as similar ones. However, on every measurement basis, as well as the rational and sentimental perceivement of the target mass, the limits of buying and recommending the brands are also gauged.

Figure 2: Millward Brown's brand equity model

Source: Millward Brown Research Company, Brand Equity Model, http://www.millwardbrown.com/solutions/slick-sheets/millwardbrown_branddynamics.aspx.

Presence is the active familiarity based on past trials, saliency, or knowledge of brand promise (Do I know about it?) **Relevance** refers to being relevant to consumer's needs, in the right price range, or in consideration set (Does it offer me something?) **Performance** is the feeling of delivering an acceptable product performance and is on the consumer's shortlist (Can it deliver?) **Advantage** is the feeling of having an emotional or rational advantage over other brands in the category (Does it offer something better than others?) **Bonding** is the rational and emotional attachments to the brand to the exclusion of most other brands (Nothing else beats it) (https://avaremy.wordpress.com/2013/11/09/brand-equity).

Figure 3: Hierarchy of brand value measurement relationships – GfK

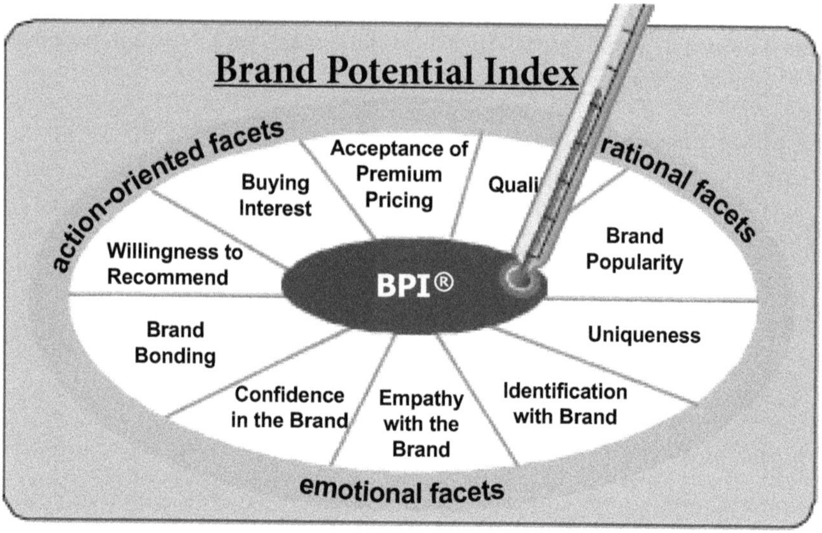

Source: GfK Research Company, Brand Potential Index Model, http://marketing.gfkamerica.com/102011-1252/GfK_Brand_Vitality_Tracking_Slip_Sheet_May_2011.pdf

GfK Research Company makes use of the chart above on gauging brand equity value measurement. In this chart, brand value is gauged in three main components, as follows: rational, sentimental, and operational limits. Each main topic enjoys sub-components. The achievement value in these components of consumer perceivement is questioned.

Figure 4: Hierarchy of brand value measurement relationships

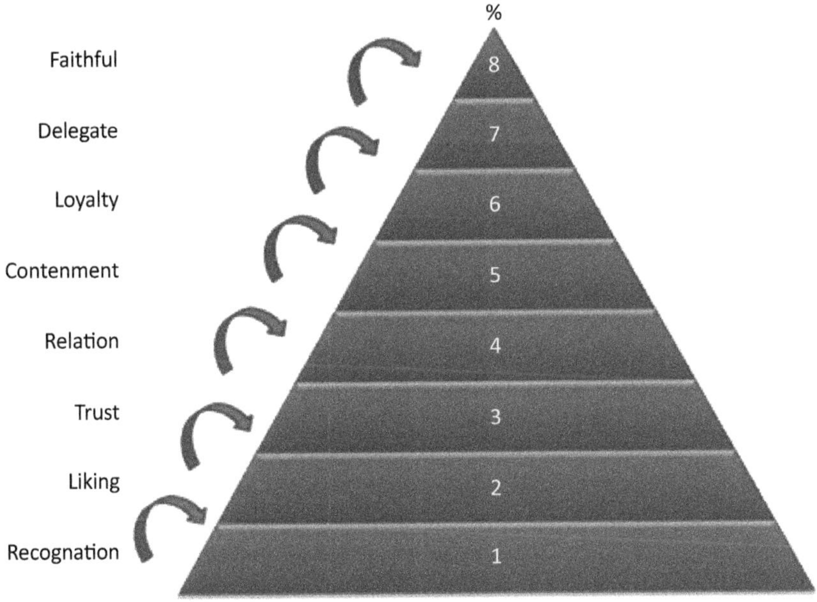

Source: Xsights Research Company, 'Perception Modeli, X-Percept', www.itibaratolyesi.com/.../Turkiye_Itibar_Endeksi_Cigdem_Penn.pptx, 2013.

Xsights Research Company makes use of triangle brand value guaging in brand equity measurement. In this triangle, the performance that these brands have in the consumer's perception is gauged. The least affecting point of the brand value is the bottom part and the most value increasing point is at the top. As you take the steps gradually towards the top, only strong brands grow can proceed increasing their rates. The questioned topics in this triangle are: recognition (knowing the brand, the name of the brand, seeing the news of the brand), liking (liking the brand, thinking highly about the brand, and liking the public relations (PR) and the commercials of the brand), trust (trusting the brand, trusting the products and the services of the brand, trusting the promises of the brand, and trusting the texts and messages of the brand), relation (preferring the brand; and buying, using, and wishing to buy it in future, if not now), contentment (the satisfaction of the brand and the satisfaction of the products and the services of the brand), loyalty (the loyalty for the brand and wishing to buy the products and the services of the brand), delegate (recommending the brand to others, talking highly about the brand to others, and letting others know about the brand), faithful (recommending the brand even when it is not mentioned in the atmosphere, carrying on using the brand, and lovers of the brand).

2.1 Internet and Social Media in Brand Equity Context

Brands are not static; they have many facets to their personality. In order to build up and retain equity as a preferred brand in the mind of the customer (Gobe, 2001:185). In the duration of brand and consumer relations, social media's structure of being able to present different experiences and opportunities and its popular and widespread usage obtain an almost unlimited break for elusion from competition and being in the foreground. Therefore, social media has become a very profitable field for advertisement companies, ad users, and for brands.

As a communication channel, social media has created significant brands for foundations, advertisements, and ad users. When social media is mentioned, it has become a reminder of a vast internet structure called Web 2.0 that provides for interactive communication. In the base of the internet and Web 2.0, social media involves a vast amount of applications such as blogs, social webs, video share sites, and RSS. According to Kaplan and Haenlein's (2010:61) statement, social media that obtains global communication for its users is the body of internet based applications that are built on an ideological and technological basis and that allow its contents to be produced, improved, and developed upon its users' base.

Provided that social media is taken into consideration from the brand communication point of view, it might as well provide a platform that improves and manages customer relationships, contributes to brand purchasing decisions, spreads sincere and correct info to the customers, informs the potential customers and the sector about what's trendy in the market and what bias the market enjoys most recently, disciplines brands, and provides a dialogue between brands and customers (Kahraman, 2010:85–86). However, social media and internet applications do not only enjoy the task of carrying the relationship between the brand and customer, but it also enjoys a product/service speciality (Scott, 2013). With billions of users, social media has gradually become a brand in itself and for this reason, it has become essential that it takes its own brand equity and evaluation into consideration as well. The research study entitled "100 Most Valuable Brand of The Globe," conducted by the International Brand Evaluation Corporation, reveals the market value of gigantic brands. According to the 2013 results, Google is in second place and Facebook is an in 52nd place (http://www.interbrand.com/en/news-room/press-releases/2013-09-30-d355afc.aspx 1 OCT 2013). As a result, it is vital that these brands that gain financial significance be approached from the brand equity point of view.

3. Research

The research section involves the target of the research study, exemplification and methodology, and research along with the data analysis.

3.1 Target of the Research Study

With its significant communicative value, social media enjoys a very effective role, especially on youngsters. It has the value of a field that shapes the youngsters' life environment and point of view, along with its communication providing facility. For this reason, it is vital that social media communication and its renewing/reshaping structure be analysed deeply. The better that this new media, which has been formed against conventional media, is analysed, the better that effective and gainful communicative activities can be formed. Within this data, the target of the research study is to create a general point of view determining the value of social media as a brand for high school students in some basic fields such as knowing the brand closely (How big the brand is?), appreciation of the brand (dynamism), pleasure of the brand, how dependable the brand is, and how advisable the brand is. In addition, we attempted to make a comparison between brands analysing social media and its applications mutually.

3.2 Methods

In gauging brand equity of social media and its applications, all the models above were analysed. The basis of brand equity determination is the hierarchy of relationships. The figure 4 involves the headlines that Aaker (1993), Keller (2001), Milward Brown Research Company, GfK Research Company, and Xsight Research Company take as the basis for brand equity determination. Taking these models as the basis, a model gauging the brand equity more elementarily and in a more result focused way in five components has been advanced. These components are as follows: knowing the brand closely, liking the brand, being satisfied about the brand, trusting the brand, and delegating for the brand voluntarily and recommending it to the others.

Although some basic criteria was taken into consideration, the association of the brand in mass perception and brand loyalty might as well be interrogated qualitatively in addition to the headlines presented above. Besides, features like concrete existence and inventory analysis of the brand were also completed in brand equity calculations. Basic headlines were taken into consideration in this research study. Five headlines were measured in order to comprehend perceptional brand equity, which was aimed not to take too much of young people's time. According to these models, the contribution effect of each component on the brand is different. The highest effect is the effect of delegating the brand voluntarily. Right next to it comes the trust for the brand. The medium effective component is being satisfied about the brand. The less effective component is liking the brand and the least effective component is knowing the brand closely. Taking this into consideration, the top contributing components have greater importance for gauging the brand equity. Besides, knowing, liking, satisfaction, and recommendation of the brand are essential to make the brand a star brand.

Figure 5: Our combination hierarchy of brand equity measurement relationships

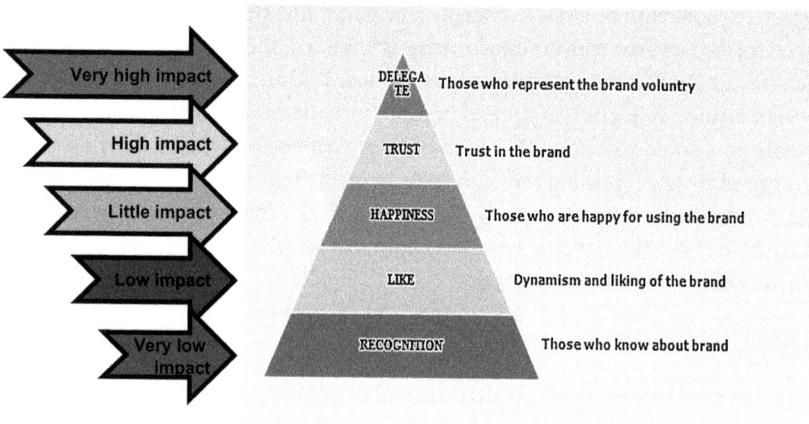

As it can be seen in this graphic, the duration that started with the recognition, the size as it were, of the brand carries on along with liking, the dynamism of the brand, and with how happy people are about the brand. Through to the top of the hierarchy, there is the trust in the brand, and on the top of this hierarchy, there is the delegation of target people which means those who represent the brand voluntarily. Those brands which are ideal targets are to improve and develop the top parts in this hierarchy. The more these areas develop, the higher the perceivable value of the brand.

3.3 The Exemplification and Methodology of the Research Study

The environment of the research study consists of high school students in Turkey. According to Turkish Statistical Corporation, Istanbul is the best representative city in Turkey with its cosmopolitan structure, having 18.2% of the whole population (13,624,240 people). Prior to the application of the research study, the project proposal and the questionnaire was presented to the Ministry of Education of Istanbul and the application of the research study was realised after getting the permission from the governorship and the Ministry of Education of Istanbul. Thus, in order to reach the target mentioned above, an effective and correct method, "quantitative research" method, and "coincidental exemplification" method have been used. When applying these methods, the questionnaire is dependent upon the prepared questionnaire with the "fill it in yourself" technique. Exemplification is determined using the "simple coincidental exemplification" method. According to the info provided by the Ministry of Education of Istanbul, there are 853 high schools with an average of 500,000 students. First, a list of all the high schools in the city of Istanbul was formed. Within this list, the "systematic coincidental exemplification method" was used to determine the high schools to conduct the application. In order to reflect the high school structure in Istanbul, eleven high schools (seven public schools and four private schools) were chosen. For each school (High School level 1 = 50 questionnaire, High School level 2 = 50 questionnaire and High school level 3 = 50 questionnaire) has 150 questionnaire application all told, which reached to 1650 students who answered the questionnaire all told. According to this, the exemplification of the research study has a 95% reliance with a ±0.02 failure rate, and it is 1650 in 500 thousand system. During the analysis of the research study, those questionnaires with mistakes and deficiency were left out and the statistical data were conducted over 1,498 questionnaires. In these chosen high schools, the questionnaires were handed out to the level one, two, and three students in the last ten minutes of the class in order to not disturb the lesson accompanied by their teachers. Students filled in/answered their questionnaire forms using the "filling it in by themselves method." They were chosen using the "simple coincidental exemplification" method. Those who attended that day in that hour made up the exemplification and thus the field study of the research was completed in March 2013.

3.4 Research Data

Of the level one, two, and three high school students, 43% of the students that participated in the research study are female students and 56.9% are male students. The range of the high schools is as follows: public high schools – 12.6%, vocational high schools – 25.5%, Anatolian (language based) high schools – 28.9%, high schools of fine arts – 8.2%, and private high schools/colleges – 24.6%. The age range of the students are as follows: between 15 and 16 years is 63.6%, between 17 and 18 years is 32.9%, and others is 3.4%.

Figure 6: Trust in foundations and the internet

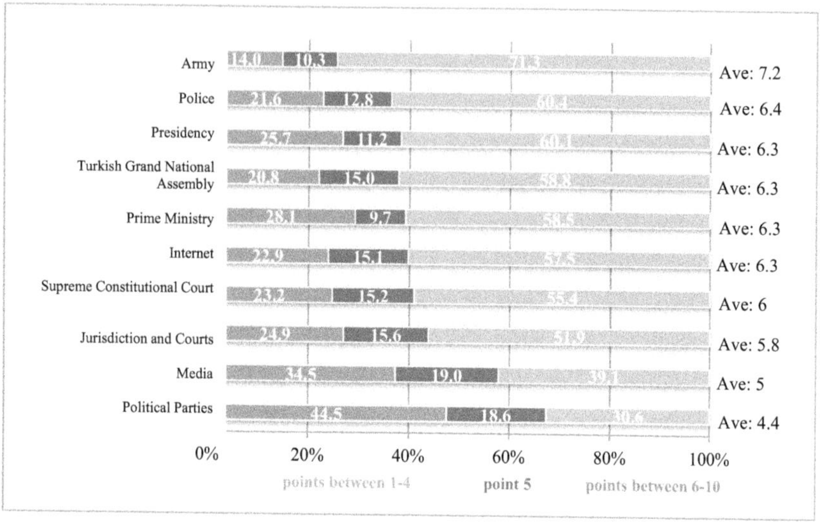

During the research study, before evaluating the brand equity of social media, the main target was to determine how much trust high school students direct to foundations and the place of the internet in this trust. The data indicates that in the credibility analysis, high school students trust army the most with a rate of 71.3%. Following this is police with 60.4%, presidency with 60.1%, Turkish Grand National Assembly with 58.8%, Prime Ministry with 58.5%, and the internet with 57.5%. The internet is in 6th place among others which indicates that the internet has a significant role on younsters. The least trusted foundations are political parties and the media. For this reason, it would not be wrong to say that traditional media no longer create reliability or interest among younsters because traditional media has lost its credibility compared to new media, and according to this opinion, it would be correct to say that youngsters tend to use new media environments more often.

Figure 7: Close recognition of the internet and social media applications

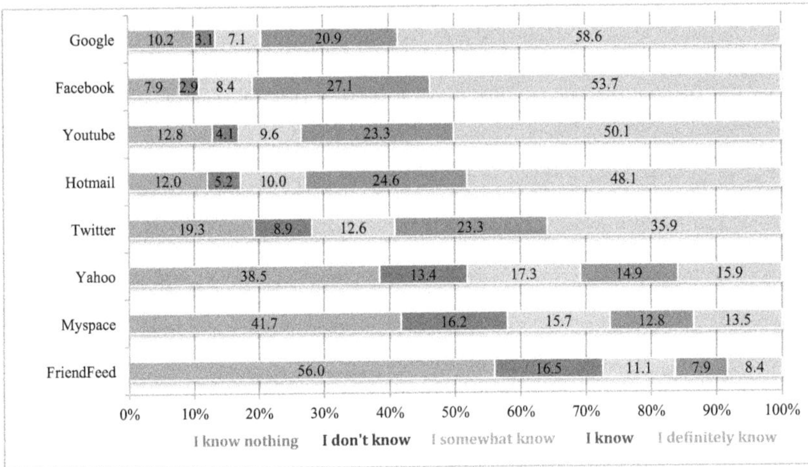

During the research study, high school students were asked how close they know the applications below, how much information they have about the applications, how they get the information about them (from media or close relationships), and how they get the information about recent news and changes for the applications. The very first component of the value of a brand is its awareness. According to the young people's "I definitely know" and "I know" answers, the "know" rate distribution is as follows: Facebook (80.8%), Google (79.5%), YouTube (73.4%), and Hotmail (72.7%). Among others, Twitter has a rate of 59.8% for young students. So it might as well be said that in spite of its increasing users in recent years, Twitter is not yet popular among high school students. In addition to this, between the two competing mail sites Hotmail and Yahoo, Hotmail is more popular among young people. In case we take the popularity as the size of the site, for young people, Google and Facebook are the biggest in their category.

Figure 8: The liking/admiration of the internet and social media applications

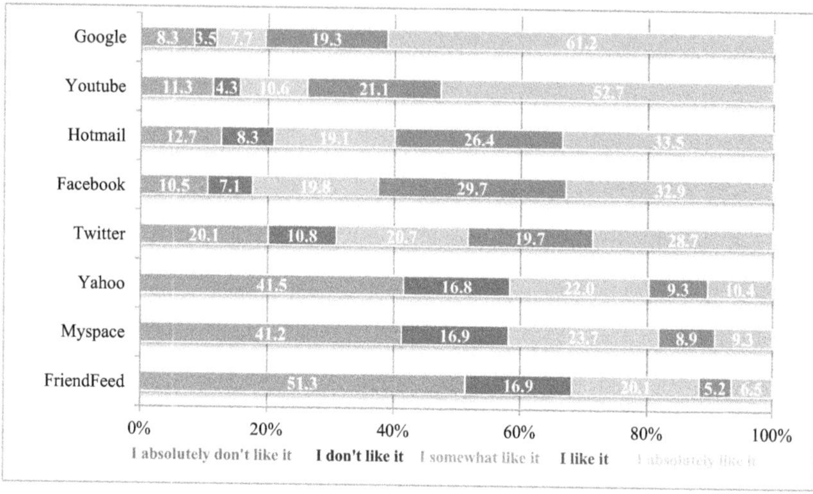

During the research study, another question was asked about how much these applications are liked. In the perceptional value of a brand, it is also important how much that brand is liked because it indicates how shiny its star is and how much it is known among its followers, which determines how dynamic the brand is. In this question, the most liked application is Google with a rate of 80.5%. Others are YouTube (73.8%), Facebook (62.6%), Hotmail (59.9%), and Twitter (48.4%). In the perceptional value of a brand, it is more important that the brand is liked rather than that it is known. For brands to be more liked is much more important than to be more known. Brands with less known value but with higher liked value are those with more potential to grow higher and with more potential to be a shining star. The main determiner in brand equity is that the liking and recognition values are either equal or the liking value is higher. Those brands are with a higher recognition but with a less liking value.

Figure 9: Recognition and liking analysis

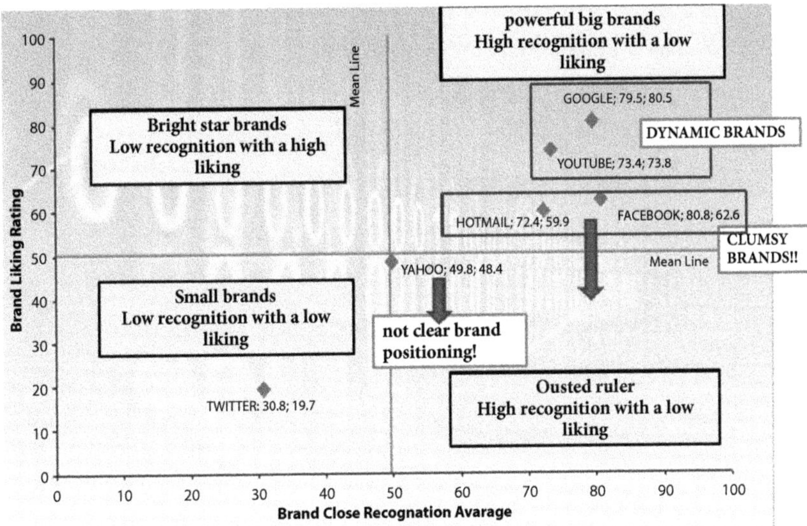

As it can be seen in the chart above, when you take the average value as the basis on the top right hand side of the chart, Google, YouTube, Facebook, and Hotmail can be categorised as "big brands" because the liking and recognition value of these brands are above the average value (50%). The significant point is that Google and YouTube are liked as much as they are known. That is something healthy for these brands. These two brands continue to grow as well as to be liked so they are perceived as dynamic brands in young people's apprehension. On the contrary, Facebook and Hotmail have less liking value compared to their recognition value which actually means that they are losing their dynamism and that they are getting clumsy. Especially in spite of its 80% recognition value, Facebook has a 62% liking value which means that it is on the way of getting a slow down and losing its brightness. If this situation continues and the difference grows larger, they have a probability of getting a place on the bottom right hand side of the chart. This part of the chart involves those brands that have a high recognition value with a low liking value. Another important finding is that Twitter is not an effective brand among young people. Yahoo is somewhere (centre of the chart) in between. Future communication activities might locate Twitter into a new position in this chart. The important thing is that it should increase its liking value.

Figure 10: Trust in the internet and social media applications

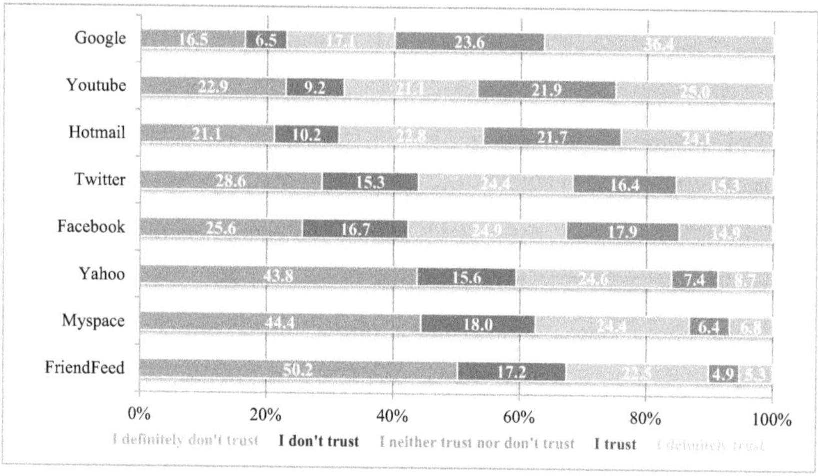

In brand equity measurement, the recognition and liking rates are usually high. Besides, trust, reliability, and advice rates are lower compared to the other values. However, the significant thing is that those brands that are considered "big" have very little or no difference between rates. When we consider how much social media creates reliability in young people's perception according to the total of "I trust" and "I definitely trust" answers, the most trusted media is Google with a rate of 60%.

Following "trust" rates are YouTube (46.9%), Hotmail (45.8%), Facebook (32.8%), Twitter (31.7%), and Yahoo (16.1%). As a result, Google is perceived as the leading brand by young people.

Figure 11: How happy the users are about the internet and social media applications

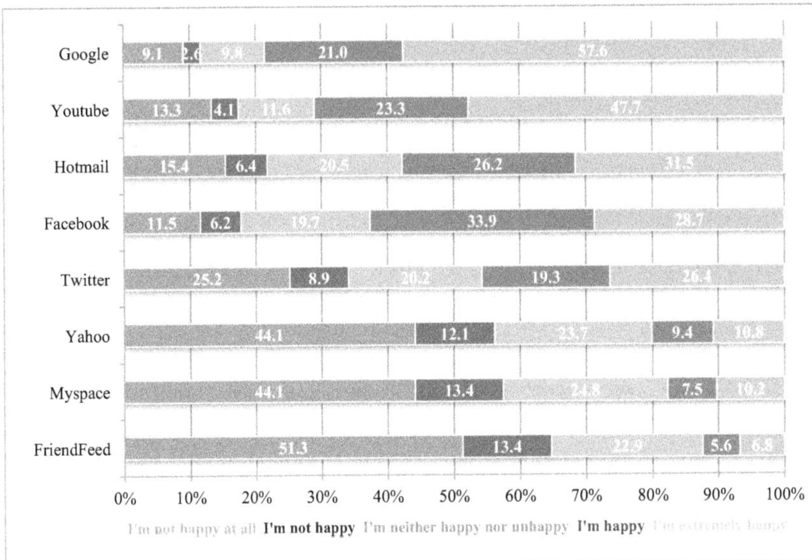

Another component determining brand equity is the level of happiness that's reflected for the brand. According to the total rate of "I'm extremely happy" and "I'm happy" answers that young people answered, they like Google the most with a rate of 78.6%, which is followed by YouTube with 71%, Facebook with 62.6%, Twitter with 45.7%, and Yahoo with 20.2%.

Figure 12: How recommendable internet and social media applications are

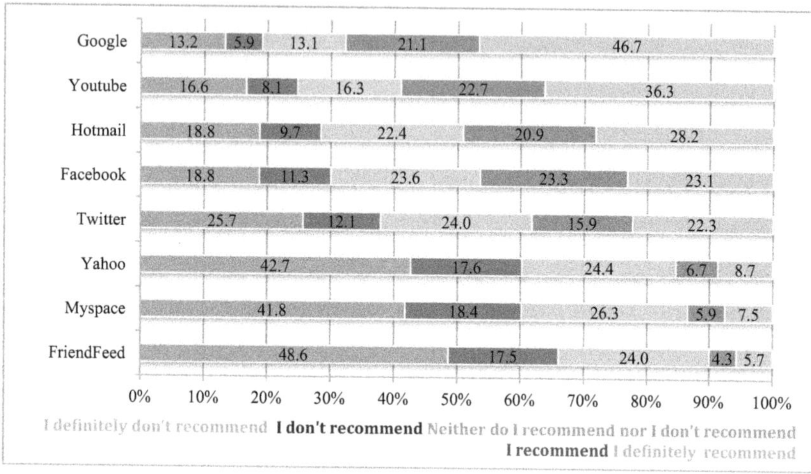

The brand equity of the triangle, the most powerful space that increases brand equity, is to recommend the brand.

In determining the brand equity along with brand recognition, liking of the brand, trust in that brand, happiness for the brand usage, and the recommendation of the brand have one step further significance. For the target group to advise brand means, different from basic customers, that those people are voluntary delegates, which indicates how much that brand is loved. For this reason, during the research study, how much the brand is recommended was also questioned. According to the total "I definitely recommend" and "I recommend" rates, Google has a rate of 67.8%. The following recommendation rates were obtained: YouTube (59%), Hotmail (49.1%), Twitter (38.2%), Facebook (46.4%), and Yahoo (14.4%). It wouldn't be wrong to say that Hotmail has a safer place than Yahoo among youngsters. Similarly, Facebook is perceived as better that Twitter by younger people. Generally, the best place is for Google, followed by YouTube.

3.5 Hierarchy of Brand Equity Measurement Relationship of the Internet and Social Media

Figure 13: Google

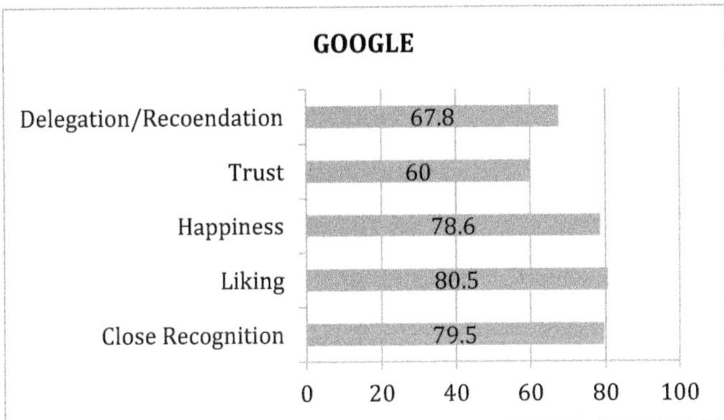

Figure 14: YouTube

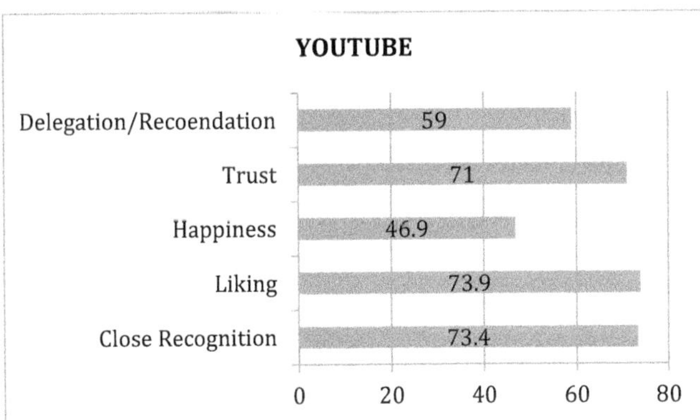

Figure 15: Facebook

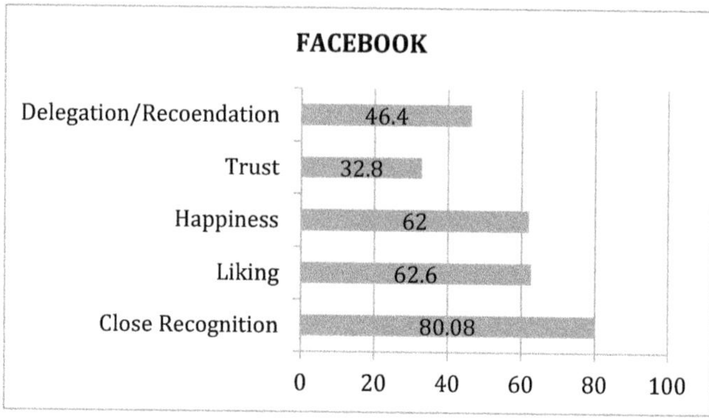

Figure 16: Hotmail

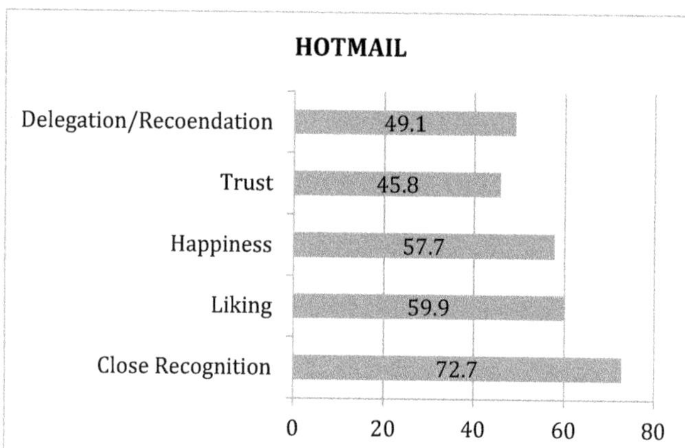

Figure 17: Yahoo

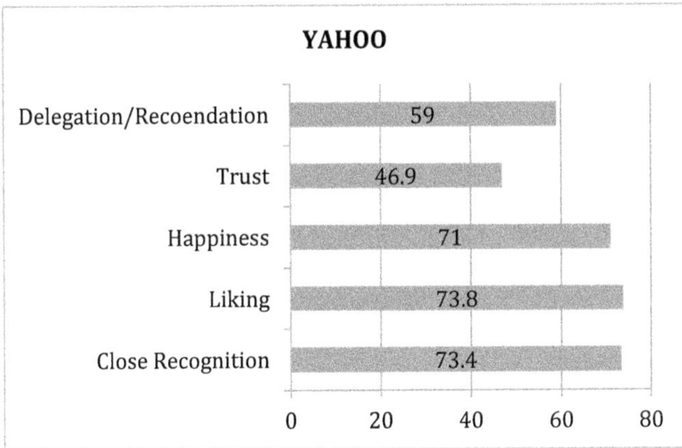

Figure 18: Twitter

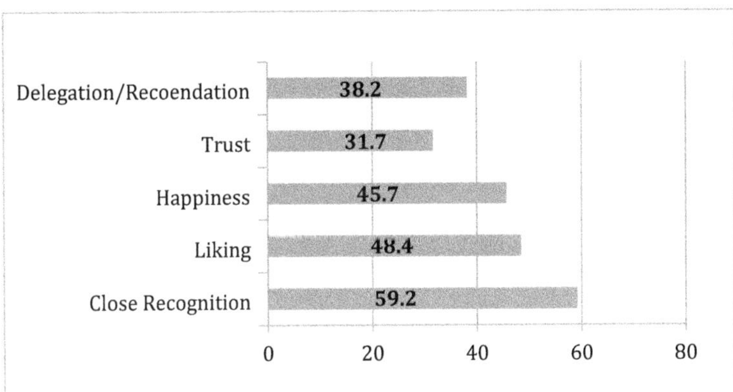

Conclusion

Today, the usage of social media and internet applications have increased a great deal due to the increasing usage of the internet and mobile devices. Social media and its applications are one of the most prolific methods in reaching the target groups for brands. Brands participate in social media in order to increase their brand equity in the perceptional dimension and to reach and touch their target group. What is significant in this sense is to be able to measure how valuable the brand is in the perception of the target group through social media and its applications. In this work, brand equity in high school students' perceptions through social media and its applications were evaluated in five basic components (close recognition of the brand (size), liking of the brand (dynamism), happiness for the brand, trust in the brand, and recommendation of the brand (delegation)). The perceptional value of a brand starts with how recognised that brand is for the target group of that brand. Close recognition is an indication of brands' size which shows how common they are. For young people, those brands that have the highest recognition are as follows: Facebook, Google, YouTube, and Hotmail. Twitter has a lower recognition value compare to Facebook. Yahoo is less valued compared to Hotmail. So it can be said that Twitter and Yahoo cannot be considered as "big" brands in young people's perception.

Another significant point that determines the brand equity is how much it is liked. The liking rate indicates the dynamism and brightness of the star of the brand. Google and YouTube are the most liked brands is this sense, in young people's perceptions. These two brands have almost the same liking rates which is to say that they are the top rated brands in the recognition and liking analysis. On the contrary, the other brands have lower liking rates which means that unless they keep their policy the way it is now, they will become clumsy, get old, lose their dynamism, and their star power will fade away. Thus, they will have low brand perceptions for their target group. Especially in spite of its 80% recognition value, Facebook has a 62% liking value which means that it is on the way to slow down and lose its brightness.

One of the important points in brand equity computation is having trust in the brand. Google, in this sense, has been found to be the most trusted brand in young people's perception. This is followed by YouTube, Facebook, and Twitter, with the rest of the brands having very low rates. One of the components that determines consumer loyalty is consumers' happiness about that brand. In addition, this happiness also determines a very important part of brand equity. The obtained data indicate that approximately 80% of high school student are happy with the Google brand. It is obvious how strong the brand image of Google is, which is directly followed by YouTube. On top of the brand equity triangle is recommendation which means that provided that people recommend the brand to other people, they are volunteer delegations of that brand. Being a delegation of a brand means that the person is on the top level of brand equity. The data that's obtained indicate that Google is on the first section of recommendation. This is followed by YouTube. The others have an average of 40% for the recommendation (delegation) rate. This means that young people feel close to social media and its applications, and for this reason, they are happy to use these brands and they voluntarily recommend the brands, becoming their natural delegations. In these kinds of research studies, the recommendation rate is usually low. This is the reason why the smallest triangle on the top of the brand equity pyramid is the recommendation (delegation) field. From this point down, it gets larger and the bottom line makes up the largest and the highest rated field which is the recommendation field. In this sense, the delegation point is the most apparent point of customer loyalty and its rate is the lowest compared to other fields. However, this research study indicates that young people often talk about social media, recommending its applications and environments, and thus become a delegation for them. Those young people take them as brands and almost half of them delegate the brands.

Another interesting point in the research study is that although the delegation rate is really high in the pyramid, the trust rate of the brands level is fairly low. This must mean that they currently do not particularly trust the internet environment. The fact that they make use of it extensively while being its volunteer delegate, not giving up using it, the internet being a part of their social life, having communication through it, and shortly living within it thoroughly does not actually mean that they have been able to build up a dependable relationship with the Internet. As a result, the reason might depend on the distrust in the brand itself as well as in the protection of confidential information that these brands enjoy within the internet atmosphere where they are located. In the article, the International Brand Evaluation Foundation, Interbrand, declares that Google has the second highest ranking of the 100 most valuable brands all over the world, revealing its financial value. Even though the work done with high school students might be considered to be a "small" or even "local" exemplification within the internet's general user environment, when you take it as the consumer based brand equity evaluation, close recognition, liking the brand, trust in the brand, happiness for the brand, recommendation of the brand, and being the volunteer delegate of the brand, Google has a pioneering location among others. In social media and its applications, YouTube can be categorised as a valuable brand because of the performance values it gained. In this work, because of the fact that there is no benchmark with another brand within the recognition/liking analysis graph, brands such as Google, YouTube, Facebook, and Hotmail, with above average performances, are considered as big brands.

This work clearly indicates that the brands examined, besides Google and YouTube, should increase their liking rate, create a brand identity, and shine their star. The brand living curve shows that having the brand only being recognised more does not actually mean that the brand is developing healthily. It means that the brand should increase its liking as it is recognised.

Resources

Aaker, David (1991). *Managing Brand Equity*, New York, Free Press.

Aktuğlu, Karpat Işıl (2004). Marka Yönetimi (Brand Management), İstanbul: İletişim Yayıncılık.

Amstrong, Gary, Philip Kotler (2009). Marketing, Pearson Prentice Hall.

Baudrillard, Jean (2008). The Consumer Society: Myths and Structures, Translated by Chris Turner, London, Sage Publication.

Gobe, Marc (2001). Emotional Branding, Allworth Press.

Kahraman, Murat (2010). *Sosyal Medya 101 (Social Media 101)*, İstanbul: MediaCat Kitapları.

Kaplan, Andreas M. and Michael Haenlein, *Users of the world, unite! The challenges and opportunities of Social Media*, Business Horizons. No: 53, 2010, ss. 59–68.

Keller, Keller L. (1993), *Conceptualizing, measuring, and managing customer-based brand equity*, Journal of Marketing, Vol. 57, pp. 1–22.

Keller, Keller L. (2003) *Strategic Brand Management, Building, Measuring and Managing Brand Equity*, Prentice Hall.

Kim H., Kim, W. and An J. A. (2003), *The effect of consumer-based brand equity on firms' financial performance*, Journal of Consumer Marketing, Vol. 20, No. 4, pp. 335–351.

Kotler, Philip and Gary Armstrong (2004). Principles of Marketing. New Jersey: Pearson-Prentice Hall.

Leone, P. Robert L., Kevin Keller vd. (2006). *Linking Brand Equity to Customer Equity*, Journal of Service Research, Vol. 9, Issue. 2, pp. 125–138.

Scott, David Meerman, (2013). The New Rules of Marketing & PR, Wiley Published.

Pelsmacker, Patrick, Maggie Geuens, Joeri Van Den Bergh (2001), *Marketing Communications*, Edinburg: Prentice Hail.

Toksarı, Murat ve Emin İnal, (2013). *Bulanık Analitik Hiyerarşisi Prosesi Yaklaşımı Kullanılarak Tüksetici Temelli Marka Değerinin Ölçümü*, International Journal of Social Science, Vol. 6, No. 1, pp. 1423–1457.

Wood, Lisa (2000). *Brands and brand equity: definition and management*, Management Desicion, Vol. 38/9, pp. 662–669.

Xsights Company, 'Perception Modeli, X-Percept',www.itibaratolyesi.com/…/Turkiye_Itibar_Endeksi_Cigdem_Penn.pptx, 20013.

GfK Research Company, Brand Potential Index Model, http://marketing.gfkamerica.com/102011-1252/GfK_Brand_Vitality_Tracking_Slip_Sheet_May_2011.pdf.

Tuğba Elmaci

Militarism in New Turkish Cinema as a Mechanism for Installing Masculinity

Introduction

Modern nation states have used nationalism and masculinity as an element of the existence while gathering the masses under one roof. Thereby, the basic tool has been militarism sitting on the ideology of nationalism as constituent elements of masculinity providing being pulled it to the centre and reproduce.

In Turkey, militarism uses masculinity both in terms of the relation of citizenship established with the state and as the most basic feature determining its relations with society. A process, such as the concept of compulsory military service, is a more important phenomenon, beyond being judicial, in terms of the relationships developed over male individuals culturally. Today, the leading role of art has an important share in encouraging the discussion of military less than in the past and it is to be rescued from an unquestionable area as a factor of establishing masculinity. Although socially militarism and to be fictionalised of masculinity in that context consist of some individual booms in daily life, the intrepidly film productions in recent term should be seen as important steps in terms of being questioned of this issue and creating public debate.

In this study, using a general framework, we discuss how to read the masculine identity installation over the language of cinema as part of new Turkey cinema and in the militarism axis *(Heads or Tails, Mountain, Thanks to Homeland, Majority, and Drag Queen)*. The study is finalised with a discussion of how masculinity shaped by militarism is reflected in daily life over the analysis of other neighbourhood kids film.

In the findings section of the study, we discuss how all of the productions of films shape and change masculinity in the militarism axis over cinema. In addition to this, the answers to questions of how it sees women and how it characterises them are sought.

Methods

Cinema is an art form taking to social life as references itself and feeding up most from this area. In this context, cinema composes a theme of all social actors' doings and makings. Consequently in this study, social structures shaping male individuals and telling them what to do and what not to do can be revealed by the method of sociological criticism. Sociological film analyses attempt to diagnose the relationships of the individual in social life with society in filmic narration (Özden 2004: 160–162). Apart from all these, it must be emphasised that sociological film criticism is open to interdisciplinary criticism. It is necessary to take advantage of psychological and psychoanalytic approaches to identify the characters and it is inevitable to take advantage of historical criticism and ideological criticism to evaluate the historical context of them.

Within the context of this study, how male individuals as social actors are shaped by militarism in social life and the fact that nationalism is the most important ideological thought revealing this reveals the necessity for multiple movie reviews.

Militarism, Nationalism, and Masculinity

To start with to explain etymological origin of militarism concept will be much easier understanding of it. *"The concept of army, which is the French equivalent militaire (English, military) is based on militar that means with regard to 'military and war' in Latin language etymologically"* (Altınay 2007). Thus, it is possible to translate the concept of militarism into Turkish as orduculuk or askercilik. It is necessary to understand militarism with the concept of nation state that emerged after the French Revolution. Militarism is a phenomenon that emerged as a mechanism to create your own armies of nation states and keep them together for the sake of an ideal. When we look at the historical context, nation states with their compulsory military applications have created a mechanism of gaining identity and belonging for male social actors. For example, after the French Revolution introduced the concept of nation state, one of the most important mechanisms transforming peasant people into the French was training and the other one was the army. The nation state found a mechanism for raising and controlling its citizens in this way. While checking citizens, the nation state laid the foundations of structure both based on severity and hierarchy (Sünbüloğlu 2009:104).

In Turkey, as well as the fact that militarism started with the effective years of The Unity and Progress Party, it is said that it was literally shaped with the Republic of Turkey. Especially with the 1930s, the most basic element internalising the state and citizenship was military. Starting with the Turkish Historical Research Society founded by Ataturk, the thesis that the Turks are the best soldiers and the understanding of the army nation are the works of those years (Altınay, Bora 2002:142). "*The military in Turkey reproduces ethicist (based on ethnicity)-an essentialist understanding of nationalism with represent himself as a carrier of eternal continuity of Turkish national identity*" (Altınay, Bora 2002:149). Thus, the army fictionalises itself as being reproduced of nationalism or the only mechanism that performs the preservation of national. As is seen in Turkey masculinity, nationalism and militarism concepts are connected to each other in such an independently from each other and all of these concepts are not interpreted and cannot be understood.

Seemingly, social gender thought not to relation with nationalism in contrast is shaped by this concept or they mutually feed up each other such as entropy. On the other hand, while militarism is a concept reproducing social gender and nationalism, it transform into an institution in the context of the army. Based on his own life practices, Barış Çoban describes this situation at a phallus centred point in his article. According to him, in the present case, *"militaristic nationalism is based on masculinity. It aims to both its protection and re-generating. Army is one of the most important mechanisms for protecting and breeding of men. In the trainings given by Army, it emphasizes that reproductive and making as many children as possible are necessary and obligatory for guaranteeing the existence of the nation against the enemy and not to fall into the minority in terms of population density, namely to be able to fight against internal enemies. Men are founder and maintainer of nation, in this sense, nationalism is phallocentric"* (Çoban 2014). All these lofty areas and tasks related to the homeland are given to men. In this sense, military service is also the area where masculinity is reproduced and reinforced.

Pınar Selek summarises the situation in his interviews on the texts named "Sürüne Sürüne Asker Olmak" compiled from reportages of the view to the military: *"Like many men environments, military is a social area that men describes himself over women and women become objective and they have developed a culture of sexuality. Men here are learning once again not just how to be a man, what acceptable gender stereotypes are. Both from there systematic training and from each other... In this environment where armed men knock each other, dominant social values are internalized again together. Acceptable gender stereotypes are learned with acceptable social-political-cultural patterns. Are also learned what to do to unadmitted... To enemy, to prostitute, to the one who making a mistake, to the weak, to the one who is out of order, to the anomalistic... it will be experienced together that in which circumstances beating, swearing, raping, harassment are legitimizing. Cannot gender issues be resolved the as long as systematic production continues? Of course cannot be solved... Therefore, militaristic mechanisms, is a problem for not only men, but also women, also for everyone who struggles against sexism"* (Selek 2014). As stated by Pinar Selek, there is actually a hierarchy string spreading to all social areas. While the women are in secondary sex positions in this hierarchy, men are subject to a hierarchy among themselves. It is precisely what R. W. Connell's hegemonic masculinity says. Domination of men in their internal ranking creates masculine hegemony (Connell, 1998:245). The situation created by militarism or compulsory military service is in fact the process of legitimisation of this hierarchy. So not only do they not receive their fair share of men in this hierarchy, at the same time, women are forced to live in the perception of command in social life dominated by the patriarchal system. The most important indicator reinforcing this entire situation is undoubtedly an element of violence. According to R. W. Connell, violence offers vital return to every man. Violence is the most basic tool determining the hierarchy among men even if they are in the same class. In this context, there is a direct relationship between male dominance and violence (Connell, 1998:151). The most basic indicator of militaristic patriarchal approach is perhaps this violent lesbianism. The social hierarchy string is directly proportional with the power to create this violence. Therefore, in general, women are in a weak position compared to men and this is the key point of discrimination in the patriarchal structure formed by social gender. The patriarchal structure is an opinion that men established dominance and it is considered that this dominance results from men's biology. By this way, women can be controlled thanks to features such as those attributed to men that are generally accepted, such as 'power, aggressiveness, and violence.' Furthermore, society can be controlled by men throughout the patriarchal system. Because it is a structure established with the belief that 'men are the strongest gender,' militarism is the best layout providing continuity of it. So, militarism provides the continuity of the order within the framework of a patriarchal order.

New Turkey Cinema and Militarism Overview

New Turkey cinema describes the cinema period that was shaped with new directors who separated from the Yeşilçam period and participated in cinema from the middle of the 1990s. This new cinema term is moving with the understanding influenced by society and everyday life.. The excess of male narratives is a conspicuous separate element in new Turkey cinema. Within the context of this study, the films taken in the near term and that offer militarism as a transformative mechanism on male individuals or that are criticising are outstanding. Here, examining these films in general, it is necessary to mention two major trends. The first is that some films look at militarism from a certain distance and criticise it, while other films reproduce existing cultural coding (Kurtlar Vadisi Irak, Deliyürek, Şah Mat, Maskeli Beşler). Outside of this category, although it is a more dominant nationalist rhetoric, there are also nationalist nostalgic masculinity fictions such as Fetih 1453 directed by Fatih Aksoy telling the military successes shown in the past glorious wars and the army nation motto.

The films that generally focus on the military concept or militarism in Turkey have followed the reflections of the low intensity war in the southeast since the 1980s. In this context, we face films like *Heads or Tails (Uğur Yücel, 2004), Thanks to Homeland (Levent Semerci, 2009),* and *Mountain (Alper Çağlar, 2012).* Mountain and Thanks to Homeland films are narratives that personally took place in the conflict zone that focus on male friendship in the conflict zone, exalting the men who sacrificed their lives for the homeland. The Heads or Tails film is namely a war veteran film, perhaps seen for the first time in Turkey cinema. The film tells the story of two soldiers who fought in the southeast region and who were injured in the conflict. It also tells the story of their adoption process to daily life after returning from the military. Although it is a different film in this sense, the *Heads or Tails* film focuses on two characters who were corrupted psychology, rather than the concept of war or militarism, because in fact, it focuses on two problematic characters. On the other hand, although it shows war, there are movies focusing on the psychology of war. Majority is the first movie in this category. This movie tells the story of a young man who is about to go to the military but not for violence, having fears but pretending to go to army with the pressures of family and his environment (Seren Yüce, 2010). The interpretation process that society ascribed on the military and those based on social gender codes are clearly reflected. Although the hero is afraid to go to the army, the military imposed it upon him as a process to complete his masculinity by his father and his father's friends. In this sense, the Majority presents a pure show of hegemonic masculinity blessing militarism. The Drag Queen movie (Caner Alper, Mehmet Binay, 2011), which focuses on the story of a gay individual who does not want to go the army, stays to a different point. The movie was quite a provocative stance taken in the period and it is told in the film to be taken the report process called 'pink discharge paper' in the military and it is humiliating the gay individuals (the humiliation over the belief that pink colour is female-specific), the report is given to gay individuals by army shown reason for their sexual orientation. According to military law, by accepting that gay individuals are sick, they are not accepted for military service. However, they also need to prove that they are gay. They must convince the military delegation with their behaviour, attire, and pictures taken of them during sex. Although the film's hero thinks hard about going abroad with his boyfriend and about how to conduct this degrading process, he had to do what the system imposed upon him. Hegemonic masculinity mentioned in the previous section comes into play here and it is a pushed down position with the most humiliating attitude by the system as a man.

As is seen in most of these films as a mechanism for establishing masculinity and that which is believed to be at a distance to militarism, to change the general opinion or settled code requires a serious social transformation. However, films such as *Heads or Tails, Thanks to Homeland,* or *Mountain* are aim to focus on people show presence as narratives that they glorify masculinity and impose extraordinary meaning to it, reproduces its own internal hierarchies and solidified this place, furthermore not to avoid women to secondary area.

Other Neighbourhood Children

It is the first feature-length and 2009 construction cinema film of Aydın Bulut. Many famous players played in the film (Mehmet Ali Nuroğlu, İsmail Hacıoğlu, Volga Sorgu, Ertan Saban, Eyşan Özhim, and Bülent İnal). The film tells the story of two close friends living in the Gazi street that have to pay the price in order to get away from the slums where they live. The movie develops with the returning of alevist young Semih who is early discharge for one month from the army due to his heroism in operations in the Southeast and he encountered his funeral of his brother when returning and then searching for brother's killer. The film can be evaluated in the 'vet' movie category, rather than as a war film. This is because the film's two main characters, Semih and Gürdal, were in conflict with the PKK in the southeast but what they live there damaged their psychology too much.

Semih almost never mentioned what they experienced while there. But those in the neighbourhood and those around him go into rhapsodies of his success in the army. For Semih, that period is the past, dividing his lives with nightmares. He wants to forget that period and he has also staying away from violence a naive personality. The current situation is even more traumatic for Gürdal and he does not want to remember; however, he is a man who continuously demonstrates violence and walks around with camouflage. Young people in the neighbourhood are fans of his representation of violence in the army and they want to tell it at the first opportunity that they find. *(Tell brother what did you live, We want action. Where did you go into and get out? How did you shot down? How many ears did you cut? Tell it brother!)*

Gürdal and Semih did what was expected of them in the military. When returning, they were two real men that everyone was afraid of and the rights of them were represented. In Serpil Sancar's book "Masculinity: Impossible Ruling," compiled from interviews with men, she tells this in one of the interviews which is given under the title of Military, Militarism and Masculinity, as follows; *"military is a place where learning masculinity... I think masculinity is built on a huge role; namely perhaps we are a gentle human our inner world, you need to be more severe due to be man. While you are able to sit concatenating legs, you're sitting astride. So you need to show that more men. [...] They're creating such a balance that they are formed a mechanism which people start to make a request internalized what people do not want to do at all not by force or severity of the opposite side"* (Sancar, 2011). Violence in the mountains continues in everyday life of heroes as part of normalised life. Semih thinks that Gürdal killed his brother and it was certain what Semih had to do when he went to meet Gürdal. The patriarchal mission loaded onto Semih was to take revenge for his brother. He performed this with his own method. In fact, the situation is not very different from life in the mountains. Masculinity is defined as man hypertrophy in the interview of "Hello Soldier" anthology, which was given by Murathan Mungan, where he tells how it went into daily life as: *"On the other hand, it is also necessary to control the inflated masculinity. (...) He both wants to blow up masculine ego until the end but also control it. There is the same contradiction in motivating success only much can be controlled in our social Dynamics. This social pattern is more stringent in the military system and is more systematic under the name of discipline. But our civilian life color is also khaki"* (Mungan 2014). Gürdal does not give up his identification tag and camouflage clothing in civilian life. His daily life also khaki and there is no turning back. For Semih and Gürdal, civilian life continued as was determined and formed in the army. But as in the evaluation of Mungan, they have remained in civilian life that is out of control. Moreover, it is impossible to control.

Women are required for the reproduction of man's representation. They are like the sword of Damocles for men who have the fear of Freud's castration. Throughout the film, women are portrayed as complementary elements or as dependent on men as a source of permanent living. In this context, "Other Neighborhood Children" is a real man's movie. For instance, in the dialogue between Gürdal and his ex-girlfriend, Gürdal tells the moment making a story in the army like that: *"It rained for days and everywhere was swamp, boots were such pricking on the bottom that you think as if you nailed. Anyway, we reached the top of the hill, no one could go more, we were finished, we were finished... the full moon in the sky was like a dish, I stare at the full moon and see you. I got G-3 monster, three kilos were thirty kilos, I wrapped the machine wrapped. I think that it was you, later I noticed a heat on my cheek. As if your lips. Then thousand of bullets and thousand of screams. My weapon is not a gun I would say in the shining full moon, rose's face shone, rose face!"* The story quite impressed Gül. She forget about her anger towards Gürdal and wanted to have sex. The symbol of masculinity has been identified with a magnificent phallic symbol. But later, the suspicion came to the mind of Gürdal that Gül had sex with others when he was in the army and he got mad. He said "*you are mine.*" Although Gül said "*I do not belong to you,*" he insistently said that you are mine. He beat Gül terribly due to her unacceptance. Therefore, he reinforced his ruling and his 'ownership' on Gül's body.

Findings

As one of the fundamental mechanisms determining individuals and thus the relationships in everyday life, reproducing militarism is required for the continuation of the patriarchal system. Military service is vital for young men because of the importance of getting married, getting a job, and gaining social prestige. As a result, they make the concept important. The repeatedly reflected militarism, as a mechanism establishing or glorifying masculinity, or the pressure on young men created by compulsory military application and trauma seems to keep Turkish cinema busy for many years.

Another important finding related to these films is that women in this film, unfortunately, are absent. For all the movies, it is seen that subordination of women in gender stereotypes is further reinforced. As is seen, women take part as an accessory complementary to masculinity in the universe of stories. All these films take us back to the reality of cinema that cinema is cultural practice which myths are produced, reproduced and these are represented on women and masculinity and also femininity and masculinity, in short, on sexual differences (Smelik 2006:1).

Looking at the narratives within new Turkey cinema, a small share of thinking is seen while reproducing the patriarchal gender codes. Despite this entire thinking share, social infrastructure is still pretty far behind at the point of questioning the content of militarism. When we look at the box office bringings of the films that we mentioned, it is seen that they cannot even come close to the box office success of male narratives forming militarism.

As is seen when we look at today's Turkish cinema, the concept of militarism began to produce new films, allowing for different readings out of perception of a localised previous period. Considering that cinema is influenced by localised perceptions and of course the settled in social structure, expecting a radical transformation would be too optimistic.

However, with the movement of the condition that art is a pioneer, it is clear that the perception of masculinity fictionalised by militarism is not exactly based on a solid basis.,

References

Altınay. A. G. (2007). *History of Nationalism* Glossary of terms-I (1. Edition). Özgür Üniversite Publishing.

Altınay, A. G., Bora T. (2002) *"Army, Militarism and Nationalism"* Nationalism in Modern Turkey, Volume 4, Istanbul: İletişim Publishing.

Connell R. W, (1998) Gender and Power, Trans. Cem Soydemir, Istanbul: Ayrıntı Publishing.

Çoban, Barış. (2014) https://www.academia.edu/8575604/Gosteri_Iktidari_ve_Militarist_Erkeklik).

Mungan, Murathan (2014) *http://vicdaniret.org/erkeklik-bitmeyen-bir-askerlik-m-mungan/.*

Özden, Zafer (2004) Film Critic, İstanbul: İmge Publishing.

Sancar, Serpil. (2011). Masculunity: Imposible Power. (2. edition). Ankara: Metis Publishing.

Selek, Pınar. (2014) *http://ataerkiyekarsierkekler.blogspot.com.tr/2012/02/pnar-selek-erkeklik-snav-hic-bitmiyor.html.*

Smelik, Anna (2006) Feminist Cinema and Film Teory, Trans. Deniz koç. Istanbul: Agora Publishing.

Sünbüloğlu, Nurseli Yeşim (2009) Media, Nationalism, Violence, Istanbul: Su Publishing.

Dinçer Atli

A New Approach to Marketing: A Literature Review on Neuromarketing

Introduction

Many different marketing approaches have been developed since the onset of marketing activities. Within historical contexts, the changes in these marketing approaches have proceeded in parallel with developments in political, social, cultural, economic, and technological fields. From this perspective, the second half of the 20th century was especially a period in which businesses utilised globalisation and high budget marketing strategies. Professional marketing teams have developed a variety of techniques and methods to conquer the hearts and minds of customers. With the great contribution of marketing, brands have started to play important roles in the lives of their customers.

In this process, as a result of the interdisciplinary study of neuroscience and psychology, marketing had first impacted neuroeconomy and behavioural finance studies. The use of studies of neuroimaging techniques that research consumers' purchase decisions bred the neuromarketing approach. What discriminates neuromarketing from the previous marketing studies and makes it significant is the discovery that consumers, while making purchasing decisions, do not decide rationally but do so out of unconscious mechanisms. These discoveries had shown that in addition to marketing and the product, price, place, and promotion, which are the components of marketing, it has become a necessity to look at previously known approaches to marketing communication, brand management, and specifically advertising from a different perspective.

Theoretical Background

If we consider the course of history that the science of marketing has gone through, marketing 1.0 was about mass producing the simple and standard products as much as possible with a product centred approach. Every product that was introduced to the market easily found a purchaser. In the period after the Second World War when people started to talk about the "information age," marketing 2.0 tried to teach the consumers whose education and expectations increased gradually to consume more and that doing so will make them happy. In order to make themselves different in the eyes of the customers, they started to make their products different and respond to the psychological needs and desires of customers who came face-to-face with many options today, with marketing, globalisation, computerisation, the change of the needs of the new generation, and the rise of the creative class. Marketing 3.0 had emerged just at that point and in addition to the consumer oriented approach of marketing 2.0, it is proceeding with a holistic attitude that requires addressing human emotions and spirit. Parallel with this, the sale-oriented approach to marketing 3.0 is to have the capacity "to produce a product or service that was pre-purchased" (Kotler et al., 2011, p. 15–17; Görgülü & Görgülü, 2010, p. 17).

Today, as a response to the need "to produce a product or service that was pre-purchased," by taking advantage of the advancements in science and technology, the notion of neuromarketing emerged as an approach that stands in the conjunction of neuroscience and marketing. In this process, the scientific developments in neuroscience and brain research caused a paradigm shift in understanding human behaviour and decision processes.

While it was thought that humans made their economic choices for rational reasons, today it has started to be understood that consumers are affected by certain unconscious mechanisms. According to research, the behaviour and decisions of people are determined by the unconscious processes in the mid and archaic brain 95% of the time. 85% of the time, the person's brain continues to record and interpret the environmental messages (Krakoff, 2010 as cited in; Giray & Girişken, 2013, p. 610). All these findings and the new discoveries of neuroscience about the brain and the mind resulted in the development of neuromarketing research by letting the science of marketing take advantage of this information.

The Concept of Neuromarketing

Our brain takes in an average of 2,000 different stimuli every day. Only a very small amount of these stimuli are consciously interpreted by the brain and most of them are consigned to the subconscious. At this point, the subconscious has a big role in affecting our behaviours and decisions (İzgören, 2006, p. 19). The scientific research in the last decade has shown that 85% of all decisions are given with the influence of the subconscious (Krakoff, 2010; Tatlı, 2013). The research not only on marketing but also on the behavioural economy and psychology showed that the studies done with surveys make it possible to only reach the customer's conscious memories and experiences; whereas, the way to reach the real thoughts and experiences of people is to understand their emotions and subconscious (Damasio, 1994; Zaltman, 2003). Thus, to develop potent marketing strategies, it is important to understand the elements that affect consciousness and subconscious of consumers (Hart, 2009, p. 32).

Parallel with this, the developments in neuroscience have started to be used in research in some fields of social sciences. The first confluence of neuroscience with social sciences started with psychology and as a result, the field of neuropsychology emerged and later the interdisciplinary convergence of economy and neuroscience gave way to the notion of neuroeconomy (Tanrıdağ 2012, s. 82–83). Being a sub category of neuroeconomy, neuromarketing emerged as a result of the use of the methods of neuroscience in market research, to understand the market behaviour of consumers (Kenning & Plassman, 2005; Giray & Girişken, 2013, p. 609; Lee et al., 2007).

As a new and developing approach, the notion of neuromarketing is defined as the use of neuroscience tools in creating marketing strategies that can be used by marketing experts, advertisers, and researchers in order to understand what affects the consciousness and subconscious of consumers (Tüzel, 2010, p. 165). Neuromarketing, in parallel with the development of neuroscience, as a result of the use of neuroimaging methods together with behavioural psychology, is defined as a marketing science that emerged in order to better understand the decision-making processes of consumers and brought new possibilities and understanding to the science of marketing (Trends E-Magazine, 2010, p. 30).

In other words, neuromarketing is the process of developing marketing strategies coherent with the consumers' choices and assumptions, by understanding what effects the consumers' consciousness or subconscious (Tüzel, 2010, p. 164–165). In neuromarketing, the approach of neuroscience to explain the structural and functional qualities of the nervous system is used for the purpose of marketing (Trends E-Magazine, 2010, p. 30). Within the field of today's application, neuromarketing is a tool for research that tries to better understand consumer behaviour by measuring the response of consumers to brands and advertisements using neuroimaging techniques (Ural, 2008, p. 425).

The first scientific study in the field of neuromarketing was first realised with the announcement of the use of a functional magnetic resonance imaging (fMRI) device in marketing research by Harvard University professor Gerry Zaltman in the first half of 1990. This study is considered as the first encounter of neuroscience and marketing. The father of the notion of "neuromarketing" is professor Ale Smidts from the Rotterdam Management Faculty of Erasmus University. Professor Smidts is an important figure in making the notion of "neuromarketing" popular in academic and popular literature. The person who enhanced the popularity of neuromarketing and made it known worldwide is the author of the book "Buyology": Martin Lindstrom (Özçiftçi, 2012). According to his three year and seven million dollar scientific neurological research project, the Danish brand consultant is claiming that people are usually lying about their purchasing decisions, but the brain tells us the truth (Lindstrom, 2008, p. 230). Similarly, neuroscientist Antonio Damasi indicates that "people make irrational decisions by using the emotional parts of their brains not the rational." People make these decisions according to emotional, impulsive, and sensory stimulus. Therefore, neuromarketing is also defined as an approach that is focused on the neurological study of the individual's responses and his or her state of mind (Özdoğan et al., 2008, p. 2).

The Neuroscientific Tools and Techniques Used in Neuromarketing

Neuromarketing benefits from neuroscience due to some essential neurophysiological mechanisms in the brain. The brain functions by electrical impulses. When the brain encounters a stimulus, in other words, when it sees an object or smells a fragrance, a signal is sent to the brain. These signals activate the neurons and the neurons transfer the energy by blood vessels. The fMRI device, which is used in neuroimaging, can detect those activities. Thus, it becomes possible to measure the activation and its degree caused by the stimulus coming from the five senses (Ataman, 2010; Yücel & Çubuk, 2013, p. 173). For example, the luminosity appearing in the frontal lobe cortexes of the brains of the subjects is an indication of the neuro activity. This area of the brain is the location where the individual makes his or her decisions. It is considered that when this area is exposed to images of a product, it promotes the consumer to purchase (Wilkinson, 2005).

In this regard, to better understand the preferences of consumers, the responses and mental activities of the consumers to the given stimulus are neurologically examined. The following devices used in neuroimaging are utilised in this examination: (1) fMRI device which shows what parts of the brain are activated when exposed to different stimuli, in other words, scans the brain by spatial mapping; (2) electroencephalography (EEG) which measures the intensity of brain wave activity by electrical methods; (3) Eye Tracking which detects where, in what sequence, and how long a person looks at a visual object; (4) Galvanic Skin Response (GSR) Device which measures the changes on the skin when exposed to stimuli; and (5) Pet-Positron Emission Tomography Device which evaluates blood flow within the cortex in order to measure the neural activities related to different tasks (www.kocaelineurofeedback.com; Ural, 2008, p. 421–432).

The fMRI and the EEG are the most commonly used tools in neuromarketing research. Usually the neuromarketing companies utilise their own instruments and methodologies. For example, Nielsen company has developed a special EEG device for neuromarketing research called the MYND, a dry wireless headset. Additionally, they use eye-tracking and galvanic skin response devices. Labiometrics

Inc. developed a set of neuromarketing instruments. Their device is named the BioNavigator and it records brain waves and galvanic skin response. Buyology Inc. has different services for each field: MindLink for strategy, Mind Measure AdMindMeasure for advertising and packaging, and Media Mind Measure techniques to test and predict the advertising effect and the impact on consumers (Ză & Tuţă, 2013, p. 100). Today, the number of companies that do neuromarketing research are rapidly increasing worldwide and make up the neuromarketing research sector. Hundreds of medical centres across the globe are using neuroimaging techniques for marketing research (Özçiftci, 2012).

Neuromarketing Research Papers

According to a research study conducted by the Texas Baylor Medical School in 2004 by using the fMRI technique, it was found that among the subjects who drank Coca-Cola and Pepsi with closed eyes, the brain's reward centre called the ventral putamen was more activated in subjects who drank Pepsi. However, when the subjects opened their eyes, they preferred the more popular brand Coca-Cola. Both taste and cultural elements are influential in choosing a soft drink (Hatip, 2008). In his article published in the Journal *Neuron* in 2004, neuroscientist Read Montague studied what beverages the subjects chose by examining brain waves. When given unspecified beverages, the brain activities showed that the subjects chose both of the beverages at rate of fifty-fifty. But when the product was specified, 75% of the subjects chose Coca-Cola. The study showed that when the consumer is in interaction with the brands, the conscious and subconscious responses of the consumer may be in conflict with each other (Cranston, 2004).

The results of some other neuromarketing research studies can be summarised as follows:

- When subjects are exposed to a favourite picture, an increase in activity in the mid frontal cortex was observed (Wahlberg, 2004).
- Attractive faces activate the reward centre of the brain more compared to unattractive faces (Senior, 2003).
- According to research by Giray and Girişken, although the subjects did not see the objects, they were able to give responses consistent with their demographic qualities (Giray & Girişken, 2013, p. 617).
- In other research on memory and information gathering conducted by using EEG, certain visual scenes activated the left frontal cortex more rapidly and thus resulted in a better definition (Rossiter et al., 2001, p. 13–21).

- On satisfaction and reward, Erk and his colleagues stated that products that have higher social value (i.e. a sports car) activate the reward centre of the brain more compared to products that have lesser social value (i.e. a small car) (Erk et al., 2002, p. 2499–2503).
- According to research conducted by Petr Milacek & Jiri Herian, it has been demonstrated that television (TV) programs stimulate different parts of the brain. Different areas of the brain are activated while watching quiz shows and reality shows, giving a clear image on how our mind functions when watching TV (Neuromarketing Science & Business Association, 2012).
- Gemma Calvert's research study showed that the warning labels on cigarette packs have no deterring effect on smokers (Lindstrom, 2013 p. 19).
- Brian Hnutson's research team from Standford University was able to accurately predict if the subjects would decide to purchase a presented item (Lynch, 2010 p. 61 as cited in in Ză & Tuță, 2013 p. 98).
- Van der Laan, de Ridder, and Viergever & Smeets's studies demonstrated that packaging has a significant role in manipulation in terms of the level of healthiness and fat of the product. The appeal of healthy products was high. Blue, green, and white were the most preferred colours. After this study it was possible to observe patterns that influence choice. (Van der Laan, et al., as cited in in Ză & Tuță, 2013 p. 98).
- Lehmann & Reimann researched the correlation of time versus money in our purchase decisions. The results of their research studies showed that when consumers are primed with time, their favourability ratings for the product increase. These investigations provide evidence on the insular activity in time-versus-money effect (Lehmann & Reimann, 2012).
- Clithero, Smith, Carter & Huettel examined the brain regions in charge of monetary rewards and social rewards. The results demonstrated that there are different patterns representing participants-specific functional organisation and the aspects of brain organisation that generalise across individuals (Clithero et al., 2011 as cited in in Ză & Tuță 2013, p. 98).
- A research study conducted by Nielsen Company investigated why a new package of a snack food product doesn't work. The tests revealed that the new package did not engage the customers emotionally and didn't have any impact on memory. There was a continuous distraction of packaging elements, higher than norms. The core product and the brand messages did not enliven the consumer opinion (Nielsen Corporation, 2013).
- SBS & Neuro-Insight Inc.'s results showed that women are attracted to different types of cars (http://www.neuro-insight.com/case-studies 2014).

Some Advantages of Measurement Methods in Neuromarketing

Companies might have some benefits from neuromarketing studies. Neuromarketing is utilised in areas like: new product development, product design, packaging, price determination, branding, advertisement perception, detection of the proper advertisement medium, political communication, the impact of the stimulus on purchasing choices, positioning, retail selling, in-store solutions or business online, measuring trust, sales meetings, and identifying the relationship between the product and the consumer and the psycho-social reasons within this relationship (Özdoğan et al., 2010, p. 4–5; Ural, 2008, p. 426–428). By taking the subconscious dynamics in many different areas that were previously not easy to collect data into consideration, neuromarketing can provide strategic advantages in developing marketing strategies.

The measurement methods utilised in neuromarketing have some advantages compared to the survey and target group meeting methods used in marketing research. The most important advantage of neuromarketing is that it helps us understand the difference between the oral response a consumer gives and what he or she really thinks. With the tools of neuromarketing, it becomes possible to understand what the consumer really thinks rather than what he or she says (Ural 2008, p. 422). Also in some research studies, the subjects may give the answer that the researcher wants to hear, be influenced by other members of the group, or be ashamed to express what he or she really thinks (Priyadarshini, 2006).

By eliminating the above-mentioned reservations, neuromarketing helps us to understand the decision-making process of the consumer at the conscious and subconscious level and develop marketing strategies accordingly. Neuromarketing research helps companies in their marketing strategies and allows for deeper consumer insights. It represents new borders in understanding consumer behaviour, gaining rapid credibility and adoption among marketing professionals (Zară & Tuță, 2013, p. 100).

Ethical Reservations in the Field of Neuromarketing

Reservations in neuromarketing usually have an ethical aspect. There are people who think that the methods in question are used by marketing experts to manipulate the consumers (Grimes, 2006; Aktaran; Ural, 2008 p. 428). For example, the Commercial Alert organisation claims that the use of fMRI devices may lead to the manipulation of the behaviour of consumers (Wilkinson, 2005). Marketing experts that do not act ethically may develop irresistible advertisements that may lead consumers to make irrational decisions and this may lead to serious ethical problems for children and adults (Dooley, 2007; Acuff, 2005, as cited in Özdoğan et al., 2008, p. 8). Other experts think that neuromarketing does not have ethical problems regarding its methods and fields of application. If we evaluate neuromarketing according to Garret's widely accepted ethical theory, the methods used by neuromarketing are considered ethical provided that they are not utilised for unethical reasons. In order to avoid unethical applications, classification of the professional and legal ethical codes and the existence of enforcement measures will result in a healthier framework in the future (Ural, 2008, p. 425; Tüzel, 2010, p. 164–165).

Furthermore, some experts claim that neuromarketing tools and methods only define what the brain does and that neuroimaging devices cannot change the behaviour of the brain and cannot induce a state in which the individual goes out and purchases an intended product (Witchalls, 2004). It is claimed that this technique only helps researchers to better understand the needs of the consumers (Shah, 2005; as cited in; Özdoğan et al., 2008, p. 8). Additionally, there are not any unities in measuring the brain activity for neuromarketing studies. Using various methodologies may result in different outputs. Due to the special technologies needed and high costs involved, only a few companies and universities are able to run such complex research. Besides, to interpret data requires highly talented professionals and researchers from different fields such as neurologists, psychologists, economists, and software engineers (Zară & Tuţă, 2013, p. 100).

Conclusion

Though in the first stages of its development, neuromarketing is a new field of science that presents a new vision that the discipline of marketing needs; however, many things still need to be improved. Neuromarketing has the potential to increase the productiveness of marketing activities of businesses. Thus, neuromarketing methods can be used for the sales oriented approach of marketing 3.0: "producing a pre-purchased product or service." In return, with products that can be maintained in the market and with the help of the marketing mix and especially applications that can be developed in terms of marketing communication, the resource dissipation can be prevented.

In this context, new studies in the field of neuromarketing are needed to be conducted in the world and in Turkey. These studies, together with classical marketing approaches, will contribute to the discipline of marketing with a new vision. The current methods of neuromarketing have started to be used complimentarily by marketing researchers. It is expected that in the coming decade, the place and importance of neuromarketing within the larger discipline of marketing will increase and the data that is collected from neuromarketing measurements will contribute by transforming this data into strategies.

References

Acuff, D. (2005). *Taking The Guesswork Out Of Responsible Marketing,* Young Consumers: Insight and Ideas for Responsible Marketers, Vol. 6, No: 4, 68.

Clithero J. A., Smith D. V., Carter R. M., Huettel S. A., (2011). Within- and Cross-Participant Classifiers Reveal Different Neural Coding of Information, National Institute of Health, *Neuroimage,* 2011 May 15, 56(2)., 699–708.

Crandall, K., (2006). *Invisible Commercials and Hidden Persuaders:* James M. Vicary and the Subliminal Advertising Controversy of 1957. Florida USA.

Damasio, *A. 1994. Descartes' Error: Emotioni Reason And The Human Brain.* New York: Grosset/Putnam.

Dooley, R., (2007)., "Neuroethics vs. Neuromarketing", http://blog.futurelab.net/2007/02/neuroethics_vs_neuromarketing.html, December 15.

Erk, S., Spitzer, Manfred, W., A. Galley, L., Walter, H. (2002)., "*Cultural Objects Modulate Reward Circuitry*", Neuroreport, Vol. 13, No: 18, 2499–2503.

Giray C., Girişken Y. (2013). Kafkas Universitesi, *18. Ulusal Pazarlama Kongresi Bildiri Kitabi,* "Yerel Ekonomilerin Uluslararasılaşmasında Küresel Pazarlamanın Katkısı" 19–22 Haziran Kars/Sarıkamış.

Görgülü, N. Ş., Güventürk G., (2010). *Pazarlama 3.0 - Yeni Çağın Pazarlama Yaklaşımı,* Pazarlama 3.0 Yayınları, Istanbul.

Grimes, A. (2006).; Are we listening and learning? Understanding the nature of hemispherical lateralization and its application to marketing, *International Journal of Market Research,* 48(4).: 439–457.

Hatip, M., Neuro Marketing, http://marketrend.wordpress.com/2008/11/16/neuro-marketing/ 07.05.2014.

Izgören, A. Ş. (2006). *Eşikaltı Büyücüleri.* Elma Yayınevi, İstanbul.

Kenning, P. and Plassmann, H., (2005). *NeuroEconomics: An Overview From An Economic Perspective.* Brain Res. Bull.

Kotler, P. (2010). Kartajaya H., Setiawan I., Çev. Kıvanç Dündar, *Pazarlama 3.0,* Optimist Yayınları, İstanbul.

Krakoff, P., (2010). 7 Ways to Market to the Subconscious Brain:The Homer Simpson Guide to Content Marketing. [online], Amerika, http://writingontheweb.com/2010/10/21/ways-market-subconscious-brain-br-homersimpson-guide-content-marketing/ (29.04.2013).

Lee, N., Broderick, A., J., and Chamberlain, L., (2007). What is 'Neuromarketing'? A Discussion And Agenda For Future Research. International Journal of Psychophysiology.

Marketing to the Human Brain, *Trends E-Magazine*, May 2010 (Trends E-Magazine 2010, s. 30).

Lehmann S., Reimann M., (2012). Neural correlates of time versus money in product evaluation, *Frontiers in Psychology,* 372(3)., 1–20.

Lindstrom M., (2013). *Buyology*, Optimist Yayınları, Istanbul.

Lynch Z., (2010). *The Neuro Revolution. How Brain Science Is Changing Our World*, St. Martin's Press, New York, 61.

Neuro-Insights, (2013). http://www.neuro-insight.com/case-studies/ 07.05.2014.

Neuromarketing Science & Business Association, (2012). *Neuromarketing. Theory & Practice Magazine*, Issue no. 2, July, 4–7, 10–11.

Nielsen Corporation, (2013). Neurofocus, http://www.neurofocus.com/pdfs/NeuroFocusExecutiveBrief_SnackFoodPackaging.pdf 07.05.2014.

Özçiftci V.M. (2015). *Cesur Yeni Dünya, http://norobilim.com/cesur-yeni-du%CC%88nya/* 09.05.2015.

Özdoğan F.B., Tolon M., Eser Z., (2008). Nöropazarlama Üzerine Kavramsal Bir Çalışma., *Üçüncü Sektör Kooperatifçilik Dergisi*, 3(5872).

Priyadarshini, K. (2006). "Brain science - Neuromarketing And The Media Maze", ESOMAR, Worldwide Multi Media Measurement (WM3)., Shanghai, June.

Rossiter, J.R., Silberstein, Richard B., Harris, P.G., Nield, G.A. (2001)., Rossiter, John R., Silberstein, Richard B., Harris, P.G., Nield, G.A. (2001)., Brain-imaging detection of visual scene encoding in long-term memory for TV commercials, *J. Advert. Res.*, Vol. 41, 13–21.

Senior, C. (2003)., "Beauty in the brain of the beholder", *Neuron,* Vol. 38, 525–528.

Shah, P. (2005)., Neuromarketing: Smart Marketing Or Jedi Mind Control Trick?, http://www.webpronews.com/topnews/2005/06/01/neuromarketing-smart-marketing-or-jedi-mind-control-trick, Published: 2005-06-01, (November 20th. 2007).

Tanrıdağ O., Sosyal Davranışların Beyinsel Altyapısı, Inside; *Pozitif Psikoloji, Çoklu Zeka Uygulamaları,* Nevzat Tarhan, Orhan Gümüşel, Aynur Sayım, Timaş Yayınları İstanbul 2012.

Tüzel N., Tüketicilerin Zihnini Okumak: Nöropazarlama ve Reklam, *Marmara İletişim Dergisi*, Sayı 16, Ocak 2010, İstanbul, pp. 163–176.

Ural T. (2008). Pazarlamada Yeni Yaklaşım: Nöropazarlama Üzerine Kuramsal Bir Değerlendirme, *Ç. Ü. Sosyal Bilimler Enstitüsü Dergisi*, Cilt 17, Sayı 2, s. 421–432.

USA Sabah Gazetesi (2010). Dr. Bülent Ataman ile Nöro Marketing Söyleşisi, Nöro Pazarlama: Beynimiz ne söylüyor? http://www.usasabah.com/Akademiden Haberler/2010/12/23/beynimiz_ne_soyluyor_2, December 23rd, 2010.

Van der Laan N. L., De Ridder T. D. and Viergever M. A., Smeets A. M. P, (2012). Appearance Matters: Neural Correlates of Food Choice and Packaging Aesthetics, PLoS ONE, 7(7)., 1–11.

Wahlberg, D., (2004)., "Advertisers Probe Brains, Raise Fears." The Atlanta Journal-Constitution, January 31st, 2004, http://www.commercialalert.org/issues/culture/neuromarketing/advertisers-probe-brains-raise-fears, 05.05.2014.

Wilkinson, (2005). *Marketing Week*, Feb., 3.

Yücel A., Çubuk F., Nöropazarlama ve Bilinçaltı Reklamcılık Yaklaşımlarının Karşılaştırılması, *Niğde Üniversitesi İİBF Dergisi*, 2013, Cilt: 6, Sayı: 2, s. 172–183.

Zaltman, G., 2003. *How Customers Think: Essential Insights Into The Mind Of The Market.* Boston: Harward Business Press.

Zară I. A. & Tuţă M., (2013). Neuromarketing Research – A Classification and Literature Review, Research Journal of Recent Sciences, Vol. 2(8)., 95–102, August.

Burak Polat & Cem Sefa Sütçü

Television Ratings Got Social: A Case Study on The Famous Turkish TV Series Muhtesem Yuzyil

Introduction

Since the 1960s, television (TV) is the primary medium of information for the masses. The global attention on TV medium generates its own system that can be simply represented with four components: audience, broadcaster, producer, and advertiser. The producer creates the content, the broadcaster televises the content, and the advertiser invests in the content; all three components rely on the audience's decision to watch the content. All three of these components, producer, broadcaster, and advertiser, have their own sub-systems. Their objectives are intersected in some points and separated in others; however, like every organisation, their fundamental objectives are survival and growth.

The survival and growth of an organisation comes with decision-making, decision-making comes with knowledge, and knowledge comes with information; thus, for better decision-making in the TV system, audience measurement is needed. TV ratings are the worldwide standard for audience measurement that basically indicates the viewership rate of TV content in a specific time span.

Since 1973 when TV ratings had been obtained on a daily basis (Celebrating 90 years of Innovation, 2013), rating of TV content refers to the percentage of TV households that watched that content and one rating point equals one percent of the total TV audience (Poltrack, D., 1983, p. 121). When taking the hundreds of billion-dollar size of the market into consideration, the accuracy and accountability of TV ratings are extremely crucial.

In December 2011, the law enforcement officials detected a TV ratings fraud scandal in Turkey. AGB Nielsen's (formerly authorised TV audience measurement company for Turkey's TV market) 1,070 subjects of approximately 2,500 households in Turkey were leaked and the rating system was open to manipulation (Hurriyet Daily News, 2011). Even the authorised company has changed; today, the Turkish TV market is still questioning the reliability of TV ratings.

For creating more effective and reliable TV audience measurement, social media has a great potential. As Housley et al. (2014) mentioned in their article titled "Big and broad social data and the sociological imagination: a collaborative response" (p. 12):

> "...Developments linked to the emergence of big and broad social data are happening rapidly, and we cannot be certain what impact it will have on research processes. It is possible that it will promote the use of computational social science methods in place of more traditional quantitative and qualitative research methods. It may also influence thinking and re-orientate social research around new objects, populations and techniques. However, we think it is most desirable that new methods be used in conjunction with the existing ones, to make research richer and more nuanced, and we have attempted to motivate this synthesis through examples of our current research summarised above. The analysis of social processes as they actually happen is bound to give researchers insights and interesting avenues to explore that are absent from the official construction of events that is available via traditional research instruments and curated datasets..."

By reference to Housley et al., with using social media as a source of big and broad social data, conventional TV audience measurement methods can be transformed.

In this paper, the transformation of viewership with the impact of social media is first emphasised. Then, for better decision-making and a reliable TV audience measurement system, social media's potential is shared. Furthermore, content analysis of tweets of a famous Turkish TV series, Muhtesem Yuzyil, is conducted. At last, the paper concludes with several discussions on social media's position for TV audience measurement.

Social Media, TV, and TV Ratings

Social media can be defined as the social interaction among people in which they create, share, or exchange information and ideas in virtual communities and networks (Ahlqvist et al., 2008). Social media is an interactive and digital new media that makes users relatively free of time and space boundaries. The attributes of social media transform passive TV audiences into active users and new conceptions rise such as "multi-screening" and "time shift."

Multi-screening is simply watching TV in company with at least one other device such as a smart phone, Tablet PC, laptop, etc. Time shift implies time independency for watching TV content. Today, individuals watch TV content whenever they want and wherever they want in company with several devices that allow them to create, share, and interact with the TV content.

The transformation in TV watching behaviours and the digital attribute of social media constitutes a great potential for audience measurement because the users reactions to TV content can be gathered and analysed. Nielsen, despite their reputation in Turkey, launched “Twitter TV Ratings” in the United States of America in October 2013. According to Nielsen’s (2013) definition, it is “the first-ever measure of the total activity and reach of TV-related conversation on Twitter, enable users to improve media planning and buying, measure effectiveness and identify true influencers.” In Turkey, there are two companies, Kimola and Somera, which are focused on social media research for the TV industry. Nielsen, Kimola, and Somera all are conducting research studies on Twitter, an online social networking and micro-blogging service that enables users to send and read short 140-character messages called tweets.

There are three main reasons to focus on Twitter as a medium for TV audience measurement in social media:

1. Multi-screeners’ & time-shifters’ tweets: Conventional methodology on TV audience measurement cannot cover the viewers that access TV content online. The tweets that are created by multi-screeners and time-shifters are creating a significant potential for audience measurement.
2. Application User Interface (API): API is a set of routines, protocols, and tools for building software applications. (Beal) Twitter API allows third parties to integrate with Twitter’s database within a set of rules and limits that allow researchers to gather data.
3. Public User Data: Twitter users, especially teens and young adults, tend to share content publicly (Madden et al., 2013). Since private data cannot be gathered, public data availability is crucial.

The metadata of a tweet and a user provide almost all the necessary data for TV ratings; however, the lack of demographic data prevents Twitter TV Ratings from fulfilling the requirements for being an alternative TV ratings system. Nevertheless, Twitter TV Ratings can be seen as complementary to conventional TV ratings with the potential of creating insights out of the data gathered.

Content Analysis on Muhtesem Yuzyil’s Twitter Data

To determine how Twitter data can be used for TV programs and audience measurement, Muhtesem Yuzyil has been chosen as one of the most famous Turkish TV series. We conducted content analysis for tweets about the program that are gathered by Kimola, one of the social media research companies that focuses on social media TV audience measurement.

Muhtesem Yuzyil (Magnificent Century) is a prime-time historical Turkish soap opera TV series with four seasons and 139 episodes based on the story of the reign of Suleiman the Magnificent. According to Turkey’s Culture and Tourism

Ministry Copyright Division (OdaTV, 2012), Muhtesem Yuzyil has 150 million viewers across 75 countries.

19,703 tweets are gathered for Muhtesem Yuzyil's last four episodes (136th –139th) during the days that the show aired from 20:00 to 00:00. The distribution of gathered tweets is shown in Table 1.

Table 1: Gathered tweets' distribution by Kimola

Date	All Tweets	Unique Tweets	Users
21.05.2014	1,152	710	943
28.05.2014	2,494	1,745	1,950
04.06.2014	5,746	3,127	4,487
11.06.2014	10,311	5,511	8,288

Content analysis on the 136th episode's tweets has been applied to visualise the tweet frequency patterns, to examine the relationship between tweets and TV program's content, to determine topics and significant phrases that users tweet about, and to determine compliments and complaints about the TV program.

Results of the content analysis

- 42% of the overall activity happened between the 22:45–23:30 timespan that also covers the last parts of the episode.
- 30% of the overall activity is directly related to the episode's plot.

Figure 1: Gray graph: tweet frequency; black graph: directly relevant tweets to the aired TV content (x-axis: timespan from 20:00 to 00:00; y-axis: tweet quantity)

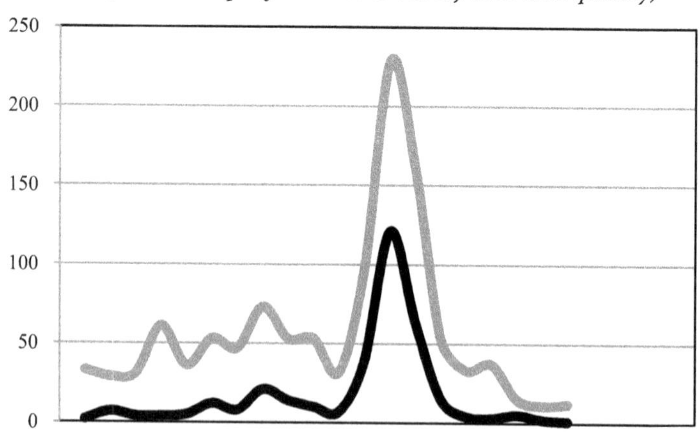

- Tweets are scored according to their positiveness and compared with the tweet frequency; a weak but positive correlation is obtained (R=0.3701, p=0.108229).
- 5% of the total users (47 users) created 22% of the overall tweets and 14% of these users do not exist now.
- 5% of the overall tweets (60 tweets) constitute 20% of the overall dataset.
- Phrases on declaration of viewing (start, follow, time, etc.) constitute 10% of the overall tweets gathered and 23% of these tweeted occurred between 20:45–21:00, just before the episode started. Tweets about the finale (139th episode) constitute 8% of the overall content and these tweets were mostly tweeted (54% of the tweets about the finale) between the 23:10 to 23:30 timespan.
- 10% of the overall content is strictly irrelevant to the TV program's content; 70% of irrelevant tweets are about TV ratings, spam links constitutes 20%, and retweet requests constitutes 10% of the overall strictly irrelevant tweets.
- As is shown in Table 2, 36% of the compliments are about the soundtracks of the show, while acting and the scenario are the secondary topics for compliments. 36% of complaints are on defective reflection of the history; the use of language and negative effect of the show on society are the other significant topics for complaints.

Table 2: Tweets with compliments and complaints

Compliments	
Soundtrack	72
Acting	66
Plot	57
Channel	4
Total	199
% of Unique Tweets	28%

Complaints	
Misinformation	28
Language	14
Nagative Effect	12
Plot	8
Acting	6
Advertisement	5
Production	3
Channel	1
Total	77
% of Unique Tweets	11%

- In the 136th episode, tweets about Prince Beyazid constitute 34% of the overall tweets on characters. Mustafa, Hürrem, and Pargalı were former strong characters of the show; however, a considerable amount of users still tweet about them.

Table 3: Tweets about characters

Rank	Characters	Percentage
1	Beyazid	33,91%
2	Süleyman	18,70%
3	Mustafa	13,04%
4	Selim	7,39%
5	Ebusuud	6,96%
6	Hürrem	6,96%
7	Mihrimmah	4,78%
8	Rüstem	2,61%
9	Fahriye	2,17%
10	Şah Sultan	1,74%
11	Lala	1,30%
12	Pargali	0,43%

Discussion

Twitter TV Ratings cannot be seen as the ultimate TV rating system, but it can be seen as complementary for TV audience measurement. The public data that Twitter users create about TV programs allow researchers to determine the impact of the TV program and also to detect insights from the audience.

The lack of demographic data is the primary issue that makes Twitter TV Ratings weak relative to conventional TV ratings, especially from the media planners' point of view. As a condition for the development of a new social media platform that is widely adopted, for providing feasible audience metrics to create a TV rating system, demographic data of users should be available.

The conventional methodology, people metre, is still a worldwide standard for TV audience measurement. Authorised TV rating research companies should monitor and analyse the chosen households' social media usage during the act of viewing. Also, converging the people metre methodology with social media measurement (User metre - Choosing social media users that watch TV, Social TV viewers, for creating an universe from these users to monitor and measure the audience) can generate an alternative TV ratings system.

Essentially, TV ratings are needed for better decision-making in the TV industry. With monitoring and measuring audiences in social media, insights will be obtained and with insights, there will better decision-making.

With fully digitalised TV infrastructure and integration with social media, there will obviously be more accurate, reliable, and effective audience measurement.

References

Ahlqvist, T., Bäck, A., Halonen, M. & Heinonen, S. (2008) *Social Media Roadmaps: Exploring the futures triggered by social media.* VTT Research Notes

Beal, V. *API – application program interface.* Retrieved September, 14, 2014 from http://www.webopedia.com/TERM/A/API.html

Celebrating 90 years of Innovation (2013). Retrieved September 12, 2014, from http://sites.nielsen.com/90years

Housley, W., Procter B., Edwards, A., Burnap, P., Williams, M., Sloan, L., Rana, O., Morgan, J., Voss, A., Greenhill, A. (2014) *Big and broad social data and the sociological imagination: a collaborative response.* Big Data & Society, Sage Journals. p. 12.

Madden, M., Lenhart, A., Cortesi, S., Gasser, U., Duggan, M. & Smith, A. (2013) Retrieved September, 14, 2014 http://www.pewinternet.org/2013/05/21/teens-social-media-and-privacy/

Nielsen Twitter TV Ratings (2013). Retrieved September 14, 2014, from http://www.nielsensocial.com/product/nielsen-twitter-tv-ratings/

Muhteşem yüzyıl'ı 150 milyon kişi izliyor. (2012) Retrieved August, 28, 2014, from http://www.odatv.com/n.php?n=telif-haklari-genel-muduru-abdurrahman-celikmuhtesem-yuzyili-150-milyon-kisi-izliyor.-2611121200

Poltrack, D. (1983) *Television Marketing: Network, Local and Cable.* Mcgraw-Hill

TV ratings may go blank as firm stops measuring. (2011) Retrieved August 28, 2014, from http://www.hurriyetdailynews.com/tv-ratings-may-go-blank--as-firm-stops-measuring.aspx?pageID=238&nID=9671&NewsCatID=341

Ceren Yegen & Baki Yegen

A Concept is Originated from Communication Technologies: "Communicative Reality" and Building Reality in Written Press

Introduction

The media has an important mission for both itself and people as part of "notification." Thus, it should inform the people and it should not move away from its mission. But today, paralleling to new media technologies and globalisation, media put aside its mission and it began to create global realities with its content according to power groups. Media's effects and actions are discussed by media reviewers.. Today, the critcal approximations deal with media effects and actions. According to a lot of critics, media creates a reality that is distinct from the phenomenon of real reality and it spread and legalised its ideologies with the power which is given on the part of citizens or societies to the media with this sort of reality. Also, media determines its content and hereby, we may talk about non-objective media. The discussions which are about media and reality get moved with the concept "communicative reality." Therefore, today, media makes up reality with its power of creating awareness and it presents some cases like reality. This reality is defined as "communicative reality" and this reality, which is made by media, led to a lot of discussions. This is because this sort of reality is an artificial thing due to it being produced by media or its power groups. In addition, this sort of reality, namely communicative reality, is also a fiction and it is a cultured phenomenon. Because of these assumptions, we can easily say that communicative reality is not an objective thing; on the contrary, it is completely partial and partisan. Some ethical problems like manipulation and disinformation can occur in the period of reporting parallel to communicative reality phenomenon. We saw some examples in the Gulf War and the Event of Soldier Jessica Dawn Lynch. It seems that how the media created its reality in these events and presented to all world. Almost everyone believed that the events happened how the media told them. In addition, we should emphasise that in this period, fake, exaggerated news, or distorted news can occur, too. Media can create objects, perceptions, and rituals like reality because people generally trust it as part of reporting. But I think this situation was changed with news media phenomenon and developing communication technologies. Thus, today, people can give news from citizen journalists and online news sites or they can make the news personally. Namely, they do not need traditional media and its news because they can reach online news more easily and faster wherever they are. Hereby, contrary to that, communicative reality is generally everywhere. At a minimum, people began to question media content and realities, they also began to believe in the news which had proof, and thanks to new media technologies and the concept of media literacy, they can easily reach the proof of news and they can question media effects like media reality. Due to the fact that media's reality, practices, and effects are topical issues, I decided to examine media's reality in written press, because like I said, media generally gives its reality with its news. Scientifist news are very important for at that point. Thus, this study's issue is to turn over the concept of communicative reality with the dimension of the written press. This study is a descriptive study and a hermeneutic method was used in the study to tell both the concept of reality and the concept of communicative reality. This study's aim is to search how the written press gives place to communicative reality in its contents. This study is important to understand how the media fictionalises reality and how the media transforms the reality to a communicative form. We can also easily say that this study is important to understand media's missions and effects on the people and the concept of reality.

The Concept of Reality

The concept of reality can be defined as all the material and moral things which exist in the world. Sometimes we have information about the concept of reality, but other times we cannot recognise or define the reality. The concept of reality is also a born and ambiguous concept that changes with eras. According to Gürkan (2009: 1), in Turkish reality, the word is derived from Kir/gir-ger origin and involves the meanings of "promise," "affiliation," "axis," "reunion," and "appearance." In the dictionary, reality is defined as "independent of consciousness, concrete and objectively existing." If we also classify the concept of reality, we can say that there are two forms of reality, known as tangible and intangible reality.

Whether social or academic, the concept of reality is always dealt with existing conditions and the reality does not change. For example, Parmenides says that *"the real world is always the same and does not change like the concept of reality"* (Koç, 1994: 235). Platon handles the concept of reality as part of art. He says that "the art imitates the reality which is perceived by emotions and hereby the art move away fromthe concept of reality" (Yarar, 2010: 6). Thus, we can say that reality is in fact a form or an entire set of forms. Social reality is defined as societies' realities and it is in front of the media reality. This kind of reality is also built by social theories which are erected in positivism. *"Critical Marxist Theory claims that the reality has an objective existence out of the individuals. Also it claims that understanding this perceptions is hindered in capitalist production relationships."* In addition, constructive social theory claims that the social reality is built up in societies (Dursun, 2013). The concept of reality is also related to mind. At this juncture, Ñaöananda (2012: 126) says that *"the luminosity of the mind is a potentiality which becomes a reality only when the necessary conditions are fulfilled." "To say the reality is such that our knowledge cannot reach it, is a claim to know reality; to urge that our knowledge is of a kind which must fail to transcend appearance, itself implies that transcendence"* (Bradley, 1897).

Media to Create Awareness and "Communicative Reality"

Media may intensively affect the consideration or behaviour systems. The primordial mass communication tool is the written press on the subject of manipulating the crowds. Generally in the world, having information and gaining contentment about the event are taken place are based on written press' news are shared by million people. According to Dijk (Duruoğlu, 2003 cited from Küçük, 1999: 370), probably another no type of discourse cannot read and share by a lot of people in the world. According to Dijk, the discourse of the news has a gigantic potential and is of vital importance to understand a lot of topics as part of the examination of the news. For example, in nearly all studies which conduct an examination of the news, the reality that the news is never a simple or pure phenomenon is emphasised. News is an evaluation of the reality, an analysis, and a selection. These studies also claim that the news is not against reality as part of partisanship and partiality (Duruoğlu, 2003: 8 cited from Küçük, 1999a:96; Dursun, 2001:124 and Çaplı, 2002:91). Today, mass communication has an impact on defining and constructing social relationships and areas. Mass communication has never been effective and strong like today (Duruoğlu, 2003: 7). According to Dursun (2013: 33), media and reality topics are the most problematic topics of today. The reality, which is built by society with interaction, transforms a reality which is provided by mass communication tools today. According to social change theory, *"real social life's activities give way to new foundation and social structures which are related to different technologies"* (Sucu, 2012: 59 cited from Han, 2010). *"If tactile communication decrease, a problem may occur about reality phenomenon's way. Thus, to have different identies can lead a reality problem in communication period"* (Sucu, 2012: 56–61). *"Media both reproductive the reality and define it. Thus media productive and support the reality definitions"* (Meder and Çeğin, 2004: 2). Luchmann thinks that media, the economy, religion, and science are social systems and that they are different from each other. According to him, nearly all systems should be reporductuve themselves. Media system's elements are not individuals, groups, or organs. Conversely, their elements are communication operations. Namely, only these operations decide what is information or what is not. Thus, the reality, which is built by media, becomes the "ordinary" one (Alver, 2007: 98–101). *"The most important critics which are directed to the media are about his role of molding public opinion. The ideas which are gave place in media, transform ideas which are shared in societies"* (İrvan, 2002: 379–380).

Potter (2005) states that the real world and the virtual world, which is fictionalised by media, are different from each other because a reality is built in the virtual world and it is not a dogma like in the real world and this kind of reality is only fiction or a dream. *"Media make mass communication and the concept of mass communication does not tell dialogue, exchange or sharing. Contrary to it tells producing content which is corporate and organized."* (Alemdar and Erdoğan, 2010: 81). Today, media does the thing which is claimed by Alemdar and Erdoğan (2010). When media creates awareness, it also builds reality. These kinds of realities, which have media content, are called "communicative reality." These kinds of realities, namely communicative reality, become people's reality and people perceive this reality like their real reality because of the trust to the media which is felt by people. According to Ricoeur (Çoban, 2007: 2), *"all communication practices in new world state the ideological practices which reproduce the people."* Namely, new media reproduce people like their attitudes. We can also say at this point, that media is a representational or symbolic system (Masterman, 2007: 27).

Reality in the News and Communicative Reality in Written Press

According to Çalışır (2012: 116), the source of the news is an event. If an event is news, it should have some principles, such as: reality/ trueness, innovation and currency, interestingness and conspicuousness, and momentousness (Çalışır, 2012: 116 cited from Tokgöz, 1981: 51; Girgin, 2009 and Dileklen, 2005: 26). In case defines the news like that: *"News is an information about an phenomenon or event."* Within this framework, news is whichever persuasion, event, or topic that is given in its time, is deal with a lot of people in the society, affect a lot of individuals again in societies. In this sense, the news for society, and thus the news, should be comprehensible (Çalışır, 2012: 116). Girgin (2009) says that news's features are: reality, innovation and currency, interestingness and conspicuousness, momentousness, and being important and being comprehensible. Hartley (1990: 11) says that "news is not an important events, contrary to news is reporting, stating, emphasising and transfering of some events, incident (Çalışır, 2012: 116). As for the reality in the news not being a real thing, it is a thing which occurred with crop of the news. Hereby, we can say that reality in news is a kind of form, too. In this situation, questions about how the reality is defined and why is has occurred gain importance. *"When we talk about reality, the concept of ideology, meaning and representation come into play. What is the reality? Is there a relationship between current politics, producing reality and building a world system? How the media's role about correlating between people and reality is realized?"* (Dursun, 2013: 33–35). According to Ersoy and Balyemez (2013: 350), in written press, news wants to show itself as an objective thing. At that point, the real aim is giving a perspective to people about its reality and trustworthiness. Hereby, an eternal trust is provided to the media, even written press. According to Yurdigül (2011: 13), the elements of the news narrative should be insightful to the reality and we can say that this claim transforms news/real and real/news polemic to a topical case in written press. According to Ersoy and Balyemez (2013: 350), when the source of news, the platform of news, and the language of news are not examined, the social and economic connections cannot occur. Hereby, individuals perceive the real news like entertainment or humour news, which are given by written press, and they can also believe them easily. As is seen, we can say that the news is taken by individuals without an examination or a period of thinking. People or societies make a shift with media content or the things which were given by the media. Namely, media content transforms the reality to the communicative reality and this kind of reality becomes a part of people's lives. Also, we should say that this kind of reality, namely communicative reality, is a form which is built by the media with its ideology or ideas. When we regard written press' power of effect, (so as Elmas and Kurban, (2011: 9) said that written press is used as an ideological tool for a long time), we can easily say that legalising the media reality is not a hard mission for written press. *"According to Bennet, when the communicative tools give news, they also give a frame about that how the people should understand the concept of reality. Hereby, media build both a reality and consciousness. And hereby news or media contents become a part of the social reality"* (Yurdigül, 2011: 16–17 cited from Day, 1997: 132). The claims which advocate that the reality, which is given by media to the people, is not a real thing, is only fiction, and is far from real life is discussed in the global world. Because, according to this claim, reality is built with lies, ideologies, prejudices etc. Thus, people believe or take a fake reality from media content or news. Also, these contents or news are not examined by people because they always trust the media and written press.

Disinformation and Manipulation as Problems of Communicative Reality

When we talk about communicative reality, we can come across some ethical problems. One of these ethical problems is "disinformation." Disinformation is made by spreading wrong, non-objective, or false news and it sometimes means the abusing of information/knowledge. With disinformation, the information can be perverted and hereby, the information becomes a lie or something that is invented. While media and the concept of reality have a close relationship, they also amalgamate with each other. According to Dursun (2013: 33), media and the concept of reality are already some of the most complicated topics of today. Also, Dolgun (2004) says that disinformation is a practice which is made for conducting people by governments or dominant classes. In the United States (US), the Bush government's announcement that Saddam Hussein had weapons of mass destruction in Iraq is the most well known example about disinformation in the media. This announcement was never proven, even after Saddam Hussein's execution. No weapons of mass destruction were found, too (Curran, 2010). Hereby, the US used disinformation and this disinformation became very popular and effective in nearly all the world. And what's more, even in August 2004, 35% of US believed that there were weapons of mass destruction in Iraq (Castells, 2009). According to İlkiz and Günaydın (2006: 9 cited form Öngören, 1998: 85–86), there is no a public welfare when a not real and not current thing or event is narrated by someone, because a thing or event which is forgotten and there is no benefit about its again incidence does not provide a benefit to anybody generally. Only when it is current and real, only then can we talk about public welfare. We should say that making or spreading disinformation media tools and technologies, which are always developed, have an important role. Paralleling to developed communication technologies, disinformation became a phenomenon which is almost propagated in virtual places, namely on the internet. For example, in social media, disinformation about Gezi Park was not banned by anyone because a lot of news was wrong or not quickly propagated in social media and social networking sites. Also, media made a lot of these news articles. As a solution of disinformation, agitators warned themselves on the internet and their individual social media accounts. But in my opinion, in Turkey especially, traditional media continued the disinformation of the events in Gezi Park (Boomerang, 2013: 2). When it comes to the communicative reality, out of the disinformation problem, the other ethical problem is "manipulation." Manipulation is an effecting practice and it is usually used in written, visual, or virtual media. According to Yılmaz, manipulation of the news is a global communicative form. The using manipulation system is deal with communication system. This structure is accessible for manipulation due to the fact that communication has fake content and elements and the phenomenon of virtuality (Yılmaz, 2013: 235 & 245 cited from Baudrillard, 2001: 93).

Conclusion and Evaluation

Consequently, we can easily say that media is still developing and changing parallel to communication technologies in our global world. This idea is clearly discussed by a lot of communities, but not anyone can escape from this claim. Written press like the media can build a lot of phenomena with its power of effect in social period, too. Written press also provides that these phenomena gain legitimacy, too. This assumption is the most important and current discussion of today because lots of academicians, scientists, critics, and even neuropsychologists sit upon the virtual or written media as part of its reality policy and effects. They perpetually interrogate media's realities and effects that how they lead to some social, professional or psychological things in the societies. They try to understand how the media changes and transforms social rituals, too. As is seen, media's reality and effects are not only about the media sector, but also deal with social life, practices, and behaviours. The concept of communicative reality, as one of the phenomena, is built by media with its own ideologies or principles. This kind of reality interprets a lot of events in its own reality and notion. This kind of reality can also change the real reality, the perception, or reality in my opinion. Thus, we can say that communicative reality is a non-objective reality kind for people because it is an organised, planned, and partial phenomenon.

References

Alemdar, K. & Erdoğan, İ. (2010). Öteki Kuram-Kitle İletişim Kuram ve Araştırmalarının Tarihsel ve Eleştirel Bir Değerlendirmesi, Ankara, Erk Publishing, 3rd Edition.

Alver, F. (2007). Gazeteciliğin Kuramsal Temelleri, Beta Publishing.

Boomerag. (2013) The Case of Gezi Park, Accessed; http://boomerangistanbul.com/wpcontent/uploads/2013/07/Boomerang-GeziParkiDosyasi.pdf, 03.03.2014.

Bradley, Francis Herbert, (1897), APPEARANCE AND REALITY A METAPHYSICAL ESSAY, Accessed: http://www.holybooks.com/wp-content/uploads/Appearance-and-Reality-by-FH-Bradley.pdf, 15.05.2014.

Castells, M. (2009). Communication Power, Oxford University Press.

Curran, J. (2009). The Future of Journalism, Journalism Studies, Vol. 11, No 4, 2010, 464–476, Routledge Taylor & Francis Group.

Çalışır, G. (2012). Küreselleşme Sürecinde Haber Kavramında Gerçekleşen Bir Dönüşüm: Küresel Haber Kavramı, *Gümüşhane University Electronic Journal of Communication Faculty*, Vol 1, No: 4, pg. 106–127.

Çoban, B. (2007). Kitle İletişim Sürecinde Toplumsal Gerçeklik ve İktidarın Kurgusu, Medya Okuryazarlığı (Ed. N. Türkoğlu & M.C. Şimşek). İstanbul, Kalemus P.

Dolgun, U. (2004). Gözetim Toplumunun Yükselişi: Enformasyon Toplumudan Gözetim Toplumuna, *Journal of Management Sciences* (1:3).

Duruoğlu, Tuba. (2003). Haber Yapmada İdeoloji Etkeni: 11 Eylül Terör Olayı Örneği Üzerine Bir İnceleme, Master Thesis was prepared at Ankara University Institute of Social Sciences Department of Public Relations and Advertisement, Ankara.

Dursun, Ç. (2013). İletişim Kuram Kritik, Ankara, İmge Bookstore.

Dursun, O. (2012). "Medyada Gerçekliğin İnşasında Okurun Rolü (Hürriyet Gazetesi Okur Yorumları Üzerine Bir Analiz)", *Hittite University Journal of Social Sciences*, Year 5, No 2, pg.1–22.

Elmas, E. & Kurban, D. (2011). Democratization Program Media Reports Series 1, "İletişimsel Demokrasi-Demokratik İletişim Türkiye'de Medya: Mevzuat, Politikalar, Aktörler", Turkey Economic and Social Studies Foundation (TESEV), İstanbul.

Ersoy, M. & Balyemez, M. (2013). GELENEKSEL VE SOSYAL MEDYANIN HABER DİLİ: "ZAYTUNG" ÖRNEĞİ, II. International Conference on Communication, Media, Technology and Design 02–04 May, pg.350–354, Famagusta – North Cyprus.

Gürkan, M. B. (2009). "GERÇEK" KAVRAMI ÜZERİNE, Anatolia ENLIGHTENMENT FOUNDATION, pg. 1–10. Accessed: http://www.anadoluaydinlanma.org/Yazilar/gercekkavrami.pdf,12.05.2014.

İlkiz, F. & Günaydın, B. (2006). Kişilik Hakları - Medyada Etik ve Yargı Kararları, *Journal of Global Communication*, Number: 2, pg. 1–15.

İrvan, S. (2002). Medya, Kültür, Siyaset, Ankara, Alp Bookstore.

Masterman, L. (2007). A Rationale for Media Education in Media Literacy in the Information Age: Information and Behavior Volume 6, Ed. Robert Kubey, Transaction Publishers, US, pg. 15–69.

Meder, M. & Çeğin, G. (2004). SEMBOLİK ŞİDDET ARENASI: TELEVİZYON VE MEDYATİK SÖYLEMİN ÖZERKLİĞİ SORUNU, *Pamukkale University Faculty of Education Journal*, Number: 15.

Ñaöanada, B. K. (2012). Concept and Reality in Early Buddhist Thought, Accessed: http://www.seeingthroughthenet.net/files/eng/books/other/concept_and_reality.pdf, 28.06.2014.

Potter, J. W. (2005). Media Literacy: Third Edition, Sage Publications, Thousand Oaks, U. S.

Sucu, İ. (2012). SOSYAL MEDYA OYUNLARINDA GERÇEKLİK OLGUSUNUN YÖN DEĞİŞTİRMESİ: SMEET OYUNU ÖRNEĞİ, *Gümüşhane University Electronic Journal of Communication Faculty, Vol.* 3, pg. 55–87.

Turkish-American Network. (2013). "Again CNN, Again Disinformation," Accessed: http://www.turkishactionalert.com/news/3360-yine-cnn-yine-dezenformasyon.html, 12.05.2014.

Yarar, C. (2010). Bertol Brecht'in ve Georgy Lukacs'ın Gerçekçilik Anlayışlarında Modern Sanatın Neliği, Ankara University Institute of Social Sciences Philosophy Department, Master Thesis, Ankara.

Yılmaz, B. M. (2013). KÜRESELLEŞME SÜRECİNDE HABERDE MANİPÜLASYON ÖRNEK OLAY: ABD-IRAK SAVAŞI, *Gümüşhane University Electronic Journal of Communication Faculty*, Vol 2, No 1, pg. 234–255.

YURDİGÜL, Y. (2011). "Kurgusal Gerçeklik Bağlamında Haber ve Gerçeklik İlişkisi", *The Journal of Atatürk Communication*, Volume: 1, pg. 13–24.

Christian Ruggiero[1]

Personalisation, Populism, and Popularisation in the European Elections of 2014: The Italian case

Abstract As a result of the peculiar political conditions at the time, the 2014 European elections represented an unusual mixture of consolidated electoral practices and innovative campaign strategies. For the three competing leaders, Matteo Renzi, Beppe Grillo, and Silvio Berlusconi, the results of the polls posed an objective of vital importance and called for election campaign communication formulas which, in spite of their differences, were made up of combinations of the same three basic ingredients, which are: personalisation of leadership, populist rhetoric, and popularisation of politics. Analysed within a setting of identical television conditions, this research study identifies the three leaders' key strategy elements using a qualitative analysis of their linguistic communication in the television political talk show *Porta a Porta*, transmitted a few days before the vote.

Keywords: Personalisation, populism, popularisation, linguistic analysis, politics in television.

1. Introduction

The European elections held on May 25th, 2014 dramatically highlighted some of the most characteristic tendencies of the "Italian case."

In so far as being considered an "intermediate" election, it offered an opportunity to check the electorate's approval of the government in power. For the Renzi government in particular, the stakes had been significantly raised. At that point, his government had been in power for less than three months and was made up of a much discussed and fragile alliance between opposing partisan forces arising from the new tri-polar mechanism sanctioned by the 2013 political elections (Lombardo and Coluccia, 2013). This surely contributed to the anomalous nature of the European Parliamentary elections held on 25 May, 2014: In no other of the

1 Researcher in Sociology of Cultural and Communicative Processes in the Department of Communication and Social Research of Sapienza University of Rome, where he teaches Formats and Styles of Broadcast Journalism and coordinates the Mediamonitor Politics Observatory - christian.ruggiero@uniroma1.it.

large European Union (EU) democracies did the vote take on such a powerful political meaning as it did in Italy. All three of the above-mentioned Italian leaders actively competed against the others, even though not one of them, *albeit* for different reasons, had in fact put themselves up as candidates.

According to a well-established pattern (Mancini, 2003; 2007), the electoral competition had taken on the character of a "for or against" referendum on the current (and unelected) prime minister. There were, however, two main differences: it was not (at least formally) a competition from which only one candidate was to emerge victorious and three players dominated the scene.

First, Matteo Renzi, who, as Prime Minister and Secretary of his political party, faced his first election since taking over the leadership of the Democratic Party. Then, there was Beppe Grillo, the "moral winner" of the 2013 election. Finally, there was Silvio Berlusconi, who suffered the highest level of political attrition following the final sentence in the trail concerning Mediaset's television (TV) rights. In light of this peculiarity, the 2014 European election became a test case for the three trends that had characterised Italian politics (and not only) in the previous decades. These trends, each in its own specific articulation, were to be found at the very centre of the campaign strategies of the three leaders. These trends are personalisation, populist rhetoric, and the popularisation of politics.

2. The «Three P» Politics

Mény and Surel's (2001: 35) definition of populism as a "one-upmanship game of democratic expectations" is offered, not as a proposal for destruction, but as one of political regeneration, "a cleaning up of all its debris and a return to its 'real' principles and values." Starting from this definition, it would appear that populism directs political action towards a noble goal; however, in contemporary political discourse, that which should be a positive interpretative category of phenomena, aimed at answering the democratic crisis, becomes a rather derogatory definition of the adversary.

As noted by Diamanti (2004), "the others are always the populists." The same term "populism" in current political debate refers to decidedly negative political experiences (fascism) or at best, to controversial connotations (the common man movement), and, as such, has been *de facto* emptied of meaning. The effects on the idea of politics that the term "populism" represents are therefore hidden and populist rhetoric, ever present in contemporary political lexicon, is expressed through the use of concepts which are not overtly populist, and, indeed so over-used as to be too drained of meaning, as "direct democracy" or "reformism."

The call for a more direct form of democracy which bypasses the greatest number of possible levels of mediation is a direct result of the acknowledgment of the crisis of the party politics model. As far back as 1995, Katz and Mair had already identified, in the disappearance of the "cartel party", a process by which political objectives were self-referential, comprehensible, and uniquely functional only to a closed circle of professionals. Political forces of different ideological orientations, which are not necessarily definable as populist *tout court*, find themselves united in protest to all forms of political and public debate oligopoly, which is to say, in denouncing the barriers created by the political forces in power aimed at maintaining the oligopoly and promoting a kind of consociativism of the elite. Condemnation of the traditional party, whether by non-organic and spontaneous forces or by internal "currents", tend to form around a leader figure, who not only represents the embodiment of authority, but also expresses values of which the "people" are the bearers.

The essence of the leadership transition, as exemplified by Berlusconi's adventure in the so-called Italian Second Republic, as well as the Northern League leader, Umberto Bossi, is that of a transition from "professional" leadership, deriving from a lengthy period of long militancy in the party, to the "populist" leadership of a "self-appointed person who bends the rules and structures to the demands and needs of the leader of the movement" (Mény and Surel 2001: 100).

Moreover, the evolution of leadership not linked to a mediating structure is, in line with the decline of the party-form organisation, not limited to explicitly populist experiences: "Symptomatic of this evolution is the propensity of leaders to distance themselves from the platform developed by their parties [...] as soon as one moves on to serious business (the election), the party leaders impose their positions and own choices (parliamentary systems) or present their proposals (presidential systems). Blair, Schröder, Jospin, D'Alema defined their programs on their own, and the parties (more or less in agreement) had to make the best of a bad situation. Clinton or Chirac presented programs designed to go beyond the base of their party, and therefore independent of this organisation" (ibid: 107). This brings to mind the process, identified by the interpretive category of "audience democracy" (Manin, 2010), according to which the parties are reduced to committees serving a leader and where representational space coincides with direct contact exchanges between the leaders and the public.

The link connecting media logic, personalisation, and populism is well illustrated in Diamanti's (2014) brief outline of contemporary Italian "populisms": The transformation of politics into communication as it undergoes a progressive identification with an environment, specifically, that of TV, is what Diamanti means by "populist." This is an environment which, in a very literal sense, "obligates leaders and politicians to behave as 'actors' in the staging of politics" (ibid: 37); populist is the language of the media, the mixture of information, entertainment, and politics that generates "populist politics in which, in order to become and remain popular, leaders must adopt a 'populist' style and language" (ibid: 39).

Diamanti's above-mentioned wordplay invokes the role of "popular" (or simply "pop") culture in the evolution of politics and that of political leaders. In what Mazzoleni and Sfardini (2009) call "pop politics," two opposite terms from the point of view of political and communication analysis, "popular" and "populist", are temporarily joined together. The process of popularisation of politics is achieved through the use of a popular register, both in the presentation of politics by the media and in the political actors' public performances in the media itself (Van Zoonen, 2005). This process, interwoven with the personalisation dimension and the ever-increasing recourse to populist rhetoric, sets out the framework of this article.

Two of the three politicians who will be considered are striking examples of populist leadership, having built their fortunes on direct contact with the "people." In the case of Berlusconi, this contact was conducted mainly through TV, while in that of Grilllo, it took place on the web. Berlusconi put policies in place to overcome parliamentary mediation, while Grilllo theorised the destruction of the parliamentary institution itself; both drew from an extra-political repertoire of experiences and used extra-political, and at times explicitly anti-political language (Prospero, 2010; Santoro, 2013). In this context, the "newcomer" Matteo Renzi is a particularly interesting competitor to study. As Diamanti (2014) noted, Renzi built his political image by openly challenging the Roman nomenclature and professional politicians, up to the point of achieving leadership in a party not traditionally identified by a personalisation of leadership. On his political ascent to Palazzo Chigi, he acted as a personal leader as he imposed himself in and on his "impersonal" party and behaved in a highly personalised fashion, bypassing party decision-making.

3. The Analysis of Political Discourse in TV: The «Three P» Politics in the Discourse of Grillo, Berlusconi, and Renzi

The three leaders, who took the field in the 2014 European election campaign, faced each other, even if *in absentia*, in the 'living room' of *Porta a Porta* in May 2014: Monday 19 (Grillo), Wednesday 21 (Berlusconi), and Thursday, May 22 (Renzi)[2].

2 The analysis of the discourses of Beppe Grillo, Silvio Berlusconi, and Matteo Renzi is part of the wider research study "European 2014" conducted by the Mediamonitor Politics Observatory of the Department of Communication and Social Research of

The communicative context in which the texts under examination occur is of particular importance. The TV transmission *Porta a Porta*, often referred to as the "Third Chamber of the Republic," is both a typical "institutional" setting for political debate, as well as a representation of the process of linguistic hybridisation characteristic of "pop politics" (Ruggiero, 2014a, 2014b). In the three 60 minute TV appearances under consideration, Grillo, Berlusconi, and Renzi were given the opportunity to concentrate on the essential part of their political offer and their "communicative surplus value" in their last TV occasion. We would argue that this "last minute" nature of these transmissions justifies the relatively small size of the corpus being analysed.

The methodology used to analyse the above-mentioned texts follows a "hermeneutic and qualitative orientation, attentive to the narrative structure of the text, the illocutionary dimension of speech acts, forms of enunciation (dialogic or monologic), the rhetorical argumentation strategies (implicit assumptions, repetition, irony, hyperbole, etc.), and the linguistic construction of patterns of orientation of thought (frames and metaphors)" (Prospero and Tani, 2008: 31). Through the analysis of short but peculiar and significant texts, we tried to identify some elements of Grillo, Berlusconi, and Renzi's storytelling strategies, and thus the "deep narrative" they used in the electoral campaign for the 2014 European Elections. We sought to understand how they described Italy in the context of the 2014 political and economic crisis and how this description interacted with the political program of the Five Star Movement, Forza Italia, and the Democratic Party. Furthermore, the analysis identified the artifices of simplification, conflictuality, and recall to the interests and prerogatives of the "people" (in line with populist rhetoric) that the three leaders used in their last chance of appleal to the voters.

3.1 Deep Narrative #1: Personalisation

The three main dimensions of personalisation, use of a populist rhetoric, and popularisation of politics can in turn be divided, for the purposes of the analysis, into "steps" (intended in the sense used by Erving Goffman). This applies in particular to the dimension of personalisation which may be divided into a strategy of self-representation and a representation of the opponent.

Sapienza University of Rome (wwww.mediamonitor-politica.it). A special thanks is due to Giorgia Gasparri and Fabio Barbera.

With regard to self-representation, with the complicity of the executive production team, as well of the show's host, Grillo tried the innovative strategy of reframing his self-representation (Lakoff and Johnson, 1998): Initially (and only initially) a serene and calm Grillo was projected onto the studio wall. However, the host immediately asked to replace this image with "the real thing." Faced with a photograph of himself as a more familiar ranting and dishevelled icon, the leader of the Five Star Movement said:

> "I'm used to this one here. If I see this one here, I'd never vote for him. It's obvious that we frighten off everyone."

He then continued the discussion with the host about the meaning of self-images and points out:

> "No, I'm not pretending to be a nice guy, and I'm not a good guy. Yet, neither am I the way they make me out to be ... terror ... they say things that are simply amazing! So I want to speak to these people to calm them down."

In a more traditional vein, and tied to a soundly consolidated modality with which he had been presenting himself to the Italians for the past 20 years, the strategy of self-presentation carried out by Silvio Berlusconi focused on the authority that the European chancelleries would attribute to him. Assuming a defensive position against Jean-Claude Junker, who as Vespa noted, had criticised the Italian political system for the presence of too many parties, Berlusconi said:

> "The Italian parties are too many because he [Junker] also thinks about all the other parties. But I say that without our parliamentarians, the Social Democratic Party would become the majority and the European People's Party the minority. For this reason, I get phone calls all the time from the Secretary of the European People's Party and its President, who phoned me just yesterday afternoon."

The reference to the use of the telephone is particularly interesting: It is a direct and informal contact, which points to a relationship of familiarity and trust in Berlusconi.

Less careful in describing himself is Matteo Renzi. Indeed, the Premier displayed a hint of self-pity when he was called upon to comment on the personalisation characterising the campaign and he said:

> "I'm not sure if I'm the one who personalised it, but from the very start of the campaign, I've been called a 'dolt.' Thank goodness if I did personalise it!"

More interesting is a reference, found again later in the analysis, to an authentic "pop" culture of mass TV which is anything but political; in responding to a question from Bruno Vespa, in which the Germans were defined as more orderly of the Italians, Renzi said:

"For goodness sake, even Zurlì the Magician[3] is more organised than me, and without doubt the Germans are more organised than the Italians. Indeed, allow me to point out that the Germans have succeeded in making their reforms."

The same reference to the culture of the small screen is found in the main assault on Grillo, which is, however, softened and made memorable by placing it in a *gaming frame*:

"... someone has decided to play this electoral campaign on fear. He has played the entire campaign by using threats; using words such as the red plague, sawn-off shotguns. If Carlo Conti were here, I would add the Black Moon[4] and then call the Green Cross[5] and carry these fear-mongers away. But just what the Hell are we talking about here?"

An attempt to discredit based on the *frame of the show* is also found embedded within the televised space of the public debate. It was a small reprimand directed at Vespa, which once again contains a poisoned fruit for the leader of the Five Star Movement:

"There was ... Vespa against Grillo or Vespa and Grillo who gave each other the high five [...] praise where it is due because both you and Beppe Grillo are two extraordinary TV professionals and I loved the quality from the point of view of the television product."

While Renzi proved himself to be perfectly capable of mastering those rhetorical tools that allowed Silvio Berlusconi in 2008 to impose his own narrative onto that of Walter Veltroni (Prospero and Ruggiero, 2010), this time the (ex) "Cavaliere" decidedly lost ground in terms of the linguistic battle. At the end of an election campaign, which was full of original ideas and a strong emotional impact, the strategic decision to de-legitimise the leader of the Five Star Movement resolved in recalling a much abused episode in Grillo's pre-political past. Berlusconi chose to tell the "truth" about the 1981 car accident in which the future Five Star Movement leader had been involved and for which he had been convicted of manslaughter:

"It was no accident. It was something he wanted, and it tells us something about his character: he saw a "no access" road sign, paid no attention on it and went ahead, along an ice-covered road running parallel a ravine. Then at the end when the car slid into the

3 Zurlì the Magician is an Italian television character created in the late 50s by Cino Tortorella and interpreted by the host himself as part of the program for youngsters *Zurlì, il mago del giovedì.*
4 Carlo Conti is a popular Italian TV host, who, in the mid-90s, conducted a TV quiz called "La Zingara" ("The Gypsy"). Actress Cloris Brosca played the Gypsy, who used to read fortune cards for the participants in the game; when the "Black Moon" card came out, the game was over and the participant lost everything.
5 The Green Cross is the local equivalent (usually municipal) of the Red Cross.

> ravine, he clambered out while the other three were trapped and died. So, don't think this can be considered an insult, it's simply a fact from the reality that Italians should know. This from a person who depicts his opponents in the way you are familiar with.

This is a strategy which is closer to the journalistic practice of "surveillance" of the public and private behaviour of politicians (Sabato, 1991) than to that of the political use of symbolic resources rhetoric makes available.

Surprisingly, in this context, the choice of a more traditional strategy to define the opponent turned out to be that of Grillo, who insisted on using his campaign mantra. As master of comic definitions, and having defined Renzi as a "dolt", Grillo limited himself to specifying the deeper meaning of this description:

> "The dolt is already washed up. I don't want to offend anyone but ... we are talking about nothing, nothing at all. About one who's been put there by the great financial and banking powers, as was Letta and, before him, Monti."

Here too the proposed policies and the quality of the opponent are not considered as being of any relevance: At the heart of Renzi's political mission, is an element which undermines it irreparably and inevitably turns him into a dull servant of the "powers that be." With a typical satirical ploy, this element is made "visible" by emphasising one aspect of the physical qualities of the Prime Minister.

3.2 Deep Narrative #2: Populism

The analytical dimension of populist rhetoric can also be split into two distinct components. The first is that of presenting one's political project as the one closest to the interests of the "people." Here, the discourse of Grillo is most interesting since it relates directly to the electoral context. Dealing with the leader of a movement that was openly critical against the EU, Vespa presented himself as a mediator with unusual force in one segment of the interview, contradicting the image of himself that he, himself, provided a little later when he referred to his ability to check up on the electoral promises of his guests ("I leave you the responsibility for what you say"):

> Vespa: "Why do you get less informed people to believe that a referendum is enough to exit the euro, when you know that it is not true?"
> Grillo: "We go to them and say: 'Dear sirs, we will not negotiate. We did not sign these treaties. Let's do away with the fiscal compact.'" Vespa: "And you think the very next day the markets will say: 'Well, that's nice?.'"
> Grillo: "Which markets? Excuse me, but I want to be the market in my own house."

This statement is paradigmatic: The extension of the electoral mandate to include the option of cancelling binding treaties signed by political forces that are considered "dead," the refusal to consider a global market as legitimate, and hinting at acting according to rules related to political and economic self-sufficiency are so brazenly populist as they seem to be stereotypical. They bring to mind those anti-euro declarations and demands for a hyper-localist identity that only the Northern League had been able to express so clearly (Cedroni, 2010) and then exaggerate those claims even further. In this particular populist part of their respective rhetorics, none of the allegations of Berlusconi or Renzi lend themselves to a comparison. However, with regard to another key word of populist rhetoric, namely '*disintermediation*' (i.e. a direct leader/electorate rapport bypassing the party hierarchy), interesting facts emerge from all three leaders under consideration.

Once again, Grillo provided the clearest examples of this disintermediation component of populist rhetoric, even though with a significant variation: The perfect identification with the movement he represents allows the leader to call into question the Five Star Movement itself or alternate the first person singular with the royal "we," leaving the sovereignty of his own actions in the hands of "his" people:

> "The Five Star Movement are citizens like these [POINTING AT THE PUBLIC], they are citizens like us. You too are a citizen. We no longer delegate anyone. The anger is this: stop delegating to a politician who then looks after his own interests.
>
> We have already won. We have done a survey, and we are at 96%, we only need to convince 4%. It will be not a victory, it will be a triumphant march. I see it from the piazzas as I travel by camper. The piazzas are even more crowded than during the political elections."
> "We did not choose Prodi, we chose the network, we chose Rodotà, before him there was a medical doctor and before that a journalist. We follow majority decisions on the internet. I do not decide anything."
>
> "For example ... I went to Renzi, I did not want to go, the web decided, and I had to go and I had to adapt. I say many things on the blog, I get contradicted by my followers who say: 'look, we see things differently.'"

The rhetoric of Berlusconi is, in every sense, more personalistic: not only as collocated within a tradition of radicalised leaderism, but also as rooted in a political history that sees the leader convey his thoughts through "emissaries," who do not fit the definition of militants, as they do not respond to the party, but rather directly to their leader.

> "...right now I'm focused on two challenges: the first is that of getting deputies to the European Parliament so as to be able to defend the interests of Italy and Italians since the others are unable to do so [...]. The second thing, to be done through direct personal contact with those of our constituents who wish to do so - we called them "missionaries of freedom" - is to explain to the Italians - to those 24 million moderates [...] who have resigned themselves to the current situation [...] – that we think we have the chance to

> win them over and indeed ensure that the party of moderates, which is a social party, becomes a political party which can win the elections hands down.

Finally, Renzi's rhetoric was more nuanced. He communicated from a decidedly post-ideological position, which allowed him to open up a dialogue with "Italians," regardless of their political affiliations, and that was based on reasons of pragmatism and interest. Regarding his post-ideological position and the dialogue with the Italians, he said:

> "If Italy were to start walking, pedalling, we will have no problem with the fiscal compact, if Italy remains in these conditions, we will be ruined. […] That's why I say, while others shout, cry out, and enjoy seeing failure, I say: Hey, we're Italians, aren't we? I am Italian before being a member of the Democratic Party. One must be Italian before one is a member of the Five Star Movement. One must be Italian before being a member of Forza Italia."

Even more interesting is the reference to disintermediation as justified by the personal interest of the electorate: This leads to the true leitmotif of the campaign, the 80 euro tax bonus promised by Renzi. This also links to the never quelled unrest of the Democratic Party, and more particularly, to Renzi's conflict with the trade unions:

> "The 80 euro bonus is a structural and definitive measure which corresponds to the largest investment ever made by an agreement with trade unions. Tell me what union has brought home 80 euros for their workers with an agreement?"

These are statements of great interest in view of focusing on a *light* and post-ideological party. They contain traces rather than clear elements of populist rhetoric, and show, especially when compared to the positions of Renzi's competitors, what one might call *populism light*.

3.3 Deep Narrative #3: Popularisation

As an element *permeating* the contemporary political discourse, the popularisation of politics is already to be found in the above-mentioned dimensions. The first is Matteo Renzi's reference to characters and objects taken from TV culture, as follows: the conductor Carlo Conti (the most immediate contact that comes to mind among those mentioned, if only because he is the only one still "in business"), the Black Moon (which evokes the famous television program *The Gypsy*), and the Cino Tortorella's TV Magician Zurlì. Then, in calling into question a recent journalistic controversy regarding the warm handshake that concluded the meeting-interview is between Vespa and Grillo three days earlier.

It is interesting to note how, only for Renzi, the popularisation dimension is fully *part of the discourse*, whereas the other two leaders interrupted the show to make room for interludes which, while having a manifestly political aims, needed to interrupt the flow of the transmission in order to be inserted into the scene.

Berlusconi for example, took advantage of his familiarity with the conductor to "defuse," with a joke, the danger of focusing on a more uncomfortable subject, the relationship between his company and government policy when he was the Prime Minister of Italy:

> "Doctor Vespa, let's escape overseas for a while. Right now, I can't, but you can. Go, find a place and then send me a postcard."

A little further on, he terminated the discussion regarding the need to move from a Letta government to a Renzi government and the various relationships between his own political party and the two leaders by "teasing" the conductor who is thought to be "guilty" of over-indulgence to recent decisions of the Democratic Party:

> "You are exaggerating because at this point, I think you are a consultant for the left which pays you."

In both cases, the goal was achieved; the talk veered in the direction imposed by the guest, who took advantage of the laughter of the audience or the momentary embarrassment of the conductor to introduce a different theme, connected to the previous one, but safely away from his painful nerve centres.

Grillo differed in his use of the popularisation of politics: not only did he resort to short jokes, but real stories as well, which contributed to an overall impression of fragmentation which is nevertheless punctuated by memorable moments:

> "They have all disappeared. Look at Monti for example: who remembers Monti? Yet it was Monti who had to sort out Italy's problems. It was Monti the man sent by JP Morgan, from the Bocconi with all the parameters to remedy the Italian finance. Then he went back to the Bocconi, and even the usher stopped him and asked him 'where are you going?.'
>
> They have three Parliaments, three! Strasbourg, Brussels and Luxembourg, and they are building another one for 400 million euros. And then they expect us to make an effort, when 4,000 of them go to Strasbourg, with all their archives for four days a month, truck-loads of documents, four days a month they go to Strasbourg! Then maybe for another five days they go to Luxembourg, meet up and then the say 'Where are you going? I don't know … am I going to go to Strasbourg or Luxembourg?.'
>
> In each criminal organisation there is a banker, a businessman, a politician, an accountant, a lawyer, a magistrate, and oftentimes there isn't even a delinquent!
> Then the super-commissioner arrives. Because we do have a super-commissioner called Cantoni, you know? A good person. An anti-corruption super commissioner. He shows up and says: 'What happened?' And showing up with him is another commissioner who says 'I didn't notice anything.'"

The dominance of pathos over logos is taken to the extreme. Not only did the politician allow himself to use a register which is, at times comical, to gain the approval of the audience, but he also expected to have the role of the "complaining" comedian, despite his firmly established change in status he still continuously used "humorous story telling" as a strategic weapon of his post-political rhetoric.

4. Conclusions

The stated aim of this paper was to identify the different mixes of personalisation, populism, and popularisation present in the communication of the three leaders, Renzi, Berlusconi, and Grillo. The initial findings confirm that all three of these elements can be indentified in each of the discourse samples analysed, to different degrees, of course.

Grillo demonstrated a willingness to radicalise all three dimensions, but, as it may have been expected, was conspicuous in his recourse to populist rhetoric. While the comedian's decision to enter into the political fray was indeed the fulfilment of the "infotainment 3.0" hypothesised by Mazzoleni and Sfardini (2009), it is also true that, perhaps because of the need to "adapt" to the more institutional setting of *Porta a Porta*, Grillo's aggressive style and "pop" communication, which finds its natural habitat on the stage of a political rally, appeared weakened, almost reduced to cliché (also because of Vespa's meta-communication, which never misses an opportunity to emphasise the exceptional nature of the circumstances in which the interview takes place). Perhaps, possibly once again because of the setting in which the discourse occurred, the personalisation dimension in Grillo, in one of its key components, was less effective than usual (i.e. the definition of the enemy). Conversely, the discourse of the leader of the Five Star Movement's self-definition was perfectly identified in a movement that wants to be, or at least presents itself as an aggregator and amplifier of the will of "the people." It is here that Grillo included a statement containing the traits of extreme localism of populism and the euro skepticism of the Northern League, when he affirmed, in front of a Vespa who played the supporting role, by expressing his complete dismay: "Which markets? Excuse me, but I want to be the market in my own house."

Berlusconi's communication appeared to be centred above all on the personalisation that has made him the centre of Italian political geography for 20 years. Although limited by the political need of reserving his attacks for only one of his competitors, the leader of Forza Italia, overtaken by both Grillo and Renzi as far as 'novelty' goes, focused in on a process of self-definition aimed at highlighting his experience and familiarity with the procedures and European government leaders, in a word, his "credibility," in the arena where the election took place, and on which the other two leaders moved with greater difficulty. This is undoubtedly a traditional strategy for the (former) "Cavaliere." This hyper-traditional strategy stands out only because it is set in a context in which references to the category of supra-political "moderates" (historically Berlusconi's "people" of reference) and "pop" elements inserted into the speech (and essentially limited to interactions with the conductor) were even less innovating.

Finally, Renzi's message turned out to be the most "pop." Precisely here, an important element of interest is found when compared to the other two, who are, for various reasons, entertainment specialists, and the latest developments of the "Italian way" to the politics of the spectacle. It is Matteo Renzi who demonstrated, in his own language, a greater harmonisation of the "pop" elements in communication. As current Prime Minister, on the one hand, he aimed at being institutional, while, on the other, being the last chance of televised contact with voters before the vote, had to muster all available rhetorical and symbolic resources in order to achieve the highest level of spectacular effect. Renzi's "popular" performances do not amuse as much as the "stories" of Grillo, but yet, compared to these, and to Berlusconi's jokes, form a coherent part of his communication, rather than as "unexpected" elements and a mirror of his rhetoric.

What characterises the words of Renzi, the Prime Minister, were the references to popular culture, particularly TV. This is made clear in the excerpts used to provide a definition of both himself and his political opponents. These references would have deserved to be placed in both spheres of discourse analysis (i.e. personalisation and popularisation). This is combined with a strategy that is more political in its intent: Being the only one to avoid the virulence with which the leaders accused each other of atrocities that affect the ethical sphere (Grillo "the murder"), nor hesitate to mock the opponent's physical appearance (Renzi "the dolt"), the Prime Minister demonstrated not only the desire to "preserve" his institutional capacity, but also the capability to be the only "man of quiet strength" (*albeit* in a sense very different from that of Mitterrand) in the electoral competition.

Finally, we deserve to mention the component of Renzi's communication that could be considered *populism light*, a new kind of political action, which combines the tones and populist rhetoric with the militancy in a traditional party and the call for a radical innovation with the attention to reassure voters with respect to a too "sharp" change. It is a strategy that may be interpreted in at least two possible ways. Lexical counterpart of his political action is seeking to seduce an electorate far beyond the limits of the left or the centrr-left, and including all those who feel "Italian" before identifying themselves with a political label, and who vote on the basis of a concrete measure, such as that of the 80 euro bonus. This bonus is a way for the head of the government to deliberately bypass any mediation, especially that of the trade unions. Or perhaps his populism light is a sign of a new balance between yesterday's "scrap dealer[6]," today's Prime Minister, and tomorrow's leader.

5. References

Campus, D. (2006). *L'antipolitica al governo. De Gaulle, Reagan, Berlusconi*. Bononia: il Mulino.

Cedroni, L. (2010). *Il linguaggio politico della transizione. Tra populismo e anti-cultura*. Rome: Armando.

Cedroni, L. e Dell'Era, T. (2002). *Il linguaggio politico*. Rome: Carocci.

Diamanti, I. (2014). *Democrazia ibrida*. Rome: Laterza.

Edelman, M. (1987). *Gli usi simbolici della politica*. Naples: Guida.

Goffman, E. (1987). *Forme del parlare*. Bononia: il Mulino.

Graber, Doris A. (1980). Mass Media and American Politics. Washington: D.C., CQ Press.

Katz, R. S., e Mair P. (1995). «Changing Models of Party Organization and Party Democracy: the emergence of the cartel party». Party Politics, 1, 1: 5–31.

Lakoff, G. e Johnson, M. (1998). *Metafore e vita quotidiana*. Milan: Bompiani.

Lombardo, C. e Coluccia C. (2013). Dal bipolarismo alla meccanica tripolare. Alcune conseguenze dei risultati elettorali del 24–25 febbraio sulla struttura del sistema politico, in M. Morcellini, M. Antenore, C. Ruggiero (eds.). *Talk& Tweet. La campagna elettorale 2013 tra Tv e Twitter*. Sant'Arcangelo di Romagna: Maggioli.

Losito, G. (2002). *L'analisi del contenuto nella ricerca sociale*. Milan: FrancoAngeli.

Mancini, P. (a cura di) (2007). *La maratona di Prodi e lo sprint di Berlusconi. La campagna elettorale 2006*, Rome: Carocci.

6 In the event that marked his conquest of the media scene, held at the Stazione Leopolda in Florence in November 2010, Renzi launched a slogan summing up the process of political renewal he wished for, as follows: the "scrapping" of old politics, becoming in journalistic narrative, the "scrap dealer." As the Treccani Encyclopedia admits, "scrap dealer" is certainly not those who work in the field of wreckage, who dismantle old machinery. Today, this epithet is given to those who want to make a clean sweep in the politics now considered out of time by getting rid of those politicians who had too long of a career and are to be replaced by new political actors who bring new ideas in politics (http://www.treccani.it/webtv/videos/pdnm_della_valle_rottamazione.html).

Mancini, P. (a cura di) (2003). *La posta in gioco. Temi, personaggi e satira della campagna elettorale 2001*. Rome: Carocci.

Mazzoleni, G. e Sfardini A. (2009). *Politica Pop. Da "Porta a Porta" a "L'isola dei famosi"*. Bolonia: il Mulino.

Manin, B. (2010). *I principi del governo rappresentativo*. Bolonia: il Mulino.

Mény, Y. e Surel, Y (2001). *Populismo e democrazia*. Bolonia: il Mulino.

Patterson, Thomas E. (1993). Out of Order. New York: Vintage Books.

Prospero, M. (2010). *Il comico della politica. Nichilismo e aziendalismo nella comunicazione di Silvio Berlusconi*. Rome: Ediesse.

Prospero, M. e Ruggiero C. (a cura di) (2010). *Le parole della politica. Personaggi, linguaggi e narrazioni nell'Italia del 2008*. Napolies: ScriptaWeb.

Prospero, M e Tani I. (2010). Introduzione, in M. Prospero, C. Ruggiero (a cura di). *Le parole della politica. Personaggi, linguaggi e narrazioni nell'Italia del 2008*. Napoles: ScriptaWeb.

Ruggiero, C. (2014a). *Le sorti della videocrazia. Tv e politica nell'Italia del Mediaevo*, Milan: Mondadori Università.

Ruggiero, C. (2014b). *La macchina della parola. Struttura, interazione, narrazione nel talk show*. Milan: FrancoAngeli.

Sabato, L. J. (1991). *Feeding Frenzy: Attack Journalism and American Politics*. New York: Free Press.

Santoro, G. (2013). *Un Grillo qualunque. Il Movimento 5 Stelle e il populismo digitale nella crisi dei partiti italiani*. Rome: Castelvecchi.

Pierre-André Taguieff (2003). *L'illusione populista*. Milan: Bruno Mondadori.

Van Zoonen, L. (2005). *Entertaining the Citizen. When Politics and Popular Culture Converge*. Lanham, MD: Rowman & Littlefield.

Bilgehan Ece Şakrak

Space-Time-Body Transformations in Monsters of Horror Genre

Introduction

In this study, it is aimed to explore the relationship between "monsters as being fantastic iconographical figures of horror movies such as vampires, werewolves, zombies, etc." and "space-time-body" transformations. The study focused on Robin Wood's question of "What does the monster stand for?" In this way, monsters as iconographical figures in relation with space-time-body transformations were evaluated in examples of both, mainstream Hollywood and Turkish horror films.

Robin Wood (1986) concentrated on "repressed" and "the return of repressed". While he mentioned "basic repression" with natural control mechanisms peculiar to living creatures such as reflex acts, he emphasizes "surplusrepression" and its formation in cultural environment. At this point, the structure of the western society that is normalized under the roof of "surplusrepression" is monogamous, heterosexual, bourgeois, male-dominated, capitalistic individuals. In this case, it is needed to seek for answer of the question, "What is repressed?" in western culture (Wood, 1986, p. 71–72).

Wood elaborates the "otherness", which is enlightened by psychoanalysis to provide perceptiveness to the concept, repression. According to the system, which idealizes the western society; "the other" people are women, proletariat, and other cultures; ethnical groups within a culture, alternative ideologies, ideological sexual deviation and children, obviously (Wood, p. 73–75).

It is usual that in the ages of social crisis, different cultural representations appear. Some of these representations develop solutions or alternatives about the crisis and idealize them, some of them produce metaphors enabling solutions, and some of them symbolize despair, giving no place to any solution (Ryan and Kellner, 2010, p. 264). The genre focusing on the repressed's/the other's dual concept prominently and dramatizing it with the "monster" figure is the horror films (Wood, s. 75). Functioning as a filter making digestible the passion and fears repressed or rejected by the consciousness returns back disguised as "monster" (Moretti, 2005, p. 130).

Method

In this study examples of the historic development of horror films in the world are analyzed according to the films and the data derived from the evaluation of the directors'/producers' opinions of the field with a qualitative research method. The study about fantastical horror films in Turkish film history is completed by the direction of this information and using the approaches appreciatively; qualitative in analysis of the films, quantitative in classifying of the fantastical monsters used in the films.

Findings

Fantastical Monsters of Horror Films and Their Development in Word Scene

Georges Meliés' *The Haunted Castle* (1896) can be counted as the first horror film with its fairy-tale, such as witchcraft, sorcery, ghost and folkloric features. Some of the first full-length horror films are pictured by the monster figures in German Expressionism, *The Cabinet of Dr. Caligari* (1920) and *Nosferatu* (1922). Caligari's doctor, at the same time an image becoming a monster functions as signifying the "other" against the "normalized" one with his time-space-body transformation and creating the fear. The first vampire of the horror film history, *Nosferatu,* as a vampire image, is one of the distinctive icons reflecting on monster representation, time-space-body transformation. The pivotal matter of this study is an initial point for later examples of codes added culturally to the image. *Nosferatu* with its long nails and teeth, living on sucking blood and in the middle of the dualities, death-live, day-night, human being-monster is a renamed German example of Bram Stoker's *Dracula* (1897) because of copyright issues.

After World War I, psychological and physical deformation of the war is represented in *The Phantom of the Opera* (1925) as monsterizing the normally accepted individual figure. *Dracula*, directed by Tod Browning in 1931 and *Frankenstein* based on Mary Shelley's novel (1818) filmed first in 1910 and secondly by James Whale in 1931, a full-length version, are the most encountered monsters of the horror films. With their narrations focusing mostly on "identities" like death and immortality, vitalizing blood, resurrection, physical transformations, re-forming of the monster image by these transformations, the darkness of the night against the daylight, the independence of the monsters from time and space as "others", these fantastical monsters created their own ideological representation-related sub-texts.

King Kong released in 1933 can be considered as a representation of the oil crisis and depression in America. Frankenstein, Dracula, werewolf, etc. are the first monsters in 1930's. Most of 1940's horror films are new versions of the ones made in 1930's (Monument, 2009). In this context as Scognamillo (2006, p. 20) states, the first golden age of horror films in Hollywood slows down in the years of the World War II; because real fears are in battle fields and concentration camps. By the peak of industrializing famous monsters begin to seem together on the screen like *Frankenstein Meets the Wolf Man* (1943) and *The House of Frankenstein* (1944). Transformation of *Invisible Man* (1933) into *Invisible Agent* in 1942 reflects the anxieties of the World War II such as distrust and paranoia that the outsider in the meaning of "the other" and this "invisible other"s capability of being everywhere.

Another fantastical monster of the horror film history is *The Wolf Man* (1941). It is important with its "genre" contributions to the werewolf tradition (Schneider, 2009, p. 77). Being Jewish in those years, equals to "the other" and the solitude feeling it created is symbolized by the loneliness of the Wolf Man. He is aware of himself as being a monster; he is cursed by someone else and transforms from a human being into a wolf at nights, inevitably (Monument, 2009). Similarly, *Cat People* (1942) tells the story of the return of the sexually repressed in *Dracula* as "the other" and this time as a woman physically turning into a wild cat with a Freudian point of view (Schneider, 2009, p. 81).

Even if in this study American films are based on, it is inevitable to mention 1950's England and Hammer Studios that starts the golden age of horror films by its "colored film" technology. *The Curse of Frankenstein* (1957) and *Horror of Dracula* (1958) are the prominent examples of this period.

Alfred Hitchcock draws attention with *Psycho* in 1960. The film is about Norman Bates' running the motel left from his dead-mother and killing the young women staying there, while he is wearing his mother's clothes. The monster image is actualized by not a physical transformation, but a cross-dressing action. With gender beyond the physical transformation, concepts like "disguising the transformation", mother-son relationship shows the necessity of psychoanalytic reading. In the film, elimination of the psychological elements that treat the male gaze in symbolic terms of "castration anxiety" in patriarchal ideology has done via annihilating the woman existence, which supports Laura Mulvay's (1975) opinion about looking from the male gaze and using the "pleasure of seeing" as a political weapon. Usage of the horror genre as a tool to express psychoanalytic themes, such as repressed sexuality, sadism, necrophilia (Carroll, 1981, p. 17) is explicit in *Psycho*. The fear in the film does not signify the fantastical monsters, but today's psychotic person. The popularity of *Psycho* paves the way for the blood scenes and following "slasher" films, containing serial killers' slaughtering their victims in bloody scenes (Anafarta, 2002, p. 2–3).

In 1968, *Rosemarys's Baby* takes a baby devoted to Satan by a husband and Satanist neighbors and the baby's mother Rosemary as the subject. Rosemary, in a male-dominated system, obeys her husband and concedes his direction. The film, combines Catholic and Satanist notions, establishes the monster image on a mother impregnated reluctantly by satanic powers and her giving birth to a satanic creature.

Night of the Living Dead (1968) as a zombie film, concepts of life and death, resurrection but symbolization of the revival as a "transformed monster" are remarkable. In relation with the social and political background, it is possible to interpret that the repression of the public comes back from the socially collective consciousness as the body of "zombie", by the reason of the USA defeat in Vietnam War. Zombies need to eat fresh human meat to survive; the survivors are their lifeblood. They can attack anyone living to survive; it can be their siblings, mothers, fathers, etc. The ones beaten by a zombie transforms into a zombie. Briefly, being a zombie is a matter of time.

The Satan, controlling the body of a female child symbolizes Christian values obviously, in *The Exorcist* (1973), to be remade later. Fathers, crucifixes, holy water and the Bible cure the thing that science cannot. Physical transformation comes true by the child's image that gets a growing satanic appearance. Similarly, the image of youngsters that transform into monsters shows up in *The Omen* (1976), which is remade later.

Another important film of 1970's is *Carrie* (1976). Carrie has telekinetic powers; she is "the other" among her high school friends, and an alone outsider. It can be considered as the pioneer of the teenage-slasher films. (Schneider, 2009, p. 229–230). Making woman the other, the film reflects the threatening side of the woman power at the same time.

George Romero's *Dawn of the Dead* (1978) is another film of the trilogy, the others are *Night of the Living Dead* (1968) and *Day of the Dead* (1985). The director's *Land of the Dead* (2005) and *Diary of the Dead* (2008) are zombie films, too. The general approach of the films is giving social messages about American society.

The first film of the series as *A Nightmare on Elm Street* (1984) is about Freddy Krueger, who kills teen-agers in their dreams by the method of using their fears. Freddy is a death image, who is burnt by his victims' parents in his life on Elm Street and he came back to revenge. In the film, horror is built by the transformation of time-space-body construction. Monster's coming back from the past signifies the time-transformation; and the ones been killed in their dreams are killed at real time simultaneously this is an explicit example of space-transformation. Resurrection of Freddy's burnt body and the physical transformation of the monster that he is immortal by the reason of his being murdered can be defined in some distinctions such as living dead, human form-deformed human, etc.

The 1980's are the years of excessiveness by the help of technological developments with special effects (Monument, 2009). *The Return of the Living Dead* (1985) a zombie film or *Gremlins* (1984) telling about monsterized little creatures are some of the examples of the age. The films like *Videodrome* (1983) and *The Fly* (1986) directed by David Cronenberg are the examples for transformation of organisms.

Candyman (1992) has a hook-hand and is a human-monster that appears after his name has been said in five times while looking at the mirror. He is Afro-American. In fact he is the fear of the callers'.

Vampirism is an excellent example for the association of fear and passion (Moretti, 2005, s.126); and Francis Ford Coppola, reinterpreted this identicalness by using the familiar image of vampire in *Bram Stoker's Dracula* (1992). Thus, the monster is back as a romantic lover. His resentment is as a result of his loss of beloved woman. In 1994 with *Interview With The Vampire,* the vampire is out of the gothic castle and in urban life. Louis is transformed into a vampire when he has a human-being, and becomes heroic in today's world; prefers animal blood instead of killing people. In 1998, the vampire in *Blade* is born as a half-vampire, half-human being. He is dedicated to killing vampires. *Blade* continues in following years with its other episodes.

The Blair Witch Project (1999) is a DV recorded film about three young students' film shooting to complete their projects in the forest and evokes today's popular genre reality-TV. It makes the conflict of reality-fiction questioned.

The vampires in *Twilight* (2008) and the other productions in the series, 2009, 2010, 2011, 2012, as a new generation for the vampire films; they are adapted themselves to the conditions of the real life of the mortals. They go to schools like anyone, they have jobs and they can go out under daylight.

It is seen that, mainstream Hollywood horror films reflect the concerns of the society with the relation of political and economical contexts in their own period. In this way, to analyze the reflections of fear elements in horror films that are produced in Turkey and what they represent, is meaningful to get an evaluation about productions between mainstream Hollywood and Turkey.

Horror Films in Turkey

The first horror film in Turkey is little known *Çığlık* (*Scream*) (1949). The oldest available Turkish horror film is *Drakula İstanbul'da* (*Dracula is in İstanbul*) (1953). It is the first version that the Dracula image is shown with fangs and walking on the ramparts (Özkaracalar, 2003, p. 206). Even though the vampire myth is originated in Christianity including folkloric features, there are no religious symbols like crucifixes, holy waters, etc. in *Drakula İstanbul'da*. Therefore, it is possible to state that the importance of the cultural differences plays a significant role on reflecting culture of horror.

Ölüler Konuşmaz ki (Deads Don't Speak) (1970) is another film hosting horror elements. Destroying of a ghost eventuates by an imam and his companies reading verses from the Koran. Affected by the sun, the ghost melts down and disappears. Likewise, the other film, in this context, the physical transformation of the ghost, in the movie including local cultural codes and religious references to Islam ends with the dying of the alive and its transforming into a ghost.

Adaptation of *The Exorcist* (1973) in 1974 as *Şeytan* (Satan) is another Turkish horror movie. In the authentic version of the film, the references to Christianity undergo some changes in *Şeytan*. The crucifixes are gone, the Bible is replaced with Koran, and holy water turns into zam-zam. In the adaptation version, a lot of cultural code in the original version is replaced with the codes targeting the audience in Turkey.

The multi-layered narrative structure and metaphor abundance of *Karanlık Sular* (*Dark Waters*) (1993) are enough to be described as the expression of "identity crisis of Turkish nation" (Özkaracalar, 2003, s.125). *Okul* (*The School*) (2003) is about a young person mocked by his friends and his death after committing suicide; in his death anniversary, the friends stand face to face with fatal incidents. The story of *Okul* is very familiar as it evokes mainstream Hollywood horror films in which the young people die one by one.

Büyü (2004) takes an archeological researcher team haunted in the archeological area by jinn as subject. With *Büyü* a new era begins for Turkey in the meaning of horror genre. This era is a kind of jinn movie rush that containing Islamic religious figures and Anatolian traditions, based on the fears originated in religious believes.

In this context it is possible to sum up the horror films produced in the last decade according to the monsters they use as in Table-1 under three categories:

Table 1: Range of Horror Films Produced in 2004–2014 According to the Monster Figures

Subject/ Year	**2004**	**2005**	**2006**	**2007**	**2008**	**2009**	**2010**	**2011**	**2012**	**2013**	**2014**
Jinn	1			1	1	1	1	1	1	3	6
Spiritual Beings			2	1			1	1	1		1
Other			2				2		1		1
TOTAL	**1**	**0**	**4**	**2**	**1**	**1**	**4**	**2**	**3**	**3**	**8**

As it is shown in Table-1, between 2010 and 2014 the movies in which monster functioning on the concept of jinn are more than other movies containing fantastical elements. They are: *Büyü* (2004), *Semum* (2008), *3 Harfliler: Marid* (2010), *Şeytan-ı Racim* (2013), *El-Cin* (2013), *Azem: Cin Karası* (2014), *Azazil: Düğüm* (2014), *Muska (2014)*, *Ammar* (2014), *Musallat* (2007), *Musallat* 2 (2011), *Dabbe 2* (2009), *Dabbe Bir Cin Vakası* (2012), *Dabbe: Cin Çarpması* (2013), *Dabbe 5: Zehr-i Cin* (2014), *Siccin* (2014).

At the second line, there are the movies containing fantastical elements, taking spiritual beings that sometimes getting closer to jinn as subject are: *Araf* (2006), *Dabbe* (2006), *Gomeda* (2007), *Cehennem 3D* (2010), *Mühürlü Köşk* (2011), *Görünmeyenler* (2012), *Reminiscence* (2014).

The third category films containing fantastical elements in which the monsters are images like zombies, goblins, human-beings transformed after been experimented on, etc. are: *Ses* (2010), *Ada Zombilerin Düğünü* (2010), *htr2b: Dönüşüm* (2012), *Gulyabani* (2014) [1]

Conclusion

During the creation of horror with using the monster image as a metaphor and the expression of horror via "the other", time-space-body transformations has remarkable contributions in fantastic horror films. These transformations break the "natural, normal and familiar" and take them out of routine. The codes idealized as "normal" are instilled in the cultural environment by the current system, in terms of ruling ideology. Thus, during the watching act in horror film, the audience reads the film – like s/he does in any other genre- by choosing the codes closest to his/her cultural universe. Therefore, representations that contain jinn as the concept of Islam have more familiar codes for the audience within the country and more effective potential to evoke horror for the audience in Turkey with comparison of the horror films that contain western codes.

Due to the ideology of the "normal" it is the product of the system within. The obscurity derived from going out of "normal" creates distrust on the audience. For

1 There are not many films except the ones categorized, containing "unfantastical" monster images. One of them is *Küçük Kıyamet* (*The Little Doom*) (2006), it gives place the earthquake happened in Turkey, in 17 August 1999 and fears about earthquake proceeding. It takes a local event and social matters as subject and this difference makes the film more remarkable among other horror films that are produced in Turkey. *Gen* (The Gene) (2006), is another film in which monster figures referee to psychological diseases doesn't host any fantastical figure.

this reason, fear comes from the "obscurity" of the "well-known" and the tension of "the anticipation" created while the unknown is known.

It is possible to see that different fantastical monsters that are produced by western horror films represent the horror and values of their periods as being "the other". On the other hand, horror films produced in Turkey used Western monster figures in first examples and could not make up original ones. In the last decade, horror films are produced in Turkey rapidly and jinn is the most-used figure in terms of the monster. Jinn as a concept and the terms it is related to, have been a part of Islamic depicts and Anatolian traditions; therefore horror films produced in Turkey recently cannot go beyond the reproduction of the concepts that are already well-known.

References

Carroll, N. (1981), "Nightmare and the Horror Film: The Symbolic Biology of Fantastic Beings", *Film Quarterly*, 34.3 (1981), pp. 16–25

Schneider, S. J. (2009), *101 Horror Movies You Must See Before You Die*, Barrons: London

Özkaracalar, K. (2003). 'Between Appropriation and Innovation: Turkish Horror Cinema', Steven Jay Schneider (ed.) *Fear Without Frontiers: Horror Cinema Across the Globe*, pp. 205–217, London: FAB Press.

Wood, R. (1986). *Hollywood From Vietnam to Reagan*, USA: Columbia University Press

Scognamillo, G. (2006). *Canavarlar Yaratıklar Manyaklar*, 2nd Ed., İstanbul: +1 Kitap

Ryan, M., Kellner, D. (2010), *Politik Kamera*, 2nd Ed., E. Özsayer (Trans.), İstanbul: Ayrıntı Yayınları

Moretti, F. (2005), "Korkunun Diyalektiği", *Mucizevi Göstergeler*, Z. Altok (Trans.), pp. 105–136

Mulvay, L. (1975), "Visual Pleasure and Narrative Cinema", *Screen*, (1975) 16 (3): 6–18

Anafarta, O. (2002), "Psycho-Sonrası Amerikan Korku Sineması 1 Slasher", *Geceyarısı Sineması*, Vol: 12 pp. 2–10

Monument, A. (Director). (2009) *Nightmares in Red, White and Blue: The Evolution of the American Horror Film* [Documentary]

İlknur Doğu Öztürk

The Effects of Culture on Positioning: An Examination of Yandex In Turkey

Abstract The self expression of the foundations has gained a huge impact on determining and positioning within contemporary competitive environment. Today environment, as we can call it customer age, the identities of the foundations are as important as the service and the products produced by these foundations. Therefore, achieving the foundational objectives on communicating with target groups plays a critical role. Informing target groups, which are very important to the foundations, form its different ways of communication.

To emphasize the positioning and to establish the reflections of the culture in marketing communication are aimed in this study. In line with this purpose, the positioning strategies the marketing communication studies carried out by Yandex, a Russian oriented search engine breaking into the Turkish market are examined and the cultural signifiers affecting brand positioning are tried to be established. From the date Yandex has broken into the Turkish market September 2011 to 2014 June, the marketing communication activities carried out by Yandex are examined and evaluated descriptively.

Keywords: Positioning, culture, public relations, advertising

Introduction

As in today's world demands, expectations and purchasing habits of the consumer differ from one group to another, even one person to another, a brand should approach to a country market and the different groups of the very country with different strategies. In the competitive environment arouse from the factors, like changing structures of the society, technological innovations, developments, a concept, brand comes into prominence as the element provides preference of the products. Creating a qualified product and a positive brand evaluation is the first step of the brand construction. Place of the concepts of quality and perception of quality is the consumer's mind (Can cited from Riesand Ries Can, 2007: 229). The name, the package, the product and the emotion awakes the consumer and are the properties help differing from competitors and branding.

If we look at the old definitions of the term, brand, we observe a link to "to burn". In fact, the word BRAND derives from ancient Scandinavian word BRANDR (to burn). In that age farmers used to sear the animals, that is the first use of "branding". The aim is to define and providing to distinguish. Today in definitions of brandwe read in dictionaries the aim is to distinguish. This is described as "the registered trademark" (Borça, 2013:4). Pointing the brand as a concept that the distinguishable part and the emotional response about the product is possible. A brand undertakes not only the distinguishing features, but different strategies. Jim Blyth (2001) lists these strategical functions as posessive sign, differentiation, functional tool, symbolic, risk reducer, shortcut tool, legal tool, strategical approach (Can cited from Blyth, 2007:227–228). It affects the positioning process by the visual differentiation from the competators and making a connection to the target group via cultural communication applications. Marx defines culture as "against the ones nature has created, the ones human has done" (Güvenç cited from Marx, 1999:100). As a combination of human made value system, morality, art, symbol, belief, custom, and tradition, the culture is one of the main factors that determine wishes and behaviours. Within a culture people are in constant interaction with their families and the other social foundations, so they develop values, preferences and perceptions (Peltekoğlu cited from Tek, 2010, 132). Culture, differing from one society to another, among groups and even in subcultures is the fact determines demands and wishes. With technological innovations and massification of communication correspondingly, the effect of culture on brand positioning increases for brands. Culture gets a higher importance in communication applications within the scope of affecting the customer's purchasing preferences and positioning the brand's differentiating features emphasized. Based on the way of how a brand is percepted, the concept of positioning comes forward as the leading concept in communication studies. As Horald and Gilson (1987:170–171) state that positioning "places brand into target group's rerefential frame", they indicate that the main theme of positioning is to differentiate the brand from its competators. On the other hand, Kotler (2006:309) argues that positioning means customers' defining of a brand according to its important and exclusive features, that is in customer's mind the criteria of the position of a brand among its competators is important. Furthermore, Kotler states that in today's competitive environment managements have to decide the target market departments and then find different positioning for each market department (Tosun cited from Harold and Gilson and Kotler, 2010, 33). The answers of the questions, who are the competators, what are the differences and similiraties between them should be considered in brand positioning process.

Brand positioning aims placing a brand in a position that has a competitive superiority in the mind of target group (Uztuğ, 2002:72). Positioning is important as in providing the determination of the brand's status in the market and the desired place for the brand by differentiating the brand from its competators. In this process of communication applications like advertisement are operative with their effect on the target group. In an environment of intensive competition and with the pressure of this competition similar "new" products are put into market, the managements send various messages to their customers and consumers via various channels (OdabaşıveOyman, 2001: 61). Advertisement, one of the communication applications used in brand positioning in the competitive environment is "the announcement of the description of a business or a commodity or a service in general broadcast media" (Kocabaş ve Elden, 1997: 12).

In advertisement, one of the elements of brand communication, the message in the form of word, picture, sound, image and symbol is transmitted in order to generate the aimed effect on the target group. The most significant communicative feature of the advertisement is that the objective effects are designed in order to set in motion the target group in related to a brand (Tosun, 2010:271). According to Tosun, advertisements are capable of not only charging a product or a brand and also a way of life and a point of view (Tosun, 2010:273).

Constructing message by using cultural and social codes such as humour, sexuality, fear or emotional attraction serves brand positioning. Creating advertisement attraction by using these emotions are used to create adistinctive and objective change, which is the desire to access the physical, psychological and social demands of the target group. According to Berger, advertisements reflect the dominant ways of thinking, points of view and trends and advertising is the process of producing attraction (Berger, 1990:131). Advertisement applications using cultural codes creating objective advertising attraction are the efficient responses of the question, how does the brand position itself, inevitably. Advertisement, consist of cultural codes and a part of brand positioning aims to place product brand in people's mind in a desired way. For this purpose using cultural codes in advertisement is inevitable. In the phase of interpretation of these codes we confront semiotics.

Semiotics began with the Swedish philologist Ferdinand de Saussure (1857–1913) and American thinker Charles Saunders Pierce (1839–1914) helps to explore the meanings beyond the visible image (Fiske, 1996:61–62). One of the most important contributors of semiotics, Barthes defines sign: A rose is only a flower; but if a young man presents it to his girlfriend it becomes a sign. The rose refers to the young man's romantical passion and this meaning is accepted by the girlfriend (Mutlu, 2004:113). Semiotics aiming to expose the syntax of signs in a text, reviews the meanings of signs and especially the generation ways of these signs and the meanings they produce. Saussure mentions two ways of arranging of the codes. The first one is paradigmatic and the second one is syntogmatic (Fiske, 1996:62). Saussure's argue about the arbitrary relationship between the signifier and signified plays a huge role in the development of semiotics. Pierce is concentrated on the three images of sign (icon, index, symbol). A movement derives from this starting point and semiological decoding spreads the world (Berger, 1996:12). Semiotics is used in all communication applications transferring meaning like advertisements, TV, newspapers, magazines. Advertising is at the top of the list of using signs definitely. Examining what a sign is, how they form and connotations they producesemiotics contributes to understand the advertising language as a communication syntax and searches the buried meanings under the surface. The main problem of semiotics is sign. There are three basic fields it studies in; the sign itself, code that signs arranged in or systems and codes and the culture the signs are treated (Fiske, 1996:62). Codes and signs are transferred between generations and cultures. People born into the culture get these codes and signs via the transferring process. Advertisement movies construct the narrative structure fictionally and include a lot of images. From the beginning of constructing process of coding the images they contain the values and elements of the cultural structure they are born in.

Method

Yandex as it has 64% marketshare and the biggest search engine in Russia is the fifth biggest Internet based product and service providing firm in the world. It reaches more than 56 billion people all around the world. It offers service in Russia, Belarus, Kazakhistan, Ukraine, the USA and in Turkey from September 2011 (http://tr.wikipedia.org/wiki/Yandex).

In this study cultural effects on advertising and using visual and linguistic codes reflecting culture as a marketing communication application and the process of brand positioning is emphasized. The objective of this study is to show the importance of the culture in brand positioning process perceptibly. With this objective, theoretic information observation on practice is run on Yandex brand. Explanations on brand and positioning are made and with the help of Pierce's Semiotic approach -icon, index, symbol- language, slogan, colours, and narration of advertisement movies from the advertisement studies with the slogan "Answers of all life questions" run in 2011 of Russian originated search engine brand Yandex. The chosen advertisement movies belong to the campaign in which year Yandex broke into Turkish market and first advertisement of Yandex in Turkey. These advertisements are downloaded to the PC from the fourth popular site in Turkey, video sharing channel Youtube (http://www.alexa.com/topsites/countries/TR).

Findings

Advertisement is formed of two parts, image and text. In the advertisement movie an image of a black frame on PC screen is in the shape of searchengine. In advertisement movies there is a Yandex text, a search bar and a find button on the background and the film goes on with the changing text.

Table 1: All visual and text frames in First advertisement movie with the slogan "answers of all the life questions"

	Sign
 Visual: Dancing robot Text: Dancing Schools	Universal and local sign (dance), Aim is access to the young target group, assertion of possessing the newest technology
 Visual: Ducklings and mother Text: Baby names	Assertion of being capable of presenting multiple choice with brand function, emphasis on family as a universal and local value, using of universal and local cultural signs
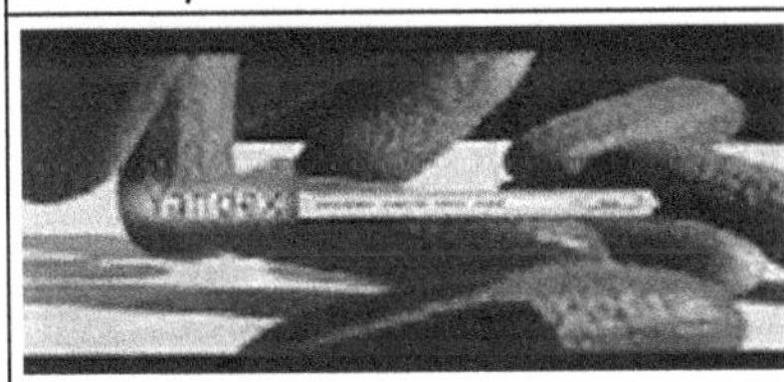 Visual: Cucumber Text: Can we be cacik?	Emphasis on food culture as a local sign with text and image
 Visual: Hippopotamus Text: Water proof mascara	Completing the text with the universal visual sign connotation,

	Sign
 Visual: Monkey Text: Compete recipe	Local and traditional public cultural sign, (this frame reminds a Turkish proverb)
 Visual: Space, planet, satellite equipment Text: How will I go home?	Assertion of being capable of showing the way to the furthest places , assertion of possessing the newest technology, assertion of navigation service (emphasis on function)

Table 2: Second advertisement movie with the slogan "Answers of all life questions"

Image	Analyse
 Visual: Running ostrich Text: Running shoes	Using universal visual sign, text in local language
 Visual: Watermelon Text: White Cheese	Emphasis on Turkish food and using local cultural sign

Image	Analyse
 Visual: Cute Cats Text: Funny person video	Using universal linguistic and visual sign,
 Visual: Undershirt and pyjamas on the clothes line Text: Picnic sites	While picnic is a universal cultural code, pyjamas belong to Turkish entertainment culture
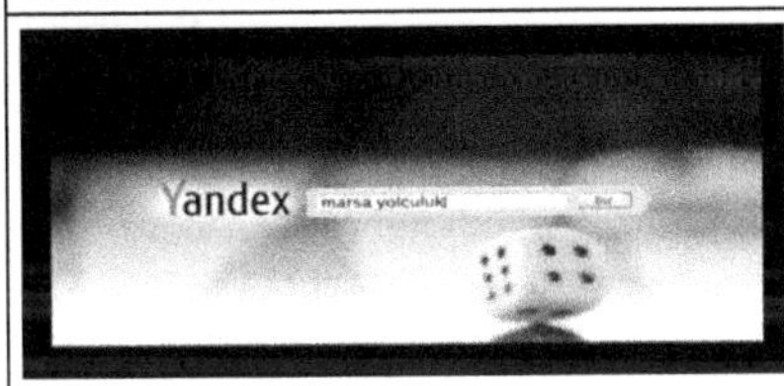 Visual: Backgammon, dice Text: Mars Travelling	A universality with a universal code in text and emphasis on locality with local code
 Visual: Shark in sea Text: Public Beaches	Textual content meaningful in local culture on an image reflecting universal culture

In the advertisement movies sound, image and music are used integrally. In the movies there was a voice over saying the slogan at the end, along with the music of advertisement campaign. At the end of the advertisement there comes a screen with brand name and the slogan and a voice over saying the slogan, "Find all the answers of all life questions" and then "Yandex, New search engine" and the brand and the slogan of the campaign is put in words.

One of the signs in advertisements is music. Music as an important element of the advertisement, it strengthenes the emotional content and provides a dramatical effect. The music in advertisements can be used both primary and supportive element. With music it is possible to call attention to the advertisement as well as to provide retention of the message in mind. Searches indicate that people find the arguments of the advertisements with music more convincing than the ones without music (Elden ve Bakır, 2010:96–97). Duck Sauce's disco-house song "Barbara Streisand" is used in the advertisement movie to boost the impressiveness as an audial element. Screen changes like blurredness or contrast or technics like shotting moves aren't used in the movies. A constant contrast setting is used all over the advertisement to emphasize only the product. Like music, colours have a language and every colour is a way of communication. According to Ünsal, using colour as an element in the advertisement derives from seven reasons (cited by Yaman, 2014:46); to call attention, to represent the scene and object as faithful to the origin, to indicate a part of the product or the message, to create some imaginations in customer's and to create a strong impression. Vivid colour signs are preferred to support the cultural signs in order to preserve the youth and energy and the humour in the local culture as well as to support the integrity of the campaign in the advertisement. By using bright and vivid colours, positive feelings like happiness are tried to be created. The Turkish advertisement movie is framed with black, the color that is explained as power and prestige in the local culture. By this way boundries are drawn to the advertisement.

At the end of the advertisement the Yandex logo on the white background and the advertisement logo appear. Black and white colours are used well balanced. The white colour mainly provides to be noticed of other colours. Therefore, it affects the recognition of the logo and the brand. In the Yandex advertisement with short words on a screen designed as it is being searched on and images contributing the textual content are used to benefit from humorous attraction. It is found that the images or text call the signs well known and recognized by audience are used in a way of completing each other. As Yandex represented by an advertisement, it is the signified in Pierce's semiotics triangle. Signifieds are the side of the part representingYandex. To direct this process, images and content especially by humour, addressing the feelings like joy and entertainment are chosen in order to convince the target group in the advertisement. The exertion of creating a younger, more cheerful and energetic image is reflected by the word "new" in the slogan, "new search engine" and significations can be made like innovation, humour and assertion. It is observed that qualities like speed, multiple choices and multi culturalism is transferred to the target group by the visual and textual signs. Advertisements show that they care about the culture of the target group by usingsigns like brand name, slogan, colour, language of the textual message. As a universal brand Yandex for example presents a universal sign like family and a sign of reflecting local culture as it can exceed to interpret the proverb, what a donkey knows about competition, together. Positioning the brand in people's minds as a search engine, which is finding all kind of answers of the audiences' possible questions, fast, young, equipped with the latest technology, facetious is aimed. Especially, there are connotions in linguistic contents in which advertisements humorous attraction is applied.

Discussion

Being a brand in order to earn the dependence and loyalty of the target group is leaned on being different. Communicative applications like advertisement influences positioning as a profession, which has effects on brands. Culture in the competitive environment transforms into stylistic, linguistic and visual signs in the form of universal-local cultural codes. It is seen that every linguistic and visual sign like a brand name and logo and slogan and colours in an advertisement movie can be interpreted by the target group and consist of universal and cultural codes. By universal codes its universality, by cultural codes its locality is emphasized. As a part of the society an individual interprets the things he sees in the advertisments by the leading of the knowledge he gets after a while in that culture. In all of the advertisement movies using signs formed of image and text to strengthen the signification, the cultural effect of the target group interpreting process of the signifers encountered before is communicated to the signified. Culture is reflected in the advertisements by using signs to access the desired positioning in the mind of the target group. Visual and linguistic signs like sound, image, music and text in the advertisements are interpreted by the audience equipped with the culture. Yandex has developed a positioning strategy, having a peculiar benefit and function.

Results

This study's conclusion is breaking into a market and brand positioning, universal cultural signs and local cultural signs must be included together in communicative applications like advertisement.

Color, music, slogan and elements in Yandex ads were built in a new way to reflect the new brand entering the country. Convenient with the Pierce's icon, sign and symbol approach, images and texts in the ads create the targeted association among the people with the specific culture. It is concluded that all messages are given in Turkish, universal and local culture signs are used, images and texts are formed as such that they complement each other and humor is benefited for a single goal to make the brand memorable. The logo, the emblem and the slogan call the target group to use the new search engine. Perception of the colours varies according to the factors like age, sex, environment, habits and the culture. Colour and music strengthen the convincing feature of the advertisement.

References

Asa Berger, A. (1996). Kitle İletişiminde Çözümleme Yöntemleri. Eskişehir: Anadolu Üniversitesi Yayınları

Berger, J. (1990). GörmeBiçimleri. İstanbul: Metis Yayınları

Borça, G. (2013). Marka ve Yönetimi. Eskişehir: Anadolu Üniversitesi Yayınları http://eogrenme.anadolu.edu.tr/eKitap/mai102u.pdfBorça Erişim T. 07.06.2014

Can, E. (2007). Marka ve Marka Yapılandırma. Marmara Üniversitesi İ.İ.B.F. Dergisi, cilt 22, No: 1. http://dosya.marmara.edu.tr/ikf/iib-dergi/2007-1/225-237-MARKA-YAPILANDIRMA.pdf Erişim T: 7.02.2014

Fiske, J. (1996). İletişim Çalışmalarına Giriş. Ankara: Bilim ve Sanat

Güvenç, B. (1999). İnsan ve Kültür. İstanbul: Remzi Kitabevi.

Kocabaş, F. ve Elden M.(1997). Reklamcılık. İstanbul: İletişim Yayıncılık.

Mutlu E. (2004). İletişim Sözlüğü. Ankara: Bilim ve Sanat

Odabaşı, Y., Oyman, M. (2002). Pazarlama İletişimi Yönetimi. İstanbul: Mediacat Yayınları.

Olgundeniz, S. S., Parsa, A. F (2014) Reklam dünyasinda imgenin gücü "Arçelik ve Vestel reklamlarinda robot karakterlerle yaratılan evren"-Journal of New World Sciences Academy April 2014 http://www.newwsa.com/download/gecici_makale_dosyalari/NWSA-7201-3375-4.pdf Erişim T. 5.06.2014

Peltekoğlu, F. B. (2010). Kavram ve Kuramlarıyla Reklam. İstanbul: Beta Yayınları

Tosun, N. B (2010). İletişim Temelli Marka Yönetimi. İstanbul: Beta Yayınları

Yaman, F. (2014) Reklamlarda Kullanılan Renkler ve Gazete Reklamlarının Nitel Analizi İletişim Kuram ve Araştırma Dergisi - Sayı 38/ Bahar 2014 Gazi Üniversitesi İletişim Fakültesi

http://www.iletisimdergisi.gazi.edu.tr/busayi/3.pdf

http://www.alexa.com/topsites/countries/TR

http://tr.wikipedia.org/wiki/Yandex

http://kliknete.com/yandex-turkiye-pazarinda.html

Remziye Kose Ozelci

Time Configuration in the Fictional Narrative in the Context of TV Series "Ben Onu Çok Sevdim"

Introduction

This work titled "Time configuration in the fictional narrative in the context of TV series "Ben Onu Çok Sevdim" is addressed with the purpose to seek an answer to the problematic proposition highlighted also by Paul Ricouer as "Can past events, whether factual or fictional, be presented without any intervention at any aspects to the narrative by the speaker?" especially in the light of the series on re-presentation of the events and political actors subject to late political history, recently broadcast on Turkish and foreign TV channels. As it may be acknowledged, fictional world of television also brings along "manufacturing consent" or "legitimization/illegitimization" as an important means of socialization. Thus, the viewer charmed by the TV language is sometimes manipulated without questioning the "factuality" and used for propaganda. The fact that the real world cannot be reflected as it is on mass media, resides above all in the obligation of "making a choice". Choosing takes place firstly at the level of facts to be communicated. Then, the elements of the communicated events are chosen. (Mutlu, 2008) In the end, regardless of the title or format, all program and image broadcast on TV are re-presented by establishing specific choosing, interpretation, construction and "narrative" codes. In this context, the TV series titled "Ben Onu Çok Sevdim" on the life of former Prime Minister of Turkey between the years 1950–1960 Adnan Menderes, who was tried at Yassiada Court established after the 1960 Military Coup and executed on September 17, 1961 will be analyzed in the framework of "narrative" theory discussed thoroughly by Paul Ricouer, who conducted studies on refiguration of history, time, and narrative through fictional narrative, in his pieces "Time and Narrative (III)", a masterwork in the field of narrative hermeneutics, to which the title of article is referred as well.

Method

Each research is conducted with the purpose of seeking answers to the questions encountered within a specific problematic proposition. Therefore, our research questions/hypotheses will gain meaning and validity within a specific problematic proposition. (Atabek, 2007) In this article too, TV series titled "Ben Onu Çok Sevdim" telling the story of the most important events and characters of our late history (The May 27, 1960 Military Coup, Yassiada Court, Executions), a trailer made by the production company of the movie with the promotional purpose, two different credits and presentation on the web site of its broadcasting channel were selected as the units of analysis of the way in which they are configured, the visual and linguistic codes used in credits, in order to seek the answers to for the following questions posed dedicated by Paul Ricouer for the differences between history and discourse. Reading two different credits, a trailer and an introductory text "in which present time, are they narrated and recalled" and "which past is regained?" The present time of the enunciation is "the essential time of discourse" since the time when narration starts is today, which is recorded in the narrative and narrator thus becomes a part of the story and his/her story is recorded as a conviction rhetoric. (Sarlo, 2012)

Findings

PANA Film[1] is the producer of the TV series, whose first episode was broadcast on September 10, 2013 on the channel ATV (national channel). Last episode of the series (15th Episode) was broadcast on January 24, 2014. The series is presented on the website of the channel it was broadcast, ATV, as follows: "***Ben Onu Çok Sevdim, in which political journey of Adnan Menderes who came to power with the Democrat party government and became prime minister in 1950, during the unsettled periods of the time, shows the audience a panorama of the political atmosphere becoming more and more challenging with Korean War, Soviet threat, process of accession to Nato and a revealed junta organization planning to topple the government. The story narrates Adnan Menderes' children and wife Berrin Menderes, to whom he was deeply committed, and who faced all difficulties and Ayhan Aydan with whom he fell in love madly. With respect to his valuable memory, we will witness the path to scaffold walked by a prime minister executed in front of his people.***" In the text communicated to the audience by the production company, ***(Sample 1)*** it is emphasized that the real and historical facts on political and personal life of the prime minister Adnan Menderes, indicated as the particular reasons of his trial before Yassiada Court would be presented

1 Pana Film was founded by Raci Şaşmaz and Bahadır Özdener in 2004. The company produced motion-picture movies addressing secret state subjects in particular and broadcast television series such as *Kurtlar Vadisi*, *Kurtlar Vadisi Pusu* as well as *Kurtlar Vadisi Irak*, *Kurtlar Vadisi Gladio* and *Kurtlar Vadisi Filistin*.

again. However, another issue, which is important and should be addressed and important one is the use of the term "witnessing". In this sense, each witnessing narration is a sort of discourse. It is because the narrator is someone involved in the events and does not pursue an external reality during enunciation. Today's stamp on any narrative about the past is unavoidable, because it is impossible to avoid the hegemony of the present time over discourse. (Sarlo, 2012) Although the story narrates the period of 1960s, the fact that expressions such as "coup, plans for toppling government, junta organization" are the statements talked frequently for supporting the discourses of current government in rule at the time when the series was broadcasted (September 2013). It is used even in the introductory text, which reinforces the view that the present time of enunciation is the essential time of discourse.

In the first trailer of 32 seconds of the series broadcast in 15 Episodes (**Sample 2**), we see one of the main characters of the series, Ayhan Aydan, sitting in front of the mirror and then turning to audience to ask "***I am Ayhan Aydan, lover, confidant, love or mistress of Prime Minister Adnan Menderes hung and killed in front his people. I never was afraid, hesitated to tell this: I loved him very much. I have courage to tell it. Do you have courage to listen?***" in a quite beautiful, cool and self-confident shape. In television series, images and their usage are effective. However, usage of words is also effective due to their functions. One of the key aspects of discourse is the fact that it addresses someone. There is another speaker, whom the discourse is directed to. Existence of a pair of speaker and listener constitutes the language as communication. (Ricouer, 2007) Therefore, scriptwriter/producer or narrator inserts what he/she wants to communicate with his/her own words into story through Ayhan Aydan. On the other hand, an enthusiastic crowd waiting for the official car of prime ministry and someone to come out of the car appears on screen. Then, the viewer catches the eyes of Adnan Menderes, who hugs the people and goes up the stairs to look at the enthusiastic crowd (also at the viewer on screen). The questions asked by Ayhan Aydan and the images shown; indicate that the main characters of the narrative story are Ayhan Aydan and Adnan Menderes. The story is a type of fictional narration with a beginning and an ending point and an organized plotline, told by someone, which covers a specific period. (Mutlu, 2008) The way the story is told in the series informs about the form of plotline. To Aristotle, who considers the characters dependent on plotline, plotline is a comprehensive concept based on events, characters and thoughts. As a matter of fact, from the first trailers of the series and in credits shown in the first 7 episodes, what is communicated that to the audience is that plotline would take place between Adnan Menderes, who was married with three kids and served as Prime Minister for 10 years, and his secret lover, Ayhan Aydan, besides some other plotlines covered. At this point, it would be good to recall Benveniste's distinction between story and discourse, as reminded by Ricouer. According to the distinction, the speaker is not involved in the story: "No one speaks here; events are shown as if they talked to themselves." Narration, on the other hand, indicates "any enunciation considering one speaker and one listener and exposing a tendency in the speaker to influence listener in any way." (Ricouer, 2012) Every story has a view in which it wants to communicate and have it adopted directly or indirectly. Another basic view this story intends to communicate is to convince the audience about the greatness and innocence of their "loves" (Adnan Menderes-Ayhan Aydan; Fatin Rüştü Zorlu-Vesamet Kutlu) although they were married, it uses the dramatic structure of the fictional world to ensure the audience to identify with it. As a matter of fact, it is possible to see this in the visual and linguistic messages provided in the sample 1–2 and 3 selected as the form of analysis. Again, in the posters prepared for the movie (poster 1 and poster 2), we can see that the story is based on love and there is a man (Adnan Menderes) torn between two women (Ayhan Aydan and Berin Menderes). There is a statement on the newsworthy photos shared on their website, with reference to the movie producer Pana Film (Photo 1) quote: "This love will be spoken about a lot. Another excellent movie from Pana Film." We can say that the narrator was a part of the events whether he/she is involved (a first-person narrative) or just witnessed (a third-person narrative) them.

Photo 1

Photo 2

Photo 3

Two credits were prepared for the series "Ben Onu Çok Sevdim." At the beginning the credits broadcast the first 6 episodes (**sample 3**), which is 1 minute and 43 seconds long. Characters shown in the credits are respectively (as characters used in the series) Adnan Menderes, Ayhan Aydan, Berin Menderes, Ayhan Aydan's mother, Ethem Menderes, Ayhan Aydan's spouse Ferit Alnar, Ayhan Aydan's friend Şadan, Ayhan Aydan's son, Yüksel Menderes, Mutlu Menderes, Aydın Menderes, Celal Bayar, Nihat Erim, the girl Yüksel Menderes loved, Fatin Rüştü Zorlu, Emel

Zorlu, Vesamet Kutlu… Characters shown in the credits mostly are Ayhan Aydan and Adnan Menderes. Scenes of Ayhan Aydan, emphasizing her musician personality and the notes, image Adnan Menderes in the parliament house. There is no image to make the audience unhappy. Following the images presented in company with the thematic music of the credits appear: "***The piece you will watch is not a biography. It is qualified as honoring historical figures. His story set with characters and events moving beyond reality, mirrors what Adnan Menderes and his friends might have felt.***" The credits are held on screen for 8 seconds. Credits are opening or ending lists containing names of the producers, directors, line producers, actors etc. who contributed to a movie, a TV show, a video track and information on making of the show, and texts identifying the movie, the show. (**Özon, p. 680**) As observed in these credits, the viewer can easily assess that the movie is based on a love story and the story is constructed on the love of Adnan Menderes and Ayhan Aydan. Such a story is quite important for Turkish viewer. This is because Adnan Menderes' secret and stirring love affair with Ayhan Aydan was featured in public sphere, on fictional TV world for the first time (apart from Yassiada Court). Turkish Opera Singer Ayhan Aydan, who lived between the years 1924–2009 took a place in our collective memory through her love affair (between the years 1951–1955) with Adnan Menderes from the Democrat Party, who served a Prime Minister between the years 1950–1960, rather than her identity as an artist. The fact that both Adnan Menderes and Ayhan Aydan are married with children; and they were spoken about over the "Baby Case" during Adnan Menderes' trial process in Yassiada Court are on the one hand, the most discussed and on the other hand, the most secret and unrevealed fact of our late history. As a matter of fact, in the trailer, the narrator's question tackled in the second sample: ***"I have courage to tell. Do you have courage to listen?"*** addressed directly to the viewer transfers the past into the "present" in order to discuss it. Therefore, in history, the basic structure of representation is performed by inserting narration into interpretation. (Ricouer, 2012)

The second credits and credits theme song of the movie is 2 minutes 15 seconds long. **(Sample 4)** These credits are used starting from episode 7 till the final episode (15). The only common aspect of the credits in question with the first one is the text ***"The piece you will watch is not a biography. It is qualified as honoring historical figures. His story set with characters and events moving beyond reality, mirrors what Adnan Menderes and his friends might have felt."*** This appears on screen after the image. Upon episode 7, the story and plotline of our fictional narration are in transition. In all the trailers and introductory texts of the first 7 episodes, the movie was constructed on the love between Ayhan Aydan- Adnan Menderes, and Fatin Rüştü Zorlu and Vesamet Kutlu as seen in the first credits and stressed in the story of movie, where the focus was on the coup, Yassiada, military junta and Berin Menderes. Credits open with the image of an envelope put on the table by someone, only whose hands are seen and thus, it is understood that he wears a military uniform. On top of the envelope, is typewritten “THIS IS TURKEY” and a stamp written the year “1960” is put in the back to close the envelope. (Photo 4) Ayhan Aydan’s expression “Ben Onu Çok Sevdim” (I Loved Him Very Much) was what she said during her defense at the Yassiada Court, which is also the movie title, appears indistinctly on the postage stamp with the map of Turkey glued on this envelope.

Photo 4

The name of Birce Akalay playing the main character of the story Ayhan Aydan is removed from the credits and the character of İdil Fırat playing Berin Menderes is made more dominant. In the episode 7, the character of Ayhan Aydan is almost ignored in the plotline and is only presented as a guest actress in the episode 7. In these credits, Adnan Menderes, Berin Menderes, İsmet İnönü, Ethem Menderes, Fatin Rüştü Zorlu, Celal Bayar, Emel Zorlu, Nihat Erim, CHP (Republican People’s Party) Deputy Ahmet, Tarık Güryay, Cemal Madanoğlu, Cemal Gürsel and many soldiers appear. Berin Menderes is in the forefront. We see that Adnan Menderes, who was happy and welcomed by the people with enthusiasm in the first credits; is now unhappy, concerned and handcuffed between soldiers’ arms. Along with these credits, we can say that the story no longer contains a chronological narration but now the relation between events within the plotline takes center stage. The viewer is drawn away from the emotional-romantic love affair (personal life) seen in the previous episodes and credits/trailers, and involved in political life (public life).

Discussion

The only means making social issues discussable and accessible in public sphere besides dramatizing these are TV movies. (Mutlu, 2008) Fictional movies draw attention of broader audience due to elements of dramatic structure such as narration, conflict, identification with character etc. Thus, fictional historical movies play an important role in formation of image on an historical era, event or person, in the memories of audience. "The time during which the fictional narration is opened and developed is not past. In order to place a narration into the past, other indications that distinguish the fact from fiction must be added to the time of the narrated world (such as creating and criticizing documents)." (Ricouer, 2012) It is an undeniable fact that main objective of both the verbal communication of the actress playing the character of Ayhan Aydan towards the audience by her own voice in the first trailer (sample 2) and the white text on black background, appeared on screen for a long time as 8 seconds in all the credits of the broadcast episodes (15 episodes) was to guide and impress the audience. In both texts, words or symbols used by the narrator were loaded with emotionality and meanings with value judgments. In this context, some words or symbols included in the trailer texts (verbal/written), the ones about love, patriotism, and ideology in particular are loaded with high level of emotionality and for this reason, and these have an almost magical power. (Gökçe, 2006) The impact function in terms of purpose is stimulated through the language used in these texts. Recently, along with development of means of mass media and increase in the level of witnessing, both in our country and in many countries of the world many political events and characters, especially coups are being revealed again. While some events and persons are made more distinguished with, due regard to the current government, others are ignored. Differently from previous broadcast fictional stories about Adnan Menderes and Yassiada Courts, the TV series "Ben Onu Çok Sevdim" has been broadcast for the first time through a national channel with such an openness that no one ever had taken the liberty to speak or write about. (Taking into consideration the close relationship of the broadcasting channel and production company, with the current government, this becomes more important.) Fictional narrator has refigured here his discourse within the narration act as the same person with the protagonist (in spite of real character and real event) with viewpoint of the present. Despite this, he changed the love story he is trying to legitimize by dramatical construction with social concerns and transformed it into a protagonist who died, was killed "for the sake of loving his homeland". In particular, on the contrary of the view stressed also by Umberto Eco for narration as he "does not say anything about this world while setting up a world with events and persons. He touches upon certain things and for the rest, he asks the reader to cooperate by filling a series of empty spaces. (Eco, 1996) told all the past-related gaps with today's viewpoint.

References

Atabek, Gülseren Ş., Ümit. (2007). Medya Metinlerini Çözümlemek, Siyasal Kitabevi, Ankara.

Eco, Umberto. (1996). Anlatı Ormanlarında Altı Gezinti, Çev. Kemal Atakay, Can Yay., İstanbul.

Gökçe, Orhan. (2006). İçerik Analizi Kuramsal ve Pratik Bilgiler, Siyasal Kitabevi, Ankara.

Mutlu, Erol. (2008).Televizyonu Anlamak, Ayraç Yay., Ankara.

Özön, Nijat. (2000). Sinema, Televizyon, Video, Bilgisayarlı Sinema Sözlüğü, Kabalcı Yay., İstanbul.

Ricouer, Paul. (2007). Yorum Teorisi, Söylem ve Artı Anlam, Paradigma Yay. İstanbul.

Ricouer, Paul. (2012). Zaman ve Anlatı: Üç; Kurmaca Anlatıda Zamanın Biçimlenişi, Çev: Mehmet Rıfat, YKY, İstanbul.

Sarlo, Beatriz. (2012). Geçmiş Zaman, Bellek Kültürü ve Özneye Dönüş Üzerine Bir Tartışma. Çev: Peral Bayaz Charum, Deniz Ekinci, Metis Yay. İstanbul.

(http://www.atv.com.tr/webtv/ben-onu-coksevdim/ozelvideo/ben-onu-coksevdim-ilk-fragmani?id=a046c003-b307-4bd7-b84c-544bf8f4a629).

Yusuf Arslan[1] & Aykut Yılmaz[2]

[1]Research Assistant, Faculty of Business and Lecturer, Vocational School of Sakarya, Sakarya University, Turkey

Online Word of Mouth Versus Personal Word of Mouth: An Application on Smart Phone Users

Abstract According to the word of mouth (WOM) literature, consumers are affected by WOM with their purchase decisions. Especially with the expansion of social media usage, online WOM (oWOM) has increasingly become important as much as personal WOM (pWOM). In this context, the purpose of this paper is to compare the effects of oWOM and pWOM on smart phone purchase decisions. The differences between oWOM and pWOM regarding message source credibility were also examined by the authors. Three main hypotheses tested in the study using the data collected from 391 smart phone owners via questionnaires. The results indicate that there is a significant difference between oWOM and pWOM respecting relative impact of oWOM and pWOM on smart phone buying decisions. According to the results, message source credibility varies between oWOM and pWOM. In addition, gender was found to be a determining factor for oWOM and pWOM. Finally, it was revealed that, oWOM is more effective for men than for women and pWOM is more effective for women than it is for men. Thus, it can be seen from the results that all three hypothesis of the study was supported.

Keywords: Word of Mouth, Online Word of Mouth, Personal Word of Mouth, Smart Phone Purchase Decisions

1. Introduction

Customers have been providing one another with information and advice for ages. Through blogs, e-mail, and online communities, people now share recommendations with thousands. It easily can be said that people trust other people more than they trust companies. As a result of this, companies have begun paying close attention to how they can use word-of mouth to achieve their purposes (Kelly, 2007).

The Word of Mouth Marketing Association (WOMMA) defines Word of mouth marketing as "giving people a reason to talk about your products and services, and making it easier for that conversation to take place. WOM communication refers to interpersonal information exchanges among adopters and potential adopters of a product (Maxham, 2001).

This type of interpersonal communication is widely believed to be more powerful than advertising and other communication tools in which the manufacturer controls the message, in part, because potential adopters tend to place more trust in information received from sources who do not benefit from the sale of one product over another (Parry et al., 2012).

The power and influence of WOM are significant, in part, because historically the source of WOM is usually from someone we know personally. This personal connection tends to make WOM recommendations more authentic and trustworthy than other forms of influence (Meuter et al., 2013). Some observers argue that, in light of the recent surge of both niche suppliers and consumer-generated content on the web, WOM is actually becoming the most essential element for economic success (Oetting, 2009).

We distinguish between two types of WOM communication, Personal Word of Mouth (pWOM) and Online Word of Mouth (oWOM). pWOM refers to communication between individuals who know each other while oWOM refers to communication between individuals who have never met in real life (Kawakomi et al., 2013)

In this paper, we examine the impact of oWOM and pWOM on smart phone purchases. We argue that the distinction between oWOM and pWOM is significant. We also concluded that the effects of oWOM and pWOM on smart phone purchase decisions were significantly different between men and women.

2. Personal Versus Online Word of Mouth

pWOM refers to the exchange of information between people, typically through conversation, and often between people who know each other (Parry et al., 2012). In contrast, oWOM involves virtual communication between consumers who have never met in real life (Park and Lee, 2009). We can define oWOM as a communication as any positive or negative statement made by customers about a product or company, which is made available to a multitude of people and institutions via the internet (Henning-Thurau et al., 2004).

pWOM has been shown to play a major role for customers' buying decisions. The advent of the Internet has extended consumers' options for gathering unbiased product information from other consumers and provides the opportunity for consumers to offer their own consumption-related advice by engaging in oWOM (Henning-Thurau et al., 2004).

The information age has paved the way to the experience economy. Consumers either try products and services first-hand or seek recommendations from others who have already done so. Since it may not be feasible or economical for consumers to test all that they hear about brands in the media, they often rely on others' reports. They talk to their neighbors, e-mail colleagues, and read online customer reviews. In the absence of direct experience, word of mouth has become one of the most valuable sources of information about brands, products, and services (Cakim, 2010).

As one facet of the aforementioned consumer empowerment in the area of online publishing, the spread of oWOM on the internet has increased significantly. oWOM provides peer-to-peer communication with a new dimension, as it enables access to WOM sources irrespective of time and place (Oetting, 2009).

3. Message Source Credibility

Source credibility refers to a message recipient's perception of the credibility of a message source, reflecting nothing about the message itself. It is defined as the extent to which an information source is perceived to be believable, competent, and trustworthy by information recipients. In addition, Eagly and Chaiken (1993) found that the persuasiveness of a message depends on the number of positive attributes the communicators possess. Information provided by highly credible sources is perceived to be useful and reliable, and thereby facilitates knowledge transfer (Cheung 2008).

Existing literature identifies "Source Expertise" and "Source Trustworthiness" as two major determinants to measure the credibility of information (e.g., Wiener. & Mowen, 1986; Whitehead, 1968). Unlike pWOM communication, oWOM message transfers between strangers, who have non-existent tie. The nature of anonymous in oWOM communication increases the difficulty of judging the credibility of source and the authenticity of the information (Cheng & Zhou, 2010).

4. Methodology

4.1 The Purpose and Hypotheses of the Study

The main objective of this study is to examine the effect of oWOM and pWOM on smart phone purchase decisions. The authors also examine the differences between oWOM and pWOM with regard to Message Source Credibility. In this study, Message Source Credibility was addressed under two sub-dimensions. These dimensions are Expertness and Trustworthiness.

The authors test three main hypotheses using data collected from 391 smart phone owners via questionnaires. Therefore, following hypotheses are offered;

H1: There is a significant difference between the effect of oWOM and pWOM on smart phone buying decisions.

H2: The effect of WOM type on smart phone buying decision varies by gender.
H3a: Relative to source expertness level, there is a significant difference between oWOM and pWOM.
H3b: Relative to source trustworthiness level, there is a significant difference between oWOM and pWOM.

4.2 Measurement

4.2.1 Personal and Online Word of Mouth

A number of the measures used in our study were drawn from prior research. East et al (2008) Kawakami et al (2012) were two main studies that we derive items to measure both oWOM and pWOM.

4.2.2 Message Source Credibility

This research focused on measuring the source credibility of oWOM and pWOM. The measurement was based on the three sub-dimensional source credibility scale developed by Ohanian (1990). Because the message sender, who sent out oWOM cannot be contacted directly, the attraction sub-dimension could not be measured. Therefore, to be able to measure both oWOM and pWOM this research only used the other two sub-dimensions, expertness and trustworthiness, to measure message source credibility. The average was used as the standard to mark high and low credibility.

4.3 Research Design

To test our hypotheses, we collected data from people, who own at least one smart phone and above the age of 18. We have chosen smart phones as a product category, because it's a technologic device most people have and it's one of the product categories people like to talk about. We collected data from 391 smart phone owners via questionnaires, using the convenience sampling method.

5. Findings

Demographic features of the participants are displayed in Table 1.

Table 1: Demographic Findings

	Gender		Age				Education Level			Income Level (Turkish Lira-TL)				Marriage Status	
	Female	*Male*	*Below 20*	*21–30*	*31–40*	*Over 41*	*Secondary Education*	*University*	*Post Graduate*	*Below 1001*	*1001–2000*	*2001–3000*	*Over 3000*	*Single*	*Married*
n	198	193	90	130	92	79	279	95	17	164	121	70	36	213	178
%	50.6	49.4	23	33.2	23.5	20,2	71,4	24.3	4.3	41.9	30.9	17.9	9.2	54.5	45.5

According to Table 1, in terms of gender the population was almost equally divided (50,6 Female – 49,4 Male). The age range of the population is equally spread between groups, except for 130 people aged 21 to 30. Most members of the population have a secondary education (279 people) and an income below 2000 TL (285 people).

Table 2: Factor Analysis

	Component		Cronbach's Alpha	Total Variance Explained
	1	2		
pWOM2	,814			
pWOM4	,793			
pWOM3	,740			33,458
pWOM1	,717		0.757	
pWOM5	,536			
oWOM3		,907		
oWOM2		,872		28,536
oWOM1		,786		

KMO: 0,747
Total Variance Explained: 61,994

Such a procedure is preferred to the application of a confirmatory factor analysis at this stage. Nine statements were extracted using the latent roots criterion and a varimax rotation. Based on literature we could have 2 separate factors for oWOM and pWOM. Both factors showed strong reliability (**α=0,76**). Table 2 contains the factor loadings for the rotated solution and Cronbach's values.

Table 3: Differences of oWOM and pWOM on Smart Phone Buying Decision

	Mean	N	Correlation	Sig.	T	df	Sig. (2-tailed)
oWOM	2,8994	391	,203	,000	−8,403	390	,000
pWOM	3,4926	391					

With regard to the relative impact of pWOM and oWOM on smart phone buying decisions, the results of paired sample *t*-test indicate that there is a significant difference between pWOM and oWOM. And because the correlation between the two structures is low, it can be said that the person affected by one of oWOM or pWOM is not necessarily affected by the other.

The results indicate that pWOM is significantly more effective than oWOM on smart phone buying decisions, thus supports H1.

Table 4: The Effect of WOM Type Comparison By Gender On Smart Phone Buying Decision

	Mean		T test		
			t	df	Sig(2-tailed)
oWOM	Men	3,0622	**2,565**	**389**	**,011**
	Women	2,7407			
pWOM	Men	3,3782	**−2,418**	**389**	**,016**
	Women	3,6040			

The results of the independent sample *t*-test indicate that the effect of WOM type on smart phone buying decisions is significantly different between Men and Women ($p<0,05$). Table 4 contains the mean values and significance values. This indicates that, on smart phone buying decision, for male and female consumer it is not the same thing to get online and personal WOM massage. While Men affected by oWOM more than Women, Women affected by pWOM more than Men. It has different effects on men and women, thus supporting H2.

Table 5: The Effect of WOM Type In Comparison To Source Expertness/Trustworthiness Level

	Mean	N	Correlation	Sig.	T	df	Sig. (2-tailed)
Online Expertness	2,9906	391	,315	,000	−4,756	390	,000
Personal Expertness	3,2984	391					
Online Trustworthiness	2,7374	391	,138	,006	−19,180	390	,000
Personal Trustworthiness	4,1756	391					

The results of the paired sample *t*-test indicate that message source credibility varies according to online and personal WOM. The means of the message source credibility dimensions were used to scale high and low message source credibility.

The result shows that the dimensions of message source credibility are significantly different for both oWOM and pWOM. This result indicates that oWOM's trustworthiness is significantly lower than pWOM'S trustworthiness. And another result is pWOM's expertness level, which is significantly higher than oWOM Expertness level, thus supports H3.

6. Discussion

In this paper, we have examined the effect of oWOM and pWOM on smart phone purchase decisions and the differences between oWOM and pWOM with regard to message source credibility. Our analysis, based on the analysis of 391 smart phone owners, supports the argument that pWOM and oWOM are affecting smart phone buying decisions. In addition we concluded that, relative to message source credibility level there is a significant difference between oWOM and pWOM. Although nowadays firms are encouraged to stimulate electronic connections with and between customers, it is still important to keep in mind the power of direct personal communications between customers, especially between women. As consumers tend to interact through a variety of these social electronic avenues, it is a key to understand the relative importance of this type of oWOM as compared to pWOM. We hope the analysis presented here will stimulate future research that expands our understanding about the effects of pWOM and oWOM.

References

Bone, P.F. (1995). Word-of-mouth effects on short-term and long-term product judgments. *Journal of Business Research*, 32(3), 213–223.

Cakim, I.M. (2010). Implementing word of mouth marketing: online strategies to identify influencers, craft stories, and draw customers. John Wiley & Sons.

Cheung, C.M.K., Lee, M.K.O., & Rabjohn, N. (2008). The impact of electronic word-of-mouth: The adoption of online opinions in online customer communities. *Internet Research*, 18(3), 229–247.

Cheng, X., & Zhou, M. (2010). *Study on effect of eWOM: A literature review and suggestions for future research.* Paper presented at the 4th International Conference on Management and Service Science (MASS 2010), Wuhan, China.

Goodman, J. A. (2009). Strategic customer service: Managing the customer experience to increase positive word of mouth, build loyalty, and maximize profits. AMACOM Div American Mgmt Assn.

Hennig-Thurau, T., Gwinner, K. P., Walsh, G., & Gremler, D. D. (2004). Electronic word-of-mouth via consumer-opinion platforms: What motivates consumers to articulate themselves on the Internet? *Journal of Interactive Marketing*, 18(1), 38–52.

Kelly, L. (2007). Beyond buzz: The next generation of word-of-mouth marketing. AMACOM Div American Mgmt Assn.

Maxham, J. G., III 2001. Service recovery's influence on consumer satisfaction, positive word-of-mouth, and purchase intentions. Journal of Business Research 54(1): 11–24.

Kawakami, T., Kishiya, K., & Parry, M. E. (2013). Personal Word of Mouth, Virtual Word of Mouth, and Innovation Use. Journal of Product Innovation Management, 30(1), 17–30.

Meuter, M. L., McCabe, D. B., & Curran, J. M. (2013). Electronic Word-of-Mouth Versus Interpersonal Word-of-Mouth: Are All Forms of Word-of-Mouth Equally Influential? *Services Marketing Quarterly*, 34(3), 240–256.

Oetting, M. (2009). *Ripple Effect*. Wiesbaden: Gabler.

Ohanian, R. (1990), "Construction and validation of a scale to measure celebrity endorsers' perceived expertise, trustworthiness, and attractiveness", Journal of Advertising, Vol. 19, pp. 39–52.

Park, C., and T. M. Lee. 2009. Information direction, website reputation and eWOM effect: A moderating role of product type. Journal of Business Research 62(1): 61–67.

Parry, M. E., Kawakami, T., & Kishiya, K. (2012). The Effect of Personal and Virtual Word-of-Mouth on Technology Acceptance. *Journal of Product Innovation Management*, 29(6), 952–966.

Phillips, R., Cordell, G., Church, G., & Jones, S. (2010). Brains on Fire: Igniting Powerful, Sustainable, Word of Mouth Movements. John Wiley & Sons.

Whitehead, J. L. (1968). Factors of source credibility. Quarterly Journal of Speech, 54(1), 59–63.

Wiener, J. L., & Mowen, J. C. (1986). Source credibility: On the independent effects of trust and expertise. Advances in Consumer Research, 13(1), 306–310.

Wu, P. C. S., & Wang, Y.-C. (2011). The influences of electronic word-of-mouth message appeal and message source credibility on brand attitude. *Asia Pacific Journal of Marketing and Logistics*, 23(4), 448–472.

www.ingramcontent.com/pod-product-compliance
Ingram Content Group UK Ltd.
Pitfield, Milton Keynes, MK11 3LW, UK
UKHW021843100926
8556IPUK00019B/1022

9 783631 666098